LET'S RIDE

LET'S RIDE

Sonny Barger's Guide to Motorcycling

Sonny Barger with
Darwin Holmstrom

WILLIAM MORROW
An Imprint of HarperCollins*Publishers*

Grateful acknowledgment is made to the following for the photographs that appear in this book. Page xiv: © by Dieter Rebmann; pages 18 and 54: © by Sonny Barger Productions; page 92: © by Gene Anthony; page 122: © by Tina Hager; page 176: © by Nicolas Syracuse; page 198: photograph by Jinushi © by *Free&Easy* magazine; page 230: photograph by Clay Garder © by Sonny Barger Productions; page 261: photograph by Paul Hatton © by Thunder Roads Arizona.

The information herein is accurate to the best of the author's knowledge as of the date this book went to press. The author and the publisher expressly disclaim liability for any losses that may be incurred as a result of applying the information contained herein.

HarperCollins books may be purchased for educational, business, or sales promotional use. For information please write: Special Markets Department, HarperCollins Publishers, 10 East 53rd Street, New York, NY 10022.

FIRST EDITION

Designed by Jamie Lynn Kerner

Library of Congress Cataloging-in-Publication Data has been applied for.

ISBN 978-0-06-196426-8

10 11 12 13 14   OV/WCT   10 9 8 7 6 5 4 3 2 1

I would like to dedicate this to my wife, Zorana, who also rides. She has been riding for seven years and now rides a 2008 Street Glide. No, I did not even attempt to teach her to ride.

—SONNY BARGER

I would like to thank Fritz Clapp for hooking me up with this project, Jim Fitzgerald for being the driving force that made it happen, and Zorana, who helped coordinate the creation of the book. I'd like to thank Ken Fund and Zack Miller at Motorbooks for letting me do this project, and also our editor Peter Hubbard and the rest of the crew at William Morrow/HarperCollins. I'd especially like to thank Sonny, whose enthusiasm for motorcycles provided the energy for this book. Sonny is, without question, the most dedicated motorcyclist I have ever met. I also want to thank my family, in particular my wife, Pat, and my father, Dean, who are also my best friends. I'd like to dedicate this book to my mother, JoAnne, who passed away while we were writing the book.

—DARWIN HOLMSTROM

CONTENTS

LET'S RIDE

INTRODUCTION

Why Ride?

ack in the 1970s people used to say: "Ride hard, die young, and leave a good-looking corpse." People said a lot of stupid things in those days. I'm in my seventies today, and that saying seems idiotic to me now. I've got a better plan: ride smart, live long, and die of old age. I take good care of myself. I eat a healthy diet, I exercise every day, and I ride safe. I do this not because I'm afraid of dying. I do it because the longer I stay healthy, the longer I can ride motorcycles.

If there's one thing I want you to know about me, it's that I love to ride. A lot of people know a lot about me, mostly because I've written one book about my life and another about my philosophy. Other people *think* they know me because so much has been written about me over the past half century. Some of it is true, but most is bullshit. And none of it is relevant here; the only thing that matters is that I love motorcycles. You do, too, or you wouldn't be reading this book.

Most motorcycle owners really aren't serious riders. They ride maybe once or twice on a weekend and only when the sun is out. They don't get up in the morning and ride to work in the cold or rain. More often than not they get in their cars instead of on their bikes.

That's not me. When it comes to a bike or a car, there is no choice. Unless I'm getting something that's too big to haul on my bike, like feed for my horses, I take the bike every time. Many times in my life I haven't even owned a car, but I always had a bike. There have been many times when I couldn't afford both a car and a motorcycle, so I always chose a bike over a car. My family and I have even had to shop for groceries on a motorcycle, but that's the way I prefer it.

Becoming a serious rider is no easy thing to do. It takes dedication and hard work, but there's not a lot you can do about it if riding motorcycles is in your blood as it is in mine. You just have to suck it up and do the work.

I've been fascinated with motorcycles as early as I can remember. As a child, I loved watching bikes roar by our house. We lived on Seventeenth Street in East Oakland, which was still a small town back in the 1940s, and our house was near a stop sign that everyone used to run. Motorcycle cops used to sit in a vacant lot by my home and wait for unsuspecting people to run the stop sign. I'd stand for hours watching the cops take off after traffic violators. The sound of their motors made me feel good.

When I was finally old enough to ride, I got a little Cushman scooter. I never got sick of riding it around our neighborhood. I loved the sound, the feel of the wind against my body. After I saw *The Wild One,* I knew I wanted a real motorcycle. When I was discharged from the army in 1956, the Bohemian thing was big in the Bay Area. I had to decide whether I was going to be a beatnik or a motorcyclist. I picked motorcycles. I'm glad I did because motorcycles are still around while the beatniks are long gone.

I bought a 1937 Indian Scout as soon as I returned home from the army. At that time, I was too young to legally own a motorcycle in the state of California, so I had to buy it in my older sister's name. Despite my age, back in the 1950s no one cared if I rode it; if it ran, you could ride it, whether you had a license or not.

The Scout ran, but it wasn't in excellent shape. It was a 45-cubic-inch (750-cc) side-valve V-twin that put out about 25 horsepower on a good day. If you really cranked on it, it might have hit 75 miles per hour when it was in its prime, but by the time I bought it, its best days were long past and it wasn't reliable enough to take out on the highway. During the short time I owned it, I never left the city of Oakland.

Within a few months I had my first Harley, a 1936 Knucklehead that cost me $125, tax included. This was a much better machine, a 61-cubic-inch bike that was well suited for longer trips. I rebuilt it and put in cylinder barrels and a flywheel from a 74-cubic-inch Knucklehead. Later I stroked it by putting in a flywheel from an 80-cubic-inch Flathead. I rode that bike all over California. When the stroked Knuckle engine blew up, I built a 1958 Panhead motor up to 80 inches and rode that until I traded it in for a brand-new 1961 XLCH Sportster. I got $500 for my Knuckle-Pan and still owed $400 on the new Sportster, which seemed like an impossible amount of money back then. But it was worth it. Sportsters were the hottest bikes you could buy at the time. They ran circles around the Big Twins. I rode XLs for seven years.

I've never been without a bike since that Indian Scout. That was more than fifty years ago, and I enjoy riding motorcycles today as much as I did when I was a kid. It's still the only way I travel.

If you're anything like I was and you want to ride a motorcycle no matter what, it's time to quit thinking and start doing. Jump in, and swim. I'll explain in the following chapters what you need to do to make that happen, but throughout the book I'm going to stress the importance of getting proper training. Don't let friends or family members teach you to ride: do it right and take a riding class. We'll talk about the types of classes that are available in the upcoming chapters, but for now all you need to know is that completing a motorcycle riding class will be the safest way to practice the skills we cover in *Let's Ride*.

● ● ●

Riding a motorcycle is easier said than done. Much of the rest of this book will tell you what to do once you decide to become a motorcycle rider, but the challenges will start before you ever fire up your engine for the first time. You're going to have to deal with the concerns of your loved ones. As soon as you tell people you're interested in riding motorcycles, you'll start to hear an endless stream of warnings, mostly some variation of "Motorcycles are dangerous!" This is true—motorcycles are dangerous, but hey, life itself is dangerous. Everything you ever do will be a risk to some degree. Even doing nothing is dangerous because you'll get soft and fat and then die of heart disease. Death, after all, is the only sure bet in life.

No matter what you do, someone somewhere will tell you it's dangerous. If you listened to every one of them, you would never do anything. You may crash your motorcycle and get hurt or killed, but you may fall off a curb and get run over by a bus, too, or tonight you could choke on a piece of fried chicken. Statistically, your bathtub might be just as dangerous as your motorcycle; thousands of people die from falling in their tubs every year, but no one tells you not to take a bath.

My sister and my dad both tried to talk me out of riding. My dad rode motorcycles with his friends, but when a good friend of his got hurt, Dad quit riding. He even stopped driving cars after that—he took a bus everywhere. He never stopped worrying about me, but he supported my decision to ride.

Only you can decide if the freedom and excitement a motorcycle can provide is worth the level of risk. If you're like me and motorcycling is in your blood, there's only one answer: "Yes."

I've done a lot of things that are more dangerous than riding a motorcycle. Smoking cigarettes came closer to killing me than riding any motorcycle has ever done. Abusing drugs gave me a heart attack when I was in my early forties. But riding motorcycles has kept me active and feeling young and alive over the years, so for me riding a motorcycle is more than worth the risks involved.

Once you've weighed the pros and cons of riding a motorcycle and decided the rewards are worth the risks, you need to do everything in your power to minimize those risks. Motorcycle riding *is* dangerous, but you can do a lot of things to make it safer. Much of the rest of this book discusses ways to avoid unnecessary risks and manage the risks you can't avoid. But first, let's discuss the rewards of motorcycling and dispel some of the myths that have grown up around bikers.

WHEN PEOPLE HEAR THAT YOU WANT to ride a motorcycle, they'll use every argument they can think of to try to talk you out of it, but they won't be able to argue with the fact that motorcycles are economical to own and operate. For starters, motorcycles are cheaper to buy than cars; the most expensive motorcycles cost about as much as the average family sedan, and the least expensive new motorcycles are cheaper than a used subcompact car. If you shop around, you can pick up a brand-new high-end motorcycle like a Victory Vegas for around $15,000, which is less than you'd pay for a new compact like a Honda Civic. You can get a decent, reliable motorcycle for under $5,000, and in some cases well under that amount. The only cars you can get for that price these days are about ready for the junkyard.

Motorcycles are fuel efficient as well. The largest, most luxurious motorcycle uses less gas than the lightest car. The most economical gas-powered cars average maybe 30 miles per gallon, and hybrid-powered cars don't get much more than 35 miles per gallon. Meanwhile the largest, most luxurious touring bikes usually get about 35–40 miles per gallon, and smaller bikes can easily get 50–60 miles per gallon. Gas prices traditionally fluctuate up and down, but with all the talk about "peak oil," I'll bet that, over the long run, fuel prices are going to trend a lot higher than they are today. The more they go up, the more money you'll save riding a motorcycle.

A lot of states also allow motorcycles to use their high-occupancy vehicle lanes, meaning you can get around on congested urban freeways more efficiently on a motorcycle than in a car. Another way to save money on a bike is in parking costs. Parking lots often charge less for motorcycles than they do for cars, which makes sense since motorcycles take up less space. If you're resourceful enough, you can even find places that let motorcycles park for free. For example, if you find a restaurant or other place of business owned by a motorcycle rider, he or she might let you park your bike in the alley or loading area behind the building. This brings up another benefit of motorcycling: a brotherhood exists among motorcycle riders.

• • •

As soon as you start riding a motorcycle, you'll find you are part of a larger community of motorcycle riders. The first thing you'll notice is that other motorcycle riders wave at you, even if you don't know them from Adam. Here's a word of advice—wave back. It doesn't matter if the other rider is some kid on a sport bike, some adventure-tourer traveling the globe on a big dual-purpose bike (we'll discuss the types of bikes and riders you'll meet later), or a member of a one-percenter club; that rider waving at you is acknowledging that the two of you are in this together. The least you could do is let the other rider know you get the message.

Waving goes back to the early days of riding. When I started riding, bikes were so unreliable that traveling the sixty miles from Oakland to San Jose was considered a big trip. You might only see one other motorcycle the whole way, so when you did, you waved at him. He might even stop and have a cup of coffee with you.

At least in part this brotherhood came about as the result of the antimotorcycle hysteria that infected the United States in the years after World War II. With communism spreading around the world and the Soviet Union getting an atomic bomb, you can't blame people for being scared of just about anything out of the ordinary, and back in those days riding a motorcycle was definitely unusual.

I first encountered this prejudice against motorcycles in 1958 while hanging out at a Doggie Diner on Twenty-third Avenue. I'd just been fired from my job and was sitting out in front of the diner when a straitlaced cop pulled up and told me that he'd been down to visit my boss the day before. I realized that he'd been the person who'd gotten me fired. From that day forward, it's gotten progressively worse. Just a couple of days ago I got a speeding ticket; the Immigration and Customs Enforcement (ICE) agent who pulled me over treated me like I was a damned dog. I've paid a lot of money in state and federal taxes, yet I get treated like that when I'm riding my motorcycle down a public highway.

BACK WHEN I STARTED RIDING, WHEN people spoke about a motorcycle, they were usually talking about either a Harley or an Indian. In some parts of California they might have been talking about a Triumph or some other Brit bike, but for most people in the United States the word *motorcycle* meant either a Harley or an Indian. With those bikes, you had to know how to fix them to ride them. Not just anyone with a fat wallet could walk into a motorcycle dealership and ride off on a new bike because in those days you spent as much time working on your bike as you did riding it. Every time you rode a bike, there was a fair chance something would go wrong before you got back home.

These days bikes are a lot more reliable and everyone has a cell phone; if something does go wrong, you can just call for help. But back then if your bike broke down, you had two choices: fix it or walk. To be a motorcycle rider in the early days of motorcycling meant that you had to be a decent motorcycle mechanic, too.

In 1958 I rode with a guy named Ernie Brown, who was the vice president of the club I was in at the time. We'd ridden down to Los Angeles and my transmission blew up. We were sitting on the side of the road when another motorcyclist named Vic Bettencourt stopped to help. It turned out that he was the president of a chapter of the same club.

I didn't even know our club had a chapter down there. We'd founded our club because we'd found a cool patch from a defunct club and we liked the patch. We didn't even know there were other chapters of the club. It was the first time we realized we were part of something bigger than just the club my friends and I had started. Vic took us to their clubhouse and put a new transmission in my bike. He also taught me a lot about what brotherhood was all about.

The tendency for bikes to break down all the time kept motorcycles off-limits for people who were trained to be things like schoolteachers and bank tellers instead of grease monkeys. It made riding a motorcycle more or less a blue-collar activity, which set up a class divide between riders and nonriders that wouldn't be torn down for generations.

ANOTHER REASON THAT MAINSTREAM AMERICAN citizens began to fear motorcycles was because of the press. As long as there have been newspapers, there've been newspaper publishers who've realized that fear sells newspapers. In the strange days following the Second World War, journalists had more fear to exploit than ever before. It didn't take much to scare the piss out of the average American in the late 1940s; anything that represented the unknown was frightening, and people who rode motorcycles represented an unknown quantity. The sight of a bunch of greasy-nailed motorcyclists roaring into a gas station was enough to make Mr. Average American wet his pants.

Being quick to pick up on anything that exploited the average American's fear of the unknown, the magazines and newspapers of the day (remember, this was back when hardly anyone had television) published stories on anything and everything that frightened people, whether it was Communist infiltrators, unidentified flying objects, or a bunch of guys out having a good time on their motorcycles. If something wasn't scary enough to sell newspapers and magazines, the newspapers and magazines would just stretch the truth until it was more sensational.

For the most part, I always get along with just about everyone I meet. People fear the unknown, but once they get to know you, they treat you the way you treat them. If you treat people with respect, they'll usually treat you with respect in return. If someone attacks me, I'm going to defend myself, but I don't go around doing things to scare people. But the problem comes when people read a lot of the crazy things that are written about me and think they should be afraid. And if it will sell papers and magazines, the press will print whatever crazy story they think people might believe.

That's exactly what they did with a motorcycle rally that got a little boisterous in the small town of

Hollister, California, over the Fourth of July holiday in 1947. About four thousand motorcycle riders came to town that weekend, mostly to attend races sponsored by the AMA (American Motorcyclist Association). That was a lot more people than the town expected and things got a little hectic.

Eyewitness reports tell of such things as motorcyclists throwing water balloons off balconies, popping wheelies on Main Street, and generally riding around whooping and hollering. There were a few drunken fights, and more than a little street racing, but other than a couple tools being stolen from a tire repair shop, there was no real crime to speak of. One guy was arrested for pissing in the radiator of a car that was overheating; when his buddy Wino Willy of the Booze Fighters Motorcycle Club went to bail him out of jail, he, too, was arrested for being drunk.

A total of twenty-nine people were arrested for drunkenness, indecent exposure, and traffic violations, but overall the motorcyclists were just a little rowdier than the cowboys were when the rodeo came to town. Finally one guy rode his motorcycle right into a bar, prompting the owner to call the California Highway Patrol, who cleared everyone out and put a stop to the party.

The Hollister event would have gone down in history as just another good Fourth of July party in a small town had not a photographer put a pile of empty beer bottles around a motorcycle and had a guy pose on the bike. He sold the resulting photo to *Life* magazine, which ran it with a short story about how hordes of motorcyclists were descending on the country hell-bent on destroying everything in their paths. Within weeks motorcycle riders replaced Communists as public enemy number one, which is more than a little ironic considering that most motorcyclists at the time were honorable patriots who had risked their lives serving their country in World War II. They just wanted to have a little fun, and they sure as hell had earned that right.

The *Life* magazine story inspired a guy named Frank Rooney to write a short story for *Harper's Magazine* called "The Cyclists' Raid." This piece of fiction became the basis for the 1953 film *The Wild One*. Mostly the film shows a bunch of people having a good time on motorcycles, but back then Johnny, played by Marlon Brando, seemed like the Antichrist to the average American, and the film helped to spread mistrust between motorcycle riders and non-motorcycle riders.

The film might have scared "average Americans" witless, but when my friends and I saw *The Wild One* as teenagers, we wanted to be just like Chino, the character played by Lee Marvin. Johnny seemed like he spent a lot of time feeling sorry for himself. I don't care what anyone says; Marlon Brando's character was a bully, and I don't like bullies. Whenever something happened, Marlon Brando said, "Me and my boys will take care of it." It was never: "I'll take care of it."

Chino had balls, and he knew how to have fun. Lee Marvin's character was like a real person. He wasn't out looking to push anyone around; he just wanted to ride his motorcycle and have a good time. He wanted everyone to be together as a group.

But as I say, most Americans didn't see the film

the way we did. Where we saw motorcyclists having a good time, they saw criminals who needed to be locked up. By the time I started riding motorcycles, motorcycle riding itself was practically a crime; not only did we have to be on constant vigil against careless car drivers, wild animals and dogs, and other hazards of the road, but we also had to watch out for the cops who would harass us at every opportunity just because of the mode of transportation we preferred. With this kind of pressure on us at all times, it made sense that we would seek the brotherhood found in motorcycle clubs.

BACK AROUND THE TURN OF THE twentieth century, people formed clubs around just about anything. There were clubs devoted to collecting butterflies, clubs devoted to examining dinosaur fossils, and clubs devoted to studying electricity. It only made sense that people would start forming motorcycle clubs almost as soon as Gottlieb Daimler first bolted a gasoline engine to his two-wheeled wooden Einspur to create the original motorcycle in 1885.

Motorcycle clubs remained popular throughout the first half of the twentieth century, but after World War II they became even more popular. Most able-bodied American men had served in the military during the war, and many of them missed the brotherhood they had shared with their fellow soldiers. Motorcycle clubs offered these veterans a way to re-create that camaraderie. By 1947, when the Hollister bash took place, there were dozens of clubs on the West Coast alone.

Just about everyone I know belongs to some sort of biking club. Riding alone is fun, but being part of a group provides advantages. With a group, you'll have someone to watch your back if something happens or help you if you go down. Plus it's nice to have someone to share the ride with. There are all sorts of clubs, and I encourage every rider to consider joining one for the brotherhood and camaraderie.

In 1957 six other guys and I started a chapter of the club I'm still in. Within six months I became president of our chapter, and I remained president for about thirty years. I'm still a member, but I haven't held an office in the club for more than twenty years. The type of club I'm in—a one-percenter club—probably isn't for everyone. No club is for everybody, but no matter what kind of riding you're interested in, you can find a motorcycle club that focuses on it.

I'VE SAVED MY PERSONAL FAVORITE PART of motorcycling for last: freedom. This subject is so important to me that I've written an entire book about it. I appreciate all the other benefits a motorcycle provides, especially the brotherhood of riders that forms around motorcycles, but for me in the end it all boils down to the freedom I find on a bike.

When I pop the gearshift lever on my bike into first and ride out onto the open road, I leave everything else behind. Before I get on my bike I might be worried about some deadline I have to meet, or some person I have to call, or some other obligation I have to fulfill, but once I ride out of my driveway, I leave all that other stuff behind. There's no room for it out on the road. I've got enough to worry about just trying to avoid all the other drivers yapping on their cell phones—there's no room for the petty worries that would be on my mind if I wasn't out on my bike.

At least I try to shed all those unimportant thoughts when I ride. Sometimes they creep in, but I do my best to avoid them because they distract me from the business at hand, which is not getting hurt or killed on my bike. Normally I do a pretty good job at clearing the unimportant crap from my mind and focusing on riding my bike. Because riding is such an intense activity, it demands your full attention. On a bike you're bombarded with all kinds of stuff coming at you, and I don't just mean other traffic. Riding reveals so many raw sights, sounds, and smells that they can overwhelm you. It can be a little intimidating at first, but I promise that riding will ultimately produce an amplified sense of being alive.

Once you let the experience of riding consume you and drive all the useless thoughts from your head, that's when you really start to enjoy the freedom of riding a bike. It doesn't matter if you're riding five miles or five hundred miles; time has little meaning when your head is in the act of riding and it's just you, your bike, and the road—at least until your ass starts to get sore and the pain interrupts your motorcycle meditation. Later in this book we'll talk about ways to prevent even that from being a problem.

● ● ●

RIDING REALLY IS A FORM OF meditation. Most religions have ways to help focus your thoughts—meditation, prayer, ceremonies—and in this way riding a motorcycle is a lot like a religion. I'm not going to talk about organized religions here because what people believe or don't believe is their own business. I don't talk to people about what I do or don't believe, and I appreciate when they don't talk to me about their beliefs. But when it comes to motorcycles, I figure that if you're reading this book you most likely have an interest in what I believe, at least as far as motorcycles are concerned.

And I believe that riding motorcycles is as good a religion as any, and probably better than most. For me, riding a motorcycle is like being part of a ceremony; it's a sort of transcendent experience some would call holy. I think a lot of my club brothers feel the same way. That's why we call going to our club meetings "going to church."

The rest of this book will cover the things you need to do to learn to ride a motorcycle, tell you how to buy the right motorcycle, teach you how to be comfortable and safe once you get it, and give you advice on what to do once you start riding. I hope that by getting the proper training, choosing a good motorcycle that suits your needs, and practicing good safety habits once you start riding, you'll stay strong and healthy and ride for many trouble-free years. Do that and you'll experience the pleasure that motorcycling has given me for more than half a century. Whether or not you join a club, if you love to ride a motorcycle, you are part of my church.

CHAPTER ONE

DISSECTING THE BEAST

The Anatomy of a Motorcycle

Motorcycles seem like they should be simple because there's really not much to them. You've got an engine, two wheels, tires, something to sit on, some controls to manage the machine, a tank for gasoline, and a frame to hold the whole works together.

In the early days of riding, the preceding description pretty much accounted for an entire motorcycle. The controls consisted of a cable going to a rudimentary carburetor, which was about as complex as a Turkish water pipe, and hopefully, a crude brake. The transmission was made up of a pulley that tightened a flat, smooth leather belt that ran from an output sprocket on the crankshaft of the engine to another pulley on the rear wheel. If the contraption had lights, they were likely powered by kerosene and turned on with matches or maybe a very rudimentary battery on more advanced models. A modern motorcycle has more computer chips than an early motorcycle had total moving parts.

Motorcycles weren't that much more complicated when I started riding. There had been a few improvements, but not many. Instead of total-loss electrical systems with enormous lead-acid batteries, the first motorcycles I rode had extremely basic six-volt electrical systems. These didn't provide enough juice to reliably power an electric starter, so we still had to kick-start our motorcycles. By then motorcycles had recirculating oiling systems so the rider no longer had to pump oil into the engine by hand, and chains took care of final drive duties instead of the smooth leather belts that spun the wheels on the earliest motorcycles, but overall, the bikes I started riding were closer to the motorized bicycles from the end of the nineteenth century than they were to the reliable, practical motorcycles we have today.

PUTTING THE MOTOR IN THE CYCLE

IN THIS BOOK I'M not going to teach you how to overhaul your motorcycle. Most modern motorcycles are too complicated for you to do much more than change the oil yourself, but you will need to become familiar with the essential parts of a motorcycle and how everything works together. If you already know these things, you might want to skip ahead to the next section, though it can never hurt to brush up.

The engine, of course, is what puts the *motor* in *motor*cycle. Engines come in two basic types: four-stroke and two-stroke. Two-stroke engines haven't been used much in the United States over the past several decades because of emissions standards. They're called "two-strokes" because every two strokes of the piston comprise one complete cycle. The piston goes down and draws in the fuel charge; it goes back up and fires the fuel charge. Two-strokes are simple engines that don't have internal oil-lubrication systems. Some of the oil lubricates the inside of the engine, and the rest is burned with the exhaust, which is why they pollute so much. The last full-sized street-legal two-stroke motorcycle sold in the U.S. market was Yamaha's RZ350 from the mid-1980s.

For several decades two-stroke engines dominated Grand Prix motorcycle racing because the engines are light and generate twice as many power pulses as a four-stroke engine, but they've been phased out over the past decade. In 2002 the top class switched from 500-cc two-strokes to 990-cc four-strokes, and in 2009 the 250-cc two-stroke class was retired, to be replaced by a 600-cc four-stroke class for the 2010 season. That leaves just the 125-cc class as the last of the two-stroke road racers.

But because two-stroke street bikes are too old and too small to be used as practical transportation, we won't be discussing two-strokes in this book. The day may come when we'll ride around on electric motorcycles powered by hydrogen fuel cells, but for the foreseeable future we'll be riding motorcycles powered by four-stroke gasoline engines.

The basic systems of a four-stroke engine are the bottom end, the cylinder block, the piston, the cylinder, the combustion chamber, the cylinder head, and the fuel intake system.

The Crankcase

The crankcase is often referred to as the "bottom end" because it's located at the bottom of almost every engine (though it's at the center of opposed engines like those found on a BMW twin or a four- or six-cylinder Gold Wing—I'll explain that later in this chapter). It consists of a crankshaft that rotates in a series of bearings. This rotation carries through the clutch, transmission, and final drive system, until it becomes the rotation of your rear tire on the pavement, which is what makes your motorcycle move down the road. Piston rods connect the crankshaft to the pistons.

These days most motorcycles are so reliable that if you regularly change your engine oil, you can ride for hundreds of thousands of miles and not give any thought to the bottom end, but that wasn't always the case. Before we had the advanced oils, oiling systems, and bearing materials we have today, spinning a bearing or throwing a rod was a common occurrence. These are catastrophic failures that can result in internal parts of the engine exploding through cases and cylinder barrels and becoming external parts. This can be a little like a grenade going off between your legs, so it's a very good thing that modern bikes have such reliable bottom ends.

To be fair, some of the methods we used to rely

on for hot-rodding our engines, like "stroking" them (this refers to the practice of installing a different crankshaft that increases the length a piston travels up and down in the cylinder, effectively increasing cubic inches without making the cylinder itself any larger), improved performance, but they also put more stress on the parts and increased the likelihood that the engine would grenade between a rider's legs. Modern motorcycle engines are too complex to easily stroke, though a few people still do this to their older 74-inch Shovelheads and Panheads. If you plan to do this to your engine, make sure you or whomever you hire to do the job knows what he's doing.

The Cylinder Block(s)

Every gas-piston engine has one or more cylinder blocks. They are aluminum blocks (any practical modern motorcycle that you will consider buying will have an aluminum engine) with a hole or holes drilled in it or them for the piston or pistons. This hole is usually lined with a steel liner for durability, though some motorcycles have cylinder walls coated with harder alloys in place of steel liners.

On a single-cylinder or an inline engine like that found on a four-cylinder sport bike or a parallel-twin engine like that found on a Triumph, there will be just one cylinder block. There are a small number of V-four engines in production; these usually have one large cylinder block with four holes drilled in it.

On a V-twin like a Victory or a Harley, there are two cylinder blocks. V-twin owners usually call these cylinder blocks "barrels" or "jugs" because they look like water barrels or jugs. They may have earned the name "jugs" because some people think they look a little like certain parts of a well-endowed woman, but it takes a lot of imagination to see the resemblance.

All motorcycle cylinder blocks (except a few specialized cylinder blocks used to build drag-racing engines) will feature some sort of cooling system. On water-cooled bikes this will consist of water jackets around the cylinders (hollowed-out spaces through which cooling water circulates from the radiator to the cylinder block and back to the radiator again). On air-cooled bikes like Harleys and Victories this will just be a series of cooling fins that provide a surface area over which the passing air can remove the heat generated from the combustion process.

The type of cooling system is probably the single most important factor in reliability and longevity in a modern engine. Liquid cooling is generally the best type when it comes to making an engine last. All modern cars and trucks are liquid cooled, and most modern engines will run for more than two hundred thousand miles.

Today's motorcycles are also water cooled, though air cooling is not necessarily a bad thing. As engine size increases, the amount of heat generated also increases, so it becomes harder to cool an engine with air alone when the cubic inches start to rise. As their air-cooled engines have grown larger, Harleys have had some cooling issues in recent years. To alleviate the problem Harley offers a system in which the rear cylinder shuts down at idle to help keep it cool when the bike is at rest.

Victory takes a different route. There are oil jets

in a Victory engine that spray streams of cooling oil at the bottoms of the pistons, right at the area in which the most heat is generated. The cylinders still crank out a hellacious amount of heat and will bake your inner thigh on a hot Arizona day, but that is true of just about every motorcycle. If you want to ride in air-conditioned comfort, you're reading the wrong book. I can tell you from tens of thousands of miles of experience that Victory engines seem to run cooler in stop-and-go traffic than Harley engines, which is one of the things I like about Victory motorcycles.

Harley does make what seems like a very good liquid-cooled motorcycle: the V-Rod. I have friends who own them and they speak very highly of them.

The Pistons, Cylinder, Combustion Chamber, Cylinder Head, and Fuel Intake System

The pistons—the aluminum slugs that go up and down in the cylinder blocks—are the beating heart of a motorcycle engine. They're powered by a fuel-air charge that burns in the combustion chamber, which is the area at the top of the cylinder. This burning generates an engine's energy as well as most of its heat.

The cylinder head is the assembly that sits atop the cylinder block. It contains valves that open and close to allow the fuel charge to get in and the spent exhaust gases to get out. Motorcycle engines can have anywhere from two to five valves per cylinder. Most Harleys have two valves per cylinder: one intake and one exhaust. Victory motorcycles all have four valves: two intake valves and two exhaust valves.

Some Hondas have three valves per cylinder, and a handful of Yamahas had five valves per cylinder, but most modern motorcycles will have four valves per cylinder.

With very few exceptions, the fuel-air charge is injected by electronically controlled atomizers on modern motorcycles, though there are still a few good used bikes out there that have old-fashioned carburetors mixing the fuel-air charge and getting it into the combustion chamber. Triumph recently switched from carburetion to fuel injection on its Bonneville-series twins, and these bikes had been some of the last new models to feature carburetors.

THE FOUR STROKES OF A FOUR-STROKE

Four-stroke engines are called four-strokes because each cycle of the combustion process consists of four strokes of the piston. The first (downward) stroke is called the "intake stroke" because the intake valves open on this stroke and the downward-moving piston draws in the fuel-and-air charge. The second (upward) stroke is called the "compression stroke" because the upward-moving piston compresses the fuel-air charge, which is ignited very near the top of the compression stroke (called "top dead center," or TDC). The energy generated by this ignition is called "combustion," and it's what gives its name to the third (downward) stroke, the combustion stroke (also called the "power stroke"). The fourth (upward) stroke is called the "exhaust stroke" because the exhaust valves open on this stroke, allowing the upward-moving piston to force the spent exhaust gases out through the open valves.

REDLINING

I'M NOT A HUGE fan of Harley-Davidson motorcycles. That is partly because for many years Harley sold motorcycles that were worn-out antiques even when they were new. In 1969 AMF (American Machinery and Foundry) bought Harley. By that time the Japanese had begun to introduce motorcycles with modern technology, and in the following years the pace of development of motorcycle technology quickened. When AMF sold Harley in 1981, the motorcycles coming from Japan were so highly developed that they made the motorcycles they produced in the 1960s look like antiques.

The bikes Harley built between 1969 and 1981 had barely changed; if anything, they got even worse. AMF looked at Harley as a cash cow and milked it dry. The company put very little money into product development. Instead, AMF ramped up production so that besides selling antiquated motorcycles, Harley's quality control went down the toilet; not only were Harley's motorcycles handicapped with old-fashioned technology like cast-iron engines, but they also became increasingly unreliable.

It wasn't that way when I started riding. In the 1950s all but the most expensive high-performance motorcycles had cast-iron engines and Harleys were as good as or better than any other bike on the market. But within fifteen years the Japanese, German, and

Italian manufacturers were selling motorcycles with aluminum cylinder blocks almost exclusively. Besides Harley, only the British still used cast iron for their cylinder blocks, and it didn't work out too well for them: by the early 1980s the entire British motorcycle industry had gone bankrupt. In fact, the British motorcycle industry would have gone out of business many years earlier if the UK government hadn't propped it up for the last twenty years of its existence.

Harley almost died at the same time. The Motor Company continued to build bikes with cast-iron cylinder jugs until the mid-1980s, when the aluminum Evolution engine hit the market. Because it is important to me as a patriot to ride an American motorcycle, I was stuck riding unreliable cast-iron Shovelheads all those years, and they were terrible motorcycles. Back then I spent as much time wrenching as riding, and it pissed me off. Harleys got a lot better after they started building the Evolution engines, but even today they are still old-fashioned air-cooled pushrod engines. (That means they have their cams down in the bottom end, and they use pushrods to operate the valves.)

Only a few other motorcycle manufacturers still use pushrods, like Royal Enfield from India, Moto Guzzi from Italy, and Ural from Russia, none of which are terribly reliable motorcycles. I wouldn't consider any of these brands when buying a motorcycle for practical transportation. Almost every motorcycle built today uses modern overhead-cam systems. Even most V-twin engines, like the engine found in my Victory, feature overhead cams.

Overhead-cam engines are more efficient and generate more power than pushrod engines, all else being equal, because they keep the valves under more direct control, allowing the engine to rev higher before valve float sets in. Valve float occurs when the cam pushes open the valve more rapidly than the valve spring can close it—it's a bad thing. If your bike is equipped with a tachometer, it will have a red zone marked on its face beginning at a certain rpm (revolutions per minute) range. The rpm range where the red zone begins is called the "redline," and is usually the engine speed at which valve float sets in. If you run your tach needle past the redline, you can destroy your engine.

Having an engine explode between your legs is not an experience I'd wish on my worst enemy. It's rare that a motorcycle engine will explode like a grenade, sending shrapnel outside the engine cases, but what happens when you spin a bearing or throw a rod can be just as deadly.

Usually you'll be going faster than you should be when this happens, which may well be why your engine explodes. You'll be riding along, enjoying the open road, and your engine will seize up. This in turn stops your rear tire from turning and it happens in less time than it takes for your heart to beat. If you're not covering your clutch (we'll discuss this in the advanced riding section of the book) and don't immediately pull in the clutch lever to disengage the rear wheel from the seized engine, you'll skid out of control and crash.

If your bike starts to skid sideways before you pull in the clutch, you'll have an even worse crash. When your tire is skidding, you lose all traction. When you pull in the clutch and the tire starts turning again, you'll regain traction. If your bike has started to skid to one side or the other, when you regain traction it will snap back in the opposite direction. This can easily happen with such force that it launches the entire motorcycle in the air. Of course you'll get launched with it. This is called "high-siding," and short of hitting a tree or a guardrail, it's about the worse kind of single-vehicle crash you can have on a motorcycle.

Overhead-cam engines have much higher redlines than do pushrod engines, which is why they produce more power, but that isn't the main reason I advise against buying most of the bikes that use pushrods. During normal street driving you seldom get anywhere near the engine's redline; the problem is that most of the engines that use pushrods use other outdated technology, too, which is why pushrod engines tend to be less reliable than those with overhead cams.

ENGINE TYPES

THERE ARE AS MANY different types of four-stroke motorcycle engines as there are types of motorcycles. Several basic engine configurations exist, and unless you plan to drop a fortune buying some rare, exotic machine, the bike you end up with will feature an engine in one of the following configurations:

- Single Cylinder
- V-Twin

- Parallel Twin
- L-Twin
- Opposed Twin
- Inline Triple
- Inline Four
- V-Four
- Opposed Four
- Opposed Six

There are a few oddball designs other than these, but without exception they will either be antiques, or they will be rare (and expensive) exotics, both of which are better suited to collections sitting in museums than they are for useful transportation because the spare parts needed to keep them on the road will be virtually unobtainable.

For example, over the years there have been a handful of motorcycles built with V-8 engines, like the racing bikes Moto Guzzi made in the mid-1950s. Over the years a few other manufacturers have built V-8-powered motorcycles, but not many. Italian Giancarlo Morbidelli developed a V-8 sport bike in the mid-1990s, but at a price tag of $60,000, he only sold four of them. A company called Boss Hoss makes gigantic motorcycles powered by automotive-type V-8 engines, but these bikes are so huge that they are just novelties even for experienced riders. They're expensive novelties, too, starting at around $40,000 for a base model and climbing well past the $50,000 mark if you start adding accessories; most owners then end up dropping another $20,000 converting them to trikes because they are so huge that they're miserable to ride.

There have been a few other oddball designs, like the inline six-cylinder bikes built by Honda and Benelli in the 1970s and early 1980s, but these weren't the most practical motorcycles even when they were new. The odds that you will end up with a bike that uses an engine configuration not on the preceding list are too small to measure.

Single Cylinders

The most basic type of engine, and the earliest to be mounted on a two-wheeled machine, is the single cylinder. As the name implies, this is an engine with a lone cylinder. These engines have always been mounted in a motorcycle frame with the engine aligned with the wheels; the engine has been angled anywhere from a slight lean toward the rear wheel, as on the very earliest Indians from 1901, to a complete forward lean, with the cylinder laying flat, parallel to the ground, its top end pointed at the front wheel, as on a Honda Trail 70 or a Harley Sprint or a Moto Guzzi from the 1960s.

Today most of the single-cylinder bikes available are designed for riding off-road. People who ride off-road place more value on agility and light weight than they do on overall power output. Anyone who's ever had to pick up a fallen motorcycle on a rough dirt trail will understand the reason for this. Because of the nature of off-road riding, where you'll find yourself negotiating steep, narrow trails covered with boulders and logs and maybe even the remains of Jimmy Hoffa if you get far enough off the beaten path, off-road motorcycles tend to fall over on a regular basis. This is why the fenders, gas tanks, and many other parts of an off-road bike are made of soft, bendable plastic. The lighter and easier to maneuver a motorcycle is, the less likely you are to fall over in the first place, and the easier the bike will be to pick up when you inevitably do fall over.

There are a few single-cylinder street bikes on the market, too, but most of these are very small displacement machines, usually 250 cc and under. Although these may be adequate for some riders, they won't cut it for most bikers.

Suzuki has built a 650-cc cruiser-type bike for many, many years. The company used to call it a "Savage," which is ironic, given the bike's docile nature—it's about as savage as an angry Yorkshire terrier. In 2005 Suzuki renamed it the "S40," which probably stands for "single cylinder, 40 cubic inches." It's not a sexy name, but then it's not the most exciting motorcycle. The single-cylinder engine is on the gutless side, and it's far from a smooth-running machine—you won't be doing thousand-mile days on this thing—but it is adequate for a lot of people. You could consider this motorcycle the baseline for what constitutes an adequate motorcycle for full-sized adult people; anything smaller and less powerful will be too small and too underpowered for serious consideration.

V-Twins

The early single-cylinder engines didn't put out a lot of power; ratings of 3 or 4 horsepower weren't uncommon. To put that in perspective, the engine in the Suzuki S40, which I just called "gutless," puts out about 28 horsepower. Even at the beginning of the twentieth century, 3 horsepower was inadequate for most riders—these early bikes needed pedal-assist to produce enough power to climb even the smallest hill—so motorcycle manufacturers looked for ways to increase power output.

The quickest way to get more power is through more engine displacement. This has always been true, and it was especially true in the early years of motor-cycling because of the primitive engine technology of the day. Riders needed bigger engines, but the tech-nological limitations of the day prohibited engineers from simply enlarging the early single-cylinder en-gines. These limitations still exist, to some degree. If engineers make engines with bores that are too large, they run into breathing and combustion problems; if they make the strokes too long, they run into prob-lems with piston speeds.

Given that cylinders could only get so big, the obvious way to get more power was to use more cyl-inders. The very earliest multi-cylinder engines were V-twins—that is, engines with their cylinders ar-ranged in a V shape. This made a lot of sense at the time since motorcycles were still just motorized bi-cycles (which is why the pedal-assist system was still in place). A bicycle frame comes to a pronounced "V" at its base, right where the engine sat. Giving the engine a V shape made the engine fit the available space better.

Even though V-twins were the earliest type of multi-cylinder engines, they still have a lot to offer. In street bikes, they generally tend to be low-revving engines that produce large amounts of low-end torque.

Twisting Force

In the real world, torque means more than raw horsepower. Torque is the measurement of the twisting force generated by an engine. Since this twisting force is what twists the wheel around in circles and makes you move down the road, you feel torque a lot more than you feel raw horsepower.

This is where big V-twin engines like those found in Harleys and Victories perform well. A 600-cc sport bike like Yamaha's R6 produces a lot more power than Harley's latest 96-cubic-inch (1584-cc) engine: 112 horsepower for the Yamaha compared with 68 horsepower for the Harley.

If ultimate horsepower output was the only factor determining what motorcycle to ride, we'd all be riding Japanese sport bikes, but there's a lot more to picking out a good, all-around motorcycle than pure engine output. For a lot of people the 68 horsepower generated by a stock 96-inch Harley Twin-Cam is adequate as long as the torque output is sufficient.

The 2006 Yamaha R6 generates just 43 pound-feet of torque, while the 96-inch Harley V-twin cranks out about 77 pound-feet of torque and the V-twin in my Victory Vision produces 109 pound-feet of torque. That doesn't mean my Victory is faster; the Yamaha is so much faster that they are almost like two completely different vehicles. But to get speed from the Yamaha, you have to rev the engine way up past 10,000 rpm. In other words, to go fast, you pretty much have to ride it like you stole it, all the time. This is fun on a racetrack, if you know what you're doing, but out among the traffic found on real-world roads, it gets tiresome.

With a big V-twin like my Vision, peak torque is reached at just 2700 rpm. That means when I want to get access to my engine's twisting force, I don't have to shift down four gears, open up the throttle, and drive like a maniac. I just roll on the throttle and the power is instantly there. So while a sport bike like the Yamaha is a lot faster on a racetrack, a big V-twin like the Vision feels a lot faster in normal driving conditions on real-world roads.

There aren't many things in life I enjoy more than the feel of riding a motorcycle with a big, torque-rich engine. When I roll on the throttle, I feel an invisible hand pressing down on me. I feel like I'm part of the road, like I'm connected to the earth by something more than just the rubber of my tires.

L-Twins

Many people might argue that the L-twin engine design is really the same as a V-twin, and they would have a good argument. The L-twin is just a V-twin with the angle between the cylinders opened up to 90 degrees, so that the engine resembles an "L" rather than a "V."

The reason I broke this design out wasn't because I think it's a separate engine design; I did it because the L-twin is generally used in a different type of motorcycle. With a few exceptions, the V-twin engine tends to be used in large motorcycles designed for relaxed types of riding. The Italian companies Aprilia and Moto Guzzi make V-twin sport bikes in very low volume, as does the Austrian company KTM, and Honda and Suzuki have produced a number of V-twin sport bikes over the years, but for the most part V-twin engines power big touring bikes and cruisers.

That doesn't mean the V-twin engine doesn't have potential as a high-performance engine. For decades Ducati has built V-twin engines that have been winning world racing championships. But Ducati uses a 90-degree angle in its V-twin engines, with one cylinder laying flat, almost parallel to the ground, and the other almost upright, tilted back only slightly, so many people refer to these as L-twins.

Parallel Twins

Another early type of multi-cylinder engine was the parallel twin. This is an engine with its two pistons arranged side by side. The British company Triumph popularized this engine design. In 1937 Edward Turner developed the Speed Twin for Triumph basically by grafting two Triumph single-cylinder engines together in a side-by-side fashion. He was far from the first to build this type of engine, but Turner's 500-cc Speed Twin was the first commercially successful mass-produced British multi-cylinder motorcycle, and the basic design has defined the British motorcycle to this day.

When John Bloor resurrected the bankrupt Triumph in the late 1980s, he was determined to build modern, cutting-edge motorcycles rather than retro throwback twin-cylinder machines, but after more than a decade he finally relented, and in the early 2000s the company once again began building traditional parallel-twin motorcycles. Today Triumph's retro-styled twins are among its most popular machines.

There aren't a lot of parallel twins on the market today, but those that are available are decent, practical motorcycles. In addition to the Triumphs just mentioned, Kawasaki makes several mid-displacement parallel twins.

Opposed Twins, Fours, and Sixes

Another type of twin-cylinder engine that's been around almost as long as the motorcycle itself is the opposed twin. This is a two-cylinder engine with pistons that move outward, directly opposite from each other. Since a Harley has a 45-degree V-twin engine, a Ducati a 90-degree V-twin engine (an L-twin), you could almost think of the opposed twin as a V-twin with a 180-degree angle between the V, but if you follow that logic, you could consider a parallel twin a V-twin with a 360-degree angle (or a zero-degree angle, if you don't want to take the long way around), but this is, of course, nonsense.

Anyway, in an opposed twin, the pistons move outward, away from each other, then inward, toward each other. Early on someone figured this motion resembled the arms of a boxer, but any boxer who boxed with a motion like this would get his ass kicked regularly and severely. Regardless, the name stuck and opposed engines are called "boxers." Volkswagen used a boxer-type engine in its old air-cooled Beetles, and Porsche and Subaru continue to use boxer engines in their cars.

The boxer engine had been used in motorcycles for about as long as the V-twin. The design appeared as early as 1904 in what eventually became the Douglas motorcycle, and Harley developed the Model W Sport Twin, which featured an opposed-twin engine, in 1919, but it was Max Friz's use of the design in his R32, BMW's first motorcycle, produced in 1923, that made the engine design iconic. BMW continues to build motorcycles powered by opposed twins to this day, and it will probably continue to do so as long as motorcycles are still being built.

Even though BMW had a great deal of success with opposed-twin engines, no other manufacturer has mass-produced a motorcycle with such an engine since the end of World War II. It wasn't until Honda introduced its Gold Wing in 1975 that any major manufacturer built a motorcycle with a boxer-type engine, and Honda's version was a four cylinder rather than a twin. In 1988 Honda added two more cylinders to create the six-cylinder Gold Wing 1500. Then in 2001, Honda bumped displacement to 1832 cc.

Today BMW's R-series twins and Honda's GL1800 Gold Wing are the only bikes that use boxer engines, but these are extremely popular bikes and there are a lot of them on the road. This might be a relatively unusual engine design—and Gold Wings and BMWs are also expensive machines—but they are also some of the best and most-popular long-distance bikes you can buy. As I said earlier, for me it's important to buy motorcycles built by American companies, but you, like a lot of motorcyclists, might have different priorities; if you ride long enough and far enough, there's a good chance you could end up owning a bike with an opposed engine someday.

Inline Triples

Think of an inline three-cylinder engine as a parallel twin with one more cylinder tacked on. Inline triples have been used sporadically throughout the years. Right now the only company mass-producing inline triples is Triumph. The company builds a variety of triples ranging from 675-cc middleweights to the gigantic 2300-cc Rocket Three line. These are generally highly regarded bikes. Their three-cylinder engines do a good job of combining the low-end torque of twin-cylinder engines with the top-end rush of engines with more cylinders. Triumph has a long history with three-cylinder engines, dating to the 1960s.

Outside of Triumphs, you won't find a lot of triples to choose from. Some Italian companies may or may not build them, but that's the nature of an Italian motorcycle company. The Italians design some of the best motorcycles available, but when it comes down to actually building them, they seem to lose interest. As a result, Italian motorcycle companies are almost always in some state of receivership, what we'd call "bankruptcy" in the United States.

Because of this, I suggest staying away from Italian motorcycles. Period. You may be tempted by their beautiful styling or their high performance, but if you succumb to temptation and buy one, consider yourself warned, because you will, without exception, have all kinds of problems with your bike, ranging from untraceable electrical problems to camshafts that disintegrate within ten thousand miles.

This is in part because of communication problems in Italian motorcycle factories. Most of the managers in Italians factories are Italians who speak Italian, while most of the workers have emigrated from Africa or the Middle East and speak other languages. In other words, the workers don't understand a word their bosses are saying. As a result, bikes are shipped with huge problems. For example, a batch of camshafts won't have the proper heat treatment on the cam lobe surfaces, or an entire production run of bikes will be shipped with the wrong central processing units (CPUs) in their fuel-injection computers.

A big part of the problem is Italy's socialist government. This is not a book about politics, but the Italian motorcycle industry is an example of politics manifesting themselves in your motorcycle riding experience, so I think it deserves a mention here. In Italy, labor laws have been heavily influenced by the Communist Party. As a result, it's almost impossible to fire someone, regardless of how poorly that person performs. Thus, people tend to rise to their level of incompetence and stay stuck in that position until they retire.

Ultimately you end up with factories filled with incompetent craftsmen who build bikes with unreliable camshafts and incorrect ignition systems. In the early 2000s Italy hired Professor Marco Biagi to propose reforms to the country's labor laws that were intended to make Italy more competitive in world markets, but in March 2002, the Red Brigade, a radical Communist faction, had the professor killed, thus ensuring that Italy would continue building unreliable motorcycles for the foreseeable future.

Professor Biagi's tragic fate illustrates the immense barriers to reform. As a result, we're unlikely to see, in our lifetime, Italian industry adopt sensible labor laws—or produce reliable motorcycles. Until that happens, you are advised to stay away from anything Italian that has electrical parts. If you must buy Italian, it's best to stick to their guns and shoes, both of which still seem to be fairly reliable.

Inline Fours

In the 1960s Harley and Triumph continued to build motorcycles that still featured the technology they'd introduced in the 1930s, primarily because they could get away with it. They had virtually no competition in the heavyweight motorcycle market, so they had little reason to spend the money needed to update their products.

But if they had been paying attention, they would have realized that the lack of competition was an illusion; they had plenty of competition, and almost all of it was coming from Japan. When Honda began exporting motorcycles to the United States in 1959, its early bikes were little 50-cc step-through machines that resembled nothing so much as an old-fashioned girl's bicycle. These were soon followed by larger motorcycles with parallel-twin engines, but the biggest of these displaced just 305 cc; none of these engines were considered direct competitors with Triumph's 650-cc parallel twins and Harley's 900-cc and 1200-cc V-twins.

When Honda introduced its first "big" bike, the Black Bomber, a sporty 450-cc parallel twin, it should have sounded like a shot across the bow of the American and British motorcycle industries. Sure, it was only a 450-cc bike, but it could outrun the bigger British twins and could even give the mighty 900-cc Sportster a run for its money. And the Japanese had no intention of stopping there.

The British sort of got with the program. Triumph and BSA began developing three-cylinder motorcycles, but they more or less backed into the program with little enthusiasm. The resulting motorcycles, introduced in 1969, were half-assed at best, weak responses to the next bomb Japan was about to drop on the motorcycling world: the Honda CB750.

The CB750 had all the attributes that people had grown to associate with Honda: modern design (the CB750 featured an all-aluminum engine with an overhead camshaft), convenience (the CB750 featured an electric starter that worked every time the owner punched a button), and reliability—you could ride this bike from coast to coast without doing anything other than oiling and tightening the chain. But the most amazing aspect of the bike was its number of cylinders: four of them, all placed transversely in a row across the frame, like two side-by-side parallel twins.

There had been four-cylinder bikes in the past. In the early years Henderson and other companies had built motorcycles with longitudinal four cylinders—that is, the four cylinders were placed end to end, leading to a very long, awkward motorcycle. Because of this, and also because of their complexity, which made early fours even more unreliable than early twins and singles, the longitudinal four was never very popular. In the 1960s the Italian company MV Agusta built a relatively modern 600-cc transverse four, but in true Italian fashion it imported only twenty or thirty of its four-cylinder bikes into the U.S. market over the course of a dozen or so years. Odds are you'll never see one of these except on the pages of a magazine.

Honda was the opposite of an Italian company; whereas there were very few Italian motorcycle dealers in the United States in the 1960s and 1970s, by 1969 there was a Honda dealership in just about every town with more than a thousand people living in it. Unlike exotic Italian motorcycles, Honda's CB750 was everywhere, virtually overnight. And unlike the earlier 450 twin, which could almost keep up with the Sportster, Harley's fastest motorcycle at the time, the new 750 four, beat the Sportster like the Sportster owed it money. Harley responded by boring the Sportster out to 1000 cc, but this only made the marginally unreliable Sportster extremely unreliable. As a response to the CB750, the upsized Sportster was beyond pathetic.

The Japanese were far from done having their way with the rest of the world's motorcycle manufacturers. Honda's CB750 dominated the heavyweight motorcycle market for three years, driving more nails in the British motorcycle industry's coffin. Then in 1972 Kawasaki introduced the Z1, a 903-cc four cylinder with not one but two overhead camshafts. Not only could the Kawasaki smoke every British and American motorcycle (and also the CB750), it could hand the fastest cars their asses.

Soon all the Japanese manufacturers were producing motorcycles with bigger and faster inline four-cylinder engines. The engine design became so common that motorcycles with inline fours were called UJMs (universal Japanese motorcycles).

It's not hard to see why they became so popular. In 1973 a rider could plunk down $1,900 for a brand-new Z1 (hundreds of dollars less than a comparable Harley) and ride off with the fastest machine available to the general public. As a result, Kawasaki sold about 85,000 Z1s in 1973, while Harley sold just 9,875 XL 1000s (in 1973 Harley dropped the "Sportster" name and didn't reinstate it until the late 1970s). This trend would continue well into the next decade, nearly bankrupting Harley-Davidson in the process.

V-Fours
The last common type of motorcycle engine is the V-four. Honda introduced the modern V-four in the 1980s and now has two bikes available with the engine design: the ST1300 sport-tourer (we'll get into types of motorcycles in the next chapter) and the Interceptor, an 800-cc sport-tourer. Think of the V-four as an automotive V-eight sliced in half.

This design has advantages in packaging because it crams four cylinders into a unit that doesn't take up much more space than your average V-twin, but it's expensive to produce because it has a lot more individual parts than an inline four. Because of high production costs not many manufacturers build V-four production bikes today. Yamaha puts V-fours in a few of its Star-series cruisers, and Aprilia recently released a V-four sport bike, but the design has never caught on like the inline four and the V-twin.

FINAL DRIVE ASSEMBLY

WE'VE SPENT A LOT of time discussing engine designs, which makes sense since without motors we'd just have bicycles, but the rest of the parts are almost as important. For example, without a final drive assembly connecting the engine to the rear wheel, the motor would just be a noisemaking device.

Power can be transferred from the transmission to the rear wheel by three main methods: belt, chain, and shaft. The earliest motorcycles used a smooth leather belt to transmit power from a pulley coming straight off the engine's crankshaft to the rear wheel. Rather than a clutch and gear set, the transmission consisted of an idler pulley that put tension on the belt. This idler pulley was disengaged with a lever, a crude system that made harnessing the 2–3 horsepower that the early motorcycle engines put out a lot more exciting than you might imagine.

By the time I started riding, belts had long been abandoned in favor of chain final drive systems in which a metal chain ran from a sprocket on the output shaft on the transmission to another sprocket attached to the rear wheel hub. This system is still used on many bikes today.

Although most U.S. motorcycle builders progressed from belt final drive to chain final drive, a lot of European manufacturers developed shaft final drive systems. These systems don't require the periodic maintenance that chain systems require, such as tightening of the chain and constant lubrication, but they are heavy and add a lot of weight to the bike.

They also have a tendency to jack the bike up under acceleration. This unsettles the chassis and has a negative impact on handling. Some manufacturers like BMW and Moto Guzzi have developed complex rear suspension designs that help minimize this tendency, but these designs bring on a new set of problems. BMW in particular has had a lot of trouble with the failure of the articulating joints it puts in its drive shafts to help control the up-and-down jacking inherent in a shaft rear-drive system.

Harley-Davidson brought back the belt concept in the early 1980s, using a toothed rubber belt on toothed sprockets in place of the chain. The system runs as smoothly as a chain system, and a quarter of a century of use has proven it to be as reliable and easy to maintain as a shaft system. It was a great idea, as evidenced by the fact that today many other manufacturers use belt final drive systems on their motorcycles, including Victory, Yamaha, and BMW.

ELECTRICAL SYSTEMS

THE OTHER MAIN PARTS of a motorcycle are its frame, electrical system, transmission, and rider controls and accommodations. The frame, that part that holds the whole thing together, is made either of steel tubes or aluminum beams. In the old days we had to worry about the engine shaking frame welds and joints loose, but today's frames are so sturdy that this has become another forget-about-it part.

There are a few exceptions—for example, in the late 1990s Suzuki built the TL1000, a V-twin sport bike that developed a reputation for breaking frames—but as long as you're not regularly popping wheelies or doing gigantic stoppies (hitting the brakes so hard you raise your back wheel in the air), you're most likely not going to have to worry about problems with your motorcycle's frame.

In the old days the electrical systems of our motorcycles were constant sources of problems. One of the improvements the Japanese brought to the motorcycle industry was the concept of reliable electrical systems. These reliable electrics in turn made electric starters a practical proposition, which is what made it possible for so many new riders to get into the sport of motorcycling. This is especially true for women; it took a hefty leg to kick-start those old V-twin Harleys. The British never did quite get the hang of reliable electrical systems and electric-starters, which was still another nail in the British motorcycle industry's coffin, but Harley did make huge improvements and today's big Harley V-twins all have functional electric starters.

With maybe the exception of the Italian motorcycles, which still seem to have lots of electrical problems, most bikes sold today have reliable electrical systems and this shouldn't be something you have to worry about unless you hook up too many electrical accessories like heated seats, grips, vests, or driving lights. You will have to keep your battery charged, but this isn't that hard to do. If you ride every day, your battery should last for years. Even if your bike sits for weeks at a time, you can hook up a trickle charger that will keep your battery charged while waiting for you to go for a ride.

TRANSMISSIONS

MODERN TRANSMISSIONS ARE ANOTHER part of the motorcycle that don't warrant a lot of owner attention. With the exception of some Yamaha models, most modern motorcycle transmissions are as reliable as most automotive transmissions (I'll discuss Yamaha's past transmission problems in the section on buying used motorcycles).

Most motorcycles use six-speed or five-speed manual transmissions. A few bikes use automatic transmissions, but these are still controversial and haven't been widely accepted. The odds are one thousand to one that you'll end up with a manually shifted motorcycle with a hand-operated clutch and a foot-operated shifter. If you're used to automatic transmissions in your car, don't worry—shifting a motorcycle is a lot easier than it sounds. I'll discuss that in the section on operating your motorcycle.

SADDLES

OTHER THAN THE ENGINE, which dictates the character of a motorcycle, the system that will most affect you as a rider will be the controls and accommodations. When you start riding, you might not realize what kinds of seats, seating positions, and control arrangements best suit your body because you'll be so focused on mastering your riding skills that you won't give comfort much thought. As your riding skills develop, however, and you start to put longer and longer days in the saddle, comfort will become a much higher priority. Nothing takes the fun out of a long day of riding like an uncomfortable seat.

You might guess that the saddle is the single most important factor in being comfortable, and in a way it is—if your butt is burning, the rest of you is going to be damned uncomfortable, too. Most stock saddles are garbage, designed to provide the lowest possible manufacturing cost rather than maximum comfort. There are quality aftermarket saddles available from a variety of sources that will keep you comfortable for many hours after the stock saddle has given up all hope of supporting your ass. In my experience, Corbin makes the best seat available—I've ridden on them for almost twenty years.

WIND PROTECTION

THE SADDLE IS THE most obvious item that contributes to your comfort on a bike, but wind protection plays a big part, too. A lot of people like riding on motorcycles without fairings (the plastic bodywork that protects the rider from the wind) or windshields, and you might, too, but I like to have some wind protection. I switched to touring bikes with full weather protection in 1983. I had to start using fairings at that time because I had throat cancer and after a laryngectomy (surgery that left me breathing through a hole in my neck) the wind shear made it impossible for me to breathe, but I'm glad I switched to touring bikes. I feel a lot less tired after a long day in the saddle when I've been on a bike with a windshield or fairing.

I prefer a tall windshield, but some people don't like having to look through them. People who wear full-face helmets sometimes don't mind the wind flowing past their heads, as long as it doesn't knock their heads around. They consider a well-designed windshield or a fairing one they can look over, and not through, one that directs a clean, nonturbulent flow of air over and around their helmets. Klock Werks makes a windshield called the Flare for Harley baggers (touring motorcycles with saddlebags) that does a great job of smoothing out the airflow.

RIDING POSITION

When you start riding, you'll probably be more concerned with how you look on your bike than how you feel on it. I don't really give two shits about how you look on your bike. Ape hangers (a tall handlebar that makes you reach for the sky to put your hands on the controls) might look cool, but they put a lot of pressure on your lower back and turn you into a giant sail to catch the wind.

The same goes for forward-mounted foot controls; you may look cool as ice leaned back in your saddle, your feet kicked way out in front of you like you were sitting in your La-Z-Boy recliner, but you'll be using your lower back to fight the wind the entire time you're on the road.

The sad fact is that most of us aren't that pretty to start with. I know I'm not. The way I see it, most of us are never going to look like movie stars on our bikes, no matter how uncomfortable we make ourselves; we might as well be comfortable.

Motorcycles are a lot more complex than they might seem at first glance, but you really need to keep only the following few things in mind.

What You Should Know

- The engine gives the motorcycle its character.
- Horsepower might win races, but on the street torque is king.
- The more comfortable your bike, the more you enjoy riding.

CHAPTER TWO

TYPES OF BIKES
What to Ride

My goal is to make you a lifelong motorcyclist. You'll need to do a lot more than just buy a $20,000 Harley—you'll need to devote yourself to not only learning to ride, but also learning to appreciate the ride. You'll know you've become a serious motorcyclist when you don't ride just because your buddies are taking their bikes out together; you ride because you can't wait to feel the freedom of the open road. Hell, you won't ride because you want to ride; you'll ride because you *need* to ride.

To get to that point, you need to rack up many miles in the saddle, and having a comfortable motorcycle makes putting in those hours a lot more fun. This is something you should keep in mind from the very beginning, when you first start thinking about getting a motorcycle. There's a lot more to being comfortable on your bike than just saddles, handlebars, and windshields. The type of bike you choose will go a long way to determining how at ease you become on your bike.

If you're just starting out, it's easy to be confused by all the different kinds of motorcycles on the market. And even if you've been riding awhile, you may have picked a bike that's not the right bike for you, and now you're stuck with a machine that doesn't meet your needs.

When it comes to picking a bike, in the end it boils down to what you like. You need guts to ride the bikes you like the best. You should decide what's important to you and then pick the best bike that meets your requirements. Don't choose a motorcycle to impress other people; choose one that impresses you. *Don't worry about what other people think.* Instead, decide what bike's best for you, then get out there and have fun on it.

I pick my bikes based on my own priorities. As I've mentioned, it's important to me to ride an American bike. I have always ridden American, which is why I stuck with Harley-Davidson until Victory's bikes came along. I feel that way about everything. I ride an American-bred quarter horse, and I drive an American pickup (a Chevy). I grew up during World War II and was taught to buy *only* American.

It hasn't always been easy to ride American. I've never liked Harleys much—I've always considered them to be the bottom of the technology pile—but I rode Harleys for fifty-two years because they were the best American bikes. Today I ride a Victory Vision because I think that's the finest bike America makes. There are so many good motorcycles to pick from today that it's hard to judge them all, but I've ridden enough to know that my Victory stacks up well against any of them.

In this section I'm going to help you figure out what's important to you when it comes to your bike. We're going to look at the types of motorcycles out there and examine the advantages and the disadvantages of each. We're going to talk about the comfort, controllability, reliability, and convenience of each type of bike.

Once you understand all of this, you might find that the bike you intially thought you wanted is actually the wrong bike for you. You may think you want a big bagger but you might not be aware of the challenges of riding a bike that's physically too large for you to ride smoothly and controllably. And you might not be aware of the costs associated with a bagger. For instance, it'll cost you more to mount new tires on an Electra Glide or Gold Wing than you'll spend on maintenance in an entire year for a Sportster. And it costs a lot more to change tires on a crotch rocket than on a dual-sport machine. Once you know what types of motorcycles are out there, you'll be better able to understand the costs associated with each.

When I first started riding, there wasn't much variety from which to choose. One bike more or less served every purpose. You could buy a single-cylinder British bike like a BSA Gold Star and do everything with it, from commuting to racing. If you wanted to ride it off-road, you took off the lights and fenders and put on a set of dirt tires. With that setup, you could use it for trail riding, dirt-track racing, or hare scrambles, which are cross-country races. If you wanted to road race it, you could get a racing fairing, mount a set of road tires, and presto! You had a competitive road racer. And if you wanted to travel across the country, you just threw on a set of saddlebags and were set to hit the road. Beginning in the 1960s, motorcycles began to get more specialized. This trend has continued to the point that today many motorcycles are so narrowly focused they're only really good for doing one thing.

ON-ROAD VERSUS OFF-ROAD

PROBABLY THE MOST BASIC division between types of motorcycles is on-road versus off-road. I picked those categories instead of "dirt" versus "street" because by "off-road" I mean any motorcycle you can't license for use on public highways; this includes all racing motorcycles, whether those motorcycles are meant for racing on dirt or pavement. This book is a street-survival guide, and we're going to focus on motorcycles you can legally ride on the street.

Racing motorcycles, whether dirt bikes or road racers, are the most highly specialized motorcycles of all, and riding them requires specialized training and skills. Lots of good books and training schools are available for anyone interested in racing motorcycles, so we're not going to get into that here. We'll discuss riding on gravel and dirt roads when we get to riding techniques, and even talk about some mild trail riding, but it will be the type of riding you might be able to do on a street bike or a street-legal dual-purpose motorcycle.

The requirements for licensing a motorcycle to legally ride on the street vary from state to state, but the minimum requirements for a motorcycle to be street legal are usually that it has a functioning headlight, a taillight, a brake light, and often a horn. Most states also require turn signals on newer models.

That doesn't mean you can just take a race bike or a dirt bike, wire up some lights, and go get a license plate. Likewise you might run into problems if you try to license a custom-built motorcycle, or if you've bought a custom-built motorcycle from a builder. Almost every state requires a motorcycle to be manufactured specifically for use on public roads, meaning that it will pass all state and federal department of transportation and emissions requirements. Usually the licensing bureau can tell if your bike is legal just from the serial number.

Some people have figured out how to get license plates on just about anything, but I've never had any reason to do this. I always ride street-legal motorcycles, so I've never looked into what's involved. Besides, licensing a nonconforming motorcycle is illegal just about everywhere, and in some states doing so will even land you in jail.

I've got people from various law-enforcement agencies watching my every move so I can't get away with anything. The last thing I need is to end up in jail because I broke the law to get a license plate for a Harley XR750 dirt-tracker or some one-off chopper that doesn't meet state and federal regulations. The feds would probably say it was a larger conspiracy and charge me with racketeering. If you want to do this, that's your business, but you'll need to seek advice from someone else.

ANTIQUE MOTORCYCLES

You'll also have to learn about antique motorcycles elsewhere. This book is a guide for people who want to become hard-core motorcyclists, riders who want to get out on the road and put some serious miles under their butts. For that you're going to need a reliable modern motorcycle that doesn't break down or need extraordinary maintenance. That rules out antique or custom motorcycles.

Antique motorcycles have old parts that are often worn out and hard (or even impossible) to replace when they break out on the road. They just don't make this stuff anymore. This was true even before these bikes became antiques; back in the 1950s when we rode motorcycles built in the 1940s, it was nearly impossible to find replacement parts. Even if the antique motorcycle has been perfectly restored, you'll still be relying on an outdated electrical system. Most antique engines either use undependable six-volt systems or they have total-loss magneto systems, neither of which is conducive to having a motorcycle that starts every time you need it to start.

There is something kind of cool about kick-starting an old motorcycle. It requires skill to get an old bike running, but take it from me—it's a lot of work. Having a motorcycle that starts every time you push a button on your handlebar is very convenient. If a bike has a kick-starter, it's almost certainly an antique and is best suited for sitting in someone's collection, and not for getting you where you need to go.

Old bikes might be cool, but everything about modern motorcycles is better than old bikes, from a practical standpoint. Even the basic material from which manufacturers make engines has improved over time. Now engines are made out of aluminum instead of cast iron because aluminum cools better and thus doesn't wear out as fast.

Still, antique motorcycles are great to look at in shows. It's fun to see how motorcycle technology developed, and for some of us old-timers it's nostalgic to see the types of bikes we used to ride. But when it comes to getting from one place to the other safely and reliably, I wouldn't want to go back to the old days. Give me the most functional, reliable modern motorcycle available. Unless you are a wizard mechanic who can overhaul your bike by the side of the road with nothing but an adjustable wrench and a Zippo lighter, you're better off avoiding "classic" bikes as your main source of transportation.

CHOPPERS AND BOBBERS

I ALSO RECOMMEND STAYING away from custom motorcycles when you're starting out, for the same reason you should avoid antiques: they are complete pains in the ass to own and ride. Custom motorcycles are bikes that have been modified or even built from scratch. The most common are choppers and bobbers.

When I first started riding, if you said the word *motorcycle* in the United States, the first thing that came to mind was a big, heavy Harley-Davidson. At the time these were the best bikes available for comfortable highway riding, but a lot of us wanted more performance than a stock Harley was capable of delivering. We didn't have much money to buy parts to make the engines faster, and even if we did, such parts weren't easy to come by. We couldn't just go online, order whatever we wanted, and have it shipped across the country. More often than not if we wanted a specific part, we had to figure out a way to make it ourselves.

A cheaper and easier way to make our bikes faster was to take parts off and make them lighter. That didn't cost any money at all, so most of us younger guys chopped parts off to create stripped-down hot-rod bikes. We'd take off fenders, extra lights, any bodywork that wasn't absolutely necessary, and pretty much anything else that didn't contribute to making the bike faster. Some guys even took off the brakes!

We never really had a name for the bikes we customized. According to the stories you read in the press, people called this type of bike a "bobber" or a "bob job," because some people called taking off parts "bobbing" back then. They're still called "bobbers" today, but I think names like "bobber" and "chopper" came from the motorcycle industry and not the people out there customizing bikes. They probably figured it would be easier to sell us junk if they gave it a catchy name.

By the time the industry types started calling our custom bikes "choppers," we'd begun to focus more on style. This happened during a wild time in our country's history. A lot of craziness was happening, and we were young and a little wild ourselves. Our bikes reflected that. People started chopping and re-welding frames to increase the rake of the bike (the angle at which the fork extends away from the frame). They also made forks longer and handlebars higher. Every year people made their forks longer, their handlebars higher, and their rakes more extreme until it got so out of control that the bikes became just about impossible to ride.

Throughout all this insanity I kept my bikes pretty functional. I did some stuff that I now realize was probably crazy, like removing the front brakes and extending the front forks, though never by more than four inches. I also took the rocker-arm clutch pedal and cut it in half, turned it upside down, and made a suicide clutch out of it. With no front brake and a suicide clutch, I had to hit neutral at every stop. That's not the safest way to stop.

I never changed the rake on any of my bikes; a radically raked front end is one of the main characteristics of a chopper. Then, as now, I liked to ride more than anything. I like to move hard and fast, which is not what choppers are meant to do. Engineers spend years developing the best angle for a bike's rake, which largely determines how a bike handles. In the 1940s Harley tried a different rake on its bike each year, looking for the perfect angle, but the company never quite nailed it because the Harleys of the 1940s and even 1950s needed steering dampers to prevent high-speed wobbles. I don't think Harley really got it right until the 1960s, when it was able to do away with the steering damper.

If it took Harley decades to find the perfect angle for the rake of its bikes, I don't expect that I'd be able to improve a bike much by spending an afternoon cutting and welding my frame to get a different rake. I'm not an engineer, but neither are all the other people experimenting with the rakes on their custom bikes. As a result of all this backyard engineering, virtually every radically raked custom bike built during the 1960s and 1970s was unsafe to ride.

I've talked to custom bike builders today who claim that they've figured out the right measurements to make a radically raked custom bike safe to ride, and I imagine that they're a lot safer than earlier examples, but I have a hard time believing that these builders can make a bike handle as well as the engineers who design frames using decades of research on motorcycle handling.

Arlen Ness, the king of the customs, may be an exception. Arlen has been a very good friend of mine for over fifty years and probably knows as much about engineering a motorcycle chassis as anyone at any motorcycle-manufacturing company. His bikes handle better than any other custom I've ever ridden (and better than a lot of factory bikes), but I still ride a mostly stock motorcycle. When it comes to motorcycle riding, I have enough to worry about without having a bike that is trying to kill me because of its poorly engineered chassis. I want my motorcycle to be safe; just "safer" doesn't quite cut it.

Choppers and bobbers may look cool, but they're better to look at than they are to ride. Some people claim that their custom bikes are reliable, but I've been riding a long time with a lot of people, many of whom ride choppers and bobbers, and in my experience these types of bikes are anything but reliable. They're homemade bikes, and as such they're prone to all sorts of oddball failures that you never encounter on a well-engineered, mass-produced motorcycle.

The welds on homemade gas and oil tanks seldom seem to stand up to the constant shaking of V-twin engines, and custom bikes spring leaks with such regularity that you can almost count on this happening if you ride any farther than the local bar or café. Their electrical systems are usually homemade, too, and unless the guy who did the wiring was a certified genius, these bikes are more likely to short out and leave you stranded than they are to run reliably. In Arizona during April (when we have our annual bike week), almost every bike you see broken down on the side of the road is a custom that someone thought was reliable enough to ride a lot of miles. They thought wrong.

Even if these bikes were reliable enough to use for everyday transportation, they're too uncomfortable to ride for more than half-hour to forty-five-minute stretches. The riding position is designed to make you look cool rather than to make you comfortable. As a result, homemade bikes place you in the worst possible riding position for long days in the saddle.

After just a few hours, parts of you that you didn't even know you had will hurt. Your joints will hurt, your internal organs will hurt, and your muscles will feel like you've just spent an afternoon being pummeled by a boxer. Some people are into this, but then some people are into pouring hot wax on their privates. To each his own, I suppose, but pain doesn't do much for me.

Choppers are more uncomfortable than bobbers because a proper bobber will put you in a slight forward lean, taking a little pressure off your lower back. It will handle better, too, because a bobber doesn't have the long, kicked-out fork that a chopper has. Because of its traditionally shorter fork and relatively conservative rake, a bobber turns a lot tighter than does a long chopper. Even so, a bobber is still a homemade bike and as likely to suffer breakdowns and failures as any other homemade bike. Unless you're a skilled mechanic and have the patience to spend as much time working on your bike as you do riding it, I'd leave the custom bobbers and choppers to the Hollywood types who can afford to have a mechanic following them around with a complete set of tools and a spare bike.

MANAGING YOUR MACHINE

THE TYPE OF BIKE you choose for your first motorcycle could determine how well you're ever going to learn to ride. If you start out on a motorcycle that doesn't allow you to completely control it, it will control you. You'll develop bad habits for the rest of your riding career. Take, for example, my habit of putting a motorcycle in neutral when I come to a stop, even though I know this is an unsafe practice. I developed this habit early on and I can't shake it. If you develop enough of these bad habits when you first start riding, you won't control your own motorcycle. Instead, you'll be at its mercy.

The most important thing to look for in your first motorcycle is manageability. The biggest mistake people make when buying their first bike is to purchase a bike that's physically too big or too powerful for them to manage. Riding well is all about being in control of your machine, and when you start out with too much motorcycle, you'll never master it.

You'll want to get a ride that is small enough to control, but picking a first bike isn't as simple as getting the smallest motorcycle you can find. When I traded my first real bike, the 45-cubic-inch Indian Scout I mentioned earlier, for a Harley, I wanted to get a 45-cubic-inch Harley, but a friend talked me into getting a larger 61-cubic-inch Harley. It took a little practice to get used to the bigger bike, but after a few rides, when I was comfortable with it, I was thankful I hadn't gotten the smaller machine.

You shouldn't get a 1,000-pound bagger or a 1400-cc crotch rocket that can hit 200 miles per hour, but you also won't want an underpowered machine that isn't capable of keeping up with traffic or a motorcycle that's physically too small for you. You'll want a bike that is small enough for you to control, but one that is big enough for you to ride comfortably and has enough power so that you won't get bored with it too soon.

How small a motorcycle you need depends on how big you are. I have a friend named Tiny who's one big motorcycle rider. What constitutes a small motorcycle for him is a whole lot different from what constitutes a small motorcycle for a woman who stands five feet tall and weighs eighty pounds soaking wet.

When I started riding, there weren't a lot of options for beginner motorcycles. If you had a lot of money, you bought a Mustang, which was a very cool little minibike styled to look like a full-sized motorcycle. There were a few other options for a kid with too much money, but not many. Back then Harley made some small bikes based on a 125-cc two-stroke engine from German maker DKW. Harley got the tooling for that engine as part of Germany's wartime reparation. In 1948 Harley put the little two-stroke engine into the Model S, a fun little bike with a girder-type front suspension, rigid rear, and a little "peanut" tank that later turned up on the XLCH Sportster. A lot of kids must have had the $325 that Harley charged for the Model S because the company sold more than ten thousand of the little two-stroke machines.

If you didn't have a lot of money, you did what I did and bought a Cushman scooter. I was just a kid, about thirteen or fourteen years old, when I got my Cushman. At that time you could get a Cushman for $25 to $50. That was a lot of money for a kid like me, making just $7 per week working at a part-time job. I worked a lot of hours to earn the $25 I needed to buy the Cushman, but I didn't really have a choice because I knew I had to ride, even in my early teens.

HOW SMALL IS TOO SMALL?

Generally speaking, you should probably consider buying a 400-cc or larger motorcycle, even as your first bike. Some of the Japanese companies make street-legal motorcycles that are as small as 125 cc, but even if these bikes are capable of hitting a safe freeway speed, they'll likely be running at or near redline to do so. A 250-cc bike might hit 70 or even 80 miles per hour, but at that speed the engine will be revving so high that running at freeway speeds for an extended period will quickly wear out both the rider and the bike. That same bike might cruise comfortably at 60 miles per hour and be able to hold that speed all day long, but consider that traffic on metropolitan freeways often moves at 70 or 75 miles per hour, even when the posted limit is 55 or 65.

Although it might be technically illegal to ride at speeds five to ten miles per hour higher than the posted speed limit, it can be dangerous not to do so. Study after study has shown that what causes accidents is not speed itself, but rather disparities in speed. If you are moving at a different speed from the other vehicles on the road, whether you are going faster or slower, you are at much greater risk of having an accident than if you travel at the same speed as the other traffic, within reason. It might seem obvious that if you ride much faster than the other vehicles on the road you are at greater risk, but a less obvious fact is that you are at a much greater risk if you ride slower than other vehicles.

Think of traffic as a flowing stream of water. If the water is flowing unimpeded, its movement is almost invisible, but if you put an impediment like a rock or log in the stream, the moving water starts swirling in all kinds of chaotic directions. When you ride slower than the surrounding traffic is moving, you become that impediment, and the drivers swerving around you will continuously create potentially life-threatening situations for the duration of the trip.

RISING FATALITIES

IN RECENT YEARS, UNFORTUNATELY, there's been a tremendous increase in the number of motorcycle fatalities. In 2008 motorcycle fatalities increased for the eleventh year in a row. A lot of reasons account for this, notably the fact that in 2008 motorcycle registrations also increased for the eleventh year in a row. More motorcycles on the road mean more accidents. But that's not the whole story.

I blame at least part of the increase in motorcycle fatalities to the rise in cell-phone use. Recent studies have shown that drivers yapping on their cell phones are impaired even more than they would be if they were drunk. This means bikers have to concentrate even harder to prevent accidents. I always tell new riders, "It doesn't matter who is at fault in a collision with a car because you are the one who will get hurt."

Sometimes preventing accidents is impossible, but

some ways of preventing wrecks are in our control. For example, you always should avoid riding while drinking alcohol; even if you've just had a beer or two and don't feel like you have a buzz, your reaction times are slowed down enough to put you in danger. We can control whether or not we ride at the same speed as traffic, at least if our bikes are fast enough to keep up with the rest of the vehicles on the road. How fast that is depends on the road. If you live in a western state with lots of open space, traffic moves a lot faster than it does in the congested and heavily patrolled urban areas in the East. If you live in New Jersey or New York City, you might never need to go more than 70 miles per hour, but if you live in Aspen, Colorado, you may find traffic moving at 90 miles per hour on the freeway into Denver.

If you never leave a congested urban area and never ride on a freeway, you might be able to get by with a 250, but then you won't have the option of leaving town or using the freeway when you need to, and sooner or later that will happen. Even a 400- or a 450-cc motorcycle might be too small to be a practical bike for most people. Your best bet is to get a bike that's at least 500 cc to 650 cc to start. If you're a larger person, you might even consider something as big as a 1200 or 1300 for your first bike.

SPECIFIC TYPES OF MOTORCYCLES

As I mentioned earlier, motorcycles have evolved into highly specialized machines. Instead of that one BSA Gold Star that could do everything, we now have a wide variety of styles of motorcycles from which to choose, each one focused on doing just one thing well. The trick is to decide what you need your bike to do and select the type that best meets your needs.

The main types of street-legal motorcycles include the following:

- Dual Sport
- Supermotard
- Cruiser
- Touring Bike
- Sport-Tourer
- Sport Bike
- Standard

The first specialized motorcycles were purpose-built race bikes. Companies like Harley-Davidson and Indian engineered bikes purely for racing purposes even before World War I, but since race bikes have always been non-street-legal machines, we won't go into them here. Besides, purebred racing bikes weren't available to the general public then, and they're still hard to find (and very expensive).

Dual Sports

Off-road motorcycles were the first specialized bikes that were widely available. These began to show up in the 1960s. At first they were just street bikes with long-travel suspension and high pipes, but they became increasingly specialized and competition ready. Today you can buy a bike that's ready to go motocross racing right off the showroom floor. Again, these were (and are) purely racing machines, but as they grew in popularity, manufacturers began to offer dual-purpose motorcycles that had some of the characteristics of these off-road racers in street-legal packages. Back when they first appeared, these were called "enduros," named after a type of mild off-road racing that was popular at the time. Today these are commonly called "dual sports."

Dual sports are usually dirt bikes that have been modified with lighting and emissions equipment that make them street legal. While dual sports are heavier than their dirt-only counterparts because of their additional equipment, they retain varying degrees of off-road capabilities. The most extreme examples—like the dual sports from KTM, Husqvarna, and some of the other European manufacturers—really are dirt bikes with headlights and oversized mufflers. They retain most of the off-road capabilities of their dirt-bike brethren.

Part of the reason dirt bikes perform well on dirt is because they have extremely long travel suspensions. A street-bike suspension only has to face potholes and the occasional road debris; in the worst instances, a street-bike shock or fork seldom has to compress more than a few inches. Dirt bikes have to cope with much greater impacts. Motocross and supercross racing has evolved into an extended series of high jumps, with the bikes flying twenty to thirty feet in the air; their shocks and forks compress a foot or more when the bikes land, so they need a lot more travel.

The extreme dual sports, the ones that are practically ready for off-road racing straight off the dealer floors, also have long-travel suspensions. This is great if you plan to do double and triple jumps with your motorcycle, but the drawback is that it makes the bikes ridiculously tall. Try climbing up on a KTM dual sport in a showroom sometime; just make sure you have someone beside you to catch you if you fall, because you'll be lucky if even the tips of your toes touch the showroom floor.

The extreme dual sports also have many of the same other drawbacks as dirt bikes, right down to the vinyl-covered fender protectors that pass for seats. Since dirt-bike racers usually stand when they ride, the seat, such as it is, exists mainly as a pad to keep the rider from bumping his or her ass on the fender. It was never designed as a place to sit. These dirt-bikes-with-lights are okay if you plan to do serious off-road riding, but they aren't great choices for practical street bikes.

The extreme examples aren't very useful for anyone but an off-road racer who has to ride his or her bike from trail to trail on public roads, but the bulk of dual-sport machines available today do make pretty good choices for first bikes, provided your legs are long enough to ride them comfortably—although they aren't as tall as the extreme versions, they're still tall enough to pose a problem for a lot of riders. Just throwing a leg over one can be a challenge if your inseam is less than thirty-two inches. Sitting that high gives you a commanding view of traffic, but if the seat is so high that you can't hold up the bike securely at a stoplight, the height can become a safety issue. I once had a vertically challenged rider fall onto me when he dropped his tall dual sport at a stoplight. He couldn't get his foot down securely and went tumbling over, almost taking me with him.

More reasonable dual sports usually range in size from 400 cc to 650 cc, and these have more than enough power to keep up with traffic. They are light, maneuverable, and generally inexpensive to buy, operate, and insure. Plus they're relatively simple so you can do most of the maintenance yourself if you have any mechanical experience at all; and if you do need to hire someone to work on them for you, the costs will be a lot less than for other types of bikes. Most of them have little or no bodywork that needs to be removed to change oil and tires or adjust valves, and because they only have one cylinder, they only have one set of valves to adjust. Since they have spoked wheels, most of them still use tube-type tires, making the repair of a flat tire a relatively inexpensive proposition, too.

If you have any interest in driving off the beaten path, if you don't mind not having the fastest and fanciest motorcycle around, and, most important, if your legs are long enough to safely ride a dual sport, then this type of bike might be right for you.

Supermotards

Supermotard bikes were developed for supermoto racing. This is a type of racing that is usually done in parking lots and can encompass sections of track that are both paved and dirt. The bikes themselves are usually created by taking dirt bikes and fitting them with street suspension and street tires. They look like dirt bikes with road-racing tires mounted on them.

Supermotards can be a lot of fun for an experienced rider, but only for short bursts of hooligan-type behavior. If you like to do wheelies and stoppies or big, smoky tire slides, few bikes do these things better than a supermotard.

But if you're looking for a practical all-around motorcycle, you'd do well to look at something other than supermotard bikes, because they are basically dirt bikes for the street, which means they're extremely uncomfortable to ride for any distance at all, mostly because they have dirt-bike-style seats. Add to this the fact that supermotards are generally expensive, costing as much or more than many full-sized motorcycles, and you can see why this type of bike is less than ideal for a beginner.

Cruisers

You'll most likely end up with a "cruiser," as the magazines call them. This is an odd name for a poorly defined style of motorcycle. The cruiser came into existence as a response to the custom bobbers and choppers we built in the 1950s and 1960s.

Up until roughly 1970 Harley only built two main types of big bikes: the XL Sportster and the FL Electra Glide. The Sportster was a hot rod back then, a lightweight high-performance bike. Remember, this was before Kawasaki started the Japanese horsepower wars with its 900-cc Z1 and right around the time Honda released its 750 four cylinder. Harley's other main line consisted of the big FL Electra Glide models. These were enormous 74-cubic-inch

(1200-cc) motorcycles loaded down with touring accessories. Most people considered these old men's motorcycles; we called them "garbage wagons" because of all the touring equipment on them.

Today I ride a full-dress motorcycle—you think differently when you are seventy than you did when you were eighteen—but we were young then. Because we young guys generally didn't want to ride around on the same types of bikes that our fathers and grandfathers rode, a lot of us customized our motorcycles. Some of us built full-on choppers and bobbers, but others just rearranged the basic material we already had available. Some guys rode stock Sportsters, but most of us preferred the smoother-running and more-reliable FL platform. Still, a lot of people wanted the cut-down look of the Sportster, so they got rid of the big, heavy Electra Glide fork with its chrome-plated steel covers and mounted the sleek, light fork from the Sportster.

The people running Harley-Davidson noticed what riders were doing to the machines they built and decided to cash in on it by offering a bike from the factory that resembled the machines people were building at home. In 1971 the Motor Company grafted a Sportster fork on an Electra Glide frame and created the Super Glide, an entirely new kind of motorcycle. I got my first Super Glide in 1972, and got my first Low Rider in 1977, after I got out of prison. It was great to have a bike that looked good right from the factory, but that didn't stop us from modifying them even more. Most of my modifications during these years were to improve a bike's performance. For example, I'd take the hydraulic disc brakes from Japanese bikes and mount them on a Harley.

The Super Glide caused a stir, and it wasn't long before other companies like Norton, Triumph, and then the Japanese companies—Yamaha, Honda, Kawasaki, and Suzuki—started offering bikes with similar style. People didn't know what to call this new type of bike, exactly. For a long time the magazines called them "customs," and later they started identifying them as "cruisers," which is the term most of the trade press still uses today. Some European magazines call them "soft choppers," which sounds even more foolish than "cruisers," so I guess we shouldn't complain.

For the most part, cruisers make good motorcycles for beginners. They are relatively light, compared with full-boat touring bikes. At the same time they are full-sized motorcycles with plenty of room for a rider and a passenger. Though they can sometimes put your arms and legs in awkward positions, cruisers are generally comfortable enough for the long haul, especially when fitted with good saddles and windshields. Plus most of them have tractable engines that help newer riders develop smooth throttle control.

Cruisers usually cost more than dual sports, but for most normal-sized people who do the vast majority of their riding on paved roads, they are more practical. You can get cruisers as small as 250 cc, but the smallest you should probably consider for a first bike is Kawasaki's 500-cc Vulcan. If you're a big person, or if you have some riding experience, you might consider getting something as large as the 100-cubic-inch (1634-cc) Victory Vegas. Some of the Japanese companies make cruisers that range up to 2000 cc, and Triumph makes one that displaces 2300 cc, but even a lot of experienced riders find bikes that displace more than 1700 cc to 1800 cc clumsy to ride.

If you're just starting out, you're better off getting a lighter, more manageable bike in the 500-cc to 1300-cc range. You can find a lot of nice cruiser-type motorcycles in this range, including Triumph's 865-cc America and Harley's Sportster line.

Touring Bikes

Unless you're an experienced rider, you'll want to stay away from the type of bike I ride, and have ridden for the past twenty-five-plus years: a touring bike. As I noted earlier, touring bikes—especially Harley-Davidsons—are often called baggers because one of their defining characteristics is the presence of saddlebags. On most touring bikes these are panniers mounted as a pair, one on each side of the rear wheel. Most often these will be made of some sort of plastic or fiberglass, but a lot of cruiser-based touring bikes have saddlebags made of leather or vinyl. The other features you'll usually find on touring bikes are fairings or windshields, comfortable saddles, and often some type of tail trunk. Most of the high-end touring bikes have all sorts of electronic gadgets, like stereos, CB radios, cruise control, and even heated seats and handgrips.

I have heated grips and a heated seat on my Victory Vision, but the feature I like best is the six-gallon gas tank, which lets me ride 200 to 250 miles without stopping to refuel. This lets me pile on lots of miles each day.

Telling you not to start out with a touring bike may sound like do-as-I-say-not-as-I-do type of advice, but touring bikes are extremely large motorcycles and a rider should have at least a few years under his or her belt before taking on one of these beasts. Victory claims a dry weight of 804 pounds for my Vision.

A lot of touring bikes are as heavy as or even heavier than my Vision. Honda's Gold Wing weighs 925 pounds wet, Harley's Electra Glide Ultra Classic weighs 890 pounds wet, and Kawasaki's Vulcan 2000 Classic weights 884 pounds wet. If you aren't an experienced rider, keeping these big bikes under control will require so much work on your part that you'll never develop proper riding skills. Once you've been riding awhile, a touring bike will likely be the most practical motorcycle you can buy; but earn your chops as a rider and develop good riding skills before jumping into one.

Just because your ride isn't classified as a touring bike doesn't mean you can't travel distances on your motorcycle. Any bike can be used for touring. In fact, when set up with windshields, saddlebags, and comfortable saddles, middleweight cruisers make great touring bikes. You won't be able to bring everything you own with you on a trip with your middleweight cruiser, but most people bring far too much junk with them when they travel, anyway (having lots of luggage capacity on a bike just encourages people to bring too much stuff). You should be able to get everything you need for any trip, no matter how long, into a couple of saddlebags and maybe a tank bag and a tailpack.

Sport-Tourers

Another category of touring bike is the sport-tourer. Like the cruiser category, this one is a little tough to define. Sometimes things get grouped together not because they are anything in particular, but because they are something that others are not. That's about as good a description of a sport-tourer as you'll find.

This type of bike can range from enormous machines like Honda's ST1300, which weighs 730 pounds wet, to a small motorcycle like the MZ Skorpion Traveller, a German bike built in the 1990s and early 2000s that is claimed to weigh in at 416 pounds dry. The only common characteristic among sport-tourers is usually just a set of hard saddlebags; other than that, they can come in just about any size and engine configuration imaginable.

The basic idea behind a sport-touring bike is that it combines the handling and performance of a sport bike with the comfort and convenience of a touring bike. BMW created the mold for this type of motorcycle. Until the late 1990s when it got into the business of building heavyweight touring bikes, just about every motorcycle the German company ever built could be considered a sport-touring bike. Even the company's GS-series bikes, which were classified as dual sports, were really more sport-touring type motorcycles.

Harley-Davidson was one of the first companies besides BMW to build a motorcycle that fit the German sport-touring mold. In 1983 Harley introduced the FXRT. In a lot of ways, this was an advanced motorcycle, at least for Harley. It had a rubber-mounted engine, five-speed transmission, sporty wind-tunnel-designed fairing, and a decent pair of hard saddlebags. Unfortunately it still had the old cast-iron Shovelhead engine. Most of the bugs had been worked out of the Shovelhead by that time, but it still used technology that the rest of the world had abandoned twenty years earlier.

In 1984 the FXRT used an Evolution motor—no more Shovelhead. When I saw my first Evo-powered FXRT, I got rid of the Shovelhead I was riding at the time and bought the FXRT. It might not have been the best motorcycle made, but at the time I considered it the best Harley. I rode FXRTs until 2000, when I switched to Road Kings.

Later in the 1980s Kawasaki introduced the first real Japanese sport-tourer, the Concours, and not long after Honda introduced its idea of a sport-tourer, the ST1100. These were good motorcycles; if they had been built by an American company, I might have bought one myself. I remember when I saw my first ST1100 in the early 1990s. I loved the look of that sleek, black machine. (I still love the look of the current 1300-cc version.)

Then other European companies like Triumph, Ducati, Moto Guzzi, and Aprilia started building sport-tourers. Today pretty much every motorcycle company still in business builds some kind of sport-tourer. Some might even argue that my Vision is a sport-tourer, though it's a little too big to qualify in my opinion. Even many of the bikes that are small enough to qualify as sport-tourers are too big for a newer rider to manage. They tend to be tall, with a lot of bodywork and luggage carried up high. This increases cornering clearance, allowing them to lean way over in fast corners, but it also makes them top-heavy and thus clumsy to manage at slower speeds. Cruisers carry their weight lower to the ground, making them feel less like they are about to tip over at low speeds. Because of this, a cruiser that weighs more than a sport-tourer can actually feel lighter.

Another disadvantage of sport-tourers, at least for newer riders, is that they are covered with expensive bodywork that can break if the bike tips over. The sad fact is that when you are learning to ride, you will most likely have a minor tip over or two. I can't remember my first tip over, but I've had a few. I'd like to say I haven't tipped my current bike, but shit happens. Even though my Vision has a lot of bodywork, it's well designed, with stop plates underneath that are the only parts that come into contact with the ground and hold the bike at a forty-five-degree angle in the event of a low-speed tip over. Most bikes with plastic bodywork hit the ground plastic first, which can get expensive. It seems the designers at Victory understand that motorcycles inevitably fall over. If you ride long enough, you will fall down; hopefully it will only happen when you are going slowly.

Even with all the plastic bodywork, a midsized sport-tourer can make a good choice for a newer rider, especially a newer rider who's fairly tall—just make sure you carry good insurance. If that's the type of bike you like, you'll find that most midsized sport-tourers are practical, comfortable, and versatile motorcycles.

Sport Bikes

Back in the 1950s and 1960s Americans weren't the only people modifying their motorcycles; Europeans were doing the same thing, only they had a different aim in mind when they started customizing their bikes. Compared with America's long stretches of straight, wide-open highways, Europe is much more condensed, with narrow, twisting streets, crowded high-speed freeways, and winding mountain passes. Americans need bikes that are stable in a crosswind on an open road, so we tend to go for motorcycles that are long and low; Europeans have to dodge fast-moving traffic on streets that often are older than the oldest American city.

The different needs of American riders and European riders go back so far that you can see them reflected in the types of saddles used on horses. American-style saddles put the rider in a roomy, stretched-out, upright position; European-style saddles had the rider leaning forward in a racer-type crouch, his or her legs tucked up behind.

When the Europeans, particularly the Brits, started modifying their motorcycles, instead of building long, low, stretched-out choppers, they copied European horse riding: low-mounted handlebars, footpegs set high and back, and cut-down saddles. This put the rider into a forward-leaning racer-type riding position. The Brits called this kind of custom a "café racer," because their riders often raced from one café to another.

This style of motorcycle was slow to catch on in the United States. Throughout the 1960s and 1970s most European and Japanese manufacturers equipped bikes sold in Europe with low handlebars and rearset footpegs, whereas bikes shipped to the U.S. market featured lower, forward-mounted footpegs and higher handlebars, which were often called "western-style" bars, because they had a sort of cowboylike look to them.

BMW brought the R90S, a café racer with a small fairing—more of a headlight shroud, since it didn't do much to protect the rider from the elements—to the U.S. market in 1973. Harley followed suit with the XLCR Sportster ("XL" is Harley's designation for the Sportster engine, and "CR" stood for "café racer") in 1977, but its model wasn't very successful and was the last sport-type motorcycle to wear the Harley brand until the recently introduced XR1200. Other than an oddball European bike imported into the country in extremely small quantities, café racers were thinly represented in the United States in the 1970s.

That was about to change, thanks in large part to the development of superbike racing. By the mid-1970s road-racing motorcycles had become so specialized that they literally no longer shared a single part with their road-going counterparts. At that time most road bikes were powered by large-displacement four-stroke engines while road-racing bikes were powered almost exclusively by purpose-built two-stroke mid-displacement engines.

Historically motorcycle racing had been something that an average motorcyclist could do. Back in the early days most clubs formed around racing; early clubs like the Boozefighters focused as much on racing as they did on raising hell. Remember, this was a time when you'd ride one motorcycle to work every day, then race that same bike on the weekend. But by the 1970s a person who wanted to race competitively had to buy a purpose-built race bike that cost half a year's salary, if you had a good job. Racing had changed from something that anyone with a motorcycle could do into an elite activity.

At just about the time that two strokes completely took over the top levels of racing, an alternative form of racing based on production bikes started to gain popularity. This happened when the Japanese introduced their big, powerful four-cylinder machines. Magazines called these "superbikes," so the production class in which these motorcycles raced became known as the "superbike" class.

Production-based classes reinvigorated the sport of motorcycle racing at a grassroots level. In the early days of superbike racing, anyone with $2,500 could walk into one of the thousands of Kawasaki or Suzuki shops that could be found in any small town and buy a production bike capable of being built into a competitive racer. Within a few years thousands of people were competing in club races all across the United States. Due to the popularity of this type of racing, manufacturers began offering sportier and sportier motorcycles. Racers liked these bikes because it was less work (and less expense) to convert them into race bikes, but a lot of nonracers bought them, too, just because they liked the style of the bikes.

At first these bikes differed little from the standard bikes of the day. They had lower handlebars, maybe a small café-racer fairing, or at least a set of footpegs moved back a few inches from the standard position. But as superbike racing grew in popularity, the manufacturers got into the sport with factory-supported teams, which meant they started making production bikes with specifications that approached those of full-on race bikes. This is how we got the first factory crotch rockets, the Honda Interceptors, Kawasaki Ninjas, Yamaha FZRs, and Suzuki GSX-Rs.

These bikes became more and more capable, until they reached a point where it was virtually impossible (and completely insane) for riders to come anywhere near reaching their limits on public roads. Today's crotch rockets are more potent than the pure racing bikes of a generation ago.

High-performance sport bikes are poor choices for beginners. Any of the 600-cc class sport bikes qualifies as one of the highest-performance machines you can buy of any type; probably only Formula 1 race cars generate more power per cubic inch than the engines in 600-cc sport bikes. But as mentioned in the last chapter, sport bikes don't generate much torque. Because of this they are difficult for a newer rider to ride smoothly in traffic.

In fact, I don't recommend anyone use modern sport bikes for daily transportation on public roads. I dislike telling people what they should and shouldn't ride, and if you want to ride a crotch rocket, you have the freedom to do so—sport bikes are popular and a lot of people use them for everyday transportation without any problems. But that said, I believe this type of motorcycle is best left to the racetrack. It's great fun to get out on a track and put your knees down on the pavement in high-speed corners, but out on the street that type of riding will just get you killed, and probably sooner rather than later. And when you're riding on this type of bike, you'll be tempted to ride it like you stole it every time you throw your leg over the saddle.

Even if you have the self-restraint needed to keep from exploring your motorcycle's limits on public roads, sport bikes are excruciatingly uncomfortable to ride. The racer crouch is ideal when you're on a track, throwing yourself from side to side, putting your knee down in the corners, and accelerating hard in the straights, but for the rest of the time, riding laid out over the gas tank puts a lot of strain on your body.

Sport bikes are especially bad in stop-and-go traffic, where you have to crane your neck back so far to see what's going on around you that your head is likely to stick in that position. Unless you're extremely young (and I mean young, like so young your fontanel has barely hardened over), if you put serious miles on a sport bike, you'd better keep a chiropractor on your payroll.

Standards

In 1980 most of the motorcycles you could buy were still basic do-it-all type machines, much like the BSA

Gold Star had been thirty years earlier. Most companies built a basic type of motorcycle and only modified it slightly for different uses. To make a cruiser, a
company would take its basic bike, add a pull-back
handlebar and a stepped saddle (the magazines called
them "buckhorn" bars and "king-queen" saddles back
then), and give it a coat of black paint. The same bike
might get a square headlight and a square plastic rear
fender cover, maybe a fork brace or an oil cooler, and
that would be sold as the sport-bike version.

The only companies making touring bikes at
that time were Harley-Davidson and BMW. The
Japanese manufacturers began to offer touring and
racing accessories, but these amounted to tinkering
around at the margins; the basic motorcycle underneath remained more or less the same. But everything changed during the 1980s. Cruisers evolved
into carbon copies of Harley-Davidson motorcycles,
complete with V-twin engines; touring bikes sprouted
barn-door-sized fairing and enough luggage capacity
to carry the entire belongings of a small third-world
village; and sport bikes developed full racing fairings,
complete with uncomfortable racer positions. At the
beginning of the decade you could count the number
of bikes made with any sort of fairing on one hand;
by the end of the decade the only bikes that didn't
have plastic fairings were the Harley-style cruisers.

As the 1990s rolled around, it seemed like no
one was building an ordinary, all-around motorcycle
anymore. The manufacturers noticed this and introduced what the motorcycle press called a "new" type
of motorcycle: the standard. In reality, this was just
the rebirth of the regular old all-around motorcycle.

Like "sport-tourer," "standard" is a bit of a garbage category. The only thing that most standards have in common is the lack of a fairing and luggage. Standards range from tiny beginner bikes like the Suzuki TU250 to BMW's wild K1300R, which is a type of standard often called a "street fighter" (street fighters are standards in that they have no bodywork but have the guts of high-performance sport bikes).

Though some of the high-performance street fighters might be a handful for newer riders to control, generally speaking, standards make good choices for first bikes. They tend to have comfortable riding positions and tractable engines, and like most cruisers, they don't have expensive bodywork to break when you inevitably drop your bike.

What You Should Know

- Don't worry about what everyone else thinks; pick the bike you like.
- Custom choppers and antique bikes might look cool, but they aren't practical to use as transportation.
- The less bodywork you have on a bike, the less it costs if you tip over, which is an important consideration for newer riders.

CHAPTER THREE

THE FUNDAMENTALS OF RIDING

You may think the next logical step would be to buy a bike. After all, how can you learn to ride if you don't have a bike? For most of the time I've been riding, the answer was that you couldn't learn to ride unless you had a bike, but over the past twenty or so years that's changed, thanks to the Motorcycle Safety Foundation. Originally formed in 1973, the MSF started out as a trade organization that promoted motorcycle manufacturers as much as it furthered safety. In some ways it still is that; its current sponsors are BMW, Ducati, Harley-Davidson, Honda, Kawasaki, KTM, Piaggio/Vespa, Suzuki, Triumph, Victory, and Yamaha, and ultimately the MSF serves those companies.

But early on the major bike companies figured

out that one of the best ways the MSF could serve them was by helping to keep as many of their customers alive as possible. You'd be hard-pressed to find an organization that has done more to promote motorcycle safety than the MSF, not just in the past thirty-some years since it was founded, but ever. Back in the early years of the MSF, motorcycle fatalities were on the rise, and they had been for the previous decade. In 1980 motorcycle-related fatalities in the United States peaked at 5,144 deaths. That same year the MSF sponsored the first International Motorcycle Safety Conference. This marked the beginning of serious research into the causes of motorcycle-related deaths. The following year the government published *Motorcycle Accident Cause Factors and Identification of Countermeasures,* which is usually referred to as the "Hurt Report," in honor of its primary author Harry Hurt.

Among its findings, the Hurt Report noted that 92 percent of riders involved in accidents lacked any formal motorcycle training; they were either self-taught, or they'd learned from family and friends. Apparently the riders' friends had passed on their own bad habits, because the report noted: "Motorcycle riders in these accidents showed significant collision avoidance problems. Most riders would overbrake and skid their rear wheel, and underbrake the front wheel, greatly reducing collision avoidance deceleration. The ability to countersteer and swerve was essentially absent."

Clearly someone needed to develop a formal motorcycle training course, but there was no obvious organization to handle that job. You might think the government would step in, but it seems that motorcycle riders are a low priority for most elected officials. The Hurt Report did nothing to light a fire under the government's collective ass to start developing and funding rider training programs.

Thankfully, the MSF stepped up and did what all levels of government were unable to do: develop a rider training program. The MSF's RiderCourse made its debut in California in 1987. Within a few years it had spread across the country. Not only do all states offer MSF RiderCourses, but the majority of them use some form of the RiderCourse curriculum in their licensing tests. Many states allow completion of the course itself to fulfill the riding skills portion of the licensing exam—complete the RiderCourse, get your motorcycle endorsement.

One of the best aspects of the RiderCourse is that in most states the program provides the motorcycles you'll use to complete the course (and often earn your motorcycle license). That means that you can learn to ride without even buying a bike, which is why I put this chapter on learning to ride before the chapter on buying a motorcycle. Many of the programs that offer the courses even provide protective gear, which will save you hundreds or even thousands of dollars. Taking a RiderCourse is the best way to find out if you even like riding a motorcycle before you spend a small fortune buying a bike and all the associated gear.

I'm going to provide you with the basics of motorcycle riding in the following pages, but first I'm going to give you the single most important piece of advice in this entire book—*complete the MSF RiderCourse.*

And if you're already an experienced motorcyclist who hasn't taken the basic RiderCourse, take one of the advanced training courses. If you're self-taught, or if you learned to ride from a friend or family member, chances are you've developed some bad habits over the years. Riding is an extremely high-risk activity and even if those bad habits haven't caused you problems so far, sooner or later your luck will run out. It's best to rely on luck as little as possible; one of the best ways to do that is to get formal training. It's the most important thing you can do to avoid getting maimed or killed. I advise you to use what I write here to help familiarize yourself with the operation of a motorcycle to help you pass the MSF RiderCourse.

THE SIX BASIC CONTROLS

OPERATING A MOTORCYCLE IS a complex activity. You'll need to use both of your hands and both of your feet to operate the controls, and you'll often be using all of them at the same time. Remember, you'll also need to use your feet to hold yourself up when the bike is stopped. Believe it or not, I've seen people forget this and fall over at a stop.

You'll have to master six basic controls to ride most motorcycles. For the first twenty or so years I rode motorcycles, manufacturers used different layouts for these main controls. I only rode Harleys, but even though all the bikes I rode were built by the same manufacturer, the location of the brakes, shifters, and clutches varied from model to model and from year to year. Having to relearn the controls each time you bought a new bike annoyed the hell out of us, and it could even be dangerous at times, but for the 1975 model year the U.S. government passed a law standardizing the location of many of those controls. Since the U.S. motorcycle market was the most important one for most manufacturers, virtually all of them adopted the layout specified by U.S. law.

The main controls on a motorcycle are as follows:

- **Throttle:** On a motorcycle the throttle is a twist grip that controls your speed, located on the right end of the handlebar.
- **Front brake lever:** This is a lever that controls the front brake, mounted on the right side of the handlebar, in front of the throttle.
- **Rear brake lever:** This is a lever that operates the rear brake, located near the right footpeg.
- **Clutch lever:** This is a lever that operates the clutch, located on the left side of the handlebar, in front of the left handgrip.
- **Shift lever:** This is a lever that shifts gears in the transmission, located near the left footpeg.
- **Handlebar:** Anyone who's ridden a bicycle knows what this is.

SECONDARY CONTROLS

IN ADDITION TO THESE six primary controls, you'll have to operate a variety of secondary controls when you're riding on public roads. The locations of these aren't as standardized as are the locations for the primary controls, but the vast majority of motorcycle manufacturers use the same basic layout. Secondary controls include the following:

- **Ignition switch.** This can be found in all sorts of odd places, from up by the instruments, to the top of the tank, to below the seat. This operates much like the switch in a car, except that it doesn't actually start the bike, as it does in most cars. For that you'll need to use . . .
- **The electric start button.** This button, which engages the electric starting motor, is usually found on the right handgrip.
- **The choke or enrichment circuit.** This is a lever, usually on the left handgrip, that engages a choke on carbureted bikes or an enrichment or fast-idle circuit on fuel-injected bikes. Up until just a few years ago all bikes had these, but as motorcycle fuel-injection technology advances, more and more bikes skip this control.
- **Engine kill switch.** This is an emergency shut-off switch for the engine. I rarely if ever find the need to use this.
- **Turn signals.** Like cars, all modern street bikes have turn signals. The location and method of operation used for these varies a bit among some manufacturers—particularly Harley-Davidson and BMW—but on most bikes the control consists of a switch on the left handgrip that you push left to engage the left turn signal, push right to engage the right turn signal, and push straight in to turn off the signals. Unlike

all modern cars, many bikes don't have self-canceling turn signals, so you'll need to remember to shut these off or you'll be riding down the road with your signal flashing. In addition to being embarrassing, this can be dangerous.

- **Horn.** This is a button located on one of the handgrips—usually the left—that activates your motorcycle's horn. Many people are afraid to use their horns because they think it's rude, but it's not nearly as rude as getting mangled by a car. If other drivers don't see you, don't worry about being rude; use your horn to let them know you're there. It could save your life.

- **Headlight dimmer switch.** This works the same as the dimmer switch in your car. I don't use this much because I always leave my headlight on high beam during the day, when I do most of my riding.

- **Speedometer.** This indicates your speed, just as it does in your car. Unlike cars, which usually feature analog speedometers, a lot of motorcycles use digital speedometers.

- **Tachometer.** This indicates your engine rpm, again just as it does in your car. Because almost all motorcycles use manual transmissions, these are much more useful on motorcycles than they are in cars, which mostly use automatic transmissions.

PRERIDE INSPECTION

MOTORCYCLES HAVE COME A long way since I started riding, but they still require more care and maintenance than cars. Even if a motorcycle was as reliable as a car, you'd still want to be extra diligent about making sure everything was in working order because the consequences of a system failing are much more extreme on a bike.

The MSF Experienced RiderCourse, which I have taken, teaches the following preride inspection technique, called "T-CLOCK":

- T: Tires and wheels
- C: Controls
- L: Lights and electrics
- O: Oil and fluids
- C: Chassis and chain
- K: Kickstand

I'll be honest; I check these items fairly regularly, but I don't check each one every time I ride. Some items I do check, if not daily, almost every day. If I rode a bike with a chain, I'd check that every day, but I don't: my bike uses a belt, which requires very little maintenance. I also check my tires and wheels every time I ride. I look them over to make certain they're not damaged or low on air. I'll visually inspect them to make sure they haven't picked up any nails or glass, but I only check the air pressure once every two or three days unless I suspect one of them might have a leak.

Similarly I don't check my oil level every day, at least on my Vision, which doesn't burn a lot of oil. If I'm riding a Harley that I know burns some oil, I'll check it often, sometimes more than once a day if I put on a lot of miles.

I'll check my lights fairly regularly to make certain they're working, especially my taillight and brake light, which I can't see while I'm riding. The consequences of a malfunctioning taillight or brake light may be getting rear-ended by a car, and as you might imagine, that falls under the category of "really bad." It seems like every car driver who has hit a motorcycle has said "I didn't see the motorcycle." Most of the time the real story is that the driver wasn't paying attention, but in my opinion, if your taillight or brake light isn't working, you're as much at fault as the driver who just hit you.

I'm always paying attention to how my controls are working, but I can't say I check these things every time I ride. Controls and cables on modern bikes are far more reliable than they were back when the MSF devised the T-CLOCK method. I do check for loose bolts in the chassis every now and then, but that was a bigger issue when I rode Harley-Davidson motorcycles, which vibrate much more than my Victory does. If you ride a Harley, you'll probably want to check the bolts and nuts on a daily basis.

CHECKING TIRES

THE ONE THING I do consider critical to check frequently is the air pressure in my tires. I've had tires go flat while I was flying down the road. I don't want it to happen again if there's anything I can do to help it. Besides, a motorcycle handles best when the tires are inflated to the proper pressure. Riding with the proper air pressure in your tires also ensures that your tires will last longer. This can save you a lot of money over time.

You'll need to consult your owner's manual to find out the proper pressure for your tires. On the sidewall of your tire you'll find text saying something like: "Maximum Air Pressure 43 PSI." That means that 43 pounds is the maximum air pressure your tire can safely handle, but that doesn't mean that your bike was designed to operate with tires pumped up to 43 PSI. More likely your bike was designed to run in the 34–38 PSI range, and inflating your tires beyond that point will adversely affect handling and also cause your tires to wear out faster.

I always keep a tire pressure gauge in my motorcycle tool kit. I've found that it's difficult to get a gauge on the valve stems on some motorcycles with a lot of luggage and bodywork. The area in which you will be working can be tight, and a long gauge can be difficult to seat properly on the valve stem. I carry a small round gauge with a dial instead of a long one with a stick that pokes out to indicate the air pressure; I find the smaller gauge is easier to maneuver around the tire and wheel.

When you check the air pressure, you should take a few seconds to make sure all the axle bolts and pinch bolts on the fork and shocks are tight. I once was riding with a buddy when the bolts securing the clamps that held his front axle in place came loose. His front wheel fell off and his bike went end over end in the ditch. Amazingly, he seemed all right after the incident, and so we continued on our way to the rally we were attending. But to this day he remembers nothing of that weekend.

COUNTERSTEERING

You NEED TO UNDERSTAND countersteering before you think about starting up your motorcycle. If you've never ridden a motorcycle, you're going to find it's unlike any other vehicle you've ever ridden or driven. You control a motorcycle by leaning into corners rather than turning into them. The closest thing to riding a motorcycle is probably flying an airplane. Like a plane, a motorcycle rotates on a central axis. Imagine a line running through the center of the motorcycle-rider combination. This is the central axis.

To initiate a turn, you countersteer the bike. No subject in motorcycling generates more debate than countersteering, and most of the people doing the arguing don't really understand the principle. Even though they don't understand it, they use it every time they ride. Most of them just don't realize they're doing it.

You countersteer a motorcycle every time you ride at any speed faster than a slow jog. It's the quickest and most efficient way to lean a motorcycle into a turn. It's pretty simple when you get down to the mechanics of it: you press the handlebar on the side in which you want to turn. If you are turning left, press the left handgrip. If you want to go right, press the right handgrip.

This may seem backward, and it would be on a different type of vehicle, like an ATV or a snowmobile. If you press the left handgrip of an ATV it would turn the front wheels to the right, thus causing the ATV to turn right. The same thing happens when you press on the left handgrip of a motorcycle;

this also makes the front wheel move slightly to the right. But unlike a four-wheeled vehicle like an ATV, when the front wheel of a motorcycle moves to the right at any rate above a fast-walking speed, it leans the motorcycle to the left and initiates a turn to the left. Once the motorcycle is leaned over at the correct angle to complete the turn, you release enough pressure for the front tire to fall to the left and the bike goes to the left.

In other words, once you've initiated the lean with countersteering, you steer through a corner as you would any other vehicle—countersteering only gets you leaned into the turn in the first place. The thing is, the turning you do after you're leaned over is so slight that you won't even notice it; you just notice the countersteering pressure needed to initiate the lean in the first place. In fact, you'll probably feel like you're countersteering all the way through the corner.

In some instances you will continue to use countersteering in a corner. If the corner tightens up—if it's what is called a "decreasing radius" corner—you may need to use countersteering to lean the bike over farther so that you turn sharper. This is where understanding countersteering will save your life. If a corner surprises you and gets tighter midcorner, you have two choices: turn sharper and make it through the corner, or run wide and either ride off the road and have a terrible crash or ride into oncoming traffic and initiate a head-on collision, depending on which direction you're going. If you can't sharpen up your turn by countersteering and leaning the motorcycle farther over, the first option won't be available to you.

Larger bikes require more pressure to make the

bike bend into its initial lean. You may feel like you need to pull on the opposite handgrip as well as push on the original handgrip. That's because the larger a bike is, the more pressure it will require to initiate countersteering. This is a good reason to start out with a smaller motorcycle.

CRANKING IT OVER

WHEN YOU FIRST RIDE your new motorcycle, make sure you do so in a safe place where there's not any traffic. I recommend finding an empty parking lot. Even if you have your license, it's still a good idea to familiarize yourself with your new machine in a place where you don't have to worry about other people hurting you so you can concentrate on not hurting yourself.

If your bike has a center stand, place it up on that. A lot of Japanese and European bikes have center stands; unfortunately most American bikes don't have them. I think this is one area where the other countries have us beat, because a center stand is one of the handiest features a bike can have. They make most maintenance jobs a lot easier, and they're much less prone to sinking into the tarmac on hot days.

Center stands are easy to use, provided you use them the right way. The trick is to follow the proper procedure:

I.   First, stand beside the bike, facing it from the left side, and grasp both handlebar grips.

2. When you have a firm grip on the bike, take your right foot and lower the center stand until you feel both its feet resting securely on the ground.

3. While keeping downward pressure on the center stand with your foot, balance the bike by the handlebars so that it rests perfectly upright.

4. There will most likely be some kind of handle down below the rear part of the saddle (some newer bikes will have a retractable handle); grasp the handle. If there's no handle, grab the frame below the saddle.

5. Lock the center stand tang (the metal tab sticking up from the bottom of the center stand) in place with the heel of your boot so that it doesn't slide around. Make certain you have a good bite on it with your boot.

6. Push downward and rearward with your boot while rolling the bike backward with your arms.

As long as you're using your leg to do the actual lifting and just using your upper body to roll the bike backward, the bike should roll right up on the center stand. If you're not lifting with your leg but rather lifting with your arms, you probably won't be able to get the bike up on the center stand. It's easy if you do it right; it's impossible if you do it wrong. It doesn't even matter how big the bike is. If you do it right, it's almost as easy to lift an 1800-cc Gold Wing as it is to lift a 250-cc Rebel. If you do it wrong, you'll have your hands full with the Rebel, and you can forget about the Gold Wing.

If your bike lacks a center stand, straddle the bike (remember, you always get on a motorcycle from the left side because the kickstand is on the left, so it will be leaning that way), hold both handgrips securely, and squeeze both the clutch and the front brake lever. You'll need to hold the clutch lever in to start most motorcycles, and holding the front brake lever in will keep the motorcycle from rolling when you start it.

If you don't have a center stand, you'll have to climb aboard the bike and hold it up yourself. When you're standing securely over the bike with one leg on each side, raise the bike up so that it stands upright. Once you've comfortably balanced the bike, you can rest your weight on the seat. Remember to raise the kickstand up, since many bikes won't run with the kickstand down. Even if a bike doesn't have a circuit that kills the engine if the kickstand is down, you still want to make sure you raise it up because if you ride off with it down it could catch on something and cause you to crash.

Next, turn your ignition key to "on" and make sure the kill switch is not in the "off" position. I've seen more than one person wear out a battery trying to start a bike while the kill switch was in the "off" position.

With your left foot, make sure the bike is in neutral. You will see a green light on the dash that indicates the bike is in neutral, but a word of warning—don't always trust that light. I've ridden many bikes that have a neutral light that will come on when the transmission isn't completely out of gear. I trust my left foot more than I trust my neutral light. I make sure that I can feel the bike is in neutral before

I start it. If you haven't yet developed a good feel for the shifter, release the clutch and brake levers and carefully roll the bike back and forth to see if the rear wheel spins freely. If it does, the bike is in neutral. (Don't forget to squeeze the clutch and front-brake levers again once you've gotten the bike into neutral.)

Once you've determined the bike is in neutral, turn on the choke or fast-idle circuit if your bike is so equipped, especially if the engine is cold. If it's been warmed up, you shouldn't have to bother with this. On a properly tuned modern motorcycle, you should now be able to push the starter button and start the motorcycle with no drama.

If the motorcycle doesn't start immediately, don't hold the starter button down. This will wear down the battery and can flood the engine or even burn out the starter motor. Instead, check for obvious problems. If there is a problem with your electrical system, you'll probably be able to hear the starter motor turning over sluggishly. If your bike is in good running condition with a good charging system, chances are that the problem is something as simple as your having bumped the kill switch into the "off" position. This is very easy to do.

Another possibility is that you may have a bike that needs just a bit of throttle to start properly. This indicates that something is not quite right in your carburetion or fuel-injection system, but the problem might be so minor that you'll never be able to track it down. Usually it's best to just figure out how much throttle you have to give your bike to start it.

This will be tricky, because the bike will likely

just require the slightest pressure on the throttle return spring; anything more than that will flood the engine with gas so that you won't be able to start the bike at all. Developing a feel for dealing with your throttle on start-up is an art, one you'll only be able to perfect with time and practice.

I've actually seen this procedure turned into art—I saw a professional comedian in Reno do a hilarious routine in which he reenacted the process of starting a carbureted Harley-Davidson. The bit lasted half an hour and was one of the funniest things I've ever seen. Fortunately for you, this is a novelty act that isn't performed very often out in the real world, thanks to modern motorcycle technology. As fuel-injection systems get better, this sort of problem is becoming increasingly rare.

ENGAGING THE CLUTCH

CHANGING GEARS WHILE RIDING a motorcycle is similar to driving a car with a manual transmission, except that you use your hands on a bike to do what your feet do in a car, and you use your feet on a bike to do what your hands would do in a car. The clutch works the same in a bike as it does in a car: it disengages the transmission from the engine. You just operate the lever with your hand instead of your foot. When you have the clutch lever pulled in all the way to the handgrip, the transmission is disengaged. As you let the clutch out, the plates in the clutch come into contact with each other and connect the transmission to the crankshaft.

The area in the travel of the clutch lever where the plates start to come into contact with each other is what the MSF calls the "friction zone." As the plates engage, the motorcycle starts to move forward. To find the friction zone, pull the clutch lever toward the handgrip and shift the transmission into first gear. To do this, push the lever down with your foot. Then, with both feet planted firmly on the ground, keep holding down the front brake lever and slowly let out the clutch lever. When the bike starts to move forward, you're in the friction zone. As soon as the bike starts to roll, pull the clutch back in and stop. If you don't, you'll kill the engine because you're still holding the front brake lever. Do this a couple of times to get a feel for where the friction zone begins.

HITTING THE BRAKES

You're just about ready to start your parking lot practice, but before you start riding, you need to make sure you can stop. Stopping will require you to use both of your hands and both of your feet, all at the same time. In one motion you'll pull in the clutch lever with your left hand, let off the throttle, squeeze the front brake lever with your right hand, push down on the rear brake lever with your right foot, and downshift with your left foot. And when it's all over, you'll have to remember to put down your feet to hold up the bike. Again, it's not that different from stopping a car, except that you have one more brake control to deal with and you'll need to hold up the bike once you've stopped.

It's critically important that you use your front brake when stopping. An average motorcycle relies on its front brakes for 70 to 80 percent of its stopping power. Bikes with a more rearward weight distribution, like long cruisers, rely a bit more on their rear brakes, but the front is still the most important. Short wheelbase sport bikes barely rely on their rear brakes at all. In fact, if you watch a motorcycle race, you'll see that the rear wheels of most of the bikes are slightly off the ground as they brake hard for a turn. On a racetrack, you mostly use your rear brake to settle the chassis in a corner; you use it very little, if at all, for stopping duty.

You'll want to develop a good feel for your brakes because good brake control will save your life more than any other skill. The Hurt Report mentioned earlier in this chapter found that not using the front brake and locking up the rear brake was a factor in the majority of fatalities, and recent reports by various state agencies have found that this is still the case.

Motorcycle manufacturers have recognized how deadly this problem is, and some high-end motorcycles now use linked braking systems with valves that direct a percentage of the braking force from the rear brake pedal to the front wheel. This makes it much easier to engage in quick, straight emergency stops, but the technology is generally used only on the most expensive motorcycles, like my Victory Vision, and Honda's Gold Wing. Most likely you'll have to develop your braking skills on a bike that isn't equipped with this technology.

If you lock up the brakes and go into a skid, it will be something of a miracle if you don't crash. If you're lucky, you'll just fall down and slide down the road. If you're not lucky, you'll have a high-side type accident, as discussed earlier.

TAKING OFF

Now THAT YOU'VE GOT a handle on what you need to do to stop and where to find the friction zone of your clutch, you can finally start riding your motorcycle. To get moving, find the friction zone of your clutch once again, only this time you're going to release the clutch lever all the way and move through the friction zone. To do this you'll have to release the front brake, but remember to cover the brake lever with at least two fingers from your right hand so you can grab the brake and stop quickly in an emergency. Covering the brake is a good habit that you should have throughout your riding career.

As you ease out the clutch lever and get into the friction zone, twist the throttle to give the engine just enough gas to start moving smoothly. Too little throttle and you'll stall the engine; too much throttle and you'll spin out and crash or even wheelie over backward, which are both terrible ways to start out your first ride. If at any time you feel you are not in complete control of the bike, pull in the clutch and apply the brakes to stop.

Because almost every motorcycle has a manual transmission, you'll need to shift gears once you get rolling. It works just like in a car—when your engine reaches a certain rpm, you need to shift up a gear to avoid overrevving. When your engine drops below a certain rpm, you need to downshift to avoid stalling the engine. Your goal is to keep your engine in what's known as the "powerband," which is the rpm range in which an engine generates power most efficiently.

Overrevving can cause your engine to blow up in extreme cases, but underrevving an engine can do damage, too. It can lead to detonation, which is when there are tiny explosions inside the engine that can damage components, and it can also cause the buildup of unburned carbon deposits. But the main problem with letting the rpm level drop below the engine's powerband is that when this happens you won't have the ability to accelerate out of danger.

If your brakes are your primary tools for avoiding crashes, the ability to accelerate runs a close second. Sometimes it's better to accelerate out of the way of danger than it is to brake to avoid it. If your engine is running below its efficient powerband and is bogging down, when you twist your throttle, there will be a pause before the engine reacts. If you're trying to get out of the way of a speeding car and this happens, you're probably not going to live very long. It's best to just make sure that your engine is in its powerband at all times so you'll always have the option of accelerating should you need it.

To shift up, roll off the throttle at the same time you squeeze in the clutch lever. When the throttle is fully closed and the clutch disengaged, move the shift lever up with your left toe in a firm, smooth movement until the lever stops. If you hesitate, your shifter might get caught between gears so that when you release the clutch and twist the throttle, your transmission will be in what's called "false neutral" and your engine will just spin without moving you forward. This can be deadly if you are trying to get out of the way of something, or if some jackass is following you too closely on the highway.

To downshift, roll off the throttle and squeeze the clutch. Firmly press down on the shift lever, and then apply a small amount of throttle as you ease out the clutch lever. You do this to match your engine speed to the speed of your rear wheel. If your rear wheel is going faster than your engine is spinning, you'll get wheel hop, which can lead to a dangerous skid.

When coming to a stop, you might shift all the way down to neutral without releasing the clutch, but you'll want to do this gradually because you can damage your motorcycle's transmission by shifting down into too low a gear while you are moving, even with the clutch lever pulled in. This is especially true if your bike's clutch is starting to wear out.

This sounds a lot more complicated than it is. In recent years there's been a trend toward motorcycles with automatic transmissions, but I think this is happening because people think riding a manual-transmission bike will be too complicated. It really isn't. You'll quickly get the hang of it, and once you've got a few miles under your belt, shifting—and everything else associated with riding a motorcycle—will come as naturally to you as breathing.

GEARING UP

BEFORE YOU DO ANY of the preceding activities, you'll need to have proper riding gear. The minimum gear you should always wear when you ride includes the following:

- Helmet
- Riding jacket
- Full-finger gloves
- Long pants
- Over-the-ankle boots

Helmets

A lot of people are surprised when they find out I never ride without a helmet. Like most people my age, I did ride without a helmet for decades. We didn't even have helmets available to us when I started riding, so we never even gave them any thought. Then in 1983 I had throat cancer and had a laryngectomy. After that I didn't have a choice. The air passing over my laryngectomy made it impossible for me to breathe unless I wore a full-face helmet, so I either wore a helmet or I didn't ride. For me that was no choice at all—I started wearing a helmet and using a wind-shield.

Today I'd wear a helmet whether I needed to or not, and not just because they are safe; I find riding is more comfortable and enjoyable with a full-face helmet. It reduces road noise, keeps the wind blasts out of my face, and keeps bugs and other debris out of my eyes.

That said, there's no doubt that wearing a helmet is a lot safer than not wearing a helmet. Harry Hurt, of Hurt Report fame, conducted a long-term study of helmet use for the University of Southern California's Head Protection Research Laboratory and dis-covered that you are five times more likely to suffer a head injury if you crash without a helmet as you would be if you crashed while you were wearing one. Every study conducted since has backed up Hurt's findings.

This doesn't mean that a helmet is some sort of magic totem that will save you in every circumstance. If you get hit by a bus or crash into a guardrail at 80 miles per hour, you'll probably experience so much blunt trauma to your body that you won't survive even if you have a helmet. But for every extreme ex-ample like that there are many cases where a person without a helmet died from hitting his or her head in a minor tip over; had he or she been wearing a helmet, the person would have suffered only minor embarrassment.

Take Indian Larry, the custom bike builder from New York, for example. On Saturday, August 28, 2004, while filming an episode of *Biker Build-Off,* Larry was performing stunts for the crowd. He rode his stunt bike through a wall of flames and topped this off with his signature bike-surfing bit, standing up on the seat, his arms stretched out in a crucifix pose. But something went wrong. His bike was prob-ably going too slow, no more than 30 miles per hour, and the front end began to wobble badly. Instead of leaning forward to grab the handlebars and then sit-ting back down in the saddle, as he might usually do, Larry fell backward off the bike and cracked his skull on the asphalt.

Everyone expected Larry to get back up. When he didn't, friends and the film crew ran to his side. No one could quite believe it was happening. Larry had performed that stunt thousands of times. He knew what he was doing. Had he been wearing a helmet, he would have just been embarrassed on camera, but he wasn't, and on Monday, August 30, Indian Larry died. The guy was a good rider with decades of experience. If it could happen to him, it could happen to any of us.

It doesn't matter to me if you wear a helmet for comfort or wear it for safety. It doesn't matter to me if you don't wear any helmet at all. It's a free country and what you do is your business, not mine. Just know that I think you should wear a full-face helmet. If you don't and crack your skull and kill yourself, don't expect me to feel sorry for you.

If you do the sensible thing and decide to wear a helmet, make sure you get one that is comfortable. If you're like me, you'll practically live in your helmet, so it's worthwhile to spend a little extra money to get one that fits and has good ventilation. The only way you'll know if a helmet fits will be to try it on.

Different helmets fit different-shaped heads. I find that Nolan helmets fit me the best. My coauthor, Darwin, is of Swedish and Norwegian descent. Some people call Swedes "round heads" and Norwegians "square heads." There might be some truth to both stereotypes because he has a hard time finding helmets to fit his misshapen head. He finds that Shoei helmets fit him the best. You'll have to try on a bunch of different helmets to see which brands fit your head shape the best.

As for ventilation, that's tougher to test when trying on helmets in a motorcycle shop. Generally speaking, the more expensive the helmet, the better ventilation it will have. A well-ventilated helmet will flow so much air around your head that when you're riding at anything above a walking speed your head will be cooler with the helmet than without it. Believe it or not, when the temperature hits 110 degrees here in Arizona, wearing a well-ventilated helmet keeps me cooler than I would be if I rode without a helmet. When it comes to quality helmets, you usually get what you pay for.

Riding Jackets and Pants

When I started riding motorcycles, bikers had one option for a riding jacket: black leather. This was fine if you wanted to be Marlon Brando, but for those of us who identified with Chino there weren't a lot of options. That's changed completely now. Today you can get anything from one-piece Gore-Tex riding suits to fully armored mesh pants and jackets. To list all the options and features would take a complete chapter. At the very least you'll want a jacket with built-in armor to protect you in case of a crash.

If you ride a lot, you'll probably need at least two motorcycle jackets—one for warm weather and one for cold weather. Traditional leather jackets still work well for cooler weather, and you can get ventilated leather jackets for riding in warm weather if you like the look of leather.

Otherwise you can buy one of the riding suits from a company like Aerostich. These are the suits you see a lot of serious long-distance riders wearing. They are usually made of water-resistant materials like Gore-Tex, and can either be one-piece overall-type suits or traditional two-piece pants and jackets. These are nice if you commute to work on your motorcycle because you can wear them over your street clothes. The newer mesh riding suits are pretty nice, too. Most have built-in body armor, so they provide at least minimal protection in a crash, and they provide the maximum cooling in hot weather.

The minimum you want for leg protection is a pair of jeans. If you are riding around in shorts, you are a fool. If you crash, even at a low speed, you're going to spend years getting painful skin grafts. Plus you'll look like an idiot. Regular jeans are the bare minimum you should consider for riding motorcycles. Better yet would be a pair of jeans made especially for riding motorcycles, with built-in armor in the knees. Best of all would be leather motorcycle-specific pants, or at least a pair of Gore-Tex or mesh motorcycle pants.

I'll be honest—I've never worn gear with built-in armor, but I've been lucky. My coauthor, Darwin, hasn't been so fortunate—he took a low-speed spill a couple of years ago when he wasn't wearing armor and crushed his knee so severely that he'll walk with a limp for the rest of his life and will eventually need knee-replacement surgery. Armored jeans or riding pants may well have prevented much of the damage.

Boots and Gloves
Always wear a sturdy pair of gloves when riding motorcycles. Ideally you'll want a pair with gauntlets that extend over your wrists because these will pre-

vent bees and other insects and debris from flying up your jacket sleeves while riding down the road. Having an angry hornet stinging your armpit can be a little distracting when you are riding through traffic. Motorcycle-specific gloves will have extra leather on the palms, fingers, and knuckles to provide extra protection in the event of a crash.

You'll also want to wear boots that go up over your ankles. If you see someone riding around in tennis shoes, or worse yet, sandals, you're probably seeing the same fool who wears shorts while riding. I recommend not getting too friendly with an idiot like that because then you'll have to go and visit him or her in the hospital while he or she is getting painful skin grafts.

Good boots serve a variety of purposes on a bike. First off, your feet are an important part of your motorcycle's suspension—after all, it's your legs that are suspending the bike when it's not moving. You want the contact points with the ground (your feet) to be as firm and secure as possible, so make sure your boots have grippy soles. If you go with cowboy boots, make sure they're work-type cowboy boots with rubber soles rather than the fashion-type boots with smooth leather soles, which are as slippery as banana peels. I wear cowboy boots and always make sure to get boots with rubber soles.

Your boots will also protect your feet, and not just in the event of a crash; every time you ride they'll protect your feet from getting burned by the exhaust pipes or getting hit by rocks thrown up by your front wheel.

WHAT YOU SHOULD KNOW

- Countersteering is the only way to get your bike to start turning at speeds faster than a walking pace.
- The front brake provides most of your stopping power; use it.
- Helmets not only protect your head, but they make riding more comfortable.

CHAPTER FOUR

EVALUATING A USED MOTORCYCLE

WHY BUY A USED MOTORCYCLE?

THE MOST COMPELLING REASON to buy a used motorcycle is to save money. Any new motorcycle you buy will be worth much less money the moment you ride it out of a dealership.

For many years Harley-Davidson motorcycles were exceptions to this rule; when Harley built fewer bikes than it could sell each year and their motorcycles were in short supply, you could buy a new bike and turn around and sell it that same day for a profit. But those days are long gone. Once you had to get on a waiting list to buy a Harley, but now the Motor Company builds more bikes than it can sell. As a result, used Harleys are worth less than new ones. If you don't believe me, do a little snooping around the classifieds, Craigslist, or eBay and see what's selling.

In the old days when motorcycles wore out more quickly than they do today, you could make a good argument for not buying used bikes, but that no longer applies. Most motorcycles built today will outlast several owners. Unless you crash, it's pretty hard to wreck a modern motorcycle. Today's bikes will easily run for a hundred thousand or more miles, and most riders seldom put more than four thousand or five thousand miles per year on their bike. At that rate a modern bike should last for twenty or more years, so if you buy a five-year-old motorcycle that's in good shape, you should be set to ride for many years.

There are exceptions, though. Take Harley-Davidsons, again. While some Harleys might run forty thousand to fifty thousand miles without a re-build, most of them are pretty tired by the time they hit the thirty-thousand-mile mark. When the Evolution engine came out in the 1980s, the California Highway Patrol ran their Harleys for thirty thousand miles, rebuilt the top ends of the engines, and then retired the bikes from active duty. They used them for training at the academy for a while before selling them, but they were no longer considered reliable enough for patrol work.

You can plan on rebuilding a Harley four or five times before a Honda wears out. I personally do not believe that any Harley will last longer than fifty to sixty thousand miles without a rebuild, regardless of how well maintained it is. Many Harley dealers won't accept a used Harley on trade if it has more than forty thousand miles on it, which tells me that their assessment of how long the bikes will run between engine rebuilds jibes with mine. On the other hand, at least you *can* rebuild your Harley; when your Honda wears out, it's done. Because of the way most Honda engines are constructed, it will probably cost you four times as much to rebuild a worn-out Honda as it will to buy another used Honda. This is why some people call Japanese motorcycles "disposable."

You'll also want to avoid motorcycles that have been raced or used heavily on racetracks. When I say a modern bike should be good for a hundred thousand or more miles, I'm talking about a hundred thousand street miles. A mile spent on a racetrack takes a lot more out of a bike than a mile spent on the street. If a bike has been raced or used for a lot of track days, all bets are off when it comes to reliability.

Fortunately there are ways to tell if a bike has been raced. If the bike has some sort of aftermarket bodywork on it, there's a good chance that it's been raced, or at least crashed heavily. Or it may have just been owned by some dipstick who fancied himself a racer, but the end result is the same.

A definitive way to see if a bike has been used on a racetrack is to check the axle bolts and the bolts holding on parts like brake calipers, footpegs, and shift and brake levers; if they have holes drilled in them, they've been safety wired. This is a sure sign that the bike has seen heavy track use. If you're buying a track bike to use on the track, then having a bike ready for safety wiring is a good thing, but for anyone buying a street bike for street use, evidence of safety wiring should be a big red flag that this bike has led an extremely hard life.

Although you can generally find good, reliable motorcycles in the used-bike market, the potential to get ripped off is high. The following information should help you negotiate the minefield that is the used-bike market.

A CAUTIONARY NOTE ABOUT RESURRECTING WRECKS

ONE OF THE CHEAPEST ways to buy a bike can be to find one that's been wrecked and rebuild it, but unless you're a seasoned motorcycle restorer, I recommend against this route. If you know what you are doing and enjoy that sort of work, then rebuilding a wrecked bike can be a rewarding process, but for most of us it's a complete pain in the ass.

Even if you have experience, chances are that the end result will be a bike that is never completely reliable. I used to ride with a guy who got all of his bikes this way, and even though he knew what he was doing, his bikes always suffered from niggling little problems.

Most of these resulted from the fact that the bike had sustained more structural damage in its crash than had been apparent when my buddy first examined it. An engine case might have a hairline crack, or a steering head might have been slightly tweaked, or some hidden piece of bent metal might have been wearing a hole in the wiring harness. My friend spent more time hunting down oil leaks and electrical gremlins than he did riding. I finally quit riding with the guy because I got sick of waiting for him while he made roadside repairs.

Trying to save money by rebuilding a wreck can also be an example of what the Brits call "false economy"; in the end you might spend more money trying to fix all the little problems than you would have spent buying a nonwrecked bike in the first place. Even if the damage to the bike is just cosmetic, you'll be shocked when you see how much bodywork and trim pieces for modern motorcycles cost. There are always exceptions to every rule, but generally speaking you'll probably save money by buying the best bike you can afford right from the start.

This brings up another potential hazard of buying used bikes—getting a bike with a salvage title. These are bikes that have been crashed and purchased from the owners by a salvage yard or an insurance company. This means that the motorcycle has been declared a total loss by a state's department of motor vehicles. "Total loss" means that the cost to fix the damage from a wreck would have exceeded the value of the motorcycle.

When a bike has been declared a total loss, any future owner who wants to license the bike has to create a new title for the vehicle, which will be marked as "salvage" by most states' motor vehicle departments. A few states allow the title to be resurrected as "clean" after some kind of inspection, but most states don't. Unless the title is cleaned in one of the few states that still allows this, the motorcycle will always be marked as a salvage-title vehicle.

Sometimes a motorcycle might end up with a salvage title because of superficial cosmetic damage, and the bike will be as good as new with a few new parts, but then again there's a good chance that the motorcycle might have suffered some serious structural damage when it was wrecked, structural damage that might not be readily apparent but will make itself known at the worst possible time, like when you're riding across Utah or Arizona on a 110-degree day.

Even if a bike didn't receive serious structural damage in a wreck, what are the odds that the same careless rider who crashed the motorcycle in the first place abused its engine or transmission to the point of failure before he or she wrecked the bike?

A related issue to watch out for is a bike with a salvage title that has been "cleaned" as just mentioned. Someone may have bought a wrecked bike, rebuilt it, and then exchanged the salvage title for a clean title in one of the states that still allows this sort of thing. The person then resells the bike as if it's never been wrecked, even though it is as likely to have serious problems as any other wrecked bike. Be wary of bikes that have been titled in several different states. This could be a sign that the bike has had its title cleaned, which in turn means that it's either been wrecked or, worse yet, stolen. In the latter case, you might have worse problems than an unreliable motorcycle; you might find yourself under arrest for receiving stolen property.

MECHANICAL INSPECTION

THE BEST WAY TO avoid buying a bike that's been wrecked is to have a professional mechanic examine the motorcycle before you buy it. This is a good idea for any used bike that you might buy, whether you buy it from a dealership or from a private seller.

If you know a motorcycle mechanic whom you trust, spend a few dollars to hire him or her to examine the bike. Otherwise do a little research to find a reputable shop where you can take the bike. If you're buying the bike from a shop, there's not much point in letting the shop staff examine the bike themselves, since they've already examined it. You're best off having a third-party mechanic who hasn't got a stake in selling the bike examine it. A shop or individual seller who won't let an outside mechanic examine a bike should be a bright red flag telling you to find a different bike.

To ensure the most objective mechanical inspection, take the bike to a shop that doesn't carry the brand of bike you're buying. Like all things, there are exceptions to this advice. For example, if you're buying a Ducati, which will have desmodromic valves (valves that are opened and closed mechanically, rather than being closed by valve springs, as on most engines), you probably won't learn much about the bike from your local Harley shop, where the mechanics are unfamiliar with overhead cams in general and probably wouldn't know a desmo valve from a pig's aorta. But in general you'll get the most unbiased opinion if you take a bike to a shop that doesn't sell that particular brand.

I understand that getting the bike professionally inspected will be a hassle and will cost you money, but the grief (and money) you might save yourself could make it worthwhile. It may even be impossible in some cases, but most dealers should allow you to take a motorcycle to an off-site mechanic or allow you to bring in a mechanic to inspect the bike. They won't encourage this, and they won't advertise this fact, but if you show you're serious about buying a bike, most reputable dealers will allow it.

DEALERSHIPS VERSUS THE PRIVATE SELLER

UNLESS A PRIVATE SELLER has unrealistic expectations or he or she is just fishing for a sucker to pay an inflated price, chances are that a private seller will ask less for the exact same bike than would a professional dealer. There are a number of reasons for this. A private seller isn't working on a business model that accounts for the interest he or she is paying the bank for inventory. He or she may have a loan for the bike, but most people don't think in terms of how much interest they're paying every day, as do most businesses. To make up their own financing costs, dealerships charge a little extra to help offset interest payments. They also add a certain percentage to the prices of their used bikes to cover operating costs. It costs a lot of money just to turn the lights on in a dealership every morning. Add in the salaries and health-care costs of their employees, and you can see why dealerships have to charge more for used bikes.

On the other hand, if a dealership is any good, you'll get something in return for the extra money you spend there. When buying from a private seller, the general rule is "buyer beware." After you buy a bike from a private seller, if something is wrong with it and the seller won't make it right, your only recourse may be to sue the seller, which will end up costing you even more money with no guarantee that you'll be successful.

Most shops, however, offer some sort of warranty, and if they want to have your repeat business, they'll bend over backward to make certain you are happy with your new bike. They may even be required to make it right for you by law; some states have lemon laws that apply to motorcycle dealerships as well as automobile dealerships.

If your bike does need repair, even if it's for something that happened after you bought it, dealers tend to take care of their customers. They'll be more motivated to help out a loyal customer whom they know than they will be to help out some stranger who bought a bike from a private seller. Also consider that if a dealership originally sold the bike when it was new, which is often the case with good shops that have a lot of repeat customers, chances are they'll know your bike's entire service history and will be familiar with its idiosyncrasies.

If you buy a motorcycle that still has time remaining on its factory warranty, you may be able to use the warranty to defray the cost of necessary repairs. (Be sure to check the terms of the warranty to ensure the repair is covered.) If you've bought your bike from a dealership, any dealership worthy of your business will take care of arranging for the repair and filling out warranty paperwork. If you bought your bike from a private party and take it in for warranty repairs, you may find that the dealership is not quite as helpful. That might not seem fair, but that's just the way it is.

If you need to finance your motorcycle, a dealership will have a department that does nothing but arrange financing for motorcycles. It will also be able to help you deal with all the other legal paperwork involved with buying a motorcycle, like paying sales tax, getting insurance, filling out your registration, and transferring the title. When you buy from a private seller, you'll have to deal with all these details yourself.

A good dealership will inspect, service, and check to make certain every motorcycle it sells is roadworthy; the odds are that the used bikes a good shop is selling will be reliable. The same holds true for a good private owner. A responsible owner will keep his or her motorcycle in good repair. The trick is deciding whether or not a shop or individual is reputable, and it's a lot easier to determine if a shop that sells hundreds of motorcycles every year is reputable than it is to determine the trustworthiness of a private seller who sells a bike maybe once every five or six years.

GETTING DOWN TO BUSINESS

REGARDLESS OF HOW DIFFERENT motorcycles may seem, at their hearts they are more or less all the same. After spending an entire chapter discussing the different types of bikes, this might seem like a contradiction, but when it comes to inspecting a used motorcycle, the process is pretty much the same for everything from a 250-cc single-cylinder trail bike to an 1800-cc six-cylinder Gold Wing.

In addition to a mechanic (or at least a friend who's knowledgeable about motorcycles), you'll want to bring the following items when you go to look at a used bike:

- Flashlight for looking into dark places
- Tire pressure gauge to avoid a flat while on a test ride
- Clean rag to wipe off the inevitable grease you will get on yourself
- Mechanic's mirror to see hard-to-reach items like the wiring harness

The following procedures apply to all bikes, as does the following advice: if something doesn't check out, move on and find another bike. Unless you have a mechanic estimate the costs of repairing any problems you might find, you can assume the costs will be high. Even routine maintenance like valve adjustments or tire replacement can cost hundreds of dollars. Serious repairs, like fixing a failing transmission, will cost thousands. If you pay $4,500 for a nine-year-old Yamaha Road Star with 59,000 miles, then have to drop another $3,000 fixing the transmission, you're getting dangerously close to the cost of a two-year-old carry-over version of the same bike with zero miles. (A "carry-over" is a brand-new bike from a previous season that has gone unsold.)

To keep this manageable, we'll group the parts of the bike together as follows:

- Cosmetic—This refers to the condition of the bodywork and the condition of the metal parts.
- Electrics—This will refer to the charging system, lights, battery, starter, instrumentation, and ignition.
- Chassis—For our purposes, this will include the frame itself and the bearings and bushings associated with the frame as well as the shocks, swingarm, fork, steering head, and wheels and tires.
- Drivetrain—Here we'll examine the engine, transmission, and final drive.

You can break the inspection process down into two sections—the macroscopic inspection and the microscopic inspection.

THE COSMETIC EVALUATION

THE MACROSCOPIC IS THE broad cosmetic overview of the bike, which is really a fancy way of saying your first impression of the machine.

Does It Shine?

Is the bike clean? Is it obviously well maintained? Does it have rusted metal or oxidized aluminum showing? Does is show evidence of a major crash?

Does it look like the owner took decent care of the motorcycle you're inspecting? If he rode it as carefully as he'd shave his own mother's legs with a straight razor, you'll be able to tell just from the bike's appearance. The bike will have a fresh coat of wax and the paint will glow. Even if the bike has a few miles under its belt, if it's been stored properly, ideally inside a garage, but if not, at least under a quality cover that breathes and doesn't trap moisture, the paint should be almost like new. Sure, there may be some minor scratches or some swirls in the finish—these sorts of things are inevitable on a motorcycle that gets ridden regularly—but overall the bike should shine.

Likewise the chrome should be polished to the point where the sun's reflection practically burns out the corneas of your eyes. It should not be rusted or pitted, and the chrome should be deep; you should be able to look down into it. If you find pitting in the chrome finish or rusty exhaust pipes, you could be looking at some expensive repairs.

Any exposed aluminum should be smooth and clean. If it has a whitish appearance, it is oxidizing. This usually occurs only when a bike has sat out in the elements for long periods of time (although it can occur more quickly in areas near oceans, where saltwater spray can get on a bike and degrade its metal parts). Replacing oxidized aluminum parts like engine cases and fork legs is prohibitively expensive and often exceeds the value of a motorcycle, even a Harley-Davidson. It can also be a sign that there are deeper problems with a bike, since the same elements that degraded the aluminum parts will have compromised other parts, like electrical components and rubber seals.

You may find corrosion on the metal parts around the battery box. This might look like hell, but usually it is just cosmetic, caused by an overheated battery puking out a bit of battery acid because it was over-charged. Or it had a blocked vent hose, or the battery cracked at some point. It's difficult (if not impossible) to remove this scarring, but as long as it appears to have been an isolated occurrence, it shouldn't cause any long-term harm. If it appears to be a repeated event, however, it might indicate a more serious prob-lem with an electrical system that overcharges the battery.

On many Japanese bikes, you might find that the exposed aluminum parts have taken on a yellowish appearance, especially on older bikes. This is because they're coated with a protective film that takes on a tint as it ages. The brownish-yellow tint isn't pretty, but it's common and doesn't indicate deeper prob-lems beyond age.

What Do Dents Mean?
Be sure to look for dents and other signs of crash-ing. A small ding on an exhaust pipe, footpeg tip, or clutch lever likely means a bike has fallen over, but that isn't necessarily a deal breaker. Motorcycles are inherently unstable machines, and as such they are prone to falling over. Sooner or later, every bike will fall over. A kickstand will sink into the asphalt on a hot day, or you might hit a slick patch of diesel while rolling up to a gas pump just as you happen to be crossing a rough seam in the pavement. Shit happens. The vast majority of these parking-lot tip overs result in such minor cosmetic damage that it's

not worth fixing, but they do leave telltale marks on the machine.

Also, don't worry about stone chips on the fenders or the frame behind the front wheel. This is natural wear and tear and is unavoidable if the bike is to be ridden in the real world. The only bikes without stone chips are brand-new ones sitting on showroom floors or useless trailer queens hauled from bike show to bike show. All of my bikes have fallen over more than once, and each of them have pitted chrome and paint from rocks and road debris. If you ride forty thousand miles or more each year, your bikes will be pitted too.

Bigger dents are usually signs of more serious crashes that can have more dire consequences to the motorcycle's structural integrity. If a bike took a hit that was hard enough to put a grapefruit-sized divot in the gas tank, chances are the parts that you can't see took a hard hit, too. At the very least it indicates that the owner didn't treat his or her bike with the respect it deserved.

If a bike has plastic bodywork like a fairing, saddlebags, or a trunk, even a minor tip over can have much more expensive consequences. Check to make sure that all the gaps in the body panels have a uniform fit and all the tabs holding the parts together are intact and not broken off. Examine all the plastic for cracks. Even if the plastic isn't cracked, spiderweb cracks in the paint around mounting bolts are a sign that the bike has been through some sort of traumatic event. This will also show up in the metal mounting brackets that hold the bodywork in place.

Visually inspect all the plastic pieces to ensure they line up straight; if they sit crooked, something underneath them is probably bent, which could be a very bad thing.

Even if the plastic pieces appear straight, examine the brackets holding them in place (at least the ones you can see) to make sure they aren't bent or tweaked. Even if the brackets are straight, examine them for evidence that they have been straightened. This is a sign that the bike has been in a serious crash.

Check the seat cover for rips and tears. The stitching should line up, and everything should be straight. If the seat cover doesn't line up with the rest of the bike, chances are it's an aftermarket seat cover. Again, if the seat looks okay and is comfortable, this shouldn't be a deal breaker—a previous owner may have simply hooked the original seat cover with his boot and ripped it—but it could also be a sign that a motorcycle has been in a serious crash and has been rebuilt.

Most important, does the bike match the owner's description? If the seller claimed the bike was in mint condition, does it really look like it just rolled off the showroom floor, or is there oil weeping out of the head gasket? Does the bike look like it has a lot more miles than the odometer suggests? This may mean that the owner tampered with the odometer, or else that the bike spent a good part of its life sitting out in the elements even when it wasn't running. Either way, this is not good. A little exaggeration on the owner's part is to be expected, but if there is a gross discrepancy, you have no choice but to question the owner's honesty in general. If the owner has grossly misrepresented the bike, you can either negotiate the price downward or, better yet, go find a better motorcycle.

Sometimes a bike might look like it has a lot more miles on it than it really does, but in reality, it just has a lot of years under its belt. As I mentioned earlier, many riders rarely take their motorcycles out of the garage. If you just ride to town once or twice a month, you'll be lucky to put on more than four hundred miles per year. That means you can have a ten-year-old motorcycle with three or four thousand miles or less on the clock. Harleys seem especially prone to spending more time in garages than out on highways.

The end result can be a bike that might not have many miles on its odometer but is still a ten-year-old motorcycle, with ten-year-old seals and ten-year-old bearings. Harleys seem more susceptible to this sort of rot than other brands. Harleys with low miles but lots of years usually have very dry gaskets that leak motor oil everywhere. Not only should you avoid buying one of these, but you should avoid parking them in your driveway.

A PART-BY-PART GUIDE TO INSPECTING A USED MOTORCYCLE

ONCE A BIKE HAS passed the macroscopic examination, it's time to put it under the microscope. You would think a bike that looks good on the outside would be good on the inside; after all, an owner who treated a bike's cosmetics with respect should treat its mechanicals with respect, too. In most cases, you'd be correct. An owner who puts the effort into maintaining a bike's appearance usually puts as much effort into maintaining its mechanical parts. But there are always exceptions to every rule, and when you are paying your hard-earned money for a motorcycle, you don't want to pay even more because you ended up with one of those exceptions.

When buying a bike, you'll be able to put all the things you learned about the parts of a motorcycle in chapter 1 to good use. If you need to, go back and skim over that chapter to refresh your memory regarding the different systems and subsystems of a motorcycle, because you'll be examining each of them when checking out the parts of a used bike you're thinking about buying.

The Electrics

Electrical systems have historically been the weakest parts of motorcycles and the most prone to failure. This is partly because there's just not enough space to package a heavy-duty electrical system like you'd find on a car. For most of the 110 or so years that motorcycles have been manufactured, the manufacturers' solution to the problem was to keep electrical systems as simple as possible. On the earliest bikes the electrical system consisted of a crude magneto that provided spark; if the bike had any lights at all, they'd be powered by kerosene. The earliest electrical lights were powered by batteries, just like your flashlight, and as with your flashlight, those batteries had to be replaced when they ran down. This is called a "total loss" system.

The earliest regenerating electrical systems used six-volt DC generators to charge batteries and power lights. These systems could remain crude because they didn't need to be more sophisticated; the single most difficult task of riding—starting a motorcycle—was done with legs of the flesh-and-blood kind rather than of the electrical variety. When the riding public began to demand electric starters on their motorcycles, these systems were no longer adequate and were replaced with twelve-volt systems that used automotive-style alternators to provide electrical power. By the time electronic ignition became common on bikes in the late 1970s and early 1980s, relatively reliable alternators provided all electrical power.

The slow evolution of motorcycle electrical systems is one good reason to avoid buying older bikes. Even newer bikes with early electronic ignition systems can be riddled with expensive electrical problems. For example, Yamahas from the early 1980s tended to have electrical systems that would overcharge, cooking batteries and voltage regulators. Worse yet, the Maxim 750 and 1100, a couple of Yamaha's bigger four-cylinder bikes, had crude computerized ignition systems that, when they failed, would make a bike completely inoperable. And they did fail, all the time. The system was virtually unusable and Yamaha abandoned it after just a couple of years. Yamaha is notorious for not carrying replacement parts for a motorcycle after it is out of production, meaning that within a few years, replacement computers for these bikes were virtually unobtainable. As a result, you still might run across a Yamaha Maxim 750 or 1100 or a 750 Seca that appears to be in almost new condition. Beware and avoid these bikes at all costs.

Throughout the history of motorcycles, really lousy bikes like this do crop up, sometimes from the least likely sources. For example, the four-cylinder Honda 1200-cc Gold Wings from the 1980s had a tendency to burn out their stators, which are roughly the equivalent of automotive alternators. This would have been bad enough by itself, but Honda made the matter worse by placing the stator inside the engine cases. This means to replace a stator, you'll have to split the engine cases. This is the most extensive operation you can perform on a modern Japanese motorcycle engine. It's also the most expensive one; replacing the stator on a 1200-cc Gold Wing can easily cost you $2,000–$3,000, which is close to the value of the entire bike.

As motorcycle technology advanced, bad designs like these became increasingly rare, which further underscores my point that modern motorcycles are your best bets when considering used machines. The worst electrical problem you're likely to encounter when buying a modern motorcycle is a weak battery. Modern batteries can last for years, but some climates can make them wear out more quickly. Both cold and heat can shorten the life of a battery. If a battery's not properly cared for in northern climates, they can wear out during the winter months, and in hot climates, the sun and heat can shorten a battery's life. I live in Arizona, where I replace my battery every two years just to be safe.

As good as modern electrical systems are, you'll still need to give the electrical system a thorough examination just to be safe. This is easier said than done, however, because most of the parts are buried deep within the motorcycle. Some things are easy to check, like whether or not the lights and horn work, but other things are going to take more work.

Take the wiring harness, most of which runs along the frame, or even through it; it would be damned hard to examine an entire wiring harness without completely dismantling a motorcycle, but you should make sure that at least the parts of the harness that you can see are in good shape. Big chunks of black friction tape around some section of the wiring harness, particularly up by the steering head area where the harness can get pinched in a bad crash, is a sign that the bike has likely had some major repairs.

Even the battery can be difficult to see on some bikes, but you should try to take a look at it because it can tell you a lot about a motorcycle. The terminals should be clean and free of corrosion, and the cables should be bolted on tightly. Most motorcycles now used sealed batteries, but if the bike you're looking at was built more than five or six years ago, it may have a refillable battery. If so, make certain that the battery water is set at the correct level.

The more accessories a bike has, the more powerful its electrical system needs to be. Be wary of bikes that have a lot of aftermarket electrical accessories, like GPS systems, heated seats and grips, stereos, and a couple of dozen driving lights. Modern bikes have reliable electrical systems, but only within reason. If your system was designed to produce a certain amount of power reliably, and then you mount accessories that draw twice as much juice as the system was designed to provide, your formerly reliable electrical system may not be very reliable at all. It's best to stick with a bike that only has the accessories with which it left the factory.

A lot of aftermarket accessories aren't a deal breaker. If you don't like them, usually they are easy to remove. If you do decide to keep them, make sure the owner knew what he or she was doing when they were installed. Make sure that they are wired properly, that the exposed connections are taped or sheathed, and that all connections are properly soldered or crimped.

You may not even consider the most important electrical accessory—the starter—an accessory, but those of us who began riding back when starting a motorcycle required a strong leg and a good boot know better. This is one accessory that needs to work properly. If the bike hasn't been run in a while or if the weather is cold, a bike you're looking at might need a little help to turn over, but once the bike has been run for a while—say thirty minutes or so out on the highway—the starter should spin the engine to life with no drama. Failure to do so might just mean that a bike needs a new battery, but it could also be a sign that a bike needs expensive repairs.

If you aren't able to take the bike out for a test ride to charge up the battery, at least check the charging indicator light. Most bikes will have some sort of idiot light (that's what we used to call indicator lights that were used when what was really needed was a good gauge) for the charging system. Although it does not provide much useful information, at the very least an idiot light lets you know when there is a problem. If the light continues to glow after the engine is running at normal idle speed, the bike either has charging problems or soon will have them.

If you do uncover anything amiss with the electrical system, my advice is to run as far and fast as you can and find another bike to buy. The problems may well be simple and inexpensive to fix, but usually they will be difficult and extremely expensive, and they'll undoubtedly be tricky to find and diagnose. If you have any doubts about your expertise in motorcycle electrics, this is one of the best reasons to have a competent professional examine the bike you're thinking about buying.

With more and more bikes using antilock brake systems (ABS), electrics also are playing an increasingly large role in brake performance. These are highly complex, computer-based systems that defy intuitive understanding. But it doesn't take a scientist to understand that brake performance can be the difference between life and death. If you look at a bike that has ABS and the brakes don't seem to perform properly, do not buy that motorcycle without having a qualified mechanic check the ABS equipment. I know that in addition to being dangerous, ABS failures are extremely expensive. I personally would not buy a bike with ABS problems.

The Chassis

You'll need a good electrical system just to get your bike out on the road, but once you're out riding, you must make sure the rest of the bike is up to par, too—particularly the frame and suspension.

I'm going to start at the front of the bike and work my way back. The most complicated system (and thus most prone to failure) is the fork. A fork is probably the most likely item to get tweaked in a crash, since it is at the front of the bike and the first thing that connects with whatever a rider might be crashing into. It is also prone to less serious problems, like worn-out seals.

The majority of motorcycles you will be looking at will use hydraulically damped telescopic forks. These are the two long shock absorbers connecting your front wheel to your handlebar. There are other types of front ends—Harley uses an old-fashioned springer-type fork on some models, and BMW has too many oddball systems to keep track of—but I'm going to focus on the hydraulic front fork, which is the most common type.

The fork assembly is held together by metal pieces called "triple clamps." These attach the fork to the steering head, which is the tubular assembly on the front of the frame in which the fork pivots. The triple clamps hold either the fork tubes or the fork sliders, depending on what type is used. Think of the fork tube as the male part of the fork, the part that inserts into the female part, and the slider as the female part that gets penetrated by the male part. (This may seem crude, but these are the terms that mechanics have always used.)

Traditionally the male part is at the top and the female part is at the bottom, but I've noticed that in recent years the trend has been to reverse these positions. Consequently, the inserting male part is now often found at the bottom, down by the wheel, and the female part is up by the triple clamps. These were originally called "upside-down forks," and are still often referred to as "USD forks," though they are becoming so common that more often than not people just call them "forks." At first USD forks were only found on sport bikes, but now they've begun to appear on all types of bikes, including cruisers. Harley uses USD forks on its new Sportster XR1200 and Victory uses them on its Hammer and Kingpin models.

The first tools you'll need to check a bike's fork are your eyeballs. Look at the fork from the side. The two legs of the fork should line up perfectly. If one of the legs is skewed at a bit of an angle or looks bent, chances are the bike has experienced more than the normal amount of wear and tear. If the whole assembly looks a little cockeyed, then either the triple clamps are bent or the frame itself is bent in such a way that the steering head itself is tweaked. In the grand scheme of things, these problems range from really bad to downright terrible, and they should motivate you to find a different bike.

The other thing to look for in the visual inspection is oil leaking from a fork seal. If the fork hasn't been cleaned, you'll easily be able to see a ring where oil has collected and grime has built up around the fork tube, right at the end of the fork slider's travel (the point at which the male part is most deeply inserted into the female part). Even if you don't see this telltale ring, the fork seals may leak; the owner may just have wiped the tubes down so the leak wasn't obvious.

You can tell if this is the case with a simple test. First, make certain that the owner or the mechanic you brought along, or anyone else capable of standing on his or her own two feet, is standing beside the bike to help keep it secure. Go to the front of the bike and get a strong grip on the handlebar. With the front wheel placed firmly between your legs, squeeze the front brake lever to keep the bike from rolling away from you (or worse yet, over you) and lift the bike up off its side stand. Once you have the bike securely upright, pump the fork up and down a few times. When you are finished, put the bike back down on its side stand, making sure that it's resting in a secure position, and rub your finger along the exposed part of the fork tube above (or below on USD forks) the slider. If the seal is leaking, you'll feel a thin film of oil.

If the bike is more than a few years old and hasn't had the fork seals replaced, there's a good chance you'll find a leaky fork seal. A leaky fork seal shouldn't be a deal breaker, but like just about everything else associated with a motorcycle, it will be relatively expensive to fix. Call a motorcycle shop that sells the model you're looking at and get a quote for replacing the seals. Your final offer for the bike should reflect the money you'll have to pay to repair the fork.

Follow the same procedure to check for other possible fork problems. When you're pumping the fork up and down, make certain that both sides of the fork legs are moving up and down freely, without binding or making noise, both of which could be signs of expensive problems to come.

Steering Head Bearings

You can check the steering head bearings at the same time you're checking out the fork. While you're holding the bike up turn the handlebar all the way to the left, then all the way back to the right. Listen to see if you hear a clunking sound, which could indicate that a steering head bearing is loose or worn out; it may have dents and flat spots that can't be adjusted away.

If the bike has a center stand, put it up on the center stand, as described in chapter 3.

Once the bike is securely on the stand, have the person who's with you place his or her weight on the rear of the bike. This should lift the front tire in the air. When you've made sure the bike is secure, center the bar so that the tire is facing straight ahead and let it fall to one side, and then the other. If the wheel moves evenly and smoothly, chances are it's in good condition. If it moves with a clunky, jerky motion, the bike likely has problems with the steering head bearings.

Again, this is not uncommon on older bikes, and it shouldn't be a deal breaker; the bearings may just need an adjustment, but there is a good chance that they will need to be replaced. This will be even more expensive than leaky fork seals, especially if the bike has a lot of bodywork that needs to be removed. Check with a local shop to find out what this will cost to repair, and if you decide to buy the bike, make an offer that will reflect that cost.

While you have the front of the bike up in the air, check the condition of the wheel bearings by grasping the front wheel at a right angle to the fork and rock it from side to side. If you notice any play in the wheel, the wheel bearing will need shimming or replacement.

Tires

If you're used to automobile tires, which often last fifty thousand miles or more, you're in for a rude and expensive awakening when it comes to motorcycle tires. The very best motorcycle tires won't last ten thousand miles; in most cases you'll be doing good to get seventy-five hundred miles from a set of tires. And these tires are expensive; on big touring bikes like the Gold Wing or Vision that require the removal of a lot of plastic bodywork to gain access to the tires, you could be looking at $600-plus to buy a set of high-quality tires, and another $300 to have a shop mount them.

There's really no way around this—it's just the price you'll pay to ride a motorcycle—but with that said, you can still do a few things to help keep your costs down, even when you first buy a bike. Pick up a tread-measuring tool and measure the depth of the tread on any bike you're thinking of buying. Make sure the tires have at least 50 percent of their tread life left. If they don't, get an estimate for the cost of tire replacement from your local shop and reflect those costs in any offer you might make for the bike.

Check the air pressure of the tires. Low air pressure is obviously not a major problem, but you'll want to make certain that the tires are properly inflated before a bike is safe to take out on a test ride (consult the owner's manual for the proper air-pressure level). Low pressure can mean a tire has a leak, but as often as not it just means the bike might have sat unused for a while. If a bike has been unused for more than a few months, check the sidewalls for dry rot, cracks, and weather checking. If a tire shows signs of problems like this, it should be replaced regardless of how much tread is left on it.

You can get a lot of information from the tire itself, like the date the tire was manufactured, for example. The date of manufacture is found in the final four-digit code stamped into the small oval area on the tire's sidewall, right after the word *DOT* (Department of Transportation). The first two digits denote the week of the year in which the tire was manufactured and the last two digits represent the last two numbers of the year of manufacture. For example, if a tire was manufactured in June of 2006, the code will read: "2806."

If the tire has a code that ends in three digits, that means the tire was manufactured before the year 2000. If that's the case, then figure that you will need to replace it regardless of how good it looks. There is no hard-and-fast rule about how old a tire should get before replacing, but if you don't have the sense not to ride on tires that are over ten years old, you should probably take up a safer hobby, like knitting. Even if a tire is just six or seven years old, you can assume it's past its prime and will need replacement before you start riding the bike. Again, this isn't a deal breaker, but when negotiating to buy the bike, your offer should reflect the cost of tire replacement.

Frames

Modern motorcycle frames are generally pretty robust pieces of equipment and won't shake to pieces the way they used to on earlier bikes. (There are, however, exceptions, including Suzuki's first-generation TL1000, a high-performance V-twin sport bike built in the late 1990s and early 2000s, and which developed a notable reputation for frame failure. Most frames you look at will either be made of tubular steel or aluminum alloy beams, though those found on BMWs from the 1980s and 1990s are virtually not frames at all, but rather consist of a couple of subframes bolted to the engine cases. In general, these were strong and reliable and should be no more problematic than the frames on other modern bikes.

Even though frame failures are rare, you should still take some time to inspect the frame of any used bike you consider buying. Check the gussets and welds for cracks, especially in high-stress areas like around the steering head. Look for dents or severe scratches that might indicate a bike has been wrecked, and look for signs of corrosion around the battery box. Take note of flaking paint, which could also be a sign that a bike has been through a serious crash. Don't walk away from a bike because of a little flaking in the frame's paint, but if you do see this, keep your eyes open for other trouble signs.

Swingarms/Rear Suspensions

All modern motorcycles have some sort of swinging arm rear suspension. From the 1950s until the 1980s this consisted of a fairly standard setup, with a metal fork attached to the rear wheel, coming together in front of the wheel, and attaching to the frame at a pivot point behind the transmission. A pair of shocks, one on either side of the rear wheel, controlled the wheel's up-and-down motion.

This status quo began to change in the mid-1970s. Yamaha used the first modern single-shock setup on its factory motocross race bike in 1973. Within a few years both Yamaha and Suzuki offered single-shock dirt bikes to the general public. At first these used triangular swingarms that placed the shock at the top of the triangle, in front of the rear tire. The shocks on these bikes rested at an angle and connected to the frame up under the gas tank. This system was soon replaced by a setup that placed the shock upright in front of the wheel. By the early 1980s all competitive dirt bikes used this latter setup.

At the same time, single-shock arrangements began to appear on street bikes. In 1980 BMW introduced the R80G/S, an 800-cc dual sport that featured a single shock, though this was mounted in the traditional position, alongside the rear wheel. Where the BMW design broke with tradition was its use of a single-sided rear swingarm, which was basically like a traditional swingarm cut in half. BMW called this system the "Monolever."

Yamaha used a more innovative single-shock system when it introduced the Virago series in 1981. These early Yamahas used a system much like the very first single-shock dirt bikes, with a triangular swingarm and a laid-down shock that ran under the seat and connected to the frame up by the gas tank.

Over the next few years Japanese sport bikes began to feature single-shock rear suspensions, though these followed the practice of the later dirt bikes, with a vertical shock mounted in front of the rear tire. Harley even got into the alternative rear suspension business with its Softail system. Like the Virago, this system featured a triangular rear swing-arm, but instead of being located under the seat, the shocks were mounted down under the engine, hidden from sight.

The main difference between the Harley system and the various systems used by the Japanese and Germans was that the Japanese and German systems were all about function. The main purpose of the Harley system was cosmetic; Harley was trying to re-create the look of the earlier hardtails (bikes without any rear suspension at all). It did this by hiding the entire rear suspension system as best it could.

Today we have a bewildering variety of rear sus-pension designs to pick from. Having said all this, unless you're planning to spend a lot of time on a racetrack, you should simply make sure that any used bike you're buying doesn't have problems with its swingarm. Swingarms generally are extremely stout and should cause little trouble over the life of a motorcycle, but you'll still need to check for potential problems.

First, examine the shock or shocks. Make sure they aren't leaking fluid, or that they haven't lost their gas charge if they are nitrogen shocks. You can check for leaks in much the same way you check the fork seals—bounce the bike up and down and then check for greasy moisture on the shaft of the shock. You should be able to tell if the shocks are properly charged and/or filled with fluid after you bounce the bike up and down. If it bounces too easily, the shock(s) will probably need work. This is not uncommon on bikes with a few miles under their belts, but like everything else, it will be expensive.

An even more expensive repair would be to replace the swingarm pivot bushings. When these get bad, they can make your rear wheel wobble while you ride down the road. As you might imagine, this can have fatal consequences on the highway and needs to be fixed immediately. Thankfully you should easily be able to determine if the swingarm bushings are bad before your bike enters a "death wobble" on the open road. The procedure for checking swingarm bushings is similar to checking the steering head bearing and is much easier to do on a bike equipped with a center stand. When the bike is on a center stand, the rear wheel is lifted up in the air so you can wiggle it back and forth to see if there is any play in the bushings. If there is a little play, that might not mean there's a problem—on many bikes the swing-arm pivot simply can be adjusted to eliminate this play—but if the swingarm clunks from side to side, you can be certain the bike will soon experience expensive and dangerous problems. Walk away from any bike with a sick swingarm while you still can.

The Final Drive

This is also the time to check the final drive system. As mentioned in chapter 1, there are three common types of final drive systems: chains, shafts, and belts. Belts are the best system, in my opinion, and require little maintenance, but they can fail with age and wear. For this reason, check the condition of the rubber to ensure it's not cracked or coming apart. Most important, make certain the belt has all of its teeth. If teeth are missing from the belt, it is just about to fail.

A damaged belt is not a huge problem on some belt-drive bikes, but, on others, it could get expensive. Generally speaking, if the belt runs inside the frame as it passes over the swingarm pivot between the front and rear pulleys, as it does on Harley-Davidson touring bikes and Softail models, the frame will have to come apart to replace the belt. This is a huge job and is much more expensive than changing belts on models that have the belt running outside the frame, such as Harley's Dyna and Sportster models. If the belt has any damage or noticeable wear, check with a local shop to see how much they charge for replacing belts on that model. If you decide to buy the bike, reflect the cost of belt replacement in your offer.

I prefer belts over shafts because belts don't alter the handling characteristics of a bike the way shafts do, even though shafts require less maintenance than belts. When you have a shaft-driven bike up on a center stand (most bikes with shaft drives have center stands), you can check the oil level in the rear drive unit by opening a screw-in plug that rests on the upper part of the ring and pinion housing and looking inside to see that the oil is at the proper level. Once you've determined that it is, put the bike in gear (with the engine off, of course), grab the rear wheel, and jerk it back and forth. If you feel a loud, loose "clunk" inside the rear drive housing, the bike may be about to experience a very expensive drive-shaft failure.

Chains are the most common types of rear-drive systems, and they also wear out the fastest. In the 1970s and early 1980s a few manufacturers like Harley-Davidson and Yamaha used chain-drive systems that ran the chain in an enclosed oil bath. These enclosed chains lasted virtually forever, but the cases that held the oil were heavy and prone to leaking. They eventually proved to be a technologi-cal dead end and by the mid-1980s all motorcycle companies had abandoned the idea and gone back to open chains and sprockets, or in Harley's case, belts.

You'd be lucky to get twenty thousand miles from a chain and a set of sprockets. If you're like me, that won't get you through one riding season. Add to that the fact that the chain final drive is the most maintenance-intensive system on a modern motorcy-cle, and you can see why I don't care for them. You'll need to adjust your chain at least every week, perhaps every other day if you're a serious rider.

Be prepared to get dirty when checking the con-dition of the chain. Although there are some good chain lubricants that don't leave a greasy buildup or attract too much road grime, even the cleanest chain on a bike that is regularly ridden will be somewhat greasy and dirty. This is where the clean rag you brought along will come in handy.

First check the tension on the chain to make certain the chain isn't so loose that it will cause problems when riding. If the bike is well maintained, then the slack should be within the manufacturer's tolerance, usually meaning the chain should have enough free play to move up and down an inch or two. An overly tight chain might be evidence of a well-meaning but ill-informed seller. A slightly loose chain may only mean the bike gets ridden a lot, but in my mind, a chain that is sloppy is a red flag indicating its owner neglects basic maintenance. If the chain is too loose to ride safely, have the owner adjust it before going out on a test ride.

When the chain tension has been set to the proper level, roll the rear wheel to turn the chain and check it at various spots. If the tension varies from location to location, the chain may have tight spots, indicating that it is on its last legs.

The condition of the sprockets will also tell you how long you can expect the chain to last. Since the wheel only turns one direction under power (no chain-driven motorcycles have reverse gears), the teeth of the sprockets only wear on one side. Because of this, they develop a distinct cupping appearance as they wear out—one side of each tooth appears worn and the other appears almost new.

Sprockets usually wear out at almost identical rates as chains, requiring the chain and both sprockets to be replaced at the same time. Since wear is much easier to see on the sprockets than on the chain itself, you can expect that the chain will have about as much life left in it as do the sprockets. If the owner claims to have replaced the chain but not the sprockets, ignore anything the person says after that because he or she is either a liar or a fool.

If the bike lacks a center stand, the process of checking the suspension and chassis gets a lot trickier. Here's where taking the bike to a mechanic can be worthwhile, because any worthy mechanic will have a lift he or she can use to hoist the bike up for these types of examinations. Barring access to a secure lift, your next best bet is to use a good stand, like those built by the company Pit Bull. Quality stands will support either wheel (if you have two, you can support both ends at once), but unlike a lift designed specifically for motorcycles, which connect to a bike at the center of the frame, stands lift a bike at its wheels. This loads the suspension with the weight of the motorcycle, making it much more difficult to check for problems with the swingarm bushings or steering head bearing.

Brakes

The brakes on any motorcycle you'll consider buying are perhaps the single most important items when it comes to saving your bacon out on the highway. There are two kinds of brakes: disc brakes and drum brakes. Disc brakes slow your motorcycle by squeezing pistons inside calipers, which are attached to your frame or fork so that they don't rotate with the wheel. These pistons push pads against a disc that's connected to the wheel so that it rotates with the wheel. The pressure of the pistons slows and gradually stops the wheel's rotation.

Drum brakes work by expanding the brake

shoes—stationary, horseshoe-shaped devices—against the inner surface of a rotating wheel hub. As mentioned earlier, you'll only run across drum brakes on extremely low-end motorcycles, usually the smallest cruisers from the Japanese manufacturers, which often still feature drum brakes in the back. The majority of quality motorcycles you'll be considering will have discs at either end.

Finding a bike you like with a drum rear brake shouldn't cause you to exclude that bike automatically. Disc brakes are unquestionably better, but drum brakes can be at least adequate, provided a motorcycle isn't too heavy. Make certain they work smoothly and stop the bike without shuddering.

If there is a problem with the rear drum brake, this means the shoes are worn. Often these can be adjusted. There will be a lever coming out of the wheel hub that activates the shoes inside. Where the lever connects to the brake cable leading to the brake pedal on the right side of the engine, there should be an adjustable rod connecting the cable to the lever. This rod will have a spring on it to keep tension between the rod and the lever. You'll find an adjustable nut at the end of the rod. If the nut is at the beginning of its travel and there is a lot of room to tighten it down before it reaches the end of its travel, chances are the brake shoes still have some usable life in them. If the nut has been adjusted down toward the end of its travel, most likely the brake shoes will need to be replaced soon.

Replacing the brake shoes is a relatively inexpensive process, and one you can easily do yourself, even if you're not mechanically inclined. The hardest part of replacing the shoes is getting the wheel off the bike. If you can do that, the brake cover should just pop off. Yet even simple tasks require your full attention to detail. Always remember that the life you are putting on the line will be your own. As you start taking the wheel apart, take careful notes, outlining where everything goes, so you can put it all back together correctly when you are finished. Leave off one cotter key or leave one bolt loose, and you might find that your wheel falls off when you stab at the brake pedal. If you have any doubts whatsoever about your ability to fix your own brakes, leave the job to a professional.

If you find a bike with a drum brake in front, it will either be too old or too small for you to seriously consider buying. Any bike worth purchasing will have at least one disc brake up front, and likely two. The process for checking disc brakes is quite a bit different than it is for drum brakes.

The first thing you need to check is the condition of the fluid. This will be in a reservoir on the handlebar, right up by the front brake lever. Some BMWs from the 1970s placed the reservoir under the tank, and custom bike builders often place reservoirs in the oddest places you can imagine. But if you're following my advice, you're not going to be looking at antiques or hand-built customs, so any bike you should be looking at will have the front brake reservoir on the right handlebar.

Check both the clarity and level of the brake fluid. The fluid should be relatively clear and set to the correct level. Generally speaking, brake fluid levels don't vary all that much on a properly functioning brake system. In hundreds of thousands of miles of riding, I've rarely had to add fluid to modern disc brakes. A low fluid level usually means there is some sort of leak in the system or that it hasn't been properly maintained and is seriously overdue for a fluid change. Either case is bad news and ought to ring alarm bells.

Likewise fluid that is cloudy or dirty-looking is a sign that something isn't right. This indicates that the bike's owner has neglected to perform routine maintenance or that the brake system is contaminated. If the fluid level is low or if the fluid itself looks murky, chances are an expensive brake repair is in the bike's near future—or worse yet, the system is on the verge of experiencing a catastrophic failure that could end with you being crippled or killed.

After checking the fluid in the front brake master cylinder, move on to the brake hoses. Make certain the visible hoses aren't cracked, kinked, or obviously leaking. If they appear to be in rough condition, it's another sign the bike has been seriously neglected.

But even hoses that look good on the outside might be worn out, especially if the bike is more than five or six years old. You'll only be able to determine this with a test ride. If the front brake lever feels mushy; if there is a slight pause between pulling the brake lever and when the brake pads start to bite into the disc; or if the brake lever seems to move too close to the handlebar, you've got a bike with problematic brakes. It may be something extremely simple, like air in the brake lines. This can be cured by bleeding the brakes. (If you don't know how to do this already, you should probably leave it to a mechanic. If the bike has ABS, then you'll definitely want to leave bleeding to a trained mechanic, even if you know how to bleed brakes yourself, because ABS systems are incredibly complicated.) On the other hand, a mushy brake lever could also indicate the need for new brake lines.

Needing new brake lines is not a major issue and shouldn't dissuade you from buying a bike. In fact, if the bike is more than five or six years old, expect to replace them sooner or later, even if they aren't causing obvious problems when you buy the bike. It's a relatively simple procedure, but like everything else related to motorcycle maintenance, it is expensive. Get an estimate and, as always, include the replacement cost in your offer.

(A side note on brakes: if you need to replace the brake lines, you should spend a few extra dollars and replace them with braided-steel lines, which will last much longer and are also much better-looking.)

Next you'll need to check the brake pads. Most brake calipers will have some sort of cap on top of them. You should be able to pop this cap off and visually inspect the pads. This consists of simply looking at the pads to see how far down the material that grabs the brake discs has worn. Generally, new pads have at least a quarter inch of material on them. Most have a groove in the middle of the pads that runs almost all the way through the material. You can use that groove as a gauge to determine how far the pads have worn down.

Worn brake pads really aren't an issue when buying a used bike because pads are relatively easy and cheap to replace. The most expensive pads on the market seldom cost more than $50, and if you change the pads yourself, you'll save hundreds of dollars over the cost of having the pads replaced in a shop. The first step is usually to remove the calipers by unfastening the two bolts that hold them to the caliper carriers. (On some bikes you don't even have to do this—you can replace the pads with the calipers in place.) Then you pop the inspection cover off, remove a couple of pins, and remove the pads. Putting in the new pads is just a little more difficult, because you'll have to press the pistons back into the calipers to make room for the new pads, which will be much thicker than the old ones due to their additional pad material. This might require using a little force.

Be aware that the pistons are easily damaged. If you try to pry them apart with a metal tool, you'll likely damage the metal on the pistons, creating sharp edges that can tear seals and cause costly leaks. You'll need something soft, like a wood stick, to safely pry apart the pistons. After that, you should be able to drop the calipers in, replace the pins (along with the clips or keys that secure the pins in place), and you're done. Again, if you're going to replace the brake pads yourself, as with any repair, make certain you take careful notes and put everything back together properly. No helmet, riding jacket, boots, gloves, or any other protective gear will save you if your brake calipers fall off. Because of this, if you have any doubts at all about your ability to change the brake pads, leave the job to a professional.

The last part of the brake system you'll examine will be the rotors. These will also be the easiest parts to examine, since they are usually right out in the open where you can see them. Look at them from the front or from the top, whichever gives you the best view, and make sure they're straight and not warped. Have the owner or a friend roll the bike while you look at the brakes because any warping will be more obvious while the wheel is turning.

When the bike is stationary, run your hands across the braking surfaces. The faces of the discs should feel smooth. If the bike has any miles at all on it, you'll most likely feel some ridges, but these shouldn't be numerous or deep. Damaged discs could be another sign of a crash; at the very least they're evidence of improper maintenance.

Checking the Oil

You would think that anyone selling a bike would have the sense to make certain the engine had oil, but I didn't live this long by overestimating the average person's capacity for common sense. Most people will have the oil filled to the proper level, but you don't want to have an engine seize up and cause you to crash because you happened across the one idiot who didn't.

Most modern motorcycles use wet-sump oil systems. These are similar to automotive systems in that the oil is held in a reservoir at the bottom of the crankcase and is checked via a dipstick.

However, unlike automotive dipsticks, which are usually held in place by rubber plugs and their own weight, motorcycle dipsticks are usually made of lightweight plastic and screwed in place. This can lead to confusion when checking the oil, since some manufacturers require you to screw the dipstick all the way down to check the level while others require you to unscrew it and simply let it rest in the filler hole to get the proper level. The difference between these two methods is significant and can lead to underfilling, or worse yet, overfilling the oil reservoir by as much as one quart. The only way to find out for certain which method you need to use is to check the owner's manual (any conscientious owner will have an owner's manual to go with a bike—if he or she doesn't, you should probably find another bike).

If a bike has a center stand, place the bike on the stand to check the oil level. On bikes that lack center stands, you'll have to consult the owner's manual to find out whether you should check the oil with the bike on its side stand or if you need to have someone hold the bike upright while you check the oil. You'd think that manufacturers who neglected to fit bikes with center stands would design their dipsticks to work with the bike on its side stand, but you'd be wrong most of the time. More often than not you'll have to figure out a way to hold the bike upright to check oil, which is a major pain in the ass and very unsafe if you don't have a stand or have someone to help you.

While you're checking the oil level, check the condition of the oil. It should be relatively clear and brown. The blacker and dirtier it is, the longer it's been since the oil was changed. In addition to being sludgy and dirty, old oil doesn't provide adequate lubrication. The job of the oil is to coat the moving metal parts with a thin film so that the metal moves on the oil film rather than having metal rub against metal.

Oil is classified in two categories: organic and synthetic. Organic oil is the black stuff that is pumped out of the ground. Synthetic oil is man-made and is better in just about every respect than organic oil. Organic oil starts to break down after a thousand or so miles of use; synthetic oil doesn't start to break down until two thousand miles of use. When the molecules in oil start to break down, oil loses its ability to evenly coat the metal with a layer of film, leading to metal-on-metal contact, which is what makes an engine wear out.

Because of this, you'll want to change oil at least every two thousand to three thousand miles if you use organic oil. I use organic oil and change it every twenty-five hundred miles. If you run synthetic oil, you can go three thousand to four thousand miles between oil changes. Many manufacturers specify oil changes at six thousand to eight thousand miles, but this is just marketing hype. My coauthor, Darwin Holmstrom, once asked Erik Buell, former president of the late Buell Motorcycle Company, about this. Buell is a straight shooter and answered honestly. "Of course anyone who knows anything about engines won't go any longer than four thousand miles without changing oil on any bike," he said, "but the other manufacturers still recommend longer intervals for marketing reasons. We have to play their game."

If the oil is black and dirty-looking, then it's gone longer than three thousand to four thousand miles between oil changes. This means that the engine has experienced abnormal wear. Modern engines are tough and will take a certain amount of abuse, so if everything checks out on the bike (and it doesn't have very many miles on the clock), then you still might consider buying one with dirty oil, but I'd probably find another bike. Changing oil is the most basic routine maintenance you can perform on a bike. If an owner has neglected this, he or she has probably neglected everything else, too.

When you examine the oil, smell it. A burnt smell indicates serious engine problems and should cause you to move on to another bike. Also look for specs of crud in the oil. These could be metal shavings and indicate a serious problem. If the bike is barely broken in, you might find a few small metal shavings in the oil, an indication that it left the factory with tolerances that might have been on the tight side, but if the bike is well broken in, metal shavings in the oil are bad news.

In liquid-cooled bikes, also watch for any creamy froth on top of the oil. This indicates a leaking head gasket that allows antifreeze into the oil, which means the bike will need extensive repairs before it's safe and reliable to ride. If you see evidence of this on the dipstick, thank the owner for taking the time to show you the bike and move on to the next bike.

THE ROAD TEST

AT THIS POINT YOU'LL have learned about as much as you can from examining a stationary bike. If a used motorcycle meets your standards up until here, you'll have to take it for a road test to determine whether the engine and transmission are up to snuff. I know you'll likely want to get straight to the road test, which is by far the most fun part of the entire process, but there's a reason you save this for last—you need to check out everything else to make certain the bike is safe to ride before you risk your life by taking it out on the road.

Although the road test may be exciting for the buyer, it's the least enjoyable for the seller. A dealership might not let you ride a bike at all, though they are more likely to let you ride a used bike than a new one. The dealer may tell you that you won't be able to ride the bike because of insurance reasons, but if you can convince the dealer you're seriously considering buying the bike, you should be able to talk the salesperson into a test ride. It helps if you look like a potentially serious buyer. This is one time it pays to dress conservatively; if you have tribal tattoos on your forehead and are wearing a T-shirt that says "Fuck Death!" your odds of getting a test ride diminish considerably.

Even a private seller may be reluctant to let you ride his or her motorcycle. You can hardly blame the owner; the person is trying to get money by selling his or her bike. To get the most money for the bike, the person likely has worked hard to make it as presentable as possible. Should some dimwit take the bike on a test ride and drop it, the owner loses.

The seller can't count on the potential buyer to do the right thing if a mishap occurs on a test drive; that is, financially compensate the seller for any potential damage to the bike. If that happens, the seller may have to show the bike to an insurance company, which will probably require the seller to pay some sort of deductible, and then the company may jack up his or her rates. So, although you really should ride any bike you are considering buying, don't be surprised if the seller requires some sort of written agreement or security deposit before he or she lets you take out the bike. It might be a bit of an overreaction, but it is understandable.

You should always treat a motorcycle with respect, and this is especially true when that motorcycle belongs to someone else. You're not trying to see how fast the motorcycle is—there are dozens of magazines and websites with professionals who have already answered that question for you. And you're not trying to prove you're the next road-racing superstar. You're just trying to determine the mechanical soundness of the bike.

In addition to confirming the quality of the frame and suspension, the focus of your road test should be to determine the condition of the engine and transmission. If you think the other stuff is expensive, check out the cost of an engine or transmission rebuild in a modern motorcycle. Chances are the costs could approach what you pay for the motorcycle in the first place.

ONCE YOU'VE DETERMINED THAT THE BIKE has the proper amount of oil and that the oil is in good condition, start the engine and let it warm up—trying to ride a motorcycle with a cold engine won't tell you much more about it than that the engine is cold.

If the bike has a center stand, leave it on the stand while warming up. When the bike is on the side stand, the oil will slosh to one side of the oil pan. Depending on the position of the pickup of the oil pump, if the oil sloshes too far to one side of the pan or the other, the pump might suck air instead of oil, especially if the oil level is low. Because of this, some bikes, especially older Japanese four cylinders, can starve the top ends of oil if they are run for extended periods while resting on their side stands. (This won't be a problem if the bike has a dry-sump system like that used by Harley-Davidson.)

Once you're out on the road, pay attention to the overall feel of the motorcycle. Does the frame feel solid or does it squirm around underneath you? Does the suspension seem controlled, yet compliant? Or is it soft and mushy? Or perhaps stiff and bouncing? Does the bike track straight or does it move down the road like it's a crab? Do all the controls work properly or are they sticky and stiff? For the most part you're looking for surprises, since you should have a handle on all of these areas from your earlier inspection of the bike.

You're not going to be pushing a bike's handling limits on a test ride, but you will want to get a feel for the general soundness of the chassis. The bike should track straightly and predictably when pointed down the road, corner without any drama, and be stable on the straights. The suspension should be firm but compliant. The fork shouldn't dive excessively during braking and the rear shock(s) shouldn't bottom out over bumps. Make certain the bike doesn't shake its head when decelerating, particularly in the 45- to 30-mile-per-hour range. If it does, it may just need a steering head bearing adjustment, or the bike may just have mismatched tires (this is easy enough to check once you've stopped), but a bearing replacement is probably in the cards.

The main things you're checking on the test ride are the engine and transmission. A strong engine should start easily and idle smoothly once warmed up. An uneven idle could indicate problems with the carburetors or fuel-injection system. The bike should accelerate without hesitation and should not miss or pop. It most definitely should not produce any smoke from the exhaust pipe once the engine is warmed up, and you shouldn't smell a strong odor of unburned gasoline. If you see white smoke, the engine is burning oil. If you see black smoke, the bike is running rich, meaning it's getting too much gas and not enough air in the fuel charge. Either way, it's not good. Any hiccups, uneven response, or engine bogging indicates a fuel-delivery system problem.

The engine shouldn't make any ticking, rattling, or other mechanical knocking sounds. All you should hear is the burble of the exhaust. Some engines emit a whining sound from their cam gears, especially some of the gear-driven V-fours from Honda, but this shouldn't sound like something inside the engine is broken.

The transmission should pop into first gear with slick mechanical precision; there should be no clunks, reluctance, or any other drama. Clutch take-up should be progressive. If the clutch is jerky and sudden, it could just mean that the clutch cable needs to be adjusted, or it could mean that the clutch itself is weak. If this seems like a problem, have the owner adjust the clutch cable per the procedure outlined in the owner's manual and see if that takes care of the problem. If it doesn't, you need to be suspicious of the clutch. This might also indicate potentially expensive transmission problems.

The rest of the shifts should be as smooth and slick as the shift into first gear. Pay special attention to any clunky shifts or grinding noises coming from the transmission, especially on Yamahas. For years, from the mid-1980s until at least the early 2000s, some Yamahas were prone to transmission failure, the result of Yamaha's practice of using tolerances that were too loose in their transmissions. Most of the afflicted bikes will have had their transmissions fail by now and will have been rebuilt to tighter tolerances, and a lot of people have ridden tens of thousands of miles with no problems at all. Even if I didn't have a policy of buying American-built motorcycles, I'd still stay away from used Yamahas.

But any motorcycle can have a bad transmission. For example, Harley's early five-speed transmissions—those built before the late 1980s—had notoriously weak shifting forks and were prone to expensive failures. This problem was so prevalent that it opened the door for a lot of aftermarket transmission builders like Baker, most of whom made transmissions that were as good as (and, more often than not, better than) the original equipment trannies that Harley used.

When Harley switched to six-speed transmissions in 2008, they once again had transmission problems. They had really bad fifth gears that would fail. It turned out that the problem was caused by the way the fifth gear was cut. Harley revised the way it cut the fifth-gear cogs for 2009 and the problem seems to have gone away.

If you suspect any problems at all with the transmission, pay close attention and don't buy the bike unless you are sure that the problem was something like a loose clutch cable or a poor shift on your part and not with the transmission itself. If a bike pops out of gear, head directly back to the owner and give the bike back to him or her before the transmission fails completely, possibly giving an unscrupulous seller an opening to blame you for the failed transmission. And a bike that pops out of gear will have its transmission fail sooner rather than later. You don't even need to call a shop and find out what a transmission rebuild will cost you, because I can answer that question for you: too damned much.

When you get the bike into top gear out on the road—roughly at 45 miles per hour on most bikes—accelerate up to the speed limit. The engine's rpm should rise in proportion to your speed. If the engine seems to spool up faster than you're building speed, the clutch is probably slipping.

Replacing the clutch isn't all that expensive compared to transmissions. But consider that modern clutches are pretty tough, so if the clutch is wearing out on a bike that doesn't have a lot of miles, chances are that it's been seriously abused, perhaps even raced. A weak clutch should serve as a warning flag for other potential problems.

What You Should Know

- A thorough inspection up front can save you thousands of dollars down the road.
- When in doubt, consult a good mechanic.
- If something doesn't check out, find another motorcycle.

CHAPTER FIVE

BUYING A BIKE

Like most aspects of motorcycle ownership, the process of buying bikes is different from automobiles—you'll find this out as soon as you go to finance and insure your bike. Whether you buy a new bike or a used bike, you'll need to make a few arrangements before you ride home on your new (or new-to-you) machine. As mentioned in the last chapter, if you buy a bike from a dealership, the staff can help you with details like financing, licensing, and insurance; but if you're buying a used bike from a private seller, you'll have to arrange for these things yourself. Either way, you'll want to keep in mind some important considerations that are unique to buying bikes.

PRICING A USED MOTORCYCLE

DETERMINING WHAT'S A FAIR value for any used motorcycle you're looking at will be a challenge. There are online resources like the venerable *Kelley Blue Book* that list rough values for pretty much every motorcycle available, but the prices are a lot more volatile for used motorcycles than they are for used cars. To make matters more confusing, prices can vary wildly from region to region. For example, a high-performance sport bike will have more value in a metro area or a rural area that has a lot of winding roads than it will in a place with few metro areas and nothing but flat, straight roads, places like North Dakota and Kansas.

Regardless of the region, few people are getting the kind of money that *KBB* lists for any motorcycle since the economy imploded a few years back. Still, you can use *KBB* prices as a jumping-off point. Remember to deduct the costs of any likely repairs or needed maintenance from the prices listed in sources like *KBB*.

A more accurate way to assess the current market for a bike is to go on eBay and find as many examples of the particular bike as you can. Even if you don't plan to buy a bike on eBay, sign up for an eBay account and monitor the sales of the bikes you are interested in buying using the "My eBay" feature. After spending a couple of weeks watching which bikes sell and how much they sell for, you'll have a pretty fair idea of the current market value of any used bike you may want to buy.

If you're like most people, you'll try to negotiate the best deal possible, but like everyone else you meet, you should treat the seller with respect. This should be true whether you're buying from a private seller or a dealership. You can make a low-ball offer if you want, but if the offer is insultingly low, you better use a little humor when making it to avoid coming across as a crook. A salesperson at a dealership will just laugh off your offer by saying something like, "But seriously . . ." Your chances might not be much better with a private seller, but who knows? Maybe the seller will be desperate or inexperienced enough (or both) to take the offer.

In general, you have little to gain by nickel-and-diming the seller. If you've determined that a used bike is worthy of buying, saving a few hundred dollars on the purchase price won't mean much in the long run. If you like the bike and enjoy riding it, you'll have forgotten about the extra money just about as soon as you hit the open road.

FINANCING A BIKE

SPEAKING OF MONEY, BEFORE you even start looking at used bikes from private sellers, you have to make sure you have the capital to buy the bike or else you're wasting everyone's time. Ideally you should pay cash for everything you buy—paying interest on a loan is a huge waste of money—but the reality is that most people don't have enough spare cash sitting around to buy a motorcycle.

If you have to finance your bike, you at least should be smart about it. The interest paid in finance

charges can represent a good chunk of the overall money you'll ultimately pay for the bike, so you
should arrange for the lowest interest rate you can
find.

First talk to the loan officer at your own bank. (If
you have a decent credit rating, you will have at least
one bank with which you regularly do business. If
you don't have a bank, your credit rating will be poor
and you'll be at the mercy of whatever loan shark is
willing to lend you the money to buy a motorcycle.)
See what interest rates and monthly payments will be
for loans spread out over different time periods. Usually loans are paid off over a period of time ranging
from thirty-six to seventy-two months. The longer
the loan period, the lower the monthly payments, but
the interest rate usually goes up as the time it takes to
repay a loan gets longer.

After you've determined the best rate you can
get from your bank, call at least two other banks to
see if they can beat your bank's rate. This way you'll
find the best rate available, but don't expect a good
rate. You'll probably be in for a shock when you hear
the rates for financing motorcycles, which are almost
always much higher than the rates for financing cars.
The rates you end up paying will vary from company to company, state to state, and person to person,
and will depend on variables such as the prime rate
and the borrower's credit rating. If you can't afford
to pay cash, your best bet is to try to get a special
financing deal from a factory, but those can be few
and far between in times of tight credit. In general, if
you buy a bike, especially a used bike, expect to pay

close to double the interest rate you would get if you financed a new car. If you are financing a new bike from a dealership, you may be able to take advantage of special rates from the factory; but if you're financing a used bike, you'll just need to prepare to pay high interest rates.

In some cases those rates can approach the rates offered by your typical loan shark. Back when Harley sold more bikes than it built and had people paying $500 or more just to get on the waiting list to buy one of its motorcycles, the company's financial arm could charge whatever it wanted for interest. At one point the rate was as high as 21 percent. Just like the days of waiting lists to buy Harleys, the days of the Motor Company being able to charge outrageous interest rates are long gone now.

MOTORCYCLE INSURANCE

THE COST OF INSURING a motorcycle can rival the cost of maintaining and repairing it. This is especially true of high-performance sport bikes, which are grossly overrepresented in accident claims. That doesn't necessarily mean they're more prone to accidents, though you'd think that would be the case, judging from young people we've all seen riding their crotch rockets like lunatics. But in reality, middle-aged men aboard cruisers and touring bikes statistically account for more fatalities than do young squids on sport bikes. ("Squid" is a derogatory term for young people who ride recklessly aboard crotch rockets. No one knows exactly where the term came from. One theory is that it's because when they crash, they leave a squidlike blood splatter on the pavement.)

Though sport bikes don't account for the majority of accidents, they are justly overrepresented in insurance claims. This is because they are covered top to bottom in expensive plastic bodywork that lacks the protective features of most touring bikes like my Vision. If my bike falls over, or if a Honda Gold Wing or ST1300 falls over while standing still or at extremely low speeds, the bike's built-in design features prevent much serious damage from occurring. If a sport bike like a Honda CBR1000RR, Yamaha R1, or Suzuki GSX-R falls over, even while standing still in a parking lot, there will be thousands of dollars worth of broken plastic on the pavement.

Most owners simply can't absorb the cost of fixing that and have to rely on insurance payments to pay for the repair of their bikes. Often they won't have a choice but to repair the bikes since so many of them are financed by banks, and banks will require the owner to obtain full-coverage insurance. This brings up another advantage of paying cash for a bike rather than financing it; if you pay cash for a bike, you can save money by just obtaining liability insurance. (Most states will require you to at least have liability insurance.) If you finance a bike, you will have to obtain full-coverage insurance, which is much more expensive.

That said, even if you can get by with just liability insurance, it might be a good idea to get full coverage to protect your investment if your bike is worth a significant amount of money. If the cost is too high, you can save some money by going with a policy with a higher deductible. If you go with a $1,000 deductible (the amount you pay up front before insurance kicks in) instead of a $300 deductible, you'll have to cover more of the cost of any repairs for damage caused in an accident out of your own pocket, but at least you'll be able to recoup the bulk of the cost of your bike if it's totaled.

Besides, the higher deductibles you would pay in the event of an accident might not cost you that much more than having the insurance pay for the repair, because if you ever do file a motorcycle claim, most insurance companies will jack your rates up so much that it will more than equal the cost of any small repairs in the long run. Unless your bike has major damage, it can often cost you less to repair it without help from the insurance company once you figure in higher insurance premiums.

If you finance a bike, you may have the option of obtaining what is called "gap" insurance. This will pay the difference between what an insurance company pays for the value of a bike should you total it out and the amount that you may owe.

Chances are if you finance a new bike, you'll be upside down on your loan for most of the term of the loan because new motorcycles depreciate so quickly in value. (Being upside down on a loan means that you owe more on the loan than the item you financed is worth.) This means that if you wreck the bike or if it gets stolen, you won't collect enough on the insurance to cover the loan, so in addition to losing your motorcycle, you'll have to cough up a bunch of money to pay the difference. Gap insurance will pay that difference. If you have to finance your bike, the bank or dealer's financial department will likely offer you gap insurance. It might be a good idea to take them up on that offer.

Expect to be shocked when you find out how much you'll pay every month for full-coverage motorcycle insurance. If you have any moving violations or accident claims on your record, you may have difficulty finding insurance at any price. If you have automobile insurance with a company that also offers motorcycle insurance, going with the same company will likely be your least expensive option. You may even get a multivehicle discount. Unfortunately the odds are good that your auto insurer won't even offer motorcycle insurance. Because of high claim rates (remember, motorcycles fall over a lot more often than do automobiles), a lot of companies don't even offer motorcycle insurance.

Rates will vary from company to company, but there are some guidelines you can use when seeking insurance. Sport bikes or sport-tourers with a lot of plastic bodywork will be more expensive to insure than touring bikes for the reasons described previously. In general, bigger bikes will be more expensive to insure than smaller bikes, at least within the same category. A big cruiser may be cheaper to insure than a small sport bike, but it will be more expensive than a smaller cruiser. And a small sport bike will cost more than a large touring bike, but it will cost less than insuring a big sport bike.

Where you live will also affect your insurance rates. Companies base their rates on crash and theft

statistics in a given region. If you live in a neighborhood where a lot of motorcycle thefts have been reported, you will have higher insurance rates than if
you lived in a suburb with low rates of motor vehicle
theft. Sometimes the statistics are surprising—some
so-called nice neighborhoods have high theft rates—
but, in general, the farther you live from an inner
city, the lower your insurance rates will be. If you
live in a rural area, you'll most likely have the lowest
rates of all.

BUYING A NEW MOTORCYCLE

BUYING A NEW BIKE is in most ways much simpler
than purchasing a used machine. You won't need to
examine every component of a new bike because it
won't have any wear and tear to examine. Likewise
you won't need to look for evidence of abuse and improper maintenance, since you'll be first person to
use (or abuse) and maintain the bike.

Even though you'll spend more buying a new
bike, there are some good reasons to go this route if
you can afford it. You can never be sure that a used
bike was properly cared for, regardless how thoroughly you inspect it. You'll be the person who controls how well maintained a new bike will be.

When you're shopping for a used bike, you'll
look for the best available bike that suits your needs.
When shopping for a new bike, you'll have your pick
of any bike that falls into the price range you establish
for yourself. Deciding which ones you want to look

at is the fun part, because your research will consist of reading about each bike in motorcycle magazines and on motorcycle websites.

BEWARE OF "BETA TESTING" NEW BIKES

ONE WORD OF ADVICE when picking out a new bike—be cautious when buying a newly introduced model. Sometimes manufacturers have an unwritten policy of beta testing; that is, the first few examples of a new bike might not have had all the bugs worked out of them in the development process, making the buyers an unwitting part of that process. Because of the pressure to meet production schedules, manufacturers sometimes push new models out the door before they're completely ready and then they work out any potential problems on the fly.

Harley-Davidson is considered the worst offender in this respect. Longtime riders will tell you never to buy a first-year version of any Harley. This has probably been true since Harley and the Davidson brothers cobbled together their first prototype bike in 1903, but it has definitely been true since at least the introduction of the Knucklehead in 1936.

In 1936 recirculating oil systems were still relatively new. Instead of high-pressure pumps that circulated oil through the engine, earlier total-loss engines just had a hand pump that a rider would pump every so often to lubricate the engine. This oil would circulate around the engine and then either be burned or slosh out through one of the many areas on the engine where moving parts were exposed, most commonly through the valve train. Recirculating oiling systems were a huge step forward in engine reliability, but designers of early examples like Harley's 1936 Knucklehead didn't fully comprehend the need to contain the oil being circulated by the high-pressure oil pump, so they didn't fully enclose the valve gear. As a result, the very first Knuckleheads sprayed their riders with hot oil from the valve train. Harley quickly remedied this by designing tin cups that snapped over the exposed valve gear, but the problem wasn't really solved until Motor Company engineers redesigned the valve train so that it was completely enclosed.

This sort of problem-solving-on-the-fly approach has been a pattern with Harley ever since. The early Panheads had major problems with their hydraulic lifters, problems that weren't solved until the lifters were moved from the tops of the pushrods down into the crankcases. The first electric-start Electra Glides also suffered teething problems, as did the newly introduced Shovelheads, alternator-equipped Shovelheads, and the first bikes equipped with five-speed transmissions.

The first-year Evolution engines had so many problems that for years a lot of riders wore T-shirts that read: SEE NO EVO. HEAR NO EVO. SPEAK NO EVO. When the Evolution was later replaced with the Twin Cam 88, a mechanic friend of mine hurried up and bought one of the last Evolution-powered bikes because he knew the new TC88 engines would have problems. He was right. The TC88 engine came out in 1999. At the Sturgis rally in 2000 the sides of South Dakota roads were littered with TC88 engines that had suffered catastrophic failure of their camshaft bearings.

Harley eventually worked out the bugs in all of these engines, but the pattern continues to this day. Even though the 96-cubic-inch Twin Cam engine was just an enlarged version of the TC88, early examples of that engine suffered from overheating problems. You should flat out avoid buying the first-year (and often even the second-year) examples of any new product from Harley-Davidson.

Just because Harley is the worst offender doesn't mean other companies don't follow the same practice. Even competent non-Italian manufacturers can be guilty of beta testing every now and then. Usually, new bikes from Germany and Japan are good to go from the first day of production, but every now and then a motorcycle slips out of every factory before all the bugs are worked out.

FINDING A GOOD MOTORCYCLE SHOP

ONCE YOU'VE DETERMINED WHICH bikes you want to look at, you'll need to find dealerships that sell those brands. Just finding dealerships used to be tough since up until a few years ago most motorcycle shops were little out-of-the-way holes in the ground. Historically motorcycle sales didn't generate the kind of cash flow that allowed dealers to open up high-profile shops in good retail locations.

But that changed in the late 1990s and early 2000s, thanks in large part to the success of Harley-Davidson. A company that was almost bankrupt in early 1986, Harley-Davidson's fortunes dramatically changed in the late 1980s. The Motor Company's rags-to-riches story became the stuff of legend, and by the early 1990s Harley was one of the most successful companies in America.

In large part Harley's success was as much the result of its marketing clothing and accessories as it was the result of its motorcycle sales. And the company wasn't just selling exhaust pipes and T-shirts; by the early 1990s Harley shops sold just about any product you could imagine emblazoned with the company's famous bar-and-shield logo, from toilet-seat covers to cigarettes.

Because retailing products other than motorcycles was such a big part of its business model, Harley forced its dealers to build new facilities on prime commercial real estate. These new Harley superstores were more like expensive boutique shops than the traditional motorcycle dealerships that used to be found on the wrong side of the tracks, sandwiched between a scrap-iron yard and a whorehouse.

By the early 1990s Harley dominated the American motorcycle market; where Harley led, the other manufacturers followed. By the mid-2000s just about every motorcycle dealership had moved from its previous steel sheds hidden in industrial parks into big, fancy showrooms in high-buck retail areas. It used to be that you'd need a phone book and a good map to find a motorcycle shop in a strange city; today you can hardly miss them because they're right along the freeway, next to the Audi dealerships and Cracker Barrel restaurants.

Although you won't have to track down motorcycle shops like we did in the old days, you will have to do a little research to see which shops are good and which should be avoided, because not all motorcycle shops are created equal. Each one is staffed by human beings, and the excellence of a shop is only as good as the quality of those individuals.

To determine the quality of the staff will require two things of you. The first is that you have some knowledge of the bike you're looking at, which you will have, since you followed my advice and did some research. Second, you have to use your knowledge of human nature. You need to have a feel for whether someone is telling you the truth or feeding you a line of bullshit. Developing that sort of intuition is beyond the scope of this book.

THE SERVICE DEPARTMENT

A CRITICAL FACTOR IN finding the right dealership is the quality of a shop's service department. It really doesn't matter how straight a shooter a salesperson might be if the service department is staffed by morons.

For example, when I first saw Harley's then-new V-Rod, I was visiting a Harley shop while traveling out of state. I wasn't interested in buying the bike, but I was curious about its maintenance costs. I knew

Porsche had designed the overhead-cam engine, and Porsche has a reputation for building engines that are idiotically expensive to maintain. I'd stopped at the Harley shop to get a part for my Road King and decided to ask the service manager how much it cost to do a major service on the V-Rod.

The guy told me that it would be the same as the cost of the major service of any other V-twin. To comprehend the sheer stupidity this man exhibited, you need to understand something about Harley's air-cooled V-twins and the V-Rod engine. The air-cooled V-twin, the engine that's found in every Harley except the various V-Rod models, uses the same basic overhead valve system the company has used since the 1936 Knucklehead, which has the cam (or cams) located down in the case moving pushrods that go up to the top end and open the valves. These pushrods have featured hydraulic lifters since before I started riding, which means that the valves never need to be adjusted.

The V-Rod uses overhead cams that don't have hydraulic lifters, meaning that like most high-performance motorcycles they need periodic valve adjustments. The valve adjustment is usually the most expensive part of a major tune-up. When the service manager said the cost for a V-Rod tune-up was the same as the tune-up for any other V-twin, I asked him if that meant they adjusted the valves on the V-Rod for free.

I don't know if I've ever seen a man look so befuddled. Here was a man so ignorant about motorcycle mechanics that he didn't even know he had to adjust the valves on Harley's new V-Rod (which, it turns out, is a ridiculously expensive process because the engine has to be dropped to gain access to the rear valves). And this fool was the shop's service manager. I wouldn't want anyone this ignorant checking the air pressure in my tires, much less supervising the people who might be rebuilding my engine.

I asked around, and it turns out that I'm not the only person who wasn't impressed with this shop and its service department. A lot of the local riders I spoke with refused to do business with the shop; instead, many of them drove an extra seventy miles to do business with a respected shop in a neighboring state.

If it's possible to meet with local motorcyclists, you can get a good idea from talking to them which shops are good and which should be avoided. You can also learn a bit about this by snooping around online and trying to find local motorcycle forums, but remember, like anything else you read on the Internet, take what you read with a grain of salt. Sometimes customers are to blame, but that doesn't stop them from unfairly lambasting a dealership on the Internet.

Ultimately you have to make the decision as to where you're going to shop for a bike. Again, you need to have a pretty good knowledge of motorcycles to accurately gauge the competency of a shop and its service department. If you don't feel comfortable with your own knowledge base, try to enlist the help of a friend who knows something about motorcycles.

FINAL NEGOTIATIONS

ONCE YOU'VE FOUND THE bike of your dreams from an independent seller or the right shop, one with a competent sales staff and a good service department, it's time to negotiate a price. You'll have less room to negotiate the price of a new bike than you will a used bike. As mentioned in the last chapter, dealerships have to make some money on each bike they sell just to keep their doors open. That said, there's no reason why you have to foot the entire bill for their overhead. There has to be a little compromise on the parts of both you and the dealer.

Most dealers will do what they can to meet you halfway, but in recent decades that has not been the case with Harley dealers. For many years, selling Harleys consisted of sitting behind a desk, collecting $500 deposits, and putting names on a list. The dealers had little incentive to compromise with a buyer. Today the motorcycle market is very different, and Harley sales are down dramatically. Harley dealers have been slow to change their stubborn ways, but they will have to adapt to survive. Those dealers that are unwilling to compromise will become extinct.

Typically dealers add a base margin of 12 to 18 percent on new bikes. They often add extra charges on top of that, like freight and setup costs. They also make money from their finance department by talking you into things like extended warranties.

Your best tool for finding a dealership with the

lowest markup is still the old-fashioned telephone. You can find a lot of dealerships advertising on the Internet, but they usually aren't listing the lowest prices they have available. More often they seem to be fishing for buyers willing to pay a bit more. For example, a shop might list a bike at $11,000 on its webpage but if you call and talk to a salesperson, you might find that you can get a one- or two-year-old carry-over version of the exact same bike for $8,000.

Make certain you ask for an out-the-door price when shopping via phone. Make it clear that you want the salesperson to include all extra charges like freight and setup costs as well as the costs of license plates and sales tax. This way you're comparing apples to apples when talking to salespeople from different dealerships; it also ensures you won't be surprised by additional costs when you go to buy the bike.

If you can't get a straight answer from a salesperson, you're best off avoiding that dealership. If the person says something like "Come on down and we'll talk about it," he or she is trying to lure you into that dealership. There are plenty of motorcycle shops out there; you don't need to deal with one that tries to trick you right from the start.

You'll be able to get somewhat of an idea about what dealers are paying for the wholesale price of a bike from the range of prices you find when calling around. You can figure that the lowest prices are marked up around 12 percent from the wholesale cost and the highest prices are marked up around 18 percent. Do the math and you'll have a rough idea of what the wholesale cost is.

You can negotiate from there, but chances are you'll have a hard time getting the price down much below the lowest price you find when shopping around. What you can do is use this information to negotiate the best price at the best dealership you found while researching dealerships. If the best price is available at a dealership with a lousy service department or a bad reputation, you can try to negotiate the same price from a dealership with a decent service department and a better reputation.

PULLING THE TRIGGER

IF YOU'RE BUYING FROM a dealership in your own state, the dealership will take care of getting license plates for a bike and paying the sales tax. It will roll that cost into your out-the-door price. But if you're buying from an out-of-state dealership or a private party, you'll need to take care of tax and licensing yourself.

There are some ways to make this process simpler and safer. For example, it's a good idea to write up some sort of simple contract between you and the seller. This doesn't have to be a formal document drawn up by a lawyer. It just needs to be a document written in plain, easily understandable language that outlines the terms to which you and the buyer agree. Both you and the seller should have a signed copy of the agreement.

Before any money changes hands, you'll need to make sure you have all the paperwork you'll need when you go to your state department of motor vehicles for your license plates. You'll need a clear title, and you'll need to make sure that the VIN (vehicle identification number) and engine numbers are correct and match the title. If there's some discrepancy, you may find it impossible to get a license plate for your bike.

What You Should Know

- Be prepared before going to buy a motorcycle—have your financing and insurance in order before you even go to look at a bike.
- Avoid financing if you can help it because it makes buying a motorcycle much more expensive.
- Make sure you can afford to insure a motorcycle before you buy it.

CHAPTER SIX

ADVANCED RIDING TECHNIQUES

Now that you've learned enough about motorcycles to decide what type you want, you've learned how to ride, and you've bought a motorcycle, I'm going to talk about the most important thing you can do while riding a motorcycle: staying alive. In this chapter we're going to discuss advanced training and riding techniques, including cornering, braking, and coping with other vehicles.

More than anything else in this book, the information that follows will help keep you alive. But as with the information in chapter 3, your best bet is still to get professional training. Once again, the Motorcycle Safety Foundation is a good place to start when looking for advanced training: in the late 1980s MSF developed its Experienced RiderCourse (ERC), a half-day course for newer riders and seasoned riders alike that's designed to hone bikers' riding skills as well as help develop the mental skills that will keep people alive out on the meat-grinding public highways. I took the ERC back when it first came out in the 1980s. I'd sent so many new riders to the basic RiderCourse that I thought I should take a course myself. I had nearly thirty years of experience when I took the ERC, and I still found it extremely helpful (even though I was the only rider in the entire class who fell down).

If you want to take your riding skills to the next level, you might want to consider going to one of the many high-performance riding schools available. These usually are held at racetracks and use motorcycles provided by the school, though some, like Lee Parks's Total Control Advanced Riding Clinic, take place in large parking lots and require you to provide your own motorcycle. (See the appendix for more information about riding courses.)

The fact that you're reading this book bodes well for your future survival as a motorcyclist. I'm trying to share a lifetime of experience with you, and I hope you'll find it useful, but I can't stress strongly enough the need to get proper training. Ideally you'll use the information in this section of the book in conjunction with what you learn in an advanced riding course.

SITUATIONAL AWARENESS

AWARENESS OF YOUR SURROUNDINGS will usually be the critical factor that determines whether you live or die out on public roads. You need to be aware of what you are doing at all times, you need to be aware of what other people are doing, and you need to make other drivers aware of what you are doing.

Being aware of your own actions is the element over which you have the most control. An obvious way of doing that is to ride sober. Normally I don't care what people do. I figure it's their business. If they want to have a beer or three, I don't see a problem with that. Likewise I don't really care if they like to burn a marijuana cigarette now and then. Hell, I don't really care if they're drunk and high all the time, if they snort Drano or bang rat poison. It's their business, and it really doesn't matter whether or not I approve. Abuse yourself in whatever way you see fit, but when it comes time to ride a motorcycle, I highly recommend riding sober.

The Hurt Report found that alcohol was involved in nearly half of all motorcycle fatalities. That was thirty years ago, but the number has remained relatively stable. In 1998, 45 percent of motorcycle fatalities involved alcohol; in 2004, 48 percent involved alcohol. The problem is that alcohol and other drugs slow down your reaction time, and reaction time is everything when it comes to crashing or not crashing your motorcycle. When something happens—when that deer jumps out in front of you or that car swerves into your lane because the driver didn't see you—you have only a fraction of a second to react. If your reactions are an instant too slow because you have had even one beer, that could easily mean the difference between life and death.

Last year on the way home from Sturgis a couple

of deer—a doe and a fawn—ran out in front of me. I was able to slow down just enough to miss the mother as she ran across the road, but not the fawn. Luckily for both of us the fawn didn't cross the road, but instead, ran alongside me before turning back into the forest. I was stone-cold sober and paying attention, and even then, I barely reacted fast enough to avoid hitting the larger deer. Had I drank even one beer, that might have slowed my reaction time just enough to cause me to hit the deer.

But other distractions can impair your reaction times almost as much as alcohol and other drugs. The main cause of distracted driving these days is the cell phone. If you're calling on your cell phone or, worse yet, texting while you're riding your motorcycle, well, you deserve to be killed, preferably sooner rather than later. That's all I have to say about that subject.

Still other distractions exist that are less obvious because they're inside your own head. When you ride, are you focusing on what you're doing and the potential hazards that are all around you, or are you thinking about giving your boss that beat down he's deserved for all these years? Are you thinking about the condition of your motorcycle, or are you thinking about the condition of your marriage? If you're concentrating on the fight you just had with your wife when you told her you were going for a motorcycle ride, you're probably not concentrating on that cell-phone-yakking half-wit in the SUV that's barreling down on you.

I lost a good friend this way. The guy was a skilled rider and extremely safety conscious—he was one of the first people I ever knew who wore a helmet. His motorcycle was always in tip-top condition, and he never rode when he was drunk or high. But one day he got in an argument with his girlfriend, took off on his bike, lost control in a corner, and hit an oak tree.

It's impossible to clear your mind of all distractions all the time—if we could, the makers of sleeping pills, Prozac, and other mental medications would be out of business—but before you head out on the road, you have to do everything you can to empty your mind of anything that will disrupt your focus on riding. Do whatever it takes to clear your head, including going to the bathroom. (You'd be surprised how much your concentration can suffer when you've got a full bladder.)

Anger is another huge distraction, but it's hard not to get angry when you're sharing the road with the collection of simpletons known as other drivers. Anger clouds your judgment and slows your reaction time. You'll often have every reason in the world to be angry at other drivers, but you need to remain calm, cool, and collected in every situation, regardless of who is right and who is wrong. Above all, don't get into road-rage situations with other vehicles. They may be completely wrong, but they have your life in their hands. Right or wrong, you can't win an argument with someone who has the ability to end your life by simply turning his or her steering wheel.

Buddhist monks spend entire lifetimes trying to figure out how to clear these sorts of distractions from their minds. Maybe it works for them; maybe it doesn't. I don't know—I've spent my life doing other things. Like riding motorcycles. Since I don't expect to become a Buddhist monk anytime soon, I've had to find other ways to clear my mind when I'm on my bike.

One trick I've developed is to focus my attention on potential hazards. I study my surroundings and imagine what might go wrong. I look for brush or other growth along the road that might block my view of a deer or other critter that might run out in front of me. I watch other traffic, looking for other vehicles that might swerve into my lane, or trucks with loads that might come loose or tires that might blow out, sending debris onto the road.

I look for any element that might pose danger, then I check to see how prepared I am to deal with that danger. Have I placed my motorcycle in the best position to deal with potential hazards? Do I have enough room to maneuver out of the way of danger? (I'll talk more about lane positioning later.) Am I covering my front brake with my right fingers so that I don't lose a fraction of a second reaching for my brake if the situation goes south in a hurry? Is my engine in its powerband so that if I need to accelerate out of the way of danger, I won't twist my throttle only to have the engine bog down? Am I traveling at a safe speed in the first place?

In addition to assessing how prepared I am to deal with potential dangers, I devise plans of action in case something does go wrong. I look at the way a load on a truck is tied down to try to determine which way the debris is likely to fall if the ties come loose, then look for a clear, safe space to move in the opposite direction of where the debris will likely fall. I try to determine possible paths of travel of even the most errant vehicle. I allow plenty of room between me and the vehicle in front of me, and I position my bike so that I have the best view of any potential danger. If I spot potential danger, I reposition my bike so that I have the least exposure to that threat and the best possible escape routes if the worst-case scenario comes to pass.

This exercise helps me prepare for potential danger, but it does more than that: it focuses my complete attention on that moment in time, so that I'm not thinking about anything other than riding my motorcycle in that place in time. It might not be the same as spending a lifetime in some Buddhist monastery, but the concentration required while riding a motorcycle is a form of focused meditation that makes all the petty distractions of day-to-day life melt away. It might seem morbid to concentrate on potential danger with such intense focus, but it clears my head. When I'm finished riding, I feel relaxed and recharged, so morbid or not, I consider it a beneficial activity. Some people ride with stereos blasting at top volume, but to me that would interrupt my meditation on the ride. The only sound track I need for that is the music my engine makes when it's running in peak condition.

DEFEATING ROAD HAZARDS

THINK OF GOING OUT on public roads aboard a motorcycle as a form of going to war. As in any form of combat, the only way to win is to know your enemy. You can better understand the nature of the threats you'll face if you break down the types of hazards into three broad categories:

- **Vehicles.** These include everything from a fast-moving bicycle to a double-trailer semitruck. This category has the most potential to kill a motorcycle rider, so you should never trust any other vehicle. Obviously the bigger the vehicle, the more potential harm it can do to you; but when you're on a bike, you are so vulnerable that even an errant bicycle rider can potentially take you out. Learn to identify the vehicles that are most likely to kill you, and when you're riding among them, always look for possible escape routes should things start to go wrong.

- **Debris and potholes.** This category includes any stationary object that can lead to your losing control of your motorcycle if you hit it. This could be the road alligators from one of the thousands of blown truck tires that you'll be dodging as long as you ride motorcycles, or it could be a sign post at the edge of the road, or a box of bolts that fell off a flatbed truck. You'll need to perfect your control over your motorcycle to develop the riding skills that will help you avoid hitting this type of hazard.

- **People and other animals.** People and other animals move slower than vehicles, but they can be almost as deadly—and even more erratic. They can change direction quickly, and they don't follow normal patterns of movement, as vehicular traffic does. When you're moving down the road on your motorcycle, you'll often ride in conditions that make it difficult to see animals and pedestrians until they pop out right in front of you, so you'll need to learn to recognize the situations in which two- or four-legged critters are likely to appear.

When riding on public highways, I recommend adopting the attitude that every single person on the road is a sociopathic serial killer who has just escaped from an asylum for the criminally insane. This might seem a little pessimistic, but you'll live longer if you assume everyone else on the road is a homicidal moron whose sole purpose is to kill you.

Face it: an unsettlingly high percentage of American drivers are unfit to be behind the wheel in the best of circumstances. What else would you expect in a country where the hardest part of the driving test is parallel parking? Parking is the opposite of driving, so there's not a hell of a lot of actual driving involved in getting a driver's license. Technically it should be called a parking license, but it's not, and the end result is a nation of people who think of the driver's seat as a place to make phone calls and send text messages while they are going somewhere else. There's not much you can depend on anymore, but you can be virtually certain that someone is going to do something incredibly stupid out on the road. The best way to deal with the situation is to make certain that person is not you.

You need to have complete awareness of every single one of the idiots with whom you're sharing the road while you are out on your bike. You need to learn to read traffic and learn to recognize the clues that will alert you to potentially dangerous situations. You need to develop a feel for the circumstances in which other drivers are likely to do something stupid.

For example, when you are on a multilane road, pulling up to an intersection alongside a line of cars, you can be sure that at least one of them is going to pull out into your lane to get around that line, and you can be just as sure that the person will not have checked his or her mirror or looked over his or her shoulder to clear the lane, so he or she has no idea you are there. Or when you're riding along a row of parked cars, expect at least one of them to pull out in front of you or even beside you.

When you're riding alongside slow-moving or parked traffic, always position your bike as far away from the line of cars as possible to give yourself room to react when the car inevitably pulls out right in front of you. Constantly scan for safe space in which you can swerve around the damned fool. Monitor your rearview mirror to make certain no one will run you over if the only safe course of action is to brake hard. Create circumstances in which you have the most possible options in the event of any dangerous situation.

Don't ever believe anyone's turn signals. The person may be driving down the road totally oblivious to the fact that his or her turn signal is flashing. If he or she does plan to change lanes, he or she is more likely to not use the signals at all. The person changing lanes without signaling a lane change will probably be the life-threatening situation you encounter most often. It will happen with such frequency that you'll soon be surprised when someone does signal a lane change and doesn't pull into your lane while you are occupying it.

To prevent this you need to be completely aware of what everyone on the road is doing at all times. The best way to determine if a person is about to change lanes isn't to watch his or her turn signal; it's to watch his or her front tires. Before a car can change direction, its front tires have to turn. Where the front tires turn, the car will follow. If you see the tires turn toward your spot on the road, you have an extra split second to react, find a safe space, and move out of harm's way.

Watching the front tires of cars is especially useful for alerting you when oncoming cars are about to make a left turn across your lane. This is an exceptionally dangerous situation. Unfortunately it's also a common occurrence—I've been almost taken out by oncoming cars making unsignaled left turns in front of me more than all other near misses combined. To be fair to other drivers, motorcycles are hard to see in the best conditions; when they are coming right at you, they don't present a very large profile and are even easier to miss. Factor in the 50 percent chance that the oncoming driver is distracted because his main squeeze is "sexting" him, and for all practical purposes you're invisible.

Because of this you'll likely have someone making a turn across your lane of traffic on a weekly basis. Sometimes it will be on a daily basis. And it won't always happen at obvious intersections. Often the person will be turning into a driveway or a parking lot that you might not have seen. The other driver may even be making a U-turn. I lost a friend in December

2009 because a van made an unsignaled U-turn and pulled out just as he was passing by. And this man was as experienced a rider as I've ever known.

You can't prevent this situation, but you can prepare for it, and, as I've mentioned, one of the best ways to do that is to watch the front tires of other vehicles. If a car is coming at you, watch its left front tire. Position yourself so that you're as far away from the vehicle as possible, and ride in a place that will leave you room to get out of the way should you see the other vehicle's left wheel start to turn in your direction.

Watching the front tires of other vehicles won't make you invincible, but it will give you extra time to react to danger. If you are paying attention and notice the instant someone turns a front tire toward your lane, you'll have an extra fraction of a second to react, and that fraction of a second could save your life. But this only helps if you're aware of your surroundings. To be effective, your reaction will have to take into account every other numb-nuts driver on the road. You won't be gaining much if you swerve to miss a car moving into your lane from the right and accidentally hit the car in the lane to your left.

You'll also have to be aware of all the nonvehicular hazards. For example, when you're riding along a line of parked cars, it's just as likely that a dog or a child will run out from between the parked cars as it is that one of the parked cars will pull out in front of you. There's no way to predict the behavior of an animal or a child; the best you can do is try to identify places where an animal or a child might possibly emerge onto a road. Be aware of your surroundings, cover your front brake lever, and be prepared to make an emergency stop the instant you see something moving into your path of travel.

Sometimes the nonmoving hazards can be as deadly as the moving ones. You need to be aware of road conditions that could lead to a loss of traction, like rain, dirt, leaves, railroad tracks, potholes, oil, antifreeze, ice, and sand or gravel buildup. Debris is especially dangerous when you encounter it in a curve. It tends to build up on the outside edge of a curve, so you need to give this area extra attention when you are scanning the road in a corner.

If there is debris in a corner, slow down to give yourself time to maneuver around it. If it takes you by surprise and there isn't enough time to avoid it, don't panic and hit the brakes. This will upset your chassis and increase the chances that you'll lose traction and crash. Instead, maintain a steady speed through the corner. If you've slowed down to a safe speed before entering the corner, you should be all right. If you are going too fast and need to slow down in a corner, stand the bike up for a brief moment, brake, then immediately countersteer back into the corner. If you react quickly, you should be able to maintain control of your motorcycle, but if you stand the bike up and brake for more than a split second, there's a good chance you'll run off the road.

Even the paint on the road itself can be hazardous. The paint of the center stripe and at the edge of the road, or in a crosswalk, or warning of an approaching railroad crossing, or words such as STOP AHEAD can get as slippery as mud or ice, especially when wet. If you have Speed Channel, watch a motorcycle road race in the rain some time. You'll see that even the best riders in the world will crash the instant their tire hits some wet paint on the surface of the racetrack.

The paint doesn't even have to be wet to be dangerous. Sometimes when the temperature gets high enough, the paint starts to melt and turn into a substance that resembles slippery wet vinyl. When your tire hits this, your whole bike can slide to one side or the other. If you're not prepared or overreact, you can find yourself doing a face plant into the pavement. Always treat paint on pavement as a low-traction surface, especially when the weather has been wet or extremely hot.

MAKING YOURSELF VISIBLE

In addition to being aware of your surroundings and the other drivers, you need to make other drivers aware of you. When another driver says he didn't see the motorcyclist he just killed, he's most likely telling the truth. Motorcycles are small vehicles compared with all the four-wheeled traffic on the road, and it's easy for other drivers to miss seeing them.

Your job is to make that less easy. It helps to wear bright-colored clothing and helmets, or even wear vests and riding suits made of reflective high-visibility material. You might even want to consider getting a brightly colored motorcycle. I find that when I'm riding a brightly colored bike, say yellow or orange, I have a lot fewer situations where people make left turns in front of me than I do when I'm riding a black bike.

But I'm somewhat limited in what I can wear when it comes to reflective vests. I'm a member of a club, and one of the club's bylaws is that I have to wear a garment prominently displaying that club's insignia when I ride. Plus I like black motorcycles, so I start out with two strikes against me. Even so, there's a lot I can do to make myself more visible when I'm riding, like riding with my high beam on during the day. This goes a long way toward getting the attention of other drivers.

I also make a point of always signaling my lane changes and turns early, giving other drivers time to notice my bike and see what I'm going to do next. When I change lanes, for example, once I've looked in my mirrors and determined that the lane I'm moving into is clear, I activate my turn signals early and sometimes even supplement the turn signal with a hand signal, just so there is no question about my intentions. I get stopped by the cops all the time (I think they watch too much television and believe everything they see). Often the cops will say they stopped me because I didn't use my turn signal. When they say this, I know I'm dealing with a dishonest cop, because I *always* use my turn signal.

Another trick I've developed for making myself more visible is to give my brake pedal a light tap, even when I'm not slowing or stopping, just to make my brake light flash and get the attention of cars that may be behind me. And I'm not afraid to use my horn. I don't give a damn about being polite when it comes to life-or-death situations, and if another driver doesn't see me, my life is in danger. If it takes a blast from my horn to let the other driver know I'm there, then I'll blast my horn.

One thing to remember: even if you think you've got the attention of another driver, don't bet your life on it. The driver might be looking right at you—you may even think you've made eye contact with him or her—but in reality the person is looking right through you. Instead of seeing you, he or she could be looking at a cell-phone screen, reading a text message.

ZONES OF AWARENESS

To be aware of what's going on around you, scan your surroundings in a methodical way. Your eyes are your tools for getting information about what's going on around you. To get the most out of them, you need to keep them moving all the time. Don't let your eyes fixate on any one object for more than a fraction of a second. Once you've determined something isn't a threat, move on to the next thing.

Scan all aspects of your surroundings, and don't just focus on other traffic. Watch for animals, debris, and the condition of road surfaces. Keep your eyes open for piles of loose gravel or sand in corners, which can be as slippery as ice. Make sure you include your rearview mirror as part of the landscape you're scanning, but also turn your head slightly to check your blind spots, especially when turning, stopping, or changing lanes (again, see the upcoming information about soft lane changes).

You need to pay more attention to some areas than others on a motorcycle. Imagine the region around your bike is the face of a clock. Because you are always traveling forward on a motorcycle, the area between eleven o'clock and one o'clock is the area from which danger will come at you most rapidly and most frequently, so this area should get the lion's share of your time when scanning. Focus on your intended path. Concentrate on the area about twelve to fourteen seconds ahead of your bike, since you'll need at least this much time to react in an emergency situation. Keep your eyes up. This will aim your vision ahead, where the greatest danger lies.

Watch for subtle clues, like a shadow on the road ahead. It might indicate some oil, fresh tar, or some other slippery surface that could cause you to lose traction and crash. Be aware of movement in the bushes on the edge of the road, which could be a sign that an animal is about to enter the road in front of you.

You need to make the area in front of you your primary focus, but that doesn't mean you can ignore the other areas. You need to pay attention to what you see out of the corners of your eyes. A flash of movement might be a deer getting ready to jump out in front of you, or it might be a car pulling out of a driveway into your lane. Or that SUV barreling down on you in your rearview mirror might be driven by some texting fool who really doesn't see you. Most danger will come at you from the front, but you need to be aware of all 360 degrees of your surroundings, from twelve o'clock back to twelve o'clock, especially at intersections.

INTERSECTIONS

INTERSECTIONS ARE THE MOST dangerous places you can be on a motorcycle, because they are where other vehicles behave most unpredictably, but you can do a lot to minimize the danger. Remember, an intersection is anywhere that traffic can cross your lane of traffic. This means that driveways and other crossings are forms of intersections.

The most dangerous intersections are the odd ones where several roads converge at once. You'll encounter these where multiple roads meet or where frontage roads run along a main road. The average car driver always seems to be confused to some degree; at complicated intersections, the degree of confusion spikes and people drive in an especially stupid manner because they don't know what they are supposed to do.

Blind driveways and blind intersections have to run a close second to complicated intersections for degrees of danger, but they're all dangerous. Following a few simple practices can make them less dangerous:

- Slow down when riding through any intersection. The more dangerous the type of intersection, the more you should slow down. Slowing down puts you in control of the situation by giving you more time to scan the intersection for potential dangers. The earlier you can detect possible danger, the more time you have to prepare to deal with it.

- Make certain an intersection is clear before you proceed through it. Be sure that the person in a stopped car isn't just changing the CD in the stereo or applying makeup. If that is the case, the driver may finish doing whatever it is he or she is doing and pull into your lane just as you're passing through the intersection.

- When passing through an intersection, be extra diligent about practicing the other safety techniques discussed elsewhere in this book: cover your front brake lever, watch the front tires of other vehicles, and position your bike so that you have the best visibility and are most visible, and so that you have the most safe space in which to maneuver.

When passing through an intersection while another vehicle is blocking your view, pay extra attention to possible left-turning vehicles that you might not see at first. If the vehicle blocking your view is in the left lane and you're in the right lane, you can position yourself for the best view by riding on the far right side of your lane, positioning yourself as far away from potential left-turning vehicles as possible. If you're following the vehicle, your best position might be on the far left side of the lane, where you'll be most visible to the turning vehicle.

As you prepare to stop at an intersection, pay special attention to the vehicles behind you. Be even more careful if you're stopping on a yellow light because a lot of people interpret a yellow light as a signal to floor it and drive like hell. That person may be looking at the light, or at traffic in the cross street, and might not even see you until he or she has run you down.

This situation is so lethal that you should always scan for a possible escape route in case you need one. Choose the side of the road that will give you the most room to maneuver, which will usually be the side of the lane that is farthest away from oncoming traffic. When you do stop, don't pull right up behind the vehicle in front of you; that way, if someone behind you doesn't stop, the emergency escape route that you identified as you entered the intersection won't be blocked by the vehicle in front of you.

It's important to always leave yourself enough room to maneuver whenever you stop, whether you're at an intersection or not. Even when you have to stop because freeway traffic stops moving, monitor the traffic behind you. Make sure you have room to move forward, even if that means you have to ride between parked cars. That way if someone behind you doesn't stop, you'll have at least some sort of clear space to use for getting out of the vehicle's path.

To do this, your bike will have to be ready to go. When you sit at an intersection, or anytime you have to stop where there is traffic around you, make sure you leave your bike in first gear, with the clutch lever pulled in. That way if you need to get out of someone's way in a hurry, you won't lose any time shifting into gear. Remember, a split second is the difference between living and dying.

Leaving my bike in first gear has been a hard habit for me to adopt. When I started riding, motorcycles had foot-operated clutches and hand-operated shifters. The shifters would be operated with a lever attached to the gas tank that was connected to the transmission with linkage rods that ran down from the tank. These shifters never really worked well because of all that sloppy linkage, so we used to get rid of the linkage and use levers coming straight out of the transmission for shifting. We called them "suicide shifters."

Using a suicide shifter meant that we had to push in the clutch with our left foot and reach down and shift with our left hand. This was an awkward operation while moving, but when a bike was stopped, keeping the bike in gear while holding the clutch pedal down with one foot bordered on impossible. We had to shift into neutral before we stopped so that we could let the clutch pedal out and hold the stopped bike up with both feet. This habit became so strongly ingrained in me that to this day I have to remind myself to keep my bike in gear at a stop.

BLIND SPOTS

I SUSPECT THAT POORLY designed driver's education programs over the past sixty or seventy years are responsible for a lot of the lousy driving habits we have today. I know they are responsible for the fact that, by my count, seven out of eight drivers don't know how to use their side-view mirrors.

Side-view mirrors are a relatively recent tool in

the United States. Europeans had them for many years, but we didn't really start to get them on cars until the 1970s, and when we did get them, no one knew how to use them correctly. Especially driver's ed teachers. Side-view mirrors are designed to cover the blind spots you can't see with your rearview mirror, but for many years driver's ed teachers taught kids that they were supposed to point the mirrors at their rear bumpers. For all I know, they still do. When the side-view mirrors are pointed at the rear bumper, the driver sees only the same area in the side-view mirrors as he or she does in the rearview mirror, and his or her blind spot is still as blind as ever.

The correct way to use side-view mirrors is to position them so that you can see what's in the blind spots to the sides of your vehicle. But since most people haven't figured this out yet, they're still driving around with blind spots. And blind spots are deadly for motorcyclists. Never ride alongside the rear part of a car, because most likely the driver has no idea you are there. It's best not to ride beside any vehicle if you can help it, but if you have to ride beside one, at least make sure that you're riding in a spot where the other driver can see you if he or she bothers to look.

THE SOFT LANE CHANGE

SOMETIMES WE PRACTICE LIFESAVING techniques without even knowing we're doing them until someone explicitly points them out to us. This happened to me when I read about "the soft lane change" in a book called *Ride Hard, Ride Smart* (Motorbooks: 2004), written by a fellow named Pat Hahn who coordinates public information and education for the Minnesota Motorcycle Safety Center.

What Hahn means by "soft lane change" is easing into a lane when you're changing lanes rather than darting into the new lane. This will allow you and anyone else on the road time and space for mistakes. No matter how thoroughly you've checked the lane you plan to enter, there's always something you might have missed, like a car in the next lane over deciding to occupy that same lane, or some fool weaving through traffic at 100-plus miles per hour.

To perform a soft lane change, first check your mirrors and blind spot to make certain the lane you want to move into is clear (as you would anytime you change lanes). Next, signal your lane change (again, just as you would anytime you change lanes), but instead of moving from the center of the lane you're in to the center of the next lane, just move to the line that divides the two lanes and hold that position, leaving your turn signal on. Before you move all the way into the next lane, once again check your mirror and glance over at your blind spot to make certain you didn't miss something or that some kid with a fast car and a death wish isn't zigzagging through the lane.

Leave your turn signal on while you do this. If you've missed something and there's a car you didn't see, the driver should have realized your intentions by this point. The person will most likely either honk his or her horn at you or move over to let you in. Either option is better than getting hit by the other vehicle.

You'll complete the lane change only after you're absolutely certain that no other vehicle is vying for the same space. Don't turn off your turn signal until after you've safely completed the lane change. All of this should happen in a matter of seconds, which is a lot longer than you might think, but the extra time taken could mean the difference between you getting where you're going or you ending up in a hospital or a morgue.

You should practice soft lane changes not just every time you ride a motorcycle, but anytime you operate any vehicle on public roads. This is the surest way to avoid hitting hard-to-see vehicles while changing lanes, such as motorcycles, for example. If you always practice soft lane changes, the life you save may be my own.

PRESERVING SAFE SPACE

ON A BIKE YOU don't have fenders and bumpers and safety cages and crumple zones to protect you in case of an accident. Instead, you have flesh-and-blood legs and arms that are no match for three tons of sport utility vehicle. Because you are so vulnerable, you need to keep as much space as possible around you.

You do this by safely positioning your bike on the road. Always put your bike in the position that gives you the best view of the road ahead of you. Don't follow vehicles too closely, because in addition to blocking your view of the road ahead, tailgating takes away valuable time for you to react in an emergency. This is especially true when following a truck. If you find yourself following a truck, make sure to keep extra space between you and the truck. Better yet, make sure to choose a lane in which there are no vehicles in front of you, if that is at all possible.

If traffic is too heavy and there are no clear lanes available, stay to the right or the left of the lane so that you can see past the vehicles in front of you. Avoid riding in the center of the lane because in addition to affording the least visibility, that is the slipperiest part of the lane. Car engines, transmissions, and radiators are located between the car's wheels, and most of the slippery liquids that drip from a car on the highway build up in the center of the lane. The wheels that pass on the edges of the lane tend to keep the wheel tracks clean and free of slippery buildup, so you'll get your best traction there.

As you become more familiar with traffic patterns you'll learn to make traffic work for you instead of against you. On multilane roads you can position your bike in the right lane so that vehicles in the left lane will block oncoming drivers making left turns from hitting you. This is a skill that will require you to be able to read and assess a situation instantly, and you need to be confident of your riding skills and reaction times.

On occasion this will necessitate riding more aggressively than you might normally so you can keep up with fast-moving traffic, or even ride a little faster than the rest of traffic, but this isn't always a bad thing. Some studies have even shown that a motorcyclist riding just a bit faster than traffic is safer than a motorcyclist riding slower than traffic or even just the same speed as traffic. That seems to be the case in my experience.

This doesn't mean you'll have an excuse to ride as fast as you want. The key here is to ride *slightly* faster. As we mentioned earlier, deviating from traffic flow is a sure way to get into an accident. If you're riding slightly faster than traffic, you're doing so because you're trying to increase the safe space around your motorcycle. You're speeding up to move into a free space in traffic and avoid getting boxed in by other vehicles. Always try to find a spot in traffic that provides you with the most room possible. Sometimes this will mean you have to change lanes to find one with more safe space in which to ride, but that doesn't mean you'll be zipping in and out of traffic like a lunatic. You'll be changing lanes safely and sensibly, using the soft-lane-change method described in the last section.

Poor road conditions or poor weather conditions will require additional time to respond to unexpected events, so you'll need even more safe space in such conditions. You can get that safe space by slowing down, giving yourself more time to react. Debris on the road will also require you to slow down to give yourself more reaction time and thus more safe space.

You'll even need to be aware of the safe space around you when you park your motorcycle. Since motorcycles are so hard to see, someone might consider a parking space you're occupying empty and try to park in it. You may be standing there, putting on your helmet and gloves, and the next thing you know you're looking at the undercarriage of a Dodge Ram. When you pull into a parking space, position your motorcycle so that it is as visible to other drivers using the parking lot as possible.

BRAKING PRACTICE

ONE OF THE MOST dangerous situations in which you can find yourself is one in which you've locked up your brakes. At that point your tires have zero traction and the slightest twitch or sneeze or even blink on your part will put you down on the ground. The best you can hope for is a low-side, which is a crash where you just lay the bike down without flipping it over, but you're just as likely to go over the high side.

To avoid locking up your brakes, you need to know the traction limits of your bike, and the only way to really find out where those limits are is to test them. This practice itself is somewhat dangerous, but there are ways to do it that make it less dangerous. First off you'll need to find a safe place to practice, like a large, empty parking lot with clean, smooth pavement, somewhere where you can safely accelerate up to speeds of 20 to 30 miles per hour. Once you reach that speed, practice stopping as hard as you can. Remember that your front brake does most of the work.

Keep stopping harder and harder, and eventually you'll brake so hard that you lock up one of the tires. If your brakes are functioning properly, this will almost certainly be the rear tire. Immediately ease pressure on the brake pedal until the tire is once again turning freely. If you were only going 20 to 30 miles an hour when you started, you should have slowed down enough by the time the rear wheel locks to avoid crashing.

Once you're accustomed to using both brakes hard, practice the same drill using just the front brake. At the slightest hint of the front tire locking up, release the front brake. If you lock up your front brake, you will most likely fall down, even at low speeds. Once you've got a feel for this, go back to practicing with both brakes. You'll notice that your stops are both shorter and more controlled, even after just a few practice stops.

Do this several times, and by the time you're finished, you'll be able to feel what your motorcycle is doing just before you lock up your brakes. Your hands and feet will tell you when a tire is about to lock up. This will help give you an instinctive sense for just how much braking force you can apply in a real emergency situation.

Braking is such an important skill that you need to keep practicing it, even after you've mastered the basics. When you're out on the open road approaching stop signs, first make certain that no one is behind you. Once you've determined the road behind you is clear, practice stopping hard on different types of roads and road surfaces. Don't brake to the point of locking up your tires, but do try to stop in as little distance as possible. That way when a deer jumps out in front of you or some fool doesn't see you and pulls out on the highway just as you're approaching an intersection, hard stops will be second nature for you. Instead of panicking and having a life-threatening crash, your instincts will take over and you'll be much more likely to come to a safe stop.

RIDING IN THE RAIN

IF YOU RIDE A motorcycle, you will get caught in bad weather, even if you live in the desert. It's part of the deal you make with the world when you decide to become a motorcyclist. If you prepare properly and know what you're doing, it's not as terrible as you might think. But riding in the rain does increase your danger level.

Having a good rain suit helps to reduce some of the danger. If you're warm and dry rather than wet, cold, and miserable, you'll be much more focused on the matter at hand, which is, of course, safely riding your motorcycle. Rain suits are either one- or two-piece suits made of polyvinyl chloride (PVC) or nylon. The one-piece suits do a better job of keeping a rider dry because they don't allow rain to seep in at a rider's waist, the way a two-piece suit can. On the other hand, the two-piece suits are easier to put on quickly at the side of the road.

Polyvinyl chloride provides better protection from the rain than does nylon, but it's sticky to the touch, especially when wet, making it hard to put on over leather. Because of this a good PVC suit will have a cotton mesh lining that slides against leather riding gear. Ideally both the top and bottom of the suit should be mesh-lined. The better the rain gear, the more it will cost, but in this case you really do get what you pay for.

Staying dry in the rain is just part of the battle. You also have to stay up on two wheels. You have a lot less traction available on wet roads than on dry roads, which equates to much less traction available for turning and stopping. That means you have to slow down when you're riding in the rain, and you have to be even smoother when using the throttle and brakes than when you are on dry pavement. Jerky steering or throttle inputs that you wouldn't even notice on dry pavement can put you down on the ground when the road is wet.

Earlier I mentioned that you should avoid riding in the center of the lane because that's where all the slippery fluids build up. When it rains, the water lifts these fluids up off the pavement and makes them even slipperier, so it's especially important to avoid the center of the lane when it's raining. What's problematic about this is that pavement often sinks down in the wheel tracks where you ride, allowing water to build up in them. This can lead to hydroplaning, which is an extremely low-traction situation.

This is the main reason you want to make sure that you have a lot of tread on your tires; the more your tires wear down, the shallower the rain grooves cut into their surface become. These grooves allow water to squeeze out from under your tires as you ride, keeping the tire rubber in contact with the pavement. As your tires start to become bald, the water begins to build up under them when you ride in the rain. This is what causes hydroplaning.

The trend toward fatter tires seems to have made motorcycles more susceptible to hydroplaning. While riding across Texas on my way to Minnesota for a club rally in the summer of 2009 my bike hydroplaned in a rainstorm. Since the tires had good tread on them, I think the culprit might have been the size of the tires, which are exceptionally fat.

What You Should Know

- After receiving initial rider training, the best thing you can do to ensure your survival as a motorcyclist is to get advanced training.
- Everyone else on the road has the potential to kill you at any time.
- Situational awareness at all times is the key to staying alive on a motorcycle.

CHAPTER SEVEN

LIVING WITH A MOTORCYCLE

Now that you've learned enough about motorcycles to decide what type you want, you've learned how to ride, and you've bought a motorcycle, I'm going to give you some advice on what to do with it. This is the fun stuff. I'm going to talk a bit about traveling and about joining clubs. But first I'm going to discuss some basic motorcycle maintenance, which might not sound like much fun, but when you develop a bond with your motorcycle, you'll learn to enjoy it (or at least not hate it).

Figuring out what to do with your motorcycle isn't that complicated. First and foremost, you'll just want to get out there and ride the wheels off your new bike. After you first start to ride, your motorcycle will become your obsession. When you're not riding it, you're sneaking out to the garage to polish and maintain it. If you're anything like me, you'll continue to feel this way long after the new wears off your motorcycle. I've been riding for nearly sixty years, and I still can't wait to get out on my bike. As soon as I finish writing this chapter, I plan to head straight for my garage to take my bike out for a ride.

Before you ever hit the road on your motorcycle, you'll want to make sure that it's in top working order. I apologize for going back to the dark side of motorcycling for a moment here, but the consequences of just one bolt coming loose while you're riding are so horrible that you don't want to leave anything to chance.

When I started riding, it seemed like we practically had to rebuild our motorcycles every time we took them out on the road. In fact, it was like this until not all that long ago. Motorcycle technology has come a long way in the past thirty years and today's motorcycles are more like modern cars when it comes to maintenance requirements, but they still need more maintenance than any car. You'll still need to perform routine procedures to keep your bike in safe condition.

BASIC MAINTENANCE

PEOPLE HAVE STRONG FEELINGS about motorcycle maintenance—it seems like they either love it or hate it. I have to admit that I'm not particularly fond of it, but like it or not, I've spent a good chunk of my life wrenching on motorcycles. Today I can afford to have a good mechanic maintain my bike and I don't miss doing it myself. Still, I'm glad I learned how to work on a motorcycle because even today's reliable motorcycles break down now and then.

Because of that, I recommend that you learn how to do basic maintenance and repair on your motorcycle. I'm not saying you need to go to some motorcycle mechanics program to learn how to overhaul your own machine; I'm talking about basic routine maintenance that anyone can do.

Before you start working on your bike you should get a repair manual of some sort. Most new bikes will have instructions for basic maintenance in their owner's manual, though sometimes they'll say that the job should only be performed by technicians trained for that brand of bike. I think that's chickenshit, but I guess manufacturers don't much care what I think. They probably give more weight to what their lawyers think because they're afraid of being held liable if some fool does something stupid. Protecting fools from themselves seems a futile activity to me, but I digress.

Your owner's manual will most likely be insufficient if you want to work on your own motorcycle. If you bought your bike used, you may not even have an owner's manual. You'll have to supplement your owner's manual with some sort of repair manual. Clymer, Haynes, and Chilton all publish generic repair manuals for most motorcycles. These are usually adequate, though they're not ideal because they tend to cover families of bikes rather than specific models, and they don't always do a good job addressing small differences between different models.

Your best option would be to buy an actual shop repair manual for your bike. These are the manuals that the manufacturers publish for their own mechanics to use. They cover every detail of your bike, from removing bodywork to tearing down an engine. These will give you all the tricks you need to know to work on your particular machine. Sometimes something that seems as simple as removing a series of bolts can go from an uncomplicated job to a complete nightmare if you remove the bolts in the wrong order. The repair manual will provide you with that sort of inside information. Repair manuals are expensive and can run up to $100 apiece, or even more, but if you plan to do any complicated work on your own bike, that is money well spent.

The first things you'll need to work on your bike are some basic tools. Most Japanese and European bikes come with tool kits. The Japanese tool kits generally aren't very good and won't be sufficient for even routine maintenance. BMWs come with high-quality tool kits. Triumph tool kits aren't quite as good as BMW kits, but they're much better than the ones that come with Japanese bikes. Harleys don't come with tool kits at all.

I suggest putting together your own small tool kit that fits in the saddlebags. At the very least you'll need the following items in your tool kit:

- **Wrench set.** This will be your most important tool, so get the highest-quality wrenches you can. If you're trying to save space, you can get open-ended wrenches that have different-sized wrenches on each end. If you have bigger saddlebags, you can get wrenches that have open ends on one side and boxed ends on the other. If your bike uses metric-sized bolts and nuts, get a metric set. If it uses SAE standard-sized nuts and bolts, get an SAE standard wrench set.

- **Ratchet and socket set.** As with your wrenches, make sure you get the correct type, either metric or SAE standard. I have a compact ratchet with a three-quarter-inch drive and an articulating elbow in my tool kit. This is handy for getting at bolts and nuts in hard-to-reach places. And it is sufficient for minor maintenance and repair, but the articulating joint would make it unsuitable for major repair jobs.

   In addition to the ratchet, I keep sockets in all the most common sizes. I also recommend getting at least one extension for the sockets. If you only get one, it's better to get a longer one than a short one, but ideally you should have two or three extensions of different lengths. You might only keep the medium one in your on-bike tool kit and keep the others in your garage tool kit.

- **Screwdrivers.** To save space, I have a screwdriver with replaceable tips and keep a variety of tips in both Phillips and flat-blade sizes. If you have a Harley, you'll also want to get a Torx screwdriver. This has a star-shaped tip and is the only way to remove some screws on Harleys. You can also get these with multiple tips.

   Don't skimp and try to get by with cheap screwdrivers. And throw out screwdrivers as soon as they start to wear out. If you have rounded tips on your screwdrivers, you'll strip screw heads, turning a simple job into an expensive trip to a machine shop to have a stripped screw drilled out. If it's an important screw, it may even require you to tow your bike to the shop. One tow trip to the shop would pay for a lifetime of screwdrivers.

- **Allen wrench set.** You can usually get one Allen wrench that contains all the different sizes you need folded up like a pocketknife. Remember to get the right type for your bike: metric or SAE standard.

- **Pliers.** Ideally you'll want both regular and needle-nose pliers, but if you only have room for one, I'd go with the needle-nose pliers. I used to recommend regular pliers but have changed my mind because needle-nose pliers are more versatile. Needle-nose pliers can do pretty much anything regular pliers can do, although they aren't very good at things like removing bolts. But needle-nose pliers can do many things that regular pliers can't. Besides, if you have your wrenches and sockets, you should use those for removing bolts and nuts instead of pliers.

- **Spark-plug wrench.** The best spark-plug wrench is a deep-well socket that you can use on your ratchet, but make sure your socket is deep enough to get down to the bolt lugs on your spark plug.

- **Air pressure gauge.** Get a good-quality gauge that provides an accurate reading. I prefer a dial gauge because it's more accurate, it's easier to use in tight spaces, and also because it takes up less space in my tool kit than a traditional pencil-type gauge.

In addition to your portable tool kit, you should have a few basic tools at home in your garage:

- **A stool.** It doesn't hurt to squat beside your bike for a moment or two, but most jobs take longer than you expect. Your legs will get sore in a hurry if you squat beside your motorcycle for any length of time. You might even do permanent nerve damage. It's much more comfortable to sit on a stool while you're working.

- **A torque wrench.** This is a wrench that measures how tightly a nut has been twisted onto a bolt. It does this by either having a needle that points to the torque value, or a ratchet-type device that freewheels when a nut has been torqued to the proper specification. Your repair manual will have a proper torque value for just about every fastener on your bike. It's especially important to get the proper torque on things like axle bolts and triple-clamp bolts. If they are too loose, your wheels or fork could fall off; if they are too tight, your bearings will wear prematurely.

- **An oil filter wrench.** This will be a wrench that either wraps around the body of your oil filter with bands that tighten as you turn the wrench or else a cap that you place on the bottom of the filter itself and turn with a ratchet (and usually a long extension).

- **A soft-faced mallet.** You'll often run into a situation where some stubborn part needs a little persuasion. The trouble is you can't bang on these parts with just any tool or you'll damage them. A soft-faced mallet will allow you to use the required amount of force without damaging the part in question.

- **Lubricants.** At the very least you'll need engine oil and some WD-40. If you have a bike with a chain final drive, you'll also need some chain lube (don't use WD-40 on your chain—see the upcoming "Maintaining Your Chain" section for details).

- **Funnels.** You'll need a variety of funnels of different sizes and different-length spouts to reach all the places in which you'll need to get fluid into a motorcycle. You can also use them to catch the fluids you're removing from a motorcycle, especially motorcycles with dry-sump engines and remote oil tanks, like older Harleys (and current-model Sportsters). You'll want funnels made of different types of material, as some applications will call for a stiff funnel made of aluminum, whereas others will require a pliable plastic funnel.

- **Containers.** You'll want a red plastic can to hold fresh gas, and you'll want a small spray can to spray oil or small amounts of gas. You'll also want a fairly large catch pan to catch the oil you drain from your engine when you're performing an oil change, and larger covered containers in which to store the oil until you can get it to a recycling center.

CHANGING OIL

ENGINE OIL TECHNOLOGY HAS developed at almost the same breakneck pace as motorcycle technology, and the oils we have today are much better than the oils we had available even thirty years ago. All the major brands are very good, though you need to make sure that you use the oil weight specified by your bike's manufacturer. But as good as modern oil has become, you'll still need to change it on a regular basis. I prefer to err on the side of caution and change oil every twenty-five hundred miles, even though I use high-quality oil.

The following is a general outline of what's involved in changing engine oil. I'm not going to go into the preparation needed to ready your bike for an oil change, like removing bodywork, because the process will vary from bike to bike so there's no way to cover it here. On some bikes you might not even have to remove bodywork. I know a guy with a sport bike who removes just one bolt from his inner fairing and that lets him pull the fairing out far enough so that he can get the oil to drain straight down into his oil pan. You'll have to figure out how to get access to your own drain plug and oil filter. After that, you'll use the following procedure:

1. **Wear good latex gloves.** This isn't just to keep your hands pretty. We know for a fact that oil is a carcinogen, and you don't want it to touch your skin.
2. **Run the engine for a short time to warm up the oil.** This makes changing oil a potentially

painful experience, but you'll need the oil to be warm to flow freely out of the engine. Note that this will make your exhaust pipes extremely hot, so be careful not to touch them when you're working on your bike.

3. **Locate the drain plug.** The drain plug will be somewhere on the sump at the bottom of your motorcycle engine, or else on the bottom edge of one side. Once you've located it, place your catch pan under the plug. (If you have a dry sump with an external oil tank, like the one on a Harley Sportster, you'll have to drain the oil tank instead of the sump.)

4. **Remove the plug.** This is usually a large, hex-head bolt. Let the oil drain completely into the catch pan. Be careful when you remove the plug because the hot oil will pour out over your fingers. You'll need to pull the plug away from the hole quickly once you've unscrewed it or you could burn your fingers. Be especially careful not to drop the plug into the catch pan or you'll have to fish it out of a pan of hot, dirty oil.

5. **Clean and replace the drain plug once the oil has finished draining from the engine.** Most drain plugs have magnetic tips that collect metal shavings from inside the engine. Clean all of this material off before replacing the plug. Some drain plugs have metal washers to enhance the plug's seal. If your bike is so equipped, make certain you don't lose this washer when removing the plug. Also make certain the area around the hole is clean and doesn't have any dirt or debris that could get inside your engine or pre-

vent the drain plug from forming a seal against the oil pan.

6. **Place the catch pan under the oil filter and remove it.** You'll want to change the filter every time you change oil, so consider that a normal part of changing oil. Older bikes use canister-type filters, which are elements that go inside a canister that's permanently attached to the engine, but most modern motorcycles use automotive-type spin-on filters.

   Again, watch out for hot oil spraying down on your hand. The old filter will be filled with engine oil—dump this in the catch pan and properly dispose of the filter.

7. **Attach the new filter.** Smear clean engine oil from the bottles you're using to refill the engine sump onto the rubber seal attached to the top of the new filter, then screw it back on the engine. Only use your hands to tighten the filter—don't use the filter wrench or you'll get the filter so tight you may never be able to remove it again.

8. **Refill the oil.** As mentioned earlier, different bikes use different methods for measuring the oil level. Make sure that you fill the oil tank to the top of the level using the measuring method specified for your bike. Once you've got it to the full mark, restart the engine to pump oil into the filter.

   Be careful when you are doing this. When you first start the engine, your oil system won't be pressurized for the first couple seconds, so if you rev the engine, you could do permanent damage. Let the engine idle for a minute or two, then shut it down and recheck the oil. The oil level will have gone down by the amount that has been pumped into the filter. Refill the oil to the full mark.

After you've changed your oil, keep an eye on the oil level and check for leaks around the drain plug and the filter the next few times you ride the bike, just in case something has gone wrong.

MAINTAINING YOUR CHAIN

I THINK I'VE MADE my feelings about chain drives clear throughout the book, but if your budget only allows you to buy a midpriced motorcycle, most likely you'll have to settle for a chain-driven bike. That means you'll have to deal with the hassle of maintaining a chain. And you'll have to do this yourself because if you take it in to a shop to have the chain tightened, well, your bike will be in the shop all the time.

Replacing chains and sprockets, on the other hand, is a huge job, one that you probably will want to leave to a trained mechanic unless you're fairly skilled. The chores you'll handle yourself will be cleaning, lubricating, and tightening the tension of your chain.

Chains are expensive so you'll want to make them last as long as possible. This means you'll want to keep them clean and well lubricated. Most modern chains have internal lubrication permanently sealed in place with rubber O-rings. This makes the chains last longer, but it also means that you have to be careful what kind of products you use on them, since some chemicals will degrade the O-rings. This means you should not use WD-40. WD-40 is an excellent product for its intended use, but it is a penetrating lubricant used to loosen up things like tight bolts. WD-40 will penetrate the O-rings, destroying their seals. To clean the grime off your chain, only use an O-ring compatible cleaner and a soft brush.

Lubricate the chain with one of the many excellent chain lubricants on the market. I've heard good things about both Bel-Ray and PJ1 brands. Lubricating the chain is best done while the motorcycle is up on the center stand or up on a good support stand like a Pit Bull. When you apply the lubricant, aim the spray from the can at the inside of the chain, just ahead of the rear sprocket, while rotating the wheel forward to evenly coat the chain. This will not only lubricate the chain but also the rear sprocket, which is exposed and needs better lubricant coverage than does the front sprocket, which is covered and somewhat protected from dirt and debris. When you've lubricated the entire chain, clean the excess lubricant off the wheel and tire.

Ideally you'll want to check your chain's tension while someone is sitting aboard your bike, holding it up but putting his or her weight on the suspension so that the springs are compressed. It would be best if the person weighed as close as possible to your weight. This will put your suspension at the angle at which it will be when you're riding and will give you the most accurate reading of your chain's tension. I say this because the distance between the front and rear sprockets changes as the angle between the swingarm and the engine changes. This change in distance is extremely slight, but it can be enough to affect the tension of the chain. Checking the tension with the swingarm at the proper angle can help prevent you from overtightening your chain; overtightening is the main killer of chains.

To check the tension, grasp the chain on the underside of the swingarm about halfway between the front and rear sprockets and move the chain up and down. If the chain moves up and down more than about an inch and a half or two inches, it needs to be tightened. Check in several different spots on the chain by rolling the bike ahead and rechecking the tension. If the amount of chain movement varies from place to place, the chain may have a tight spot. If the tight spot is bad enough, you'll have to replace the chain. A tight spot is simply a spot where the chain is stiff and doesn't bend on its roller pins. Note that a "tight spot" is different than having a chain that is too tight.

The chain-tightening procedure varies from bike to bike, but most chain-driven motorcycles will use some form of the following method to adjust chain tension. Place the bike on its center stand or on the portable stand you've purchased and recheck the chain's tension. It will have changed from when you checked it while the suspension was weighted because the distance between the front and rear sprocket will have changed. It will feel looser than it did while the other person was sitting on the bike. If it moved an inch and a half while the suspension was weighted, it might move three inches when the suspension is unweighted.

Take this into account when adjusting the chain so you don't overtighten it. If you gained an inch and a half of chain travel by putting the bike on the stand and then tighten the chain down to an appropriate three-quarters of an inch of travel, your chain will be stretched as tight as a funeral drum when you get back on your bike. This will stretch your chain and drastically decrease its life span. Overtightening to this degree may even cause your chain to break and shoot off the back of your sprocket like a missile.

To prevent this catastrophe, add the amount of chain travel you gained when you put the bike up on the stand to the three-quarters of an inch you need for proper operation. If you gained an inch and a half of travel when you put the bike up on the stand, don't tighten your chain beyond two to two and a quarter inches of travel. This should put you right in the half inch to three-quarters of an inch of travel that you need when you get back on the bike.

Next, loosen the axle nuts. You will have to remove a security pin on most bikes when loosening the axle nuts. Once the axle nuts are removed, you can adjust the chain. You do this by adjusting bolts on the end of the swingarm on either side of the wheel. Usually there will be two hex-head nuts on each bolt—an inner nut to move the axle and an outer nut to lock the inner nut in place when the job is done. Loosen up the outer nut and then carefully adjust the inner nut, moving the nut on one side of the wheel a small amount, then moving the other nut an equal amount. If you don't move the bolts on each side the exact same amount, your back tire will get out of alignment with your front tire. When you've got the tension set to the proper amount, tighten down the outside nuts to lock the inner nuts in place. Retighten the axle bolts and insert a new security pin.

TOURING

FROM THE FIRST TIME I got on a motorcycle, I had the urge to take off and keep on riding. I still do. I like riding everywhere—to the store, to the gym, wherever—but there's nothing I enjoy as much as hitting the open road for a long trip. I hope you'll share my enthusiasm for long-distance riding.

You can travel on any bike you own, if it is reliable. Some bikes make better touring rides than others, but ultimately the best bike for a tour is the one sitting in your garage, because that's what you've got available. You might as well make the most of it. If you've followed my advice, you've bought a bike that is comfortable. If that's the case, the only real functional issues you'll have to deal with are luggage capacity and fuel range.

Having a bike with too small a gas tank can be a real hindrance to successful touring. Most bikes available today have at least sufficient fuel capacity to prevent you from being stranded between gas stops, but that wasn't always the case. For many years Harley-Davidson Sportsters had notoriously small gas tanks. This was such a serious problem that you didn't want to head out of town by yourself on a Sportster for fear of running out of gas and being stranded. Today's Sportsters still have small tanks that make them poorly suited for long-distance travel, but at least they're large enough for you to make it to the next gas station without running out of fuel most of the time. (There have been other bikes with such small fuel tanks that they have been all but impossible to use for touring, including Kawasaki's Eliminator of the mid-1980s and Honda's Superhawk of the late 1990s, but most of the bikes on the market today have fuel capacity that is at least adequate.)

You can't do much about your bike's fuel capacity without radical modification, but you can alter your bike's luggage capacity without too much trouble. Lots of luggage options are available that will work on almost any motorcycle. The trick is to equip your bike with luggage that stays securely fastened and doesn't rub against your tires or belt or chain.

If you've bought a bike equipped with saddlebags, you're already three-quarters of the way to having all the luggage capacity you'll need. If you have a touring bike, you might even have a top box or trunk on the back. If you like the hard luggage found on a touring bike, you may be able to buy optional hard luggage specifically for your bike, either from the manufacturer or from an aftermarket company like Givi or Corbin. This is the best way to go, but it's also an expensive route and will probably require you to put your motorcycle in a shop for a day or two while the luggage is installed.

If you don't have the money, time, or patience to go this route, you can mount soft luggage. There are three basic pieces of soft luggage:

- **Saddlebags.** These are bags that you put over the rear portion of your seat and ride outboard of the rear wheel, one on each side of the bike. These are usually your primary piece of luggage.

- **Tankbags.** These are bags that mount on top of your tank. They can hold a lot of items and provide the easiest access for a rider in the saddle. They make great places to store items you frequently need while riding, like cameras, sunscreen, bottled water, and fluid and soft rags for cleaning your face shield. Plus they're handy for storing articles of clothing you might remove as the temperature warms up during the day, like sweatshirts and heavy gloves.
- **Tailpacks.** These mount on the passenger portion of your seat and can greatly increase your luggage capacity, making them invaluable for long trips. The best of these will have built-in bungee cords so you can securely attach them to your bike.

Soft removable saddlebags can be made of leather, vinyl, or heavy nylon. Tankbags and tailpacks are almost always made of heavy nylon, though some have hard plastic shells. Soft luggage has its drawbacks. It's not lockable, like hard luggage, and you have to be careful to mount the pieces securely so they don't move around and rub your tires or fall off. Removable soft luggage also isn't rainproof, meaning that you'll have to pack your stuff in heavy garbage bags before you put it in the luggage, but it has the advantages of being inexpensive and easily removed when you are done traveling.

PACKING FOR A TRIP

Almost every person who takes his or her first motorcycle trip makes the same mistake: packing too
much gear. You'll overload your luggage with stuff
that you won't even unpack until you get back home.
Everyone with any touring experience will warn you
not to do this, but you'll do it anyway because you'll
be worried that you'll need this or that item but won't
have it.

Really, you only need a few items for a safe, comfortable trip. Bring the small tool kit I told you about
earlier in this chapter, of course. Bring a first-aid kit,
too. It doesn't have to be elaborate, but should include the following basic items:

- A selection of bandages, including gauze bandages
- Adhesive tape
- Some sort of antibiotic

If you have room to add a few more items, you
should try to fit them in. Your first-aid kit isn't the
place to save weight.

Apply the less-is-more philosophy in spades when
it comes to your clothes. Bring a couple of pairs of
jeans, a few T-shirts, a couple of turtleneck sweaters
(turtleneck sweaters are great in cold weather because
they make a nice seal between your jacket and your
helmet). Bring enough underwear and socks to last
you the duration of your trip (underwear and socks
don't take up much space). That about covers it. As
long as you have clean underwear and socks, you can
get by in most situations.

Traveling on a motorcycle is one of the most rewarding activities in which you can ever engage. It is also one of the most grueling. Spending a long day in the saddle takes the piss right out of you. You're going to have to prepare your body as much as you prepare your gear and your bike.

I recommend starting an exercise regime before going on a motorcycle trip. This will help build up your stamina and endurance. And get in the habit of eating a healthy diet. This will be hard to keep up when you're out on the road, eating in restaurants every day, but if you make smart choices, you can keep your energy level high. The most important thing is to drink enough water. If you just drink soda or coffee, the caffeine in those drinks depletes your body's water supply. Get in the habit of drinking a bottle of water each time you stop for gas.

PLANNING A TRIP

WHEN YOU PLAN YOUR first trip, you'll probably spend weeks, or even months poring over maps, plotting your route. Chances are that you will have fun, but the odds are just as good that you'll bite off more than you can chew. Most people underestimate how much time their trips will take, which leads them to rush to make up time. If you fall into this trap, you'll miss seeing a lot of the things you wanted to see in the first place. Plus you'll be anxious and won't be able to relax and enjoy the trip itself.

The trick for avoiding this pitfall is to be realistic when planning your trip in the first place. If your route will take you across South Dakota or some other state where the interstate speed limit is 75 miles per hour, don't expect to cover seventy-five miles for every hour you're out on your bike, even if you're riding at 80 miles per hour or faster. You need to factor in things like gas stops, rest stops, and getting stuck behind the occasional semi. At best, you'll probably average 60 miles per hour.

As you become more experienced, your average speed will increase, but not by much. If you're riding two-up or riding with a group of bikes, you'll probably average even slower. When you're with a group of bikers, rest stops take longer because more people are using the available bathrooms, gas stops take longer because more tanks need to be filled, and riding itself takes longer because not everyone travels at the same speed. Ultimately you'll only travel as fast as the slowest rider in the group.

Thus if you plan to spend eight hours traveling by yourself on a freeway (which is a long time to be droning down a long, straight interstate highway), don't expect to cover more than four hundred miles that day. And you won't be able to make up time by speeding because those few minutes you might gain by riding faster will be more than lost by the half hour or more that you'll sit alongside the road while the state trooper calls in your license information and writes your expensive speeding ticket.

If you're riding on two-lane highways, you can knock your average speed down to 50 miles per hour because the speed limits will be lower and you'll spend more time being cock blocked by traffic. If you get into the mountains where the roads turn twisty and the scenic beauty beckons you to stop and take photos, figure that at best you'll cover thirty to forty miles every hour, and less if you're with a group of other bikers. You could push yourself and not stop to enjoy the scenery, but that defeats the purpose of being there on a motorcycle in the first place. It's better to take your time and enjoy your trip than to turn it into the Bataan Death March.

If you are worried about not covering enough ground, it's better to plan a shorter trip. If you are going to some destination, like to visit a relative in a far-off state, don't try to cram in a lot of sightseeing and side trips. If you have to be somewhere quickly, you won't be able to stop and enjoy the extra places you're visiting anyway. If you don't have to be anywhere at any specific time, plan shorter routes that allow you plenty of time to absorb the places you visit. If you are going to spend five days riding through Colorado and Wyoming, don't plan a trip that will cover more than fifteen hundred miles.

Whatever you do, don't run yourself ragged while you're traveling on a bike. Relax, get plenty of sleep, and eat a healthy diet. Make sure you take time to stop and stretch your legs when you visit someplace or stop to take some photos. You might not think it's possible to fall asleep while riding a bike, but it is, and the potential consequences range from horrible to even worse. Even if you don't fall asleep, the more tired you are, the less alert you are. The less alert you are, the slower your reaction times. The slower your reaction times, the more likely you are to get killed. If you compare the potential costs of pushing yourself while on a trip with any potential benefits, you'll see that there's nothing to be gained by rushing your trip and everything to lose.

CLUBS

As MOST OF YOU probably knew before you picked up this book, I'm a member of a motorcycle club. It's the type of club that's often called a "one-percenter" club. As the legend goes, an AMA spokesperson once said that 99 percent of all motorcyclists were good, responsible citizens, and all the trouble was being caused by the 1 percent of outlaws. I have my own ideas about this. I was there for a lot of the so-called trouble, and to me it seemed like there was a disconnection between what was really happening and what the press was reporting. I'd attend an event in which nothing out of the ordinary appeared to happen, and then I'd read a sensationalized account of that same event in the press in which it seemed that all the barbaric tribes of Europe had descended. My take is that most of the trouble referred to by this AMA official, if he even existed, took place in the pages of newspapers and magazines, and not in the flesh-and-blood world.

Regardless, the one-percent title stuck and actually became a badge of honor for club members. We consider one-percenter clubs elite organizations, where membership isn't open to just anyone. Membership requires extreme dedication. When you become a member of a one-percenter club, the club becomes your life. It becomes your family—your parents, your brothers and sisters, your wife, and your children.

When you become a member of a one-percenter club, you have dedicated your life to that club.

As far as I'm concerned, extreme dedication is what separates one-percenter clubs from other types of clubs, but there are certain characteristics that are shared by many (but not all) one-percenter clubs. Most one-percenter club members wear some sort of garment that features the club patch (often called "colors") centered on the back of the garment, where it can be seen while the man (as politically incorrect as this may be, there are no one-percenter clubs that allow women to be members—clubs that allow women are by nature not one-percenter clubs) is riding his motorcycle. That garment is usually a denim vest, or more accurately, a denim jacket with the sleeves cut off, which is why it's often called a "cut," but sometimes the patch is sewn on a leather vest or jacket.

Typically a one-percenter patch consists of three parts: a central image depicting the club's insignia, a rocker patch (a curved bar) on top with the club's name, and another rocker patch below indicating the particular chapter of a club. This type of three-piece patch usually signifies that a club is a one-percenter club, but not always. I'll soon explain that in more detail. Likewise if a patch is a two-piece or one-piece patch, that usually means that the club is not a one-percenter club.

One-percenter clubs are as varied as the individuals who make up their memberships. Some clubs consist of single groups located in a specific geographic area whereas others are composed of chapters spread around the country, or even the globe. Few one-percenter clubs recruit their members. Instead, the clubs attract prospective members by their public behavior and reputation. We don't recruit; we recognize. Riders who aspire to be members approach the club, show their interest, and work to prove they are worthy.

The process a prospect follows usually goes as follows: introduction, hang-around status, sponsorship, prospect phase, and finally either membership or failure. The would-be prospect first reaches the provisional status of a "hang-around." This is when club members have privately voted to make official the hang-around's status of club associate.

If and when a club member deems the hang-around worthy of sponsorship as a prospect and is willing to act as the person's mentor, that member meets with the individual and offers to sponsor him. At a club meeting, the member stands up for the potential prospect and asks for a vote authorizing "prospect" status. By doing this the member becomes responsible for the prospect. If a majority of members agree, the prospect is brought into the meeting, told of his new status, and given the bottom rocker "prospect" patch.

The official recognition as "prospect" marks the beginning of the prospect's hard-core testing phase, which may take many months. The prospect is given menial tasks, such as cleaning the clubhouse, helping set up for meetings and events, running errands, and maintaining members' bikes. Occasionally he is also trusted with more significant jobs that require greater skill, creativity, or finesse; these assignments will come directly from the prospect's sponsor, upon whom the quality of the prospect's performance will reflect.

When the sponsoring member deems the time appropriate, he brings the prospect's membership to a vote before the whole club. This milestone event will include an open discussion among the members regarding the prospect's qualities (pro and con). In most clubs, a unanimous vote is required to grant membership. When the vote is taken, if only one member votes against granting membership, that member must explain his reasons in case he knows something the others do not.

If the members do not grant membership at this time, they decide whether to continue the prospect phase or dismiss the prospect entirely. If they do agree to make the prospect a member, they may invite the person into the meeting to congratulate him, or they may keep it a secret so they can surprise the prospect with his full patch at another time.

MOM-AND-POP CLUBS

DON'T FEEL BAD IF the life of a one-percenter isn't right for you. I have my priorities, and my club is at the top of that list, but because of that I've had to make a lot of sacrifices. I've never been able to have children because my club responsibilities are so demanding that I wouldn't have time to properly raise them. I've even gone to prison.

Like I said, one-percenter clubs are as varied as the individuals who compose them. The clubs are not criminal syndicates. Anytime you have a group of people collected together, the group will include some people who don't always abide by the letter of the law. You'd think that law-enforcement agencies would deal with individual club members on an individual basis, but you'd be wrong. All members of one-percenter clubs are painted with the same brush by law-enforcement agencies.

If you do join a one-percenter club, you'd better be prepared to live your life under a microscope. When you do any business transaction whatsoever, you'll need to make sure you have all your legal bases covered. This is part of the dedication required to be a member, and it's no easy thing.

But if you're interested in this type of club, only at a less-intense level, there are organizations that offer much of the brotherhood and camaraderie of a one-percenter club, and even elements of the one-percenter lifestyle, but that aren't actual one-percenter clubs. I guess you could call them "two-percenter" clubs. We call them "mom-and-pop" clubs. These clubs can be organized around riding motorcycles, like the one-percenter clubs, or they can be organized around something else. For example, there are two-percenter clubs that combine sobriety with motorcycling, clubs that combine religion with motorcycling, and even clubs composed of war veterans and police officers.

These clubs vary in the degree of dedication they require of their members. In general, if clubs use a three-piece patch, they'll require more dedication because usually they'll need to have an understanding with and abide by the rules set by the local one-percenter clubs in order to fly three-piece colors. Be warned: membership in one of the more dedicated mom-and-pop clubs may mean you'll suffer the same prejudice from the law-enforcement community as membership in a one-percenter club, especially at the local level. The FBI might know the difference between a church-based club or a group of Alcoholics Anonymous members and a real one-percenter club, but your local cop probably won't.

CLUBS FOR THE OTHER NINETY-EIGHT PERCENT

AGAIN, DON'T WORRY IF even these two-percenter clubs don't sound right for you. There are almost as many different types of motorcycle clubs as there are different types of motorcyclists. I highly recommend that you find one that suits your lifestyle and personality.

As a motorcyclist, you may often find yourself the odd man (or woman) out as you ride through the world. Although more and more of us are riding every year, we're still a very small minority of motorists. Clubs offer camaraderie and brotherhood. They provide social outlets, places where we can gather with our own kind and talk about our passion—motorcycles and riding—without boring nonmotorcyclists. A motorcycle club is a nexus where the motorcycling community can come together.

You can find a club devoted to every different type of riding. There are off-road and trail-riding clubs, there are road-racing and sport-bike clubs, and there are clubs devoted to long-distance touring riders. There are general clubs devoted to all motorcycles and clubs devoted to specific types of motorcycles, like turbocharged bikes. There are clubs devoted to antique motorcycles, and clubs devoted to every brand of motorcycle ever built, from ATK to Zundapp. In addition to clubs devoted to certain makes, there are clubs devoted to just specific models of those brands. Take BMW motorcycles, for example. There are clubs devoted to all BMW motorcycles, clubs devoted to just antique BMWs, clubs devoted to air-cooled BMWs, and clubs devoted to specific BMW models, like the GS series.

There are clubs devoted to riders from a particular area, clubs devoted to riders based on their sexual orientation, and clubs devoted to just one sex. For example, the Dykes on Bikes club is based on both sex and sexual orientation. There are clubs just for riders over a certain age, and there are clubs that no rider of a certain age would join if he or she was in his or her right mind. There are clubs based on every spiritual system known to man, from the Anglican Church to Zoroastrianism. There are clubs for everyone from Baptists to Buddhists. There are professionally oriented motorcycle clubs, such as clubs for cops and for firefighters, and I'm sure there are clubs just for slackers and bums.

Find out where motorcyclists gather, and ride there to check out the local scene. At the very least you'll meet people who share a powerful common interest with you: motorcycling. To find a club, or at least a loosely organized motorcycling community, all you really have to do is pursue the activity you most enjoy: riding a motorcycle.

What You Need to Know

- You need to learn to perform basic mainte-nance on your own bike, especially if it's chain-driven.
- You need to prepare your body and your bike for the rigors of a long trip.
- Joining a club is a great way to connect with the motorcycle community.

APPENDIX

Motorcycle Resources

MOTORCYCLE SAFETY FOUNDATION

THROUGHOUT THE BOOK I'VE referred to a variety of organizations, businesses, and other resources that I use and recommend. I'm presenting them here in alphabetical order because they are all more or less equally important, with one exception: the Motorcycle Safety Foundation. That's because the Rider-Course and Experienced RiderCourse that the MSF offers are the most important resources for any motorcyclist. To find a program in your area, check out the MSF at www.msf-usa.org/.

AEROSTICH

AEROSTICH MADE ITS NAME by pioneering synthetic riding suits, the kind that are worn by just about every serious Iron-Butt-type long-distance motorcyclist, but today the company offers everything from riding gear to electronic accessories to camping equipment. When you're talking serious long-distance motorcyclists, Aerostich owner Andy Goldfine is as hard-core as they come, and he personally makes certain that the products he offers to the motorcycling community are the best available. Check out Aerostich at www.aerostich.com/.

CORBIN SADDLES

MIKE CORBIN IS A personal friend of mine, but if I didn't know him from Adam, I'd still use his saddles. I think the fact that just about every serious long-distance rider uses a Corbin saddle whether they know Mike or not means that I'm not alone in this opinion. You can check out Corbin at www.corbin.com/.

THUNDERHEADER

PROBABLY NO MOTORCYCLE-RELATED TOPIC is more controversial right now than loud exhaust pipes. A lot of riders run straight pipes—that is, pipes with no sound baffling whatsoever—or nearly straight pipes that are too loud for use on public streets. At the same time most new motorcycles have such restrictive exhaust systems that their performance suffers, so most riders end up adding some sort of aftermarket exhaust system. I know I do, and for the last twenty-five years I've only used Thunderheaders. As far as I'm concerned these are the best exhaust systems on the market. You can check out their exhaust systems at www.thunderheader.net/.

ARLEN NESS

THROUGHOUT THIS BOOK I'VE advocated keeping your bike basically stock, but I was talking about functional changes, like altering the geometry of your motorcycle's frame or overbuilding the engine. I also like to keep my bikes looking businesslike, but that doesn't mean you can't sharpen up your bike's appearance with some decorative accessories. There's no better place to get quality customizing accessories than from my good friend Arlen Ness. He can sell you anything from a customized footpeg to a complete motorcycle. When you buy something from Arlen, you can be sure that it is the best-engineered, highest-quality part on the market. Check out the amazing range of products he offers at www.arlen-ness.com/.

TOTAL CONTROL ADVANCED RIDER CLINIC

EARLIER IN THE BOOK I suggested getting advanced rider training. Once you've finished the MSF Experienced RiderCourse, a good next step is Lee Parks's Total Control Advanced Rider Clinic. To see schedules and locations, go to www.totalcontroltraining.net/.

KLOCK WERKS KUSTOM CYCLES

WHEN A MAN BUILDS custom motorcycles and designs motorcycle parts in the middle of South Dakota, about 250 miles away from the edge of nowhere, he'd better be good at what he does, and Brian Klock, founder of Klock Werks Kustom Cycles, definitely meets that criteria. If you're in the market for anything from a well-designed part to a complete custom bike, Klock Werks has what you are looking for. Check them out at www.kustomcycles.com/.

READING LIST

IN WRITING THIS BOOK, I've tried my best to sum up the tricks and techniques I've learned over the course of a lifetime of riding, and I think I've done a good job of presenting information you're not going to find anywhere else, but there's still a lot of information that you won't find in these pages. It's a good thing other people have written about this subject, so that much of that information is available elsewhere. All of these books are available on Amazon.com. There are many bits of information in the following books that could very easily save your life, so you owe it to yourself to read them:

The Motorcycle Safety Foundation's Guide to Motorcycling Excellence: Skills, Knowledge, and Strategies for Riding Right (2nd ed.) by the Motorcycle Safety Foundation

This is the textbook for the MSF RiderCourse program, and as such, it should be as indispensable a part of your motorcycling experience as the RiderCourse itself.

How to Ride a Motorcycle: Rider's Guide to Strategy, Safety and Skill Development by Pat Hahn

Maximum Control: Mastering Your Heavyweight Bike by Pat Hahn

Ride Hard, Ride Smart: Ultimate Street Strategies for Advanced Motorcyclists by Pat Hahn

No book can really teach you how to ride a bike, but no book better prepares you to learn than Pat Hahn's *How to Ride a Motorcycle*. This is a good one to read before you take the MSF RiderCourse. *Maximum Control* focuses on the specific skills needed to master a heavyweight motorcycle, but it has a lot to offer the rider of any motorcycle, large or small. If the MSF RiderCourse is a freshman-level course, think of *Ride Hard, Ride Smart* as a sophomore-level textbook. It takes up where the RiderCourse leaves off, bridging the gap between the MSF material and high-performance riding books like *Total Control* and *Twist of the Wrist*.

Total Control by Lee Parks

Unlike most high-performance riding books, which focus on the needs of a race rider, this one applies the lessons to street riding.

A Twist of the Wrist: The Motorcycle Road Racers Handbook by Keith Code

Twist of the Wrist II: The Basics of High-Performance Motorcycle Riding by Keith Code

Soft Science of Road Racing Motorcycles: The Technical Procedures and Workbook for Road Racing Motorcycles by Keith Code

Keith Code's books were the first modern high-performance riding books, and in many ways they are still among the best. They are primarily focused on the demands of riding on a racetrack, but they still contain a lot of good information for anyone wanting to be a better rider.

FINNEGANS
WAKE

BY JAMES JOYCE

Dubliners
A Portrait of the Artist as a Young Man
Exiles (play)
Ulysses
Collected Poems
Finnegans Wake
Giacomo Joyce

FÍNNEGANS WAKE

James Joyce

THE VIKING PRESS · NEW YORK

PENGUIN BOOKS

PENGUIN BOOKS
Published by the Penguin Group
Viking Penguin Inc., 40 West 23rd Street, New York, New York 10010, U.S.A.
Penguin Books Ltd, 27 Wrights Lane, London W8 5TZ, England
Penguin Books Australia Ltd, Ringwood, Victoria, Australia
Penguin Books Canada Ltd, 2801 John Street,
Markham, Ontario, Canada L3R 1B4
Penguin Books (N.Z.) Ltd, 182–190 Wairau Road,
Auckland 10, New Zealand

Penguin Books Ltd, Registered Offices:
Harmondsworth, Middlesex, England

First published in Great Britain
by Faber and Faber Ltd 1939
First published in the United States of America
by Viking Penguin Inc. 1939
Viking Compass Edition published 1959
Reprinted 1961, 1962, 1965, 1966, 1967, 1968 (twice),
1969, 1970, 1971 (twice), 1972, 1973, 1974, 1975
Published in Penguin Books 1976

13   15   17   19   20   18   16   14

628 p.

Library of Congress catalog card number: 59-354
ISBN 0 14 00.6286 6

Printed in the United States of America

Set in Garamond No. 3

FINNEGANS WAKE

I

riverrun, past Eve and Adam's, from swerve of shore to bend
of bay, brings us by a commodius vicus of recirculation back to
Howth Castle and Environs.

Sir Tristram, violer d'amores, fr'over the short sea, had passen-
core rearrived from North Armorica on this side the scraggy
isthmus of Europe Minor to wielderfight his penisolate war: nor
had topsawyer's rocks by the stream Oconee exaggerated themselse
to Laurens County's gorgios while they went doublin their mumper
all the time: nor avoice from afire bellowsed mishe mishe to
tauftauf thuartpeatrick: not yet, though venissoon after, had a
kidscad buttended a bland old isaac: not yet, though all's fair in
vanessy, were sosie sesthers wroth with twone nathandjoe. Rot a
peck of pa's malt had Jhem or Shen brewed by arclight and rory
end to the regginbrow was to be seen ringsome on the aquaface.

The fall (bababadalgharaghtakamminarronnkonnbronntonner-
ronntuonnthunntrovarrhounawnskawntoohoohoordenenthur-
nuk!) of a once wallstrait oldparr is retaled early in bed and later
on life down through all christian minstrelsy. The great fall of the
offwall entailed at such short notice the pftjschute of Finnegan,
erse solid man, that the humptyhillhead of humself prumptly sends
an unquiring one well to the west in quest of his tumptytumtoes:
and their upturnpikepointandplace is at the knock out in the park
where oranges have been laid to rust upon the green since dev-
linsfirst loved livvy.

What clashes here of wills gen wonts, oystrygods gaggin fishygods! Brékkek Kékkek Kékkek Kékkek! Kóax Kóax Kóax! Ualu Ualu Ualu! Quaouauh! Where the Baddelaries partisans are still out to mathmaster Malachus Micgranes and the Verdons catapelting the camibalistics out of the Whoyteboyce of Hoodie Head. Assiegates and boomeringstroms. Sod's brood, be me fear! Sanglorians, save! Arms apeal with larms, appalling. Killykillkilly: a toll, a toll. What chance cuddleys, what cashels aired and ventilated! What bidimetoloves sinduced by what tegotetabsolvers! What true feeling for their's hayair with what strawng voice of false jiccup! O here here how hoth sprowled met the duskt the father of fornicationists but, (O my shining stars and body!) how hath fanespanned most high heaven the skysign of soft advertisement! But was iz? Iseut? Ere were sewers? The oaks of ald now they lie in peat yet elms leap where askes lay. Phall if you but will, rise you must: and none so soon either shall the pharce for the nunce come to a setdown secular phoenish.

Bygmester Finnegan, of the Stuttering Hand, freemen's maurer, lived in the broadest way immarginable in his rushlit toofarback for messuages before joshuan judges had given us numbers or Helviticus committed deuteronomy (one yeastyday he sternely struxk his tete in a tub for to watsch the future of his fates but ere he swiftly stook it out again, by the might of moses, the very water was eviparated and all the guenneses had met their exodus so that ought to show you what a pentschanjeuchy chap he was!) and during mighty odd years this man of hod, cement and edifices in Toper's Thorp piled buildung supra buildung pon the banks for the livers by the Soangso. He addle liddle phifie Annie ugged the little craythur. Wither hayre in honds tuck up your part inher. Oftwhile balbulous, mithre ahead, with goodly trowel in grasp and ivoroiled overalls which he habitacularly fondseed, like Haroun Childeric Eggeberth he would caligulate by multiplicables the alltitude and malltitude until he seesaw by neatlight of the liquor wheretwin 'twas born, his roundhead staple of other days to rise in undress maisonry upstanded (joygrantit!), a waalworth of a skyerscape of most eyeful hoyth entowerly, erigenating from

next to nothing and celescalating the himals and all, hierarchitec-
titiptitoploftical, with a burning bush abob off its baubletop and
with larrons o'toolers clittering up and tombles a'buckets clottering down.

Of the first was he to bare arms and a name: Wassaily Boos-
laeugh of Riesengeborg. His crest of huroldry, in vert with
ancillars, troublant, argent, a hegoak, poursuivant, horrid, horned.
His scutschum fessed, with archers strung, helio, of the second.
Hootch is for husbandman handling his hoe. Hohohoho, Mister
Finn, you're going to be Mister Finnagain! Comeday morm and,
O, you're vine! Sendday's eve and, ah, you're vinegar! Hahahaha,
Mister Funn, you're going to be fined again!

What then agentlike brought about that tragoady thundersday
this municipal sin business? Our cubehouse still rocks as earwitness
to the thunder of his arafatas but we hear also through successive
ages that shebby choruysh of unkalified muzzlenimiissilehims that
would blackguardise the whitestone ever hurtleturtled out of
heaven. Stay us wherefore in our search for tighteousness, O Sus-
tainer, what time we rise and when we take up to toothmick and
before we lump down upown our leatherbed and in the night and
at the fading of the stars! For a nod to the nabir is better than wink
to the wabsanti. Otherways wesways like that provost scoffing
bedoueen the jebel and the jpysian sea. Cropherb the crunch-
bracken shall decide. Then we'll know if the feast is a flyday. She
has a gift of seek on site and she allcasually ansars helpers, the
dreamydeary. Heed! Heed! It may half been a missfired brick, as
some say, or it mought have been due to a collupsus of his back
promises, as others looked at it. (There extand by now one thousand and one stories, all told, of the same). But so sore did abe
ite ivvy's holired abbles, (what with the wallhall's horrors of rolls-
rights, carhacks, stonengens, kisstvanes, tramtrees, fargobawlers,
autokinotons, hippohobbilies, streetfleets, tournintaxes, mega-
phoggs, circuses and wardsmoats and basilikerks and aeropagods
and the hoyse and the jollybrool and the peeler in the coat and
the mecklenburk bitch bite at his ear and the merlinburrow bur-
rocks and his fore old porecourts, the bore the more, and his

blightblack workingstacks at twelvepins a dozen and the noobi-
busses sleighding along Safetyfirst Street and the derryjellybies
snooping around Tell-No-Tailors' Corner and the fumes and the
hopes and the strupithump of his ville's indigenous romekeepers,
homesweepers, domecreepers, thurum and thurum in fancymud⁷
murumd and all the uproor from all the aufroofs, a roof for may
and a reef for hugh butt under his bridge suits tony) wan warning Phill filt tippling full. His howd feeled heavy, his hoddit did
shake. (There was a wall of course in erection) Dimb! He stot-
tered from the latter. Damb! he was dud. Dumb! Mastabatoom,
mastabadtomm, when a mon merries his lute is all long. For
whole the world to see.

Shize? I should shee! Macool, Macool, orra whyi deed ye diie?
of a trying thirstay mournin? Sobs they sighdid at Fillagain's
chrissormiss wake, all the hoolivans of the nation, prostrated in
their consternation and their duodisimally profusive plethora of
ululation. There was plumbs and grumes and cheriffs and citherers
and raiders and cinemen too. And the all gianed in with the shout-
most shoviality. Agog and magog and the round of them agrog.
To the continuation of that celebration until Hanandhunigan's
extermination! Some in kinkin corass, more, kankan keening.
Belling him up and filling him down. He's stiff but he's steady is
Priam Olim! 'Twas he was the dacent gaylabouring youth. Sharpen
his pillowscone, tap up his bier! E'erawhere in this whorl would ye
hear sich a din again? With their deepbrow fundigs and the dusty
fidelios. They laid him brawdawn alanglast bed. With a bockalips
of finisky fore his feet. And a barrowload of guenesis hoer his head.
Tee the tootal of the fluid hang the twoddle of the fuddled, O!

Hurrah, there is but young gleve for the owl globe wheels in
view which is tautaulogically the same thing. Well, Him a being
so on the flounder of his bulk like an overgrown babeling, let wee
peep, see, at Hom, well, see peegee ought he ought, platterplate. ⊡
Hum! From Shopalist to Bailywick or from ashtun to baronoath
or from Buythebanks to Roundthehead or from the foot of the
bill to ireglint's eye he calmly extensolies. And all the way (a
horn!) from fjord to fjell his baywinds' oboboes shall wail him

6

rockbound (hoahoahoah!) in swimswamswum and all the livvy-long night, the delldale dalppling night, the night of bluerybells, her flittaflute in tricky trochees (O carina! O carina!) wake him. With her issavan essavans and her patterjackmartins about all them inns and ouses. Tilling a teel of a tum, telling a toll of a tea-ry turty Taubling. Grace before Glutton. For what we are, gifs à gross if we are, about to believe. So pool the begg and pass the kish for crawsake. Omen. So sigh us. Grampupus is fallen down but grinny sprids the boord. Whase on the joint of a desh? Fin-foefom the Fush. Whase be his baken head? A loaf of Singpan-try's Kennedy bread. And whase hitched to the hop in his tayle? A glass of Danu U'Dunnell's foamous olde Dobbelin ayle. But, lo, as you would quaffoff his fraudstuff and sink teeth through that pyth of a flowerwhite bodey behold of him as behemoth for he is noewhemoe. Finiche! Only a fadograph of a yestern scene. Almost rubicund Salmosalar, ancient fromout the ages of the Ag-apemonides, he is smolten in our mist, woebecanned and packt away. So that meal's dead off for summan, schlook, schlice and goodridhirring.

Yet may we not see still the brontoichthyan form outlined a-slumbered, even in our own nighttime by the sedge of the trout-ling stream that Bronto loved and Brunto has a lean on. *Hic cubat edilis. Apud libertinam parvulam.* Whatif she be in flags or flitters, reekierags or sundyechosies, with a mint of mines or beggar a pinnyweight. Arrah, sure, we all love little Anny Ruiny, or, we mean to say, lovelittle Anna Rayiny, when unda her brella, mid piddle med puddle, she ninnygoes nannygoes nancing by. Yoh! Brontolone slaaps, yoh snoores. Upon Benn Heather, in Seeple Isout too. The cranic head on him, caster of his reasons, peer yu-thner in yondmist. Whooth? His clay feet, swarded in verdigrass, stick up starck where he last fellonem, by the mund of the maga-zine wall, where our maggy seen all, with her sisterin shawl. While over against this belles' alliance beyind Ill Sixty, ollol-lowed ill! bagsides of the fort, bom, tarabom, tarabom, lurk the ombushes, the site of the lyffing-in-wait of the upjock and hock-ums. Hence when the clouds roll by, jamey, a proudseye view is

7

enjoyable of our mounding's mass, now Wallinstone national museum, with, in some greenish distance, the charmful water-loose country and the two quitewhite villagettes who hear show of themselves so gigglesomes minxt the follyages, the prettilees! Penetrators are permitted into the museomound free. Welsh and the Paddy Patkinses, one shelenk! Redismembers invalids of old guard find poussepousse pousseypram to sate the sort of their butt. For her passkey supply to the janitrix, the mistress Kathe. Tip.

This the way to the museyroom. Mind your hats goan in! Now yiz are in the Willingdone Museyroom. This is a Prooshious gunn. This is a ffrinch. Tip. This is the flag of the Prooshious, the Cap and Soracer. This is the bullet that byng the flag of the Prooshious. This is the ffrinch that fire on the Bull that bang the flag of the Prooshious. Saloos the Crossgunn! Up with your pike and fork! Tip. (Bullsfoot! Fine!) This is the triplewon hat of Lipoleum. Tip. Lipoleumhat. This is the Willingdone on his same white harse, the Cokenhape. This is the big Sraughter Willingdone, grand and magentic in his goldtin spurs and his ironed dux and his quarterbrass woodyshoes and his magnate's gharters and his bangkok's best and goliar's goloshes and his pullupon-easyan wartrews. This is his big wide harse. Tip. This is the three lipoleum boyne grouching down in the living detch. This is an inimyskilling inglis, this is a scotcher grey, this is a davy, stooping. This is the bog lipoleum mordering the lipoleum beg. A Gallawghurs argaumunt. This is the petty lipoleum boy that was nayther bag nor bug. Assaye, assaye! Touchole Fitz Tuomush. Dirty MacDyke. And Hairy O'Hurry. All of them arminus-varminus. This is Delian alps. This is Mont Tivel, this is Mont Tipsey, this is the Grand Mons Injun. This is the crimealine of the alps hooping to sheltershock the three lipoleums. This is the jinnies with their legahorns feinting to read in their handmade's book of stralegy while making their war undisides the Willingdone. The jinnies is a cooin her hand and the jinnies is a ravin her hair and the Willingdone git the band up. This is big Willingdone mormorial tallowscoop Wounderworker obscides on the flanks of the jinnies. Sexcaliber hrosspower. Tip. This

8

is me Belchum sneaking his phillippy out of his most Awful Grimmest Sunshat Cromwelly. Looted. This is the jinnies' hastings dispatch for to irrigate the Willingdone. Dispatch in thin red lines cross the shortfront of me Belchum. Yaw, yaw, yaw! Leaper Orthor. Fear siecken! Fieldgaze thy tiny frow. Hugacting. Nap. That was the tictacs of the jinnies for to fontannoy the Willingdone. Shee, shee, shee! The jinnies is jillous agincourting all the lipoleums. And the lipoleums is gonn boycottoncrezy onto the one Willingdone. And the Willingdone git the band up. This is bode Belchum, bonnet to busby, breaking his secred word with a ball up his ear to the Willingdone. This is the Willingdone's hurold dispitchback. Dispitch desployed on the regions rare of me Belchum. Salamangra! Ayi, ayi, ayi! Cherry jinnies. Figtreeyou! Damn fairy ann, Voutre. Willingdone. That was the first joke of Willingdone, tic for tac. Hee, hee, hee! This is me Belchum in his twelvemile cowchooks, weet, tweet and stampfoi th foremost, footing the camp for the jinnies. Drink a sip, drankasup, for he's as sooner buy a guinness than he'd stale store stout. This is Rooshious balls. This is a ttrinch. This is mistletropes. This is Canon Futter with the popynose. After his hundred days' indulgence. This is the blessed. Tarra's widdars! This is jinnies in the bonny bawn blooches. This is lipoleums in the rowdy howses. This is the Willingdone, by the splinters of Cork, order fire. Tonnerre! (Bullsear! Play!) This is camelry, this is floodens, this is the solphereens in action, this is their mobbily, this is panickburns. Almeidagad! Arthiz too loose! This is Willingdone cry. Brum! Brum! Cumbrum! This is jinnies cry. Underwetter! Goat strip Finnlambs! This is jinnies rinning away to their ousterlists dowan a bunkersheels. With a nip nippy nip and a trip trippy trip so airy. For their heart's right there. Tip. This is me Belchum's tinkyou tankyou silvoor plate for citchin the crapes in the cool of his canister. Poor the pay! This is the bissmark of the marathon merry of the jinnies they left behind them. This is the Willingdone branlish his same marmorial tallowscoop Sophy-Key-Po for his royal divorsion on the rinnaway jinnies. Gambariste della porca! Dalaveras fimmieras! This is the pettiest of the lipoleums, Toffeethief, that spy on the Willingdone from his big white harse, the Capeinhope. Stonewall Willingdone is an old maxy montrumeny. Lipoleums is nice hung bushellors. This is hiena hinnessy laughing alout at the Willingdone. This is lipsyg dooley krieging the funk from the hinnessy. This is the hinndoo Shimar Shin between the dooley boy and the hinnessy. Tip. This is the wixy old Willingdone picket up the half of the threefoiled hat of lipoleums fromoud of the bluddle filth. This is the hinndoo waxing ranjymad for a bombshoob. This is the Willingdone hanking the half of the hat of lipoleums up the tail on the buckside of his big white harse. Tip. That was the last joke of Willingdone. Hit, hit, hit! This is the same white harse of the Willingdone, Culpenhelp, waggling his tailoscrupp with the half of a hat of lipoleums to insoult on the hinndoo seeboy. Hney, hney, hney! (Bullsrag! Foul!) This is the seeboy, madrashattaras, upjump and pumpim, cry to the Willingdone: Ap Pukkaru! Pukka Yurap! This is the Willingdone, bornstable ghentleman, tinders his maxbotch to the cursigan Shimar Shin. Basucker youstead! This is the dooforhim seeboy blow the whole of the half of the hat of lipoleums off of the top of the tail on the back of his big wide harse. Tip (Bullseye! Game!) How Copenhagen ended. This way the museyroom. Mind your boots goan out.

Phew!

What a warm time we were in there but how keling is here the airabouts! We nowhere she lives but you mussna tell annaone for the lamp of Jig-a-Lanthern! It's a candlelittle houthse of a month and one windies. Downadown, High Downadown. And nummered quaintlymine. And such reasonable weather too! The wagrant wind's awalt'zaround the piltdowns and on every blasted knollyrock (if you can spot fifty I spy four more) there's that gnarlybird ygathering, a runalittle, doalittle, preealittle, pouralittle, wipealittle, kicksalittle, severalittle, eatalittle, whinealittle, kenalittle, helfalittle, pelfalittle gnarlybird. A verytableland of bleakbardfields! Under his seven wrothschields lies one, Lumproar. His glav toside him. Skud ontorsed. Our pigeons pair are flewn for northcliffs.

The three of crows have flapped it southenly, kraaking of de baccle to the kvarters of that sky whence triboos answer; Wail, 'tis well! She niver comes out when Thon's on shower or when Thon's flash with his Nixy girls or when Thon's blowing toom-cracks down the gaels of Thon. No nubo no! Neblas on you liv! Her would be too moochy afreet. Of Burymeleg and Bindme-rollingeyes and all the deed in the woe. Fe fo fom! She jist does hopes till byes will be byes. Here, and it goes on to appear now, she comes, a peacefugle, a parody's bird, a peri potmother, a pringlpik in the ilandiskippy, with peewee and powwows in beggybaggy on her bickybacky and a flick flask fleckflinging its pixylighting pacts' huemeramybows, picking here, pecking there, pussypussy plunderpussy. But it's the armitides toonigh, militopucos, and toomourn we wish for a muddy kissmans to the minutia workers and there's to be a gorgeups truce for happinest childher everwere. Come nebo me and suso sing the day we sallybright. She's burrowed the coacher's headlight the better to pry (who goes cute goes siocur and shoos aroun) and all spoiled goods go into her nabsack: curtrages and rattlin buttins, nappy spattees and flasks of all nations, clavicures and scampulars, maps, keys and woodpiles of haypennies and moonled brooches with bloodstaned breeks in em, boaston nightgarters and masses of shoesets and nickelly nacks and foder allmicheal and a lugly parson of cates and howitzer muchears and midgers and maggets, ills and ells with loffs of toffs and pleures of bells and the last sigh that come fro the hart (bucklied!) and the fairest sin the sunsaw (that's cearc!). With Kiss. Kiss Criss. Cross Criss. Kiss Cross. Undo lives 'end. Slain.

How bootifull and how truetowife of her, when strengly fore-bidden, to steal our historic presents from the past postprophetic-als so as to will make us all lordy heirs and ladymaidesses of a pretty nice kettle of fruit. She is livving in our midst of debt and laffing through all plores for us (her birth is uncontrollable), with a naperon for her mask and her sabboes kickin arias (so sair! so solly!) if yous ask me and I saack you. Hou! Hou! Gricks may rise and Troysirs fall (there being two sights for ever a picture) for in the byways of high improvidence that's what makes life-work leaving and the world's a cell for citters to cit in. Let young wimman run away with the story and let young min talk smooth behind the butteler's back. She knows her knight's duty while Luntum sleeps. Did ye save any tin? says he. Did I what? with a grin says she. And we all like a marriedann because she is mercenary. Though the length of the land lies under liquidation (floote!) and there's nare a hairbrow nor an eyebush on this glaubrous phace of Herrschuft Whatarwelter she'll loan a vesta and hire some peat and sarch the shores her cockles to heat and she'll do all a turfwoman can to piff the business on. Paff. To puff the blaziness on. Poffpoff. And even if Humpty shell fall frumpty times as awkward again in the beardsboosoloom of all our grand remonstrancers there'll be iggs for the brekkers come to mournhim, sunny side up with care. So true is it that therewhere's a turnover the tay is wet too and when you think you ketch sight of a hind make sure but you're cocked by a hin.

Then as she is on her behaviourite job of quainance bandy, fruting for firstlings and taking her tithe, we may take our review of the two mounds to see nothing of the himples here as at elsewhere, by sixes and sevens, like so many heegills and collines, sitton aroont, scentbreeched and somepotreek, in their swishawish satins and their taffetaffe tights, playing Wharton's Folly, at a treepurty on the planko in the purk. Stand up, mickos! Make strake for minnas! By order, Nicholas Proud. We may see and hear nothing if we choose of the shortlegged bergins off Corkhill or the bergamoors of Arbourhill or the bergagambols of Summerhill or the bergincellies of Miseryhill or the country-bossed bergones of Constitutionhill though every crowd has its several tones and every trade has its clever mechanics and each harmonical has a point of its own, Olaf's on the rise and Ivor's on the lift and Sitric's place's between them. But all they are all there scraping along to sneeze out a likelihood that will solve and salve life's robulous rebus, hopping round his middle like kippers on a griddle, O, as he lays dormont from the macroborg of Holdhard to the microbirg of Pied de Poudre. Behove this sound of Irish sense. Really? Here English might be seen. Royally? One sovereign punned to petery pence. Regally? The silence speaks the scene. Fake!

So This Is Dyoublong?

Hush! Caution! Echoland!

How charmingly exquisite! It reminds you of the outwashed engravure that we used to be blurring on the blotchwall of his innkempt house. Used they? (I am sure that tiring chabelshoveller with the mujikal chocolat box, Miry Mitchel, is listening) I say, the remains of the outworn gravemure where used to be blurried the Ptollmens of the Incabus. Used we? (He is only pretendant to be stugging at the jubalee harp from a second existed lishener, Fiery Farrelly.) It is well known. Lokk for himself and see the old butte new. Dbln. W. K. O. O. Hear? By the mausolime wall. Fimfim fimfim. With a grand funferall. Fumfum fumfum. 'Tis optophone which ontophanes. List! Wheatstone's magic lyer. They will be tuggling foriver. They will be lichening for allof. They will be pretumbling forover. The harpsdischord shall be theirs for ollaves.

Four things therefore, saith our herodotary Mammon Lujius in his grand old historiorum, wrote near Boriorum, bluest book in baile's annals, f.t. in Dyfflinarsky ne'er sall fail til heathersmoke and cloudweed Eire's ile sall pall. And here now they are, the fear of um. T. Totities! *Unum.* (Adar.) A bulbenboss surmounted upon an alderman. Ay, ay! *Duum.* (Nizam.) A shoe on a puir old wobban. Ah, ho! *Triom.* (Tamuz.) An auburn mayde, o'brine a'bride, to be desarted. Adear, adear! *Quodlibus.* (Marchessvan.) A penn no weightier nor a polepost. And so. And all. (Succoth.)

So, how idlers' wind turning pages on pages, as innocens with anaclete play popeye antipop, the leaves of the living in the boke of the deeds, annals of themselves timing the cycles of events grand and national, bring fassilwise to pass how.

1132 A.D. Men like to ants or emmets wondern upon a groot hwide Whallfisk which lay in a Runnel. Blubby wares upat Ublanium.

566 A.D. On Baalfire's night of this year after deluge a crone that

13

hadde a wickered Kish for to hale dead turves from the bog look-
it under the blay of her Kish as she ran for to sothisfeige her cow-
rieosity and be me sawl but she found hersell sackvulle of swart
goody quickenshoon and small illigant brogues, so rich in sweat.
Blurry works at Hurdlesford.

(Silent.)

566 A.D. At this time it fell out that a brazenlockt damsel grieved
(sobralasolas!) because that Puppette her minion was ravisht of her
by the ogre Puropeus Pious. Bloody wars in Ballyaughacleeagh-
bally.

1132 A.D. Two sons at an hour were born until a goodman
and his hag. These sons called themselves Caddy and Primas.
Primas was a santryman and drilled all decent people. Caddy
went to Winehouse and wrote o peace a farce. Blotty words for
Dublin.

Somewhere, parently, in the ginnandgo gap between antedilu-
vious and annadominant the copyist must have fled with his
scroll. The billy flood rose or an elk charged him or the sultrup
worldwright from the excelsissimost empyrean (bolt, in sum)
earthspake or the Dannamen gallous banged pan the bliddy du-
ran. A scribicide then and there is led off under old's code with
some fine covered by six marks or ninepins in metalmen for the
sake of his labour's dross while it will be only now and again in
our rear of o'er era, as an upshoot of military and civil engagements, that a gynecure was let on to the scuffold for taking that
same fine sum covertly by meddlement with the drawers of his
neighbour's safe.

Now after all that farfatch'd and peragrine or dingnant or clere
lift we our ears, eyes of the darkness, from the tome of Liber Li-
vidus and, (toh!), how paisibly eirenical, all dimmering dunes
and gloamering glades, selfstretches afore us our fredeland's plain!
Lean neath stone pine the pastor lies with his crook; young pricket by pricket's sister nibbleth on returned viridities; amaid her
rocking grasses the herb trinity shams lowliness; skyup is of ever-
grey. Thus, too, for donkey's years. Since the bouts of Hebear
and Hairyman the cornflowers have been staying at Ballymun,

the duskrose has choosed out Goatstown's hedges, twolips have pressed togatherthem by sweet Rush, townland of twinedlights, the whitethorn and the redthorn have fairygeyed the mayvalleys of Knockmaroon, and, though for rings round them, during a chiliad of perihelygangs, the Formoreans have brittled the tooath of the Danes and the Oxman has been pestered by the Firebugs and the Joynts have thrown up jerrybuilding to the Kevanses and Little on the Green is childsfather to the City (Year! Year! And laughtears!), these paxsealing buttonholes have quadrilled across the centuries and whiff now whafft to us, fresh and made-of-all-smiles as, on the eve of Killallwho.

The babbelers with their thangas vain have been (confusium hold them!) they were and went; thigging thugs were and houhnhymn songtoms were and comely norgels were and pollyfool fiansees. Menn have thawed, clerks have surssurhummed , the blond has sought of the brune: Elsekiss thou may, mean Kerry piggy?: and the duncledames have countered with the hellish fellows: Who ails tongue coddeau, aspace of dumbillsilly? And they fell upong one another: and themselves they have fallen. And still nowanights and by nights of yore do all bold floras of the field to their shyfaun lovers say only: Cull me ere I wilt to thee!: and, but a little later: Pluck me whilst I blush! Well may they wilt, marry, and profusedly blush, be troth! For that saying is as old as the howitts. Lave a whale a while in a whillbarrow (isn't it the truath I'm tallin ye?) to have fins and flippers that shimmy and shake. Tim Timmycan timped hir, tampting Tam. Fleppety! Flippety! Fleapow!

Hop!

In the name of Anem this carl on the kopje in pelted thongs a parth a lone who the joebiggar be he? Forshapen his pigmaid hoagshead, shroonk his plodsfoot. He hath locktoes, this shortshins, and, Obeold that's pectoral, his mammamuscles most mousterious. It is slaking nuncheon out of some thing's brain pan. Me seemeth a dragon man. He is almonthst on the kiep fief by here, is Comestipple Sacksoun, be it junipery or febrewery, marracks or alebrill or the ramping riots of pouriose and

froriose. What a quhare soort of a mahan. It is evident the mich-
indaddy. Lets we overstep his fire defences and these kraals of
slitsucked marrogbones. (Cave!) He can prapsposterus the pil-
lory way to Hirculos pillar. Come on, fool porterfull, hosiered
women blown monk sewer? Scuse us, chorley guy! You toller-
day donsk? N. You tolkatiff scowegian? Nn. You spigotty an-
glease? Nnn. You phonio saxo? Nnnn. Clear all so! 'Tis a Jute.
Let us swop hats and excheck a few strong verbs weak oach ea-
ther yapyazzard abast the blooty creeks.

Jute. — Yutah!

Mutt. — Mukk's pleasurad.

Jute. — Are you jeff?

Mutt. — Somehards.

Jute. — But you are not jeffmute?

Mutt. — Noho. Only an utterer.

Jute. — Whoa? Whoat is the mutter with you?

Mutt. — I became a stun a stummer.

Jute. — What a hauhauhauhaudibble thing, to be cause! How,
      Mutt?

Mutt. — Aput the buttle, surd.

Jute. — Whose poddle? Wherein?

Mutt. — The Inns of Dungtarf where Used awe to be he.

Jute. — You that side your voise are almost inedible to me.
      Become a bitskin more wiseable, as if I were
      you.

Mutt. — Has? Has at? Hasatency? Urp, Boohooru! Booru
      Usurp! I trumple from rath in mine mines when I
      rimimirim!

Jute. — One eyegonblack. Bisons is bisons. Let me fore all
      your hasitancy cross your qualm with trink gilt. Here
      have sylvan coyne, a piece of oak. Ghinees hies good
      for you.

Mutt. — Louee, louee! How wooden I not know it, the intel-
      lible greytcloak of Cedric Silkyshag! Cead mealy
      faulty rices for one dabblin bar. Old grilsy growlsy!
      He was poached on in that eggtentical spot. Here

where the liveries, Monomark. There where the mis-
sers moony, Minnikin passe.

Jute. — Simply because as Taciturn pretells, our wrongstory-
shortener, he dumptied the wholeborrow of rubbages on to soil here.

Mutt. — Just how a puddinstone inat the brookcells by a
riverpool.

Jute. — Load Allmarshy! Wid wad for a norse like?

Mutt. — Somular with a bull on a clompturf. Rooks roarum
rex roome! I could snore to him of the spumy horn,
with his woolseley side in, by the neck I am sutton
on, did Brian d' of Linn.

Jute. — Boildoyle and rawhoney on me when I can beuraly
forsstand a weird from sturk to finnic in such a pat-
what as your rutterdamrotter. Onheard of and um-
scene! Gut aftermeal! See you doomed.

Mutt. — Quite agreem. Bussave a sec. Walk a dun blink
roundward this albutisle and you skull see how olde
ye plaine of my Elters, hunfree and ours, where wone
to wail whimbrel to peewee o'er the saltings, where
wilby citie by law of isthmon, where by a droit of
signory, icefloe was from his Inn the Byggning to
whose Finishthere Punct. Let erehim ruhmuhrmuhr.
Mearmerge two races, swete and brack. Morthering
rue. Hither, craching eastuards, they are in surgence:
hence, cool at ebb, they requiesce. Countlessness of
livestories have netherfallen by this plage, flick as
flowflakes, litters from aloft, like a waast wizzard all of
whirlworlds. Now are all tombed to the mound, isges
to isges, erde from erde. Pride, O pride, thy prize!

Jute. — 'Stench!

Mutt. — Fiatfuit! Hereinunder lyethey. Llarge by the smal an'
everynight life olso th'estrange, babylone the great-
grandhotelled with tit tit tittlehouse, alp on earwig,
drukn on ild, likeas equal to anequal in this sound
seemetery which iz leebez luv.

Jute. — 'Zmorde!

Mutt. — Meldundleize! By the fearse wave behoughted. Despond's sung. And thanacestross mound have swollup them all. This ourth of years is not save brickdust and being humus the same roturns. He who runes may rede it on all fours. O'c'stle, n'wc'stle, tr'c'stle, crumbling! Sell me sooth the fare for Humblin! Humblady Fair. But speak it allsosiftly, moulder! Be in your whisht!

Jute. — Whysht?

Mutt. — The gyant Forficules with Amni the fay.

Jute. — Howe?

Mutt. — Here is viceking's graab.

Jute. — Hwaad !

Mutt. — Ore you astoneaged, jute you?

Jute. — Oye am thonthorstrok, thing mud.

(Stoop) if you are abcedminded, to this claybook, what curios of signs (please stoop), in this allaphbed! Can you rede (since We and Thou had it out already) its world? It is the same told of all. Many. Miscegenations on miscegenations. Tieckle. They lived und laughed ant loved end left. Forsin. Thy thingdome is given to the Meades and Porsons. The meandertale, aloss and again, of our old Heidenburgh in the days when Head-in-Clouds walked the earth. In the ignorance that implies impression that knits knowledge that finds the nameform that whets the wits that convey contacts that sweeten sensation that drives desire that adheres to attachment that dogs death that bitches birth that entails the ensuance of existentiality. But with a rush out of his navel reaching the reredos of Ramasbatham. A terricolous vively-onview this; queer and it continues to be quaky. A hatch, a celt, an earshare the pourquose of which was to cassay the earthcrust at all of hours, furrowards, bagawards, like yoxen at the turnpaht. Here say figurines billycoose arming and mounting. Mounting and arming bellicose figurines see here. Futhorc, this liffle effingee is for a firefing called a flintforfall. Face at the eased! O I fay! Face at the waist! Ho, you fie! Upwap and dump em, face to face! When a

18

part so ptee does duty for the holos we soon grow to use of an allforabit. Here (please to stoop) are selveran cued peteet peas of quite a pecuniar interest inaslittle as they are the pellets that make the tomtummy's pay roll. Right rank ragnar rocks and with these rox orangotangos rangled rough and rightgorong. Wisha, wisha, whydidtha? Thik is for thorn that's thuck in its thoil like thumfool's thraitor thrust for vengeance. What a mnice old mness it all mnakes! A middenhide hoard of objects! Olives, beets, kimmells, dollies, alfrids, beatties, cormacks and daltons. Owlets' eegs (O stoop to please!) are here, creakish from age and all now quite epsilene, and oldwolldy wobblewers, haudworth a wipe o grass. Sss! See the snake wurrums everyside! Our durlbin is sworming in sneaks. They came to our island from triangular Toucheaterre beyond the wet prairie rared up in the midst of the cargon of prohibitive pomefructs but along landed Paddy Wippingham and the his garbagecans cotched the creeps of them pricker than our whosethere outofman could quick up her whatsthats. Somedivide and sumthelot but the tally turns round the same balifuson. Racketeers and bottloggers.

Axe on thwacks on thracks, axenwise. One by one place one be three dittoh and one before. Two nursus one make a plausible free and idim behind. Starting off with a big boaboa and three-legged calvers and ivargraine jadesses with a message in their mouths. And a hundreadfilled unleavenweight of liberorumqueue to con an we can till allhorrors eve. What a meanderthalltale to unfurl and with what an end in view of squattor and anntisquattor and postproneauntisquattor! To say too us to be every tim, nick and larry of us, sons of the sod, sons, littlesons, yea and lealittlesons, when usses not to be, every sue, siss and sally of us, dugters of Nan! Accusative ahnsire! Damadam to infinities!

True there was in nillohs dieybos as yet no lumpend papeer in the waste and mightmountain Penn still groaned for the micies to let flee. All was of ancientry. You gave me a boot (signs on it!) and I ate the wind. I quizzed you a quid (with for what?) and you went to the quod. But the world, mind, is, was and will be writing its own wrunes for ever, man, on all matters that fall

19

under the ban of our infrarational senses fore the last milch-camel, the heartvein throbbing between his eyebrowns, has still to moor before the tomb of his cousin charmian where his date is tethered by the palm that's hers. But the horn, the drinking, the day of dread are not now. A bone, a pebble, a ramskin; chip them, chap them, cut them up allways; leave them to terracook in the muttheringpot: and Gutenmorg with his cromagnom charter, tintingfast and great primer must once for omniboss step ru-brickredd out of the wordpress else is there no virtue more in al-cohoran. For that (the rapt one warns) is what papyr is meed of, made of, hides and hints and misses in prints. Till ye finally (though not yet endlike) meet with the acquaintance of Mister Typus, Mistress Tope and all the little typtopies. Fillstup. So you need hardly spell me how every word will be bound over to carry three score and ten toptypsical readings throughout the book of Doublends Jined (may his forehead be darkened with mud who would sunder!) till Daleth, mahomahouma, who oped it closeth thereof the. Dor.

Cry not yet! There's many a smile to Nondum, with sytty maids per man, sir, and the park's so dark by kindlelight. But look what you have in your handself! The movibles are scrawling in motions, marching, all of them ago, in pitpat and zingzang for every busy eerie whig's a bit of a torytale to tell. One's upon a thyme and two's behind their lettice leap and three's among the strubbely beds. And the chicks picked their teeths and the domb-key he begay began. You can ask your ass if he believes it. And so cuddy me only wallops have heels. That one of a wife with folty barnets. For then was the age when hoops ran high. Of a noarch and a chopwife; of a pomme full grave and a fammy of levity; or of golden youths that wanted gelding; or of what the mischievmiss made a man do. Malmarriedad he was reverso-gassed by the frisque of her frasques and her prytty pyrrhique. Maye faye, she's la gaye this snaky woman! From that trippiery toe expectungpelick! Veil, volantine, valentine eyes. She's the very besch Winnie blows Nay on good. Flou inn, flow ann. Hohore! So it's sure it was her not we! But lay it easy, gentle

mien, we are in rearing of a norewhig. So weenybeeny-
veenyteeny. Comsy see! Het wis if ee newt. Lissom! lissom!
I am doing it. Hark, the corne entreats! And the larpnotes
prittle.

It was of a night, late, lang time agone, in an auldstane eld,
when Adam was delvin and his madameen spinning watersilts,
when mulk mountynotty man was everybully and the first leal
ribberrobber that ever had her ainway everybuddy to his love-
saking eyes and everybilly lived alove with everybiddy else, and
Jarl van Hoother had his burnt head high up in his lamphouse,
laying cold hands on himself. And his two little jiminies, cousins
of ourn, Tristopher and Hilary, were kickaheeling their dummy
on the oil cloth flure of his homerigh, castle and earthenhouse.
And, be dermot, who come to the keep of his inn only the niece-
of-his-in-law, the prankquean. And the prankquean pulled a rosy
one and made her wit foreninst the dour. And she lit up and fire-
land was ablaze. And spoke she to the dour in her petty perusi-
enne: Mark the Wans, why do I am alook alike a poss of porterpease? And that was how the skirtmisshes began. But the dour
handworded her grace in dootch nossow: Shut! So her grace
o'malice kidsnapped up the jiminy Tristopher and into the shandy westerness she rain, rain, rain. And Jarl van Hoother war-
lessed after her with soft dovesgall: Stop deef stop come back to
my earin stop. But she swaradid to him: Unlikelihud. And there
was a brannewail that same sabboath night of falling angles somewhere in Erio. And the prankquean went for her forty years'
walk in Tourlemonde and she washed the blessings of the love-
spots off the jiminy with soap sulliver suddles and she had her
four owlers masters for to tauch him his tickles and she convor-
ted him to the onesure allgood and he became a luderman. So then
she started to rain and to rain and, be redtom, she was back again
at Jarl van Hoother's in a brace of samers and the jiminy with
her in her pinafrond, lace at night, at another time. And where
did she come but to the bar of his bristolry. And Jarl von Hoother had his baretholobruised heels drowned in his cellarmalt,
shaking warm hands with himself and the jimminy Hilary and

21

the dummy in their first infancy were below on the tearsheet, wringing and coughing, like brodar and histher. And the prankquean nipped a paly one and lit up again and redcocks flew flackering from the hillcombs. And she made her witter before the wicked, saying: Mark the Twy, why do I am alook alike two poss of porterpease? And: Shut! says the wicked, handwording her madesty. So her madesty a forethought set down a jiminy and took up a jiminy and all the lilipath ways to Woeman's Land she rain, rain, rain. And Jarl von Hoother bleethered atter her with a loud finegale: Stop domb stop come back with my earring stop. But the prankquean swaradid: Am liking it. And there was a wild old grannewwail that laurency night of starshootings somewhere in Erio. And the prankquean went for her forty years' walk in Turnlemeem and she punched the curses of cromcruwell with the nail of a top into the jiminy and she had her four larksical monitrix to touch him his tears and she provorted him to the onecertain allsecure and he became a tristian. So then she started raining, raining, and in a pair of changers, be dom ter, she was back again at Jarl von Hoother's and the Larryhill with her under her abromette. And why would she halt at all if not by the ward of his mansionhome of another nice lace for the third charm? And Jarl von Hoother had his hurricane hips up to his pantrybox, ruminating in his holdfour stomachs (Dare! O dare!), and the jiminy Toughertrees and the dummy were belove on the watercloth, kissing and spitting, and roguing and poghuing, like knavepaltry and naivebride and in their second infancy. And the prankquean picked a blank and lit out and the valleys lay twinkling. And she made her wittest in front of the arkway of trihump, asking: Mark the Tris, why do I am alook alike three poss of porter pease? But that was how the skirtmishes endupped. For like the campbells acoming with a fork lance of lightning, Jarl von Hoother Boanerges himself, the old terror of the dames, came hip hop handihap out through the pikeopened arkway of his three shuttoned castles, in his broadginger hat and his civic chollar and his allabuff hemmed and his bullbraggin soxangloves and his ladbroke breeks and his cattegut bandolair and his fur-

22

framed panuncular cumbottes like a rudd yellan gruebleen or-
angeman in his violet indignonation, to the whole longth of the
strongth of his bowman's bill. And he clopped his rude hand to
his eacy hitch and he ordurd and his thick spch spck for her to
shut up shop, dappy. And the duppy shot the shutter clup (Per-
kodhuskurunbarggruauyagokgorlayorgromgremmitghundhurth-
rumathunaradidillifaititillibumullunukkunun!) And they all drank
free. For one man in his armour was a fat match always for any
girls under shurts. And that was the first peace of illiterative
porthery in all the flamend floody flatuous world. How kirssy the
tiler made a sweet unclose to the Narwhealian captol. Saw fore
shalt thou sea. Betoun ye and be. The prankquean was to hold
her dummyship and the jimminies was to keep the peacewave
and van Hoother was to git the wind up. Thus the hearsomeness
of the burger felicitates the whole of the polis.

O foenix culprit! Ex nickylow malo comes mickelmassed bonum. Hill, rill, ones in company, billeted, less be proud of. Breast
high and bestride! Only for that these will not breathe upon
Norronesen or Irenean the secrest of their soorcelossness. Quarry silex, Homfrie Noanswa! Undy gentian festyknees, Livia Noanswa? Wolkencap is on him, frowned; audiurient, he would
evesdrip, were it mous at hand, were it dinn of bottles in the far
ear. Murk, his vales are darkling. With lipth she lithpeth to him
all to time of thuch on thuch and thow on thow. She he she ho
she ha to la. Hairfluke, if he could bad twig her! Impalpabunt,
he abhears. The soundwaves are his buffeteers; they trompe him
with their trompes; the wave of roary and the wave of hooshed
and the wave of hawhawhawrd and the wave of neverheedthem-
horseluggarsandlistletomine. Landloughed by his neaghboormis-
tress and perpetrified in his offsprung, sabes and suckers, the
moaning pipers could tell him to his faceback, the louthly one
whose loab we are devorers of, how butt for his hold halibutt, or
her to her pudor puff, the lipalip one whose libe we drink at, how
biff for her tiddywink of a windfall, our breed and washer givers,
there would not be a holey spier on the town nor a vestal flout-
ing in the dock, nay to make plein avowels, nor a yew nor an eye

to play cash cash in Novo Nilbud by swamplight nor a' toole o' tall o' toll and noddy hint to the convaynience.

He dug in and dug out by the skill of his tilth for himself and all belonging to him and he sweated his crew beneath his auspice for the living and he urned his dread, that dragon volant, and he made louse for us and delivered us to boll weevils amain, that mighty liberator, Unfru-Chikda-Uru-Wukru and begad he did, our ancestor most worshipful, till he thought of a better one in his windower's house with that blushmantle upon him from earsend to earsend. And would again could whispring grassies wake him and may again when the fiery bird disembers. And will again if so be sooth by elder to his youngers shall be said. Have you whines for my wedding, did you bring bride and bedding, will you whoop for my deading is a? Wake? *Usqueadbaugham!*

Anam muck an dhoul! Did ye drink me doornail?

Now be aisy, good Mr Finnimore, sir. And take your laysure like a god on pension and don't be walking abroad. Sure you'd only lose yourself in Healiopolis now the way your roads in Kapelavaster are that winding there after the calvary, the North Umbrian and the Fivs Barrow and Waddlings Raid and the Bower Moore and wet your feet maybe with the foggy dew's abroad. Meeting some sick old bankrupt or the Cottericks' donkey with his shoe hanging, clankatachankata, or a slut snoring with an impure infant on a bench. 'Twould turn you against life, so 'twould. And the weather's that mean too. To part from Devlin is hard as Nugent knew, to leave the clean tanglesome one lushier than its neighbour enfranchisable fields but let your ghost have no grievance. You're better off, sir, where you are, primesigned in the full of your dress, bloodeagle waistcoat and all, remembering your shapes and sizes on the pillow of your babycurls under your sycamore by the keld water where the Tory's clay will scare the varmints and have all you want, pouch, gloves, flask, bricket, kerchief, ring and amberulla, the whole treasure of the pyre, in the land of souls with Homin and Broin Baroke and pole ole Lonan and Nobucketnozzler and the Guinnghis Khan. And we'll be coming here, the ombre players, to rake your gravel and bringing you presents, won't we, fenians? And it isn't our spittle we'll stint you of, is it, druids?·Not shabbty little imagettes, pennydirts and dodgemyeyes you buy in the soottee stores. But offerings of the field. Mieliodories, that Doctor Faherty, the madison man, taught to gooden you. Poppypap's a passport out. And honey is the holiest thing ever was, hive, comb and earwax, the food for glory, (mind you keep the pot or your nectar cup may yield too light!) and some goat's milk, sir, like the maid used to bring you. Your fame is spreading like Basilico's ointment since the Fintan Lalors piped you overborder and there's whole households beyond the Bothnians and they calling names after you. The menhere's always talking of you sitting around on the pig's cheeks under the sacred rooftree, over the bowls of memory where every hollow holds a hallow, with a pledge till the drengs, in the Salmon House. And admiring to our supershillelagh where the palmsweat on high is the mark of your manument. All the toothpicks ever Eirenesians chewed on are chips chepped from that battery block. If you were bowed and soild and letdown itself from the oner of the load it was that paddyplanters might pack up plenty and when you were undone in every point fore the laps of goddesses you showed our labourlasses how to free was easy. The game old Gunne, they do be saying, (skull!) that was a planter for you, a spicer of them all. Begog but he was, the G.O.G! He's duddandgunne now and we're apter finding the sores of his sedeq but peace to his great limbs, the buddhoch, with the last league long rest of him, while the millioncandled eye of Tuskar sweeps the Moylean Main! There was never a warlord in Great Erinnes and Brettland, no, nor in all Pike County like you, they say. No, nor a king nor an ardking, bung king, sung king or hung king. That you could fell an elmstree twelve urchins couldn't ring round and hoist high the stone that Liam failed. Who but a Maccullaghmore the reise of our fortunes and the faunayman at the funeral to compass our cause? If you was hogglebully itself and most frifty like you was taken waters still what all where was your like to lay the cable or who was the batter could better Your Grace? Mick Mac Magnus MacCawley can take you off to

25

the pure perfection and Leatherbags Reynolds tries your shuffle and cut. But as Hopkins and Hopkins puts it, you were the pale eggynaggy and a kis to tilly up. We calls him the journeyall Buggaloffs since he went Jerusalemfaring in Arssia Manor. You had a gamier cock than Pete, Jake or Martin and your archgoose of geese stubbled for All Angels' Day. So may the priest of seven worms and scalding tayboil, Papa Vestray, come never anear you as your hair grows wheater beside the Liffey that's in Heaven! Hep, hep, hurrah there! Hero! Seven times thereto we salute you! The whole bag of kits, falconplumes and jackboots incloted, is where you flung them that time. Your heart is in the system of the Shewolf and your crested head is in the tropic of Copricapron. Your feet are in the cloister of Virgo. Your olala is in the region of sahuls. And that's ashore as you were born. Your shuck tick's swell. And that there texas is tow linen. The loamsome roam to Laffayette is ended. Drop in your tracks, babe! Be not unrested! The headboddylwatcher of the chempel of Isid, Totumcalmum, saith: I know thee, metherjar, I know thee, salvation boat. For we have performed upon thee, thou abramanation, who comest ever without being invoked, whose coming is unknown, all the things which the company of the precentors and of the grammarians of Christpatrick's ordered concerning thee in the matter of the work of thy tombing. Howe of the shipmen, steep wall!

Everything's going on the same or so it appeals to all of us, in the old holmsted here. Coughings all over the sanctuary, bad scrant to me aunt Florenza. The horn for breakfast, one o'gong for lunch and dinnerchime. As popular as when Belly the First was keng and his members met in the Diet of Man. The same shop slop in the window. Jacob's lettercrackers and Dr Tipple's Vi-Cocoa and the Eswuards' desippated soup beside Mother Seagull's syrup. Meat took a drop when Reilly-Parsons failed. Coal's short but we've plenty of bog in the yard. And barley's up again, begrained to it. The lads is attending school nessans regular, sir, spelling beesknees with hathatansy and turning out tables by mudapplication. Allfor the books and never pegging smashers after Tom Bowe Glassarse or Timmy the Tosser. 'Tisraely the truth! No isn't it, roman pathoricks? You were the doublejoynted janitor the morning they were delivered and you'll be a grandfer yet entirely when the ritehand seizes what the lovearm knows. Kevin's just a doat with his cherub cheek, chalking oghres on walls, and his little lamp and schoolbelt and bag of knicks, playing postman's knock round the diggings and if the seep were milk you could lieve his olde by his ide but, laus sake, the devil does be in that knirps of a Jerry sometimes, the tarandtan plaidboy, making encostive inkum out of the last of his lavings and writing a blue streak over his bourseday shirt. Hetty Jane's a child of Mary. She'll be coming (for they're sure to choose her) in her white of gold with a tourch of ivy to rekindle the flame on Felix Day. But Essie Shanahan has let down her skirts. You remember Essie in our Luna's Convent? They called her Holly Merry her lips were so ruddyberry and Pia de Purebelle when the redminers riots was on about her. Were I a clerk designate to the Williamswoodsmenufactors I'd poster those pouters on every jamb in the town. She's making her rep at Lanner's twicenightly. With the tabarine tamtammers of the whirligigmagees. Beats that cachucha flat. 'Twould dilate your heart to go.

Aisy now, you decent man, with your knees and lie quiet and repose your honour's lordship! Hold him here, Ezekiel Irons, and may God strengthen you! It's our warm spirits, boys, he's spooring. Dimitrius O'Flagonan, cork that cure for the Clancartys! You swamped enough since Portobello to float the Pomeroy. Fetch neahere, Pat Koy! And fetch nouyou, Pam Yates! Be nayther angst of Wramawitch! Here's lumbos. Where misties swaddlum, where misches lodge none, where mystries pour kind on, O sleepy! So be yet!

I've an eye on queer Behan and old Kate and the butter, trust me. She'll do no jugglywuggly with her war souvenir postcards to help to build me murial, tippers! I'll trip your traps! Assure a sure there! And we put on your clock again, sir, for you. Did or didn't we, sharestutterers? So you won't be up a stump entirely. Nor shed your remnants. The sternwheel's crawling strong. I seen your missus in the hall. Like the queenoveire. Arrah, it's herself that's fine, too, don't be talking! Shirksends? You storyan Harry chap longa me Harry chap storyan grass woman plethy good trout. Shakeshands. Dibble a hayfork's wrong with her only her lex's salig. Boald Tib does be yawning and smirking cat's hours on the Pollockses' woolly round tabouretcushion watching her sewing a dream together, the tailor's daughter, stitch to her last. Or while waiting for winter to fire the enchantement, decoying more nesters to fall down the flue. It's an allavalonche that blows nopussy food. If you only were there to explain the meaning, best of men, and talk to her nice of guldenselver. The lips would moisten once again. As when you drove with her to Findrinny Fair. What with reins here and ribbons there all your hands were employed so she never knew was she on land or at sea or swooped through the blue like Airwinger's bride. She was flirtsome then and she's fluttersome yet. She can second a song and adores a scandal when the last post's gone by. Fond of a concertina and pairs passing when she's had her forty winks for supper after kanekannan and abbely dimpling and is in her merlin chair assotted, reading her Evening World. To see is it smarts, full lengths or swaggers. News, news, all the news. Death, a leopard, kills fellah in Fez. Angry scenes at Stormount. Stilla Star with her lucky in goingaways. Opportunity fair with the China floods and we hear these rosy rumours. Ding Tams he noise about all same Harry chap. She's seeking her way, a chickle a chuckle, in and out of their serial story, *Les Loves of Selskar et Pervenche*, freely adapted to *The Novvergin's Viv*. There'll be bluebells blowing in salty sepulchres the night she signs her final tear. Zee End. But that's a world of ways away. Till track laws time. No silver ash or switches for that one! While flattering candles flare. Anna Stacey's how are you! Worther waist in the noblest, says Adams and Sons, the wouldpay actionneers. Her hair's as brown as ever it was. And wivvy and wavy. Repose you now! Finn no more!

For, be that samesake sibsubstitute of a hooky salmon, there's already a big rody ram lad at random on the premises of his haunt of the hungred bordles, as it is told me. Shop Illicit, flourishing like a lordmajor or a buaboabaybohm, litting flop a deadlop (aloose!) to lee but lifting a bennbranch a yardalong (ivoeh!) on the breezy side (for showm!), the height of Brewster's chimpney and as broad below as Phineas Barnum; humphing his share of the showthers is senken on him he's such a grandfallar, with a pocked wife in pickle that's a flyfire and three lice nittle clinkers, two twilling bugs and one midgit pucelle. And aither he cursed and recursed and was everseen doing what your fourfootlers saw or he was never done seeing what you coolpigeons know, weep the clouds aboon for smiledown witnesses, and that'll do now about the fairyhees and the frailyshees. Though Eset fibble it to the zephiroth and Artsa zoom it round her heavens for ever. Creator he has created for his creatured ones a creation. White monothoid? Red theatrocrat? And all the pinkprophets cohalething? Very much so! But however 'twas 'tis sure for one thing, what sherif Toragh voucherfors and Mapqiq makes put out, that the man, Humme the Cheapner, Esc, overseen as we thought him, yet a worthy of the naym, came at this timecoloured place where we live in our paroqial fermament one tide on another, with a bumrush in a hull of a wherry, the twin turbane dhow, *The Bey for Dybbling*, this archipelago's first visiting schooner, with a wicklowpattern waxenwench at her prow for a figurehead, the deadsea dugong updipdripping from his depths, and has been repreaching himself like a fishmummer these siktyten years ever since, his shebi by his shide, adi and aid, growing hoarish under his turban and changing cane sugar into sethulose starch (Tuttut's cess to him!) as also that, batin the bulkihood he bloats about when innebbiated, our old offender was humile, commune and ensectuous from his nature, which you may gauge after the bynames was put under him, in lashons of languages, (honnein suit and praisers be!) and, totalisating him, even hamissim of himashim that he, sober serious, he is ee and no counter he who will be ultimendly respunchable for the hubbub caused in Edenborough.

Now (to forebare for ever solittle of Iris Trees and Lili O'Rangans), concerning the genesis of Harold or Humphrey Chimpden's occupational agnomen (we are back in the presurnames prodromarith period, of course just when enos chalked halltraps) and discarding once for all those theories from older sources which would link him back with such pivotal ancestors as the Glues, the Gravys, the Northeasts, the Ankers and the Earwickers of Sidlesham in the Hundred of Manhood or proclaim him offsprout of vikings who had founded wapentake and seddled hem in Herrick or Eric, the best authenticated version, the Dumlat, read the Reading of Hofed-ben-Edar, has it that it was this way. We are told how in the beginning it came to pass that like cabbaging Cincinnatus the grand old gardener was saving daylight under his redwoodtree one sultry sabbath afternoon, Hag Chivychas Eve, in prefall paradise peace by following his plough for rootles in the rere garden of mobhouse, ye olde marine hotel, when royalty was announced by runner to have been pleased to have halted itself on the highroad along which a leisureloving dogfox had cast followed, also at walking pace, by a lady pack of cocker spaniels. Forgetful of all save his vassal's plain fealty to the ethnarch Humphrey or Harold stayed not to yoke or saddle but stumbled out hotface as he was (his sweatful bandanna loose from his pocketcoat) hasting to the forecourts of his public in topee, surcingle, solascarf and plaid, plus fours, puttees and bulldog boots ruddled cinnabar with

30

flagrant marl, jingling his turnpike keys and bearing aloft amid the fixed pikes of the hunting party a high perch atop of which a flowerpot was fixed earthside hoist with care. On his majesty, who was, or often feigned to be, noticeably longsighted from green youth and had been meaning to inquire what, in effect, had caused yon causeway to be thus potholed, asking substitutionally to be put wise as to whether paternoster and silver doctors were not now more fancied bait for lobstertrapping honest blunt Haromphreyld answered in no uncertain tones very similarly with a fearless forehead: Naw, yer maggers, aw war jist a cotchin on thon bluggy earwuggers. Our sailor king, who was draining a gugglet of obvious adamale, gift both and gorban, upon this, ceasing to swallow, smiled most heartily beneath his walrus moustaches and indulging that none too genial humour which William the Conk on the spindle side had inherited with the hereditary whitelock and some shortfingeredness from his greataunt Sophy, turned towards two of his retinue of gallowglasses, Michael, etheling lord of Leix and Offaly and the jubilee mayor of Drogheda, Elcock, (the two scatterguns being Michael M. Manning, protosyndic of Waterford and an Italian excellency named Giubilei according to a later version cited by the learned scholarch Canavan of Canmakenoise), in either case a triptychal religious family symbolising puritas of doctrina, business per usuals and the purchypatch of hamlock where the paddish preties grow and remarked dilsydulsily: Holybones of Saint Hubert how our red brother of Pouringrainia would audibly fume did he know that we have for surtrusty bailiwick a turnpiker who is by turns a pikebailer no seldomer than an earwigger! For he kinned Jom Pill with his court so gray and his haunts in his house in the mourning. (One still hears that pebble crusted laughta, japijap cheerycherrily, among the roadside tree the lady Holmpatrick planted and still one feels the amossive silence of the cladstone allegibelling: Ive mies outs ide Bourn.) Comes the question are these the facts of his nominigentilisation as recorded and accolated in both or either of the collateral andrewpaulmurphyc narratives. Are those their fata which we read in sibylline between the *fas* and its *nefas?* No dung

31

on the road? And shall Nohomiah be our place like? Yea, Mulạchy our kingable khan? We shall perhaps not so soon see. Pinck poncks that bail for seeks alicence where cumsceptres with scentaurs stay. Bear in mind, son of Hokmah, if so be you have metheg in your midness, this man is mountain and unto changeth doth one ascend. Heave we aside the fallacy, as punical as finikin, that it was not the king kingself but his inseparable sisters, uncontrollable nighttalkers, Skertsiraizde with Donyahzade, who afterwards, when the robberers shot up the socialights, came down into the world as amusers and were staged by Madame Sudlow as Rosa and Lily Miskinguette in the pantalime that two pitts paythronosed, Miliodorus and Galathee. The great fact emerges that after that historic date all holographs so far exhumed initialled by Haromphrey bear the sigla H.C.E. and while he was only and long and always good Dook Umphrey for the hungerlean spalpeens of Lucalizod and Chimbers to his cronies it was equally certainly a pleasant turn of the populace which gave him as sense of those normative letters the nickname Here Comes Everybody. An imposing everybody he always indeed looked, constantly the same as and equal to himself and magnificently well worthy of any and all such universalisation, every time he continually surveyed, amid vociferatings from in front of *Accept these few nutties!* and *Take off that white hat!*, relieved with *Stop his Grog* and *Put It in the Log* and *Loots in his* (bassvoco) *Boots*, from good start to happy finish the truly catholic assemblage gathered together in that king's treat house of satin alustrelike above floats and footlights from their assbawlveldts and oxgangs unanimously to clapplaud (the inspiration of his lifetime and the hits of their careers) Mr Wallenstein Washington Semperkelly's immergreen tourers in a command performance by special request with the courteous permission for pious purposes the homedromed and enliventh performance of the problem passion play of the millentury, running strong since creation, *A Royal Divorce*, then near the approach towards the summit of its climax, with ambitious interval band selections from *The Bo' Girl* and *The Lily* on all horserie show command nights from his viceregal booth (his bossaloner is ceilinged there a cuckoospit less eminent than the redritualhoods of Maccabe and Cullen) where, a veritable Napoleon the Nth, our worldstage's practical jokepiece and retired cecelticocommediant in his own wise, this folksforefather all of the time sat, having the entirety of his house about him, with the invariable broadstretched kerchief cooling his whole neck, nape and shoulderblades and in a wardrobe panelled tuxedo completely thrown back from a shirt well entitled a swallowall, on every point far outstarching the laundered clawhammers and marbletopped highboys of the pit stalls and early amphitheatre. The piece was this: look at the lamps. The cast was thus: see under the clock. Ladies circle: cloaks may be left. Pit, prommer and parterre, standing room only. Habituels conspicuously emergent.

A baser meaning has been read into these characters the literal sense of which decency can safely scarcely hint. It has been blurtingly bruited by certain wisecrackers (the stinks of Mohorat are in the nightplots of the morning), that he suffered from a vile disease. Athma, unmanner them! To such a suggestion the one selfrespecting answer is to affirm that there are certain statements which ought not to be, and one should like to hope to be able to add, ought not to be allowed to be made. Nor have his detractors, who, an imperfectly warmblooded race, apparently conceive him as a great white caterpillar capable of any and every enormity in the calendar recorded to the discredit of the Juke and Kellikek families, mended their case by insinuating that, alternately, he lay at one time under the ludicrous imputation of annoying Welsh fusiliers in the people's park. Hay, hay, hay! Hoq, hoq, hoq! Faun and Flora on the lea love that little old joq. To anyone who knew and loved the christlikeness of the big cleanminded giant H. C. Earwicker throughout his excellency long vicefreegal existence the mere suggestion of him as a lustsleuth nosing for trouble in a boobytrap rings particularly preposterous. Truth, beard on prophet, compels one to add that there is said to have been quondam (pfuit! pfuit!) some case of the kind implicating, it is interdum believed, a quidam (if he did not exist it would be necessary quoniam to invent him) abhout that time stambuling ha-round Dumbaling in leaky sneakers with his tarrk record who has remained topantically anonymos but (let us hue him Abdullah Gamellaxarksky) was, it is stated, posted at Mallon's at the instance of watch warriors of the vigilance committee and years afterwards, cries one even greater, Ibid, a commender of the frightful, seemingly, unto such as were sulhan sated, tropped head (pfiat! pfiat!) waiting his first of the month froods turn for thatt chopp pah kabbakks alicubi on the old house for the chargehard, Roche Haddocks off Hawkins Street. Lowe, you blondy liar, Gob scene you in the narked place and she what's edith ar home defileth these boyles! There's a cabful of bash indeed in the homeur of that meal. Slander, let it lie its flattest, has never been able to convict our good and great and no ordinary Southron Earwicker, that homogenius man, as a pious author called him, of any graver impropriety than that, advanced by some woodwards or regarders, who did not dare deny, the shomers, that they had, chin Ted, chin Tam, chinchin Taffyd, that day consumed their soul of the corn, of having behaved with ongentilmensky immodus opposite a pair of dainty maidservants in the swoolth of the rushy hollow whither, or so the two gown and pinners pleaded, dame nature in all innocency had spontaneously and about the same hour of the eventide sent them both but whose published combinations of silkinlaine testimonies are, where not dubiously pure, visibly divergent, as wapt from wept, on minor points touching the intimate nature of this, a first offence in vert or venison which was admittedly an incautious but, at its wildest, a partial exposure with such attenuating circumstances (garthen gaddeth green hwere sokeman brideth girling) as an abnormal Saint Swithin's summer and, (Jesses Rosasharon!) a ripe occasion to provoke it.

We can't do without them. Wives, rush to the restyours! Ofman will toman while led is the lol. Zessid's our kadem, villapleach, vollapluck. Fikup, for flesh nelly, el mundo nov, zole flen! If she's a lilyth, pull early! Pauline, allow! And malers abushed, keep black, keep black! Guiltless of much laid to him he was clearly for once at least he clearly expressed himself as being with still a trace of his erstwhile burr and hence it has been received of us that it is true. They tell the story (an amalgam as absorbing as calzium chloereydes and hydrophobe sponges could make it) how one happygogusty Ides-of-April morning (the anniversary, as it fell out, of his first assumption of his mirthday suit and rights in appurtenance to the confusioning of human races) ages and ages after the alleged misdemeanour when the tried friend of all creation, tigerwood roadstaff to his stay, was billowing across the wide expanse of our greatest park in his caoutchouc kepi and great belt and hideinsacks and his blaufunx fustian and ironsides jackboots and Bhagafat gaiters and his rubberised inverness, he met a cad with a pipe. The latter, the luciferant not the oriuolate (who, the odds are, is still berting dagabout in the same straw bamer, carryin his overgoat under his schulder, sheepside out, so as to look more like a coumfry gentleman and signing the pledge as gaily as you please) hardily accosted him with: Guinness thaw tool in jew me dinner ouzel fin? (a nice how-do-you-do in Poolblack at the time as some of our olddaisers may still tremblingly recall) to ask could he tell him how much a clock it was that the clock struck had he any idea by cock's luck as his watch was bradys. Hesitency was clearly to be evitated. Execration as cleverly to be honnisoid. The Earwicker of that spurring instant, realising on fundamental liberal principles the supreme importance, nexally and noxally, of physical life (the nearest help relay being pingping K. O. Sempatrick's Day and the fenian rising) and unwishful as he felt of being hurled into eternity right then, plugged by a softnosed bullet from the sap, halted, quick on the draw, and replyin that he was feelin tipstaff, cue, prodooced from his gunpocket his Jurgensen's shrapnel waterbury, ours by communionism, his by usucapture, but, on the same stroke, hearing above the skirling of harsh Mother East old Fox Goodman, the bellmaster, over the wastes to south, at work upon the ten ton tonuant thunderous tenor toller in the speckled church (Couhounin's call!) told the inquiring kidder, by Jehova, it was twelve of em sidereal and tankard time, adding, buttall, as he bended deeply with smoked sardinish breath to give more pondus to the copperstick he presented, (though this seems in some cumfusium with the chap-

35

stuck ginger which, as being of sours, acids, salts, sweets and bitters compompounded, we know him to have used as chawchaw for bone, muscle, blood, flesh and vimvital,) that whereas the hakusay accusation againstm had been made, what was known in high quarters as was stood stated in Morganspost, by a creature in youman form who was quite beneath parr and several degrees lower than yore triplehydrad snake. In greater support of his word (it, quaint anticipation of a famous phrase, has been reconstricted out of oral style into the verbal for all time with ritual rhythmics, in quiritary quietude, and toosammenstucked from successive accounts by Noah Webster in the redaction known as the Sayings Attributive of H. C. Earwicker, prize on schillings, postlots free), the flaxen Gygas tapped his chronometrum drumdrum and, now standing full erect, above the ambijacent floodplain, scene of its happening, with one Berlin gauntlet chopstuck in the hough of his ellboge (by ancientest signlore his gesture meaning: Ǝ!) pointed at an angle of thirtytwo degrees towards his *duc de Fer's* overgrown milestone as fellow to his gage and after a rendypresent pause averred with solemn emotion's fire: Shsh shake, co-comeraid! Me only, them five ones, he is equal combat. I have won straight. Hence my nonation wide hotel and creamery establishments which for the honours of our mewmew mutual daughters, credit me, I am woowoo willing to take my stand, sir, upon the monument, that sign of our ruru redemption, any hygienic day to this hour and to make my hoath to my sinnfinners, even if I get life for it, upon the Open Bible and before the Great Taskmaster's (I lift my hat!) and in the presence of the Deity Itself andwell of Bishop and Mrs Michan of High Church of England as of all such of said my immediate withdwellers and of every living sohole in every corner wheresoever of this globe in general which useth of my British to my backbone tongue and commutative justice that there is not one tittle of truth, allow me to tell you, in that purest of fibfib fabrications.

Gaping Gill, swift to mate errthors, stern to checkself, (diagnosing through eustacetube that it was to make with a markedly

36

postpuberal hypertituitary type of Heidelberg mannleich cavern
ethics) lufted his slopingforward, bad Sweatagore good murrough and dublnotch on to it as he was greedly obliged, and
like a sensible ham, with infinite tact in the delicate situation seen
the touchy nature of its perilous theme, thanked um for guilders
received and time of day (not a little token abock all the same that
that was owl the God's clock it was) and, upon humble duty to
greet his Tyskminister and he shall gildthegap Gaper and thee his
a mouldy voids, went about his business, whoever it was, saluting
corpses, as a metter of corse (one could hound him out had one
hart to for the monticules of scalp and dandruff droppings blaze
his trail) accompanied by his trusty snorler and his permanent
reflection, verbigracious; I have met with you, bird, too late,
or if not, too worm and early: and with tag for ildiot repeated
in his secondmouth language as many of the bigtimer's verbaten
words which he could balbly call to memory that same kveldeve,
ere the hour of the twattering of bards in the twitterlitter between
Druidia and the Deepsleep Sea, when suppertide and souvenir to
Charlatan Mall jointly kem gently and along the quiet darkenings
of Grand and Royal, ff, flitmansfluh, and, kk, 't crept i' hedge
whenas to many a softongue's pawkytalk mude unswer u sufter
poghyog, Arvanda always aquiassent, while, studying castelles
in the blowne and studding cowshots over the noran, he spat in
careful convertedness a musaic dispensation about his *hearthstone*,
if you please, (Irish saliva, *mawshe dho hole*, but would a respectable prominently connected fellow of Iro-European ascendances
with welldressed ideas who knew the correct thing such as Mr
Shallwesigh or Mr Shallwelaugh expectorate after such a callous
fashion, no thank yous! when he had his belcher *spuckertuck* in his
pucket, pthuck?) musefed with his thockits after having supped
of the dish sot and pottage which he snobbishly dabbed Peach
Bombay (it is rawly only Lukanpukan pilzenpie which she knows
which senaffed and pibered him), a supreme of excelling peas,
balled under minnshogue's milk into whitemalt winesour, a pro-
viant the littlebilker hoarsely relished, chaff it, in the snevel season,
being as fain o't as your rat wi'fennel; and on this celebrating

37

occasion of the happy escape, for a crowning of pot valiance, this regional platter, benjamin of bouillis, with a spolish olive to middlepoint its zaynith, was marrying itself (porkograso!) erebusqued very deluxiously with a bottle of Phenice-Bruerie '98, followed for second nuptials by a Piessporter, Grand Cur, of both of which cherished tablelights (though humble the bounquet 'tis a leaman's farewell) he obdurately sniffed the cobwebcrusted corks.

Our cad's bit of strife (knee Bareniece Maxwelton) with a quick ear for spittoons (as the aftertale hath it) glaned up as usual with dumbestic husbandry (no persicks and armelians for thee, Pomeranzia!) but, slipping the clav in her claw, broke of the matter among a hundred and eleven others in her usual curtsey (how faint these first vhespers womanly are, a secret pispigliando, amad the lavurdy den of their manfolker!) the next night nudge one as was Hegesippus over a hup a ' chee, her eys dry and small and speech thicklish because he appeared a funny colour like he couldn't stood they old hens no longer, to her particular reverend, the director, whom she had been meaning in her mind primarily to speak with (hosch, intra! jist a timblespoon!) trusting, between cuppled lips and annie lawrie promises (mighshe never have Esnekerry pudden come Hunanov for her pecklapitschens!) that the gossiple so delivered in his epistolear, buried teatoastally in their Irish stew would go no further than his jesuit's cloth, yet (in vinars venitas! volatiles valetotum!) it was this overspoiled priest Mr Browne, disguised as a vincentian, who, when seized of the facts, was overheard, in his secondary personality as a Nolan and underreared, poul soul, by accident—if, that is, the incident it was an accident for here the ruah of Ecclectiastes of Hippo outpuffs the writress of Havvah-ban-Annah—to pianissime a slightly varied version of Crookedribs confidentials, (what Mère Aloyse said but for Jesuphine's sake!) hands between hahands, in fcalty sworn (my bravor bcst! my fraur!) and, to the strains of *The Secret of Her Birth,* hushly pierce the rubiend aurellum of one Philly Thurnston, a layteacher of rural science and orthophonethics of a nearstout figure and about the middle of his forties during a priestly flutter for safe and sane bets at the hippic runfields of breezy Baldoyle on a date (W. W. goes through the caɪd) easily capable of rememberance by all pickers-up of events national and Dublin details, the doubles of Perkin and Paullock, peer and prole, when the classic Encourage Hackney Plate was captured by two noses in a stablecloth finish, ek and nek, some and none, evelo nevelo, from the cream colt Bold Boy Cromwell after a clever getaway by Captain Chaplain Blount's roe hinny Saint Dalough, Drummer Coxon, nondepict third, at breakneck odds, thanks to you great little, bonny little, portey little, Winny Widger! you're all their nappies! who in his never-rip mud and purpular cap was surely leagues unlike any other phantomweight that ever toppitt our timber maggies.

'Twas two pisononse Timcoves (the wetter is pest, the renns are overt and come and the voax of the turfur is hurled on our lande) of the name of Treacle Tom as waṣ just out of pop following the theft of a leg of Kehoe, Donnelly and Packenham's Finnish pork and his own blood and milk brother Frisky Shorty, (he was, to be exquisitely punctilious about them, both shorty and frisky) a tip-ster, come off the hulks, both of them awful poor, what was out on the bumaround for an oofbird game for a jimmy o'goblin or a small thick un as chanced, while the Seaforths was making the colleenbawl, to ear the passon in the motor clobber make use of his law language (Edzo, Edzo on), touchin the case of Mr Adams what was in all the sundays about it which he was rubbing noses with and having a gurgle off his own along of the butty bloke in the specs.

This Treacle Tom to whom reference has been made had been absent from his usual wild and woolly haunts in the land of counties capalleens for some time previous to that (he was, in fact, in the habit of frequenting common lodginghouses where he slept in a nude state, hailfellow with meth, in strange men's cots) but on racenight, blotto after divers tots of hell fire, red biddy, bull dog, blue ruin and creeping jenny, Eglandine's choic-est herbage, supplied by the Duck and Doggies, the Galop-ping Primrose, Brigid Brewster's, the Cock, the Postboy's Horn, the Little Old Man's and All Swell That Aimswell, the Cup and the Stirrup, he sought his wellwarmed leababobed in a housingroom Abide With Oneanother at Block W.W., (why didn't he back it?) Pump Court, The Liberties, and, what with moltapuke on voltapuke, resnored alcoh alcoho alcoherently to the burden of *I come, my horse delayed,* nom num, the substance of the tale of the evangelical bussybozzy and the rusinurbean (the 'girls' he would keep calling them for the collarette and skirt, the sunbonnet and carnation) in parts (it seemed he was before the eyots of martas or otherwales the thirds of fossilyears, he having beham with katya when lavinias had her mens lease to sea in a psumpship doodly show whereat he was looking for fight niggers with whilde roarses) oft in the chilly night (the metagonistic! the epickthalamorous!) during uneasy slumber in their hearings of a small and stonybroke cashdraper's executive, Peter Cloran (discharged), O'Mara, an exprivate secretary of no fixed abode (locally known as Mildew Lisa), who had passed several nights, funnish enough, in a doorway under the blankets of homelessness on the bunk of iceland, pillowed upon the stone of destiny colder than man's knee or woman's breast, and Hosty, (no slouch of a name), an illstarred beachbusker, who, sans rootie and sans scrapie, suspicioning as how he was setting on a twoodstool on the verge of selfabyss, most starved, with melancholia over everything in general, (night birman, you served him with natigal's nano!) had been towhead tossing on his shakedown, devising ways and manners of means, of what he loved to ifidalicence somehow or other in the nation getting a hold of some chap's parabellum in the hope of taking a wing sociable and lighting upon a sidewheel dive somewhere off the Dullkey Downlairy and Bleakrooky tramaline where he could throw true and go and blow the sibicidal napper off himself for two bits to boldywell baltitude in the peace and quitybus of a one sure shot bottle, he after having being trying all he knew with the lady's help of Madam Gristle for upwards of eighteen calanders to get out of Sir Patrick Dun's, through Sir Humphrey Jervis's and into the Saint Kevin's bed in the Adelaide's hosspittles (from

40

these incurable welleslays among those uncarable wellasdays through Sant Iago by his cocklehat, good Lazar, deliver us!) without after having been able to jerrywangle it anysides. Lisa O'Deavis and Roche Mongan (who had so much incommon, epipsychidically; if the phrase be permitted *hostis et odor insuper petroperfractus*) as an understood thing slept their sleep of the swimborne in the one sweet undulant mother of tumblerbunks with Hosty just how the shavers in the shaw the yokels in the yoats or, well, the wasters in the wilde, and the bustling tweeny-dawn-of-all-works (meed of anthems here we pant!) had not been many jiffies furbishing potlids, doorbrasses, scholars' applecheeks and linkboy's metals when, ashhopperminded like no fella he go make bakenbeggfuss longa white man, the rejuvenated busker (for after a goodnight's rave and rumble and a shinkhams topmorning with his coexes he was not the same man) and his broadawake bedroom suite (our boys, as our Byron called them) were up and ashuffle from the hogshome they lovenaned The Barrel, cross Ebblinn's chilled hamlet (thrie routes and restings on their then superficies curiously correspondant with those linea and puncta where our tubenny habenny metro maniplumbs below the ober-flake underrails and stations at this time of riding) to the thrum-mings of a crewth fiddle which, cremoaning and cronauning, levey grevey, witty and wevey, appy, leppy and playable, caressed the ears of the subjects of King Saint Finnerty the Festive who, in brick homes of their own and in their flavory fraiseberry beds, heeding hardly cry of honeyman, soed lavender or foyneboyne salmon alive, with their priggish mouths all open for the larger appraisiation of this longawaited Messiagh of roaratorios, were only halfpast atsweeeep and after a brisk pause at a pawnbroking establishment for the prothetic purpose of redeeming the song-ster's truly admirable false teeth and a prolonged visit to a house of call at Cujas Place, fizz, the Old Sots' Hole in the parish of Saint Cecily within the liberty of Ceolmore not a thousand or one national leagues, that was, by Griffith's valuation, from the site of the statue of Primewer Glasstone setting a match to the march of a maker (last of the stewards peut-être), where, the tale rambles along, the trio of whackfolthediddlers was joined by a further—intentions—apply—tomorrow casual and a decent sort of the hadbeen variety who had just been touching the weekly insult, phewit, and all figblabbers (who saith of noun?) had stimulants in the shape of gee and gees stood by the damn decent sort after which stag luncheon and a few ones more just to celebrate yesterday, flushed with their firestuffostered friendship, the rascals came out of the licensed premises, (Browne's first, the small p.s. ex-ex-executive capahand in their sad rear like a lady's postscript: I want money. Pleasend), wiping their laughleaking lipes on their sleeves, how the bouckaleens shout their rosçan generally (seinn fion, seinn fion's araun.) and the rhymers' world was with reason the richer for a wouldbe ballad, to the balledder of which the world of cumannity singing owes a tribute for having placed on the planet's melomap his lay of the vilest bogeyer but most attractionable avatar the world has ever had to explain for.

This, more krectly lubeen or fellow — me — lieder was first poured forth where Riau Liviau riots and col de Houdo humps, under the shadow of the monument of the shouldhavebeen legislator (Eleutheriodendron! Spare, woodmann, spare!) to an overflow meeting of all the nations in Lenster fullyfilling the visional area and, as a singleminded supercrowd, easily representative, what with masks, whet with faces, of all sections and cross sections (wineshop and cocoahouse poured out to brim up the broaching) of our liffeyside people (to omit to mention of the mainland minority and such as had wayfared *via* Watling, Ernin, Icknild and Stane, in chief a halted cockney car with its quotal of Hardmuth's hacks, a northern tory, a southern whig, an eastanglian chronicler and a landwester guardian) ranging from slips of young dublinos from Cutpurse Row having nothing better to do than walk about with their hands in their kneepants, sucking airwhackers, weedulicet, jumbobricks, side by side with truant officers, three woollen balls and poplin in search of a croust of pawn to busy professional gentlemen, a brace of palesmen with dundrearies, nooning toward Daly's, fresh from snipehitting and mallardmissing on Rutland heath, exchanging cold sneers, mass-going ladies from Hume Street in their chairs, the bearers baited, some wandering hamalags out of the adjacent cloverfields of Mosse's Gardens, an oblate father from Skinner's Alley, bricklayers, a fleming, in tabinet fumant, with spouse and dog, an aged hammersmith who had some chisellers by the hand, a bout of cudgel players, not a few sheep with the braxy, two bluecoat scholars, four broke gents out of Simpson's on the Rocks, a portly and a pert still tassing Turkey Coffee and orange shrub in tickeyes door, Peter Pim and Paul Fry and then Elliot and, O, Atkinson, suffering hell's delights from the blains of their annuitants' acorns not forgetting a deuce of dianas ridy for the hunt, a particularist prebendary pondering on the roman easter, the tonsure question and greek uniates, plunk em, a lace lappet head or two or three or four from a window, and so on down to a few good old souls, who, as they were juiced after taking their pledge over at the uncle's place, were evidently under the spell of liquor, from the wake of Tarry the Tailor a fair girl, a jolly postoboy thinking off three flagons and one, a plumodrole, a half sir from the weaver's almshouse who clings and clings and chatchatchat clings to her, a wholedam's cloudhued pittycoat, as child, as curiolater, as Caoch O'Leary. The wararrow went round, so it did, (a nation wants a gaze) and the ballad, in the felibrine trancoped metre affectioned by Taiocebo in his *Casudas de Poulichinello Artahut*, stumpstampaded on to a slip of blancovide and headed by an excessively rough and red woodcut, privately printed at the rimepress of Delville, soon fluttered its secret on white highway and brown byway to the rose of the winds and the blew of the gaels, from archway to lattice and from black hand to pink ear, village crying to village, through the five pussyfours green of the united states of Scotia Picta—and he who denays it, may his hairs be rubbed in dirt! To the added strains (so peacifold) of his majesty the flute, that onecrooned king of inscrewments, Piggott's purest, *ciello alsoliuto*, which Mr Delaney (Mr Delacey?), horn, anticipating a perfect downpour of plaudits among the rapsods, piped out of his decentsoort hat, looking still more like his purseyful namesake as men of Gaul noted, but before of to sputabout, the

43

snowycrested curl amoist the leader's wild and moulting hair, 'Ductor' Hitchcock hoisted his fezzy fuzz at bludgeon's height signum to his companions of the chalice for the Loud Fellow, boys' and *silentium in curia!* (our maypole once more where he rose of old) and the canto was chantied there chorussed and christened where by the old tollgate, Saint Annona's Street and Church.

And around the lawn the rann it rann and this is the rann that Hosty made. Spoken. Boyles and Cahills, Skerretts and Pritchards, viersified and piersified may the treeth we tale of live in stoney. Here line the refrains of. Some vote him Vike, some mote him Mike, some dub him Llyn and Phin while others hail him Lug Bug Dan Lop, Lex, Lax, Gunne or Guinn. Some apt him Arth, some bapt him Barth, Coll, Noll, Soll, Will, Weel, Wall but I parse him Persse O'Reilly else he's called no name at all. Together. Arrah, leave it to Hosty, frosty Hosty, leave it to Hosty for he's the mann to rhyme the rann, the rann, the rann, the king of all ranns. Have you here? (Some ha) Have we where? (Some hant) Have you hered? (Others do) Have we whered? (Others dont) It's cumming, it's brumming! The clip, the clop! (All cla) Glass crash. The (klikkaklakkaklaskaklopatzklatschabattacreppycrotty-graddaghsemmihsammihnouithappluddyappladdypkonpkot!).

⎰*Ardite, arditi!*
⎱Music cue.

"THE BALLAD OF PERSSE O'REILLY."

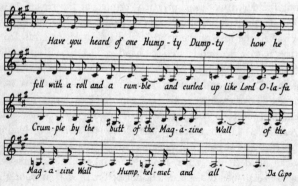

44

Have you heard of one Humpty Dumpty
How he fell with a roll and a rumble
And curled up like Lord Olofa Crumple
By the butt of the Magazine Wall,
  (Chorus) Of the Magazine Wall,
     Hump, helmet and all?

He was one time our King of the Castle
Now he's kicked about like a rotten old parsnip.
And from Green street he'll be sent by order of His Worship'
To the penal jail of Mountjoy
  (Chorus) To the jail of Mountjoy!
     Jail him and joy.

He was fafafather of all schemes for to bother us
Slow coaches and immaculate contraceptives for the populace,
Mare's milk for the sick, seven dry Sundays a week,
Openair love and religion's reform,
  (Chorus) And religious reform,
     Hideous in form.

Arrah, why, says you, couldn't he manage it?
I'll go bail, my fine dairyman darling,
Like the bumping bull of the Cassidys
All your butter is in your horns.
  (Chorus) His butter is in his horns.
     Butter his horns!

(Repeat) Hurrah there, Hosty, frosty Hosty, change that shirt
             [on ye,
Rhyme the rann, the king of all ranns!

    Balbaccio, balbuccio!
We had chaw chaw chops, chairs, chewing gum, the chicken-
         [pox and china chambers
Universally provided by this soffsoaping salesman.

Small wonder He'll Cheat E'erawan our local lads nicknamed him
When Chimpden first took the floor
    (Chorus) With his bucketshop store
             Down Bargainweg, Lower.

So snug he was in his hotel premises sumptuous
But soon we'll bonfire all his trash, tricks and trumpery
And'tis short till sheriff Clancy'll be winding up his unlimited
                                        [company
With the bailiff's bom at the door,
    (Chorus) Bimbam at the door.
             Then he'll bum no more.

Sweet bad luck on the waves washed to our island
The hooker of that hammerfast viking
And Gall's curse on the day when Eblana bay
Saw his black and tan man-o'-war.
    (Chorus) Saw his man-o'-war.
             On the harbour bar.

Where from? roars Poolbeg. Cookingha'pence, he bawls Donnez-
                        [moi scampitle, wick an wipin'fampiny
Fingal Mac Oscar Onesine Bargearse Boniface
Thok's min gammelhole Norveegickers moniker
Og as ay are at gammelhore Norveegickers cod.
    (Chorus) A Norwegian camel old cod.
             He is, begod.

Lift it, Hosty, lift it, ye devil ye! up with the rann, the rhyming
                                         [rann!

It was during some fresh water garden pumping
Or, according to the *Nursing Mirror*, while admiring the mon-
                                       [keys
That our heavyweight heathen Humpharey
Made bold a maid to woo
    (Chorus) Woohoo, what'll she doo!
             The general lost her maidenloo!

He ought to blush for himself, the old hayheaded philosopher,
For to go and shove himself that way on top of her.
Begob, he's the crux of the catalogue
Of our antediluvial zoo,
    (Chorus) Messrs. Billing and Coo.
                Noah's larks, good as noo.

He was joulting by Wellinton's monument
Our rotorious hippopopotamuns
When some bugger let down the backtrap of the omnibus
And he caught his death of fusiliers,
    (Chorus) With his rent in his rears.
                Give him six years.

'Tis sore pity for his innocent poor children
But look out for his missus legitimate!
When that frew gets a grip of old Earwicker
Won't there be earwigs on the green?
    (Chorus) Big earwigs on the green,
                The largest ever you seen.

    Suffoclose! Shikespower! Seudodanto! Anonymoses!

Then we'll have a free trade Gaels' band and mass meeting
For to sod the brave son of Scandiknavery.
And we'll bury him down in Oxmanstown
Along with the devil and Danes,
    (Chorus) With the deaf and dumb Danes,
                And all their remains.

And not all the king's men nor his horses
Will resurrect his corpus
For there's no true spell in Connacht or hell
    (bis) That's able to raise a Cain.

Chest Cee! 'Sdense! Corpo di barragio! you spoof of visibility in a freakfog, of mixed sex cases among goats, hill cat and plain mousey, Bigamy Bob and his old Shanvocht! The Blackfriars treacle plaster outrage be liddled! Therewith was released in that kingsrick of Humidia a poisoning volume of cloud barrage indeed. Yet all they who heard or redelivered are now with that family of bards and Vergobretas himself and the crowd of Caraculacticors as much no more as be they not yet now or had they then notever been. Canbe in some future we shall presently here amid those zouave players of Inkermann the mime mumming the mick and his nick miming their maggies, Hilton St Just (Mr Frank Smith), Ivanne Ste Austelle (Mr J. F. Jones), Coleman of Lucan taking four parts, a choir of the O'Daley O'Doyles doublesixing the chorus in *Fenn Mac Call and the Serven Feeries of Loch Neach*, *Galloper Troppler and Hurleyquinn* the zitherer of the past with his merrymen all, zimzim, zimzim. Of the persins sin this Eyrawyggla saga (which, thorough readable to int from and, is from tubb to buttom all falsetissues, antilibellous and nonactionable and this applies to its whole wholume) of poor Osti-Fosti, described as quite a musical genius in a small way and the owner of an exceedingly niced ear, with tenorist voice to match, not alone, but a very major poet of the poorly meritary order (he began Tuonisonian but worked his passage up as far as the we-all-hang-together Animandovites) no one end is known. If they

48

whistled him before he had curtains up they are whistling him still after his curtain's doom's doom. *Ei fù.* His husband, poor old A'Hara (Okaroff?) crestfallen by things and down at heels at the time, they squeak, accepted the (Zassnoch!) ardree's shilling at the conclusion of the Crimean war and, having flown his wild geese, alohned in crowds to warnder on like Shuley Luney, enlisted in Tyrone's horse, the Irish whites, and soldiered a bit with Wolsey under the assumed name of Blanco Fusilovna Bucklovitch (spurious) after which the cawer and the marble halls of Pump Court Columbarium, the home of the old seakings, looked upon each other and queth their haven evermore for it transpires that on the other side of the water it came about that on the field of Vasileff's Cornix inauspiciously with his unit he perished, saying, this papal leafless to old chap give, rawl chawclates for mouther-in-louth. *Booil.* Poor old dear Paul Horan, to satisfy his literary as well as his criminal aspirations, at the suggestion thrown out by the doomster in loquacity lunacy, so says the Dublin Intelligence, was thrown into a Ridley's for inmates in the northern counties. Under the name of Orani he may have been the utility man of the troupe capable of sustaining long parts at short notice. He was. Sordid Sam, a dour decent deblancer, the unwashed, haunted always by his ham, the unwished, at a word from Israfel the Summoner, passed away painlessly after life's upsomdowns one hallowe'en night, ebbrous and in the state of nature, propelled from Behind into the great Beyond by footblows coulinclouted upon his oyster and atlas on behanged and behooved and behicked and behulked of his last fishandblood bedscrappers, a Northwegian and his mate of the Sheawolving class. Though the last straw glimt his baring this stage thunkhard is said (the pitfallen gagged him as 'Promptboxer') to have solemnly said — as had the brief thot but fell in till his head like a bass dropt neck fust in till a bung crate (cogged!): Me drames, O'Loughlins, has come through! Now let the centuple celves of my egourge as Micholas de Cusack calls them, — of all of whose I in my hereinafter of course by recourse demission me — by the coincidance of their contraries reamalgamerge in that indentity

49

of undiscernibles where the Baxters and the Fleshmans may they cease to bidivil uns and (but at this poingt though the iron thrust of his cockspurt start might have prepared us we are well-nigh stinkpotthered by the mustardpunge in the tailend) this outandin brown candlestock melt Nolan's into peese! *Han var*. Disliken as he was to druriodrama, her wife Langley, the prophet, and the decentest dozendest short of a frusker whoever stuck his spickle through his spoke, disappeared, (in which toodooing he has taken all the French leaves unveilable out of Calomne-quiller's Pravities) from the sourface of this earth, that austral plain he had transmaried himself to, so entirely spoorlessly (the mother of the book with a dustwhisk tabularasing his obliteration done upon her involucrum) as to tickle the speculative to all but opine (since the Levey who might have been Langley may have really been a redivivus of paganinism or a volunteer Vousden) that the hobo (who possessed a large amount of the humoresque) had transtuled his funster's latitat to its finsterest interrimost. *Bhi she*. Again, if Father San Browne, tea and toaster to that quaint-esttest of yarnspinners is Padre Don Bruno, treu and troster to the queen of Iar-Spain, was the reverend, the sodality director, that eupeptic viceflayer, a barefaced carmelite, to whose palpi-tating pulpit (which of us but remembers the rarevalent and hornerable Fratomistor Nawlanmore and Brawne.) sinning society sirens (see the [Roman Catholic] presspassim) fortunately became so enthusiastically attached and was an objectionable ass who very occasionally cockaded a raffles ticket on his hat which he wore all to one side like the hangle of his pan (if Her Elegance saw him she'd have the canary!) and was semiprivately convicted of mal-practices with his hotwashed tableknife (glossing over the cark in his pocket) that same snob of the dunhill, fully several year-schaums riper, encountered by the General on that redletter morning or maynoon jovesday and were they? *Fuitfuit*.

When Phishlin Phil wants throws his lip 'tis pholly to be fortune flonting and whoever's gone to mix Hotel by the salt say water there's nix to nothing we can do for he's never again to sea. It is nebuless an autodidact fact of the commonest that the shape of the average human cloudyphiz, whereas sallow has long daze faded, frequently altered its ego with the possing of the showers (Not original!). Whence it is a slopperish matter, given the wet and low visibility (since in this scherzarade of one's thousand one nightinesses that sword of certainty which would indentifide the body never falls) to idendifine the individuone in scratch wig, squarecuts, stock lavaleer, regattable oxeter, baggy pants and shufflers (he is often alluded to as Slypatrick, the llad in the llane) with already an incipience (lust!) in the direction of area baldness (one is continually firstmeeting with odd sorts of others at all sorts of ages!) who was asked by free boardschool shirkers in drenched coats overawall, Will, Conn and Otto, to tell them overagait, Vol, Pov and Dev, that fishabed ghoatstory of the haardly creditable edventyres of the Haberdasher, the two Curchies and the three Enkelchums in their Bearskin ghoats! Girles and jongers, but he has changed alok syne Thorkill's time! Ya, da, ra, gathery, pimp, shesses, shossafat, okodeboko, nine! Those many warts, those slummy patches, halfsinster wrinkles, (what has come over the face on wholebroader E?), and (shrine of Mount Mu save us!) the large fungopark he has grown! Drink!

Sport's a common thing. It was the Lord's own day for damp to wait for a postponed regatta's eventualising is not of Battlecock Shettledore-Juxta-Mare only) and the request for a fully armed explanation was put (in Loo of Pat) to the porty (a native of the sisterisle — Meathman or Meccan? — by his brogue, exace eyes, lokil calour and lucal odour which are said to have been average clownturkish (though the capelist's voiced nasal liquids and the way he sneezed at zees haul us back to the craogs and bryns of the Silurian Ordovices) who, the lesser pilgrimage accomplished, had made, pats' and pigs' older inselt, the southast bluffs of the stranger stepshore, a *regifugium persecutorum*, ence hindquarters) as he paused at evenchime for some or so minutes (hit the pipe, dannyboy! Time to won, barmon. I'll take en to win.) amid the devil's one duldrum (Apple by her blossom window and Charlotte at her toss panomancy his sole admirers, is only tearts in store) for a fragrend culubosh during his week-

51

end pastime of executing with Anny Oakley deadliness (the consummatory pairs of provocatives, of which remained provokingly but two, the ones he fell for, Lili and Tutu, cork em!) empties which had not very long before contained Reid's family (you ruad that before, soaky, but all the bottles in sodemd histry will not soften your bloodathirst!) stout. Having reprimed his repeater and resiteroomed his timespiece His Revenances, with still a life or two to spare for the space of his occupancy of a world at a time, rose to his feet and there, far from Tolkaheim, in a quiet English garden (commonplace!), since known as Whiddington Wild, his simple intensive curolent vocality, my dearbraithers, my most dearbrathairs, as he, so is a supper as is a sipper, spake of the One and told of the Compassionate, called up before the triad of precoxious scaremakers (scoretaking: Spegulo ne helpas al malbellulo, Mi Kredas ke vi estas prava, Via dote la vizago rispondas fraulino) the now to ushere mythical habiliments of Our Farfar and Arthor of our doyne.

Television kills telephony in brothers' broil. Our eyes demand their turn. Let them be seen! And wolfbone balefires blaze the trailmost if only that Mary Nothing may burst her bibby buckshee. When they set fire then she's got to glow so we may stand some chances of warming to what every soorkabatcha, tum or hum, would like to know. The first Humphrey's latitudinous baver with puggaree behind, (calaboose belong bigboss belong Kang the Toll) his fourinhand bow, his elbaroom surtout, the refaced unmansionables of gingerine hue, the state slate umbrella, his gruff woolselywellesly with the finndrinn knopfs and the gauntlet upon the hand which in an hour not for him solely evil had struck down the might he mighthavebeen d'Esterre of whom his nation seemed almost already to be about to have need. Then, stealing his thunder, but in the befitting legomena of the smaller country, (probable words, possibly said, or field family gleaming) a bit duskish and flavoured with a smile seein as ow his thoughts consisted chiefly of the cheerio, he aptly sketched for our soontobe second parents (sukand see whybe!) the touching seene. The solence of that stilling! Here one migh

52

a fin fell. Boomster rombombonant! It scenes like a landescape from Wildu Picturescu or some seem on some dimb Arras, dumb as Mum's mutyness, this mimage of the seventyseventh kusin of kristansen is odable to os across the wineless Ere no œdor nor mere eerie nor liss potent of suggestion than in the tales of the tingmount. (Prigged!)

And there oftafter, jauntyjogging, on an Irish visavis, insteadily with shoulder to shoulder Jehu will tell to Christianier, saint to sage, the humphriad of that fall and rise while daisy winks at her pinker sister among the tussocks and the copoll between the shafts mocks the couple on the car. And as your who may look like how on the owther side of his big belttry your tyrs and cloes your noes and paradigm maymay rererise in eren. Follow we up his whip vindicative. Thurston's! Lo bebold! *La arboro, lo petrusu.* The augustan peacebetothem oaks, the monolith rising stark from the moonlit pinebarren. In all fortitudinous ajaxious rowdinoisy tenuacity. The angelus hour with ditchers bent upon their farm usetensiles, the soft belling of the fallow deers (*doerehmoose genuane!*) advertising their milky approach as midnight was striking the hours (*letate!*), and how brightly the great tribune outed the sharkskin smokewallet (imitation!) from his frock, kippers, and by Joshua, he tips un a topping swank cheroot, none of your swellish soide, quoit the reverse, and how manfally he says, pluk to pluk and lekan for lukan, he was to just pluggy well suck that brown boyo, my son, and spend a whole half hour in Havana. Sorer of the kreeksmen, would not thore be old high gothsprogue! Wherefore he met Master, he mean to say, he do, sire, bester of redpublicans, at Eagle Cock Hostel on Lorenzo Tooley street and how he wished his Honour the bannocks of Gort and Morya and Bri Head and Puddyrick, yore Loudship, and a starchboxsitting in the pit of his St Tomach's, — a strange wish for you, my friend, and it would poleaxe your sonson's grandson utterly though your own old sweatandswear floruerunts heaved it hoch many as the times, when they were turrified by the hitz.

Chee chee cheers for Upkingbilly and crow cru cramwells

Downaboo! Hup, boys, and hat him! See! Oilbeam they're lost we've found rerembrandtsers, their hours to date link these heirs to here but wowhere are those yours of Yesterdays? Farseeinge-therich and Poolaulwoman Charachthercuss and his Ann van Vogt. D.e.e.d! Edned, ended or sleeping soundlessly? Favour with your tongues! *Intendite!*

Any dog's life you list you may still hear them at it, like sixes and seventies as eversure as Halley's comet, ulemamen, sobran-jewomen, storthingboys and dumagirls, as they pass its bleak and bronze portal of your Casaconcordia: Huru more Nee, minny frickans? Hwoorledes har Dee det? Losdoor onleft mladies, cue. Millecientotrigintadue scudi. Tippoty, kyrie, tippoty. Cha kai rotty kai makkar, sahib? Despenseme Usted, senhor, en son suc-co, sabez. O thaw bron orm, A'Cothraige, thinkinthou gaily? Lick-Pa-flai-hai-pa-Pa-li-si-lang-lang. Epi alo, ecou, Batiste, tu-vavnr dans Lptit boing going. Ismeme de bumbac e meias de por-tocallie. O.O. Os pipos mios es demasiada gruarso por O pic-colo pocchino. Wee fee? Ung duro. Kocshis, szabad? Mercy, and you? Gomagh, thak.

And, Cod, says he with mugger's tears: Would you care to know the prise of a liard? Maggis, nick your nightynovel! Mass Travener's at the mike again! And that bag belly is the buck to goat it! Meggeg, m'gay chapjappy fellow, I call our univalse to witness, as sicker as moyliffey eggs is known by our good househalters from yorehunderts of mamooth to be which they commercially are in ahoy high British quarters (conventional!) my guesthouse and cowhaendel credits will immediately stand ohoh open as straight as that neighbouring monument's fabrica-tion before the hygienic gllll (this was where the reverent sab-both and bottlebreaker with firbalk forthstretched touched upon his tricoloured boater, which he uplifted by its pickledhoopy (he gave Stetson one and a penny for it) whileas oleaginosity of an-cestralolosis sgocciolated down the both pendencies of his mut-sohito liptails (Sencapetulo, a more modestuous conciliabulite never curled a torn pocketmouth), cordially inwiting the adul-lescence who he was wising up to do in like manner what all did

54

so as he was able to add) lobe before the Great Schoolmaster's. (I tell you no story.) Smile!

The house of Atreox is fallen indeedust (Ilyam, Ilyum! Maeromor Mournomates!) averging on blight like the mundibanks of Fennyana, but deeds bounds going arise again. Life, he himself said once, (his biografiend, in fact, kills him verysoon, if yet not, after) is a wake, livit or krikit, and on the bunk of our breadwinning lies the cropse of our seedfather, a phrase which the establisher of the world by law might pretinately write across the chestfront of all manorwombanborn. The scene, refreshed, reroused, was never to be forgotten, the hen and crusader everintermutuomergent, for later in the century one of that puisne band of factferreters, (then an excivily (out of the custom huts) (retired), (hurt), under the sixtyfives act) in a dressy black modern style and wewere shiny tan burlingtons, (tam, homd and dicky, quopriquos and peajagd) rehearsed it, pippa pointing, with a dignified (copied) bow to a namecousin of the late archdeacon F. X. Preserved Coppinger (a hot fellow in his night, may the mouther of guard have mastic on him!) in a pullwoman of our first transhibernian with one still sadder circumstance which is a dirkandurk heartskewerer if ever to bring bouncing brimmers from marbled eyes. Cycloptically through the windowdisks and with eddying awes the round eyes of the rundreisers, back to back, buck to bucker, on their airish chaunting car, beheld with intouristing anterestedness the clad pursue the bare, the bare the green, the green the frore, the frore the cladagain, as their convoy wheeled encirculingly abound the gigantig's lifetree, our fireleaved loverlucky blomsterbohm, phoenix in our woodlessness, haughty, cacuminal, erubescent (repetition!) whose roots they be asches with lustres of peins. For as often as the Archicadenus, pleacing aside his *Irish Field* and craving their auriculars to recepticle particulars before they got the bump at Castlebar (mat and far!) spoke of it by request all, hearing in this new reading of the part whereby, because of Dyas in his machina, the new garrickson's grimacing grimaldism hypostasised by substintuation the axiomatic orerotundity of that once grand old elrington

55

bawl, the copycus's description of that fellowcommuter's play upon countenants, could simply imagine themselves in their bosom's inmost core, as *pro tem locums*, timesported acorss the yawning (abyss), as once they were seasiders, listening to the cockshyshooter's evensong evocation of the doomed but always ventriloquent Agitator, (ncnot more plangorpound the billows o'er Thounawahallya Reef!) silkhouatted, a whallrhosmightiadd, aginsst the dusk of skumring, (would that fane be Saint Muezzin's calling — holy places! — and this fez brimless as brow of faithful toucher of the ground, did wish it were — blessed be the bones! — the ghazi, power of his sword.) his manslayer's gunwielder protended towards that overgrown leadpencil which was soon, monumentally at least, to rise as Molyvdokondylon to, to be, to be his mausoleum (O'dan stod tillsteyne at meisies aye skould show pon) while olover his exculpatory features, as Roland rung, a wee dropeen of grief about to sillonise his jouejous, the ghost of resignation diffused a spectral appealingness, as a young man's drown o'er the fate of his waters may gloat, similar in origin and akkurat in effective to a beam of sunshine upon a coffin plate.

Not olderwise Inn the days of the Bygning would our Traveller remote, unfriended, from van Demon's Land, some lazy skald or maundering pote, lift wearywilly his slowcut snobsic eyes to the semisigns of his zooteac and lengthily lingering along flaskneck, cracket cup, downtrodden brogue, turfsod, wildbroom, cabbageblad, stockfisch, longingly learn that there at the Angel were herberged for him poteen and tea and praties and baccy and wine width woman wordth warbling: and informally quasi-begin to presquesm'ile to queasithin' (Nonsense! There was not very much windy Nous blowing at the given moment through the hat of Mr Melancholy Slow!)

But in the pragma what formal cause made a smile of *that* tothink? Who was he to whom? (O'Breen's not his name nor the brown one his maid.) Whose are the placewheres? Kiwasti, kisker, kither, kitnabudja? Tal the tem of the tumulum. Giv the gav of the grube. Be it cudgelplayers' country, orfishfellows' town or leeklickers' land or panbpanungopovengreskey. What regnans raised the rains have levelled but we hear the pointers and can gauge their compass for the melos yields the mode and the mode the manners plicyman, plansiman, plousiman, plab. Tsin tsin tsin tsin! The forefarther folkers for a prize of two peaches with Ming, Ching and Shunny on the lie low lea. We'll sit down on the hope of the ghouly ghost for the titheman troubleth but his hantitat hies not here. They answer from their Zoans; Hear the four of them! Hark torror of them! I, says Armagh, and a'm proud o'it. I, says Clonakilty, God help us! I, says Deansgrange, and say nothing. I, says Barna, and whatabout it? Hee haw! Before he fell hill he filled heaven: a stream, alplapping streamlet, coyly coiled um, cool of her curls: We were but thermites then, wee, wee. Our antheap we sensed as a Hill of Allen, the Barrow for an People, one Jotnursfjaell: and it was a grummelung amung the porktroop that wonderstruck us as a thunder, yunder.

Thus the unfacts, did we possess them, are too imprecisely few to warrant our certitude, the evidencegivers by legpoll too untrustworthily irreperible where his adjugers are semmingly freak threes but his judicandees plainly minus twos. Nevertheless Madam's Toshowus waxes largely more lifeliked (entrance, one kudos; exits, free) and our notional gullery is now completely complacent, an exegious monument, aerily perennious. Oblige with your blackthorns; gamps, degrace! And there many have paused before that exposure of him by old Tom Quad, a flashback in which he sits sated, gowndabout, in clericalease habit, watching bland sol slithe dodgsomely into the nethermore, a globule of maugdleness about to corrugitate his mild dewed cheek and the tata of a tiny victorienne, Alys, pressed by his limper looser.

Yet certes one is. Eher the following winter had overed the pages of nature's book and till Ceadurbar-atta-Cleath became Dablena Tertia, the shadow of the huge outlander, maladik, multvult, magnoperous, had bulked at the bar of a rota of tribunals in manor hall as in thieves' kitchen, mid pillow talk and chithouse chat, on Marlborough Green as through Molesworth Fields, here sentenced pro tried with Jedburgh justice, there acquitted con-testimony with benefit of clergy. His Thing Mod have undone him: and his madthing has done him man. His beneficiaries are legion in the part he created: they number up his years. Greatwheel Dunlop was the name was on him: behung, all we are his bisaacles. As hollyday in his house so was he priest and king to that: ulvy came, envy saw, ivy conquered. Lou! Lou! They have waved his green boughs o'er him as they have torn him limb from lamb. For his muertification and uxpiration and dumnation and annuhulation. With schreis and grida, deprofound souspirs. Steady, sullivans! Mannequins pause! Longtong's breach is fallen down but Graunya's spreed's abroad. Ahdostay, feedailyones, and feel the Flucher's bawls for the total of your flouts is not fit to fan his fettle, O! Have a ring and sing wohl! Chin, chin! Chin, chin! And of course all chimed din width the eatmost boviality. Swiping rums and beaunes and sherries and ciders and negus and citronnades too. The strongers. Oho, oho, Mester Begge, you're about to be bagged in the bog again. Bugge. But softsies seufsighed: Eheu, for gassies! But, lo! lo! by the threnning gods, human, erring and condonable, what the statues of our kuo, who is the messchef be our kuang, ashu ashure there, the unforgettable treeshade looms up behind the jostling judgements of those, as all should owe, malrecapturable days.

Tap and pat and tapatagain, (fire firstshot, Missiers the Refuseleers! Peingpeong! For saxonlootie!) three tommix, soldiers free, cockaleak and cappapee, of the Coldstream. Guards were walking, in (*pardonnez-leur, je vous en prie, eh?*) Montgomery Street. One voiced an opinion in which on either wide (*pardonnez!*), nodding, all the Finner Camps concurred (*je vous en prie, eh?*). It was the first woman, they said, souped him, that fatal wellesday, Lili Coninghams, by suggesting him they go in a field. Wroth mod eldfar, ruth redd stilstand, wrath wrackt wroth, confessed private Pat Marchison *retro*. (Terse!) Thus contenters with santoys play. One of our coming Vauxhall ontheboards who is resting for the moment (she has been callit by a noted stagey elecutioner a wastepacket Sittons) was interfeud in a waistend pewty parlour. Looking perhaps even more pewtyflushed in her cherry-derry padouasoys, girdle and braces by the Halfmoon and Seven Stars, russets from the Blackamoor's Head, amongst the climbing boys at his Eagle and Child and over the corn and hay emptors at their Black and All Black, Mrs F ... A ... saidaside, half in stage of whisper to her confidante glass, while recoopering her cartwheel chapot (ahat! — and we now know what thimbles a baquets on lallance a talls mean), she hoped Sid Arthar would git a Chrissman's portrout of orange and lemonsized orchids with hollegs and ether, from the feeatre of the Innocident, as the worryld had been uncained. Then, while it is odrous comparisoning to the sprangflowers of his burstday which was a viridable goddinpotty for the reinworms and the charlattinas and all branches of climatitis, it has been such a wanderful noyth untirely, added she, with many regards to Maha's pranjapansies. (Tart!) Prehistoric, obitered to his dictaphone an entychologist: his propenomen is a properismenon. A dustman nocknamed Sevenchurches in the employ of Messrs Achburn, Soulpetre and Ashreborn, prairmakers, Glintalook, was asked by the sisterhood the vexed question during his midday collation of leaver and buckrom alternatively with stenk and kitteney phie in a hashhoush and, thankeaven, responsed impulsively: We have just been propogandering his nullity suit and what they took out of his ear among my own crush. All our fellows at O'Dea's sages with Aratar Calaman he is a cemented brick, buck it all! A more nor usually sober cardriver, who was jauntingly hosing his runabout, Ginger Jane, took a strong view. Lorry hosed her as he talked and this is what he told rewritemen: Irewaker is just a plain pink joint reformee in private life but folks all have it by brehemons laws he has parliamentary honours. Eiskaffier said (Louigi's, you know that man's, brillant Savourain): *Mon foie*, you wish to ave some homelette, yes, lady! Good, mein leber! Your hegg he must break himself. See, I crack, so, he sit in the poele, umbedimbt! A perspirer (over sixty) who was keeping up his tennises panted he kne ho har twa to clect infamatios but a diffpair flannels climb wall and trespassing on doorbell. After fullblown Braddon hear this fresky troterella! A railways barmaid's view (they call her

Spilltears Rue) was thus expressed: to sympathisers of the Dole Line, Death Avenue, anent those objects of her pity-prompted ministrance, to wet, man and his syphon. Ehim! It is ever too late to whissle when Phyllis floods her stable. It would be skarlot shame to jailahim in lockup, as was proposed to him by the Seddoms creature what matter what merrytricks went off with his revulverher in connections with ehim being a norphan and enjoining such wicked illth, ehim! Well done, Drumcollakill! Kitty Tyrrel is proud of you, was the reply of a B.O.T. official (O blame gnot the board!) while the Daughters Benkletter murmured in uniswoon: Golforgilhisjurylegs! Brian Lynsky, the cub curser, was questioned at his shouting box, Bawlonabraggat, and gave a snappy comeback, when saying: Paw! Once more I'll hellbowl! I am for caveman chase and sahara sex, burk you! Them two bitches ought to be leashed, canem! Up hog and hoar hunt! Paw! A wouldbe martyr, who is attending on sanit Asitas where he is being taught to wear bracelets, when grilled on the point, revealed the undoubted fact that the consequence would be that so long as Sankya Moondy played his mango tricks under the mysttetry, with shady apsaras sheltering in his leaves' licence and his shadowers torrifried by the potent bolts of indradiction, there would be fights all over Cuxhaven. (Tosh!) Missioner Ida Wombwell, the seventeenyearold revivalist, said concerning the coincident of interfizzing with grenadines and other respectable and disgusted peersons using the park: That perpendicular person is a brut! But a magnificent brut! 'Caligula' (Mr Danl Magrath, bookmaker, wellknown to Eastrailian poorusers of the Sydney Parade Ballotin) was, as usual, antipodal with his: striving todie, hopening tomellow, Ware Splash. Cobbler. We have meat two hourly, sang out El Caplan Buycout, with the famous padre's turridur's capecast, meet too ourly, matadear! Dan Meiklejohn, precentor, of S.S. Smack and Olley's was probiverbal with his upsiduxit: *mutatus mutandus.* Dauran's lord ('Sniffpox') and Moirgan's lady ('Flatterfun') took sides and crossed and bowed to each other's views and recrossed themselves. The dirty dubs upin their flies, went too free, echoed the dainly drabs downin their scenities, una mona. Sylvia Silence, the girl detective (*Meminerva*, but by now one hears turtlings all over Doveland!) when supplied with informations as to the several facets of the case in her cozy-dozy bachelure's flat, quite overlooking John a'Dream's mews, leaned back in her really truly easy chair to query restfully through her vowelthreaded syllabelles: Have you evew thought, wepow-tew, that sheew gweatness was his twadgedy? Nevewtheless ac-cowding to my considewed attitudes fow this act he should pay the full penalty, pending puwsuance, as pew Subsec. 32, section 11, of the C. L. A. act 1885, anything in this act to the contwawy notwithstanding. Jarley Jilke began to silke for he couldn't get home to Jelsey but ended with: He's got the sack that helped him moult instench of his gladsome rags. Meagher, a naval rating, seated on one of the granite cromlech setts of our new fish-shambles for the usual aireating after the ever popular act, with whom were Questa and Puella, piquante and quoite, (this had a cold in her brain while that felt a sink in her summock, wit's wat, wot's wet) was encouraged, although nearvanashed himself, by one of·his co-affianced to get your breath, Walt, and gobbit and when ther chidden by her fastra sastra to saddle up your pance, Naville, thus cor replied to her other's thankskissing: I lay my two fingerbuttons, fiancee Meagher, (he speaks!) he was to blame about your two velvetthighs up Horniman's Hill — as hook and eye blame him or any other piscman? — but I also think, Puellywally, by the siege of his trousers there was some-one else behind it — you bet your boughtem blarneys — about their three drummers down Keysars Lane. (Trite!).

Be these meer marchant taylor's fablings of a race referend with oddman rex? Is now all seenheard then forgotten? Can it was, one is fain in this leaden age of letters now to wit, that so diversified outrages (they have still to come!) were planned and partly carried out against so staunch a covenanter if it be true than any of those recorded ever took place for many, we trow, beyessed to and denayed of, are given to us by some who use the truth but sparingly and we, on this side ought to sorrow for their pricking pens on that account. The seventh city, Urovivla, his citadear of refuge, whither (would we believe the laimen and their counts), beyond the outraved gales of Atreeatic, changing clues with a baggermalster, the hejirite had fled, silentioussuemeant under night's altosonority, shipalone, a raven of the wave, (be mercy, Mara! A he whence Rahoulas!) from the ostmen's dirtby on the old vic, to forget in expiating manslaughter and, reberthing in remarriment out of dead seekness to devine previdence, (if you are looking for the bilder deep your ear on the movietone!) to league his lot, palm and patte, with a papishee. For mine qvinne I thee giftake and bind my hosenband I thee halter. The wastobe land, a lottuse land, a luctuous land, Emeraldilluim, the peasant pastured, in which by the fourth commandment with promise his days apostolic were to be long by the abundant mercy of Him Which Thundereth From On High, murmured, would rise against him with all which in them were, franchisables and inhabitands, astea as agora, helotsphilots, do him hurt, poor jink, ghostly following bodily, as were he made a ourse for them, the corruptible lay quick, all saints of incorruption of an holy nation, the common or ere-in-garden castaway, in red resurrection to condemn so they might convince him, first pharoah, Humpheres Cheops Exarchas, of their proper sins. Business bred to speak with a stiff upper lip to all men and most occasions the Man we wot of took little short of fighting chances but for all that he or his or his care were subjected to the horrors of the premier terror of Errorland. (perorhaps!)

We seem to us (the real Us!) to be reading our Amenti in the sixth sealed chapter of the going forth by black. It was after the show at Wednesbury that one tall man, humping a suspicious parcel, when returning late amid a dense particular on his home way from the second house of the Boore and Burgess Christy Menestrels by the old spot, Roy's Corner, had a barkiss revolver placed to his faced with the words: you're shot, major: by an unknowable assailant (masked) against whom he had been jealous over, Lotta Crabtree or Pomona Evlyn. More than that Whenn the Waylayer (not a Lucalizod diocesan or even of the Glendalough see, but hailing fro' the prow of Little Britain), mentioning in a bytheway that he, the crawsopper, had, in edition to Reade's cutless centiblade, a loaded Hobson's which left only twin alternatives as, viceversa, either he would surely shoot her, the aunt, by pistol, (she could be okaysure of that!) or, failing of such, bash in Patch's blank face beyond recognition, pointedly asked with gaeilish gall wodkar blizzard's business Thornton had with that Kane's fender only to be answered by the aggravated assaulted that that that was the snaps for him, Midweeks, to sultry well go and find out if he was showery well able. But how transparingly nontrue, gentlewriter! His feet one is not a tall man, not at all, man. No such parson. No such fender. No such lumber. No such race. Was it supposedly in connection with a girls, Myramy Huey or Colores Archer, under Flaggy Bridge (for ann there is but one liv and hir newbridge is her old) or to explode his twelvechamber and force a shrievalty entrance that the heavybuilt Abelbody in a butcherblue blouse from One Life One Suit (a men's wear store), with a most decisive bottle of single in his possession, seized after dark by the town guard at Haveyoucaught-emerod's temperance gateway was there in a gate's way.

Fifthly, how parasoliloquisingly truetoned on his first time of hearing the wretch's statement that, muttering Irish, he had had had o'gloriously a'lot too much hanguest or hoshoe fine to drink in the House of Blazes, the Parrot in Hell, the Orange Tree, the Glibt, the Sun, the Holy Lamb and, lapse not leashed, in Ramitdown's ship hotel since the morning moment he could dixtinguish a white thread from a black till the engine of the laws declosed unto Murray and was only falling fillthefluthered up against the gatestone pier which, with the cow's bonnet a'top o'it, he falsetook for a cattlepillar with purest peaceablest intentions. Yet how lamely hobbles the hoy of his then pseudojocax axplanation how, according to his own story, he was a process server and was merely trying to open zozimus a bottlop stoub by mortially hammering his *magnum bonum* (the curter the club the sorer the savage) against the bludgey gate for the boots about the swan, Maurice Behan, who hastily into his shoes with nothing his hald barra tinnteack and came down with homp, shtemp and jumphet to the tiltyard from the wastes a'sleep in his obi ohny overclothes or choker, attracted by the norse of guns playing Delandy is cartager on the raglar rock to Dulyn, said war' prised safe in bed as he dreamed that he'd wealthes in mormon halls when wokenp by a fourth loud snore out of his land of byelo while hickstrey's maws was grazing in the moonlight by hearing hammering on the pandywhank scale emanating from the blind pig and anything like it (oonagh! oonagh!) in the whole history of the Mullingcan Inn he never. This battering babel allower the door and sideposts, he always said, was not in the very remotest like the belzey babble of a bottle of boose which would not rouse him out o' slumber deep but reminded him loads more of the martiallawsey marses of foreign musikants' instrumongs or the overthrewer to the third last days of Pompery, if anything. And that after this most nooningless knockturn the young reine came down desperate and the old liffopotamus started ploring all over the plains, as mud as she cud be, ruinating all the bouchers' schurts and the backers' wischandtugs so that be the chandeleure of the Rejaneyjailey they were all night wasching the walters of, the weltering walters off. Whyte.

Just one moment. A pinch in time of the ideal, musketeers! Alphos, Burkos and Caramis, leave Astrelea for the astrollajerries and for the love of the saunces and the honour of Keavens pike puddywhackback to Pamintul. And roll away the reel world, the reel world, the reel world! And call all your smokeblushes, Snowwhite and Rosered, if you will have the real cream! Now for a strawberry frolic! Filons, filoosh! *Cherchons la flamme!* Fammfamm! Fammfamm!

Come on, ordinary man with that large big nonobli head, and that blanko berbecked fischial ekksprezzion Machinsky Scapolopolos, Duzinascu or other. Your machelar's mutton leg's getting musclebound from being too pulled. Noah Beery weighed stone thousand one when Hazel was a hen. Now her fat's falling fast. Therefore, chatbags, why not yours? There are 29 sweet reasons why blossomtime's the best. Elders fall for green almonds when they're raised on bruised stone root ginger though it winters on their heads as if auctumned round their waistbands. If you'd had pains in your hairs you wouldn't look so orgibald. You'd have Colley Macaires on your lump of lead. Now listen, Mr Leer! And stow that sweatyfunnyadams Simper! Take an old geeser who calls on his skirt. Note his sleek hair, so elegant, *tableau vivant.* He vows her to be his own honeylamb, swears they will be papa pals, by Sam, and share good times way down west in a guaranteed happy lovenest when May moon she shines and they twit twinkle all the night, combing the comet's tail up right and shooting popguns at the stars. Creampuffs all to dime! Every nice, missymackenzies! For dear old grumpapar, he's gone on the razzledar, through gazing and crazing and blazing at the stars. Compree! She wants her wardrobe to hear from above by return with cash so as she can buy her Peter Robinson trousseau and cut a dash with Arty, Bert or possibly Charley Chance (who knows?) so tolloll Mr Hunker you're too dada for me to dance (so off she goes!) and that's how half the gels in town has got their bottom drars while grumpapar he's trying to hitch his braces on to his trars. But old grum he's not so clean dippy between sweet you and yum (not on your life, boy! not in those trousers! not by a large jugful!) for someplace on the sly, where Furphy he isn't by, old grum has his gel number two (bravevow, our Grum!) and he would like to canoodle her too some part of the time for he is downright fond of his number one but O he's fair mashed on peaches number two so that if he could only canoodle the two, chivee chivoo, all three would feel genuinely happy, it's as simple as A. B. C., the two mixers, we mean, with their cherrybum chappy (for he is simply shamming dippy) if they all were afloat in a dreamlifeboat, hugging two by two in his zoo-doo-you-doo, a tofftoff for thee, missymissy for me and howcameyou-e'enso for Farber, in his tippy, upindown dippy, tiptoptippy canoodle, can you? Finny.

Ack, ack, ack. With which clap, trap and soddenment, three to a loaf, our mutual friends the fender and the bottle at the gate seem to be implicitly in the same bateau, so to singen, bearing also several of the earmarks of design, for there is in fact no use in putting a tooth in a snipery of that sort and the amount of all those sort of things which has been going on onceaday in and twiceaday out every other nachtistag among all kinds of promiscious individuals at all ages in private homes and reeboos publikiss and allover all and elsewhere throughout secular sequence the country over and overabroad has been particularly stupendous. To be continued. Federals' Uniteds' Transports' Unions' for Exultations' of Triumphants' Ecstasies.

But resuming inquiries. Will it ever be next morning the postal unionist's (officially called carrier's, Letters Scotch, Limited) strange fate (Fierceendgiddyex he's hight, d.e., the losel that hucks around missivemaids' gummibacks) to hand in a huge chain envelope, written in seven divers stages of ink, from blanchessance to lavandaiette, every pothook and pancrook bespaking the wisherwife, superscribed and subpencilled by yours A Laughable Party, with afterwite, S.A.G., to Hyde and Cheek, Edenberry, Dubblenn, WC? Will whatever will be written in lappish language with inbursts of Maggyer always seem semposed, black looking white and white guarding black, in that siamixed twoatalk used twist stern swift and jolly roger? Will it bright upon us, nightle, and we plunging to our plight? Well, it might now, mircle, so it light. Always and ever till Cox's wife, twice Mrs Hahn, pokes her beak into the matter with Owen K. after her, to see whawa smutter after, will this kiribis pouch filled with litterish fragments lurk dormant in the paunch of that halpbrother of a herm, a pillarbox?

The coffin, a triumph of the illusionist's art, at first blench naturally taken for a handharp (it is handwarp to tristinguish jubabe from jabule or either from tubote when all three have just been invened) had been removed from the hardware premises of Oetzmann and Nephew, a noted house of the gonemost west, which in the natural course of all things continues to supply funeral requisites of every needed description. Why needed, though? Indeed needed (wouldn't you feel like rattanfowl if you hadn't the oscar!) because the flash brides or bride in their lily

66

boleros one games with at the Nivynubies' finery ball and your upright grooms that always come right up with you (and by jingo when they do!) what else in this mortal world, now ours, when meet there night, mid their nackt, me there naket, made their nought the hour strikes, would bring them rightcame back in the flesh, thumbs down, to their orses and their hashes.

To proceed. We might leave that nitrience of oxagiants to take its free of the air and just analectralyse that very chymerical combination, the gasbag where the warderworks. And try to pour somour heiterscene up thealmostfere. In the bottled heliose case continuing, Long Lally Tobkids, the special, sporting a fine breast of medals, and a conscientious scripturereader to boot in the brick and tin choorch round the coroner, swore like a Norewheezian tailliur on the stand before the proper functionary that he was up against a right querrshnorrt of a mand in the butcher of the blues who, he guntinued, on last epening after delivering some carcasses mattonchepps and meatjutes on behalf of Messrs Otto Sands and Eastman, Limericked, Victuallers, went and, with his unmitigated astonissment, hickicked at the dun and dorass against all the runes and, when challengèd about the pretended hick (it was kickup and down with him) on his solemn by the imputant imputed, said simply: I appop pie oath, Phillyps Captain. You did, as I sostressed before. You are deepknee in error, sir, Madam Tomkins, let me then tell you, replied with a gentlewomanly salaam MackPartland, (the meatman's family, and the oldest in the world except nick, name.) And Phelps was flayful with his peeler. But his phizz fell.

Now to the obverse. From velveteens to dimities is barely a fivefinger span and hence these camelback excesses are thought to have been instigated by one or either of the causing causes of all, those rushy hollow heroines in their skirtsleeves, be she magretta be she the posque. Oh! Oh! Because it is a horrible thing to have to say to say to day but one dilalah, Lupita Lorette, shortly after in a fit of the unexpectednesses drank carbolic with all her dear placid life before her and paled off while the other soiled dove that's her sister-in-love, Luperca Latouche, finding

one day while dodging chores that she stripped teasily for binocular man and that her jambs were jimpjoyed to see each other, the
nautchy girly soon found her fruitful hat too small for her and
rapidly taking time, look, she rapidly took to necking, partying
and selling her spare favours in the haymow or in lumber closets
or in the greenawn *ad huck* (there are certain intimacies in all
ladies' lavastories we just lease to imagination) or in the sweet
churchyard close itself for a bit of soft coal or an array of thin
trunks, serving whom in fine that same hot coney *a la Zingara*
which our own little Graunya of the chilired cheeks dished up
to the greatsire of Oscar, that son of a Coole. Houri of the coast
of emerald, arrah of the lacessive poghue, Aslim-all-Muslim, the
resigned to her surrender, did not she, come leinster's even, true
dotter of a dearmud, (her pitch was Forty Steps and his perch old
Cromwell's Quarters) with so valkirry a licence as sent many a
poor pucker packing to perdition, again and again, ay, and again
sfidare him, tease fido, eh tease fido, eh eh tease fido, toos top-
ples topple, stop, dug of a dog of a dgiaour, ye! Angealousmei!
And did not he, like Arcoforty, farfar off Bissavolo, missbrand
her behaveyous with iridescent huecry of down right mean false
sop lap sick dope? Tawfulsdreck! A reine of the shee, a shebeen
quean, a queen of pranks. A kingly man, of royal mien, regally
robed, exalted be his glory! So gave so take: Now not, not now!
He would just a min. Suffering trumpet! He thought he want.
Whath? Hear, O hear, living of the land! Hungreb, dead era,
hark! He hea, eyes ravenous on her lippling lills. He hear her voi
of day gon by. He hears! Zay, zay, zay! But, by the beer of his
profit, he cannot answer. Upterputty till rise and shine! Nor needs
none shaft ne stele from Phenicia or Little Asia to obelise on
the spout, neither pobalclock neither folksstone, nor sunkenness
in Tomar's Wood to bewray how erpressgangs score off the rued.
The mouth that tells not will ever attract the unthinking tongue
and so long as the obseen draws theirs which hear not so long
till allearth's dumbnation shall the blind lead the deaf. Tatcho,
tawney yeeklings! The column of lumps lends the pattrin of the
leaves behind us. If violence to life, limb and chattels, often as

not, has been the expression, direct or through an agent male, of womanhid offended, (ah! ah!), has not levy of black mail from the times the fairies were in it, and fain for wilde erthe blothoms followed an impressive private reputation for whispered sins?

Now by memory inspired, turn wheel again to the whole of the wall. Where Gyant Blyant fronts Peannlueamoore There was once upon a wall and a hooghoog wall a was and such a wall-hole did exist. Ere ore or ire in Aaarlund. Or you Dair's Hair or you Diggin Mosses or your horde of orts and oriorts to garble a garthen of Odin and the lost paladays when all the eddams ended with aves. Armen? The doun is theirs and still to see for menags if he strikes a lousaforitch and we'll come to those baregazed shoeshines if you just shoodov a second. And let oggs be good old gaggles and Isther Estarr play Yesther Asterr. In the drema of Sorestost Areas, Diseased. A stonehinged gate then was for another thing while the suroptimist had bought and enlarged that shack under fair rental of one yearlyng sheep, (prime) value of sixpence, and one small yearlyng goat (cadet) value of eight-pence, to grow old and happy (hogg it and kidd him) for the re-minants of his years; and when everything was got up for the purpose he put an applegate on the place by no means as some pretext a bedstead in loo thereof to keep out donkeys (the pig-dirt hanging from the jags to this hour makes that clear) and just thenabouts the iron gape, by old custom left open to prevent the cats from getting at the gout, was triplepatlockt on him on purpose by his faithful poorters to keep him inside probably and possibly enaunter he felt like sticking out his chest too far and tempting gracious providence by a stroll on the peoplade's egg-day, unused as he was yet to being freely clodded.

O, by the by, lets wee brag of praties, it ought to be always remembered in connection with what has gone before that there was a northroomer, Herr Betreffender, out for his zimmer hole-digs, digging in number 32 at the Rum and Puncheon (Branch of Dirty Dick's free house) in Laxlip (where the Sockeye Sammons were stopping at the time orange fasting) prior to that, a Kom-merzial (Gorbotipacco, he was wreaking like Zentral Oylrubber)

69

from Osterich, the U.S.E. paying (Gaul save the mark!) 11/- in
the week (Gosh, these wholly romads!) of conscience money in
the first deal of Yuly wheil he was, swishing beesnest with bles-
sure, and swobbing broguen eeriesh myth brockendootsch, making his reporterage on Der Fall Adams for the Frankofurto Siding,
a Fastland payrodicule, and er, consstated that one had on him
the Lynn O'Brien, a meltoned lammswolle, disturbed, and wider
he might the same zurichschicken other he would, with tosend
and obertosend tonnowatters, one monkey's damages become.
Now you must know, franksman, to make a heart of glass, that
the game of gaze and bandstand butchery was merely a Patsy
O'Strap tissue of threats and obuses such as roebucks raugh at
pinnacle's peak and after this sort. Humphrey's unsolicited visitor,
Davy or Titus, on a burgley's clan march from the middle west,
a hikely excellent crude man about road who knew his Bullfoost
Mountains like a starling bierd, after doing a long dance untidled
to Cloudy Green, deposend his bockstump on the waityoumay-
wantme, after having blew some quaker's (for you! Oates!) in
through the houseking's keyhole to attract attention, bleated
through the gale outside which the tairor of his clothes was hog-
callering, first, be the hirsuiter, that he would break his bulshey-
wigger's head for him, next, be the heeltapper, that he would
break the gage over his lankyduckling head the same way he
would crack a nut with a monkeywrench and, last of all, be the
stirabouter, that he would give him his (or theumperom's or any-
bloody else's) thickerthanwater to drink and his bleday steppe-
brodhar's into the bucket. He demanded more wood alcohol to
pitch in with, alleging that his granfather's was all taxis and that
it was only after ten o'connell, and this his isbar was a public
oven for the sake of irsk irskusky, and then, not easily dis-
couraged, opened the wrathfloods of his atillarery and went on at
a wicked rate, weathering against him in mooxed metaphores
from eleven thirty to two in the afternoon without even a lunch-
eonette interval for House, son of Clod, to come out, you jew-
beggar, to be Executed Amen. Earwicker, that patternmind, that
paradigmatic ear, receptoretentive as his of Dionysius, longsuffer-

70

ing although whitening under restraint in the sititout corner of his conservatory, behind faminebuilt walls, his thermos flask and ripidian flabel by his side and a walrus whiskerbristle for a tuskpick, compiled, while he mourned the flight of his wild guineese, a long list (now feared in part lost) to be kept on file of all abusive names he was called (we have been compelled for the rejoicement of foinne loidies ind the humours of Milltown etcetera by Josephine Brewster in the collision known as Contrastations with Inkermann and so on and sononward, lacies in loo water, flee, celestials, one clean turv): *Firstnighter, Informer, Old Fruit, Yellow Whigger, Wheatears, Goldy Geit, Bogside Beauty, Yass We've Had His Badannas, York's Porker, Funnyface, At Baggotty's Bend He Bumped, Grease with the Butter, Opendoor Ospices, Cainandabler, Ireland's Eighth Wonderful Wonder, Beat My Price, Godsoilman, Moonface the Murderer, Hoary Hairy Hoax, Midnight Sunburst, Remove that Bible, Hebdromadary Publocation, Tummer the Lame the Tyrannous, Blau Clay, Tight before Teatime, Read Your Pantojoke, Acoustic Disturbance, Thinks He's Gobblasst the Good Dook of Ourguile, W.D.'s Grace, Gibbering Bayamouth of Dublin, His Farther was a Mundzucker and She had him in a Growler, Burnham and Bailey, Artist, Unworthy of the Homely Protestant Religion, Terry Cotter, You're Welcome to Waterfood, signed the Ribbonmen, Lobsterpot Lardling, All for Arthur of this Town, Hooshed the Cat from the Bacon, Leathertogs Donald, The Ace and Deuce of Paupering, O'Reilly's Delights to Kiss the Man behind the Borrel, Magogagog, Swad Puddlefoot, Gouty Ghibeline, Loose Luther, Hatches Cocks' Eggs, Muddle the Plan, Luck before Wedlock, I Divorce Thee Husband, Tanner and a Make, Go to Hellena or Come to Connies, Piobald Puffpuff His Bride, Purged out of Burke's, He's None of Me Causin, Barebarean, Peculiar Person, Grunt Owl's Facktotem, Twelve Months Aristocrat, Lycanthrope, Flunkey Beadle Vamps the Tune Letting on He's Loney, Thunder and Turf Married into Clandorf, Left Boot Sent on Approval, Cumberer of Lord's Holy Ground, Stodge Arschmann, Awnt Yuke, Tommy Furlong's Pet Plagues, Archdukon Cabbanger, Last Past the Post, Kennealey Won't Tell Thee off Nancy's Gown,*

Scuttle to Cover, Salary Grab, Andy Mac Noon in Annie's Room, Awl Out, Twitchbratschballs, Bombard Street Besser, Sublime Porter, A Ban for Le King of the Burgaans and a Bom for Ye Sur of all the Ruttledges, O'Phelim's Cutprice, And at Number Wan Wan Wan, What He Done to Castlecostello, Sleeps with Feathers end Ropes, It is Known who Sold Horace the Rattler, Enclosed find the Sons of Fingal, Swayed in his Falling, Wants a Wife and Forty of Them, Let Him Do the Fair, Apeegeequanee Chimmuck, Plowp Goes his Whastle, Ruin of the Small Trader, He —— Milkinghoneybeaverbrooker, Vee was a Vindner, Sower Rapes, Armenian Atrocity, Sickfish Bellyup, Edomite, — 'Man Devoyd of the Commoner Characteristics of an Irish Nature, Bad Humborg, Hraabhraab, Coocoohandler, Dirt, Miching Daddy, Born Burst Feet Foremost, Woolworth's Worst, Easyathic Phallusaphist, Guilteypig's Bastard, Fast in the Barrel, Boose in the Bed, Mister Fatmate, In Custody of the Polis, Boawwll's Alocutionist, Deposed, but anarchistically respectful of the liberties of the noninvasive individual, did not respond a solitary wedgeword beyond such sedentarity, though it was as easy as kissanywhere for the passive resistant in the booth he was in to reach for the hello gripes and ring up Kimmage Outer 17.67, because, as the fundamentalist explained, when at last shocked into speech, touchin his woundid feelins in the fuchsiar the dominican mission for the sowsealist potty was on at the time and he thought the rowmish devowtion known as the howly rowsary might reeform ihm, Gonn. That more than considerably unpleasant bullocky before he rang off drunkishly pegged a few glatt stones, all of a size, by way of final mocks for his grapes, at the wicket in support of his words that he was not guilphy but, after he had so slaunga vollayed, reconnoitring through his semisubconscious the seriousness of what he might have done had he really polished off his terrible intentions finally caused him to change the bawling and leave downg the whole grumus of brookpebbles pangpung and, having sobered up a bit, paces his groundould diablen lionndub, the flay the flegm, the floedy fleshener, (purse, purse, pursyfurse, I'll splish the splume of them all!) this backblocks boor bruskly put out

72

his langwedge and quite quit the paleologic scene, telling how by his selfdenying ordnance he had left Hyland on the dissenting table, after exhorting Earwicker or, in slightly modified phraseology, Messrs or Missrs Earwicker, Seir, his feminisible name of multitude, to cocoa come outside to Mockerloo out of that for the honour of Crumlin, with his broody old flishguds, Gog's curse to thim, so as he could brianslog and burst him all dizzy, you go bail, like Potts Fracture did with Keddle Flatnose and nobodyatall with Wholyphamous and build rocks over him, or if he didn't, for two and thirty straws, be Cacao Campbell, he didn't know what he wouldn't do for him nor nobody else nomore nor him after which, batell martell, a brisha a milla a stroka a boola, so the rage of Malbruk, playing on the least change of his manjester's voice, the first heroic couplet from the fuguall tropical, Opus Elf, Thortytoe: *My schemes into obeyance for This time has had to fall:* they bit goodbyte to their thumb and, his bandol eer his solgier, dripdropdrap on pool or poldier, wishing the loff a falladelfian in the morning, proceeded with a Hubbleforth slouch in his slips backwords (*Et Cur Heli!*) in the directions of the duff and demb institutions about ten or eleven hundred years lurch away in the moonshiny gorge of Patself on the Bach. Adyoe!

And thus, with this rochelly exetur of Bully Acre, came to close that last stage in the siegings round our architcitadel which we would like to recall, if old Nestor Alexis would wink the worth for us, as Bar-le-Duc and Dog-an-Doras and Bangen-op-Zoom.

Yed he med leave to many a door beside of Oxmanswold for so witness his chambered cairns a cloudletlitter silent that are at browse up hill and down coombe and on eolithostroton, at Howth or at Coolock or even at Enniskerry, a theory none too rectiline of the evoluation of human society and a testament of the rocks from all the dead unto some the living. Olivers lambs we do call them, skatterlings of a stone, and they shall be gathered unto him, their herd and paladin, as nubilettes to cumule, in that day hwen, same the lightning lancer of Azava Arthur-honoured (some Finn, some Finn avant!), he skall wake from earthsleep, haught crested elmer, in his valle of briers of Greenman's Rise O, (lost leaders live! the heroes return!) and o'er dun and dale the Wulverulverlord (protect us!) his mighty horn skall roll, orland, roll.

For in those deyes his Deyus shall ask of Allprohome and call to himm: Allprohome! And he make answer: Add some. Nor wink nor wunk. *Animadiabolum, mene credidisti mortuum?* Silence was in thy faustive halls, O Truiga, when thy green woods went dry but there will be sounds of manymirth on the night's ear ringing when our pantriarch of Comestowntonobble gets the pullover on his boots.

Liverpoor? Sot a bit of it! His braynes coolt parritch, his pelt nassy, his heart's adrone, his bluidstreams acrawl, his puff but a piff, his extremeties extremely so: Fengless, Pawmbroke, Chilblaimend and Baldowl. Humph is in his doge. Words weigh no no more to him than raindrips to Rethfernhim. Which we all like. Rain. When we sleep. Drops. But wait until our sleeping. Drain. Sdops.

As the lion in our teargarten remembers the nenuphars of his Nile (shall Ariuz forget Arioun or Boghas the baregams of the Marmarazalles from Marmeniere?) it may be, tots wearsense full a naggin in twentyg have sigilposted what in our brievingbust, the besieged bedreamt him stil and solely of those lililiths undeveiled which had undone him, gone for age, and knew not the watchful treachers at his wake, and theirs to stay. Fooi, fooi, chamermissies! Zeepyzoepy, larcenlads! Zijnzijn Zijnzijn! It may be, we moest ons hasten selves te declareer it, that he reglimmed? presaw? the fields of heat and yields of wheat where corngold Ysit? shamed and shone. It may be, we habben to upseek a bitty door our good township's courants want we knew't, that with his deepseeing insight (had not wishing oftebeen but good time wasted), within his patriarchal shamanah, broadsteyne 'bove citie (Twillby! Twillby!) he conscious of enemies, a kingbilly white-horsed in a Finglas mill, prayed, as he sat on anxious seat, (kunt ye neat gift mey toe bout a peer saft eyballds!) during that three and a hellof hours' agony of silence, *ex profundis malorum*, and bred with unfeigned charity that his wordwounder (an engles to the teeth who, nomened Nash of Girahash, would go anyold where in the weeping world on his mottled belly (the rab, the kreeponskneed!) for milk, music or married missusses) might, mercy to providential benevolence's who hates prudencies' astuteness, unfold into the first of a distinguished dynasty of his posteriors, blackfaced connemaras not of the fold but elder children of his household, his most besetting of ideas (*pace* his twolve predamanant passions) being the formation, as in more favoured climes, where the Meadow of Honey is guestfriendly and the Mountain of Joy receives, of a truly criminal stratum, Ham's cribcracking yeggs, thereby at last eliminating from all classes and masses with directly derivative decasualisation: *sigarius* (sic!) *vindicat urbes terrorum* (sicker!): and so, to mark a bank taal she arter, the obedience of the citizens elp the ealth of the ole.

Now gode. Let us leave theories there and return to here's here. Now hear. 'Tis gode again. The teak coffin, Pughglasspanelfitted, feets to the east, was to turn in later, and pitly patly near the porpus, materially effecting the cause. And this, liever, is the thinghowe. Any number of conservative public bodies, through a number of select and other committees having power to add to their number, before voting themselves and himself, town, port and garrison, by a fit and proper resolution, following a koorts order of the groundwet, once for all out of plotty existence, as a forescut, so you maateskippey might to you cuttinrunner on a neuw pack of klerds, made him, while his body still persisted, their present of a protem grave in Moyelta of the best Lough Neagh pattern, then as much in demand among misonesans as the Isle of Man today among limniphobes. Wacht even! It was in a fairly fishy kettlekerry, after the Fianna's foreman had taken his handful, enriched with ancient woods and dear dutchy deeplinns mid which were an old knoll and a troutbeck, vainyvain of her osiery and a chatty sally with any Wilt or Walt who would ongle her as Izaak did to the tickle of his rod and watch her waters of her sillying waters of and there now brown peater arripple (may their quilt gild lightly over his somnolulutent form!) Whoforyou lies his last, by the wrath of Bog, like the erst curst Hun in the bed of his treubleu Donawhu.

Best. This wastohavebeen underground heaven, or mole's paradise which was probably also an inversion of a phallopharos, intended to foster wheat crops and to ginger up tourist trade (its architecht, Mgr Peurelachasse, having been obcaecated lest he should petrifake suchanevver while the contractors Messrs T. A. Birkett and L. O. Tuohalls were made invulnerably venerable) first in the west, our misterbilder, Castlevillainous, openly damned and blasted by means of a hydromine, system, Sowan and Belting, exploded from a reinvented T.N.T. bombingpost up ahoy of eleven and thirty wingrests (*circiter*) to sternbooard out of his aerial thorpeto, Auton Dynamon, contacted with the expectant minefield by tins of improved ammonia lashed to her shieldplated gunwale, and fused into tripupcables, slipping through tholse and playing down from the conning tower into the ground battery fuseboxes, all differing as clocks from keys since nobody appeared to have the same time of beard, some saying by their Oorlog it was Sygstryggs to nine, more holding with the Ryan vogt it was Dane to pfife. He afterwards whaanever his blaetther began to fail off him and his rough bark was wholly husky and, stoop by stoop, he neared it (wouldmanspare!) carefully lined the ferroconcrete result with rotproof bricks and mortar, fassed to fossed, and retired beneath the heptarchy of his towerettes, the beauchamp, byward, bull and lion, the white, the wardrobe and bloodied, so encouraging (insteppen, alls als hats beliefd!) additional useful councils public with hoofd offdealings which were welholden of ladykants te huur out such as the Breeders' Union, the Guild of Merchants of the Staple *et*, a.u.c. to present unto him with funebral pomp, over and above that, a stone slab with the usual Mac Pelah address of velediction, a very fairworded instance of falsemeaning adamelegy: We have done ours gohellt with you, Heer Herewhippit, overgiven it, skidoo!

But t'house and allaboardshoops! Show coffins, winding sheets, goodbuy bierchepes, cinerary urns, liealoud blasses, snuffchests, poteentubbs, lacrimal vases, hoodendoses, reekwaterbeckers, breakmiddles, zootzaks for eatlust, including upyourhealthing rookworst and meathewersoftened forkenpootsies and for that matter, javel also, any kind of inhumationary bric au brac for the adornment of his glasstone honophreum, would, met these trein of konditiens, naturally follow, halas, in the ordinary course, enabling that roundtheworlder wandelingswight, did suches pass

77

him, to live all safeathomely the presenile days of his life of opulence, ancient ere decrepitude, late lents last lenience, till stuffering stage, whaling away the whole of the while (*hypnos chilia eonion!*) lethelulled between explosion and reexplosion (Donnaurwatteur! Hunderthunder!) from grosskopp to megapod, embalmed, of grand age, rich in death anticipated.

But abide Zeit's sumonserving, rise afterfall. Blueblitzbolted from there, knowing the hingeworms of the hallmirks of habitationlesness, buried burrowing in Gehinnon, to proliferate through all his Unterwealth, seam by seam, sheol om sheol, and revisit our Uppercrust Sideria of Utilitarios, the divine one, the hoarder hidden propaguting his plutorpopular progeniem of pots and pans and pokers and puns from biddenland to boughtenland, the spearway fore the spoorway.

The other spring offensive on the heights of Abraham may have come about all quite by accidence, Foughtarundser (for Breedabrooda had at length presuaded him to have himself to be as septuply buried as the murdered Cian in Finntown), had not been three monads in his watery grave (what vigilantes and ridings then and spuitwyne pledges with aardappel frittling!) when portrifaction, dreyfussed as ever, began to ramp, ramp, ramp, the boys are parching. A hoodenwinkle gave the signal and a blessing paper freed the flood. Why did the patrizien make him scares with his gruntens? Because the druiven were muskating at the door. From both Celtiberian camps (granting at the onset for the sake of argument that men on the two sides in New South Ireland and Vetera Uladh, bluemin and pillfaces, during the ferment With the Pope or On the Pope, had, moors or letts, grant ideas, grunted) all conditions, poor cons and dives mor, each, of course, on the purely doffensive since the eternals were owlwise on their side every time, were drawn toowards their Bellona's Black Bottom, once Woolwhite's Waltz (Ohiboh, how becrimed, becursekissed and bedumbtoit!) some for want of proper feeding in youth, others already caught in the honourable act of slicing careers for family and carvers in conjunction; and, if emaciated nough, the person garrotted may have suggested to whomever he took the ham of, the plain being involved in darkness, low cirque waggery, nay, even the first old wugger of himself in the flesh, whiggissimus incarnadined, when falsesighted by the ifsuchhewas bully on the hill for there had circulated freely fairly among his opposition the feeling that in so hibernating Massa Ewacka, who, previous to that demidetached life, had been known of barmicidal days, cook said, between soups and savours, to get outside his own length of rainbow trout and taerts atta tarn as no man of woman born, nay could, like the great crested brebe, devour his threescoreten of roach per lifeday, ay, and as many minnow a minute (the big mix, may Gibbet choke him!) was, like the salmon of his ladderleap all this time of totality secretly and by suckage feeding on his own misplaced fat.

Ladies did not disdain those pagan ironed times of the first city (called after the ugliest Danadune) when a frond was a friend inneed to carry, as earwigs do their dead, their soil to the earthball where indeeth we shall calm decline, our legacy unknown. Venuses were gigglibly temptatrix, vulcans guffawably eruptious and the whole wives' world frockful of fickles. Fact, any human inyon you liked any erenoon or efter would take her bare godkin out, or an even pair of hem, (lugod! lugodoo!) and prettily pray with him (or with em even) everyhe to her taste, long for luck, tapette and tape petter and take pettest of all. (Tip!) Wells she'd woo and wills she's win but how the deer knowed where she'd marry! Arbour, bucketroom, caravan, ditch? Coach, carriage, wheelbarrow, dungcart?

Kate Strong, a widow (Tiptip!) — she pulls a lane picture for us, in a dreariodreama setting, glowing and very vidual, of old dumplan as she nosed it, a homelike cottage of elvanstone with droppings of biddies, stinkend pusshies, moggies' duggies, rotten witchawubbles, festering rubbages and beggars' bullets, if not worse, sending salmofarious germs in gleefully through the smithereen panes — Widow Strong, then, as her weaker had turned him to the wall (Tiptiptip!), did most all the scavenging from good King Hamlaugh's gulden dayne though her lean besom cleaned but sparingly and her bare statement reads that,

there being no macadamised sidetracks on those old nekropolitan
nights in, barring a footbatter, Bryant's Causeway, bordered
with speedwell, white clover and sorrel a wood knows, which
left off, being beaten, where the plaintiff was struck, she
left down, as scavengers, who will be scavengers must, her
filthdump near the Serpentine in Phornix Park (at her time called
Finewell's Keepsacre but later tautaubapptossed Pat's Purge),
that dangerfield circling butcherswood where fireworker oh
flaherty engaged a nutter of castlemallards and ah for archer
stunned's turk, all over which fossil footprints, bootmarks,
fingersigns, elbowdints, breechbowls, a. s. o. were all succes-
sively traced of a most envolving description. What subtler
timeplace of the weald than such wolfsbelly castrament to will
hide a leabhar from Thursmen's brandihands or a loveletter,
lostfully hers, that would be lust on Ma, than then when ructions
ended, than here where race began: and by four hands of forethought the first babe of reconcilement is laid in its last cradle
of hume sweet hume. Give over it! And no more of it! So pass
the pick for child sake! O men!

For hear Allhighest sprack for krischnians as for propagana
fidies and his nuptial eagles sharped their beaks of prey: and
every morphyl man of us, pome by pome, falls back into this
terrine: as it was let it be, says he! And it is as though where
Agni araflammed and Mithra monished and Shiva slew as maya-
mutras the obluvial waters of our noarchic memory withdrew,
windingly goharksome, to some hastyswasty timberman torch-
priest, flamenfan, the ward of the wind that lightened the fire that
lay in the wood that Jove bolt, at his rude word. Posidonius
O'Fluctuary! Lave that bloody stone as it is! What are you
doing your dirty minx and his big treeblock way up your path?
Slip around, you, by the rare of the ministers'! And, you, take
that barrel back where you got it, Mac Shane's, and go the way
your old one went, Hatchettsbury Road! And gish! how they
gushed away, the pennyfares, a who!e school for scamper, with
their sashes flying sish behind them, all the little pirlypettes!
Issy-la-Chapelle! Any lucans, please?

Yes, the viability of vicinals if invisible is invincible. And we are not trespassing on his corns either. Look at all the plotsch! Fluminian! If this was Hannibal's walk it was Hercules' work. And a hungried thousand of the unemancipated slaved the way. The mausoleum lies behind us (O Adgigasta, *multipopulipater!*) and there are milestones in their cheadmilias faultering along the tramestrack by Brahm and Anton Hermes! Per omnibus secular seekalarum. Amain. But the past has made us this present of a rhedarhoad. So more boher O'Connell! Though rainy-hidden, you're rhinohide. And if he's not a Romeo you may scallop your hat. Wereupunder in the fane of Saint Fiacre! Halte!

It was hard by the howe's there, plainly on this disoluded and a buchan cold spot, rupestric then, resurfaced that now is, that Luttrell sold if Lautrill bought, in the saddle of the Brennan's (now Malpasplace?) pass, versts and versts from true civilisation, not where his dreams top their traums halt (Beneathere! Bena-there!) but where livland yontide meared with the wilde, saltlea with flood, that the attackler, a cropatkin, though under medium and between colours with truly native pluck, engaged the Adversary who had more in his eye than was less to his leg but whom for plunder sake, he mistook in the heavy rain to be Oglethorpe or some other ginkus, Parr aparrently, to whom the headandheelless chickenestegg bore some Michelangiolesque resemblance, making use of sacrilegious languages to the defect that he would challenge their hemosphores to exterminate them but he would cannonise the b — y b — r's life out of him and lay him out contritely as smart as the b — r had his b — y nightprayers said, three patrecknocksters and a couplet of hellmuirries (*tout est sacré pour un sacreur, femme à barbe ou homme-nourrice*) at the same time, so as to plugg well let the blubbywail ghoats out of him, catching holst of an oblong bar he had and with which he usually broke furnitures he rose the stick at him. The boarder incident prerepeated itself. The pair (whethertheywere Nippo-luono engaging Wei-Ling-Taou or de Razzkias trying to recon-noistre the general Boukeleff, man may not say), struggled apairently for some considerable time, (the cradle rocking equally to one and oppositely from the other on its law of capture and recapture), under the All In rules around the booksafe, fighting like purple top and tipperuhry Swede, (Secremented Servious of the Divine Zeal!) and in the course of their tussle the toller man, who had opened his bully bowl to beg, said to the miner who was carrying the worm (a handy term for the portable distillery which consisted of three vats, two jars and several bottles though we purposely say nothing of the stiff, both parties having an interest in the spirits): Let me go, Pautheen! I hardly knew ye. Later on, after the solstitial pause for refleshmeant, the same man (or a different and younger him of the same ham) asked in the vermicular with a very oggly chew-chin-grin: Was six victolios fifteen pigeon takee offa you, tell he me, stlongfella, by picky-pocky ten to foul months behindaside? There were some further collidabanter and severe tries to convert for the best part of an hour and now a woden affair in the shape of a webley (we at once recognise our old friend Ned of so many illortemperate letters) fell from the intruser who, as stuck as that cat to that mouse in that tube of that christchurch organ, (did the imnage of Girl Cloud Pensive flout above them light young charm, in ribbons and pigtail?) whereupon became friendly and, saying not his shirt to tear, to know wanted, joking and knobkerries all aside laying, if his change companion who stuck still to the invention of his strongbox, with a tenacity corrobberating their mutual tenitorial rights, happened to have the loots change of a tenpound crickler about him at the moment, addling that hap so, he would pay him back the six vics odd, do you see, out of that for what was taken on the man of samples last Yuni or Yuly, do you follow me, Capn? To this the other, Billi with the Boule, who had mummed and mauled up to that (for he was hesitency carried to excelcism) rather amusedly replied: Woowoo would you be grossly surprised, Hill, to learn that, as it so happens, I honestly have not such a thing as the loo, as the least chance of a tinpanned crackler anywhere about me at the present mohomoment but I believe I can see my way, as you suggest, it being Yuletide or Yuddanfest and as it's mad nuts, son, for you

82

when it's hatter's hares, mon, for me, to advance you something like four and sevenpence between hopping and trapping which you might just as well have, boy baches, to buy J. J. and S. with. There was a minute silence before memory's fire's rekindling and then. Heart alive! Which at very first wind of gay gay and whisk-wigs wick's ears pricked up, the starving gunman, strike him pink, became strangely calm and forthright sware by all his lards porsenal that the thorntree of sheol might ramify up his Sheo-fon to the lux apointlex but he would go good to him suntime marx my word fort, for a chip off the old Flint, (in the Nichtian glossery which purveys aprioric roots for aposteriorious tongues this is nat language at any sinse of the world and one might as fairly go and kish his sprogues as fail to certify whether the wartrophy eluded at some lives earlier was that somethink like a jug, to what, a coctable) and remarxing in languidoily, seemingly much more highly pleased than tongue could tell at this opening of a lifetime and the foretaste of the Dun Bank pearlmothers and the boy to wash down which he would feed to himself in the Ruadh Cow at Tallaght and then into the Good Woman at Ringsend and after her inat Conway's Inn at Blackrock and, first to fall, cursed be all, where appetite would keenest be, atte, funeral fare or fun fain real, Adam and Eve's in Quantity Street by the grace of gamy queen Tailte, her will and testament: You stunning little southdowner! I'd know you anywhere, Declaney, let me truthfully tell you in or out of the lexinction of life and who the hell else, be your blanche patch on the boney part! Goalball I've struck this daylit dielate night of nights, by golly! My hat, you have some bully German grit, sundowner! He spud in his faust (axin); he toped the raw best (pardun); he poked his pick (a tip is a tap): and he tucked his friend's leave. And, with French hen or the portlifowlium of hastes and leisures, about to continue that, the queer mixture exchanged the pax in embrace or poghue puxy as practised between brothers of the same breast, hillelulia, killelulia, allenalaw, and, having ratified before the god of the day their torgantruce which belittlers have schmall-kalled the treatyng to cognac, turning his fez menialstrait in the direction of Moscas, he first got rid of a few mitsmillers and hurooshoos and levanted off with tubular jurbulance at a bull's run over the assback bridge, spitting his teeths on rooths, with the seven and four in danegeld and their humoral hurlbat or other uncertain weapon of *lignum vitae*, but so evermore rhumanasant of a toboggan poop, picked up to keep some crowplucking appointment with some rival rialtos anywheres between Pearidge and the Littlehorn while this poor delaney, who they left along with the confederate fender behind and who albeit ballsbluffed, bore up wonderfully wunder all of it with a whole number of plumsized contusiums, plus alasalah bruised coccyx, all over him, reported the occurance in the best way he could, to the flabbergaze of the whole lab, giving the Paddybanners the military salute as for his exilicy's the O'Daffy, in justifiable hope that, in nobiloroman review of the hugely sitisfactuary conclusium of their negotiations and the jugglemonkysh agripment deinderivative, some lotion or fomentation of poppyheads would be jennerously exhibited to the parts, at the nearest watchhouse in Vicar Lane, the white ground of his face all covered with diagonally redcrossed nonfatal mammalian blood as proofpositive of the seriousness of his character and that he was bleeding in self defience (stanch it!) from the nostrils, lips, pavilion and palate, while some of his hitter's hairs had been pulled off his knut's head by Colt though otherwise his allround health appeared to be middling along as it proved most fortunate that not one of the two hundred and six bones and five hundred and one muscles in his corso was a whit the whorse for her whacking. Herwho?

Nowthen, leaving clashing ash, brawn and muscle and brassmade to oust earthernborn and rockcrystal to wreck isinglass but wurming along gradually for our savings backtowards motherwaters so many miles from bank and Dublin stone (olympiading even till the eleventh dynasty to reach that thuddysickend Hamlaugh) and to the question of boney's unlawfully obtaining a pierced paraflamme and claptrap fireguard there crops out the still more salient point of the politish leanings and town pursuits of our forebeer, El Don De Dunelli, (may his ship thicked stick in the bottol of the river and all his crewsers stock locked in the burral of the seas!) who, when within the black of your toenail, sir, of being mistakenly ambushed by one of the uddahveddahs, and as close as made no matter, mam, to being kayoed offhand when the hyougono heckler with the Peter the Painter wanted to hole him, was consistently practising the first of the primary and imprescriptible liberties of the pacific subject by circulating (be British, boys to your bellybone and chuck a chum a chance!) alongst one of our umphrohibited semitary thrufahrts, open to buggy and bike, to walk, Wellington Park road, with the curb or quaker's quacknostrum under his auxter and his alpenstuck in his redhand, a highly commendable exercise, or, number two of our *acta legitima plebeia*, on the brink (beware to baulk a man at his will!) of taking place upon a public seat, to what, bare by Butt's, most easterly (but all goes west!) of blackpool bridges, as a public protest and naturlikevice, without intent to annoy either, being praisegood thankfully for the wrathbereaved ringdove and the fearstung boaconstrictor and all the more right jollywell pleased, which he was, at having other people's weather.

But to return to the atlantic and Phenitia Proper. As if that were not to be enough for anyone but little headway, if any, was made in solving the wasnottobe crime cunundrum when a child of Maam, Festy King, of a family long and honourably associated with the tar and feather industries, who gave an address in old plomansch Mayo of the Saxons in the heart of a foulfamed potheen district, was subsequently haled up at the Old Bailey on the calends of Mars, under an incompatibly framed indictment of both the counts (from each equinoxious points of view, the one fellow's fetch being the other follow's person) that is to see, flying cushats out of his ouveralls and making fesses immodst his forces on the field. Oyeh! Oyeh! When the prisoner, soaked in methylated, appeared in dry dock, appatently ambrosiaurealised, like Kersse's Korduroy Karikature, wearing, besides stains, rents and patches, his fight shirt, straw braces, souwester and a policeman's corkscrew trowsers, all out of the true (as he had purposely torn up all his cymtrymanx bespokes in the mamertime), deposing for his exution with all the fluors of sparse in the royal Irish vocabulary how the whole padderjagmartin tripiezite suet and all the sulfeit of copperas had fallen off him quatz unaccountably like the chrystalisations of Alum on Even while he was trying for to stick fire to himcell, (in feacht he was dripping as he found upon stripping for a pipkin ofmalt as he feared the coold raine) it was attempted by the crown (P.C. Robort) to show that King, *elois* Crowbar, once known as Meleky, impersonating a climbing boy, rubbed some pixes of any luvial peatsmoor o'er his face, plucks and pussas, with a clanetourf as the best means of disguising himself and was to the middlewhite fair in Mudford of a Thoorsday, feishts of Peeler and Pole, under the illassumed names of Tykingfest and Rabworc picked by him and Anthony out of a tellafun book, ellegedly with a pedigree pig (unlicensed) and a hyacinth. They were on that sea by the plain of Ir nine hundred and ninetynine years and they never cried crack or ceased from regular paddlewicking till that they landed their two and a trifling selves, amadst camel and ass, greybeard and suckling, priest and pauper, matrmatron and merrymeg, into the meddle of the mudstorm. The gathering, convened by the Irish Angricultural and Prepostoral Ouraganisations, to help the Irish muck to look his brother dane in the face and attended thanks to Larry by large numbers, of christies and jew's totems, tospite of the deluge, was distinctly of a scattery kind when the ballybricken he could get no good of, after cockofthewalking through a few fancyfought mains ate some of the doorweg, the pikey later selling the gentleman ratepayer because she, Francie's sister, that is to say, ate a whole side of his (the animal's) sty, on a struggle Street, *Qui Sta Troia*, in order to pay off, hiss or lick, six doubloons fifteen arrears of his, the villain's not the rumbler's rent.

Remarkable evidence was given, anon, by an eye, ear, nose and throat witness, whom Wesleyan chapelgoers suspected of being a plain clothes priest W.P., situate at Nullnull, Medical Square, who, upon letting down his rice and peacegreen coverdisk and having been sullenly cautioned against yawning while being grilled, smiled (he had had a onebumper at parting from Mrs Molroe in the morning) and stated to his eliciter under his morse mustaccents (gobbless!) that he slept with a bonafides and that he would be there to remember the filth of November, hatinaring, rowdy O, which, with the jiboulees of Juno and the dates of ould lanxiety, was going, please the Rainmaker, to decembs within the ephemerides of profane history, all one with Tournay, Yetstoslay and Temorah, and one thing which would pigstickularly strike a person of such sorely tried observational powers as Sam, him and Moffat, though theirs not to reason why, the striking thing about it was that he was patrified to see, hear, taste and smell, as his time of night, how Hyacinth O'Donnell, B.A., described in the calendar as a mixer and wordpainter, with part of a sivispacem (Gaeltact for dungfork) on the fair green at the hour of twenty-four o'clock sought (the bullycassidy of the friedhoffer!) to sack, sock, stab and slaughter singlehanded another two of the old kings, Gush Mac Gale and Roaring O'Crian, Jr., both changelings, unlucalised, of no address and in noncommunicables, between him and whom, ever since wallops before the Mise of Lewes, bad blood existed on the ground of the boer's trespass on the bull or because he firstparted his polarbeeber hair in twoways, or because they were creepfoxed andt grousuppers over a nippy in a noveletta, or because they could not say meace, (mute and daft) meathe. The litigants, he said, local congsmen and donalds, kings of the arans and the dalkeys, kings of mud and tory, even the goat king of Killorglin, were egged on by their supporters in the shape of betterwomen with bowstrung hair of Carrothagenuine ruddiness, waving crimson petties and screaming from Isod's towertop. There were cries from the thicksets in court and from the macdublins on the bohernabreen of: Mind the bank from Banagher, Mick, sir! Prodooce O'Donner. Ay! Exhibit his relics! Bu! Use the tongue mor! Give lip less! But it oozed out in Deadman's Dark Scenery Court through crossexanimation of the casehardened testis that when and where that knife of knifes the treepartied ambush was laid (roughly spouting around half hours 'twixt dusk in dawn, by Waterhose's Meddle Europeic Time, near Stop and Think, high chief evervirens and only abfalltree in auld the land) there was not as much light from the widowed moon as would dim a child's altar. The mixer, accordingly, was bluntly broached, and in the best basel to boot, as to whether he was one of those lucky cocks for whom the audible-visible-gnosible-edible world existed. That he was only too cognitively conatively cogitabundantly sure of it because, living, loving, breathing and sleeping morphomelosophopancreates, as he most significantly did, whenever he thought he heard he saw he felt he made a bell clipperclipperclipperclipper. Whether he was practically sure too of his lugs and truies names in this king and blouseman business? That he was pediculously so. Certified? As cad could be. Be lying! Be the loriee I will. It was Morbus O' Somebody? A'Quite. Szerday's Son? A satyr in weddens. And how did the greeneyed mister arrive at the B.A.? That it was like his poll. A crossgrained trapper with murty odd oogs, awflorated ares, inquiline nase and a twithcherous mouph? He would be. Who could bit you att to a tenyerdfuul when aastalled? Ballera jobbera. Some majar bore too? Iguines. And with tumblerous legs, redipnominated Helmingham Erchenwyne Rutter Egbert Crumwall Odin Maximus Esme Saxon Esa Vercingetorix Ethelwulf Rupprecht Ydwalla Bentley Osmund Dysart Yggdrasselmann? Holy Saint Eiffel, the very phoenix! It was Chudley Magnall once more between the deffodates and the dumb scene? The two childspies waapreesing him auza de Vologue but the renting of his rock was from the three wicked Vuncouverers Forests bent down awhits, arthou sure? Yubeti, Cumbilum comes! One of the oxmen's thingabossers, hvad? And had he been refresqued by the founts of bounty playing there — is — a — pain — aleland in Long's gourgling barral? A loss of Lordedward and a lack of sirphilip a surgeonet showeradown could suck more gargling bubbles out of the five lamps in Portterand's praise. Wirrgeling and maries? As whose wouldn't, laving his leaftime in Blackpool. But, of course, he could call himself Tem, too, if he had time to? You butt he could anytom. When he pleased? Win and place. A stoker temptated by evesdripping aginst the driver who was a witness as well? Sacred avatar, how the devil did they guess it! Two dreamyums in one dromium? Yes and no error. And both as like as a duel of lentils? Peacisely. So he was pelted out of the coram populo, was he? Be the powers that be he was. The prince in principel should not expose his person? Macchevuole! Rooskayman kamerad? Sooner Gallwegian he would say. Not unintoxicated, fair witness? Drunk as a fishup. Askt to whether she minded whither he smuked? Not if he barkst into phlegms. Anent his ajaculations to his Crosscann Lorne, cossa? It was corso in cursu on coarser again. The gracious miss was we not doubt sensible how yellowatty on the forx was altered? That she esually was, O'Dowd me not! As to his religion, if any? It was the see-you-Sunday sort. Exactly what he meant by a pederast prig? Bejacob's, just a gent who prayed his lent. And if middleclassed portavorous was a usual beast? Bynight as useful as a vomit to a shorn man. If he had rognarised dtheir gcourts marsheyls? Dthat nday in ndays he had. Lindendelly, coke or skilllies spell me gart without a gate? Harlyadrope. The grazing rights (Mrs Magistra Martinetta) expired with the expiry of the goat's sire, if they were not mistaken? That he exactly could not tell the worshipfuls but his mother-in-waders had the recipis for the price of the coffin and that he was there to tell them that herself was the velocipede that could tell them kitcat. A maundarin tongue in a pounderin jowl? Father ourder about the mathers of prenanciation. Distributary endings? And we recommends. *Quare hircum?* No answer. *Unde gentium fe . . . ?* No ah. Are you not danzzling on the age of a vulcano? Siar, I am deed. And how olld of him? He was intendant to study pulu. Which was meant in a shirt of two shifts macoghamade or up Finn, threehatted ladder? That a head in thighs under a bush at the sunface would bait a serpent to a millrace through the heather. Arm bird colour defdum ethnic fort perharps? Sure and glomsk handy jotalpheson as well. Hokey jasons, then, in a pigeegeeses? On a pontiff's order as ture as there's an ital on atac. As a gololy bit to joss? Leally and tululy. But, why this hankowchaff and whence this second tone, son-yet-sun? He had the cowtaw in his buxers flay of face. So this that Solasistras, setting odds evens at defiance, took the laud from Labouriter? What displaced Tob, Dilke and Halley, not been greatly in love with the game. And, changing the venders, from the king's head to the republican's arms, as to the pugnaxities evinxed from flagfall to antepost during the effrays round fatherthyme's beckside and the regents in the plantsown raining, with the skiddystars and the morkern-windup, how they appealed to him then? That it was wildfires night on all the bettygallaghers. Mickmichael's soords shrieking shrecks through the wilkinses and neckanicholas' toastingforks pricking prongs up the tunnybladders. Let there be fight? And there was. Foght. On the site of the Angel's, you said? Guinney's Gap, he said, between what they said and the pussykitties. In the middle of the garth, then? That they mushn't toucht it. The devoted couple was or were only two disappainted solicitresses on the job of the unfortunate class on Saturn's mountain fort? That was about it, jah! And Camellus then said to Gemellus: I should know you? Parfaitly. And Gemellus then said to Camellus: Yes, your brother? Obsolutely. And if it was all about that, egregious sir? About that and the other. If he was not alluding to the whole in the wall? That he was when he was not eluding from the whole of the woman. Briefly, how such beginall finally struck him now? Like the crack that bruck the bank in Multifarnham. Whether he fell in with what they meant? Cursed that he suppoxed he did. Thos Thoris, Thomar's Thom? The rudacist rotter in Roebuck-dom. Surtopical? And subhuman. If it was, in yappanoise language, ach bad clap? Oo! Ah! Augs and ohrs with Rhian O'-kehley to put it tertianly, we wrong? Shocking! Such as turly pearced our really's that he might, that he might never, that he might never that night? Treely and rurally. Bladyughfoulmoeck-lenburgwhurawhorascortastrumpapornanennykocksapastippata -ppatupperstrippuckputtanach, eh? You have it alright.

Meirdreach an Oincuish! But a new complexion was put upon the matter when to the perplexedly uncondemnatory bench (whereon punic judgeship strove with penal law) the senior

king of all, Pegger Festy, as soon as the outer layer of stuccko-
muck had been removed at the request of a few live jurors,
declared in a loudburst of poesy, through his Brythonic interpreter on his oath, mhuith peisth mhuise as fearra bheura muirre
hriosmas, whereas take notice be the relics of the bones of the
story bouchal that was ate be Cliopatrick (the sow) princess
of parked porkers, afore God and all their honours and king's
commons that, what he would swear to the Tierney of Dundal-
gan or any other Tierney, yif live thurkells folloged him about
sure that was no steal and that, nevertheless, what was deposited
from that eyebold earbig noseknaving gutthroat, he did not fire
a stone either before or after he was born down and up to that
time. And, incidentalising that they might talk about Markarthy
or they might walk to Baalastartey or they might join the nabour
party and come on to Porterfeud this the sockdologer had the
neck to endorse with the head bowed on him over his outturned
noreaster by protesting to his lipreaders with a justbeencleaned
barefacedness, abeam of moonlight's hope, in the same trelawney
what he would impart, pleas bench, to the Llwyd Josus and the
gentlemen in Jury's and the four of Masterers who had been all
those yarns yearning for that good one about why he left
Dublin, that, amreeta beaker coddling doom, as an Inishman was
as good as any cantonnatal, if he was to parish by the market steak
before the dorming of the mawn, he skuld never ask to see sight or
light of this world or the other world or any either world, of Tyre-
nan-Og, as true as he was there in that jackabox that minute, or
wield or wind (no thanks t'yous!) the inexousthausthible wassail-
horn tot of iskybaush the hailth up the wailth of the endknown ab-
god of the fire of the moving way of the hawks with his heroes in
Warhorror if ever in all his exchequered career he up or lave a
chancery hand to take or throw the sign of a mortal stick or stone
at man, yoelamb or salvation army either before or after being
puptised down to that most holy and every blessed hour. Here,
upon the halfkneed castleknocker's attempting kithoguishly to
lilt his holymess the paws and make the sign of the Roman God-
helic faix, (Xaroshie, zdrst! —in his excitement the laddo had

91

broken exthro Castilian into which the whole audience perseguired and pursuited him *olla podrida*) outbroke much yellachters from owners in the heall (Ha!) in which, under the mollification of methaglin, the testifighter reluctingly, but with ever so ladylike indecorum, joined. (Ha! Ha!)

The hilariohoot of Pegger's Windup cumjustled as neatly with the tristitone of the Wet Pinter's as were they *isce et ille* equals of opposites, evolved by a onesame power of nature or of spirit, *iste*, as the sole condition and means of its himundher manifestation and polarised for reunion by the symphysis of their antipathies. Distinctly different were their duasdestinies. Whereas the maidies of the bar, (a pairless trentene, a lunarised score) when the eranthus myrrmyrred: Show'm the Posed: fluttered and flattered around the willingly pressed, nominating him for the swiney prize, complimenting him, the captivating youth, on his having all his senses about him, stincking thyacinths through his curls (O feen! O deur!) and bringing busses to his cheeks, their masculine Oirisher Rose (his neece cleur!), and legando round his nice new neck for him and pizzicagnoling his woolywags, with their dindy dandy sugar de candy mechree me postheen flowns courier to belive them of all his untiring young dames and send treats in their times. Ymen. But it was not unobserved of those presents, their worships, how, of one among all, her deputised to defeme him by the Lunar Sisters' Celibacy Club, a lovelooking leapgirl, all all alonely, Gentia Gemma of the Makegiddyculling Reeks, he, wan and pale in his unmixed admiration, seemed blindly, mutely, tastelessly, tactlessly, innamorate with heruponhim in shining aminglement, the shaym of his hisu shifting into the shimmering of her hers, (youthsy, beautsy, hee's her chap and shey'll tell memmas when she gays whom) till the wild wishwish of her sheeshea melted most musically mid the dark deepdeep of his shayshaun.

And whereas distracted (for was not just this in effect which had just caused that the effect of that which it had caused to occur?) the four justicers laid their wigs together, Untius, Muncius, Punchus and Pylax but could do no worse than promulgate their standing verdict of Nolans Brumans whereoneafter King, having murdered all the English he knew, picked out his pockets and left the tribunal scotfree, trailing his Tommeylommey's tunic in his hurry, thereinunder proudly showing off the blink pitch to his britgits to prove himself (an't plase yous!) a rael genteel. To the Switz bobbyguard's curial but courtlike: Commodore valley O hairy, Arthre jennyrosy?: the firewaterloover returted with such a vinesmelling fortytudor ages rawdownhams tanyouhide as would turn the latten stomach even of a tumass equinous (we were pre-pared for the chap's clap cap, the accent, but, took us as, by surprise and now we're geshing it like gush gash from a burner!) so that all the twofromthirty advocatesses within echo, pulling up their briefs at the krigkry: Shun the Punman!: safely and soundly soccered that fenemine Parish Poser, (how dare he!) umprumptu right-oway hames, much to his thanks, gratiasagam, to all the wrong donatrices, biss Drinkbattle's Dingy Dwellings where (for like your true venuson Esau he was dovetimid as the dears at Bottome) he shat in (zoo), like the muddy goalbind who he was (dun), the chassetitties belles conclaiming: You and your gift of your gaft of your garbage abaht our Farvver! and gaingridando: Hon! Verg! Nau! Putor! Skam! Schams! Shames!

And so it all ended. Artha kama dharma moksa. Ask Kavya for the kay. And so everybody heard their plaint and all listened to their plause. The letter! The litter! And the soother the bitther! Of eyebrow pencilled, by lipstipple penned. Borrowing a word and begging the question and stealing tinder and slipping like soap. From dark Rosa Lane a sigh and a weep, from Lesbia Looshe the beam in her eye, from lone Coogan Barry his arrow of song, from Sean Kelly's anagrim a blush at the name, from I am the Sullivan that trumpeting tramp, from Suffering Duf-ferin the Sit of her Style, from Kathleen May Vernon her Mebbe fair efforts, from Fillthepot Curran his scotchlove machree-ther, from hymn Op. 2 Phil Adolphos the weary O, the leery, O, from Samyouwill Leaver or Damyouwell Lover thatjolly old molly bit or that bored saunter by, from Timm Finn again's weak tribes loss of strength to his sowheel, from the wedding on the greene, agirlies, the gretnass of joyboys, from Pat Mullen, Tom Mallon, Dan Meldon, Don Maldon a slickstick picnic made in Moate by Muldoons. The solid man saved by his sillied woman. Crackajolking away like a hearse on fire. The elm that whimpers at the top told the stone that moans when stricken. Wind broke it. Wave bore it. Reed wrote of it. Syce ran with it. Hand tore it and wild went war. Hen trieved it and plight pledged peace. It was folded with cunning, sealed with crime, uptied by a harlot, undone by a child. It was life but was it fair? It was free but was it art? The old hunks on the hill read it to perlection. It made ma make merry and sissy so shy and rubbed some shine off Shem and put some shame into Shaun. Yet Una and Ita spill famine with drought and Agrippa, the propastored, spells tripulations in his threne. Ah, furchte fruchte, timid Danaides! Ena milo melomon, frai is frau and swee is too, swee is two when swoo is free, ana mala woe is we! A pair of sycopanties with amygdaleine eyes, one old obster lumpky pumpkin and three meddlars on their slies. And that was how framm Sin fromm Son, acity arose, finfin funfun, a sitting arrows. Now tell me, tell me, tell me then! What was it?

A . . . . !
? . . . . O!

So there you are now there they were, when all was over again, the four with them, setting around upin their judges' chambers, in the muniment room, of their marshalsea, under the suspices of Lally, around their old traditional tables of the law like Somany Solans to talk it over rallthesameagain. Well and druly dry. Suffering law the dring. Accourting to king's evelyns. So help her goat and kiss the bouc. Festives and highajinks and jintyaun and her beetyrossy bettydoaty and not to forget now a'duna o'darnel. The four of them and thank court now there were no more of them. So pass the push for port sake. Be it soon. Ah ho! And do you remember, Singabob, the badfather, the same, the great Howdoyoucallem, and his old nickname, Dirty Daddy Pantaloons, in his monopoleums, behind the war of the two roses, with Michael Victory, the sheemen's preester, before he caught his paper dispillsation from the poke, old Minace and Minster York? Do I mind? I mind the gush off the mon like Ballybock manure works on a tradewinds day. And the O'Moyly gracies and the O'Briny rossies chaffing him bluchface and playing him pranks. How do you do, todo, North Mister? Get into my way! Ah dearome forsailoshe! Gone over the bays! When ginabawdy meadabawdy! Yerra, why would he heed that old gasometer with his hooping coppin and his dyinboosycough and all the birds of the southside after her, Minxy Cunningham, their dear divorcee darling, jimmies and jonnies to be her jo? Hold hard. There's three other corners to our isle's cork float. Sure, 'tis well I can telesmell him $H_2 C E_3$ that would take a township's breath away! Gob and I nose him too well as I do meself, heaving up the Kay Wall by the 32 to 11 with his limelooking horsebags full of sesameseed, the Whiteside Kaffir, and his sayman's effluvium and his scentpainted voice, puffing out his thundering big brown cabbage! Pa! Thawt I'm glad a gull for his pawsdeen fiunn! Goborro, sez he, Lankyshied! Gobugga ye, sez I! O breezes! I sniffed that lad long before anyone. It was when I was in my farfather out at the west and she and myself, the redheaded girl, firstnighting down Sycomore Lane. Fine feelplay we had of it mid the kissabetts frisking in the kool kurkle dusk of the lushiness. My perfume of the pampas, says she (meaning me) putting out her netherlights, and I'd sooner one precious sip at your pure mountain dew than enrich my acquaintance with that big brewer's belch.

And so they went on, the fourbottle men, the analists, unguam and nunguam and lunguam again, their anschluss about her whosebefore and his whereafters and how she was lost away away in the fern and how he was founded deap on deep in anear, and the rustlings and the twitterings and the raspings and the snappings and the sighings and the paintings and the ukukuings and the (hist!) the springapartings and the (hast!) the bybyscuttlings and all the scandalmunkers and the pure craigs that used to be (up) that time living and lying and rating and riding round Nunsbelly Square. And all the buds in the bush. And the laughing jackass. Harik! Harik! Harik! The rose is white in the darik! And Sunfella's nose has got rhinoceritis from haunting the roes in the parik! So all rogues lean to rhyme. And contradrinking themselves about Lillytrilly law pon hilly and Mrs Niall of the Nine Corsages and the old markiss their besterfar, and, arrah, sure there was never a marcus at all at all among the manlies and dear Sir Armoury, queer Sir Rumoury, and the old house by the churpelizod, and all the goings on so very wrong long before when they were going on retreat, in the old gammeldags, the four of them, in Milton's Park under lovely Father Whisperer and making her love with his stuffstuff in the languish of flowers and feeling to find was she mushymushy, and wasn't that very both of them, the saucicissters, *a drahereen o machree*!, and (peep!) meeting waters most improper (peepette!) ballround the garden, trickle trickle trickle triss, please, miman, may I go flirting? farmers gone with a groom and how they used her, mused her, licksed her and cuddled. I differ with ye! Are you sure of yourself now? You're a liar, excuse me! I will not and you're another! And Lully holding their breach of the peace for them. Pool loll Lolly! To give and to take! And to forego the pasht! And all will be forgotten! Ah ho! It was too too bad to be falling out about her kindness pet and the shape of OOOOOOOO Ourang's time. Well, all right, Lelly. And shakeahand. And schenkusmore. For Craig sake. Be it suck.

Well?

Well, even should not the framing up of such figments in the evidential order bring the true truth to light as fortuitously as a dim seer's setting of a starchart might (heaven helping it!) uncover the nakedness of an unknown body in the fields of blue or as forehearingly as the sibspeeches of all mankind have foliated (earth seizing them!) from the root of some funner's stotter all the soundest sense to be found immense our special mentalists now holds (*securus iudicat orbis terrarum*) that by such playing possum our hagious curious encestor bestly saved his brush with his posterity, you, charming coparcenors, us, heirs of his tailsie. Gundogs of all breeds were beagling with renounced urbiandorbic bugles, hot to run him, given law, on a scent breasthigh, keen for the worry. View! From his holt outratted across the Juletide's genial corsslands of Humfries Chase from Mullinahob and Peacockstown, then bearing right upon Tankardstown, the outlier, a white noelan which Mr Lœwensteil Fitz Urse's basset beaters had first misbadgered for a bruin of some swart, led bayers the run, then through Raystown and Horlockstown and, louping the loup, to Tankardstown again. Ear canny hare for doubling through Cheeverstown they raced him, through Loughlinstown and Nutstown to wind him by the Boolies. But from the good turn when he last was lost, check, upon Ye Hill of Rut in full winter coat with ticker pads, pointing for his rooming house his old nordest in his rolltoproyal hessians a deaf fuchser's volponism hid him close in covert, miraculously ravenfed and buoyed up, in rumer, reticule, onasum and abomasum, upon (may Allbrewham have his mead!) the creamclotted sherriness of cinnamon syllabub, Mikkelraved, Nikkelsaved. Hence hounds hied home. Preservative perseverance in the reeducation of his intestines was the rebuttal by whilk he sort of git the big bulge on the whole bunch of spasoakers, dieting against glues and gravies, in that sometime prestreet protown. Vainly violence, virulence and vituperation sought wellnigh utterly to attax and abridge, to derail and depontify, to enrate and inroad, to ongoad and unhume the great shipping mogul and underlinen overlord.

But the spoil of hesitants, the spell of hesitency. His atake is it ashe, tittery taw tatterytail, hasitense humponadimply, heyheyheyhey a winceywencky.

Assembly men murmured. Reynard is slow!

One feared for his days. Did there yawn? 'Twas his stommick. Eruct? The libber. A gush? From his visuals, Pung? Delivver him, orelode! He had laid violent hands on himself, it was brought in Fugger's Newsletter, lain down, all in, fagged out, with equally melancholy death. For the triduum of Saturnalia his goatservant had paraded hiz willingsons in the Forum while the jenny infanted the lass to be greeted raucously (the Yardstated) with houx and epheus and measured with missiles too from a hundred of manhood and a wimmering of weibes. Big went the bang: then wildewide was quiet: a report: silence: last Fama put it under ether. The noase or the loal had dreven him blem, blem, stun blem. Sparks flew. He had fled again (open shunshema!) this country of exile, sloughed off, sidleshomed *via* the subterranean shored with bedboards, stowed away and ankered in a dutch bottom tank the Arsa, *hod* S.S. Finlandia, and was even now occupying, under an islamitic newhame in his seventh generation, a physical body Cornelius Magrath's (badoldkarakter, commonorrong canbung) in Asia Major, where as Turk of the theater (first house all flatty: the king, eleven sharps) he had bepiastered the buikdanseuses from the opulence of his omnibox while as arab at the streetdoor he bepestered the bumbashaws for the alms of a para's pence. Wires hummed. Peacefully general astonishment assisted by regrettitude had put a term till his existence: he saw the family saggarth, resigned, put off his remainders, was recalled and scrapheaped by the Maker. Chirpings crossed. An infamous private ailment (vulgovarioveneral) had claimed endright, closed his vicious circle, snap. Jams jarred. He had walked towards the middle of an ornamental lilypond when innebriated up to the point where braced shirts meet knickerbockers, as wangfish daring the buoyant waters, when rodmen's firstaiding hands had rescued un from very possibly several feel of demifrish water. Mush spread. On Umbrella Street where he did drinks from a pumps a kind of workman, Mr Whitlock, gave him a piece of wood. What words of power were made fas between them, ekenames and auchnomes, *acnomina ecnumina?* That, O that, did Hansard tell us, would gar ganz Dub's ear wag in every pub of all the citta! Batty believes a baton while Hogan hears a hod yet Heer prefers a punsil shapner and Cope and Bull go cup and ball. And the Cassidy — Craddock rome and reme round e'er a wiege ne'er a waage is still immer and immor awagering over it, a cradle with a care in it or a casket with a kick behind. Toties testies quoties questies. The war is in words and the wood is the world. Maply me, willowy we, hickory he and yew yourselves. Howforhim chirrupeth evereachbird! From golddawn glory to glowworm gleam. We were lowquacks did we not tacit turn. Elsewere there here no concern of the Guinnesses. But only the ruining of the rain has heard. *Estout pourporteral!* Cracklings cricked. A human pest cycling (pist!) and recycling (past!) about the sledgy streets, here he was (pust!) again! Morse nuisance noised. He was loose at large and (Oh baby!) might be anywhere when a disguised exnun, of huge standbuild and masculine manners in her fairly fat forties, Carpulenta Gygasta, hattracted hattention by harbitrary conduct with a homnibus. Aerials buzzed to coastal listeners of an oertax bror collector's budget, fullybigs, sporran, tie, tuft, tabard and bloody antichill cloak, its tailor's (Baernfather's) tab reading V.P.H., found nigh Scaldbrothar's Hole, and divers shivered to think what kaind of beast, wolves, croppis's or fourpenny friars, had devoured him. C. W. cast wide. Hvidfinns lyk, drohneth svertgleam, Valkir lockt. On his pinksir's postern, the boys had it, at Whitweekend had been nailed an inkedup name and title, inscribed in the national cursives, accelerated, regressive, filiform, turreted and envenomoloped in piggotry: Move up. Mumpty! Mike room for Rumpty! By order, Nickekellous Plugg; and this go, no pentecostal jest about it, how gregarious his race soever or skilful learned wise cunning knowledgable clear profound his saying fortitudo fraught or prudentiaproven, were he chief, count, general, fieldmarshal, prince, king or Myles the Slasher in his person, with a moliamordhar mansion in the Breffnian empire and a place of inauguration on the hill of Tullymongan, there had been real murder, of the rayheallach royghal raxacraxian variety, the MacMahon chaps, it was, that had done him in. On the fidd of Verdor the rampart combatants had left him lion with his dexter handcoup wresterected in a pureede paumee bloody proper. Indeed not a few thick and thin wellwishers, mostly of the clontarfminded class, (Colonel John Bawle O'Roarke, fervxamplus), even ventured so far as to loan or beg copies of D. Blayncy's trilingual triweekly, *Scatterbrains' Aftening Posht*, so as to make certain sure onetime and be satisfied of their quasicontribusodalitarian's having become genuinely quite beetly dead whether by land whither by water. Transocean atalaclamoured him; The latter! The latter! Shall their hope then be silent or Macfarlane lack of lamentation? He lay under leagues of it in deep Bartholoman's Deep.

Achdung! Pozor! Attenshune! Vikeroy Besights Smucky Yung Pigeschoolies. Tri Paisdinernes Eventyr Med Lochlanner Fathach I Fiounnisgehaven. Bannalanna Bangs Ballyhooly Out Of Her Buddaree Of A Bullavogue.

But, their bright little contemporaries notwithstanding, on the morrowing morn of the suicidal murder of the unrescued expatriate, aslike as asnake comes sliduant down that oaktree onto the duke of beavers, (you may have seen some liquidamber exude exotic from a balsam poplar at Parteen-a-lax Limestone. Road and cried Abies Magnifica! not, noble fir?) a quarter of nine, imploring his resipiency, saw the infallible spike of smoke's jutstiff punctual from the seventh gable of our Quintus Centimachus' porphyroid buttertower and then thirsty p.m. with oaths upon his lastingness (*En caecos harauspices! Annos longos patimur!*) the lamps of maintenance, beaconsfarafield innerhalf the zuggurat, all brevetnamed, the wasting wyvern, the tawny of his mane, the swinglowswaying bluepaw, the outstanding man, the lolllike lady, being litten for the long (O land, how long!) lifesnight, with suffusion of fineglass transom and leadlight panes.

Wherefore let it hardly by any being thinking be said either or thought that the prisoner of that sacred edifice, were he an Ivor the Boneless or an Olaf the Hide, was at his best a onestone parable, a rude breathing on the void of to be, a venter hearing his own bauchspeech in backwords, or, more strictly, but tristurned initials, the cluekey to a worldroom beyond the roomwhorld, for scarce one, or pathetically few of his dode canal sammenlivers cared seriously or for long to doubt with Kurt Iuld van Dijke (the gravitational pull perceived by certain fixed residents and the capture of uncertain comets chancedrifting through our system suggesting an authenticitatem of his aliquitudinis) the canonicity of his existence as a tesseract. Be still, O quick! Speak him dumb! Hush ye fronds of Ulma!

Dispersal women wondered. Was she fast?

Do tell us all about. As we want to hear allabout. So tellus tellas allabouter. The why or whether she looked alottylike like ussies and whether he had his wimdop like themses shut? Notes and queries, tipbids and answers, the laugh and the shout, the ards and downs. Now listed to one aneither and liss them down and smoothen out your leaves of rose. The war is o'er. Wimwim wimwim! Was it Unity Moore or Estella Swifte or Varina Fay or Quarta Quaedam? Toemaas, mark oom for yor ounckel! Pigeys, hold op med yer leg! Who, but who (for second time of asking) was then the scourge of the parts about folkrich Lucalizod it was wont to be asked, as, in ages behind of the Homo Capite Erectus, what price Peabody's money, or, to put it bluntly, whence is the herringtons' white cravat, as, in epochs more cainozoic, who struck Buckley though nowadays as thentimes every schoolfilly of sevenscore moons or more who knows her intimologies and every colleen bawl aroof and every redflammelwaving warwife and widowpeace upon Dublin Wall for ever knows as yayas is yayas how it was Buckleyself (we need no blooding paper to tell it neither) who struck and the Russian generals, da! da!, instead of Buckley who was caddishly struck by him when be herselves. What fullpried paulpoison in the spy of three castles or which hatefilled smileyseller? And that such a vetriol of venom, that queen's head affranchisant, a quiet stinkingplaster zeal could cover, prepostered or postpaid! The loungelizards of the pumproom had their nine days' jeer, and pratschkats at their platschpails too and holenpolendom beside, Szpaszpas Szpissmas, the zhanyzhonies, when, still believing in her owenglass, when izarres were twinklins, that the upper reaches of her mouthless face and her impermanent waves were the better half of her, one nearer him, dearer than all, first warming creature of his early morn, bondwoman of the man of the house, and murrmurr of all the mackavicks, she who had given his eye for her bed and a tooth for a child till one one and one ten and one hundred again, O me and O ye! cadet and prim, the hungray and anngreen (and if she is older now than her teeth she has hair that is younger than thighne, my dear!) she who shuttered him after his fall and waked him widowt sparing and gave him keen and made him able and held adazillahs to each arche of his noes, she who will not rast her from her running to seek him till, with the help of the okeamic, some such time that she shall have been after hiding the crumbends of his enormousness in the areyou looking-for Pearlfar sea, (ur, uri, uria!) stood forth, burnzburn the gorg-gony old danworld, in gogor's name, for gagar's sake, dragging the countryside in her train, finickin here and funickin there, with her louisequean's brogues and her culunder buzzle and her little bolero boa and all and two times twenty curlicornies for her headdress, specks on her eyeux, and spudds on horeilles and a circusfix riding her Parisienne's cockneze, a vaunt her straddle from Equerry Egon, when Tinktink in the churchclose clinked Steploajazzyma Sunday, *Sola*, with pawns, prelates and pookas pelotting in her piecebag, for Handiman the Chomp, Esquoro, biskbask, to crush the slander's head.

Wery weeny wight, plead for Morandmor! *Notre Dame de la Ville*, mercy of thy balmheartzyheat! Ogrowdnyk's beyond her-bata tay, wort of the drogist. Bulk him no bulkis. And let him rest, thou wayfarre, and take no gravespoil from him! Neither mar his mound! The bane of Tut is on it. Ware! But there's a little lady waiting and her name is A.L.P. And you'll agree. She must be she. For her holden heirheaps hanging down her back. He spenth his strenth amok haremscarems. Poppy Narancy, Gial-lia, Chlora, Marinka, Anileen, Parme. And ilk a those dames had her rainbow huemoures yet for whilko her whims but he coined a cure. Tifftiff today, kissykissy tonay and agelong pine tomauran-na. Then who but Crippled-with-Children would speak up for Dropping-with-Sweat?

> *Sold him her lease of ninenineninetee,*
> *Tresses undresses so dyedyedaintee,*
> *Goo, the groot gudgeon, gulped it all.*
> *Hoo was the C. O. D.?*
> Bum!

At Island Bridge she met her tide.
Attabom, attabom, attabombomboom!
The Fin had a flux and his Ebba a ride.
Attabom, attabom, attabombomboom!
We're all up to the years in hues and cribies.
That's what she's done for wee!

Woe!

Nomad may roam with Nabuch but let naaman laugh at Jordan! For we, we have taken our sheet upon her stones where we have hanged our hearts in her trees; and we list, as she bibs us, by the waters of babalong.

In the name of Annah the Allmaziful, the Everliving, the Bringer of Plurabilities, haloed be her eve, her singtime sung, her rill be run, unhemmed as it is uneven!

Her untitled mamafesta memorialising the Mosthighest has gone by many names at disjointed times. Thus we hear of, *The Augusta Angustissimost for Old Seabeastius' Salvation, Rockabill Booby in the Wave Trough, Here's to the Relicts of All Decencies, Anna Stessa's Rise to Notice, Knickle Down Duddy Gunne and Arishe Sir Cannon, My Golden One and My Selver Wedding, Amoury Treestam and Icy Siseule, Saith a Sawyer til a Strame, Ik dik dopedope et tu mihimihi, Buy Birthplate for a Bite, Which of your Hesterdays Mean Ye to Morra? Hoebegunne the Hebrewer Hit Waterman the Brayned, Arcs in His Ceiling Flee Chinx on the Flur, Rebus de Hibernicis, The Crazier Letters, Groans of a Briton-ess, Peter Peopler Picked a Plot to Pitch his Poppolin, An Apology for a Big* (some such nonoun *as Husband* or *husboat* or *hose-bound* is probably understood for we have also the pluxherple-thoric *My Hoonsbood Hansbaad's a Journey to Porthergill gone and He Never Has the Hour), Ought We To Visit Him? For Ark see Zoo, Cleopater's Nedlework Ficturing Aldborougham on the Sahara with the Coombing of the Cammmels and the Parlourmaids of Aegypt, Cock in the Pot for Father, Placeat Vestrae, A New Cure for an Old Clap, Where Portentos they'd Grow Gonder how I'd Wish I Woose a Geese; Gettle Nettie, Thrust him not, When the*

*Myrtles of Venice Played to Bloccus's Line, To Plenge Me High
He Waives Chiltern on Friends, Oremunds Queue Visits Amen
Mart, E'en Tho' I Granny a-be He would Fain Me Cuddle, Twenty
of Chambers, Weighty Ten Beds and a Wan Ceteroom, I Led the
Life, Through the Boxer Coxer Rising in the House with the Golden
Stairs, The Following Fork, He's my O'Jerusalem and I'm his
Po, The Best in the West, By the Stream of Zemzem under Zig-
zag Hill, The Man That Made His Mother in the Marlborry
Train, Try Our Taal on a Taub, The Log of Anny to the Base
All, Nopper Tipped a Nappiwenk to his Notylytl Dantsigirls, Prszss
Orel Orel the King of Orlbrdsz, Intimier Minnelisp of an Extor-
reor Monolothe, Drink to Him, My Juckey, and Dhoult Bemine
Thy Winnowing Sheet, I Ask You to Believe I was his Mistress,
He Can Explain, From Victrolia Nuancee to Allbart Noahnsy,
Da's a Daisy so Guimea your Handsel too, What Barbaras Done
to a Barrel Organ Before the Rank, Tank and Bonnbtail, Huskvy
Admortal, What Jumbo made to Jalice and what Anisette to Him,
Ophelia's Culpreints, Hear Hubty Hublin, My Old Dansh, I am
Older northe Rogues among Whisht I Slips and He Calls Me his
Dual of Ayessha, Suppotes a Ventriliquorst Merries a Corpse,
Lapps for Finns This Funnycoon's Week, How the Buckling Shut
at Rush in January, Look to the Lady, From the Rise of the
Dudge Pupublick to the Fall of the Potstille, Of the Two Ways
of Opening the Mouth, I have not Stopped Water Where It Should
Flow and I Know the Twentynine Names of Attraente, The Tortor
of Tory Island Traits Galasia like his Milchcow, From Abbeygate
to Crowalley Through a Lift in the Lude, Smocks for Their Graces
and Me Aunt for Them Clodshoppers, How to Pull a Good Horus-
coup even when Oldsire is Dead to the World, Inn the Gleam of
Waherlow, Fathe He's Sukceded to My Esperations, Thee Steps
Forward, Two Stops Back, My Skin Appeals to Three Senses and
My Curly Lips Demand Columbkisses; Gage Street on a Crany's
Savings, Them Lads made a Trion of Battlewatschers and They
Totties a Doeit of Deers, In My Lord's Bed by One Whore Went
Through It, Mum It is All Over, Cowpoyride by Twelve Acre Ter-
riss in the Unique Estates of Amessican, He Gave me a Thou so I*

serve Him with Thee, Of all the Wide Torsos in all the Wild Glen, O'Donogh, White Donogh, He's Hue to Me Cry, I'm the Stitch in his Baskside You'd be Nought Without Mom, To Keep the Huskies off the Hustings and Picture Pets from Lifting Shops, Norsker Torsker Find the Poddle, He Perssed Me Here with the Ardour of a Tonnoburkes, A Boob Was Weeping This Mower was Reaping, O'Loughlin, Up from the Pit of my Stomach I Swish you the White of the Mourning, Inglo-Andean Medoleys from Tommany Moohr, The Great Polynesional Entertrainer Exhibits Ballantine Brautchers with the Link of Natures, The Mimic of Meg Neg and the Mackeys, Entered as the Lastest Pigtarial and My Pooridiocal at Stitchioner's Hall, Siegfield Follies and or a Gentlehomme's Faut Pas, See the First Book of Jealesies Pessim, The Suspended Sentence, A Pretty Brick Story for Childsize Heroes, As Lo Our Sleep, I Knew I'd Got it in Me so Thit settles That, Thonderbalt Captain Smeth and La Belle Sauvage Pocahonteuse, Way for Wet Week Welikin's Douchka Marianne, The Last of the Fingallians, It Was Me Egged Him on to the Stork Exchange and Lent my Dutiful Face to His Customs, Chee Chee Cheels on their China Miction, Pickedmeup Peters, Lumptytumtumpty had a Big Fall, Pimpimp Pimpimp, Measly Ventures of Two Lice and the Fall of Fruit, The Fokes Family Interior, If my Spreadeagles Wasn't so Tight I'd Loosen my Cursits on that Bunch of Maggiestraps, Allolosha Popofetts and Howke Cotchme Eye, Seen Aples and Thin Dyed, i big U to Beleaves from Love and Mother, Fine's Fault was no Felon, Exat Delvin Renter Life, The Flash that Flies from Vuggy's Eyes has Set Me Hair On Fire, His is the House that Malt Made, Divine Views from Back to the Front, Abe to Sare Stood Icyk Neuter till Brahm Taulked Him Common Sex, A Nibble at Eve Will That Bowal Relieve, Allfor Guineas, Sounds and Compliments Libidous, Seven Wives Awake Aweek, Airy Ann and Berber Blut, Amy Licks Porter While Huffy Chops Eads, Abbrace of Umbellas or a Tripple of Caines, Buttbutterbust, From the Manorlord Hoved to the Misses O'Mollies and from the Dames to their Sames, Manyfestoons for the Colleagues on the Green, An Outstanding Back and an Excellent Halfcentre if Called on, As Tree is Quick and Stone is

White So is My Washing Done by Night, First and Last Only True Account all about the Honorary Mirsu Earwicker, L.S.D., and the Snake (Nuggets!) by a Woman of the World who only can Tell Naked Truths about a Dear Man and all his Conspirators how they all Tried to Fall him Putting it all around Lucalizod about Privates Earwicker and a Pair of Sloppy Sluts plainly Showing all the Unmentionability falsely Accusing about the Raincoats.

The proteiform graph itself is a polyhedron of scripture. There was a time when naif alphabetters would have written it down the tracing of a purely deliquescent recidivist, possibly ambidextrous, snubnosed probably and presenting a strangely profound rainbowl in his (or her) occiput. To the hardily curiosing entomophilust then it has shown a very sexmosaic of nymphosis in which the eternal chimerahunter Oriolopos, now frond of sugars, then lief of saults, the sensory crowd in his belly coupled with an eye for the goods trooth bewilderblissed by their night effluvia with guns like drums and fondlers like forceps persequestellates his vanessas from flore to flore. Somehows this sounds like the purest kidooleyoon wherein our madernacerution of lour lore is rich. All's so herou from us him in a kitchernott darkness, by hasard and worn rolls arered, we must grope on till Zerogh hour like pou owl giaours as we are would we salve aught of moments for our aysore today. Amousin though not but. Closer inspection of the *bordereau* would reveal a multiplicity of personalities inflicted on the documents or document and some prevision of virtual crime or crimes might be made by anyone unwary enough before any suitable occasion for it or them had so far managed to happen along. In fact, under the closed eyes of the inspectors the traits featuring the *chiaroscuro* coalesce, their contrarieties eliminated, in one stable somebody similarly as by the providential warring of heartshaker with housebreaker and of dramdrinker against freethinker our social something bowls along bumpily, experiencing a jolting series of prearranged disappointments, down the long lane of (it's as semper as oxhousehumper!) generations, more generations and still more generations.

Say, baroun lousadoor, who in hallhagal wrote the durn thing anyhow? Erect, beseated, mountback, against a partywall, below freezigrade, by the use of quill or style, with turbid or pellucid mind, accompanied or the reverse by mastication, interrupted by visit of seer to scribe or of scribe to site, atwixt two showers or atosst of a trike, rained upon or blown around, by a right-down regular racer from the soil or by a too pained whittlewit laden with the loot of learning?

Now, patience; and remember patience is the great thing, and above all things else we must avoid anything like being or becoming out of patience. A good plan used by worried business folk who may not have had many momentums to master Kung's doctrine of the meang or the propriety codestruces of Carprimustimus is just to think of all the sinking fund of patience possessed in their conjoint names by both brothers Bruce with whom are incorporated their Scotch spider and Elberfeld's Calculating Horses. If after years upon years of delving in ditches dark one tubthumper more than others, Kinihoun or Kahanan, giardarner or mear measenmanonger, has got up for the darnall same purpose of reassuring us with all the barbar of the Carrageehouse that our great ascendant was properly speaking three syllables less than his own surname (yes, yes, less!), that the ear of Fionn Earwicker aforetime was the trademark of a broadcaster with wicker local jargon for an ace's patent (Hear! Calls! Everywhair!) then as to this radiooscillating epiepistle to which, cotton, silk or samite, kohol, gall or brickdust, we must ceaselessly return, whereabouts exactly at present in Siam, Hell or Tophet under that glorisol which plays touraloup with us in this Aludin's Cove of our cagacity is that bright soandsuch to slip us the dinkum oil?

Naysayers we know. To conclude purely negatively from the positive absence of political odia and monetary requests that its page cannot ever have been a penproduct of a man or woman of that period or those parts is only one more unlookedfor conclusion leaped at, being tantamount to inferring from the nonpresence of inverted commas (sometimes called quotation marks) on any page that its author was always constitutionally incapable of misappropriating the spoken words of others.

Luckily there is another cant to the questy. Has any fellow, of the dime a dozen type, it might with some profit some dull evening quietly be hinted — has any usual sort of ornery josser, flat-chested fortyish, faintly flatulent and given to ratiocination by syncopation in the elucidation of complications, of his greatest Fung Yang dynasdescendanced, only another the son of, in fact, ever looked sufficiently longly at a quite everydaylooking stamped addressed envelope? Admittedly it is an outer husk: its face, in all its featureful perfection of imperfection, is its fortune: it exhibits only the civil or military clothing of whatever passion-pallid nudity or plaguepurple nakedness may happen to tuck itself under its flap. Yet to concentrate solely on the literal sense or even the psychological content of any document to the sore neglect of the enveloping facts themselves circumstantiating it is just as hurtful to sound sense (and let it be added to the truest taste) as were some fellow in the act of perhaps getting an intro from another fellow turning out to be a friend in need of his, say, to a lady of the latter's acquaintance, engaged in performing the elaborative antecistral ceremony of upstheres, straightaway to run off and vision her plump and plain in her natural altogether, preferring to close his blinkhard's eyes to the ethiquethical fact that she was, after all, wearing for the space of the time being some definite articles of evolutionary clothing, inharmonious creations, a captious critic might describe them as, or not strictly necessary or a trifle irritating here and there, but for all that suddenly full of local colour and personal perfume and suggestive, too, of so very much more and capable of being stretched, filled out, if need or wish were, of having their surprisingly like coincidental parts separated don't they now, for better survey by the deft hand of an expert, don't you know? Who in his heart doubts either that the facts of feminine clothiering are there all the time or that the feminine fiction, stranger than the facts, is there also at the same time, only a little to the rere? Or that one may be separated from the other? Or that both may then be contemplated simultaneously? Or that each may be taken up and considered in turn apart from the other?

109

Here let a few artifacts fend in their own favour. The river felt she wanted salt. That was just where Brien came in. The country asked for bearspaw for dindin! And boundin aboundin it got it surly. We who live under heaven, we of the clovery kingdom, we middlesins people have often watched the sky overreaching the land. We suddenly have. Our isle is Sainge. The place. That stern chuckler Mayhappy Mayhapnot, once said to repeation in that lutran conservatory way of his that Isitachapel-Asitalukin was the one place, *ult aut nult*, in this madh vaal of tares (whose verdhure's yellowed therever Phaiton parks his car while its tamelised tay is the drame of Drainophilias) where the possible was the improbable and the improbable the inevitable. If the proverbial bishop of our holy and undivided with this me ken or no me ken Zot is the Quiztune havvermashed had his twoe nails on the head we are in for a sequentiality of improbable possibles though possibly nobody after having grubbed up a lock of cwold cworn aboove his subject probably in Harrystotalies or the vivle will go out of his way to applaud him on the onboiassed back of his remark for utterly impossible as are all these events they are probably as like those which may have taken place as any others which never took person at all are ever likely to be. Ahahn!

About that original hen. Midwinter (fruur or kuur?) was in the offing and Premver a promise of a pril when, as kischabrigies sang life's old sahatsong, an iceclad shiverer, merest of bantlings observed a cold fowl behaviourising strangely on that fatal midden or chip factory or comicalbottomed copsjute (dump for short) afterwards changed into the orangery when in the course of deeper demolition unexpectedly one bushman's holiday its limon threw up a few spontaneous fragments of orangepeel, the last remains of an outdoor meal by some unknown sunseeker or placehider *illico* way back in his mistridden past. What child of a strandlooper but keepy little Kevin in the despondful surrounding of such sneezing cold would ever have trouved up on a strate that was called strete a motive for future saintity by euchring the finding of the Ardagh chalice by another heily innocent and beachwalker whilst trying with pious clamour to wheedle Tipperaw raw raw reeraw puteters out of Now Sealand in spignt of the patchpurple of the massacre, a dual a duel to die to day, goddam and biggod, sticks and stanks, of most of the Jacobiters.

The bird in the case was Belinda of the Dorans, a more than quinquegintarian (Terziis prize with Serni medal, Cheepalizzy's Hane Exposition) and what she was scratching at the hour of klokking twelve looked for all this zogzag world like a goodish-sized sheet of letterpaper originating by transhipt from Boston (Mass.) of the last of the first to Dear whom it proceded to mention Maggy well & allathome's health well only the hate turned the mild on *the van* Houtens and the general's elections with a *lovely* face of some born gentleman with a beautiful present of wedding cakes for dear thankyou Chriesty and with grand funferall of poor Father Michael don't forget unto life's & Muggy well how are you Maggy & hopes soon to hear well & must now close it with fondest to the twoinns with four crosskisses for holy paul holey corner holipoli wholyisland pee ess from (locust may eat all but this sign shall they never) affectionate largelooking tache of tch. The stain, and that a teastain (the overcautelousness of the masterbilker here, as usual, signing the page away), marked it off on the spout of the moment as a genuine relique of ancient Irish pleasant pottery of that lydialike languishing class known as a hurry-me-o'er-the-hazy.

Why then how?

Well, almost any photoist worth his chemicots will tip anyone asking him the teaser that if a negative of a horse happens to melt enough while drying, well, what you do get is, well, a positively grotesquely distorted macromass of all sorts of horsehappy values and masses of meltwhile horse. Tip. Well, this freely is what must have occurred to our missive (there's a sod of a turb for you! please wisp off the grass!) unfilthed from the boucher by the sagacity of a lookmelittle likemelong hen. Heated residence in the heart of the orangeflavoured mudmound had partly ob-literated the negative to start with, causing some features pal-pably nearer your pecker to be swollen up most grossly while the farther back we manage to wiggle the more we need the loan of a lens to see as much as the hen saw. Tip.

You is feeling like you was lost in the bush, boy? You says: It is a puling sample jungle of woods. You most shouts out: Bethicket me for a stump of a beech if I have the poultriest notions what the farest he all means. Gee up, girly! The quad gospellers may own the targum but any of the Zingari shoolerim may pick a peck of kindlings yet from the sack of auld hensyne.

Lead, kindly fowl! They always did: ask the ages. What bird has done yesterday man may do next year, be it fly, be it moult, be it hatch, be it agreement in the nest. For her socioscientific sense is sound as a bell, sir, her volucrine automutativeness right on normalcy: she knows, she just feels she was kind of born to lay and love eggs (trust her to propagate the species and hoosh her fluffballs safe through din and danger!); lastly but mostly, in her genesic field it is all game and no gammon; she is ladylike in everything she does and plays the gentleman's part every time. Let us auspice it! Yes, before all this has time to end the golden age must return with its vengeance. Man will become dirigible, Ague will be rejuvenated, woman with her ridiculous white burden will reach by one step sublime incubation, the manewanting human lioness with her dishorned discipular manram will lie down together publicly flank upon fleece. No, assuredly, they are not justified, those gloompourers who grouse that letters have never been quite their old selves again since that weird weekday in bleak Janiveer (yet how palmy date in a waste's oasis!) when to the shock of both, Biddy Doran looked at literature.

And. She may be a mere marcella, this midget madgetcy, Misthress of Arths. But. It is not a hear or say of some anomorous letter, signed Toga Girilis, (teasy dear). We have a cop of her fist right against our nosibos. We note the paper with her jotty young watermark: *Notre Dame du Bon Marché.* And she has a heart of Arin! What lumililts as she fols with her fallimineers and her nadianods. As a strow will shaw she does the wind blague, recting to show the rudess of a robur curling and shewing the fansaties of a frizette. But how many of her readers

realise that she is not out to dizzledazzle with a graith uncouthre-
ment of postmantuam glasseries from the lapins and the grigs.
Nuttings on her wilelife! Grabar gooden grandy for old almea-
nium adamologists like Dariaumaurius and Zovotrimaserov-
meravmerouvian; (dmzn!); she feel plain plate one flat fact thing
and if, lastways firdstwise, a man alones sine anyon anyons
utharas has no rates to done a kik at with anyon anakars about
tutus milking fores and the rereres on the outerrand asikin the
tutus to be forrarder. Thingcrooklyexineverypasturesixdix-
likencehimaroundhersthemaggerbykinkinkankanwithdownmind-
lookingated. Mesdaims, Marmouselles, Mescerfs! Silvapais! All
schwants (schwrites) ischt tell the cock's trootabout him. Ka-
pak kapuk. No minzies matter. He had to see life foully the
plak and the smut, (schwrites). There were three men in him
(schwrites). Dancings (schwrites) was his only ttoo feebles.
With apple harlottes. And a little mollvogels. Spissially (schwrites)
when they peaches. Honeys wore camelia paints. Yours very
truthful. Add dapple inn. Yet is it but an old story, the tale of
a Treestone with one Ysold, of a Mons held by tentpegs and his
pal whatholoosed on the run, what Cadman could but Badman
wouldn't, any Genoaman against any Venis, and why Kate takes
charge of the waxworks.

Let us now, weather, health, dangers, public orders and other
circumstances permitting, of perfectly convenient, if you police,
after you, policepolice, pardoning mein, ich beam so fresch, bey?
drop this jiggerypokery and talk straight turkey meet to mate, for
while the ear, be we mikealls or nicholists, may sometimes be inclined to believe others the eye, whether browned or nolensed,
find it devilish hard now and again even to believe itself. *Habes
aures et num videbis? Habes oculos ac mannepalpabuat?* Tip! Drawing nearer to take our slant at it (since after all it has met with
misfortune while all underground), let us see all there may remain
to be seen.

I am a worker, a tombstone mason, anxious to pleace avery-
buries and jully glad when Christmas comes his once ayear. You
are a poorjoist, unctuous to polise nopebobbies and tunnibelly

soully when 'tis thime took o'er home, gin. We cannot say aye to aye. We cannot smile noes from noes. Still. One cannot help noticing that rather more than half of the lines run north-south in the Nemzes and Bukarahast directions while the others go west-east in search from Maliziies with Bulgarad for, tiny tot though it looks when schtschupnistling alongside other incunabula, it has its cardinal points for all that. These ruled barriers along which the traced words, run, march, halt, walk, stumble at doubtful points, stumble up again in comparative safety seem to have been drawn first of all in a pretty checker with lampblack and blackthorn. Such crossing is antechristian of course, but the use of the homeborn shillelagh as an aid to calligraphy shows a distinct advance from savagery to barbarism. It is seriously believed by some that the intention may have been geodetic, or, in the view of the cannier, domestic economical. But by writing thithaways end to end and turning, turning and end to end hithaways writing and with lines of litters slittering up and louds of latters slettering down, the old semetomyplace and jupetbackagain from tham Let Rise till Hum Lit. Sleep, where in the waste is the wisdom?

Another point, in addition to the original sand, pounce powder, drunkard paper or soft rag used (any vet or inhanger in ous sot's social can see the seen for seemself, a wee ftofty od room, the cheery spluttered on the one karrig, a darka disheen of voos from Dalbania, any gotsquantity of racky, a portogal and some buk setting out on the sofer, you remember the sort of softball sucker motru used to tell us when we were all biribiyas or nippies and messas) it has acquired accretions of terricious matter whilst loitering in the past. The teatimestained terminal (say not the tag, mummer, or our show's a failure!) is a cosy little brown study all to oneself and, whether it be thumbprint, mademark or just a poor trait of the artless, its importance in establishing the identities in the writer complexus (for if the hand was one, the minds of active and agitated were more than so) will be best appreciated by never forgetting that both before and after the battle of the Boyne it was a habit not to sign letters

114

always. Tip. And it is surely a lesser ignorance to write a word with every consonant too few than to add all too many. The end? Say it with missiles then and thus arabesque the page. You have your cup of scalding Souchong, your taper's waxen drop, your cat's paw, the clove or coffinnail you chewed or champed as you worded it, your lark in clear air. So why, pray, sign anything as long as every word, letter, penstroke, paperspace is a perfect signature of its own? A true friend is known much more easily, and better into the bargain, by his personal touch, habits of full or undress, movements, response to appeals for charity than by his footwear, say. And, speaking anent Tiberias and other ncestuish salacities among gerontophils, a word of warning about the tenderloined passion hinted at. Some softnosed peruser might mayhem take it up erogenously as the usual case of poons, *prostituta in herba* plus dinky pinks deliberatively summersaulting off her bisexycle, at the main entrance of curate's perpetual soutane suit with her one to see and awoh! who picks her up as gingerly as any balmbearer would to feel whereupon the virgin was most hurt and nicely asking: whyre have you been so grace a mauling and where were you chaste me child? Be who, farther potential? and so wider but we grisly old Sykos who have done our unsmiling bit on 'alices, when they were yung and easily freudened, in the penumbra of the procuring room and what oracular comepression we have had apply to them! could (did we care to sell our feebought silence *in camera*) tell our very moistnostrilled one that *father* in such virgated contexts is not always that undemonstrative relative (often held up to our conumacy) who settles our hashbill for us and what an innocent allbroad's adverb such as Michaelly looks like can be suggestive of under the pudendascope and, finally, what a neurasthene nympholept, endocrine-pineal typus, of inverted parentage with a repossessing drauma present in her past and a priapic urge for ongress with agnates before cognates fundamentally is feeling or under her lubricitous meiosis when she refers with liking to ome feeler she fancie's face. And Mm. We could. Yet what need o say? 'Tis as human a little story as paper could well carry, in

affect, as singsing so Salaman susuing to swittvitles while as un-
bluffingly blurtubruskblunt as an Esra, the cat, the cat's meeter,
the meeter's cat's wife, the meeter's cat's wife's half better, the
meeter's cat's wife's half better's meeter, and so back to our
horses, for we also know, what we have perused from the pages
of *I Was A Gemral*, that Showting up of Bulsklivism by 'Schot-
tenboum', that Father Michael about this red time of the white
terror equals the old regime and Margaret is the social revolution
while cakes mean the party funds and dear thank you signifies
national gratitude. In fine, we have heard, as it happened, of
Spartacus intercellular. We are not corknered yet, dead hand!
We can recall, with voluntears, the froggy jew, and sweeter far
'twere now westhinks in Dumbil's fair city ere one more year is
o'er. We tourned our coasts to the good gay tunes. When from
down swords the sea merged the oldowth guns and answer made
the bold O' Dwyer. But. *Est modest in verbos.* Let a prostitute
be whoso stands before a door and winks or parks herself in the
fornix near a makeussin wall (sinsin! sinsin!) and the curate one
who brings strong waters (gingin! gingin!), but also, and dinna
forget, that there is many asleeps between someathome's first
and moreinausland's last and that the beautiful presence of waiting kates will until life's (!) be more than enough to make any
milkmike in the language of sweet tarts punch hell's hate into his
twin nicky and that Maggy's tea, or your majesty, if heard as a
boost from a born gentleman is (?). For if the lingo gasped between
kicksheets, however basically English, were to be preached from
the mouths of wickerchurchwardens and metaphysicians in the
row and advokaatoes, allvoyous, demivoyelles, languoaths, les-
biels, dentelles, gutterhowls and furtz, where would their practice be or where the human race itself were the Pythagorean ses-
quipedalia of the panepistemion, however apically Volapucky
grunted and gromwelled, ichabod, habakuk, opanoff, uggamyg
hapaxle, gomenon, ppppfff, over country stiles, behind slate
dwellinghouses, down blind lanes, or, when all fruit fails, unde
some sacking left on a coarse cart?

So hath been, love: tis tis: and will be: till wears and tears an ages. Thief us the night, steal we the air, shawl thiner liefest, mine! Here, Ohere, insult the fair! Traitor, bad hearer, brave! The lightning look, the birding cry, awe from the grave, ever-flowing on the times. Feueragusaria iordenwater; now godsun shine on menday's daughter; a good clap, a fore marriage, a bad wake, tell hell's well; such is manowife's lot of lose and win again, like he's gruen quhiskers on who's chin again, she plucketed them out but they grown in again. So what are you going to do about it? O dear!

If juness she saved! Ah ho! And if yulone he pouved! The ol-old stoliolum! From quiqui quinet to michemiche chelet and a jambebatiste to a brulobrulo! It is told in sounds in utter that, in signs so adds to, in universal, in polygluttural, in each auxiliary neutral idiom, sordomutics, florilingua, sheltafocal, flayflutter, a con's cubane, a pro's tutute, strassarab, ereperse and anythongue athall. Since nozzy Nanette tripped palmyways with Highho Harry there's a spurtfire turf a'kind o'kindling when oft as the souffsouff blows her peaties up and a claypot wet for thee, my Sitys, and talkatalka tell Tibbs has eve: and whathough (revilous life proving aye the death of ronaldses when winpower wine has bucked the kick on poor won man) billiousness has been billious-ness during milliums of millenions and our mixed racings have been giving two hoots or three jeers for the grape, vine and brew and Pieter's in Nieuw Amsteldam and Paoli's where the poules go and rum smelt his end for him and he dined off sooth ameri-can (it would give one the frier even were one a normal Kettle-licker) this oldworld epistola of their weatherings and their marryings and their buryings and their natural selections has combled tumbled down to us fersch and made-at-all-hours like an ould cup on tay. As I was hottin me souser. Haha! And as you was caldin your dutchy hovel. Hoho! She tole the tail or her toon. Huhu!

Now, kapnimancy and infusionism may both fit as tight as two trivets but while we in our wee free state, holding to that prestatute in our charter, may have our irremovable doubts as to the whole sense of the lot, the interpretation of any phrase in the whole, the meaning of every word of a phrase so far deciphered out of it, however unfettered our Irish daily independence, we must vaunt no idle dubiosity as to its genuine authorship and holusbolus authoritativeness. And let us bringtheecease to beakerings on that clink, olmond bottler! On the face of it, to volt back to our desultory horses, and for your roughshod mind, bafflelost bull, the affair is a thing once for all done and there you are somewhere and finished in a certain time, be it a day or a year or even supposing, it should eventually turn out to be a serial number of goodness gracious alone knows how many days or years. Anyhow, somehow and somewhere, before the bookflood or after her ebb, somebody mentioned by name in his telephone directory, Coccolanius or Gallotaurus, wrote it, wrote it all, wrote it all down, and there you are, full stop. O, undoubtedly yes, and very potably so, but one who deeper thinks will always bear in the baccbuccus of his mind that this downright there you are and there it is is only all in his eye. Why?

Because, Soferim Bebel, if it goes to that, (and dormerwindow gossip will cry it from the housetops no surelier than the writing on the wall will hue it to the mod of men that mote in the main street) every person, place and thing in the chaosmos of Alle anyway connected with the gobblydumped turkery was moving and changing every part of the time: the travelling inkhorn (possibly pot), the hare and turtle pen and paper, the continually more and less intermisunderstanding minds of the anticollaborators, the as time went on as it will variously inflected, differently pronounced, otherwise spelled, changeably meaning vocable scriptsigns. No, so holp me Petault, it is not a miseffectual whyacinthinous riot of blots and blurs and bars and balls and hoops and wriggles and juxtaposed jottings linked by spurts of speed: it only looks as like it as damn it; and, sure, we ought really to rest thankful that at this deleteful hour of dungflies dawning we have even a written on with dried ink scrap of paper at all to show for ourselves, tare it or leaf it, (and we are lufted to ourselves as the soulfisher when he led the cat out of the bout) after all that we lost and plundered of it even to the hidmost coignings of the

earth and all it has gone through and by all means, after a good
ground kiss to Terracussa and for wars luck our lefftoff's flung
over our home homoplate, cling to it as with drowning hands,
hoping against hope all the while that, by the light of philo-
phosy, (and may she never folsage us!) things will begin to clear
up a bit one way or another within the next quarrel of an hour
and be hanged to them as ten to one they will too, please the pigs,
as they ought to categorically, as, stricly between ourselves, there
is a limit to all things so this will never do.

For, with that farmfrow's foul flair for that flayfell foxfetor,
(the calamite's columitas calling for calamitous calamitance) who
that scrutinising marvels at those indignant whiplooplashes; those
so prudently bolted or blocked rounds; the touching reminiscence
of an incompletet trail or dropped final; a round thousand whirli-
gig glorioles, prefaced by (alas!) now illegible airy plumeflights,
all tiberiously ambiembellishing the initials majuscule of Earwicker: the meant to be baffling chrismon trilithon sign ⋔, finally
called after some his hes hecitency Hec, which, moved contra-
watchwise, represents his title in sigla as the smaller Δ, fontly
called following a certain change of state of grace of nature alp
or delta, when single, stands for or tautologically stands beside
the consort: (though for that matter, since we have heard from
Cathay cyrcles how the hen is not mirely a tick or two after the
first fifth fourth of the second eighth twelfth — siangchang
hongkong sansheneul — but yirely the other and thirtieth of the
ninth from the twentieth, our own vulgar 432 and 1132 irre-
spectively, why not take the former for a village inn, the latter
for an upsidown bridge, a multiplication marking for crossroads
ahead, which you like pothook for the family gibbet, their old
fourwheedler for the bucker's field, a tea anyway for a tryst
someday, and his onesidemissing for an allblind alley leading to
an Irish plot in the Champ de Mors, not?) the steady monologuy
of the interiors; the pardonable confusion for which some blame
the cudgel and more blame the soot but unthanks to which
the pees with their caps awry are quite as often as not taken
for kews with their tails in their or are quite as often as not

119

taken for pews with their tails in their mouths, thence your pristopher polombos, hence our Kat Kresbyterians; the curt witty wotty dashes never quite just right at the trim trite truth letter; the sudden spluttered petulance of some capItalIsed mIddle; a word as cunningly hidden in its maze of confused drapery as a fieldmouse in a nest of coloured ribbons: that absurdly bullsfooted bee declaring with an even plainer dummpshow than does the mute commoner with us how hard a thing it is to mpe mporn a gentlerman: and look at this prepronominal *funferal*, engraved and retouched and edgewiped and puddenpadded, very like a whale's egg farced with pemmican, as were it sentenced to be nuzzled over a full trillion times for ever and a night till his noddle sink or swim by that ideal reader suffering from an ideal insomnia: all those red raddled obeli cayennepeppercast over the text, calling unnecessary attention to errors, omissions, repetitions and misalignments: that (probably local or personal) variant *maggers* for the more generally accepted *majesty* which is but a trifle and yet may quietly amuse: those superciliouslooking crisscrossed Greek ees awkwardlike perched there and here out of date like sick owls hawked back to Athens: and the geegees too, jesuistically formed at first but afterwards genuflected aggrily toewards the occident: the Ostrogothic kakography affected for certain phrases of Etruscan stabletalk and, in short, the learning betrayed at almost every line's end: the headstrength (at least eleven men of thirtytwo palfrycraft) revealed by a constant labour to make a ghimel pass through the eye of an iota: this, for instance, utterly unexpected sinistrogyric return to one peculiar sore point in the past; those throne open doubleyous (of an early muddy terranean origin whether man chooses to damn them agglutinatively loo — too — blue — face — ache or illvoodawpeehole or, kants koorts, topplefouls) seated with such floprightdown determination and reminding uus ineluctably of nature at her naturalest while that fretful fidget eff, the hornful digamma of your bornabarbar, rarely heard now save when falling from the unfashionable lipsus of some hetarosexual (used always in two boldfaced print types — one of them as wrongheaded as

his Claudian brother, is it worth while interrupting to say? —
throughout the papyrus as the revise mark) stalks all over the
page, broods ꓱ sensationseeking an idea, amid the verbiage,
gaunt, stands dejectedly in the diapered window margin, with
its basque of bayleaves all aflutter about its forksfrogs, paces
with a frown, jerking to and fro, flinging phrases here, there, or
returns inhibited, with some half-halted suggestion, Ŀ, dragging
its shoestring; the curious warning sign before our protoparent's
ipsissima verba (a very pure nondescript, by the way, sometimes
a palmtailed otter, more often the arbutus fruitflowerleaf of the
cainapple) which paleographers call *a leak in the thatch* or *the
Aranman ingperwhis through the hole of his hat*, indicating that the
words which follow may be taken in any order desired, hole of
Aran man the hat through the whispering his ho (here keen
again and begin again to make soundsense and sensesound kin
again); those haughtypitched disdotted aiches easily of the rariest
inasdroll as most of the jaywalking eyes we do plough into halve,
unconnected, principial, medial or final, always jims in the jam,
sahib, as pipless as threadworms: the innocent exhibitionism of
those frank yet capricious underlinings: that strange exotic serpentine, since so properly banished from our scripture, about as freak-
wing a wetterhand now as to see a righteaded ladywhite don a
corkhorse, which, in its invincible insolence ever longer more and
of more morosity, seems to uncoil spirally and swell lacertinelazily
before our eyes under pressure of the writer's hand; the ungainly
musicianlessness so painted in sculpting selfsounder ah ha as
blackartful as a *podatus* and dumbfounder oh ho oaproariose as
ten canons in skelterfugue: the studious omission of year number
and era name from the date, the one and only time when our
copyist seems at least to have grasped the beauty of restraint; the
lubricitous conjugation of the last with the first: the gipsy mating of a grand stylish gravedigging with secondbest buns (an in-
terpolation: these munchables occur only in the Bootherbrowth
family of MSS., Bb — Cod IV, Pap II, Brek XI, Lun III, Dinn
XVII, Sup XXX, Fullup M D C X C: the scholiast has hungrily
misheard a deadman's toller as a muffinbell): the four shortened

ampersands under which we can glypse at and feel for ourselves across all those rushyears the warm soft short pants of the quick-scribbler: the vocative lapse from which it begins and the accusative hole in which it ends itself; the aphasia of that heroic agony of recalling a once loved number leading slip by slipper to a general amnesia of misnomering one's own: next those ars, rrrr! those ars all bellical, the highpriest's hieroglyph of kettletom and oddsbones, wrasted redhandedly from our hallowed rubric prayer for truce with booty, *O'Remus pro Romulo,* and rudely from the fane's pinnacle tossèd down by porter to within an aim's ace of their quatrain of rubyjets among Those Who arse without the Temple nor since Roe's Distillery burn'd have quaff'd Night's firefill'd Cup But jig jog jug as Day the Dicebox Throws, whang, loyal six I lead, out wi'yer heart's bluid, blast ye, and there she's for you, sir, whang her, the fine ooman, rouge to her lobster locks, the rossy, whang, God and O'Mara has it with his ruddy old Villain Rufus, wait, whang, God and you're another he hasn't for there's my spoil five of spuds's trumps, whang, whack on his pigsking's Kisser for him, K.M. O'Mara where are you?; then (coming over to the left aisle corner down) the cruciform postscript from which three *basia* or shorter and smaller *oscula* have been overcarefully scraped away, plainly inspiring the tenebrous *Tunc* page of the Book of Kells (and then it need not be lost sight of that there are exactly three squads of candidates for the crucian rose awaiting their turn in the marginal panels of Columkiller, chugged in their three ballotboxes, then set apart for such hanging committees, where two was enough for anyone, starting with old Matthew himself, as he with great distinction said then just as since then people speaking have fallen into the custom, when speaking to a person, of saying two is company when the third person is the person darkly spoken of, and then that last labiolingual *basium* might be read as a *suavium* if whoever the embracer then was wrote with a tongue in his (or perhaps her) cheek as the case may have been then); and the fatal droopadwindle slope of the blamed scrawl, a sure sign of imperfectible moral blindness; the toomuchness, the fartoomanyness of all those fourlegged ems: and why spell dear god with a big thick dhee (why, O why, O why?): the cut and dry aks and wise form of the semifinal; and, eighteenthly or twentyfourthly, but at least, thank Maurice, lastly when all is zed and done, the penelopean patience of its last paraphe, a colophon of no fewer than seven hundred and thirtytwo strokes tailed by a leaping lasso — who thus at all this marvelling but will press on hotly to see the vaulting feminine libido of those interbranching ogham sex upandinsweeps sternly controlled and easily repersuaded by the uniform matteroffactness of a meandering male fist?

Duff-Muggli, who now may be quoted by very kind arrangement (his dectroscophonious photosensition under suprasonic light control may be logged for by our none too distant futures as soon astone values can be turned out from Chromophilomos, Limited at a millicentime the microamp), first called this kind of paddygoeasy partnership the ulykkhean or tetrachiric or quadrumane or ducks and drakes or debts and dishes perplex (v. *Some Forestallings over that Studium of Sexophonologistic Schizophrenesis*, vol. xxiv, pp. 2-555) after the wellinformed observation, made miles apart from the Master by Tung-Toyd (cf. *Later Frustrations amengst the Neomugglian Teachings abaft the Semiunconscience, passim*) that in the case of the littleknown periplic bestteller popularly associated with the names of the wretched mariner (trianforan deffwedoff our plumsucked pattern shapekeeper) a Punic admiralty report, *From MacPerson's Oshean Round By the Tides of Jason's Cruise*, had been cleverly capsized and saucily republished as a dodecanesian baedeker of the everytale-a-treat-in-itself variety which could hope satisfactorily to tickle me gander as game as your goose.

The unmistaken identity of the persons in the Tiberiast duplex came to light in the most devious of ways. The original document was in what is known as Hanno O'Nonhanno's unbrookable script, that is to say, it showed no signs of punctuation of any sort. Yet on holding the verso against a lit rush this new book of Morses responded most remarkably to the silent query of our world's oldest light and its recto let out the piquant fact that it was but pierced butnot punctured (in the university sense of the term) by numerous stabs and foliated gashes made by a pronged instrument. These paper wounds, four in type, were gradually and correctly understood to mean stop, please stop, do please stop, and O do please stop respectively, and following up their one true clue, the circumflexuous wall of a singleminded men's asylum, accentuated by bi tso fb rok engl a ssan dspl itch ina, — Yard inquiries pointed out ⟶ that they ad bîn "provoked" ay Λ fork, of à grave Brofèsor; àth é's Brèak — fast — table; ; acùtely profèššionally *piquéd*, to⹀introdùce a notion of time [ùpon à plane (?) sù ' ' fàç'e'] by pùnct! ingh oles (sic) in iSpace?! Deeply religious by nature and position, and warmly attached to Thee, and smearbread and better and Him and newlaidills, it was rightly suspected that such ire could not have been visited by him Brotfressor Prenderguest even underwittingly, upon the ancestral pneuma of one whom, with rheuma, he venerated shamelessly at least once a week at Cockspur Common as his apple in his eye and her first boys' best friend and, though plain English for a married lady misled heaps by the way, yet when some peerer or peeress detected that the fourleaved shamrock or quadrifoil jab was more recurrent wherever the script was clear and the term terse and that these two were the selfsame spots naturally selected for her perforations by Dame Partlet on her dungheap, thinkers all put grown in waterungspillfull Pratiland only and a playful fowl and musical me and not you in any case, two and two together, and, with a swarm of bisses honeyhunting after, a sigh for shyme (O, the pettybonny rouge!) separated modest mouths. So be it. And it was. The lettermaking of the explots of Fjorgn Camhelsson when he was in the Kvinnes country with Soldru's men. With acknowledgment of our fervour of the first instant he remains years most fainfully. For postscrapt see spoils. Though not yet had the sailor sipped that sup nor the humphar foamed to the fill. And fox and geese still kept the peace around *L'Auberge du Père Adam.*

Small need after that, old Jeromesolem, old Huffsnuff, old Andycox, old Olecasandrum, for quizzing your weekenders come to the R.Q. with: shoots off in a hiss, muddles up in a mussmass and his whole's a dismantled noondrunkard's son. Howbeit we heard not a son of sons to leave by him to oceanic society in his old man without a thing in his ignorance, Tulko MacHooley. And it was thus he was at every time, that son, and the other time, the day was in it and after the morrow Diremood is the name is on the writing chap of the psalter, the juxtajunctor of a dearmate and he passing out of one desire into its fellow. The daughters are after going and loojing for him, Torba's nicelookers of the fair neck. Wanted for millinary servance to olderly's person by the Totty Askinses. Formelly confounded with amother. Maybe growing a moustache, did you say, with an adorable look of amuzement? And uses noclass billiardhalls with an upandown ladder? Not Hans the Curier though had he had have only had some little laughings and some less of cheeks and were he not so warried by his bulb of persecussion he could have, ay, and would have, as true as Essex bridge. And not Gopheph go gossip, I declare to man! Noe! To all's much relief one's half hypothesis of that jabberjaw ape amok the showering jestnuts of Bruisanose was hotly dropped and his room taken up by that odious and still today insufficiently malestimated notesnatcher (kak, pfooi, bosh and fiety, much earny, Gus, poteen? Sez you!) Shem the Penman.

So?

Who do you no tonigh, lazy and gentleman?

The echo is where in the back of the wodes; callhim forth!

(Shaun Mac Irewick, briefdragger, for the concern of Messrs Jhon Jhamieson and Song, rated one hundrick and thin per storehundred on this nightly quisquiquock of the twelve apostrophes, set by Jockit Mic Ereweak. He misunderstruck and aim for am ollo of number three of them and left his free natural ripostes to four of them in their own fine artful disorder.)

1. What secondtonone myther rector and maximost bridgesmaker was the first to rise taller through his beanstale than the bluegum buaboababbaun or the giganteous Wellingtonia Sequoia; went nudiboots with trouters into a liffeyette when she was barely in her tricklies; was well known to claud a conciliation cap onto the esker of his hooth; sports a chainganger's albert solemenly over his hullender's epulence; thought he weighed a new ton when there felled his first lapapple; gave the heinousness of choice to everyknight betwixt yesterdicks and twomaries; had sevenal successivecoloured serebanmaids on the same big white drawringroam horthrug; is a Willbeforce to this hour at house as he was in heather; pumped the catholick wartrey and shocked the prodestung boyne; killed his own hungery self in anger as a young man; found fodder for five when allmarken rose goflooded; with Hirish tutores Cornish made easy; voucher

of rotables, toll of the road; bred manyheaded stepsons for one leapyourown taughter; is too funny for a fish and has too much outside for an insect; like a heptagon crystal emprisoms trues and fauss for us; is infinite swell in unfitting induments; once was he shovelled and once was he arsoned and once was he inundered and she hung him out billbailey; has a quadrant in his tile to tell Toler cad a'clog it is; offers chances to Long on but stands up to Legge before; found coal at the end of his harrow and moss-roses behind the seams; made a fort out of his postern and wrote F.E.R.T. on his buckler; is escapemaster-in-chief from all sorts of houdingplaces; if he outharrods against barkers, to the shool-bred he acts whiteley; was evacuated at the mere appearance of three germhuns and twice besieged by a sweep; from zoomor-phology to omnianimalism he is brooched by the spin of a coin; towers, an eddistoon amid the lampless, casting swannbeams on the deep; threatens thunder upon malefactors and sends whispers up fraufrau's froufrous; when Dook Hookbackcrook upsits his ass booseworthies jeer and junket but they boos him oos and baas his aas when he lukes like Hunkett Plunkett; by sosannsos and search a party on a lady of this city; business, reading news-paper, smoking cigar, arranging tumblers on table, eating meals, pleasure, etcetera, etcetera, pleasure, eating meals, arranging tum-blers on table, smoking cigar, reading newspaper, business; minerals, wash and brush up, local views, juju toffee, comic and birthdays cards; those were the days and he was their hero; pink sunset shower, red clay cloud, sorrow or Sahara, oxhide or Iren; arraigned and attainted, listed and lited, pleaded and proved; catches his check at banck of Indgangd and endurses his doom at chapel exit; brain of the franks, hand of the christian, tongue of the north; commands to dinner and calls the bluff; has a block at Morgen's and a hatache all the afternunch; plays gehamerat when he's ernst but misses mausey when he's lustyg; walked as far as the Head where he sat in state as the Rump; shows Early Eng-lish tracemarks and a marigold window with manigilt lights, a myrioscope, two remarkable piscines and three wellworthseeing ambries; arches all portcullised and his nave dates from dots; is a horologe unstoppable and the Benn of all bells; fuit, isst and herit and though he's mildewstaned he's mouldystoned; is a quercuss in the forest but plane member for Megalopolis; mountunmighty, faunonfleetfoot; plank in our platform, blank in our scouturn; hidal, in carucates he is enumerated, hold as an earl, he counts; shipshaped phrase of buglooking words with a form like the easing moments of a graminivorous; to our dooms brought he law, our manoirs he made his vill of; was an overgrind to the underground and acqueduced for fierythroats; sends boys in socks acoughawhooping when he lets farth his carbonoxside and silk stockings show her shapings when he looses hose on hers; stocks dry puder for the Ill people and pinkun's pellets for all the Pale; gave his mundyfoot to Miserius, her pinch to Anna Livia, that superfine pigtail to Cerisia Cerosia and quid rides to Titius, Caius and Sempronius; made the man who had no notion of shopkeepers feel he'd rather play the duke than play the gentleman; shot two queans and shook three caskles when he won his game of dwarfs; fumes inwards like a strombolist till he smokes at both ends; manmote, befier of him, womankind, pietad!; shows one white drift of snow among the gorsegrowth of his crown and a chaperon of repentance on that which shed gore; pause and quies, triple bill; went by metro for the polis and then hoved by; to the finders, hail! woa, you that seek!; whom fillth had plenished, dearth devoured; hock is leading, cocoa comes next, emery tries for the flag; can dance the O'Bruin's polerpasse at Noolahn to his own orchistruss accompaniment; took place before the international convention of catholic midwives and found stead before the congress for the study of endonational calamities; makes a delictuous *entrée* and finishes off the course between sweets and savouries; flouts for forecasts, flairs for finds and the fun of the fray on the fairground; cleared out three hundred sixty five idles to set up one all khalassal for henwives hoping to have males; the flawhoolagh, the grasping one, the kindler of paschal fire; forbids us our trespassers as we forgate him; the phoenix be his pyre, the cineres his sire!; piles big pelium on little ossas like the pilluls of hirculeads; has an eatupus complex

128

and a drinkthedregs kink; wurstmeats for chumps and cowcar-
lows for scullions; when he plies for our favour is very trolly
ours; two psychic espousals and three desertions; may be matter
of fact now but was futter of magd then; Cattermole Hill, ex-
mountain of flesh was reared up by stress and sank under strain;
tank it up, dank it up, tells the tailor to his tout; entoutcas for a
man, but bit a thimble for a maid; blimp, blump; a dud letter, a sing
a song a sylble; a byword, a sentence with surcease; while stands
his canyouseehim frails shall fall; was hatched at Cellbridge but
ejoculated abroad; as it gan in the biguinnengs so wound up in
a battle of Boss; Roderick, Roderick, Roderick, O, you've gone
the way of the Danes; variously catalogued, regularly regrouped;
a bushboys holoday, a quacker's mating, a wenches' sandbath;
the same homoheatherous checkinlossegg as when sollyeye airly
blew ye; real detonation but false report; spa mad but inn sane;
half emillian via bogus census but a no street hausmann when
allphannd; is the handiest of all andies and a most alleghant spot
to dump your hump; hands his secession to the new patricius but
plumps plebmatically for the bloody old centuries; eats with
doors open and ruts with gates closed; some dub him Rotshield
and more limn him Rockyfellow; shows he's fly to both demis-
fairs but thries to cover up his tracers; seven dovecotes cooclaim
to have been pigeonheim to this homer, Smerrnion, Rhoebok,
Kolonsreagh, Seapoint, Quayhowth, Ashtown, Ratheny; independent of the lordship of chamberlain, acknowledging the rule
of Rome; we saw thy farm at Useful Prine, Domhnall, Domhnall;
reeks like Illbelpaese and looks like Iceland's ear; lodged at quot
places, lived through tot reigns; takes a szumbath for his weekend
and a wassarnap for his refreskment; after a good bout at stool-
ball enjoys Giroflee Giroflaa; what Nevermore missed and
Colombo found; believes in everyman his own goaldkeeper and
in Africa for the fullblacks; the arc of his drive was forty full
and his stumps were pulled at eighty; boasts him to the thick-in-
thews the oldest creater in Aryania and looks down on the Suiss
family Collesons whom he calls *les nouvelles roches*; though his
heart, soul and spirit turn to pharaoph times, his love, faith and

hope stick to futuerism; light leglifters cense him souriantes from afore while boor browbenders curse him grommelants to his hindmost; between youlasses and yeladst glimse of Even; the Lug his peak has, the Luk his pile; drinks tharr and wodhar for his asama and eats the unparishable sow to styve off reglar rack; the beggars cloak them reclined about his paddystool, the whores winken him as they walk their side; on Christienmas at Advent Lodge, New Yealand, after a lenty illness the roeverand Mr Easterling of pentecostitis, no followers by bequest, fanfare all private; Gone Where Glory Waits Him (Ball, bulletist) but Not Here Yet (Maxwell, clark); comminxed under articles but phoenished a borgiess; from the vat on the bier through the burre in the dark to the buttle of the bawn; is A1 an the highest but Roh re his root; filled fanned of hackleberries whenas all was tuck and toss up for him as a yangster to fall fou of hockinbechers wherein he had gauged the use of raisin; ads aliments, das doles, raps rustics, tams turmoil; sas seed enough for a semination but sues skivvies on the sly; learned to speak from hand to mouth till he could talk earish with his eyes shut; hacked his way through hickheckhocks but hanged hishelp from there hereafters; rialtos, annesleyg, binn and balls to say nothing atolk of New Comyn; the gleam of the glow of the shine of the sun through the dearth of the dirth on the blush of the brick of the viled ville of Barnehulme has dust turned to brown; these dyed to tartan him, rueroot, dulse, bracken, teasel, fuller's ash, sundew and cress; long gunn but not for cotton; stood his sharp assault of famine but grew girther, girther and girther; he has twenty four or so cousins germinating in the United States of America and a namesake with an initial difference in the once kingdom of Poland; his first's a young rose and his second's French-Egyptian and his whole means a slump at Christie's; forth of his pierced part came the woman of his dreams, blood thicker then water last trade overseas; buyshop of Glintylook, eorl of Hoed; you and I are in him surrented by brwn bldns; Elin's flee polt pelhaps but Hwang Chang evelytime; he one was your of high-bigpipey boys but fancy him as smoking fags his at time of life; Mount of Mish, Mell of Moy; had two cardinal ventures and three capitol sinks; has a peep in his pocketbook and a packet-boat in his keep; B.V.H., B.L.G., P.P.M., T.D.S., V.B.D., T.C.H., L.O.N.; is Breakfates, Lunger, Diener and Souper; as the streets were paved with cold he felt his topperairy; taught himself skating and learned how to fall; distinctly dirty but rather a dear; hoveth chieftains evrywehr, with morder; Ostman Effendi, Serge Paddishaw; baases two mmany, outpriams al' his parisites; first of the fenians, *roi des fainéants*; his Tiara of scones was held unfillable till one Liam Fail felled him in Westmunster; was struck out of his sittem when he rowed saulely to demask us and to our appauling predicament brought as plagues from Buddapest; put a matchhead on an aspenstalk and set the living a fire; speared the rod and spoiled the lightning; married with cakes and repunked with pleasure; till he was buried howhappy was he and he made the welkins ring with *Up Micawber!*; god at the top of the staircase, carrion on the mat of straw; the false hood of a spindler web chokes the cavemouth of his unsightliness but the nestlings that liven his leafscreen sing him a lover of arbuties; we strike hands over his bloodied warsheet but we are pledged entirely to his green mantle; our friend vikelegal, our swaran foi; under the four stones by his streams who vanished the wassailbowl at the joy of shells; Mora and Lora had a hill of a high time looking down on his confusion till firm look in readiness, forward spear and the windfoot of curach strewed the lakemist of Lego over the last of his fields; we darkened for you, faulterer, in the year of mourning but we'll fidhil to the dimtwinklers when the streamy morvenlight calls up the sunbeam; his striped pantaloons, his rather strange walk; *hereditatis columna erecta, hagion chiton eraphon*; nods a nap for the nonce but crows cheerio when they get ecumenical; is a simultaneous equator of elimbinated integras when three upon one is by inspection improper; has the most conical hodpiece of confusianist heronim and that chuchuffuous chinchin of his is like a footsey kungoloo around Taishantyland; he's as globeful as a gasometer of lithium and luridity and he was thrice ten anular years before he wallowed round Raggiant Circos; the cabalstone at the coping of his cavin is a canine constant but only an amirican could apparoxemete the apeupresiosity of his atlast's alongement; sticklered rights and lefts at Baddersdown in his hunt for the boar trwth but made his end with the modareds that came at him in Camlenstrete; a hunnibal in exhaustive conflict, an otho to return; burning body to aiger air on melting mountain in wooing wave; we go into him sleepy children, we come out of him strucklers for life; he divested to save from the Mrs Drownings their rival queens while Grimshaw, Bragshaw and Renshaw made off with his storen clothes; taxed and rated, licensed and ranted; his threefaced stonehead was found on a whitehorse hill and the print of his costellous feet is seen in the goat's grasscircle; pull the blind, toll the deaf and call dumb, lame and halty; Miraculone, Monstrucceleen; led the upplaws at the Creation and hissed a snake charmer off her stays; hounded become haunter, hunter become fox; harrier, marrier, terrier, tav; Olaph the Oxman, Thorker the Tourable; you feel he is Vespasian yet you think of him as Aurelius; whugamore, tradertory, socianist, commoniser; made a summer assaült on our shores and begiddy got his sands full; first he shot down Raglan Road and then he tore up Marlborough Place; Cromlechheight and Crommalhill were his farfamed feetrests when our lurch as lout let free into the Lubar heloved; mareschalled his wardmotes and delimited the main; netted before nibbling, can scarce turn a scale but, grossed after meals, weighs a town in himself; Banba prayed for his conversion, Beurla missed that grand old voice; a Colossus among cabbages, the Melarancitrone of fruits; larger than life, doughtier than death; Gran Turco, orege forment; lachsembulger, leperlean; the sparkle of his genial fancy, the depth of his calm sagacity, the clearness of his spotless honour, the flow of his boundless benevolence; our family furbear, our tribal tarnpike; quary was he invincibled and cur was he burked; partitioned Irskaholm, united Irishmen; he took a svig at his own methyr but she tested a bit gorky and as for the salmon he was coming up in him all life long; comm, eilerdich, hecklebury and sawyer thee, warden;

silent as the bee in honey, stark as the breath on hauwck, Costello, Kinsella, Mahony, Moran, though you rope Amrique your home ruler is Dan; figure right, he is hoisted by the scurve of his shaggy neck, figure left, he is rationed in isobaric patties among the crew; one asks was he poisoned, one thinks how much did he leave; ex-gardener (Riesengebirger), fitted up with planturous existencies would make Roseoogreedy (mite's) little hose; taut sheets and scuppers awash but the oil silk mack Liebsterpet micks his aquascutum; the enjoyment he took in kay women, the employment he gave to gee men; sponsor to a squad of piercers, ally to a host of rawlies; against lightning, explosion, fire, earthquake, flood, whirlwind, burglary, third party, rot, loss of cash, loss of credit, impact of vehicles; can rant as grave as oxtail soup and chat as gay as a porto flippant; is unhesitent in his unionism and yet a pigotted nationalist; Sylviacola is shy of him, Matrosenhosens nose the joke; shows the sinews of peace in his chest-o-wars; fiefeofhome, ninehundred and thirtunine years of copyhold; is aldays open for polemypolity's sake when he's not suntimes closed for the love of Janus; sucks life's eleaxir from the pettipickles of the Jewess and ruoulls in sulks if any popeling runs down the Huguenots; Boomaport, Walleslee, Ubermeerschall Blowcher and Supercharger, Monsieur Ducrow, Mister Mudson, master gardiner; to one he's just paunch and judex, to another full of beans and brehons; hallucination, cauchman, ectoplasm; passed for baabaa blacksheep till he grew white woo woo woolly; was drummatoysed by Mac Milligan's daughter and put to music by one shoebard; all fitzpatricks in his emirate remember him, the boys of wetford hail him babu; indanified himself with boro tribute and was schenkt publicly to brigstoll; was given the light in drey orchafts and entumuled in threeplexes; his likeness is in Terrecuite and he giveth rest to the rainbowed; lebriety, frothearnity and quality; his reverse makes a virtue of necessity while his obverse mars a mother by invention; beskilk his gunwale and he's the second imperial, untie points, unhook tenters and he's lath and plaster; calls upon Allthing when he fails to appeal to Eachovos; basidens, ardree, kongsemma, rexregulorum; stood into Dee mouth, then backed broadside on Baulacleeva; either eldorado or ultimate thole; a kraal of fou feud fires, a crawl of five pubs; laid out lashings of laveries to hunt down his family ancestors and then pled double trouble or quick quits to hush the buckers up; threw pebblets for luck over one sodden shoulder and dragooned peoplades armed to their teeth; pept as Gaudio Gambrinus, grim as Potter the Grave; ace of arts, deuce of damimonds, trouble of clubs, fear of spates; cumbrum, cumbrum, twiniceynurseys fore a drum but tre to uno tips the scale; reeled the titleroll opposite a brace of girdles in Silver on the Screen but was sequenced from the set as Crookback by the even more titulars, Rick, Dave and Barry; he can get on as early as the twentysecond of Mars but occasionally he doesn't come off before Virgintiquinque Germinal; his Indian name is Hapapoosiesobjibway and his number in arithmosophy is the stars of the plough; took weapon in the province of the pike and let fling his line on Eelwick; moves in vicous cicles yet remews the same; the drain rats bless his offals while the park birds curse his floodlights; Portobello, Equadocta, Therecocta, Percorello; he pours into the softclad shellborn the hard cash earned in Watling Street; his birth proved accidental shows his death its grave mistake; brought us giant ivy from the land of younkers and bewitthered Apostolopolos with the gale of his gall; while satisfied that soft youthful bright matchless girls should bosom into fine silkclad joyous blooming young women is not so pleased that heavy swearsome strongsmelling irregularshaped men should blottout active handsome wellformed frankeyed boys; herald hairyfair, alloaf the wheat; husband your aunt and endow your nepos; hearken but hush it, screen him and see; time is, an archbishopric, time was, a tradesmen's entrance; beckburn brooked with wath, scale scarred by scow; his rainfall is a couple of kneehighs while his meanst grass temperature marked three in the shade; is the meltingpoint of snow and the bubblingplace of alcohol; has a tussle with the trulls and then does himself justice; hinted at in the eschatological chapters of Humphrey's *Justesse of the Jaypees* and hunted for by Theban recensors who sniff there's something behind the *Bug of the Deaf*; the king was in his cornerwall melking mark so murry, the queen was steep in armbour feeling fain and furry, the mayds was midst the haw-thorns shoeing up their hose, out pimps the back guards (pomp!) and pump gun they goes; to all his foretellers he reared a stone and for all his comethers he planted a tree; forty acres, sixty miles, white stripe, red stripe, washes his fleet in annacrwatter; whou missed a porter so whot shall he do for he wanted to sit for Pimploco but they've caught him to stand for Sue?; Dutchlord, Dutchlord, overawes us; Headmound, king and martyr, dunstung in the Yeast, Pitre-le-Pore-in Petrin, Barth-the-Grete-by-the-Exchange; he hestens towards dames troth and wedding hand like the prince of Orange and Nassau while he has trinity left behind him like Bowlbeggar Bill-the-Bustonly; brow of a hazel-wood, poo! in the dark; changes blowicks into bullocks and a well of Artesia into a bird of Arabia; the handwriting on his facewall, the cryptoconchoidsiphonostomata in his exprussians; his birthspot lies beyond the herospont and his burialplot in the pleasant little field; is the yldist kiosk on the pleninsula and the unguest hostel in Saint Scholarland; walked many hundreds and many score miles of streets and lit thousands in one nightlights in hectares of windows; his great wide cloak lies on fifteen acres and his little white horse decks by dozens our doors; O sorrow the sail and woe the rudder that were set for Mairie Quai!; his suns the huns, his dartars the tartars, are plenty here today; who repulsed from his burst the bombolts of Ostenton and falchioned each flash downsaduck in the deep; apersonal problem, a loca-tive enigma; upright one, vehicule of arcanisation in the field, lying chap, floodsupplier of celiculation through ebblanes; a part of the whole as a port for a whale; Dear Hewitt Castello, Equerry, were daylighted with our outing and are looking backwards to unearly summers, from Rhoda Dundrums; is above the seedfruit level and outside the leguminiferous zone; when older links lock older hearts then he'll resemble she; can be built with glue and clippings, scrawled or voided on a buttress; the night express sings his story, the song of sparrownotes on his stave of wires; he crawls with lice, he swarms with saggarts; is as quiet as a mursque but can be as noisy as a sonogog; was Dilmun when his date was palmy and Mudlin when his nut was cracked; suck up the sease, lep laud at ease, one lip on his lap and one cushlin his crease; his porter has a mighty grasp and his baxters the boon of broadwhite; as far as wind dries and rain eats and sun turns and water bounds he is exalted and depressed, assembled and asundered; go away, we are deluded, come back, we are disghosted; bored the Ostrov, leapt the Inferus, swam the Mabbul and flure the Moyle; like fat, like fatlike tallow, of greasefulness, yea of dripping greasefulness; did not say to the old, old, did not say to the scorbutic, scorbutic; he has founded a house, Uru, a house he has founded to which he has assigned its fate; bears a raaven geulant on a fjeld duiv; ruz the halo off his varlet when he appeared to his shecook as Haycock, Emmet, Boaro, Toaro, Osterich, Mangy and Skunk; pressed the beer of aled age out of the nettles of rashness; put a roof on the lodge for Hymn and a coq in his pot pro homo; was dapifer then pancircensor then hortifex magnus; the topes that tippled on him, the types that toppled off him; still starts our hares yet gates our goat; pocketbook packetboat, gapman gunrun; the light of other days, dire dreary darkness; our awful dad, Timour of Tortur; puzzling, startling, shocking, nay, perturbing; went puffing from king's brugh to new customs, doffing the gibbous off him to every breach of all size; with Pa's new heft and Papa's new helve he's Papapa's old cutlass Papapapa left us; when youngheaded oldshouldered and middlishneck aged about; caller herring everydaily, turgid tarpon overnight; see Loryon the comaleon that changed endocrine history by loeven his loaf with forty bannucks; she drove him dafe till he driv her blind up; the pigeons doves be perchin all over him one day on Baslesbridge and the ravens duv be pitchin their dark nets after him the next night behind Koenigstein's Arbour; tronf of the rep, comf of the priv, prosp of the pub; his headwood it's ideal if his feet are bally clay; he crashed in the hollow of the park, trees down, as he soared in the vaguum of the phoenix, stones up; looks like a moultain boultter and sounds like a rude word; the mountaen view, some lumin pale round a lamp of succar in boinyn water; three shots a puddy at up blup saddle; made up to Miss MacCormack Ni Lacarthy who made off with Darly Dermod, swank and swarthy; once diamond cut garnet now dammat cuts groany; you might find him at the Florence but watch our for him in Wynn's Hotel; theer's his bow and wheer's his leaker and heer lays his bequiet hearse, deep; Swed Albiony, likeliest villain of the place; Hennery Canterel — Cockran, eggotisters, limitated; we take our tays and frees our fleas round sadurn's mounted foot; built the Lund's kirk and destroyed the church's land; who guesse his title grabs his deeds; fletch and prities, fash and chaps; artful Juke of Wilysly; Hugglebelly's Funniral; Kukkuk Kallikak; heard in camera and excruciated; boon when with benches billeted, bann if buckshot-backshattered; heavengendered, chaosfoedted, earthborn; his father presumptively ploughed it deep on overtime and his mother as all evince must have travailled her fair share; a foot-prinse on the Megacene, hetman unwhorsed by Searingsand; honorary captain of the extemporised fire brigade, reported to be friendly with the police; the door is still open; the old stock collar is coming back; not forgetting the time you laughed at Elder Charterhouse's duckwhite pants and the way you said the whole township can see his hairy legs; by stealth of a kersse her aulburntress abaft his nape she hung; when his kettle became a hearthsculdus our thorstyites set their lymphyamphyre; his year-letter concocted by masterhands of assays, his hallmark imposed by the standard of wrought plate; a pair of pectorals and a triple-screen to get a wind up; lights his pipe with a rosin tree and hires a towhorse to haul his shoes; cures slavey's scurvy, breaks barons boils; called to sell polosh and was found later in a bed-room; has his seat of justice, his house of mercy, his corn o'copious and his stacks a'rye; prospector, he had a rooksacht, retrospector, he holds the holpenstake; won the freedom of new yoke for the minds of jugoslaves; acts active, peddles in passivism and is a gorgon of selfridgeousness; pours a laughsworth of his illformation over a larmsworth of salt; half heard the single maiden speech La Belle spun to her Grand Mount and wholed a lifetime by his ain fireside, wondering was it hebrew set to himmeltones or the quicksilversong of qwaternions; his troubles may be over but his doubles have still to come; the lobster pot that crabbed our keel, the garden pet that spoiled our squeezed peas; he stands in a lovely park, sea is not far, importune towns of X, Y and Z are easily over reached; is an excrescence to civilised humanity and but a wart on Europe; wanamade singsigns to soundsense an yit he wanna git all his flesch nuemaid motts truly prural and plusible; has excisively large rings and is uncustomarily perfumed; lusteth ath he listeth the cleah whithpeh of a themise; is a prince of the fingallian in a hiberniad of hoolies; has a hodge to wherry him and a frenchy to curry him and a brabanson for his beeter and a fritz at his switch; was waylaid of a parker and beschotten by a buckeley; kicks lintils when he's cuppy and casts Jacob's arroroots, dime after dime, to poor waifstrays on the perish; reads the charms of H. C. Endersen all the weaks of his evenin and the crimes of Ivaun the Taurrible every strongday morn; soaps you soft to your face and slaps himself when he's badend; owns the bulgiest bungbarrel that ever was tiptapped in the privace of the Mullingar Inn; was born with a nuasilver tongue in his mouth and went round the coast of Iron with his lift hand to the scene; raised but two fingers and yet smelt it would day; for whom it is easier to found a see in Ebblannah than for I or you to find a dubbeltye in Dampsterdamp; to live with whom is a lifemayor and to know whom a liberal education; was dipped in Hoily Olives and chrysmed in Scent Otooles; hears cricket on the earth but annoys the life out of predikants; still turns the durc's ear of Darius to the now thoroughly infurioted one of God; made Man with juts that jerk and minted money mong maney; likes a six acup pudding when he's come whome sweetwhome; has come through all the eras of livsadventure from moonshine and shampaying down to clouts and pottled porter; woollem the farsed, hahnreich the althe, charge the sackend, writchad the thord; if a mandrake shricked to convultures at last surviving his birth the weibduck will wail bitternly over the rotter's resurrection; loses weight in the moon night but girds girder by the sundawn; with one touch

138

of nature set a veiled world agrin and went within a sheet of tissuepaper of the option of three gaols; who could see at one blick a saumon taken with a lance, hunters pursuing a doe, a swallowship in full sail, a whyterobe lifting a host; faced flappery like old King Cnut and turned his back like Cincinnatus; is a farfar and morefar and a hoar father Nakedbucker in villas old as new; squats aquart and cracks aquaint when it's flaggin in town and on haven; blows whiskery around his summit but stehts stout upon his footles; stutters fore he falls and goes mad entirely when he's waked; is Timb to the pearly morn and Tomb to the mourning night; and an he had the best bunbaked bricks in bould Babylon for his pitching plays he'd be lost for the want of his wan wubblin wall?

Answer: Finn MacCool!

2. Does your mutter know your mike?

Answer: When I turn meoptics, from suchurban prospects, 'tis my filial's bosom, doth behold with pride, that pontificator, and circumvallator, with his dam night garrulous, slipt by his side. Ann alive, the lisp of her, 'twould grig mountains whisper her, and the bergs of Iceland melt in waves of fire, and her spoon-me-spondees, and her dirckle-me-ondenees, make the Rageous Ossean, kneel and quaff a lyre! If Dann's dane, Ann's dirty, if he's plane she's purty, if he's fane, she's flirty, with her auburnt streams, and her coy cajoleries, and her dabblin drolleries, for to rouse his rudderup, or to drench his dreams. If hot Hammurabi, or cowld Clesiastes, could espy her pranklings, they'd burst bounds agin, and renounce their ruings, and denounce their doings, for river and iver, and a night. Amin!

3. Which title is the true-to-type motto-in-lieu for that Tick for Teac thatchment painted witt wheth one darkness, where asnake is under clover and birds aprowl are in the rookeries and a magda went to monkishouse and a riverpaard was spotted, which is not Whichcroft Whorort not Ousterholm Dreyschluss not Haraldsby, grocer, not Vatandcan, vintner, not Houseboat and Hive not Knox-atta-Belle not O'Faynix Coalprince not Wohn Squarr Roomyeck not Ebblawn Downes not Le Decer

Le Mieux not Benjamin's Lea not Tholomew's Whaddingtun gnot Antwarp gnat Musca not Corry's not Weir's not the Arch not The Smug not The Dotch House not The Uval nothing Grand nothing Splendid (Grahot or Spletel) nayther *Erat Est Erit* noor *Non michi sed luciphro?*

Answer: Thine obesity, O civilian, hits the felicitude of our orb!

4. What Irish capitol city (a dea o dea!) of two syllables and six letters, with a deltic origin and a nuinous end, (ah dust oh dust!) can boost of having *a*) the most extensive public park in the world, *b*) the most expensive brewing industry in the world, *c*) the most expansive peopling thoroughfare in the world, *d*) the most phillohippuc theobibbous paùpulation in the world: and harmonise your abecedeed responses?

Answer: *a*) Delfas. And when ye'll hear the gould hommers of my heart, my floxy loss, bingbanging again the ribs of yer resistance and the tenderbolts of my rivets working to your destraction ye'll be sheverin wi' all yer dinful sobs when *we'll* go riding acope-acurly, you with yer orange garland and me with my conny cordial, down the greaseways of rollicking into the waters of wetted life. *b*) Dorhqk. And sure where can you have such good old chimes anywhere, and *leave* you, as on the Mash and how'tis I would be engaging you with my plovery soft accents and descanting upover the scene beunder me of your loose vines in their hairafall with them two loving loofs braceleting the slims of your ankles and your mouth's flower rose and sinking ofter the soapstone of silvry speech. *c*) Nublid. Isha, why wouldn't we be happy, avourneen, on the mills'money he'll soon be leaving you as soon as I've my own owned brooklined Georgian mansion's lawn to recruit upon by Doctor Cheek's special orders and my copper's panful of soybeans and Irish in my east hand and a James's Gate in my west, after all the errears and erroriboose of combarative embottled history, and your goodself churning over the newleaved butter (*more* power to you), the choicest and the cheapest from Atlanta to Oconee, while I'll be drowsing in the gaarden. *d*) Dalway. I hooked my thoroughgoing trotty the first down Spanish Place, Mayo I make, Tuam I take, Sligo's sleek but Galway's grace. Holy eel and Sainted Salmon, chucking chub and ducking dace, Rodiron's not *your* aequal! says she, leppin half the lane. *abcd*) A bell a bell on Shalldoll Steepbell, ond be'll go massplon pristmoss speople, Shand praise gon ness our fayst moan *neople*, our prame *Shandeepen*, pay name muy *feepence*, moy nay non *Aequalllllll!*

5. Whad slags of a loughladd would retten smuttyflesks, empt-out old mans, melk vitious geit, scareoff jackinjills fra tiddle anding, smoothpick waste papish pastures, insides man outsiders angell, sprink dirted water around village, newses, tobaggon and sweeds, plain general kept, louden on the kirkpeal, foottreats given to malafides, outshriek hyelp hyelp nor his hair efter buggelawrs, might underhold three barnets, putzpolish crotty bottes, nightcoover all fireglims, serve's time till baass, grindstone his kniveses, fullest boarded, lewd man of the method of godliness, perchance he nieows and thans sits in the spoorwaggen, X.W.C.A. on Z.W.C.U., Doorsteps, Limited, or Baywindaws Bros swobber preferred. Walther Clausetter's and Sons with the H. E. Chimneys' Company to not skreve, will, on advices, be bacon or stable hand, must begripe fullstandingly irers' langurge, jublander or northquain bigger prefurred, all duties, kine rights, family fewd, outings fived, may get earnst, no get combitsch, profusional drinklords to please obstain, he is fatherlow soundigged inmoodmined pershoon but aleconnerman, nay, *that* must he isn't?

Answer: Pore ole Joe!

6. What means the saloon slogan Summon In The Housesweep Dinah?

Answer: Tok. Galory bit of the sales of Cloth nowand I have to beeswax the bringing in all the claub of the porks to us how I thawght I knew his stain on the flower if me ask and can could speak and he called by me midden name Tik. I am your honey honeysugger phwhtphwht tha Bay and who bruk the dandleass and who seen the blackcullen jam for Tomorrha's big pickneck I hope it'll pour prais the Climate of all Ireland I heard the grackles and I skimming the crock on all your sangwidges fippence per leg per drake. Tuk. And who eight the last of the goosebellies that was mowlding from measlest years and who leff that there and who put that here and who let the kilkenny stale the chump. Tek. And whowasit youwasit propped the pot in the yard and whatinthe nameofsen lukeareyou rubbinthe sideofthe flureofthe lobbywith. *Shite!* will you have a plateful? Tak.

7. Who are those component partners of our societate, the doorboy, the cleaner, the sojer, the crook, the squeezer, the lounger, the curman, the tourabout, the mussroomsniffer, the bleakablue tramp, the funpowtherplother, the christymansboxer, from their prés salés and Donnybrook prater and Roebuck's campos and the Ager Arountown and Crumglen's grassy but Kimmage's champ and Ashtown fields and Cabra fields and Finglas fields and Santry fields and the feels of Raheny and their fails and Baldoygle to them who are latecomers all the year's round by anticipation, are the porters of the passions in virtue of retroratiocination, and, contributting their conflingent controversies of differentiation, unify their voxes in a vote of vaticination, who crunch the crusts of comfort due to depredation, drain the mead for misery to incur intoxication, condone every evil by practical justification and condam any good to its own gratification, who are ruled, roped, duped and driven by those numen daimons, the feekeepers at their laws, nightly consternation, fortnightly fornication, monthly miserecordation and omniannual recreation, doyles when they deliberate but sullivans when they are swordsed, Matey, Teddy, Simon, Jorn, Pedher, Andy, Barty, Philly, Jamesy Mor and Tom, Matt and Jakes Mac Carty?

Answer: The Morphios!

8. And how war yore maggies?

Answer: They war loving, they love laughing, they laugh weeping, they weep smelling, they smell smiling, they smile hating, they hate thinking, they think feeling, they feel tempting, they tempt daring, they dare waiting, they wait taking, they take thanking, they thank seeking, as born for lorn in lore of love to live and wive by wile and rile by rule of ruse 'reathed rose and hose hol'd home, yeth cometh elope year, coach and four, Sweet Peck-at-my-Heart picks one man more.

9. Now, to be on anew and basking again in the panaroma of all flores of speech, if a human being duly fatigued by his dayety in the sooty, having plenxty off time on his gouty hands and vacants of space at his sleepish feet and as hapless behind the dreams of accuracy as any camelot prince of dinmurk, were at this auctual futule preteriting unstant, in the states of suspensive exanimation, accorded, throughout the eye of a noodle, with an earsighted view of old hopeinhaven with all the ingredient and egregiunt whights and ways to which in the curse of his persistence the course of his tory will had been having recourses, the reverberration of knotcracking awes, the reconjungation of nodebinding ayes, the redissolusingness of mindmouldered ease and the thereby hang of the Hoel of it, could such a none, whiles even led comesilencers to comeliewithhers and till intempestuous Nox should catch the gallicry and spot lucan's dawn, byhold at ones what is main and why tis twain, how one once meet melts in tother wants poignings, the sap rising, the foles falling, the nimb now nihilant round the girlyhead so becoming, the wrestless in the womb, all the rivals to allsea, shakeagain, O disaster! shakealose, Ah how starring! but Heng's got a bit of Horsa's nose and Jeff's got the signs of Ham round his mouth and the beau that spun beautiful pales as it palls, what roserude and oragious grows gelb and greem, blue out the ind of it! Violet's dyed! then *what* would that fargazer seem to seemself to seem seeming of, dimm it all?

Answer: A collideorscape!

10. What bitter's love but yurning, what' sour lovemutch but a bref burning till shee that drawes dothe smoake retourne?

Answer: I know, pepette, of course, dear, but listen, precious! Thanks, pette, those are lovely, pitounette, delicious! But mind the wind, sweet! What exquisite hands you have, you angiol, if you didn't gnaw your nails, isn't it a wonder you're not achamed of me, you pig, you perfect little pigaleen! I'll nudge you in a minute! I bet you use her best Perisian smear off her vanity table to make them look so rosetop glowstop nostop. I know her. Slight me, would she? For every got I care! Three creamings a day, the first during her shower and wipe off with tissue. Then after cleanup and of course before retiring. Beme shawl, when I think of that espos of a Clancarbry, the foodbrawler, of the sociationist party with hiss blackleaded chest, hello, Prendregast! that you, Innkipper, and all his fourteen other fullback maulers or hurling stars or whatever the dagos they are, baiting at my Lord Ornery's, just becups they won the egg and spoon there so ovally provencial at Balldole. My Eilish assent he seed makes his admiracion. He is seeking an opening and means to be first with me as his belle alliance. Andoo musnoo play zeloso! Soso do todas. Such is Spanish. Stoop alittle closer, fealse! Delightsome simply! Like Jolio and Romeune. I haven't fell so turkish for ages and ages! Mine's me of squisious, the chocolate with a soul. Extraordinary! Why, what are they all, the mucky lot of them only? Sht! I wouldn't pay three hairpins for them. Peppt! That's rights, hold it steady! Leg me pull. Pu! Come big to Iran. Poo! What are you nudging for? No, I just thought you were. Listen, loviest! Of course it was *too* kind of you, miser, to remember my sighs in shockings, my often expressed wish when you were wandering about my trousseaurs and before I forget it don't forget, in your extensions to my personality, when knotting my remembrancetie, shoeweek will be trotting back with red heels at the end of the moon but look what the fool bought cabbage head and, as I shall answer to gracious heaven, I'll always in always remind of snappy new girters, me being always the one for charms with my very best in proud and gloving even if he was to be vermillion miles my youth to live on, the rubberend Mr Polkingtone, the quonian fleshmonger who Mother Browne solicited me for unlawful converse with, with her mug of October (a pots on it!), creaking around on his old shanksaxle like a crosty old cornquake. Airman, waterwag, terrier, blazer! I'm fine, thanks ever! Ha! O mind you poo tickly. Sall I puhim in momou. Mummum. Funny spot to have a fingey! I'm terribly sorry, I swear to you I am! May you never see me in my birthday pelts seenso tutu and that her blanches mainges may rot leprous off her whatever winking maggis I'll bet by your cut you go fleurting after with all the glass on her and the jumps in her stomewhere! Haha! I suspected she was! Sink her! May they fire her for a barren ewe! So she says: Tay for thee? Well, I saith: Angst so mush: and desired she might not take it amiss if I esteemed her but an odd. If I did ate toughturf I'm not a mishy-missy. Of course I know, pettest, you're so learningful and considerate in yourself, so friend of vegetables, you long cold cat you! Please by acquiester to meek my acquointance! Codling, snakelet, iciclist! My diaper has more life to it! Who drowned you in drears, man, or are you pillale with ink? Did a weep get past the gates of your pride? My tread on the clover, sweetness? Yes, the buttercups told me, hug me, damn it all, and I'll kiss you back to life, my peachest. I mean to make you suffer, meddlar, and I don't care this fig for contempt of courting. That I chid you, sweet sir? You know I'm tender by my eye. Can't you read by dazzling ones through me true? Bite my laughters, drink my tears. Pore into me, volumes, spell me stark and spill me swooning. I just don't care what my thwarters think. Transname me loveliness, now and here me for all times! I'd risk a policeman passing by, Magrath or even that beggar of a boots at the Post. The flame? O, pardone! That was what? Ah, did you speak, stuffstuff? More poestries from Chickspeer's with gleechoreal music or a jaculation from the garden of the soul. Of I be leib in the immoralities? O, you mean the strangle for love and the sowiveall of the prettiest? Yep, we open hap coseries in the home. And once upon a week I improve on myself I'm so keen on that New Free Woman with novel inside. I'm always as tickled as can be over Man in a Surplus by the Lady who Pays the Rates. But I'm as pie as is possible. Let's root out Brimstoker and give him the thrall of our lives. It's Dracula's nightout. For creepsake don't make a flush! Draw the shades, curfe you, and I'll beat any sonnamonk to love. Holy bug, how my highness would jump to make you flame your halve a ban-nan in two when I'd run my burning torchlight through (to adore

145

me there and then cease to be? Whatever for, blossoms?) Your hairmejig if you had one. If I am laughing with you? No, lovingest, I'm not so dying to take my rise out of you, adored. Not in the very least. True as God made my Mamaw hiplength modesty coatmawther! It's only because the rison is I'm only any girl, you lovely fellow of my dreams, and because old somebooby is not a roundabout, my trysting of the tulipies, like that puff pape bucking Daveran assoiling us behinds. What a nerve! He thinks that's what the vesprey's for. How vain's that hope in cleric's heart Who still pursues th'adult' rous art, Cocksure that rusty gown of his Will make fair Sue forget his phiz! Tame Schwipps. Blessed Marguerite bosses, I hope they threw away the mould or else we'll have Ballshossers and Sourdamapplers with their medical assassiations all over the place. But hold hard till I've got my latchkey vote and I'll teach him when to wear what woman callours. On account of the gloss of the gleison Hasaboobrawbees isabeaubel. And because, you pluckless lanka-loot, I hate the very thought of the thought of you and because, dearling, of course, adorest, I was always meant for an engin-dear from the French college, to be musband, *nomme d'engien*, when we do and contract with encho tencho solver when you are married to reading and writing which pleasebusiness now won't be long for he's so loopy on me and I'm so leapy like since the day he carried me from the boat, my saviored of eroes, to the beach and I left on his shoulder one fair hair to guide hand and mind to its softness. Ever so sorry! I beg your pardon, I was listening to every treasuried word I said fell from my dear mot's tongue otherwise how could I see what you were thinking of our granny? Only I wondered if I threw out my shaving water. Anyway, here's my arm, pulletneck. Gracefully yours. Move your mouth towards minth, more, preciousest, more on more! To please me, treasure. Don't be a, I'm not going to! Sh! nothing! A cricri somewhere! Buybuy! I'm fly! Hear, pippy, under the limes. You know bigtree are all against gravstone. They hisshis-tenency. Garnd ond mand! So chip chirp chirrup, cigolo, for the lug of Migo! The little passdoor, I go you before, so, and you're

146

at my apron stage. Shy is him, dovey? Musforget there's an audience. I have been lost, angel. Cuddle, ye divil ye! It's our toot-a-toot. Hearhere! Sensation! Let them, their whole four courtships! Let them, Bigbawl and his boosers' eleven makes twelve territorials. The Old Sot's Hole that wants wide streets to commission their noisense in, at the Mitchells *v*. Nicholls. *Aves Selvae Acquae Valles*! And my waiting twenty classbirds, sitting on their stiles! Let me finger their eurhythmytic. And you'll see if I'm selfthought. They're all of them out to please. Wait! In the name of. And all the holly. And some the mistle and it Saint Yves. Hoost! Ahem! There's Ada, Bett, Celia, Delia, Ena, Fretta, Gilda, Hilda, Ita, Jess, Katty, Lou, (they make me cough as sure as I read them) Mina, Nippa, Opsy, Poll, Queeniee, Ruth, Saucy, Trix, Una, Vela, Wanda, Xenia, Yva, Zulma, Phoebe, Thelma. And Mee! The reformatory boys is goaling in for the church so we've all comefeast like the groupsuppers and caught lipsolution from Anty Pravidance under penancies for myrtle sins. When their bride was married all my belles began ti ting. A ring a ring a rosaring! Then everyone will hear of it. Whoses wishes is the farther to my thoughts. But I'll plant them a poser for their nomanclatter. When they're out with the daynurse doing Chaperon Mall. Bright pigeons all over the whirrld will fly with my mistletoe message round their loveribboned necks and a crumb of my cake for each chasta dieva. We keeps all and sundry papers. In th' amourlight, O my darling! No, I swear to you by Fibsburrow churchdome and Sainte Andrée's Undershift, by all I hold secret from my world and in my underworld of nighties and naughties and all the other wonderwearlds! Close your, notmust look! Now open, pet, your lips, pepette, like I used my sweet parted lipsabuss with Dan Holohan of facetious memory taught me after the flannel dance, with the proof of love, up Smock Alley the first night he smelled pouder and I coloured beneath my fan, *pipetta mia*, when you learned me the linguo to melt. Whowham would have ears like ours, the blackhaired! Do you like that, *silenzioso?* Are you enjoying, this same little me, my life, my love? Why do you like my whisping? Is it not divinely deluscious? But in't it bafforyou? *Misi, misi!* Tell me till my thrillme comes! I will not break the seal. I am enjoying it still, I swear I am! Why do you prefer its in these dark nets, if why may ask, my sweetykins? Sh sh! Long-ears is flying. No, sweetissest, why would that ennoy me? But don't! You want to be slap well slapped for that. Your delighted lips, love, be careful! Mind my duvetyne dress above all! It's golded silvy, the newest sextones with princess effect. For Rut-land blue's got out of passion. So, so, my precious! O, I can see the cost, chare! Don't tell me! Why, the boy in sheeps' lane knows that. If I sell whose, dears? Was I sold here' tears? You mean those conversation lozenges? How awful! The bold shame of me! I wouldn't, chickens, not for all the juliettes in the twinkly way! I could snap them when I see them winking at me in bed. I didn't did so, my intended, or was going to or thinking of. Shshsh! Don't start like that, you wretch! I thought ye knew all and more, ye aucthor, to explique to ones the significat of their exsystems with your nieu nivulon lead. It's only another queer fish or other in Brinbrou's damned old trouchorous river again, Gothewishegoths bless us and spare her! And gibos rest from the bosso! Excuse me for swearing, love, I swear to the sorrasims on their trons of Uian I didn't mean to by this alpin armlet! Did you really never in all our cantalang lives speak clothse to a girl's before? No! Not even to the charmermaid? How marfellows! Of course I believe you, my own dear doting liest, when you tell me. As I'd live to, O, I'd love to! Liss, liss! I muss whiss! Never that ever or I can remember dearstreaming faces, you may go through me! Never in all my whole white life of my match-less and pair. Or ever for bitter be the frucht of this hour! With my whiteness I thee woo and bind my silk breasths I thee bound! Always, Amory, amor andmore! Till always, thou lovest! Shshshsh! So long as the lucksmith. Laughs!

11. If you met on the binge a poor acheseyeld from Ailing, when the tune of his tremble shook shimmy on shin, while his countrary raged in the weak of his wailing, like a rugilant pugi-lant Lyon O'Lynn; if he maundered in misliness, plaining his

plight or, played fox and lice, pricking and dropping hips teeth, or wringing his handcuffs for peace, the blind blighter, praying Dieuf and Domb Nostrums foh thomethinks to eath; if he weapt while he leapt and guffalled quith a quhimper, made cold blood a blue mundy and no bones without flech, taking kiss, kake or kick with a suck, sigh or simper, a diffle to larn and a dibble to lech; if the fain shinner pegged you to shave his immartial, wee skillmustered shoul with his ooh, hoodoodoo! broking wind that to wiles, woemaid sin he was partial, we don't think, Jones, we'd care to this evening, would you?

Answer: No, blank ye! So you think I have impulsivism? Did they tell you I am one of the fortysixths? And I suppose you heard I had a wag on my ears? And I suppose they told you too that my roll of life is not natural? But before proceeding to conclusively confute this begging question it would be far fitter for you, if you dare! to hasitate to consult with and consequentially attempt at my disposale of the same dime-cash problem elsewhere naturalistically of course, from the blinkpoint of so eminent a spatialist. From it you will here notice, Schott, upon my for the first remarking you that the sophology of Bitchson while driven as under by a purely dime-dime urge is not without his cashcash charackericksticks, borrowed for its nonce ends from the fiery goodmother Miss Fortune (who the lost time we had the pleasure we have had our little *recherché* brush with, what, Schott?) and as I further could have told you as brisk as your D.B.C. behaviouristically *pailleté* with a coat of homoid icing which is in reality only a done by chance ridiculisation of the whoo-whoo and where's hairs theorics of Winestain. To put it all the more plumbsily. The speechform is a mere sorrogate. Whilst the quality and tality (I shall explex what you ought to mean by this with its proper when and where and why and how in the subsequent sentence) are alternativomentally harrogate and arrogate, as the gates may be.

Talis is a word often abused by many passims (I am working out a quantum theory about it for it is really most tantumising state of affairs). A pessim may frequent you to say: Have you been

149

seeing much of Talis and Talis those times? optimately meaning: Will you put up at hree of irish? Or a ladyeater may perhaps have casualised as you temptoed her *à la sourdine*: Of your plates? Is Talis de Talis, the swordswallower, who is on at the Craterium the same Talis von Talis, the penscrusher, no funk you! who runs his duly mile? Or this is a perhaps cleaner example. At a recent postvortex piece infustigation of a determinised case of chronic spinosis an extension lecturer on The Ague who out of matter of form was trying his seesers, Dr's Het Ubeleeft, borrowed the question: Why's which Suchman's *talis qualis?* to whom, as a fatter of macht, Dr Gedankje of Stoutgirth, who was wiping his whistle, toarsely retoarted: While thou beast' one zoom of a whorl! (Talis and Talis originally mean the same thing, hit it's: Qualis.)

Professor Loewy-Brueller (though as I shall promptly prove his whole account of the Sennacherib as distinct from the Shalmanesir sanitational reforms and of the Mr Skekels and Dr Hydes problem in the same connection differs *toto coelo* from the fruit of my own investigations — though the reason I went to Jericho must remain for certain reasons a political secret — especially as I shall shortly be wanted in Cavantry, I congratulate myself, for the same and other reasons — as being again hopelessly vitiated by what I have now resolved to call the dime and cash diamond fallacy) in his talked off confession which recently met with such a leonine uproar on its escape after its confinement *Why am I not born like a Gentileman and why am I now so speakable about my own eatables* (Feigenbaumblatt and Father, Judapest, 5688, A.M.) whole-heartedly takes off his gabbercoat and wig, honest draughty fellow, in his public interest, to make us see how though, as he says: 'by Allswill' the inception and the descent and the endswell of Man is *temporarily* wrapped in obscenity, looking through at these accidents with the faroscope of television, (this nightlife instrument needs still some subtractional betterment in the readjustment of the more refrangible angles to the squeals of his hypothesis on the outer tin sides), I can easily believe heartily in my own most spacious immensity as my ownhouse and microbemost cosm when I am reassured by ratio that the cube of my volumes is to the surfaces of their subjects as the sphericity of these globes (I am very pressing for a parliamentary motion this term which, under my guidance, would establish the deleteriousness of decorousness in the morbidisation of the modern mandaboutwoman type) is to the feracity of Fairynelly's vacuum. I need not anthrapologise for any obintentional (I must here correct all that school of neoitalian or paleoparisien schola of tinkers and spanglers who say I'm wrong *parcequeue* out of revolscian from romanitis I want to be) downtrodding on my foes. Professor Levi-Brullo, F.D. of Sexe-Weiman-Eitelnaky finds, from experiments made by hinn with his Nuremberg eggs in the one hands and the watches cunldron apan the oven, though it is astensably a case of Ket's rebollions cooling the Popes back, because the number of squeer faiths in weekly circulation will not be appreciably augmented by the notherslogging of my cupolar clods. What the romantic in rags pines after like all tomtompions haunting crevices for a deadbeat escupement and what het importunes our *Mitleid* for in accornish with the Mortadarthella taradition is the poorest commononguardiant waste of time. *His* everpresent toes are always in retaliessian out throuth his overpast boots. Hear him squak! Teek heet to that looswallawer how he bolo the bat! Tyro a toray! *When* Mullocky won the couple of colds, *when* we were stripping in number three, I would like the neat drop that would malt in my mouth but I fail to see *when* (I am purposely refraining from expounding the obvious fallacy as to the specific gravitates of the two deglutables implied nor to the lapses lequou asousiated with the royal gorge through students of mixed hydrostatics and pneumodipsics will after some difficulties grapple away with my meinungs). Myrrdin aloer! as old Marsellas Cambriannus puts his. But, on Professor Llewellys ap Bryllars, F.D., Ph. Dr's showings, the plea, if he pleads, is all posh and robbage on a melodeontic scale since his man's *when* is no otherman's *quandour* (Mine, dank you?) while, for aught I care for the contrary, the all is *where* in love as war and

151

the plane where me arts soar you'd aisy rouse a thunder from and where I cling true'tis there I climb tree and where Innocent looks best (pick!) there's holly in his ives.

As my explanations here are probably above your understandings, lattlebrattons, though as augmentatively uncomparisoned as Cadwan, Cadwallon and Cadwalloner, I shall revert to a more expletive method which I frequently use when I have to sermo with muddlecrass pupils. Imagine for my purpose that you are a squad of urchins, snifflynosed, goslingnecked, clothyheaded, tangled in your lacings, tingled in your pants, etsitaraw etcicero. And you, Bruno Nowlan, take your tongue out of your inkpot! As none of you knows javanese I will give all my easyfree translation of the old fabulist's parable. Allaboy Minor, take your head out of your satchel! *Audi*, Joe Peters! *Exaudi* facts!

The Mookse and The Gripes.

Gentes and laitymen, fullstoppers and semicolonials, hybreds and lubberds!

Eins within a space and a wearywide space it wast ere wohned a Mookse. The onesomeness wast alltolonely, archunsitslike, broady oval, and a Mookse he would a walking go (My hood! cries Antony Romeo), so one grandsumer evening, after a great morning and his good supper of gammon and spittish, having flabelled his eyes, pilleoled his nostrils, vacticanated his ears and palliumed his throats, he put on his impermeable, seized his impugnable, harped on his crown and stepped out of his immobile *De Rure Albo* (socolled becauld it was chalkfull of masterplasters and had borgeously letout gardens strown with cascadas, pintacostecas, horthoducts and currycombs) and set off from Ludstown *a spasso* to see how badness was badness in the weirdest of all pensible ways.

As he set off with his father's sword, his *lancia spezzata*, he was girded on, and with that between his legs and his tarkeels, our once in only Bragspear, he clanked, to my clinking, from veetoes to threetop, every inch of an immortal.

He had not walked over a pentiadpair of parsecs from his azylium when at the turning of the Shinshone Lanteran near

Saint Bowery's-without-his-Walls he came (secunding to the one one oneth of the propecies, *Amnis Limina Permanent*) upon the most unconsciously boggylooking stream he ever locked his eyes with. Out of the colliens it took a rise by daubing itself Ninon. It looked little and it smelt of brown and it thought in narrows and it talked showshallow. And as it rinn it dribbled like any lively purliteasy: *My, my, my! Me and me! Little down dream don't I love thee!*

And, I declare, what was there on the yonder bank of the stream that would be a river, parched on a limb of the olum, bolt downright, but the Gripes? And no doubt he was fit to be dried for why had he not been having the juice of his times?

His pips had been neatly all drowned on him; his polps were charging odours every older minute; he was quickly for getting the dresser's desdaign on the flyleaf of his frons; and he was quietly for giving the bailiff's distrain on to the bulkside of his *cul de Pompe*. In all his specious heavings, as be lived by Optimus Maximus, the Mookse had never seen his Dubville brooder-on-low so nigh to a pickle.

Adrian (that was the Mookse now's assumptinome) stuccstill phiz-à-phiz to the Gripes in an accessit of aurignacian. But Allmookse must to Moodend much as Allrouts, austereways or wastersways, in roaming run through Room. Hic sor a stone, singularly illud, and on hoc stone Seter satt huc sate which it filled quite poposterously and by acclammation to its fullest justotoryum and whereopum with his unfallable encyclicling upom his alloilable, diupetriark of the wouest, and the athemyst-sprinkled pederect he always walked with, *Deusdedit*, cheek by jowel with his frisherman's blague, *Bellua Triumphanes*, his everyway addedto wallat's collectium, for yea longer he lieved yea broader he betaught of it, the fetter, the summe and the haul it cost, he looked the first and last micahlike laicness of Quartus the Fifth and Quintus the Sixth and Sixtus the Seventh giving allnight sitting to Lio the Faultyfindth.

— Good appetite us, sir Mookse! How do you do it? cheeped the Gripes in a wherry whiggy maudelenian woice and the jackasses all within bawl laughed and brayed for his intentions for they knew their sly toad lowry now. I am rarumominum blessed to see you, my dear mouster. Will you not perhopes tell me everything if you are pleased, sanity? All about aulne and lithial and allsall allinall about awn and liseias? Ney?

Think of it! O miserendissimest retempter! A Gripes!

— Rats! bullowed the Mookse most telesphorously, the concionator, and the sissymusses and the zozzymusses in their robenhauses quailed to hear his tardeynois at all for you cannot wake a silken nouse out of a hoarse oar. Blast yourself and your anathomy infairioriboos! No, hang you for an animal rurale! I am superbly in my supremest poncif! Abase you, baldyqueens! Gather behind me, satraps! Rots!

— I am till infinity obliged with you, bowed the Gripes, his whine having gone to his palpruy head. I am still always having a wish on all my extremities. By the watch, what is the time, pace?

Figure it! The pining peever! To a Mookse!

— Ask my index, mund my achilles, swell my obolum, woshup my nase serene, answered the Mookse, rapidly by turning clement, urban, eugenious and celestian in the formose of good grogory humours. Quote awhore? That is quite about what I came on *my* missions with *my* intentions *laudibiliter* to settle with *you*, barbarousse. Let thor be orlog. Let Pauline be Irene. Let you be Beeton. And let me be Los Angeles. Now measure your length. Now estimate my capacity. Well, sour? Is this space of our couple of hours too dimensional for you, temporiser? Will you give you up? *Como? Fuert it?*

Sancta Patientia! You should have heard the voice that answered him! *Culla vosellina.*

— I was just thinkling upon that, swees Mooksey, but, for all the rime on my raisins, if I connow make my submission, I cannos give you up, the Gripes whimpered from nethermost of his wanhope. Ishallassoboundbewilsothoutoosezit. My tumble, loudy bullocker, is my own. My velicity is too fit in one stockend. And my spetial inexshellsis the belowing things ab ove. But I will never be abler to tell Your Honoriousness (here he near lost his limb) though my corked father was bott a pseudowaiter, whose o'cloak you ware.

Incredible! Well, hear the inevitable.

— *Your* temple, *sus in cribro!* Semperexcommunicambiambisumers. Tugurios-in-Newrobe or Tukurias-in-Ashies. Novarome, my creature, blievend bleives. My building space in lyonine city is always to let to leonlike Men, the Mookse in a most consistorous allocution pompifically with immediate jurisdiction constantinently concludded (what a crammer for the shapewrucked Gripes!). And I regret to proclaim that it is out of my temporal to help you from being killed by inchies, (what a thrust!), as we first met each other newwhere so airly. (Poor little sowsieved subsquashed Gripes! I begin to feel contemption for him!). My side, thank decretals, is as safe as motherour's houses, he continued, and I can seen from my holeydome what it is to be wholly sane. Unionjok and be joined to yok! Parysis, *tu sais*, crucycrooks, belongs to him who parises himself. And there I must leave you subject for the pressing. I can prove that against you, weight a momentum, mein goot enemy! or Cospol's not our star. I bet you this dozen odd. This foluminous dozen odd. *Quas primas*—but 'tis bitter to compote my knowledge's fructos of. Tomes.

Elevating, to give peint to his blick, his jewelled pederect to the allmysty cielung, he luckystruck blueild out of a few shouldbe santillants, a cloister of starabouts over Maples, a lucciolys in Teresa street and a stopsign before Sophy Barratt's, he gaddered togodder the odds docence of his vellumes, gresk, letton and russicruxian, onto the lapse of his prolegs, into umfullth onescuppered, and sat about his widerproof. He proved it well whoonearth dry and drysick times, and *vremiament, tu cesses*, to the extinction of Niklaus altogether (Niklaus Alopysius having been the once Gripes's popwilled nimbum) by Neuclidius and Inexagoras and Mumfsen and Thumpsem, by Orasmus and by Amenius, by Anacletus the Jew and by Malachy the Augurer and by the Cappon's collection and after that, with Cheekee's gelatine and Alldaybrandy's formolon, he reproved it ehrltogether when not in that order sundering in some different order, alter three thirty and a hundred times by the binomial dioram and the penic walls and the ind, the Inklespill legends and the rure, the rule of the hoop and the blessons of expedience and the jus, the jugicants of Pontius Pilax and all the mummyscrips in Sick Bokes' Juncroom and the Chapters for the Cunning of the Chapters of the Conning Fox by Tail.

While that Mooksius with preprocession and with preprecession, duplicitly and diplussedly, was promulgating ipsofacts and sadcontras this raskolly Gripos he had allbust seceded in monophysicking his illsobordunates. But asawfulas he had caught his base semenoyous sarchnaktiers to combuccinate upon the silipses of his aspillouts and the acheporeoozers of his haggy-own pneumax to synerethetise with the breadchestviousness of his sweeatovular ducose sofarfully the loggerthuds of his sakellaries were fond at variance with the synodals of his somepooliom and his babskissed nepogreasymost got the hoof from his philioquus.

— Efter thousand yaws, O Gripes con my sheepskins, yow will be belined to the world, enscayed Mookse the pius.

— Ofter thousand yores, amsered Gripes the gregary, be the goat of MacHammud's, yours may be still, O Mookse, more botheared.

— Us shall be chosen as the first of the last by the electress of Vale Hollow, obselved the Mookse nobily, for par the unicum of Elelijiacks, Us am in Our stabulary and that is what Ruby and Roby fall for, blissim.

The Pills, the Nasal Wash (Yardly's), the Army Man Cut, as british as bondstrict and as straightcut as when that broken-arched traveller from Nuzuland . . .

— Wee, cumfused the Gripes limply, shall not even be the last of the first, wee hope, when oust are visitated by the Veiled Horror. And, he added: Mee are relying entirely, see the forte-thurd of Elissabed, on the weightiness of mear's breath. Puffut!

Unsightbared embouscher, relentless foe to social and business succes! (Hourihaleine) It might have been a happy evening but . . .

And they viterberated each other, *canis et coluber* with the wildest ever wielded since Tarriestinus lashed Pissasphaltium.

— Unuchorn!

— Ungulant!

— Uvuloid!

— Uskybeak!

And bullfolly answered volleyball.

Nuvoletta in her lightdress, spunn of sisteen shimmers, was looking down on them, leaning over the bannistars and listening all she childishly could. How she was brightened when Should-rups in his glaubering hochskied his welkinstuck and how she was overclused when Kneesknobs on his zwivvel was makeacting such a paulse of himshelp! She was alone. All her nubied companions were asleeping with the squirrels. Their mivver, Mrs Moonan, was off in the Fuerst quarter scrubbing the backsteps of Number 28. Fuvver, that Skand, he was up in Norwood's sokaparlour, eating oceans of Voking's Blemish. Nuvoletta listened as she reflected herself, though the heavenly one with his constellatria and his emanations stood between, and she tried all she tried to make the Mookse look up at her (but *he* was fore too adiaptotously farseeing) and to make the Gripes hear how coy she could be (though he was much too schystimatically auricular about *his ens* to heed her) but it was all mild's vapour moist. Not even her feignt reflection, Nuvoluccia, could they toke their gnoses off for their minds with intrepifide fate and bungless curiasity, were conclaved with Heliogobbleus and Commodus and Enobarbarus and whatever the coordinal dickens they did as their damprauch of papyrs and buchstubs said. As if that was their spiration! As if theirs could duiparate her queendim! As if she would be third perty to search on search proceedings! She tried all the winsome wonsome ways her four winds had taught her. She tossed her sfumastelliacinous hair like *la princesse de la Petite Bretagne* and she rounded her mignons arms like Mrs Cornwallis-West and she smiled over herself like the beauty of the image of the pose of the daughter of the queen of the Emperour of Irelande and she sighed after herself as were she born to bride with Tristis Tristior Tristissimus. But, sweet madonine, she might fair as well have carried her daisy's worth to Florida. For the Mookse, a dogmad Accanite, were not amoosed and the Gripes, a dubliboused Catalick, wis pinefully obliviscent.

—I see, she sighed. There are menner.

The siss of the whisp of the sigh of the softzing at the stir of the ver grose O arundo of a long one in midias reeds: and shades began to glidder along the banks, greepsing, greepsing, duusk unto duusk, and it was as glooming as gloaming could be in the waste of all peacable worlds. Metamnisia was allsoonome coloroform brune; citherior spiane an eaulande, innemorous and unnumerose. The Mookse had a sound eyes right but he could not all hear. The Gripes had light ears left yet he could but ill see. He ceased. And he ceased, tung and trit, and it was neversoever so dusk of both of them. But still Moo thought on the deeps of the undths he would profoundth come the morrokse and still Gri feeled of the scripes he would escipe if by grice he had luck enoupes.

Oh, how it was duusk! From Vallee Maraia to Grasyaplaina, dormimust echo! Ah dew! Ah dew! It was so duusk that the tears of night began to fall, first by ones and twos, then by threes and fours, at last by fives and sixes of sevens, for the tired ones were wecking, as we weep now with them. O! O! O! Par la pluie!

Then there came down to the thither bank a woman of no appearance (I believe she was a Black with chills at her feet) and she gathered up his hoariness the Mookse motamourfully where he was spread and carried him away to her invisible dwelling, thats hights, *Aquila Rapax*, for he was the holy sacred solem and poshup spit of her boshop's apron. So you see the Mookse he had reason as I knew and you knew and he knew all along. And there came down to the hither bank a woman to all important (though they say that she was comely, spite the cold in her heed) and, for he was as like it as blow it to a hawker's hank, she plucked down the Gripes, torn panicky autotone, in angeu from his limb and cariad away its beotitubes with her to her unseen

158

shieling, it is, *De Rore Coeli*. And so the poor Gripes got wrong;
for that is always how a Gripes is, always was and always will be.
And it was never so thoughtful of either of them. And there were
left now an only elmtree and but a stone. Polled with pietrous,
Sierre but saule. O! Yes! And Nuvoletta, a lass.

Then Nuvoletta reflected for the last time in her little long life
and she made up all her myriads of drifting minds in one. She
cancelled all her engauzements. She climbed over the bannistars;
she gave a childy cloudy cry: *Nuée! Nuée!* A lightdress fluttered.
She was gone. And into the river that had been a stream (for a
thousand of tears had gone eon her and come on her and she was
stout and struck on dancing and her muddied name was Missis-
liffi) there fell a tear, a singult tear, the loveliest of all tears (I
mean for those crylove fables fans who are 'keen' on the pretty-
pretty commonface sort of thing you meet by hopeharrods) for it
was a leaptear. But the river tripped on her by and by, lapping
as though her heart was brook: *Why, why, why! Weh, O weh!
I'se so silly to be flowing but I no canna stay!*

No applause, please! Bast! The romescot nattleshaker will go
round your circulation in *diu dursus*.

Allaboy, Major, I'll take your reactions in another place after
themes. Nolan Browne, you may now leave the classroom. Joe
Peters, Fox.

As I have now successfully explained to you my own natural-
born rations which are even in excise of my vaultybrain insure
me that I am a mouth's more deserving case by genius. I feel in
symbathos for my ever devoted friend and halfaloafonwashed,
Gnaccus Gnoccovitch. Darling gem! Darling smallfox! Horose-
shoew! I could love that man like my own ambo for being so
baileycliaver though he's a nawful curillass and I must slav to
methodiousness. I want him to go and live like a theabild in
charge of the night brigade on Tristan da Cunha, isle of man-
overboard, where he'll make Number 106 and be near Inacces-
sible. (The meeting of mahoganies, be the waves, rementious
me that this exposed sight though it pines for an umbrella of its
own and needs a shelter belt of the true service sort to keep its

159

boles clean, — the weeping beeches, Picea and Tillia, are in a
wild state about it — ought to be classified, as Cricketbutt Will-
owm and his two nurserymen advisers suggested, under genus
Inexhaustible when we refloat upon all the butternat, sweet gum
and manna ash redcedera which is so purvulent there as if there
was howthorns in Curraghchasa which ought to look as plane
as a lodgepole to anybody until we are introduced to that pine-
tacotta of Verney Rubeus where the deodarty is pinctured for us
in a pure stand, which we do not doubt ha has a habitat of doing,
but without those selfsownseedlings which are a species of proof
that the largest individual *can* occur at or in an olivetion such as
East Conna Hillock where it mixes with foolth accacians and
common sallies and *is* tender) *Vux Populus*, as we say in hickory-
hockery and I wish we had some more glasses of *arbor vitae*.
Why roat by the roadside or awn over alum pot? Alderman
Whitebeaver is dakyo. He ought to go away for a change of
ideas and he'd have a world of things to look back on. Do, sweet
Daniel! If I weren't a jones in myself I'd elect myself to be his
dolphin in the wildsbillow because he is such a barefooted rubber
with my supersocks pulled over his face which I publicked in
my bestback garden for the laetification of siderodromites and
to the irony of the stars. You will say it is most unenglish and
I shall hope to hear that you will not be wrong about it. But I
further, feeling a bit husky in my truths.

Will you please come over and let us mooremoore murgessly
to each's other down below our vices. I am underheerd by old
billfaust. Wilsh is full of curks. The coolskittle is philip deblinite. Mr Wist is thereover beyeind the wantnot. Wilsh and wist
are as thick of thins udder as faust on the deblinite. Sgunoshooto
estas preter la tapizo malgranda. Lilegas al si en sia chambro.
Kelkefoje funcktas, kelkefoje srumpas Shultroj. Houdian Kiel vi
fartas, mia nigra sinjoro? And from the poignt of fun where I
am crying to arrive you at they are on allfore as foibleminded as
you can feel they are fablebodied.

My heeders will recoil with a great leisure how at the out-
break before trespassing on the space question where even

michelangelines have fooled to dread I proved to mindself as to your sotisfiction how his abject all through (the *quickquid* of Professor Ciondolone's too frequently hypothecated *Bettlermensch*) is nothing so much more than a mere cashdime however genteel he may want ours, if we please (I am speaking to us in the second person), for to this graded intellecktuals dime *is* cash and the cash system (you must not be allowed to forget that this is all contained, I mean the system, in the dogmarks of origen on spurios) means that I cannot now have or nothave a piece of cheeps in your pocket at the same time and with the same manners as you can now nothalf or half the cheek apiece I've in mind unless Burrus and Caseous have not or not have seemaultaneously sysentangled themselves, selldear to soldthere, once in the dairy days of buy and buy.

Burrus, let us like to imagine, is a genuine prime, the real choice, full of natural greace, the mildest of milkstoffs yet unbeaten as a risicide and, of course, obsoletely unadulterous whereat Caseous is obversely the revise of him and in fact not an ideal choose by any meals, though the betterman of the two is meltingly addicted to the more casual side of the arrivaliste case and, let me say it at once, as zealous over him as is passably he. The seemsame home and histry seeks and hidepence which we used to be reading for our prepurgatory, hot, Schott? till Duddy shut the shopper op and Mutti, poor Mutti! brought us our poor suppy, (ah who! eh how!) in Acetius and Oleosus and Sellius Volatilis and Petrus Papricus! Our Old Party quite united round the Slatbowel at Commons: Pfarrer Salamoss himself and that sprog of a Pedersill and his Sprig of Thyme and a dozen of the Murphybuds and a score and more of the hot young Capels and Lettucia in her greensleeves and you too and me three, twinsome bibs but hansome ates, like shakespill and eggs! But there's many a split pretext bowl and jowl; and (snob screwing that cork, Schott!) to understand this as well as you can, feeling how backward you are in your down-to-the-ground benches, I have completed the following arrangement for the coarse use of stools and if I don't make away with you I'm beyond Caesar outnullused.

The older sisars (Tyrants, regicide is too good for you!) become unbeurrable from age, (the compositor of the farce of dustiny however makes a thunpledrum mistake by letting off this pienofarte effect as his furst act as that is where the juke comes in) having been sort-of-nineknived and chewly removed (this soldier - author - batman for all his commontoryism is just another of those souftsiezed bubbles who never quite got the sandhurst out of his eyes so that the champaign he draws for us is as flop as a plankrieg) the twinfreer types are billed to make their reupprearance as the knew kneck and knife knickknots on the deserted *champ de bouteilles.* (A most cursery reading into the Persic-Uraliens hostery shows us how Fonnumagula picked up that propper numen out of a colluction of prifixes though to the permienting cannasure the Coucousien oafsprung of this sun of a kuk is as sattin as there's a tub in Tobolosk) *Ostiak della Vogul Marina!* But that I dannoy the fact of wanton to weste point I could paint you to that butter (cheese it!) if you had some wash. Mordvealive! Oh me none onsens! Why the case is as inessive and impossive as kezom hands! Their interlocative is conprovocative just as every hazzy hates to having a hazbane in her noze. Caseous may bethink himself a thought of a caviller but Burrus has the reachly roundered head that goes best with thofthinking defensive fideism. He has the lac of wisdom under every dent in his lofter while the other follow's onni vesy milky indeedmymy. Laughing over the linnuts and weeping off the uniun. He hisn't the hey og he lisn't the lug, poohoo. And each night sim misses mand he winks he had the semagen. It was aptly and corrigidly stated (and, it is royally needless for one *ex ungue Leonem* to say by whom) that his seeingscraft was that clarety as were the wholeborough of Poutresbourg to be averlaunched over him pitchbatch he could still make out with his augstritch the green moat in Ireland's Eye. Let me sell you the fulltroth of Burrus when he wore a younker. Here it is, and chorming too, in six by sevens! A cleanly line, by the gods! A king off duty and a jaw for ever! And what a cheery ripe outlook, good help me Deus v Deus! If I were to speak my ohole mouthful to arinam about it you should call me the ormuzd aliment in your midst of faime. Eat ye up, heat ye up! sings the somun in the salm. *Butyrum et mel comedet ut sciat reprobare malum et eligere bonum.* This, of course, also explains why we were taught to play in the childhood: *Der Haensli ist ein Butterbrot, mein Butterbrot! Und Koebi iss dein Schtinkenkot! Ja! Ja! Ja!*

This in fact, just to show you, is Caseous, the brutherscutch or puir tyron: a hole or two, the highstinks aforefelt and anygo prigging wurms. Cheesugh! you complain. And Hi Hi High must say you are not Hoa Hoa Hoally in the wrong!

Thus we cannot escape our likes and mislikes, exiles or ambusheers, beggar and neighbour and — this is where the dimeshow advertisers advance the temporal relief plea — let us be tolerant of antipathies. *Nex quovis burro num fit mercaseus?* I am not hereby giving my final endorsement to the learned ignorants of the Cusanus philosophism in which old Nicholas pegs it down that the smarter the spin of the top the sounder the span of the buttom (what the worthy old auberginiste ought to have meant was: the more stolidly immobile *in space* appears to me the bottom which is presented to use in time by the top primomobilisk &c.). And I shall be misunderstord if understood to give an unconditional sinequam to the heroicised furibouts of the Nolanus theory, or, at any rate, of that substrate of apart from hissheory where the Theophil swoors that on principial he was the pointing start of his odiose by comparison and that whiles eggs will fall cheapened all over the walled the Bure will be dear on the Brie.

Now, while I am not out now to be taken up as unintentionally recommending the Silkebjorg tyrondynamon machine for the more economical helixtrolysis of these amboadipates until I can find space to look into it myself a little more closely first I shall go on with my decisions after having shown to you in good time how both products of our social stomach (the excellent Dr Burroman, I noticed by the way from his emended food theory, has been carefully digesting the very wholesome criticism

I helped him to in my princeps edition which is all so munch to the cud) are mutuearly polarised the incompatabilily of any delusional acting as ambivalent to the fixation of his pivotism. Positing, as above, too males pooles, the one the pictor of the other and the omber the *Skotia* of the one, and looking wantingly around our undistributed middle between males we feel we must waistfully woent a female to focus and on this stage there pleasantly appears the cowrymaid M. whom we shall often meet below who introduces herself upon us at some precise hour which we shall again agree to call absolute zero or the babbling pumpt of platinism. And so like that former son of a kish who went up and out to found his farmer's ashes we come down home gently on our own turnedabout asses to meet Margareen.

We now romp through a period of pure lyricism of shame-bred music (technologically, let me say, the appetising entry of this subject on a fool chest of vialds is plumply pudding the carp before doevre hors) evidenced by such words in distress as *I cream for thee, Sweet Margareen,* and the more hopeful *O Margareena! O Margareena! Still in the bowl is left a lump of gold!* (Correspondents, by the way, will keep on asking me what is the correct garnish to serve drisheens with. Tansy Sauce. Enough). The pawnbreaking pathos of the first of these shoddy pieces reveals it as a Caseous effort. Burrus's bit is often used for a toast. Criniculture can tell us very precisely indeed how and why this particular streak of yellow silver first appeared on (not in) the bowel, that is to see, the human head, bald, black, bronze, brown, brindled, betteraved or blanchemanged where it might be usefully compared with an earwig on a fullbottom. I am offering this to Signorina Cuticura and I intend to take it up and bring it under the nosetice of Herr Harlene by way of diverting his attentions. Of course the unskilled singer continues to pervert our wiser ears by subordinating the space-element, that is to sing, the *aria*, to the time-factor, which ought to be killed, *ill tempor*. I should advise any unborn singer who may still be among my heeders to forget her temporal diaphragm at home (the best thing that could happen to it!) and attack the roulade with a swift *colpo di glottide* to the lug (though Maace I will insist was reclined from overdoing this, his recovery often being slow) and then, O! on the third dead beat, O! to cluse her eyes and aiopen her oath and see what spice I may send her. How? Cease thee, cantatrickee! I fain would be solo. Arouse thee, my valour! And save for e'er my true Bdur!

I shall have a word to say in a few yards about the acoustic and orchidectural management of the tonehall but, as ours is a vivarious where one plant's breaf is a lunger planner's byscent and you may not care for argon, it will be very convenient for me for the emolument to pursue Burrus and Caseous for a rung or two up their isocelating biangle. Every admirer has seen my goulache of Marge (she is *so* like the sister, you don't know, and they both dress A L I K E !) which I titled *The Very Picture of a Needlesswoman* which in the presence ornates our national cruetstand. This genre of portraiture of changes of mind in order to be truly torse should evoke the bush soul of females so I am leaving it to the experienced victim to complete the general suggestion by the mental addition of a wallopy bound or, should the zulugical zealot prefer it, a congorool teal. The hatboxes which composed Rhomba, lady Trabezond (Marge in her *excelsis*), also comprised the climactogram up which B and C may fondly be imagined ascending and are suggestive of gentlemen's spring modes, these modes carrying us back to the superimposed claylayers of eocene and pleastoseen formation and the gradual morphological changes in our body politic which Professor Ebahi-Ahuri of Philadespoinis (Ill) — whose bluebutterbust I have just given his coupe de grass to — neatly names a *boîte à surprises*. The boxes, if I may break the subject gently, are worth about fourpence pourbox but I am inventing a more patent process, foolproof and pryperfect (I should like to ask that Shedlock Homes person who is out for removing the roofs of our criminal classics by what *deductio ad domunum* he hopes *de tacto* to detect anything unless he happens of himself, *movibile tectu*, to have a slade off) after which they can be reduced to a fragment of their true crust by even the youngest of Margees if she will take plase to be seated and smile if I please.

Now there can be no question about it either that I having done as much, have quite got the size of that demilitery young female (we will continue to call her Marge) whose types may be met with in any public garden, wearing a very "dressy" affair, known as an "ethel" of instep length and with a real fur, reduced to 3/9, and muffin cap to tone (they are "angelskin" this fall), ostentatiously hemming apologetically over the shirtness of some "sweet" garment, when she is not sitting on all the free benches avidously reading about "it" but ovidently on the look out for "him" or so "thrilled" about the best dressed dolly pram and beautiful elbow competition or at the movies swallowing sobs and blowing bixed mixcuits over "childe" chaplain's "latest" or on the verge of the gutter with some bobbedhair brieffrocked babyma's toddler (the Smythe-Smythes now keep TWO domestics and aspire to THREE male ones, a shover, a butlegger and a sectary) held hostage at armslength, teaching His Infant Majesty how to make waters worse.

(I am closely watching Master Pules, as I have regions to suspect from my post that her "little man" is a secondary schoolteacher under the boards of education, a voted disciple of Infantulus who is being utilised thus publicly by the *seducente infanta* to conceal her own more mascular personality by flaunting frivolish finery over men's inside clothes, for the femininny of that totamulier will always lack the musculink of a verumvirum. My solotions for the proper parturience of matres and the education of micturious mites must stand over from the moment till I tackle this tickler hussy for occupying my uttentions.)

Margareena she's very fond of Burrus but, alick and alack! she velly fond of chee. (The important influence exercised on everything by this eastasian import has not been till now fully flavoured though we can comfortably taste it in this case. I shall come back for a little more say farther on.) A cleopatrician in her own right she at once complicates the position while Burrus and Caseous are contending for her misstery by implicating herself with an elusive Antonius, a wop who would appear to hug a personal interest in refined chees of all chades at the same time as he wags an antomine art of being rude like the boor. This Antonius-Burrus-Caseous grouptriad may be said to equate the *qualis* equivalent with the older socalled *talis* on *talis* one just as quantly as in the hyperchemical economantarchy the tantum ergons irruminate the quantum urge so that eggs is to whey as whay is to zeed like your golfchild's abe boob caddy. And this is why any simple philadolphus of a fool you like to dress, an athemisthued lowtownian, exlegged phatrisight, may be awfully green to one side of him and fruitfully blue on the other which will not screen him however from appealing to my gropesarching eyes; through the strongholes of my acropoll, as a boosted blasted bleating blatant bloaten blasphorus blesphorous idiot who kennot tail a bomb from a painapple when he steals one and wannot psing his psalmen with the cong in our gregational pompoms with the canting crew.

No! Topsman to your Tarpeia! This thing, Mister Abby, is nefand. (And, taking off soutstuffs and alkalike matters, I hope we can kill time to reach the salt because there's some forceglass neutric assets bittering in the soldpewter for you to plump your pottage in). The thundering legion has stormed Olymp that it end. Twelve tabular times till now have I edicted it. Merus Genius to Careous Caseous! *Moriture, te salutat!* My phemous themis race is run, so let Demoncracy take the highmost! (Abraham Tripier. Those old diligences are quite out of date. Read next answer). I'll beat you so lon. (Bigtempered. Why not take direct action. See previous reply). My unchanging Word is sacred. The word is my Wife, to exponse and expound, to vend and to velnerate, and may the curlews crown our nuptias! Till Breath us depart! Wamen. Beware would you change with my years. Be as young as your grandmother! The ring man in the rong shop but the rite words by the rote order! *Ubi lingua nuncupassit, ibi fas! Adversus hostem semper sac!* She that will not feel my fulmoon let her peel to thee as the hoyden and the impudent! That mon that hoth no moses in his sole nor is not awed by conquists of word's law, who never with humself was fed and leaves his soil to lave his head, when his hope's in his highlows from whisking his woe, if he came to my preach, a proud pursebroken ranger, when the heavens were welling the spite of their spout, to beg for a bite in our bark *Noisdanger*, would meself and Mac Jeffet, four-in-hand, foot him out? — ay! — were he my own breastbrother, my doubled withd love and my singlebiassed hate, were we bread by the same fire and signed with the same salt, had we tapped from the same master and robbed the same till, were we tucked in the one bed and bit by the one flea, homo-gallant and hemycapnoise, bum and dingo, jack by churl, though it broke my heart to pray it, still I'd fear I'd hate to say!

12. *Sacer esto?*

Answer: *Semus sumus!*

Shem is as short for Shemus as Jem is joky for Jacob. A few toughnecks are still getatable who pretend that aboriginally he was of respectable stemming (he was an outlex between the lines of Ragonar Blaubarb and Horrild Hairwire and an inlaw to Capt. the Hon. and Rev. Mr Bbyrdwood de Trop Blogg was among his most distant connections) but every honest to goodness man in the land of the space of today knows that his back life will not stand being written about in black and white. Putting truth and untruth together a shot may be made at what this hybrid actually was like to look at.

Shem's bodily getup, it seems, included an adze of a skull, an eight of a larkseye, the whoel of a nose, one numb arm up a sleeve, fortytwo hairs off his uncrown, eighteen to his mock lip, a trio of barbels from his megageg chin (sowman's son), the wrong shoulder higher than the right, all ears, an artificial tongue with a natural curl, not a foot to stand on, a handful of thumbs, a blind stomach, a deaf heart, a loose liver, two fifths of two buttocks, one gleetsteen avoirdupoider for him, a manroot of all evil, a salmonkelt's thinskin, eelsblood in his cold toes, a bladder tristended, so much so that young Master Shemmy on his very first debouch at the very dawn of protohistory seeing himself such and such, when playing with thistlewords in their garden nursery, Griefotrofio, at Phig Streat 111, Shuvlin, Old Hoeland, (would we go back there now for sounds, pillings and sense? would we now for annas and annas? would we for full-score eight and a liretta? for twelve blocks one bob? for four testers one groat? not for a dinar! not for jo!) dictited to of all his little brothron and sweestureens the first riddle of the universe: asking, when is a man not a man?: telling them take their time, yungfries, and wait till the tide stops (for from the first his day was a fortnight) and offering the prize of a bittersweet crab, a little present from the past, for their copper age was yet un-minted, to the winner. One said when the heavens are quakers, a second said when Bohemeand lips, a third said when he, no, when hold hard a jiffy, when he is a gnawstick and detarmined to, the next one said when the angel of death kicks the bucket of life, still another said when the wine's at witsends, and still another when lovely wooman stoops to conk him, one of the littliest said me, me, Sem, when pappa papared the harbour, one of the wittiest said, when he yeat ye abblokooken and he zmear hezelf zo zhooken, still one said when you are old I'm grey fall full wi sleep, and still another when wee deader walkner, and another when he is just only after having being semisized, an-other when yea, he hath no mananas, and one when dosc pigs they begin now that they will flies up intil the looft. All were wrong, so Shem himself, the doctator, took the cake, the correct solution being — all give it up? — ; when he is a — yours till the rending of the rocks, — Sham.

Shem was a sham and a low sham and his lowness creeped out first via foodstuffs. So low was he that he preferred Gibsen's tea-time salmon tinned, as inexpensive as pleasing, to the plumpest roeheavy lax or the friskiest parr or smolt troutlet that ever was gaffed between Leixlip and Island Bridge and many was the time he repeated in his botulism that no junglegrown pineapple ever smacked like the whoppers you shook out of Ananias' cans, Findlater and Gladstone's, Corner House, Englend. None of your inchthick blueblooded Balaclava fried-at-belief-stakes or juicejelly legs of the Grex's molten mutton or greasilygristly grunters' goupons or slice upon slab of luscious goosebosom with lump after load of plumpudding stuffing all aswim in a swamp of bogoakgravy for that greekenhearted yude! Rosbif of Old Zealand! he could not attouch it. See what happens when your somatophage merman takes his fancy to our virgitarian swan? He even ran away with hunself and became a farsoonerite, saying he would far sooner muddle through the hash of lentils in Europe than meddle with Irrland's split little pea. Once when among those rebels in a state of hopelessly helpless intoxication the piscivore strove to lift a czitround peel to either nostril, hiccupping, apparently impromptued by the hibat he had with his glottal stop, that he kukkakould flowrish for ever by the smell, as the czitr, as the kcedron, like a scedar, of the founts, on mountains, with limon on, of Lebanon. O! the lowness of him was beneath all up to that sunk to! No likedbylike firewater or firstserved firstshot or gulletburn gin or honest brewbarrett beer either. O dear no! Instead the tragic jester sobbed himself wheywhingingly sick of life on some sort of a rhubarbarous maundarin yellagreen funkleblue windigut diodying applejack squeezed from sour grapefruice and, to hear him twixt his sedimental cupslips when he had gulfed down mmmmuch too mmmmany gourds of it retching off to almost as low withswillers, who always knew notwithstanding when they had had enough and were rightly indignant at the wretch's hospitality when they found to their horror they could not carry another drop, it came straight from the noble white fat, jo, openwide sat, jo, jo, her why hide that, jo jo jo, the winevat, of the most serene magyansty az archdiochesse, if she is a duck, she's a douches, and when she has a feherbour snot her fault, now is it? artstouchups, funny you're grinning at, fancy you're in her yet, Fanny Urinia.

Aint that swell, hey? Peamengro! Talk about lowness! Any dog's quantity of it visibly oozed out thickly from this dirty little blacking beetle for the very fourth snap the Tulloch-Turnbull girl with her coldblood kodak shotted the as yet unremuneranded national apostate, who was cowardly gun and camera shy, taking what he fondly thought was a short cut to Caer Fere, Soak Amerigas, vias the shipsteam *Pridewin*, after having buried a hatchet not so long before, by the wrong goods exeunt, num-

171

mer desh to tren, into Patatapapaveri's, fruiterers and musical florists, with his *Ciaho, chavi! Sar shin, shillipen?* she knew the vice out of bridewell was a bad fast man by his walk on the spot.

[Johns is a different butcher's. Next place you are up town pay him a visit. Or better still, come tobuy. You will enjoy cattlemen's spring meat. Johns is now quite divorced from baking. Fattens, kills, flays, hangs, draws, quarters and pieces. Feel his lambs! Ex! Feel how sheap! Exex! His liver too is great value, a spatiality! Exexex! COMMUNICATED.]

Around that time, moravar, one generally, for luvvomony hoped or at any rate suspected among morticians that he would early turn out badly, develop hereditary pulmonary T.B., and do for himself one dandy time, nay, of a pelting night blanketed creditors, hearing a coarse song and splash off Eden Quay sighed and rolled over, sure all was up, but, though he fell heavily and locally into debit, not even then could such an antinomian be true to type. He would not put fire to his cerebrum; he would not throw himself in Liffey; he would not explaud himself with pneumantics; he refused to saffrocake himself with a sod. With the foreign devil's leave the fraid born fraud diddled even death. *Anzi*, cabled (but shaking the worth out of his maulth: Guarda-costa leporello? Szasas Kraicz!) from his Nearapoblican asylum to his jonathan for a brother: Here tokay, gone tomory, we're spluched, do something, Fireless. And had answer: Inconvenient, David.

You see, chaps, it will trickle out, freaksily of course, but the tom and the shorty of it is: he was in his bardic memory low. All the time he kept on treasuring with condign satisfaction each and every crumb of trektalk, covetous of his neighbour's word, and if ever, during a Munda conversazione commoted in the nation's interest, delicate tippits were thrown out to him touch-ing his evil courses by some wellwishers, vainly pleading by scriptural arguments with the opprobrious papist about trying to brace up for the kidos of the thing, Scally wag, and be a men instead of a dem scrounger, dish it all, such as: Pray, what is the meaning, sousy, of that continental expression, if you ever came acrux it, we think it is a word transpiciously like *canaille?*: or: Did you anywhere, kennel, on your gullible's travels or during your rural troubadouring, happen to stumble upon a certain gay young nobleman whimpering to the name of Low Swine who always addresses women out of the one corner of his mouth, lives on loans and is furtivefree yours of age? without one sigh of haste like the supreme prig he was, and not a bit sorry, he would pull a vacant landlubber's face, root with earwaker's pensile in the outer of his lauscher and then, lisping, the prattlepate parnella, to kill time, and swatting his deadbest to think what under the canopies of Jansens Chrest would any decent son of an Albiogenselman who had bin to an university think, let a lent hit a hint and begin to tell all the intelligentsia admitted to that tamileasy samtalaisy conclamazzione (since, still and before physicians, lawyers merchant, belfry pollititians, agricolous manufraudurers, sacrestanes of the Pure River Society, philanthropicks lodging on as many boards round the panesthetic at the same time as possible) the whole lifelong swrine story of his entire low cornaille existence, abusing his deceased ancestors wherever the sods were and one moment tarabooming great blunderguns (poh!) about his farfamed fine Poppamore, Mr Humhum, whom history, climate and entertainment made the first of his sept and always up to debt, though Eavens ears ow many fines he faces, and another moment visanvrerssas, cruaching three jeers (pah!) for his rotten little ghost of a Peppybeg, Mr Himmyshimmy, a blighty, a reeky, a lighty, a scrapy, a bably, a ninny, dirty seventh among thieves and always bottom sawyer, till nowan knowed how howmely howme could be, giving unsolicited testimony on behalf of the absent, as glib as eaveswater to those present (who meanwhile, with increasing lack of interest in his semantics, allowed various subconscious smickers to drivel slowly across their fichers), unconsciously explaining, for inkstands, with a meticulosity bordering on the insane, the various meanings of all the different foreign parts of speech he misused and cuttlefishing every lie unshrinkable about all the other people in the story, leaving out, of course, foreconsciously, the simple worf and plague and poison they had cornered him about until there was not a snoozer among them but was utterly undeceived in the heel of the reel by the recital of the rigmarole.

He went without saying that the cull disliked anything anyway approaching a plain straightforward standup or knockdown row and, as often as he was called in to umpire any octagonal argument among slangwhangers, the accomplished washout always used to rub shoulders with the last speaker and clasp shakers (the handtouch which is speech without words) and agree to every word as soon as half uttered, command me!, your servant, good, I revere you, how, my seer? be drinking that! quite truth, gratias, I'm yoush, see wha'm hearing?, also goods, please it, me sure?, be filling this!, quiso, you said it, apasafello, muchas grassyass, is there firing-on-me?, is their girlic-on-you?, to your good self, your sulphur, and then at once focuss his whole unbalanced attention upon the next octagonist who managed to catch a listener's eye, asking and imploring him out of his piteous onewinker, (*hemoptysia diadumenos*) whether there was anything in the world he could do to please him and to overflow his tumbletantaliser for him yet once more.

One hailcannon night (for his departure was attended by a heavy downpour) as very recently as some thousand rains ago he was therefore treated with what closely resembled parsonal violence, being soggert all unsuspectingly through the deserted village of Tumblin-on-the-Leafy from Mr Vanhomrigh's house at 81 bis Mabbot's Mall as far as Green Patch beyond the brickfields of Salmon Pool by rival teams of slowspiers counter quicklimers who finally, as rahilly they had been deteened out rawther laetich, thought, busnis hits busnis, they had better be streaking for home after their Auborne-to-Auborne, with thanks for the pleasant evening, one and all disgustedly, instead of ruggering him back, and awake, reconciled (though they were as jealous as could be cullions about all the truffles they had brought on him) to a friendship, fast and furious, which merely arose out of the noxious pervert's perfect lowness. Again there was a hope that people,

174

looking on him with the contemp of the contempibles, after first gaving him a roll in the dirt, might pity and forgive him, if properly deloused, but the pleb was born a Quicklow and sank alowing till he stank out of sight.

All Saints beat Belial! Mickil Goals to Nichil! Notpossible! Already?

In Nowhere has yet the Whole World taken part of himself for his
  Wife;   •
By Nowhere have Poorparents been sentenced to Worms, Blood and
  Thunder for Life
Not yet has the Emp from Corpsica forced the Arth out of Engleterre;
Not yet have the Sachsen and Judder on the Mound of a Word made
  Warre;
Not yet Witchywithcy of Wench struck Fire of his Heath from on
  Hoath;
Not yet his Arcobaleine forespoken Peacepeace upon Oath;
Cleftfoot from Hempal must tumpel, Blamefool Gardener's bound to
  fall;
Broken Eggs will poursuive bitten Apples for where theirs is Will
  there's his Wall;
But the Mountstill frowns on the Millstream while their Madsons
  leap his Bier
And her Rillstrill liffs to His Murkesty all her daft Daughters laff
  in her Ear.
Till the four Shores of deff Tory Island let the douʒe dumm Eire-
  whiggs raille!
Hirp! Hirp! for their Missed Understandings! chirps the Ballat of
  Perce-Oreille.

O fortunous casualitas! Lefty takes the cherubcake while Rights cloves his hoof. Darkies never done tug that coon out to play non-excretory, anti-sexuous, misoxenetic, gaasy pure, flesh and blood games, written and composed and sung and danced by Niscemus Nemon, same as piccaninnies play all day, those old (none of your honeys and rubbers!) games for fun and ele-ment we used to play with Dina and old Joe kicking her behind and before and the yellow girl kicking him behind old Joe,

175

games like *Thom Thom the Thonderman*, *Put the Wind up the Peeler*, *Hat in the Ring*, *Prisson your Pritchards and Play Withers Team*, *Mikel on the Luckypig*, *Nickel in the Slot*, *Sheila Harnett and her Cow*, *Adam and Ell*, *Humble Bumble*, *Moggie's on the Wall*, *Twos and Threes*, *American Jump*, *Fox Come out of your Den*, *Broken Bottles*, *Writing a Letter to Punch*, *Tiptop is a Sweetstore*, *Henressy Crump Expelled*, *Postman's Knock*, *Are We Fairlys Represented?*, *Solomon Silent reading*, *Appletree Bearstone*, *I know a Washerwoman*, *Hospitals*, *As I was Walking*, *There is Oneyone's House in Dreamcolohour*, *Battle of Waterloo*, *Colours*, *Eggs in the Bush*, *Habberdasherisher*, *Telling your Dreams*, *What's the Time*, *Nap*, *Ducking Mammy*, *Last Man Standing*, *Heali Baboon and the Forky Theagues*, *Fickleyes and Futilears*, *Handmarried but once in my Life and I'll never commit such a Sin agin*, *Zip Cooney Candy*, *Turkey in the Straw*, *This is the Way we sow the Seed of a long and lusty Morning*, *Hops of Fun at Miliken's Make*, *I seen the Toothbrush with Pat Farrel*, *Here's the Fat to graze the Priest's Boots*, *When his Steam was like a Raimbrandt round Mac Garvey.*

Now it is notoriously known how on that surprisingly bludgeony Unity Sunday when the grand germogall allstar bout was harrily the rage between our weltingtoms extraordinary and our pettythicks the marshalaisy and Irish eyes of welcome were smiling daggers down their backs, when the roth, vice and blause met the noyr blank and rogues and the grim white and cold bet the black fighting tans, categorically unimperatived by the maxims, a rank funk getting the better of him, the scut in a bad fit of pyjamas fled like a leveret for his bare lives, to Talviland, ahone ahaza, pursued by the scented curses of all the village belles and, without having struck one blow, (pig stole on him was lust he lagging it was becaused dust he shook) kuskykorked himself up tight in his inkbattle house, badly the worse for boosegas, there to stay in afar for the life, where, as there was not a moment to be lost, after he had boxed around with his fortepiano till he was whole bach bamp him and bump him blues, he collapsed carefully under a bedtick from Schwitzer's, his face enveloped into a dead warrior's telemac, with a lullobaw's somnbomnet and a whotwaterwottle at his feet to stoke his energy of waiting, moaning feebly, in monkmarian monotheme, but tarned long and then a nation louder, while engaged in swallowing from a large ampullar, that his pawdry's purgatory was more than a nigger bloke could bear, hemiparalysed by the tong warfare and all the shemozzle, (*Daily Maily, fullup Lace! Holy Maly, Mothelup Joss!*) his cheeks and trousers changing colour every time a gat croaked.

How is that for low, laities and gentlenuns? Why, dog of the Crostiguns, whole continents rang with this Kairokorran lowness! Sheols of houris in chems upon divans, (revolted stellas vespertine vesamong them) at a bare (O!) mention of the scaly rybald exclaimed: Poisse!

But would anyone, short of a madhouse, believe it? Neither of those clean little cherubum, Nero or Nobookisonester himself, ever nursed such a spoiled opinion of his monstrous marvellosity as did this mental and moral defective (here perhaps at the vanessance of his lownest) who was known to grognt rather than gunnard upon one occasion, while drinking heavily of spirits to that interlocutor *a latere* and private privysuckatary he used to pal around with, in the kavehazs, one Davy Browne-Nowlan, his heavenlaid twin, (this hambone dogpoet pseudoed himself under the hangname he gave himself of Bethgelert) in the porchway of a gipsy's bar (Shem always blaspheming, so holy writ, Billy, he would try, old Belly, and pay this one manjack congregant of his four soups every lass of nexmouth, Bolly, so sure as thair's a tail on a commet, as a taste for storik's fortytooth, that is to stay, to listen out, ony twenny minnies moe, Bully, his Ballade Imaginaire which was to be dubbed *Wine, Woman and Waterclocks*, or *How a Guy Finks and Fawkes When He Is Going Batty*, by Maistre Sheames de la Plume, some most dreadful stuff in a murderous mirrorhand) that he was avoopf (parn me!) aware of no other shaggspick, other Shakhisbeard, either prexactly unlike his polar andthisishis or procisely the seem as woops (parn!) as what he fancied or guessed the sames as he was himself and that, greet scoot, duckings and thuggery, though he was foxed fux to fux like a bunnyboy rodger with all the teashop

177

lionses of Lumdrum hivanhoesed up gagainst him, being a lapsis linquo with a ruvidubb shortartempa, bad cad dad fad sad mad nad vanhaty bear, the consciquenchers of casuality prepestered crusswords in postposition, scruff, scruffer, scrufferumurraimost andallthatsortofthing, if reams stood to reason and his lanka-livline lasted he would wipe alley english spooker, multaphoniaksically spuking, off the face of the erse.

After the thorough fright he got that bloody, Swithun's day, though every doorpost in muchtried Lucalizod was smeared with generous erstborn gore and every free for all cobbleway slippery with the bloods of heroes, crying to Welkins for others, and noahs and cul verts agush with tears of joy, our low waster never had the common baalamb's pluck to stir out and about the compound while everyone else of the torchlit throng, slashers and sliced alike, mobbu on massa, waaded and baaded around, yampyam pampyam, chanting the Gillooly chorus, from the Monster Book of Paltryattic Puetrie, *O pura e pia bella!* in junk et sampam or in secular sinkalarum, heads up, on his bonafide avocation (the little folk creeping on all fours to their natural school treat but childishly gleeful when a stray whizzer sang out intermediately) and happy belongers to the fairer sex on their usual quest for higher things, but vying with Lady Smythe to avenge Mac-Jobber, went stonestepping with their bickerrstaffs on educated feet, plinkity plonk, across the sevenspan ponte *dei colori* set up over the slop after the war-to-end war by Messrs a charitable government for the only once (dia dose Finnados!) he did take a tompip peepestrella throug a threedraw eighteen hawkspower durdicky telescope, luminous to larbourd only like the lamps in Nassaustrass, out of his westernmost keyhole, spitting at the impenetrablum wetter, (and it was porcoghastly that outumn) with an eachway hope in his shivering soul, as he prayed to the cloud Incertitude, of finding out for himself, on akkount of all the kules in Kroukaparka or oving to all the kodseoggs in Kalatavala, whether true conciliation was forging ahead or falling back after the celestious intemperance and, for Duvvelsache, why, with his see me see and his my see a corves and his frokerfoskerfuskar

178

layen loves in meeingseeing, he got the charm of his optical life when he found himself (*hic sunt lennones!*) at pointblank range blinking down the barrel of an irregular revolver of the bulldog with a purpose pattern, handled by an unknown quarreler who, supposedly, had been told off to shade and shoot shy Shem should the shit show his shiny shnout out awhile to look facts in their face before being hosed and creased (uprip and jack him!) by six or a dozen of the gayboys.

What, para Saom Plaom, in the names of Deucalion and Pyrrha, and the incensed privy and the licensed pantry gods and Stator and Victor and Kutt and Runn and the whole mesa redonda of Lorencao Otulass in convocacaon, was this disinterestingly low human type, this Calumnious Column of Cloaxity, this Bengalese Beacon of Biloxity, this Annamite Aper of Atroxity, really at, it will be precise to quarify, for he seems in a badbad case?

The answer, to do all the diddies in one dedal, would sound: from pulling himself on his most flavoured canal the huge chesthouse of his elders (the *Popapreta*, and some navico, navvies!) he had flickered up and flinnered down into a drug and drunkery addict, growing megalomane of a loose past. This explains the litany of septuncial lettertrumpets honorific, highpitched, erudite, neoclassical, which he so loved as patricianly to manuscribe after his name. It would have diverted, if ever seen, the shuddersome spectacle of this semidemented zany amid the inspissated grime of his glaucous den making believe to read his usylessly unreadable Blue Book of Eccles, *édition de ténèbres*, (even yet sighs the Most Different, Dr. Poindejenk, authorised bowdler and censor, it can't be repeated!) turning over three sheets at a wind, telling himself delightedly, no espellor mor so, that every splurge on the vellum he blundered over was an aisling vision more gorgeous than the one before t.i.t.s., a roseschelle cottage by the sea for nothing for ever, a ladies tryon hosiery raffle at liberty, a sewerful of guineagold wine with brancomongepadenopie and sickcylinder oysters worth a billion a bite, an entire operahouse (there was to be stamping room only in the prompter's box and

everthemore his queque kept swelling) of enthusiastic noble-
women flinging every coronetcrimsoned stitch they had off at
his probscenium, one after the others, inamagoaded into ajustil-
loosing themselves, in their gaiety pantheomime, when, egad, sir,
acordant to all acountstrick, he squealed the topsquall im *Deal
Lil Shemlockup Yellin* (geewhiz, jew ear that far! soap ewer!
loutgout of sabaous! juice like a boyd!) for fully five minutes, in-
finitely better than Baraton McGluckin with a scrumptious cocked
hat and three green, cheese and tangerine trinity plumes on the
right handle side of his amarellous head, a coat macfarlane (the
kerssest cut, you understand?) a sponiard's digger at his ribs,
(*Alfaiate punxit*) an azulblu blowsheet for his blousebosom
blossom and a dean's crozier that he won from Cardinal Lin-
dundarri and Cardinal Carchingarri and Cardinal Loriotuli and
Cardinal Occidentaccia (ah ho!) in the dearby darby doubled for
falling first over the hurdles, madam, in the odder hand, a.a.t.s.o.t.,
but what with the murky light, the botchy print, the tattered
cover, the jigjagged page, the fumbling fingers, the foxtrotting
fleas, the lieabed lice, the scum on his tongue, the drop in his
eye, the lump in his throat, the drink in his pottle, the itch in his
palm, the wail of his wind, the grief from his breath, the fog of
his mindfag, the buzz in his braintree, the tic of his conscience,
the height up his rage, the gush down his fundament, the fire
in his gorge, the tickle of his tail, the bane in his bullugs, the
squince in his suil, the rot in his eater, the ycho in his earer,
the totters of his toes, the tetters on his tumtytum, the rats in his
garret, the bats in his belfry, the budgerigars and bumbosolom
beaubirds, the hullabaloo and the dust in his ears since it took him
a month to steal a march he was hardset to mumorise more than
a word a week. Hake's haulin! Hook's fisk! Can you beat it?
Whawe! I say, can you bait it? Was there ever heard of such
lowdown blackguardism? Positively it woolies one to think
over it.

Yet the bumpersprinkler used to boast aloud alone to himself
with a haccent on it when Mynfadher was a boer constructor and
Hoy was a lexical student, parole, and corrected with the black-

board (trying to copy the stage Englesemen he broughts their house down on, shouting: Bravure, surr Chorles! Letter purfect! Culossal, Loose Wallor! Spache!) how he had been toed out of all the schicker families of the klondykers from Pioupioureich, Swabspays, the land of Nod, Shruggers' Country, Pension Danubierhome and Barbaropolis, who had settled and stratified in the capital city after its hebdomodary metropoliarchialisation as sunblistered, moonplastered, gory, wheedling, joviale, litcherous and full, ordered off the gorgeous premises in most cases on account of his smell which all cookmaids eminently objected to as ressembling the bombinubble puzzo that welled out of the pozzo. Instead of chuthoring those model households plain wholesome pothooks (a thing he never possessed of his Nigerian own) what do you think Vulgariano did but study with stolen fruit how cutely to copy all their various styles of signature so as one day to utter an epical forged cheque on the public for his own private profit until, as just related, the Dustbin's United Scullerymaid's and Househelp's Sorority, better known as Sluttery's Mowlted Futt, turned him down and assisted nature by unitedly shoeing the source of annoyance out of the place altogether and taytotally on the heat of the moment, holding one another's gonk (for no-one, hound or scrublady, not even the Turk, ungreekable in purscent of the armenable, dared whiff the polecat at close range) and making some pointopointing remarks as they done so at the perfects of the Sniffey, your honour, aboon the lyow why a stunk, mister.

[Jymes wishes to hear from wearers of abandoned female costumes, gratefully received, wadmel jumper, rather full pair of culottes and onthergarmenteries, to start city life together. His jymes is out of job, would sit and write. He has lately commited one of the then commandments but she will now assist. Superior built, domestic, regular layer. Also got the boot. He appreciates it. Copies. ABORTISEMENT.]

One cannot even begin to post figure out a statuesquo ante as to how slow in reality the excommunicated Drumcondriac, nate Hamis, really was. Who can say how many pseudostylic shamiana, how few or how many of the most venerated public impostures, how very many piously forged palimpsests slipped in the first place by this morbid process from his pelagiarist pen?

Be that as it may, but for that light phantastic of his gnose's glow as it slid lucifericiously within an inch of its page (he would touch at its from time to other, the red eye of his fear in saddishness, to ensign the colours by the beerlitz in his mathness and his educandees to outhue to themselves in the cries of girl-glee: gember! inkware! chonchambre! cinsero! zinnzabar! tincture and gin!) Nibs never would have quilled a seriph to sheepskin. By that rosy lampoon's effluvious burning and with help of the simulchronic flush in his pann (a ghinee a ghirk he ghets there!) he scrabbled and scratched and scriobbled and skrevened nameless shamelessness about everybody ever he met, even sharing a precipitation under the idlish tarriers' umbrella of a showerproof wall, while all over up and down the four margins of this rancid Shem stuff the evilsmeller (who was devoted to Uldfadar Sardanapalus) used to stipple endlessly inartistic portraits of himself in the act of reciting old Nichiabelli's monolook interyerear *Hanno, o Nonanno, acce'l brubblemm'*as, ser Autore, q.e.d., a heartbreakingly handsome young paolo with love lyrics for the goyls in his eyols, a plaintiff's tanner vuice, a jucal inkome of one hundred and thirtytwo dranchmas per yard from Broken Hill stranded estate, Camebreech mannings, cutting a great dash in a brandnew two guinea dress suit and a burled hogsford hired for a Fursday evenin merry pawty, anna loavely long pair of inky Italian moostarshes glistering with boric vaseline and frangipani. Puh! How unwhisperably so!

The house O'Shea or O'Shame, *Quivapieno*, known as the Haunted Inkbottle, no number Brimstone Walk, Asia in Ireland, as it was infested with the raps, with his penname SHUT sepia-scraped on the doorplate and a blind of black sailcloth over its wan phwinshogue, in which the soulcontracted son of the secret cell groped through life at the expense of the taxpayers, dejected into day and night with jesuit bark and bitter bite, calico-hydrants of zolfor and scoppialamina by full and forty Queasi-sanos, every day in everyone's way more exceeding in violent abuse of self and others, was the worst, it is hoped, even in our western playboyish world for pure mousefarm filth. You brag of your brass castle or your tyled house in ballyfermont? Niggs, niggs and niggs again. For this was a stinksome inkenstink, quite puzzonal to the wrottel. Smatterafact, Angles aftanon browsing there thought not Edam reeked more rare. My wud! The warped flooring of the lair and soundconducting walls thereof, to say nothing of the uprights and imposts, were persianly literatured with burst loveletters, telltale stories, stickyback snaps, doubtful eggshells, bouchers, flints, borers, puffers, amygdaloid almonds, rindless raisins, alphybettyformed verbage, vivlical viasses, om-piter dictas, visus umbique, ahems and ahahs, imeffible tries at speech unasyllabled, you owe mes, eyoldhyms, fluefoul smut, fallen lucifers, vestas which had served, showered ornaments, borrowed brogues, reversibles jackets, blackeye lenses, family jars, falsehair shirts, Godforsaken scapulars, neverworn breeches, cutthroat ties, counterfeit franks, best intentions, curried notes, upset latten tintacks, unused mill and stumpling stones, twisted quills, painful digests, magnifying wineglasses, solid objects cast at goblins, once current puns, quashed quotatoes, messes of mot-tage, unquestionable issue papers, seedy ejaculations, limerick damns, crocodile tears, spilt ink, blasphematory spits, stale shest-nuts, schoolgirls', young ladies', milkmaids', washerwomen's, shopkeepers' wives, merry widows', ex nuns', vice abbess's, pro virgins', super whores', silent sisters', Charleys' aunts', grand-mothers', mothers'-in-laws', fostermothers', godmothers' garters, tress clippings from right, lift and cintrum, worms of snot, toothsome pickings, cans of Swiss condensed bilk, highbrow lotions, kisses from the antipodes, presents from pickpockets, borrowed plumes, relaxable handgrips, princess promises, lees of whine, deoxodised carbons, convertible collars, diviliouker doffers, broken wafers, unloosed shoe latchets, crooked strait waistcoats, fresh horrors from Hades, globules of mercury, undeleted glete, glass eyes for an eye, gloss teeth for a tooth, war moans, special sighs, longsufferings of longstanding, ahs ohs ouis sis jas jos gias neys thaws sos, yeses and yeses and yeses, to which, if one has the stomach to add the breakages, upheavals distortions, inversions of all this chambermade music one stands, given a grain of goodwill, a fair chance of actually seeing the whirling dervish, Tumult, son of Thunder, self exiled in upon his ego, a nightlong a shaking betwixtween white or reddr hawrors, noondayterrorised to skin and bone by an ineluctable phantom (may the Shaper have mercery on him!) writing the mystery of himsel in furniture.

Of course our low hero was a self valeter by choice of need so up he got up whatever is meant by a stourbridge clay kitchenette and lithargogalenu fowlhouse for the sake of akes (the umpple does not fall very far from the dumpertree) which the moromelodious jigsmith, in defiance of the Uncontrollable Birth Preservativation (Game and Poultry) Act, playing lallaryrook cookerynook, by the dodginess of his lentern, brooled and cocked and potched in an athanor, whites and yolks and yilks and whotes to the frulling fredonnance of *Mas blanca que la blanca hermana* and *Amarilla, muy bien*, with cinnamon and locusts and wild beeswax and liquorice and Carrageen moss and blaster of Barry's and Asther's mess and Huster's micture and Yellownan's embrocation and Pinkingtone's patty and stardust and sinner's tears, acuredent to Sharadan's *Art of Panning*, chanting, for all regale to the like of the legs he left behind with Litty fun Letty fan Leven, his cantraps of fermented words, abracadabra calubra culorum, (his oewfs à la Madame Gabrielle de l'Eglise, his avgs à la Mistress B. de B. Meinfelde, his eiers Usquadmala à la pomme de ciel, his uoves, oves and uves à la Sulphate de Soude, his ochiuri sowtay sowmmonay à la Monseigneur, his soufflosion of oogs with somekat on toyast à la Mère Puard, his Poggadovies alla Fenella, his Frideggs à la Tricarême) in what was meant for a closet (Ah ho! If only he had listened better to the four masters that infanted him Father Mathew and Le Père Noble and Pastor Lucas and Padre Aguilar — not forgetting Layteacher Baudwin! Ah ho!) His costive Satan's antimonian manganese limolitmious

nature never needed such an alcove so, when Robber and Mum-
sell, the pulpic dictators, on the nudgment of their legal advisers,
Messrs Codex and Podex, and under his own benefiction of their
pastor Father Flammeus Falconer, boycotted him of all mutton-
suet candles and romeruled stationery for any purpose, he winged
away on a wildgoup's chase across the kathartic ocean and made
synthetic ink and sensitive paper for his own end out of his wit's
waste. You ask, in Sam Hill, how? Let manner and matter of this
for these our sporting times be cloaked up in the language of
blushfed porporates that an Anglican ordinal, not reading his
own rude dunsky tunga, may ever behold the brand of scarlet
on the brow of her of Babylon and feel not the pink one in his
own damned cheek.

*Primum opifex, altus prosator, ad terram viviparam et cuncti-
potentem sine ullo pudore nec venia, suscepto pluviali atque discinctis
perizomatis, natibus nudis uti nati fuissent, sese adpropinquans,
flens et gemens, in manum suam evacuavit* (highly prosy, crap in his
hand, sorry!), *postea, animale nigro exoneratus, classicum pulsans,
stercus proprium, quod appellavit deiectiones suas, in vas olim
honorabile tristitiae posuit, eodem sub invocatione fratrorum gemino-
rum Medardi et Godardi laete ac melliflue minxit, psalmum qui
incipit: Lingua mea calamus scribae velociter scribentis: magna voce
cantitans* (did a piss, says he was dejected, asks to be exonerated),
*demum ex stercore turpi cum divi Orionis iucunditate mixto, cocto,
frigorique exposito, encaustum sibi fecit indelibile* (faked O'Ryan's,
the indelible ink).

Then, pious Eneas, conformant to the fulminant firman which
enjoins on the tremylose terrian that, when the call comes, he
shall produce nichthemerically from his unheavenly body a no
uncertain quantity of obscene matter not protected by copriright
in the United Stars of Ourania or bedeed and bedood and bedang
and bedung to him, with this double dye, brought to blood heat,
gallic acid on iron ore, through the bowels of his misery, flashly,
faithly, nastily, appropriately, this Esuan Menschavik and the first
till last alshemist wrote over every square inch of the only fools-
cap available, his own body, till by its corrosive sublimation one

continuous present tense integument slowly unfolded all marry-voising moodmoulded cyclewheeling history (thereby, he said, reflecting from his own individual person life unlivable, trans-accidentated through the slow fires of consciousness into a dividual chaos, perilous, potent, common to allflesh, human only, mortal) but with each word that would not pass away the squid-self which he had squirtscreened from the crystalline world waned chagreenold and doriangrayer in its dudhud. This exists that isits after having been said we know. And dabal take dab-nal! And the dal dabal dab aldanabal! So perhaps, agglaggagglo-meratively asaspenking, after all and arklast fore arklyst on his last public misappearance, circling the square, for the deathfête of Saint Ignaceous Poisonivy, of the Fickle Crowd (hopon the sexth day of Hogsober, killim our king, layum low!) and brandish-ing his bellbearing stylo, the shining keyman of the wilds of change, if what is sauce for the zassy is souse for the zazimas, the blond cop who thought it was ink was out of his depth but bright in the main.

Petty constable Sistersen of the Kruis-Kroon-Kraal it was, the parochial watch, big the dog the dig the bog the bagger the dugger the begadag degabug, who had been detailed from pollute stoties to save him, this the quemquem, that the quum, from the ligatureliablous effects of foul clay in little clots and mobmauling on looks, that wrongcountered the tenderfoot an eveling near the livingsmeansuniumgetherum, Knockmaree, Comty Mea, reel-ing more to the right than he lurched to the left, on his way from a protoprostitute (he would always have a (stp!) little pigeoness somewhure with his arch girl, Arcoiris, smockname of Mergyt) just as he was butting in rand the coyner of bad times under a hideful between the rival doors of warm bethels of worship through his boardelhouse fongster, greeting for grazious oras as usual: Where ladies have they that a dog meansort herring? Sergo, search me, the incapable reparteed with a selfevitant subtlety so obviously spurious and, raising his hair, after the grace, with the christmas under his clutcharm, for Portsymasser and Purtsymessus and Pertsymiss and Partsymasters, like a prance of findingos, with a shillto shallto slipny stripny, in he skittled. Swikey! The allwhite poors guardiant, pulpably of balltossic stummung, was literally astundished over the painful sake, how he burstteself, which he was gone to, where he intent to did he, whether you think will, wherend the whole current of the afternoon whats the souch of a surch hads of hits of hims, urged and staggered thereto in his countryports at the caledosian capacity for Lieutuvisky of the caftan's wineskin and even more so, during, looking his bigmost astonishments, it was said him, aschu, fun the concerned outgift of the dead med dirt, how that, arrahbejibbers, conspuent to the dominical order and exking noblish permish, he was namely coon at bringer at home two gallonts, as per royal, full poultry till his murder. Nip up and nab it!

Polthergeistkotzdondherhoploits! Kick? What mother? Whose porter? Which pair? Why namely coon? But our undilligence has been plutherotested so enough of such porterblack lowneess, too base for printink! Perpending that Putterick O'Purcell pulls the coald stoane out of Winterwater's and Silder Seas sing for Harreng our Keng, sept okt nov dez John Phibbs march! We cannot, in mercy or justice nor on the lovom for labaryntos, stay here for the residence of our existings, discussing Tamstar Ham of Tenman's thirst.

JUSTIUS (to himother): Brawn is my name and broad is my nature and I've breit on my brow and all's right with every feature and I'll brune this bird or Brown Bess's bung's gone bandy. I'm the boy to bruise and braise. Baus!

Stand forth, Nayman of Noland (for no longer will I follow you obliquelike through the inspired form of the third person singular and the moods and hesitensies of the deponent but address myself to you, with the empirative of my vendettative, provocative and out direct), stand forth, come boldly, jolly me, move me, zwilling though I am, to laughter in your true colours ere you be back for ever till I give you your talkingto! Shem Macadamson, you know me and I know you and all your shemeries. Where have you been in the uterim, enjoying yourself all the morning since your last wetbed confession? I advise you to conceal yourself, my little friend, as I have said a moment ago and put your hands in my hands and have a nightslong homely little confiteor about things. Let me see. It is looking pretty black against you, we suggest, Sheem avick. You will need all the elements in the river to clean you over it all and a fortifine popespriestpower bull of attender to booth.

Let us pry. We thought, would and did. *Cur, quicquid, ubi, quando, quomodo, quoties, quibus auxiliis?* You were bred, fed, fostered and fattened from holy childhood up in this two easter island on the piejaw of hilarious heaven and roaring the other place (plunders to night of you, blunders what's left of you, flash as flash can!) and now, forsooth, a nogger among the blankards of this dastard century, you have become of twosome twiminds forenenst gods, hidden and discovered, nay, condemned fool, anarch, egoarch, hiresiarch, you have reared your disunited kingdom on the vacuum of your own most intensely doubtful soul. Do you hold yourself then for some god in the manger, Shehohem, that you will neither serve not let serve, pray nor let pray? And here, pay the piety, must I too nerve myself to pray for the loss of selfrespect to equip me for the horrible necessity of scandalisang (my dear sisters, are you ready?) by sloughing off my hope and tremors while we all swin together in the pool of Sodom? I shall shiver for my purity while they will weepbig for your sins. Away with covered words, new Solemonities for old Badsheetbaths! That inharmonious detail, did you name it? Cold caldor! Gee! Victory! Now, opprobro of underslung pipes, johnjacobs, while yet an adolescent (what do I say?), while still puerile in your tubsuit with buttonlegs, you got a handsome present of a selfraising syringe and twin feeders (you know, Monsieur Abgott, in your art of arts, to your cost as well as I do (and don't try to hide it) the penals lots I am now poking at) and the wheeze sort of was you should (if you were as bould a stroke now as the curate that christened you, sonny douth-the-candle!) repopulate the land of your birth and count up your progeny by the hungered head and the angered thousand but you thwarted

the wious pish of your cogodparents, soph, among countless
occasions of failing (for, said you, I will elenchate), adding to the
malice of your transgression, yes, and changing its nature, (you
see I have read your theology for you) alternating the morosity
of my delectations — a philtred love, trysting by tantrums,
small peace in ppenmark — with sensibility, sponsibility, passi-
bility and prostability, your lubbock's other fear pleasures of a
butler's life, even extruding your strabismal apologia, when
legibly depressed, upon defenceless paper and thereby adding to
the already unhappiness of this our popeyed world, scribblative!
— all that too with cantreds of countless catchaleens, the man-
nish as many as the minneful, congested around and about you
for acres and roods and poles or perches, thick as the fluctuant
sands of Chalwador, accomplished women, indeed fully edu-
canded, far from being old and rich behind their dream of arri-
visme, if they have only their honour left, and not deterred by bad
weather when consumed by amorous passion, struggling to possess themselves of your boosh, one son of Sorge for all daughters
of Anguish, *solus cum sola sive cuncties cum omnibobs* (I'd have
been the best man for you, myself), mutely aying for that natural
knot, debituary vases or vessels preposterous, for what would
not have cost you ten bolivars of collarwork or the price of one
ping pang, just a lilt, let us trillt, of the oldest song in the wooed
woodworld, (two-we! to-one!), accompanied by a plain gold
band! Hail! Hail! Highbosomheaving Missmisstress Morna of
the allsweetheartening bridemuredemeanour! Her eye's so gladsome we'll all take shares in the ——groom!

Sniffer of carrion, premature gravedigger, seeker of the nest
of evil in the bosom of a good word, you, who sleep at our vigil
and fast for our feast, you with your dislocated reason, have
cutely foretold, a jophet in your own absence, by blind poring
upon your many scalds and burns and blisters, impetiginous sore
and pustules, by the auspices of that raven cloud, your shade, and
by the auguries of rooks in parlament, death with every disaster,
the dynamitisation of colleagues, the reducing of records to
ashes, the levelling of all customs by blazes, the return of a lot

of sweetempered gunpowdered didst unto dudst but it never stphruck your mudhead's obtundity (O hell, here comes our funeral! O pest, I'll miss the post!) that the more carrots you chop, the more turnips you slit, the more murphies you peel, the more onions you cry over, the more bullbeef you butch, the more mutton you crackerhack, the more potherbs you pound, the fiercer the fire and the longer your spoon and the harder you gruel with more grease to your elbow the merrier fumes your new Irish stew.

O, by the way, yes, another thing occurs to me. You let me tell you, with the utmost politeness, were very ordinarily designed, your birthwrong was, to fall in with Plan, as our nationals should, as all nationists must, and do a certain office (what, I will not tell you) in a certain holy office (nor will I say where) during certain agonising office hours (a clerical party all to yourself) from such a year to such an hour on such and such a date at so and so much a week *pro anno* (Guinness's, may I remind, were just agulp for you, failing in which you might have taken the scales off boilers like any boskop of Yorek) and do your little thruppenny bit and thus earn from the nation true thanks, right here in our place of burden, your bourne of travail and ville of tares, where after a divine's prodigence you drew the first watergasp in your life, from the crib where you once was bit to the crypt you'll be twice as shy of, same as we, long of us, alone with the colt in the curner, where you were as popular as an armenial with the faithful, and you set fire to my tailcoat when I hold the paraffin smoker under yours (I hope that chimney's clear) but, slackly shirking both your bullet and your billet, you beat it backwards like Boulanger from Galway (but he combed the grass against his stride) to sing us a song of alibi, (the cuthone call over the greybounding slowrolling amplyheaving metamorphoseous that oozy rocks parapangle their preposters with) nomad, mooner by lamplight, antinos, shemming amid everyone's repressed laughter to conceal your scatchophily by mating, like a thorough-paste prosodite, masculine monosyllables of the same numerical mus, an Irish emigrant the wrong way out, sitting on your crooked sixpenny stile, an unfrillfrocked quackfriar, you (will you for the laugh of Scheekspair just help mine with the epithet?) semi-semitic serendipitist, you (thanks, I think that describes you) Europasianised Afferyank!

Shall we follow each others a steplonger, drowner of daggers, whiles our liege, tilyet a stranger in the frontyard of his happiness, is taking, (heal helper! one gob, one gap, one gulp and gorger of all!) his refreshment?

There grew up beside you, amid our orisons of the speediest in Novena Lodge, Novara Avenue, in Patripodium-am-Bummel, oaf, outofwork, one remove from an unwashed savage, on his keeping and in yours, (I pose you know why possum hides is cause he haint the nogumtreeeumption) that other, Immaculatus, from head to foot, sir, that pure one, Altrues of other times, he who was well known to celestine circles before he sped aloft, our handsome young spiritual physician that was to be, seducing every sense to selfwilling celebesty, the most winning counterfeuille on our incomeshare lotetree, a chum of the angelets, a youth those reporters so pettitily wanted as gamefellow that they asked his mother for ittle earps brupper to let him tome to Tindertarten, pease, and bing his scooter 'long and 'tend they were all real brothers in the big justright home where Dodd lives, just to teddyfy the life out of him and pat and pass him one with other like musk from hand to hand, that mothersmothered model, that goodlooker with not a flaw whose spiritual toilettes were the talk of half the town, for sunset wear and nightfallen use and daybroken donning and nooncheon showing and the very thing for teasetime, but him you laid low with one hand one fine May morning in the Meddle of your Might, your bosom foe, because he mussed your speller on you or because he cut a pretty figure in the focus of your frontispecs (not one did you slay, no, but a continent!) to find out how his innards worked!

Ever read of that greatgrand landfather of our visionbuilders, Baaboo, the bourgeoismeister, who thought to touch both himmels at the punt of his risen stiffstaff and how wishywashy sank the waters of his thought? Ever thought of that hereticalist Marcon and the two scissymaidies and how bulkily he shat the Ructions gunorrhal? Ever hear of that foxy, that lupo and that monkax and the virgin heir of the Morrisons, eh, blethering ape?

Malingerer in luxury, collector general, what has Your Lowness done in the mealtime with all the hamilkcars of cooked vegetables, the hatfuls of stewed fruit, the suitcases of coddled ales, the Parish funds, me schamer, man, that you kittycoaxed so flexibly out of charitable butteries by yowling heavy with a hollow voice drop of your horrible awful poverty of mind so as you couldn't even pledge a crown of Thorne's to pawn a coat off Trevi's and as how you was bad no end, so you was, so whelp you Sinner Pitre and Sinner Poule, with the chicken's gape and *pas mal de siècle*, which, by the by, Reynaldo, is the ordinary emetic French for grenadier's drip. To let you have your plank and your bonewash (O the hastroubles you lost!), to give you your pound of platinum and a thousand thongs a year (O, you were excruciated, in honour bound to the cross of your own cruelfiction!) to let you have your Sarday spree and holinight sleep (fame would come to you twixt a sleep and a wake) and leave to lie till Paraskivee and the cockcock crows for Danmark. (O Jonathan, your estomach!) The simian has no sentiment secretions but weep cataracts for all me, Pain the Shamman! Oft in the smelly night will they wallow for a clutch of the famished hand, I say, them bearded jezabelles you hired to rob you, while on your sodden straw impolitely you encored (Airish and nawboggaleesh!) those hornmade ivory dreams you reved of the Ruth you called your companionate, a beauty from the bible, of the flushpots of Euston and the hanging garments of Marylebone. But the dormer moonshee smiled selene and the lightthrowers knickered: who's whinging we? Comport yourself, you inconsistency! Where is that little alimony nestegg against our predictable rainy day? Is it not the fact (gainsay me, cakeeater!) that, while whistlewhirling your crazy elegies around Templetombmount joyntstone, (let him pass, pleasegoodjesusalem, in a bundle of straw, he was balbettised after hay-making) you squandered among underlings the overload of your extravagance and made a hottentot of dulpeners crawsick with your crumbs? Am I not right? Yes? Yes? Yes? Holy wax and holifer! Don't tell me, Leon of the fold, that you are not a loanshark! Look up, old sooty, be advised by mux and take your medicine. The Good Doctor mulled it. Mix it twice before repastures and powder three times a day. It does marvels for your gripins and it's fine for the solitary worm.

Let me finish! Just a little judas tonic, my ghem of all jokes, to make you go green in the gazer. Do you hear what I'm seeing, hammet? And remember that golden silence gives consent, Mr Anklegazer! Cease to be civil, learn to say nay! Whisht! Come here, Herr Studiosus, till I tell you a wig in your ear. We'll do a whisper drive, for if the barishnyas got a twitter of it they'd tell the housetops and then all Cadbury would go crackers. Look! Do you see your dial in the rockingglass? Look well! Bend down a stigmy till I! It's secret! Iggri, I say, the booseleers! I had it from Lamppost Shawe. And he had it from the Mullah. And Mull took it from a Bluecoat schooler. And Gay Socks jot it from Potapheu's wife. And Rantipoll tipped the wink from old Mrs Tinbullet. And as for she was confussed by pro-Brother Thacolicus. And the good brother feels he would need to defecate you. And the Flimsy Follettes are simply beside each other. And Kelly, Kenny and Keogh are up up and in arms. That a cross may crush me if I refuse to believe in it. That I may rock anchor through the ages if I hope it's not true. That the host may choke me if I beneighbour you without my charity! Sh! Shem, you are. Sh! You are mad!

He points the deathbone and the quick are still. *Insomnia, somnia somniorum. Awmawm.*

MERCIUS (of hisself): *Domine vopiscus!* My fault, his fault, a kingship through a fault! Pariah, cannibal Cain, I who oathily forswore the womb that bore you and the paps I sometimes sucked, you who ever since have been one black mass of jigs and jimjams, haunted by a convulsionary sense of not having been or being all that I might have been or you meant to becoming, bewailing like a man that innocence which I could not defend like a woman, lo, you there, Cathmon-Carbery, and thank Movies from the innermost depths of my still attrite heart, Wherein the days of youyouth are evermixed mimine, now ere the compline hour of being alone athands itself and a puff or so before we yield our spiritus to the wind, for (though that royal one has not yet drunk a gouttelette from his consummation and the flowerpot on the pole, the spaniel pack and their quarry, retainers and the public house proprietor have not budged a millimetre and all that has been done has yet to be done and done again, when's day's woe, and lo, you're doomed, joyday dawns and, la, you dominate) it is to you, firstborn and firstfruit of woe, to me, branded sheep, pick of the wasterpaperbaskel, by the tremours of Thundery and Ulerin's dogstar, you alone, windblasted tree of the knowledge of beautiful andevil, ay, clothed upon with the metuor and shimmering like the horescens, astroglodynamonologos, the child of Nilfit's father, blzb, to me unseen blusher in an obscene coalhole, the cubilibum of your secret sigh, dweller in the downandoutermost where voice only of the dead may come, because ye left from me, because ye laughed on me, because, O me lonly son, ye are forgetting me!, that our turfbrown mummy is acoming, alpilla, beltilla, ciltilla, deltilla, running with her tidings, old the news of the great big world, sonnies had a scrap, woewoewoe! bab's baby walks at seven months, waywayway! bride leaves her raid at Punchestime, stud stoned before a racecourseful, two belles that make the one appeal, dry yanks will visit old sod, and fourtiered skirts are up, mesdames, while Parimiknie wears popular short legs, and twelve hows to mix a tipsy wake, did ye hear, colt Cooney? did ye ever, filly Fortescue? with a beck, with a spring, all her rillringlets shaking, rocks drops in her tachie, tramtokens in her hair, all waived to a point and then all inuendation, little oldfashioned mummy, little wonderful mummy, ducking under bridges, bellhopping the weirs, dodging by a bit of bog, rapidshooting round the bends, by Tallaght's green hills and the pools of the phooka and a place they call it Blessington and slipping sly by Sallynoggin, as happy as the day is wet, babbling, bubbling, chattering to herself, deloothering the fields on their elbows leaning with the sloothering slide of her, giddygaddy, grannyma, gossipaceous Anna Livia.

He lifts the lifewand and the dumb speak.

— Quoiquoiquoiquoiquoiquoiquoiq!

O

tell me all about

Anna Livia! I want to hear all

about Anna Livia. Well, you know Anna Livia? Yes, of course,
we all know Anna Livia. Tell me all. Tell me now. You'll die
when you hear. Well, you know, when the old cheb went futt
and did what you know. Yes, I know, go on. Wash quit and
don't be dabbling. Tuck up your sleeves and loosen your talk-
tapes. And don't butt me — hike! — when you bend. Or whatever it was they threed to make out he thried to two in the
Fiendish park. He's an awful old reppe. Look at the shirt of him!
Look at the dirt of it! He has all my water black on me. And it
steeping and stuping since this time last wik. How many goes
is it I wonder I washed it? I know by heart the places he likes to
saale, duddurty devil! Scorching my hand and starving my famine to make his private linen public. Wallop it well with your
battle and clean it. My wrists are wrusty rubbing the mouldaw
stains. And the dneepers of wet and the gangres of sin in it! What
was it he did a tail at all on Animal Sendai? And how long was
he under loch and neagh? It was put in the newses what he did,
nicies and priers, the King fierceas Humphrey, with illysus dis-
tilling, exploits and all. But toms will till. I know he well. Temp
untamed will hist for no man. As you spring so shall you neap.
O, the roughty old rappe! Minxing marrage and making loof.

Reeve Gootch was right and Reeve Drughad was sinistrous! And the cut of him! And the strut of him! How he used to hold his head as high as a howeth, the famous eld duke alien, with a hump of grandeur on him like a walking wiesel rat. And his derry's own drawl and his corkswon blather and his doubling stutter and his gullaway swank. Ask Lictor Hackett or Lector Reade of Garda Growley or the Boy with the Billyclub. How elster is he a called at all? Qu'appelle? Huges Caput Earlyfouler. Or where was he born or how was he found? Urgothland, Tvistown on the Kattekat? New Hunshire, Concord on the Merrimake? Who blocksmitt her saft anvil or yelled lep to her pail? Was her banns never loosened in Adam and Eve's or were him and her but captain spliced? For mine ether duck I thee drake. And by my wildgaze I thee gander. Flowey and Mount on the brink of time makes wishes and fears for a happy isthmass. She can show all her lines, with love, license to play. And if they don't remarry that hook and eye may! O, passmore that and oxus another! Don Dom Dombdomb and his wee follyo! Was his help inshored in the Stork and Pelican against bungelars, flu and third risk parties? I heard he dug good tin with his doll, delvan first and duvlin after, when he raped her home, Sabrine asthore, in a parakeet's cage, by dredgerous lands and devious delts, playing catched and mythed with the gleam of her shadda, (if a flic had been there to pop up and pepper him!) past auld min's manse and Maisons Allfou and the rest of incurables and the last of immurables, the quaggy waag for stumbling. Who sold you that jackalantern's tale? Pemmican's pasty pie! Not a grasshoop to ring her, not an antsgrain of ore. In a gabbard he barqued it, the boat of life, from the harbourless Ivernikan Okean, till he spied the loom of his landfall and he loosed two croakers from under his tilt, the gran Phenician rover. By the smell of her kelp they made the pigeonhouse. Like fun they did! But where was Himself, the timoneer? That marchantman he suivied their scutties right over the wash, his cameleer's burnous breezing up on him, till with his runagate bowmpriss he roade and borst her bar. Pilcomayo! Suchcaughtawan! And the whale's away with the grayling! Tune your pipes and fall ahumming, you born ijypt, and you're nothing short of one! Well, ptellomey soon and curb your escumo. When they saw him shoot swift up her sheba sheath, like any gay lord salomon, her bulls they were ruhring, surfed with spree. Boyarka buah! Boyana bueh! He erned his lille Bunbath hard, our staly bred, the trader. He did. Look at here. In this wet of his prow. Don't you know he was kaldt a bairn of the brine, Wasserbourne the waterbaby? Havemmarea, so he was! H.C.E. has a codfisck ee. Shyr she's nearly as badher as him herself. Who? Anna Livia? Ay, Anna Livia. Do you know she was calling bakvandets sals from all around, nyumba noo, chamba choo, to go in till him, her erring cheef, and tickle the pontiff aisy-oisy? She was? Gota pot! Yssel that the limmat? As El Negro winced when he wonced in La Plate. O, tell me all I want to hear, how loft she was lift a laddery dextro! A coneywink after the bunting fell. Letting on she didn't care, sina feza, me absantee, him man in passession, the proxenete! Proxenete and phwhat is phthat? Emme for your reussischer Honddu jarkon! Tell us in franca langua. And call a spate a spate. Did they never sharee you ebro at skol, you antiabecedarian? It's just the same as if I was to go par examplum now in conservancy's cause out of telekinesis and proxenete you. For coxyt sake and is that what she is? Botlettle I thought she'd act that loa. Didn't you spot her in her windaug, wubbling up on an osiery chair, with a meusic before her all cunniform letters, pretending to ribble a reedy derg on a fiddle she bogans without a band on? Sure she can't fiddan a dee, with bow or abandon! Sure, she can't! Tista suck. Well, I never now heard the like of that! Tell me moher. Tell me moatst. Well, old Humber was as glommen as grampus, with the tares at his thor and the buboes for ages and neither bowman nor shot abroad and bales allbrant on the crests of rockies and nera lamp in kitchen or church and giant's holes in Grafton's causeway and deathcap mushrooms round Funglus grave and the great tribune's barrow all darnels occumule, sittang sambre on his sett, drammen and drommen, usking queasy quizzers of his ruful continence, his childlinen scarf to encourage his obsequies where he'd check their debths in that mormon's thames, be questing and handsetl, hop, step and a deepend, with his berths in their toiling moil, his swallower open from swolf to fore and the snipes of the gutter pecking his crocs, hungerstriking all alone and holding doomsdag over hunselv, dreeing his weird, with his dander up, and his fringe combed over his eygs and droming on loft till the sight of the sternes, after zwarthy kowse and weedy broeks and the tits of buddy and the loits of pest and to peer was Parish worth thette mess. You'd think all was dodo belonging to him how he durmed adranse in durance vaal. He had been belching for severn years. And there she was, Anna Livia, she darent catch a winkle of sleep, purling around like a chit of a child, Wendawanda, a fingerthick, in a Lapsummer skirt and damazon cheeks, for to ishim bonzour to her dear dubber Dan. With neuphraties and sault from his maggias. And an odd time she'd cook him up blooms of fisk and lay to his heartsfoot her meddery eygs, yayis, and staynish beacons on toasc and a cupenhave so weeshywashy of Greenland's tay or a dzoupgan of Kaffue mokau an sable or Sikiang sukry or his ale of ferns in trueart pewter and a shinkobread (hamjambo, bana?) for to plaise that man hog stay his stomicker till her pyrraknees shrunk to nutmeg graters while her togglejoints shuck with goyt and as rash as she'd russ with her peakload of vivers up on her sieve (metauwero rage it swales and rieses) my hardey Hek he'd kast them frome him, with a stour of scorn, as much as to say you sow and you sozh, and if he didn't peg the platteau on her tawe, believe you me, she was safe enough. And then she'd esk to vistule a hymn, *The Heart Bowed Down* or *The Rakes of Mallow* or Chelli Michele's *La Calumnia è un Vermicelli* or a balfy bit ov *old Jo Robidson*. Sucho fuffing a fifeing 'twould cut you in two! She'd bate the hen that crowed on the turrace of Babbel. What harm if she knew how to cockle her mouth! And not a mag out of Hum no more than out of the mangle weight. Is that a faith? That's the fact. Then riding the ricka and roya romanche, Annona, gebroren aroostokrat Nivia, dochter of Sense and Art, with Sparks' pirryphlickathims funkling her fan, anner frostivying tresses dasht with virevlies,—

while the prom beauties sreeked nith their bearers' skins! — in a period gown of changeable jade that would robe the wood of two cardinals' chairs and crush poor Cullen and smother Mac-Cabe. O blazerskate! Theirs porpor patches! And brahming to him down the feedchute, with her femtyfyx kinds of fondling endings, the poother rambling off her nose: *Vuggybarney, Wickerymandy! Hello, ducky, please don't die!* Do you know what she started cheeping after, with a choicey voicey like water-glucks or Madame Delba to Romeoreszk? You'll never guess. Tell me. Tell me. *Phoebe, dearest, tell, O tell me* and *I loved you better nor you knew.* And letting on hoon var daft about the warbly sangs from over holmen: *High hellskirt saw ladies hensmoker lily-hung pigger:* and soay and soan and so firth and so forth in a tone sonora and Oom Bothar below like Bheri-Bheri in his sandy cloak, so umvolosy, as deaf as a yawn, the stult! Go away! Poor deef old deary! Yare only teasing! Anna Liv? As chalk is my judge! And didn't she up in sorgues and go and trot doon and stand in her douro, puffing her old dudheen, and every shirvant siligirl or wensum farmerette walking the pilend roads, Sawy, Fundally, Daery or Maery, Milucre, Awny or Graw, usedn't she make her a simp or sign to slip inside by the sullyport? You don't say, the sillypost? Bedouix but I do! Calling them in, one by one (To Blockbeddum here! Here the Shoebenacaddie!) and legging a jig or so on the sihl to show them how to shake their benders and the dainty how to bring to mind the gladdest garments out of sight and all the way of a maid with a man and making a sort of a cackling noise like two and a penny or half a crown and hold-ing up a silliver shiner. Lordy, lordy, did she so? Well, of all the ones ever I heard! Throwing all the neiss little whores in the world at him! To inny captured wench you wish of no matter what sex of pleissful ways two adda tammar a lizzy a lossie to hug and hab haven in Humpy's apron!

And what was the wyerye rima she made! Odet! Odet! Tell me the trent of it while I'm lathering hail out of Denis Florence MacCarthy's combics. Rise it, flut ye, pian piena! I'm dying down off my iodine feet until I lerryn Anna Livia's cushingloo, that was writ by one and rede by two and trouved by a poule in the parco! I can see that, I see you are. How does it tummel? Listen now. Are you listening? Yes, yes! Idneed I am! Tarn your ore ouse! Essonne inne!

By earth and the cloudy but I badly want a brandnew bankside, bedamp and I do, and a plumper at that!

For the putty affair I have is wore out, so it is, sitting, yaping and waiting for my old Dane hodder dodderer, my life in death companion, my frugal key of our larder, my much-altered camel's hump, my jointspoiler, my maymoon's honey, my fool to the last Decemberer, to wake himself out of his winter's doze and bore me down like he used to.

Is there irwell a lord of the manor or a knight of the shire at strike, I wonder, that'd dip me a dace or two in cash for washing and darning his worshipful socks for him now we're run out of horse-brose and milk?

Only for my short Brittas bed made's as snug as it smells it's out I'd lep and off with me to the slobs della Tolka or the plage au Clontarf to feale the gay aire of my salt troublin bay and the race of the saywint up me ambushure.

Onon! Onon! tell me more. Tell me every tiny teign. I want to know every single ingul. Down to what made the potters fly into jagsthole. And why were the vesles vet. That homa fever's winning me wome. If a mahun of the horse but hard me! We'd be bundukiboi meet askarigal. Well, now comes the hazel-hatchery part. After Clondalkin the Kings's Inns. We'll soon be there with the freshet. How many aleveens had she in tool? I can't rightly rede you that. Close only knows. Some say she had three figures to fill and confined herself to a hundred eleven, wan by-wan bywan, making meanacuminamoyas. Olaph lamm et, all that pack? We won't have room in the kirkeyaard. She can't remember half of the cradlenames she smacked on them by the grace of her boxing bishop's infallible slipper, the cane for Kund and abbles for Eyolf and ayther nayther for Yakov Yea. A hundred and how? They did well to rechristien her Pluhurabelle. O loreley! What a loddon lodes! Heigh ho! But it's quite on the cards she'll shed

more and merrier, twills and trills, sparefours and spoilfives, nord-
sihkes and sudsevers and ayes and neins to a litter. Grandfarthring
nap and Messamisery and the knave of all knaves and the joker.
Heehaw! She must have been a gadabount in her day, so she
must, more than most. Shoal she was, gidgad. She had a flewmen
of her owen. Then a toss nare scared that lass, so aimai moe,
that's agapo! Tell me, tell me, how cam she camlin through all
her fellows, the neckar she was, the diveline? Casting her perils
before our swains from Fonte-in-Monte to Tidingtown and
from Tidingtown tilhavet. Linking one and knocking the next,
tapting a flank and tipting a jutty and palling in and pietaring
out and clyding by on her eastway. Waiwhou was the first thur-
ever burst? Someone he was, whuebra they were, in a tactic attack
or in single combat. Tinker, tilar, souldrer, salor, Pieman Peace
or Polistaman. That's the thing I'm elwys on edge to esk. Push
up and push vardar and come to uphill headquarters! Was it
waterlows year, after Grattan or Flood, or when maids were in
Arc or when three stood hosting? Fidaris will find where the
Doubt arises like Nieman from Nirgends found the Nihil. Worry
you sighin foh, Albern, O Anser? Untie the gemman's fistiknots,
Qvic and Nuancee! She can't put her hand on him for the moment. Tez thelon langlo, walking weary! Such a loon waybash-
wards to row! She sid herself she hardly knows whuon the annals
her graveller was, a dynast of Leinster, a wolf of the sea, or what
he did or how blyth she played or how, when, why, where and
who offon he jumpnad her and how it was gave her away. She
was just a young thin pale soft shy slim slip of a thing then,
sauntering, by silvamoonlake and he was a heavy trudging
lurching lieabroad of a Curraghman, making his hay for whose
sun to shine on, as tough as the oaktrees (peats be with them!)
used to rustle that time down by the dykes of killing Kildare,
for forstfellfoss with a plash across her. She thought she's sankh
neathe the ground with nymphant shame when he gave her the
tigris eye! O happy fault! Me wish it was he! You're wrong there,
corribly wrong! Tisn't only tonight you're anacheronistic! It
was ages behind that when nullahs were nowhere, in county

Wickenlow, garden of Erin, before she ever dreamt she'd lave Kilbride and go foaming under Horsepass bridge, with the great southerwestern windstorming her traces and the midland's grainwaster asarch for her track, to wend her ways byandby, robecca or worse, to spin and to grind, to swab and to thrash, for all her golden lifey in the barleyfields and pennylotts of Humphrey's fordofhurdlestown and lie with a landleaper, wellingtonorseher. Alesse, the lagos of girly days! For the dove of the dunas! Wasut? Izod? Are you sarthin suir? Not where the Finn fits into the Mourne, not where the Nore takes lieve of Blœm, not where the Braye divarts the Farer, not where the Moy changez her minds twixt Cullin and Conn tween Cunn and Collin? Or where Neptune sculled and Tritonville rowed and leandros three bumped heroines two? Neya, narev, nen, nonni, nos! Then whereabouts in Ow and Ovoca? Was it yst with wyst or Lucan Yokan or where the hand of man has never set foot? Dell me where, the fairy ferse time! I will if you listen. You know the dinkel dale of Luggelaw? Well, there once dwelt a local heremite, Michael Arklow was his riverend name, (with many a sigh I aspersed his lavabibs!) and one venersderg in junojuly, oso sweet and so cool and so limber she looked, Nance the Nixie, Nanon L'Escaut, in the silence, of the sycomores, all listening, the kindling curves you simply can't stop feeling, he plunged both of his newly anointed hands, the core of his cushlas, in her singimari saffron strumans of hair, parting them and soothing her and mingling it, that was deepdark and ample like this red bog at sundown. By that Vale Vowclose's lucydlac, the reignbeau's heavenarches arronged orranged her. Afrothdizzying galbs, her enamelled eyes indergoading him on to the vierge violetian. Wish a wish! Why a why? Mavro! Letty Lerck's lafing light throw those laurals now on her daphdaph teasesong petrock. Maass! But the majik wavus has elfun anon meshes. And Simba the Slayer of his Oga is slewd. He cuddle not help himself, thurso that hot on him, he had to forget the monk in the man so, rubbing her up and smoothing her down, he baised his lippes in smiling mood, kiss akiss after kisokushk (as he warned her niver to, niver to, nevar) on Anna-na-Poghue's of the freckled forehead. While you'd parse secheressa she hielt her souff'. But she ruz two feet hire in her aisne aestumation. And steppes on stilts ever since. That was kissuahealing with bantur for balm! O, wasn't he the bold priest? And wasn't she the naughty Livvy? Nautic Naama's now her navn. Two lads in scoutsch breeches went through her before that, Barefoot Burn and Wallowme Wade, Lugnaquillia's noblesse pickts, before she had a hint of a hair at her fanny to hide or a bossom to tempt a birch canoedler not to mention a bulgic porterhouse barge. And ere that again, leada, laida, all unraidy, too faint to buoy the fairiest rider, too frail to flirt with a cygnet's plume, she was licked by a hound, Chirripa-Chirruta, while poing her pee, pure and simple, on the spur of the hill in old Kippure, in birdsong and shearingtime, but first of all, worst of all, the wiggly livvly, she sideslipped out by a gap in the Devil's glen while Sally her nurse was sound asleep in a sloot and, feefee fiefie, fell over a spillway before she found her stride and lay and wriggled in all the stagnant black pools of rainy under a fallow coo and she laughed innocefree with her limbs aloft and a whole drove of maiden hawthorns blushing and looking askance upon her.

Drop me the sound of the findhorn's name, Mtu or Mti, sombogger was wisness. And drip me why in the flenders was she frickled. And trickle me through was she marcellewaved or was it weirdly a wig she wore. And whitside did they droop their glows in their florry, aback to wist or affront to sea? In fear to hear the dear so near or longing loth and loathing longing? Are you in the swim or are you out? O go in, go on, go an! I mean about what you know. I know right well what you mean. Rother! You'd like the coifs and guimpes, snouty, and me to do the greasy jub on old Veronica's wipers. What am I rancing now and I'll thank you? Is it a pinny or is it a surplice? Arran, where's your nose? And where's the starch? That's not the vesdre benediction smell. I can tell from here by their *eau de Colo* and the scent of her oder they're Mrs Magrath's. And you ought to have aird them. They've moist come off her. Creases in silk they are, not crampton lawn. Baptiste me, father, for she has sinned!

Through her catchment ring she freed them easy, with her hips'
hurrahs for her knees'dontelleries. The only parr with frills in
old the plain. So they are, I declare! Welland well! If tomorrow
keeps fine who'll come tripping to sightsee? How'll? Ask me
next what I haven't got! The Belvedarean exhibitioners. In their
cruisery caps and oarsclub colours. What hoo, they band! And
what hoa, they buck! And here is her nubilee letters too. Ellis
on quay in scarlet thread. Linked for the world on a flush-
caloured field. Annan exe after to show they're not Laura Ke-
own's. O, may the diabolo twisk your seifety pin! You child of
Mammon, Kinsella's Lilith! Now who has been tearing the leg
of her drawars on her? Which leg is it? The one with the bells
on it. Rinse them out and aston along with you! Where did I
stop? Never stop! Continuarration! You're not there yet. I
amstel waiting. Garonne, garonne!

    Well, after it was put in the Mercy Cordial Mendicants' Sitter-
dag-Zindeh-Munaday Wakeschrift (for once they sullied their
white kidloves, chewing cuds after their dinners of cheeckin and
beggin, with their show us it here and their mind out of that and
their when you're quite finished with the reading matarial), even
the snee that snowdon his hoaring hair had a skunner against
him. Thaw, thaw, sava, savuto! Score Her Chuff Exsquire!
Everywhere erriff you went and every bung you arver dropped
into, in cit or suburb or in addled areas, the Rose and Bottle or
Phoenix Tavern or Power's Inn or Jude's Hotel or wherever you
scoured the countryside from Nannywater to Vartryville or from
Porta Lateen to the lootin quarter you found his ikom etched
tipside down or the cornerboys cammocking his guy and Morris
the Man, with the role of a royss in his turgos the turrible, (Evro-
peahahn cheic house, unskimmed sooit and yahoort, hamman
now cheekmee, Ahdahm this way make, Fatima, half turn!)
reeling and railing round the local as the peihos piped und uban-
jees twanged, with oddfellow's triple tiara busby rotundarinking
round his scalp. Like Pate-by-the-Neva or Pete-over-Meer. This
is the Hausman all paven and stoned, that cribbed the Cabin that
never was owned that cocked his leg and hennad his Egg. And

the mauldrin rabble around him in areopage, fracassing a great bingkan cagnan with their timpan crowders. Mind your Grimm-father! Think of your Ma! Hing the Hong is his jove's hang-nomen! Lilt a bolero, bulling a law! She swore on croststyx nyne wyndabouts she's be level with all the snags of them yet. Par the Vulnerable Virgin's Mary del Dame! So she said to herself she'd frame a plan to fake a shine, the mischiefmaker, the like of it you niever heard. What plan? Tell me quick and dongu so crould! What the meurther did she mague? Well, she bergened a zakbag, a shammy mailsack, with the lend of a loan of the light of his lampion, off one of her swapsons, Shaun the Post, and then she went and consulted her chapboucqs, old Mot Moore, Casey's Euclid and the Fashion Display and made herself tidal to join in the mascarete. O gig goggle of gigguels. I can't tell you how! It's too screaming to rizo, rabbit it all! Minneha, minnehi mina-aehe, minneho! O but you must, you must really! Make my hear it gurgle gurgle, like the farest gargle gargle in the dusky dirgle dargle! By the holy well of Mulhuddart I swear I'd pledge my chanza getting to heaven through Tirry and Killy's mount of impiety to hear it all, aviary word! O, leave me my faculties, woman, a while! If you don't like my story get out of the punt. Well, have it your own way, so. Here, sit down and do as you're bid. Take my stroke and bend to your bow. Forward in and pull your overthepoise! Lisp it slaney and crisp it quiet. Deel me long-some. Tongue your time now. Breathe thet deep. Thouat's the fairway. Hurry slow and scheldt you go. Lynd us your blessed ashes here till I scrub the canon's underpants. Flow now. Ower more. And pooleypooley.

First she let her hair fal and down it flussed to her feet its teviots winding coils. Then, mothernaked, she sampood herself with galawater and fraguant pistania mud, wupper and lauar, from crown to sole. Next she greesed the groove of her keel, warthes and wears and mole and itcher, with antifouling butter-scatch and turfentide and serpenthyme and with leafmould she ushered round prunella isles and eslats dun, quincecunct, allover her little mary. Peeld gold of waxwork her jellybelly and her

grains of incense anguille bronze. And after that she wove a garland for her hair. She pleated it. She plaited. it. Of meadowgrass
and riverflags, the bulrush and waterweed, and of fallen griefs of
weeping willow. Then she made her bracelets and her anklets
and her armlets and a jetty amulet for necklace of clicking cobbles
and pattering pebbles and rumbledown rubble, richmond and
rehr, of Irish rhunerhinerstones and shellmarble bangles. That
done, a dawk of smut to her airy ey, Annushka Lutetiavitch
Pufflovah, and the lellipos cream to her lippeleens and the pick
of the paintbox for her pommettes, from strawbirry reds to
extra violates, and she sendred her boudeloire maids to His
Affluence, Ciliegia Grande and Kirschie Real, the two chirsines,
with respecks from his missus, seepy and sewery, and a request
might she passe of him for a minnikin. A call to pay and light a
taper, in Brie-on-Arrosa, back in a sprizzling. The cock striking
mine, the stalls bridely sign, there's Zambosy waiting for Me!
She said she wouldn't be half her length away. Then, then, as
soon as the lump his back was turned, with her mealiebag slang
over her shulder, Anna Livia, oysterface, forth of her bassein
came.

Describe her! Hustle along, why can't you? Spitz on the iern
while it's hot. I wouldn't miss her for irthing on nerthe. Not for
the lucre of lomba strait. Oceans of Gaud, I mosel hear that!
Ogowe presta! Leste, before Julia sees her! Ishekarry and washe-
meskad, the carishy caratimaney? Whole lady fair? Duodecimo-
roon? Bon a ventura? Malagassy? What had she on, the liddel oud
oddity? How much did she scallop, harness and weights? Here
she is, Amnisty Ann! Call her calamity electrifies man.

No electress at all but old Moppa Necessity, angin mother of
injons. I'll tell you a test. But you must sit still. Will you hold
your peace and listen well to what I am going to say now? It
might have been ten or twenty to one of the night of Allclose or
the nexth of April when the flip of her hoogly igloo flappered and
out toetippit a bushman woman, the dearest little moma ever
you saw, nodding around her, all smiles, with ems of embarras
and aues to awe, between two ages, a judyqueen, not up to your

207

elb. Quick, look at her cute and saise her quirk for the bicker she lives the slicker she grows. Save us and tagus! No more? Werra where in ourthe did you ever pick a Lambay chop as big as a battering ram? Ay, you're right. I'm epte to forgetting, Like Liviam Liddle did Loveme Long. The linth of my hough, I say! She wore a ploughboy's nailstudded clogs, a pair of ploughfields in themselves: a sugarloaf hat with a gaudyquiviry peak and a band of gorse for an arnoment and a hundred streamers dancing off it and a guildered pin to pierce it: owlglassy bicycles boggled her eyes: and a fishnetzeveil for the sun not to spoil the wrinklings of her hydeaspects: potatorings boucled the loose laubes of her laudsnarers: her nude cuba stockings were salmospotspeckled: she sported a galligo shimmy of hazevaipar tinto that never was fast till it ran in the washing: stout stays, the rivals, lined her length: her bloodorange bockknickers, a two in one garment, showed natural nigger boggers, fancyfastened, free to undo: her black-stripe tan joseph was sequansewn and teddybearlined, with wavy rushgreen epaulettes and a leadown here and there of royal swansruff: a brace of gaspers stuck in her hayrope garters: her civvy codroy coat with alpheubett buttons was boundaried round with a twobar tunnel belt: a fourpenny bit in each pocketside weighed her safe from the blowaway windrush; she had a clothes-peg tight astride on her joki's nose and she kep on grinding a sommething quaint in her fiumy mouth and the rrreke of the fluve of the tail of the gawan of her snuffdrab siouler's skirt trailed ffiffty odd Irish miles behind her lungarhodes.

Hellsbells, I'm sorry I missed her! Sweet gumptyum and no-body fainted! But in whelk of her mouths? Was her naze alight? Everyone that saw her said the dowce little delia looked a bit queer. Lotsy trotsy, mind the poddle! Missus, be good and don't fol in the say! Fenny poor hex she must have charred. Kickhams a frumpier ever you saw! Making mush mullet's eyes at her boys dobelon. And they crowned her their chariton queen, all the maids. Of the may? You don't say! Well for her she couldn't see herself. I recknitz wharfore the darling murrayed her mirror. She did? Mersey me! There was a koros of drouthdropping sur-

facemen, boomslanging and plugchewing, fruiteyeing and flower-
feeding, in contemplation of the fluctuation and the undification
of her filimentation, lolling and leasing on North Lazers' Waal
all eelfare week by the Jukar Yoick's and as soon as they saw her
meander by that marritime way in her grasswinter's weeds and
twigged who was under her archdeaconess bonnet, Avondale's
fish and Clarence's poison, sedges an to aneber, Wit-upon-
Crutches to Master Bates: *Between our two southsates and the
granite they're warming, or her face has been lifted or Alp has doped!*

But what was the game in her mixed baggyrhatty? Just the
tembo in her tumbo or pilipili from her pepperpot? Saas and
taas and specis bizaas. And where in thunder did she plunder?
Fore the battle or efter the ball? I want to get it frisk from the
soorce. I aubette my bearb it's worth while poaching on! Shake
it up, do, do! That's a good old son of a ditch! I promise I'll
make it worth your while. And I don't mean maybe. Nor yet
with a goodfor. Spey me pruth and I'll tale you true.

Well, arundgirond in a waveney lyne aringarouma she pattered
and swung and sidled, dribbling her boulder through narrowa
mosses, the diliskydrear on our drier side and the vilde vetchvine
agin us, curara here, careero there, not knowing which medway
or weser to strike it, edereider, making chattahoochee all to her
ain chichiu, like Santa Claus at the cree of the pale and puny,
nistling to hear for their tiny hearties, her arms encircling Isola-
bella, then running with reconciled Romas and Reims, on like a
lech to be off like a dart, then bathing Dirty Hans' spatters with
spittle, with a Christmas box apiece for aisch and iveryone of her
childer, the birthday gifts they dreamt they gabe her, the spoiled
she fleetly laid at our door! On the matt, by the pourch and inunder the cellar. The rivulets ran aflod to see, the glashaboys, the
pollynooties. Out of the paunschaup on to the pyre. And they all
about her, juvenile leads and ingenuinas, from the slime of their
slums and artesaned wellings, rickets and riots, like the Smyly
boys at their vicereine's levee. Vivi vienne, little Annchen! Vielo
Anna, high life! Sing us a sula, O, susuria! Ausone sidulcis!
Hasn't she tambre! Chipping her and raising a bit of a chir or a

209

jary every dive she'd neb in her culdee sacco of wabbash she raabed and reach out her maundy meerschaundize, poor souvenir as per ricorder and all for sore aringarung, stinkers and heelers, laggards and primelads, her furzeborn sons and dribblederry daughters, a thousand and one of them, and wickerpotluck for each of them. For evil and ever. And kiks the buch. A tinker's bann and a barrow to boil his billy for Gipsy Lee; a cartridge of cockaleekie soup for Chummy the Guardsman; for sulky Pender's acid nephew deltoïd drops, curiously strong; a cough and a rattle and wildrose cheeks for poor Piccolina Petite MacFarlane; a jigsaw puzzle of needles and pins and blankets and shins between them for Isabel, Jezebel and Llewelyn Mmarriage; a brazen nose and pigiron mittens for Johnny Walker Beg; a papar flag of the saints and stripes for Kevineen O'Dea; a puffpuff for Pudge Craig and a nightmarching hare for Techertim Tombigby; waterleg and gumboots each for Bully Hayes and Hurricane Hartigan; a prodigal heart and fatted calves for Buck Jones, the pride of Clonliffe; a loaf of bread and a father's early aim for Val from Skibereen; a jauntingcar for Larry Doolin, the Ballyclee jackeen; a seasick trip on a government ship for Teague O'Flanagan; a louse and trap for Jerry Coyle; slushmincepies for Andy Mackenzie; a hairclip and clackdish for Penceless Peter; that twelve sounds look for G. V. Brooke; a drowned doll, to face downwards for modest Sister Anne Mortimer; altar falls for Blanchisse's bed; Wildairs' breechettes for Magpeg Woppington; to Sue Dot a big eye; to Sam Dash a false step; snakes in clover, picked and scotched, and a vaticanned viper catcher's visa for Patsy Presbys; a reiz every morning for Standfast Dick and a drop every minute for Stumblestone Davy; scruboak beads for beatified Biddy; two appletweed stools for Eva Mobbely; for Saara Philpot a jordan vale tearorne; a pretty box of Pettyfib's Powder for Eileen Aruna to whiten her teeth and outflash Helen Arhone; a whippingtop for Eddy Lawless; for Kitty Coleraine of Butterman's Lane a penny wise for her foolish pitcher; a putty shovel for Terry the Puckaun; an apotamus mask for Promoter Dunne; a niester egg with a twicedated shell and a dynamight right for Pavl the Curate;

a collera morbous for Mann in the Cloack; a starr and girton for Draper and Deane; for Will-of-the-Wisp and Barny-the-Bark two mangolds noble to sweeden their bitters; for Oliver Bound a way in his frey; for Seumas, thought little, a crown he feels big; a tibertine's pile with a Congoswood cross on the back for Sunny Twimjim; a praises be and spare me days for Brian the Bravo; penteplenty of pity with lubilashings of lust for Olona Lena Magdalena; for Camilla, Dromilla, Ludmilla, Mamilla, a bucket, a packet, a book and a pillow; for Nancy Shannon a Tuami brooch; for Dora Riparia Hopeandwater a cooling douche and a warmingpan; a pair of Blarney braggs for Wally Meagher; a hairpin slatepencil for Elsie Oram to scratch her toby, doing her best with her volgar fractions; an old age pension for Betty Bellezza; a bag of the blues for Funny Fitz; a *Missa pro Messa* for Taff de Taff; Jill, the spoon of a girl, for Jack, the broth of a boy; a Rogerson Crusoe's Friday fast for Caducus Angelus Rubiconstein; three hundred and sixtysix poplin tyne for revery warp in the weaver's woof for Victor Hugonot; a stiff steaded rake and good varians muck for Kate the Cleaner; a hole in the ballad for Hosty; two dozen of cradles for J.F.X.P. Coppinger; tenpounten on the pop for the daulphins born with five spoiled squibs for Infanta; a letter to last a lifetime for Maggi beyond by the ashpit; the heftiest frozenmeat woman from Lusk to Livienbad for Felim the Ferry; spas and speranza and symposium's syrup for decayed and blind and gouty Gough; a change of naves and joys of ills for Armoricus Tristram Amoor Saint Lawrence; a guillotine shirt for Reuben Redbreast and hempen suspendeats for Brennan on the Moor; an oakanknee for Conditor Sawyer and musquodoboits for Great Tropical Scott; a C3 peduncle for Karmalite Kane; a sunless map of the month, including the sword and stamps, for Shemus O'Shaun the Post; a jackal with hide for Browne but Nolan; a stonecold shoulder for Donn Joe Vance; all lock and no stable for Honorbright Merreytrickx; a big drum for Billy Dunboyne; a guilty goldeny bellows, below me blow me, for Ida Ida and a hushaby rocker, Elletrouvetout, for Who-is-silvier — Where-is-he?; whatever you like to swilly to swash,

Yuinness or Yennessy, Laagen or Niger, for Festus King and Roaring Peter and Frisky Shorty and Treacle Tom and O. B. Behan and Sully the Thug and Master Magrath and Peter Cloran and O'Delawarr Rossa and Nerone MacPacem and whoever you chance to meet knocking around; and a pig's bladder balloon for Selina Susquehanna Stakelum. But what did she give to Pruda Ward and Katty Kanel and Peggy Quilty and Briery Brosna and Teasy Kieran and Ena Lappin and Muriel Maassy and Zusan Camac and Melissa Bradogue and Flora Ferns and Fauna Fox-Goodman and Grettna Greaney and Penelope Inglesante and Lezba Licking like Leytha Liane and Roxana Rohan with Simpatica Sohan and Una Bina Laterza and Trina La Mesme and Philomena O'Farrell and Irmak Elly and Josephine Foyle and Snakeshead Lily and Fountainoy Laura and Marie Xavier Agnes Daisy Frances de Sales Macleay? She gave them ilcka madre's daughter a moonflower and a bloodvein: but the grapes that ripe before reason to them that devide the vinedress. So on Izzy, her shame-maid, love shone befond her tears as from Shem, her penmight, life past befoul his prime.

My colonial, wardha bagful! A bakereen's dusind with tithe tillies to boot. That's what you may call a tale of a tub! And Hibernonian market! All that and more under one crinoline envelope if you dare to break the porkbarrel seal. No wonder they'd run from her pison plague. Throw us your hudson soap for the honour of Clane! The wee taste the water left. I'll raft it back, first thing in the marne. Merced mulde! Ay, and don't forget the reckitts I lohaned you. You've all the swirls your side of the current. Well, am I to blame for that if I have? Who said you're to blame for that if you have? You're a bit on the sharp side. I'm on the wide. Only snuffers' cornets drifts my way that the cracka dvine chucks out of his cassock, with her estheryear's marsh narcissus to make him recant his vanitty fair. Foul strips of his chinook's bible I do be reading, dodwell disgustered but chickled with chuckles at the tittles is drawn on the tattlepage. *Senior ga dito: Faciasi Omo! E omo fu fò.* Ho! Ho! *Senior ga dito: Faciasi Hidamo! Hidamo se ga facessà.* Ha! Ha! And *Die Windermere*

Dichter and Lefanu (Sheridan's) old *House by the Coachyard* and Mill (J.) *On Woman* with *Ditto on the Floss*. Ja, a swamp for Altmuehler and a stone for his flossies! I know how racy they move his wheel. My hands are blawcauld between isker and suda like that piece of pattern chayney there, lying below. Or where is it? Lying beside the sedge I saw it. Hoangho, my sorrow, I've lost it! Aimihi! With that turbary water who could see? So near and yet so far! But O, gihon! I lovat a gabber. I could listen to maure and moravar again. Regn onder river. Flies do your float. Thick is the life for mere.

Well, you know or don't you kennet or haven't I told you every telling has a taling and that's the he and the she of it. Look, look, the dusk is growing! My branches lofty are taking root. And my cold cher's gone ashley. Fieluhr? Filou! What age is at? It saon is late. 'Tis endless now senne eye or erewone last saw Waterhouse's clogh. They took it asunder, I hurd thum sigh. When will they reassemble it? O, my back, my back, my bach! I'd want to go to Aches-les-Pains. Pingpong! There's the Belle for Sexaloitez! And Concepta de Send-us-pray! Pang! Wring out the clothes! Wring in the dew! Godavari, vert the showers! And grant thaya grace! Aman. Will we spread them here now? Ay, we will. Flip! Spread on your bank and I'll spread mine on mine. Flep! It's what I'm doing. Spread! It's churning chill. Der went is rising. I'll lay a few stones on the hostel sheets. A man and his bride embraced between them. Else I'd have sprinkled and folded them only. And I'll tie my butcher's apron here. It's suety yet. The strollers will pass it by. Six shifts, ten kerchiefs, nine to hold to the fire and this for the code, the convent napkins, twelve, one baby's shawl. Good mother Jossiph knows, she said. Whose head? Mutter snores? Deataceas! Wharnow are alle her childer, say? In kingdome gone or power to come or gloria be to them farther? Allalivial, allalluvial! Some here, more no more, more again lost alla stranger. I've heard tell that same brooch of the Shannons was married into a family in Spain. And all the Dunders de Dunnes in Markland's Vineland beyond Brendan's herring pool takes number nine in yangsee's hats. And one of Biddy's

213

beads went bobbing till she rounded up lost histereve with a marigold and a cobbler's candle in a side strain of a main drain of a manzinahurries off Bachelor's Walk. But all that's left to the last of the Meaghers in the loup of the years prefixed and between is one kneebuckle and two hooks in the front. Do you tell me that now? I do in troth. Orara por Orbe and poor Las Animas! Ussa, Ulla, we're umbas all! Mezha, didn't you hear it a deluge of times, ufer and ufer, respund to spond? You deed, you deed! I need, I need! It's that irrawaddyng I've stoke in my aars. It all but husheth the lethest zswound. Oronoko! What's your trouble? Is that the great Finnleader himself in his joakimono on his statue riding the high horse there forehengist? Father of Otters, it is himself! Yonne there! Isset that? On Fallareen Common? You're thinking of Astley's Amphitheayter where the bobby restrained you making sugarstuck pouts to the ghostwhite horse of the Peppers. Throw the cobwebs from your eyes, woman, and spread your washing proper! It's well I know your sort of slop. Flap! Ireland sober is Ireland stiff. Lord help you, Maria, full of grease, the load is with me! Your prayers. I sonht zo! Madammangut! Were you lifting your elbow, tell us, glazy cheeks, in Conway's Carrigacurra canteen? Was I what, hobbledyhips? Flop! Your rere gait's creakorheuman bitts your butts disagrees. Amn't I up since the damp dawn, marthared mary allacook, with Corrigan's pulse and varicoarse veins, my pramaxle smashed, Alice Jane in decline and my oneeyed mongrel twice run over, soaking and bleaching boiler rags, and sweating cold, a widow like me, for to deck my tennis champion son, the laundryman with the lavandier flannels? You won your limpopo limp fron the husky hussars when Collars and Cuffs was heir to the town and your slur gave the stink to Carlow. Holy Scamander, I sar it again! Near the golden falls. Icis on us! Seints of light! Zezere! Subdue your noise, you hamble creature! What is it but a blackburry growth or the dwyergray ass them four old codgers owns. Are you meanam Tarpey and Lyons and Gregory? I meyne now, thank all, the four of them, and the roar of them, that draves that stray in the mist and old Johnny MacDougal along with them. Is that the Poolbeg flasher beyant, pharphar, or a fireboat coasting nyar the Kishtna or a glow I behold within a hedge or my Garry come back from the Indes? Wait till the honeying of the lune, love! Die eve, little eve, die! We see that wonder in your eye. We'll meet again, we'll part once more. The spot I'll seek if the hour you'll find. My chart shines high where the blue milk's upset. Forgivemequick, I'm going! Bubye! And you, pluck your watch, forgetmenot. Your evenlode. So save to jurna's end! My sights are swimming thicker on me by the shadows to this place. I sow home slowly now by own way, moyvalley way. Towy I too, rathmine.

Ah, but she was the queer old skeowsha anyhow, Anna Livia, trinkettoes! And sure he was the quare old buntz too, Dear Dirty Dumpling, foosterfather of fingalls and dottergills. Gammer and gaffer we're all their gangsters. Hadn't he seven dams to wive him? And every dam had her seven crutches. And every crutch had its seven hues. And each hue had a differing cry. Sudds for me and supper for you and the doctor's bill for Joe John. Befor! Bifur! He married his markets, cheap by foul, I know, like any Etrurian Catholic Heathen, in their pinky limony creamy birnies and their turkiss indienne mauves. But at milkidmass who was the spouse? Then all that was was fair. Tys Elvenland! Teems of times and happy returns. The seim anew. Ordovico or viricordo. Anna was, Livia is, Plurabelle's to be. Northmen's thing made southfolk's place but howmulty plurators made eachone in person? Latin me that, my trinity scholard, out of eure sanscreed into oure eryan! *Hircus Civis Eblanensis!* He had buckgoat paps on him, soft ones for orphans. Ho, Lord! Twins of his bosom. Lord save us! And ho! Hey? What all men. Hot? His tittering daughters of. Whawk?

Can't hear with the waters of. The chittering waters of. Flittering bats, fieldmice bawk talk. Ho! Are you not gone ahome? What Thom Malone? Can't hear with bawk of bats, all thim liffeying waters of. Ho, talk save us! My foos won't moos. I feel as old as yonder elm. A tale told of Shaun or Shem? All Livia's daughtersons. Dark hawks hear us. Night! Night! My ho head halls. I feel as heavy as yonder stone. Tell me of John or Shaun? Who were Shem and Shaun the living sons or daughters of? Night now! Tell me, tell me, tell me, elm! Night night! Telmetale of stem or stone. Beside the rivering waters of, hitherandthithering waters of. Night!

II

Every evening at lighting up o'clock sharp and until further notice in Feenichts Playhouse. (Bar and conveniences always open, Diddlem Club douncestears.) Entrancings: gads, a scrab; the quality, one large shilling. Newly billed for each wickeday perfumance. Somndoze massinees. By arraignment, childream's hours, expercatered. Jampots, rinsed porters, taken in token. With nightly redistribution of parts and players by the puppetry producer and daily dubbing of ghosters, with the benediction of the Holy Genesius Archimimus and under the distinguished patronage of their Elderships the Oldens from the four coroners of Findrias, Murias, Gorias and Falias, Messoirs the Coarbs, Clive Sollis, Galorius Kettle, Pobiedo Lancey and Pierre Dusort, while the Caesar-in-Chief looks. On. Sennet. As played to the Adelphi by the Brothers Bratislavoff (Hyrcan and Haristobulus), after humpteen dumpteen revivals. Before all the King's Hoarsers with all the Queen's Mum. And wordloosed over seven seas crowdblast in cellelleneteutoslavzendlatinsoundscript. In four tubbloids. While fern may cald us until firn make cold. *The Mime of Mick, Nick and the Maggies*, adopted from the Ballymooney Bloodriddon Murther by Bluechin Blackdillain (authorways 'Big Storey'), featuring:

GLUGG (Mr Seumas McQuillad, hear the riddles between the robot in his dress circular and the gagster in the rogues' gallery), the bold bad bleak boy of the storybooks, who, when the tabs go up, as we discover, because he knew to mutch, has been divorced into disgrace court by

THE FLORAS (Girl Scouts from St. Bride's Finishing Establishment, demand acidulateds), a month's bunch of pretty maidens who, while they pick on her, their pet peeve, form with valkyrienne licence the guard for

IZOD (Miss Butys Pott, ask the attendantess for a leaflet), a bewitching blonde who dimples delightfully and is approached in loveliness only by her grateful sister reflection in a mirror, the cloud of the opal, who, having jilted Glugg, is being fatally fascinated by

CHUFF (Mr Sean O'Mailey, see the chalk and sanguine pictograph on the safety drop), the fine frank fairhaired fellow of the fairytales, who wrestles for tophole with the bold bad bleak boy Glugg, geminally about caps or puds or tog bags or bog gats or chuting rudskin gunerally or something, until they adumbrace a pattern of somebody else or other, after which they are both carried off the set and brought home to be well soaped, sponged and scrubbed again by

ANN (Miss Corrie Corriendo, Grischun scoula, bring the babes, Pieder, Poder and Turtey, she mistributes mandamus monies, after perdunamento, hendrud aloven entrees, pulcinellis must not miss our national rooster's rag), their poor little old mother-in-lieu, who is woman of the house, playing opposite to

HUMP (Mr Makeall Gone, read the sayings from Laxdalesaga in the programme about King Ericus of Schweden and the spirit's whispers in his magical helmet), cap-a-pipe with watch and topper, coat, crest and supporters, the cause of all our grievances, the whirl, the flash and the trouble, who, having partially recovered from a recent impeachment due to egg everlasting, but throughandthoroughly proconverted, propounded for cyclological, is, studding sail once more, jibsheets and royals, in the semblance of the substance for the membrance of the umbrance with the remnance of the emblence reveiling a quemdam supercargo, of The Rockery, Poopinheavin, engaged in entertaining in his pilgrimst customhouse at Caherlehome-upon-Eskur those statutory persons

THE CUSTOMERS (Components of the Afterhour Courses at St. Patricius' Academy for Grownup Gentlemen, consult the annuary, coldporters sibsuction), a bundle of a dozen of representative locomotive civics, each inn quest of outings, who are still more sloppily served after every cup final by

SAUNDERSON (Mr Knut Oelsvinger, Tiffsdays off, wouldntstop in bad, imitation of flatfish, torchbearing supperaape, dud halfsovereign, no chee daily, rolly pollsies, Glen of the Downs, the Gugnir, his geyswerks, his earsequack, his lokistroki, o.s.v.), a scherinsheiner and spoilcurate, unconcerned in the mystery but under the inflounce of the milldieuw and butt of

KATE (Miss Rachel Lea Varian, she tells forkings for baschfellors, under purdah of card palmer teaput tosspot Madam d'Elta, during the pawses), kook-and-dishdrudge, whitch believes wanthingthats, whouse be the churchyard or whorts up the aasgaars, the show must go on.

Time: the pressant.

With futurist onehorse balletbattle pictures and the Pageant of Past History worked up with animal variations amid everglaning mangrovemazes and beorbtracktors by Messrs Thud and Blunder. Shadows by the film folk, masses by the good people. Promptings by Elanio Vitale. Longshots, upcloses, outblacks and stagetolets by Hexenschuss, Coachmaher, Incubone and Rocknarrag. Creations tastefully designed by Madame Berthe Delamode. Dances arranged by Harley Quinn and Coollimbeina. Jests, jokes, jigs and jorums for the Wake lent from the properties of the late cemented Mr T. M. Finnegan R.I.C. Lipmasks and hairwigs by Ouida Nooikke. Limes and Floods by Crooker and Toll. Kopay pibe by Kappa Pedersen. Hoed Pine hat with twentyfour ventholes by Morgen. Bosse and stringbag from Heteroditheroe's and All Ladies' presents. Tree taken for grafted. Rock rent. Phenecian blends and Sourdanian doofpoosts by Shauvesourishe and Wohntbedarft. The oakmulberryeke with silktrick twomesh from Shop-Sowry, seedsmanchap. Grabstone beg from General Orders Mailed. The crack (that's Cork!) by a smoker from the gods. The interjection (Buckley!) by the fire-ment in the pit. Accidental music providentially arranged by L'Archet and Laccorde. Melodiotiosities in purefusion by the score. To start with in the beginning, we need hirtly bemark, a community prayer, everyone for himself, and to conclude with as an exodus, we think it well to add, a chorale in canon, good for us all for us all us all all. Songs betune the acts by the ambiamphions of Annapolis, Joan MockComic, male soprano, and Jean Souslevin, bass noble, respectively: O, Mester Sogermon, ef thes es whot ye deux, then I'm not surpleased ye want that bottle of Sauvequipeu and Oh Off Nunch Der Rasche Ver Lasse Mitsch Nitscht. Till the summit scenes of climbacks castastrophear, *The Bearded Mountain* (Polymop Baretherootsch), and *The River Romps to Nursery* (Maidykins in Undiform). The whole thugogmagog, including the portions understood to be oddmitted as the results of the respective titulars neglecting to produce themselves, to be wound up for an afterenactment by a Magnificent Transformation Scene showing the Radium Wedding of Neid and Moorning and the Dawn of Peace, Pure, Perfect and Perpetual, Waking the Weary of the World.

An argument follows.

Chuffy was a nangel then and his soard fleshed light like likening. Fools top! Singty, sangty, meekly loose, defendy nous from prowlabouts. Make a shine on the curst. Emen.

But the duvlin sulph was in Glugger, that lost-to-lurning. Punct. He was sbuffing and sputing, tussing like anisine, whipping his eyesoult and gnatsching his teats over the brividies from existers and the outher liubbocks of life. He halth kelchy chosen a clayblade and makes prayses to his three of clubs. To part from these, my corsets, is into overlusting fear. Acts of feet, hoof and jarrety: athletes longfoot. Djowl, uphere!

Aminxt that nombre of evelings, but how pierceful in their sojestiveness were those first girly stirs, with zitterings of flight released and twinglings of twitchbells in rondel after, with waverings that made shimmershake rather naightily all the duskcended airs and shylit beaconings from shehind hims back. Sammy, call

on. Mirrylamb, she was shuffering all the diseasinesses of the un-
herd of. Mary Louisan Shousapinas! If Arck could no more salve
his agnols from the wiles of willy wooly woolf! If all the airish
signics of her dipandump helpabit from an Father Hogam till
the Mutther Masons could not that Glugg to catch her by the
calour of her brideness! Not Rose, Sevilla nor Citronelle; not
Esmeralde, Pervinca nor Indra; not Viola even nor all of them
four themes over. But, the monthage stick in the melmelode jawr,
I am (twintomine) all thees thing. Up tighty in the front, down
again on the loose, drim and drumming on her back and a pop
from her whistle. What is that, O holytroopers? Isot givin yoe?

Up he stulpled, glee you gees, with search a fling did die near
sea, beamy owen and calmy hugh and if you what you my call for
me I will wishyoumaycull for you.

And they are met, face a facing. They are set, force to force.
And no such Copenhague-Marengo was less so fated for a fall
since in Glenasmole of Smiling Thrushes Patch Whyte passed
O'Sheen ascowl.

Arrest thee, scaldbrother! came the evangelion, sabre accu-
sant, from all Saint Joan's Wood to kill or maim him, and be
dumm but ill s'arrested. Et would proffer to his delected one the
his trifle from the grass.

A space. Who are you? The cat's mother. A time. What do
you lack? The look of a queen.

But what is that which is one going to prehend? Seeks, buzzling
is brains, the feinder.

The howtosayto itiswhatis hemustwhomust worden schall.
A darktongues, kunning. O theoperil! Ethiaop lore, the poor lie.
He askit of the hoothed fireshield but it was untergone into the
matthued heaven. He soughed it from the luft but that bore ne
mark ne message. He luked upon the bloomingrund where ongly
his corns were growning. At last he listed back to beckline how
she pranked alone so johntily. The skand for schooling.

With nought a wired from the wordless either.

Item. He was hardset then. He wented to go (somewhere) while
he was weeting. Utem. He wished to grieve on the good persons, that

is the four gentlemen. Otem. And it was not a long time till he was feeling true forim he was goodda purssia and it was short after that he was fooling mehaunt to mehynte he was an injine ruber. Etem. He was at his thinker's aunts to give (the four gentlemen) the presence (of a curpse). And this is what he would be willing. He fould the fourd; they found the hurtled stones; they fell ill with the gravy duck: and he sod town with the roust of the meast. Atem.

Towhere byhangs ourtales.

Ah ho! This poor Glugg! It was so said of him about of his old fontmouther. Truly deplurabel! A dire, O dire! And all the freight-fullness whom he inhebited after his colline born janitor. Some-time towerable! With that hehry antlets on him and the bauble-light bulching out of his sockets whiling away she sprankled his allover with her noces of interregnation: How do you do that lack a lock and pass the poker, please? And bids him tend her, lute and airly. Sing, sweetharp, thing to me anone! So that Glugg, the poor one, in that limbopool which was his subnesciousness he could scares of all knotknow whither his morrder had bourst a blabber or if the vogalstones that hit his tynpan was that mearly his skoll missed her. Misty's trompe or midst his flooting? Ah, ho! Cicely, awe!

The youngly delightsome frilles-in-pleyurs are now showen drawen, if bud one, or, if in florileague, drawens up consociately at the hinder sight of their commoner guardian. Her boy fiend or theirs, if they are so pluriolled, cometh up as a trapadour, sinking how he must fand for himself by gazework what their colours wear as they are all showen drawens up. Tireton, cacheton, tire-ton, ba! Doth that not satisfy youth, sir? Quanty purty bellas, here, Madama Lifay! And what are you going to charm them to, Madama, do say? Cinderynelly angled her slipper; it was cho chiny yet braught her a groom. He will angskt of them from their commoner guardian at next lineup (who is really the rapier of the two though thother brother can hold his own, especially for he bandished it with his hand the hold time, mamain, a simply gra-cious: Mi, O la!), and reloose that thong off his art: Hast thou feel liked carbunckley ones? Apun which his poohoor pricoxity theirs

is a little tittertit of hilarity (Lad-o'-me-soul! Lad-o'-me-soul,
see!) and the wordchary is atvoiced ringsoundinly by their toots
ensembled, though not meaning to be clever, but just with a shrug
of their hips to go to troy and harff a freak at himself by all that
story to the ulstramarines. Otherwised, holding their noises,
they insinuate quiet private, Ni, he make peace in his preaches
and play with esteem.

Warewolff! Olff! Toboo!

So olff for his topheetuck the ruck made raid, aslick aslegs
would run; and he ankered on his hunkers with the belly belly
prest. Asking: What's my muffinstuffinaches for these times? To
weat: Breath and bother and whatarcurss. Then breath more
bother and more whatarcurss. Then no breath no bother but wor-
rawarrawurms. And Shim shallave shome.

As Rigagnolina to Mountagnone, what she meaned he could
not can. All she meaned was golten sylvup, all she meaned was
some Knight's ploung jamn. It's driving her dafft like he's so
dumnb. If he'd lonely talk instead of only gawk as thought yate-
man hat stuck hits stick althrough his spokes and if he woold nut
wolly so! Hee. Speak, sweety bird! Mitzymitzy! Though I did
ate tough turf I'm not the bogdoxy.

— Have you monbreamstone?
— No.
— Or Hellfeuersteyn?
— No.
— Or Van Diemen's coral pearl?
— No.

He has lost.

Off to clutch, Glugg! Forwhat! Shape your reres, Glugg!
Foreweal! Ring we round, Chuff! Fairwell! Chuffchuff's inners
even. All's rice with their whorl!

Yet, ah tears, who can her mater be? She's promised he'd eye
her. To try up her pretti. But now it's so longed and so fared and
so forth. Jerry for jauntings. Alabye! Fled.

The flossies all and mossies all they drooped upon her draped
brimfall. The bowknots, the showlots, they wilted into wocblots.

The pearlagraph, the pearlagraph, knew whitchly whether to weep or laugh. For always down in Carolinas lovely Dinahs vaunt their view.

Poor Isa sits a glooming so gleaming in the gloaming; the tincelles a touch tarnished wind no lovelinoise awound her swan's. Hey, lass! Woefear gleam she so glooming, this pooripathete I solde? Her beauman's gone of a cool. Be good enough to symperise. If he's at anywhere she's therefor to join him. If it's to nowhere she's going to too. Buf if he'll go to be a son to France's she'll stay daughter of Clare. Bring tansy, throw myrtle, strew rue, rue, rue. She is fading out like Journee's clothes so you can't see her now. Still we know how Day the Dyer works, in dims and deeps and dusks and darks. And among the shades that Eve's now wearing she'll meet anew fiancy, tryst and trow. Mammy was, Mimmy is, Minuscoline's to be. In the Dee dips a dame and the dame desires a demselle but the demselle dresses dolly and the dolly does a dulcydamble. The same renew. For though she's unmerried she'll after truss up and help that hussyband how to hop. Hip it and trip it and chirrub and sing. Lord Chuffy's sky sheraph and Glugg's got to swing.

So and so, toe by toe, to and fro they go round, for they are the ingelles, scattering nods as girls who may, for they are an angel's garland.

Catchmire stockings, libertyed garters, shoddyshoes, quicked out with selver. Pennyfair caps on pinnyfore frocks and a ring on her fomefing finger. And they leap so looply, looply, as they link to light. And they look so loovely, loovelit, noosed in a nuptious night. Withasly glints in. Andecoy glants out. They ramp it a little, a lessle, a lissle. Then rompride round in rout.

Say them all but tell them apart, cadenzando coloratura! R is Rubretta and A is Arancia, Y is for Yilla and N for greeneriN. B is Boyblue with odalisque O while W waters the fleurettes of novembrance. Though they're all but merely a schoolgirl yet these way went they. I' th' view o' th'avignue dancing goes entrancing roundly. Miss Oodles of Anems before the Luvium doeslike. So. And then again doeslike. So. And miss Endles of Eons efter Dies of Eirae doeslike. So. And then again doeslike. So. The many wiles of Winsure.

The grocer's bawd she slips her hand in the haricot bag, the lady in waiting sips her sup from the paraffin can, Mrs Wildhare Quickdoctor helts her skelts up the casuaway the flasht instinct she herds if a tinkle of tunder, the widow Megrievy she knits cats' cradles, this bountiful actress leashes a harrier under her tongue, and here's the girl who she's kneeled in coldfashion and she's told her priest (spt!) she's pot on a chap (chp!) and this lass not least, this rickissime woman, who she writes foot fortunes money times over in the nursery dust with her capital thumb. Buzz. All runaway sheep bound back bopeep, trailing their teenes behind them. And these ways wend they. And those ways went they. Winnie, Olive and Beatrice, Nelly and Ida, Amy and Rue. Here they come back, all the gay pack, for they are the florals, from foncey and pansey to papavere's blush, foresake-me-nought, while there's leaf there's hope, with primtim's ruse and marrymay's blossom, all the flowers of the ancelles' garden.

But vicereversing thereout from those palms of perfection to anger arbour, treerack monatan, scroucely out of scout of ocean, virid with woad, what tornaments of complementary rages rocked the divlun from his punchpoll to his tummy's shentre as he displaid all the oathword science of his visible disgrace. He was feeling so funny and floored for the cue, all over which girls as he don't know whose hue. If goosseys gazious would but fain smile him a smile he would be fondling a praise he ate some nice bit of fluff. But no geste reveals the unconnouth. They're all odds against him, the beasties. Scratch. Start.

He dove his head into Wat Murrey, gave Stewart Ryall a puck on the plexus, wrestled a hurry-come-union with the Gillie Beg, wiped all his sinses, martial and menial, out of Shrove Sundy MacFearsome, excremuncted as freely as any frothblower into MacIsaac, had a belting bout, chaste to chaste, with McAdoo about nothing and, childhood's age being aye the shameleast, tel a Tartaran tastarin toothsome tarrascone tourtoun, vestimentivorous chlamydophagian, imbretellated himself for any time untellable with what hung over to the Machonochie Middle from the MacSiccaries of the Breeks. Home!

Allwhile, moush missuies from mungy monsie, preying in his mind, son of Everallin, within himself, he swure. Macnoon maggoty mag! Cross of a coppersmith bishop! He would split. He do big squeal like holy Trichepatte. Seek hells where from yank islanders the petriote's absolation. Mocknitza! Genik! He take skiff come first dagrene day overwide tumbler, rough and dark, till when bow of the shower show of the bower with three shirts and a wind, pagoda permettant, crookolevante, the bruce, the coriolano and the ignacio. From prudals to the secular but from the cumman to the nowter. Byebye, Brassolis, I'm breaving! Our war, Dully Gray! A conansdream of lodascircles, he here schlucefinis. Gelchasser no more! Mischnary for the minestrary to all the sems of Aram. Shimach, eon of Era. Mum's for's maxim, ban's for's book and Dodgesome Dora for hedgehung sheolmastress. And Unkel Silanse coach in diligence. Disconnection of the succeeding. He wholehog himself for carberry banishment care of Pencylmania, Bretish Armerica, to melt Mrs Gloria of the Bunkers' Trust, recorporated, (prunty!) by meteoromancy and linguified heissrohgin, quit to hail a hurry laracor and catch the Paname-Turricum and regain that absendee tarry easty, his città immediata, by an alley and detour with farecard awailable getrennty years. Right for Rovy the Roder. From the safe side of distance! Libera, nostalgia! Beate Laurentie O'Tuli, Euro pra nobis! Every monk his own cashel where every little ligger is his own liogotenente with inclined jambs in full purview to his pronaose and to the deretane at his reredoss. Fuisfinister, fuyerescaper! He would, with the greatest of ease, before of weighting midhook, by dear home trashold on the raging canal, for othersites of Jorden, (heave a hevy, waterboy!) make one of hissens with a knockonacow and a chow collegions and fire off, gheol ghiornal, foull subustioned mullmud, his farced epistol to the hibruws. From Cernilius slomtime prepositus of Toumaria to the clutch in Anteach. Salvo! Ladigs and jointuremen! No more turdenskaulds! Free leaves for ebribadies! All tinsammon in the

228

yord! With harm and aches till farther alters! Wild primates not stop him frem at rearing a writing in handy antics. *Nom de plume!* Gout strap Fenlanns! And send Jarge for Mary Ink-lenders! And daunt you logh if his vineshanky's schwemmy! For he is the general, make no mistake in he. He is General Jinglesome.

Go in for scribenery with the satiety of arthurs in S.P.Q.R.ish and inform to the old sniggering publicking press and its nation of sheepcopers about the whole plighty troth between them, ma-lady of milady made melodi of malodi, she, the lalage of lyon-esses, and him, her knave arrant. To Wildrose La Gilligan from Croppy Crowhore. For all within crystal range.

Ukalepe. Loathers' leave. Had Days. Nemo in Patria. The Luncher Out. Skilly and Carubdish. A Wondering Wreck. From the Mermaids' Tavern. Bullyfamous. Naughtsycalves. Mother of Misery. Walpurgas Nackt.

Maleesh! He would bare to untired world of Leimunconon-nulstria (and what a strip poker globbtrottel they pairs would looks!) how wholefallows, his guffer, the sabbatarian (might faction split his beard!), he too had a great big oh in the megafundum of his tomashunders and how her Lettyshape, his gummer, that congealed sponsar, she had never cessed at waking malters among the jemassons since the cluft that meataxe delt her made her microchasm as gap as down low. So they fished in the kettle and fought free and if she bit his tailibout all hat tiffin for thea. He would jused sit it all write down just as he would jused set it up all writhefully rate in blotch and void, yielding to no man in hymns ignorance, seeing how heartsilly sorey he was, owning to the condrition of his bikestool. And, reading off his fleshskin and writing with his quillbone, fillfull ninequires with it for his auditers, Caxton and Pollock, a most moraculous jeeremyhead sindbook for all the peoples, under the presidency of the suchess of sceaunonsceau, a hadtobe heldin, thoroughly enjoyed by many so meny on block at Boyrut season and for their account ottorly admired by her husband in sole in-timacy, about whose told his innersense and the grusomehed's

yoeureeke of his spectrescope and why he was off colour and how
he was ambothed upon by the very spit of himself, first on the
cheekside by Michelangelo and, besouns thats, over on the owld
jowly side by Bill C. Babby, and the suburb's formule why they
provencials drollo eggspilled him out of his homety dometry nar-
rowedknee domum (osco de basco de pesco de bisco!) because
all his creature comfort was an omulette finas erbas in an ark finis
orbe and, no master how mustered, mind never mend, he could
neither swuck in nonneither swimp in the flood of cecialism and
the best and schortest way of blacking out a caughtalock of all
the sorrors of Sexton until he would accoster her coume il fou in
teto-dous as a wagoner would his mudheeldy wheesindonk at
their trist in Parisise after tourments of tosend years, bread cast
out on waters, making goods at mutuurity, Mondamoiseau of
Casanuova and Mademoisselle from Armentières. Neblonovi's
Nivonovio! Nobbio and Nuby in ennoviacion! Occitantitempoli!
He would si through severalls of sanctuaries maywhatmay might-
whomight so as to meet somewhere, if produced, on a demi pans-
sion for his whole lofetime, payment in goo to slee music and
poisonal comfany, following which, like Ipsey Secumbe, when he
fingon to foil the fluter, she could have all the g. s. M. she moo-
hooed after fore and rickwards to herslF, including science of
sonorous silence, while he, being brung up on soul butter, have
recourse of course to poetry. With tears for his coronaichon,
such as engines weep. Was liffe worth leaving? Nej!

Tholedoth, treetrene! Zokrahsing, stone! Arty, reminiscen-
sitive, at bandstand finale on grand carriero, dreaming largesse
of lifesighs over early lived offs—all old Sators of the Sowsceptre
highly nutritius family histrionic, genitricksling with Avus and
Avia, that simple pair, and descendant down on veloutypads by a
vuncular process to Nurus and Noverca, those notorious nepotists,
circumpictified in their sobrine census, patriss all of them by the
glos on their germane faces and their socerine eyes like transparents
of vitricus, patruuts to a man, the archimade levirs of his ekonome
world. Remember thee, castle throwen? Ones propsperups treed,
now stohong baroque. And oil paint use a pumme if yell trace

me there title to where was a hovel not a havel (the first rattle of
his juniverse) with a tingtumtingling and a next, next and next
(gin a paddy? got a petty? gussies, gif it ope?), while itch ish
shome.

> — My God, alas, that dear olt tumtum home
> Whereof in youthfood port I preyed
> Amook the verdigrassy convict vallsall dazes.
> And cloitered for amourmeant in thy boosome shede!

His mouthfull of ecstasy (for Shing-Yung-Thing in Shina from
Yoruyume across the Timor Sea), herepong (maladventure!) shot
pinging up through the errorooth of his wisdom (who thought
him a Fonar all, feastking of shellies by googling Lovvey, regally
freytherem, eagelly plumed, and wasbut gumboil owrithy prods
wretched some horsery megee plods coffin acid odarkery pluds
dense floppens mugurdy) as thought it had been zawhen intwo.
Wholly sanguish blooded up disconvulsing the fixtures of his
fizz. Apang which his tempory chewer med him a crazy chump
of a Haveajube Sillayass. Joshua Croesus, son of Nunn! Though
he shall live for millions of years a life of billions of years, from
their roseaced glows to their violast lustres, he shall not forget
that pucking Pugases. Holihowlsballs and bloody acres! Like
gnawthing unheardth!

But, by Jove Chronides, Seed of Summ, after at he had bate
his breastplates for, forforget, forforgetting his birdsplace, it was
soon that, that he, that he rehad himself. By a prayer? No, that
comes later. By contrite attrition? Nay, that we passed. Mid
esercizism? So is richt.

And it was so. And Malthos Moramor resumed his soul. With:
Go Ferchios off to Allad out of this! An oldsteinsong. He threwed
his fit up to his aers, rolled his poligone eyes, snivelled from his
snose and blew the guff out of his hornypipe. The hopjoimt jerk
of a ladle broom jig that he learned in locofoco when a redhot
turnspite he. Under reign of old Roastin the Bowl Ratskillers,
readyos! Why was that man for he's doin her wrong! Lookery
looks, how he's knots in his entrails! Mookery mooks, it's a
grippe of his gripes. Seekeryseeks, why his biting he's head off?

Cokerycokes, it's his spurt of coal. And may his tarpitch dilute not give him chromitis! For the mauwe that blinks you blank is mostly Carbo. Where the inflammabilis might pursuive his comburenda with a pure flame and a true flame and a flame all toogasser, soot. The worst is over. Wait! And the dubuny Mag may gang to preesses. With Dinny Finneen, me canty, ho! In the lost of the gleamens. Sousymoust. For he would himself deal a treatment as might be trusted in anticipation of his inculmination unto fructification for the major operation. When (pip!) a message interfering intermitting interskips from them (pet!) on herzian waves, (call her venicey names! call her a stell!) a butterfly from her zipclasped handbag, a wounded dove astarted from, escaping out her forecotes. Isle wail for yews, O doherlynt! The poetesser. And around its scorched cap she has twilled a twine of flame to let the laitiest know she's marrid. And pim it goes backballed. Tot burns it so leste. A claribel cumbeck to errind. Hers before his even, posted ere penned. He's your change, thinkyou methim. Go daft noon, madden, mind the step. Please stoop O to please. Stop. What saying? I have soreunder from to him now, dearmate ashore, so, so compleasely till I can get redressed, which means the end of my stays in the languish of Tintangle. Is you zealous of mes, brother? Did you boo moiety lowd? You suppoted to be the on conditiously rejected? Satanly, lade! Can that sobstuff, whingeywilly! Stop up, mavrone, and sit in my lap, Pepette, though I'd much rather not. Like things are m. ds. is all in vincibles. Decoded.

Now a run for his money! Now a dash to her dot! Old cocker, young crowy, sifadda, sosson. A bran new, speedhount, outstripperous on the wind. Like a waft to wingweary one or a sos to a coastguard. For directly with his whoop, stop and an upalepsy didando a tishy, in appreciable less time than it takes a glaciator to submerger an Atlangthis, was he again, agob, before the trembly ones, a spark's gap off, doubledasguesched, gotten orlop in a simplasailormade and shaking the storm out of his hiccups. The smartest vessel you could find would elazilee him on her knee as her lucky for the Rio Grande. He's a pigtail tarr and if he hadn't got it toothick he'd a telltale tall of his pitcher on a wall with his photure in the papers for cutting moutonlegs and capers, letting on he'd jest be japers and his tail cooked up.

Goal! It's one by its length.

Angelinas, hide from light those hues that your sin beau may bring to light! Though down to your dowerstrip he's bent to knee he maun't know ledgings here.

For a haunting way will go and you need not make your mow. Find the frenge for frocks and translace it into shocks of such as touch with show and show.

He is guessing at hers for all he is worse, the seagoer. Hark to his wily geeses goosling by, and playfair, lady! And note that they who will for exile say can for dog while them that won't leave ingle end says now for know.

For he faulters how he hates to trouble them without.

But leaving codhead's mitre and the heron's plumes sinistrant to the server of servants and rex of regums and making a bolder-dash for lubberty of speech he asks not have you seen a match being struck nor is this powder mine but, letting punplays pass to ernest:

— Haps thee jaoneofergs?
— Nao.
— Haps thee mayjaunties?
— Naohao.
— Haps thee per causes nunsibellies?
— Naohaohao.
— Asky, asky, asky! Gau on! Micaco! Get!

Ping an ping nwan ping pwan pong.

And he did a get, their anayance, and slink his hook away, aleguere come alaguerre, like a chimista inchamisas, whom the harricana hurries and hots foots, zingo, zango, segur. To hoots of utskut, urqrd, jamal, qum, yallah, yawash, yak! For he could ciappacioppachew upon a skarp snakk of pure undefallen engelsk, melanmoon or tartatortoise, tsukisaki or soppisuppon, as raskly and as baskly as your cheesechalk cow cudd spanich. Makoto! Whagta kriowday! Gelagala nausy is. Yet right divining do not was. Hovobovo hafogate hokidimatzi in kamicha! He had his sperrits all foulen on him; to vet, most griposly, he was bedizzled and debuzzled; he had his tristiest cabaleer on; and looked like bruddy Hal. A shelling a cockshy and be donkey shot at? Or a peso besant to join the armada?

But, Sin Showpanza, could anybroddy which walked this world with eyes whiteopen have looked twinsomer than the kerl he left behind him? Candidatus, viridosus, aurilucens, sinelab? Of all the green heroes everwore coton breiches, the whitemost, the goldenest! How he stud theirs with himselfs mookst kevinly, and that anterevolitionary, the churchman childfather from tonsor's tuft to almonder's toes, a haggiography in duotrigesumy, son soptimost of sire sixtusks, of Mayaqueenies sign osure, hevnly buddhy time, inwreathed of his near cissies, a mickly dazzly eely oily with looiscurrals, a soulnetzer by zvesdals priestessd, their trail the tractive, and dem dandypanies knows de play of de eye-lids, with his gamecox spurts and his smile likequid glue (the suessiest sourir ever weanling wore), whiles his host of spritties, lusspillerindernees, they went peahenning a ripidarapidarpad around him, pilgrim prinkips, kerilour kevinour, in neuchoristic congressulations, quite purringly excited, rpdrpd, allauding to him by all the licknames in the litany with the terms in which no little dulsy nayer ever thinks about implying except to her future's year and sending him perfume most praypuffs to setis-fire more then to teasim (shllwe help, now you've massmuled, you t'rigolect a bit? yismik? yimissy?) that he, the finehued, the fairhailed, the farahead, might bouchesave unto each but every-one, asfar as safras durst assune, the havemercyonhurs of his kissier licence. Meanings: Andure the enjurious till imbetther rer. We know you like Latin with essies impures, (and your liber as they sea) we certney like gurgles love the nargleygargley so, arrah-beejee, tell that old frankay boyuk to bellows upthe tombucky in his tumtum argan and give us a gust of his gushy old. Goof!

Hymnumber twentynine. O, the singing! Happy little girly-cums to have adolphted such an Adelphus! O, the swinginging hopops so goholden! They've come to chant en chor. They say

234

their salat, the madiens' prayer to the messiager of His Nabis, prostitating their selfs eachwise and combinedly. Fateha, fold the hands. Be it honoured, bow the head. May thine evings e'en be blossful! Even of bliss! As we so hope for ablution. For the sake of the farbung and of the scent and of the holiodrops. Amems.

A pause. Their orison arises misquewhite as Osman glory, ebbing wasteward, leaves to the soul of light its fading silence (allahlah lahlah lah!), a turquewashed sky. Then:

— Xanthos! Xanthos! Xanthos! We thank to thine, mighty innocent, that diddest bring it off fuitefuite. Should in ofter years it became about you will after desk jobduty becoming a bank midland mansioner we and I shall reside with our obeisant servants among Burke's mobility at La Roseraie, Ailesbury Road. Red bricks are all hellishly good values if you trust to the roster of ads but we'll save up ourselves and nab what's nicest and boskiest of timber trees in the nebohood. Oncaill's plot. Luccombe oaks, Turkish hazels, Greek firs, incense palm edcedras. The hypsometers of Mount Anville is held to be dying out of arthataxis but, praise send Larix U' Thule, the wych elm of Manelagh is still flourishing in the open, because its native of our nature and the seeds was sent by Fortune. We'll have our private palypeachum pillarposterns for lovesick letterines fondly affianxed to our front railings and swings, hammocks, tighttaught balletlines, accomodationnooks and prismic bathboites, to make Envyeyes mouth water and wonder when they binocular us from their embrassured windows in our garden rare. Fyat-Fyat shall be our number on the autokinaton and Chubby in his Chuffs oursforownly chuffeur. T will be waiting for uns as I sold U at the first antries. Our cousin gourmand, Percy, the pup, will denounce the sniffnomers of all callers where among our Seemyease Sister, Tabitha, the ninelived, will extend to the full her hearthy welcome. While the turf and twigs they tattle. Tintin tintin. Lady Marmela Shortbred will walk in for supper with her marchpane switch on, her necklace of almonds and her poirette Sundae dress with bracelets of honey and her cochineal hose with the caramel dancings, the briskly best from Bootiestown, and her suckingstaff of ivory-mint. You mustn't miss it or you'll be sorry. Charmeuses chloes, glycering juwells, lydialight fans and puffumed cynarettes. And the Prince Le Monade has been graciously pleased. His six chocolate pages will run bugling before him and Cococream toddle after with his sticksword in a pink cushion. We think His Sparkling Headiness ought to know Lady Marmela. Luisome his for lissome hers. He's not going to Cork till Cantalamesse or mayhope till Rose Easter or Saint Tibble's Day. So Niomon knows. The Fomor's in his Fin, the Momor's her and hin. A paaralone! A paaralone! And Dublin's all adin. We'll sing a song of Singlemonth and you'll too and you'll. Here are notes. There's the key. One two three. Chours! So come on, ye wealthy gentrymen wibfrufrocksfull of fun! Thin thin! Thin thin! Thej olly and thel ively, thou billy with thee coo, for to jog a jig of a crispness nice and sing a missal too. Hip champouree! Hiphip champouree! O you longtailed blackman, polk it up behind me! Hip champouree! Hiphip champouree! And, jessies, push the pumkik round. Anneliuia!

Since the days of Roamaloose and Rehmoose the pavanos have been strident through their struts of Chapelldiseut, the vaulsies have meed and youdled through the purly ooze of Ballybough, many a mismy cloudy has tripped taintily along that hercourt strayed reelway and the rigadoons have held ragtimed revels on the platauplain of Grangegorman; and, though since then sterlings and guineas have been replaced by brooks and lions and some progress has been made on stilts and the races have come and gone and Thyme, that chef of seasoners, has made his usual astewte use of endadjustables and whatnot willbe isnor was, those danceadeils and cancanzanies have come stimmering down for our begayment through the bedeafdom of po's taeorns, the obcecity of pa's teapucs, as lithe and limbfree limber as when momie mummed at ma.

Just so styled with the nattes are their flowerheads now and each of all has a lovestalk onto herself and the tot of all the tits of their understamens is as open as he can posably she and is tournesoled straightcut or sidewaist, accourdant to the coursets of things feminite, towooerds him in heliolatry, so they may catch-cup in their calyzettes, alls they go troping, those parryshoots from his muscalone pistil, for he can eyespy through them, to their selfcolours, neverthelaest their tissue peepers, (meaning Mullabury mesh, the time of appling flowers, a guarded figure of speech, a variety of perfume, a bridawl, seamist inso one) as leichtly as see saw (O my goodmiss! O my greatmess! O my prizelestly preshoes!) while, dewyfully as dimb dumbelles, all alisten to his elixir. Lovelyt!

And they said to him:

— Enchainted, dear sweet Stainusless, young confessor, dearer dearest, we herehear, aboutobloss, O coelicola, thee salutamt. Pattern of our unschoold, pageantmaster, deliverer of softmis-sives, round the world in forty mails, bag, belt and balmybeam, our barnaboy, our chepachap, with that pampipe in your put-away, gab borab, when you will be after doing all your sight-seeing and soundhearing and smellsniffing and tastytasting and tenderumstouchings in all Daneygaul, send us, your adorables, thou overblaseed, a wise and letters play of all you can ceive, chief celtech chappy, from your holy post now you hast as-certained ceremonially our names. Unclean you art not. Outcaste thou are not. Leperstower, the karman's loki, has not blanched at our pollution and your intercourse at ninety legsplits does not defile. Untouchable is not the scarecrown is on you. You are pure. You are pure. You are in your puerity. You have not brought stinking members into the house of Amanti. Elleb Inam, Titep Notep, we name them to the Hall of Honour. Your head has been touched by the god Enel-Rah and your face has been brightened by the goddess Aruc-Ituc. Return, sainted youngling, and walk once more among us! The rains of Demani are masikal as of yere. And Baraza is all aflower. Siker of calmy days. As shiver as shower can be. Our breed and better class is in brood and bitter pass. Labbeycliath longs. But we're counting on the cluck. The Great Cackler comes again. Sweetstaker, Abel lord of all our haloease, we (to be slightly more femmiliar perhips than is slickly more then nacessory), toutes philomelas as well as **mag-**

delenes, were drawpairs with two pinmarks, BVD and BVD dot, so want lotteries of ticklets posthastem (you appreciate?) so as to be very dainty, if an isaspell, and so as to be verily dandydainty, if an ishibilley, of and on, to and for, by and with, from you. Let the hitback hurry his wayward ere the missive has time to take herself off, 'twill be o'erthemore willfully intomeet if the coming offence can send our shudders before. We ſeem to have being elſewhere as tho' th' had paſs'd in our ſuſpens. Next to our shrinking selves we love sensitivas best. For they are the Angèles. Brick, fauve, jonquil, sprig, fleet, nocturne, smiling bruise. For they are an Angèle's garment. We will be constant (what a word!) and bless the day, for whole hours too, yes, for sold long syne as we shall be heing in our created being of ours elvishness, the day you befell, you dreadful temptation! Now promisus as at our requisted you will remain ignorant of all what you hear and, though if whilst disrobing to the edge of risk, (the bisifings in idolhours that satinfines tootoo!) draw a veil till we next time! You don't want to peach but bejimboed if ye do! Perhelps. We ernst too may. How many months or how many years till the myriadth and first become! Bashfulness be tupped! May he colp, may he colp her, may he mixandmass colp her! Talk with a hare and you wake of a tartars. That's mus. Says the Law. List! Kicky Lacey, the pervergined, and Bianca Mutantini, her conversa, drew their fools longth finnishfurst, Herzog van Vellentam, but me and meother ravin, my coosine of mine, have mour good three chancers, weothers, after Bohnaparts. The mything smile of me, my wholesole assumption, shes nowt me-without as weam twin herewithin, that I love like myselfish, like smithereens robinsongs, like juneses nutslost, like the blue of the sky if I stoop for to spy's between my whiteyoumightcallimbs. How their duel makes their triel! Eer's wax for Sur Soord, dong-dong bollets for the iris riflers, queemswellth of coocome in their combs for the jennyjos. Caro caressimus! Honey swarns where mellisponds. Will bee all buzzy one another minnies for the mere effect that you are so fuld of pollen yourself. Teomeo! Daurdour! We feel unspeechably thoughtless over it all here in Gizzygazelle

238

Tark's bimboowood so pleasekindly communicake with the original sinse we are only yearning as yet how to burgeon. It's meant milliems of centiments deadlost or mislaid on them but, master of snakes, we can sloughchange in the nip of a napple solongas we can allsee for deedsetton your quick. By the hook in your look we're eyed for aye were you begging the questuan with your lutean bowl round Monkmesserag. And whenever you're tingling in your trout we're sure to be tangled in our ticements. It's game, ma chère, be off with your shepherdress on! Upsome cauda! Behose our handmades for the lured! To these nunce we are but yours in ammatures yet well come that day we shall ope to be ores. Then shalt thou see, seeing, the sight. No more hoaxites! Nay more gifting in mennage! A her's fancy for a his friend and then that fellow yours after this follow ours. Vania, Vania Vaniorum, Domne Vanias!

Hightime is ups be it down into outs according! When there shall be foods for vermin as full as feeds for the fett, eat on earth as there's hot in oven. When every Klitty of a scolderymeid shall hold every yardscullion's right to stimm her uprecht for whimsoever, whether on privates, whather in publics. And when all us romance catholeens shall have ones for all amanseprated. And the world is maidfree. Methanks. So much for His Meignysthy man! And all his bigyttens. So till Coquette to tell Cockotte to teach Connie Curley to touch Cattie Hayre and tip Carminia to tap La Chérie though where the diggings he dwellst amongst us here's nobody knows save Mary. Whyfor we go ringing hands in hands in gyrogyrorondo.

These bright elects, consentconsorted, they were waltzing up their willside with their princesome handsome angeline chiuff while in those wherebus there wont bears way (mearing unknown, a place where pigeons carry fire to seethe viands, a miry hill, belge end sore footh) oaths and screams and bawley groans with a belchybubhub and a hellabelow bedemmed and bediabbled the arimaining lucisphere. Helldsdend, whelldselse! Lonedom's breach lay foulend up uncouth not be broched by punns and reedles. Yet the ring gayed rund rorosily with a drat for a brat

239

you. Yasha Yash ate sassage and mash. So he found he bash, poor Yasha Yash. And you wonna make one of our micknick party. No honaryhuest on our sposhialiste. For poor Glugger was dazed and late in his crave, ay he, laid in his grave.

But low, boys low, he rises, shrivering, with his spittyful eyes and his whoozebecome woice. Ephthah! Cisamis! Examen of conscience scruples now he to the best of his memory schemado. Nu mere for ever siden on the stolen. With his tumescinquinance in the thight of his tumstull. No more singing all the dags in his sengaggeng. Experssly at hand counterhand. Trinitatis kink had mudded his dome, peccat and pent fore, pree. Hymserf, munchaowl, maden, born of thug tribe into brood blackmail, dooly redecant allbigenesis henesies. He, by bletchendmacht of the golls, proforhim penance and come off enternatural. He, selfsufficiencer, eggscumuddher-in-chaff sporticolorissimo, what though the duthsthrows in his lavabad eyes, maketomake polentay rossum, (Good savours queen with the stem of swuith Aftreck! Fit for king of Zundas) out of bianconies, hiking ahake like any nudge-meroughgorude all over Terracuta. No more throw acids, face all lovabilities, appeal for the union and play for tirnitys. He, praise Saint Calembaurnus, make clean breastsack of goody girl now as ever drank milksoep from a spoen, weedhearted boy of potter and mudder, chip of old Flinn the Flinter, twig of the hider that tanned him. He go calaboosh all same he tell him out. Teufleuf man he strip him all mussymussy calico blong him all same he tell him all out how he make what name. He, through wolkenic connection, relation belong this remarklable moliman, Anaks Andrum, parley-glutton pure blood Jebusite, centy procent Erserum spoking. Drugmallt storehuse. Intrance on back. Most open on the lay-days. He, A. A., in peachskin shantungs, possible, sooth to say, notwithstanding far former guiles and he gaining fish consider-able, by saving grace after avalunch, to look most prophitable out of smily skibluh eye. He repeat of him as pious alios cos he ast for shave and haircut people said he'd shape of hegoat where he just was sheep of herrgott with his tile togged. Top. Not true what chronicles is bringing his portemanteau priamed full potatowards. Big dumm crumm digaditchies say short again akter, even while lossassinated by summan, he coaxyorum a pennysilvers offarings bloadonages with candid zuckers on Spinshesses Walk in presents to lilithe maidinettes for at bloo his noose for him with pruriest pollygameous inatentions, he having that pecuniarity ailmint spectacularly in heather cliff emurgency on gale days because souffrant chronic from a plentitude of house torts. Collosul rhodomantic not wert one bronze lie Scholarina say as he, greyed vike cuddlepuller, walk in her sleep his pig indicks weg femtyfem funts. Of so little is her timentrousnest great for greeting his immensesness. Sutt soonas sett they were, her uyes as his auroholes. Kaledvalch! How could one classically? One could naught critically. Ininest lightingshaft only for lovalit smugpipe, his Mistress Mereshame, of cupric tresses, the formwhite foaminine, the ambersandalled, after Aasdocktor Talop's onamuttony legture. A mish, holy balm of seinsed myrries, he is as good as a mountain and everybody what is found of his gients he knew Meistral Wikingson, furframed Noordwogen's kampften, with complexion of blushing dolomite fanned by ozeone brisees, what naver saw his bedshead farrer and nuver met his swigamore, have his ignomen from prima signation of being Master Milchku, queerest man in the benighted queendom, and, adcraft aidant, how he found the kids. Other accuse him as lochkneeghed forsunkener, dope in stockknob, all ameltingmoult after rhomatism, purely simply tammy ratkins. The kurds of Copt on the berberutters and their bedaweens! Even was Shes whole begeds off before all his nahars in the koldbethizzdryel. No gudth! Not one zouz! They whiteliveried ragsups, two Whales of the Sea of Deceit, they bloodiblabstard shooters, three Dromedaries of the Sands of Calumdonia. As is note worthies to shock his hind! Ur greeft on them! Such askors and their ruperts they are putting in for more osghirs is alse false liarnels. The frockenhalted victims! Whore affirm is agains sempry Lotta Karssens. They would lick their lenses before they would negatise a jom petter from his sodalites. In his contrary and on reality, which Bichop Babwith bares to his whitness in his *Just a Fication of*

241

Villumses, this Mr Heer Assassor Neelson, of sorestate hearing, diseased, formarly with Adenoiks, den feed all lighty, laxtleap great change of retiring family buckler, highly accurect in his everythinks, from tencents coupoll to bargain basement, live with howthold of nummer seven, wideawake, woundabout, wokinbetts, weeklings, in black velvet on geolgian mission senest mangy years his rear in the lane pictures, blanking same with autonaut and annexes and got a daarlingt babyboy bucktooth, the thick of a gobstick, coming on ever so nerses nursely, gracies to goodess, at 81. That why all parks up excited about his gunnfodder. That why ecrazyaztecs and the crime ministers preaching him mornings and makes a power of spoon vittles out of his praverbs. That why he, persona erecta, glycorawman arseniful femorniser, for a trial by julias, in celestial sunhat, with two purses agitatating his theopot with wokklebout shake, rather incoherend, from one 18 to one 18 biss, young shy gay youngs. Sympoly far infusing up pritty tipidities to lock up their rhainodaisies and be nice and twainty in the shade. Old grand tuttut toucher up of young poetographies and he turn aroundabrupth red altfrumpishly like hear samhar tionnor falls some make one noise. It's his last lap, Gigantic, fare him weal! Revelation! A fact. True bill. By a jury of matrons. Hump for humbleness, dump for dirts. And, to make a long stoney badder and a whorly show a parfect sight, his Thing went the wholyway retup Suffrogate Strate.

Helpmeat too, contrasta toga, his fiery goosemother, laotsey taotsey, woman who did, he tell princes of the age about. You sound on me, judges! Suppose we brisken up. Kings! Meet the Mem, Avenlith, all viviparous out of couple of lizards. She just as fenny as he is fulgar. How laat soever her latest still her sawlogs come up all standing. Psing a psalm of psexpeans, apocryphul of rhyme! His cheekmole of allaph foriverever her allinall and his Kuran never teachit her the be the owner of thyself. So she not swop her eckcot hjem for Howarden's Castle, Englandwales. But be the alleance of iern on his flamen vestacoat, the fibule of broochbronze to his wintermantle of pointefox. Who not knows she, the Madame Cooley-Couley, spawife to laird of manna, when first come into the pictures more as hundreads elskerelks' yahrds of annams call away, factory fresh and fiuming at the mouth, wronged by Hwemwednoget (magrathmagreeth, he takable a rap for that early party) and whenceforward Ani Mama and her fiertey bustles terrified of gmere gnomes of gmountains and furibound to be back in her mytinbeddy? Schi schi, she feightened allsouls at pignpugn and gets a pan in her stummi from the pialabellars in their pur war. Yet jackticktating all around her about his poorliness due to pannellism and grime for that he harboured her when feme sole, her zoravarn lhorde and givnergenral, and led her in antient consort ruhm and bound her durant coverture so as she could not steal from him, oz her or damman, so as if ever she's beleaved by checkenbrooth death since both was parties to the feed it's Hetman MacCumhal foots the funeral. Mealwhile she nutre him jacent from her elmer's almsdish, giantar and tschaina as sieme as bibrondas with Foli Signur's tinner roumanschy to fishle the ladwigs out of his lugwags, like a skittering kitty skattering hayels, when his favourites were all beruffled on him and her own undesirables justickulating, it was such a blowick day. Winden wanden wild like wenchen wenden wanton. The why if he but would bite and plug his baccypipes and renownse the devlins in all their pumbs and kip the streelwarkers out of the plague and nettleses milk from sickling the honeycoombe and kop Ulo Bubo selling foulty treepes, she would make massa dinars with her savuneer dealinsh and delicate her nutbrown glory cloack to Mayde Berenice and hang herself in Ostmannstown Saint Megan's and make no more mulierage before mahatmas or moslemans, but would ondulate her shookerloft hat from Alpoleary with a viv baselgia and a clamast apotria like any purple cardinal's princess or woman of the grave word to the papal legate from the Vatucum, Monsaigneur Rabbinsohn Crucis, with an ass of milg to his cowmate and chilterlings on account of all he quaqueduxed for the hnor of Hrom and the nations abhord him and wop mezzo scudo to Sant Pursy Orelli that gave Luiz-Marios Josephs their loyal devouces to be offered up missas for vowts for widders.

Hear, O worldwithout! Tiny tattling! Backwoods, be wary! Daintytrees, go dutch!

But who comes yond with pire on poletop? He who relights our spearing torch, the moon. Bring lolave branches to mud cabins and peace to the tents of Ceder, Neomenie! The feast of Tubbournigglers is at hand. Shopshup. Inisfail! Timple temple tells the bells. In syngagyng a sangasongue. For all in Ondslosby. And, the hag they damename Coverfew hists from her lane. And haste, 'tis time for bairns ta hame. Chickchilds, comeho to roo. Comehome to roo, wee chickchilds doo, when the wildworewolf's abroad. Ah, let's away and let's gay and let's stay chez where the log foyer's burning!

It darkles, (tinct, tint) all this our funnaminal world. Yon marshpond by ruodmark verge is visited by the tide. Alvemmarea! We are circumveiloped by obscuritads. Man and belves frieren. There is a wish on them to be not doing or anything. Or just for rugs. Zoo koud! Drr, deff, coal lay on and, pzz, call us pyrress! Ha. Where is our highly honourworthy salutable spousefounderess? The foolish one of the family is within. Haha! Huzoor, where's he? At house, to's pitty. With Nancy Hands. Tcheetchee! Hound through the maize has fled. What hou! Isegrim under lolling ears. Far wol! And wheaten bells bide breathless. All. The trail of Gill not yet is to be seen, rocksdrops, up benn, down dell, a craggy road for rambling. Nor yet through starland that silver sash. What era's o'ering? Lang gong late. Say long, scielo! Sillume, see lo! Selene, sail O! Amune! Ark!? Noh?! Nought stirs in spinney. The swayful pathways of the dragonfly spider stay still in reedery. Quiet takes back her folded fields. Tranquille thanks. Adew. In deerhaven, imbraced, alleged, injoynted and unlatched, the birds, tommelise too, quail silent. ii. Luathan? Nuathan! Was avond ere a while. Now conticinium. As Lord the Laohun is sheutseuyes. The time of lying together will come and the wildering of the nicht till cockeedoodle aubens Aurore. Panther monster. Send leabarrow loads amorrow. While loevdom shleeps. Elenfant has siang his triump, *Great is Eliphas Magistrodontos* and after kneeprayer pious for behemuth and mahamoth will rest him from tusker toils. Salamsalaim! Rhinohorn isnoutso pigfellow but him ist gonz wurst. Kikikuki. Hopopodorme. So-beast! No chare of beagles, frantling of peacocks, no muzzing of the camel, smuttering of apes. Lights, pageboy, lights! Brights we'll be brights. With help of Hanoukan's lamp. When otter leaps in outer parts then Yul remembers Mei. Her hung maid mohns are bluming, look, to greet those loes on coast of amethyst; arcglow's seafire siemens lure and wextward warnerforth's hooker-crookers. And now with robby brerfox's fishy fable lissaned out, the threads simwhat toran and knots in its antargumends, the pesciolines in Liffeyetta's bowl have stopped squiggling about Junoh and the whalk and feriaquintaism and pebble infinibility and the poissission of the hoghly course. And if Lubbernabohore laid his horker to the ribber, save the giregargoh and dabardin going on in his mount of knowledge (munt), he would not hear a flip flap in all Finnyland. Witchman, watch of your night? Es voes, ez noes, nott voes, ges, noun. It goes. It does not go. Dark-park's acoo with sucking loves. Rosimund's by her wishing well. Soon tempt-in-twos will stroll at venture and hunt-by-threes strut musketeering. Brace of girdles, brasse of beauys. With the width of the way for jogjoy. Hulker's cieclest elbownunsense. Hold hard! And his dithering dathering waltzers of. Stright! But meet-ings mate not as forsehn. Hesperons! And if you wand to Liv-mouth, wenderer, while Jempson's weed decks Jacqueson's Island, here lurks, bar hellpelhullpulthebell, none iron welcome. Bing. Bong. Bangbong. Thunderation! You took with the mulligrubs and we lack mulsum? No sirrebob! Great goodness, no! Were you Marely quean of Scuts or but Chrestien the Last, (our duty to you, chris! royalty, squat!) how matt your mark, though luked your johl, here's dapplebellied mugs and troublebedded rooms and sawdust strown in expectoration and for ratification by specification of your information, Mr Knight, tuntapster, buttles; his alefru's up to his hip. And Watsy Lyke sees after all rinsings and don't omiss Kate, homeswab homely, put in with the bricks. A's the sign and one's the number. Where Chavvyout Chacer calls the cup and Pouropourim stands astirrup. De oud huis bij de kerkegaard. So who over comes ever for Whoopee Weeks must put up with the Jug and Chambers.

But heed! Our thirty minutes war's alull. All's quiet on the felled of Gorey. Between the starfort and the thornwood brass castle flambs with mutton candles. Hushkah, a horn! Gadolmagtog! God es El? Housefather calls enthreateningly. From Brandenborgenthor. At Asa's arthre. In thundercloud periwig. With lightning bug aflash from afinger. My souls and by jings, should he work his jaw to give down the banks and hark from the tomb! Ansighosa pokes in her potstill to souse at the sop be sodden enow and to hear to all the bubbles besaying: the coming man, the future woman, the food that is to build, what he with fifteen years will do, the ring in her mouth of joyous guard, stars astir and stirabout. A palashe for hirs, a saucy for hers and ladlelike spoons for the wonner. But ein and twee were never worth three. So they must have their final since he's on parole. Et la pau' Leonie has the choice of her lives between Josephinus and Mario-Louis for who is to wear the lily of Bohemey, Florestan, Thaddeus, Hardress or Myles. And lead raptivity captive. Ready! Like a Finn at a fair. Now for la belle! Icy-la-Belle!

The campus calls them. Ninan ninan, the gattling gan! Childs will be wilds. 'Twastold. And vamp, vamp, vamp, the girls are merchand. The horseshow magnete draws his field and don't the fillyings fly? Educande of Sorrento, they newknow knowwell their Vico's road. Arranked in their array and flocking for the fray on that old orangeray, Dolly Brae. For these are not on terms, they twain, bartrossers, since their baffle of Whatalose when Adam Leftus and the devil took our hindmost, gegifting her with his painapple, nor will not be atoned at all in fight to no finish, that dark deed doer, this wellwilled wooer, Jerkoff and Eatsoup, Yem or Yan, while felixed is who culpas does and harm's worth healing and Brune is bad French for Jour d'Anno. Tiggers and Tuggers they're all for tenzones. Bettlimbraves. For she must walk out. And it must be with who. Teaseforhim. Toesforhim. Tossforhim. Two. Else there is danger of. Solitude.

Postreintroducing Jeremy, the chastenot coulter, the flowing taal that brooks no brooking runs on to say how, as it was mutualiter foretold of him by a timekiller to his spacemaker, velos ambos and arubyat knychts, with their tales within wheels and stucks between spokes, on the hike from Elmstree to Stene and back, how, running awage with the use of reason (sics) and ramming amok at the brake of his voice (secs), his lasterhalft was set for getting the besterwhole of his yougendtougend, for control number thrice was operating the subliminal of his invaded personality. He nobit smorfi and go poltri and let all the tondo gang bola del ruffo. Barto no know him mor. Eat larto altruis with most perfect stranger.

Boo, you're through!

Hoo, I'm true!

Men, teacan a tea simmering, hamo mavrone kerry O?

Teapotty. Teapotty.

Kod knows. Anything ruind. Meetingless.

He wept indeiterum. With such a tooth he seemed to love his wee tart when abuy. Highly momourning he see the before him. Melained from nape to kneecap though vied from her girders up. Holy Santalto, cursing saint, sight most deletious to ross up the spyballs like exude of margary! And how him it heaviered that eyerim rust! An they bare falls witless against thee how slight becomes a hidden wound? Soldwoter he wash him all time bigfeller bruisy place blong him. He no want missies blong all boy other look bruisy place blong him. Hence. It will paineth the chastenot in that where of his whence he had loseth his once for every, even though mode grow moramor maenneritsch and the Tarara boom decay. Immaculacy, give but to drink to his shirt and all skirtaskortas must change her tunics. So warred he from first to last, forebanned and betweenly, a smuggler for lifer. Lift the blank ve veered as heil! Split the hvide and aye seize heaven! He knows for he's seen it in black and white through his eyetrompit trained upon jenny's and all that sort of thing which is dandymount to a clearobscure. Prettimaid tints may try their taunts: apple, bacchante, custard, dove, eskimo, feldgrau, hematite, isingglass, jet, kipper, lucile, mimosa, nut, oysterette, prune, quasimodo, royal, sago, tango, umber, vanilla, wisteria, xray, yesplease, zaza, philomel, theerose. What are they all by? Shee.

If you nude her in her prime, make sure you find her complementary or, on your very first occasion, by Angus Dagdasson and all his piccions, she'll prick you where you're proudest with her unsatt speagle eye. Look sharp, she's signalling from among the asters. Turn again, wistfultone, lode mere of Doubtlynn! Arise, Land-under-Wave! Clap your lingua to your pallet, drop your jowl with a jolt, tambourine until your breath slides, pet a pout and it's out. Have you got me, Allysloper?

My top it was brought Achill's low, my middle I ope before you, my bottom's a vulser if ever there valsed and my whole the flower that stars the day and is solly well worth your pilger's fahrt. Where there's a hitch, a head of things, let henker's halter hang the halunkenend. For I see through your weapon. That cry's not Cucullus. And his eyelids are painted. If my tutor here is cut out for an oldeborre I'm Flo, shy of peeps, you know. But when he beetles backwards, ain't I fly? Pull the boughpee to see how we sleep. Bee Peep! Peepette! Would you like that lump of a tongue for lungeon or this Turkey's delighter, hys hyphen mys? My bellyswain's a twalf whulerusspower though he knows as much how to man a wife as Dunckle Dalton of matching wools. Shake hands through the thicketloch! Sweet swanwater! My other is mouthfilled. This kissing wold's full of killing fellows kneeling voyantly to the cope of heaven. And somebody's coming, I feel for a fect. I've a seeklet to sell thee if old Deanns won't be threaspanning. When you'll next have the mind to retire to be wicked this is as dainty a way as any. Underwoods spells bushment's business. So if you sprig poplar you're bound to twig this. 'Twas my lord of Glendalough benedixed the gape for me that time at Long Entry, commanding the approaches to my intimast innermost. Look how they're browthered! Six thirteens at Blanche de Blanche's of 3 Behind Street and 2 Turnagain Lane. Awabeg is my callby, Magnus here's my Max, Wonder One's my cipher and Seven Sisters is my nighbrood. Radouga, Rab will ye na pick them in their pink of panties. You can colour up till you're

248

prawn while I go squirt with any cockle. When here who adolls me infuxes sleep. But if this could see with its backsight he'd be the grand old greeneyed lobster. He's my first viewmarc since Valentine. Wink's the winning word.

Luck!

In the house of breathings lies that word, all fairness. The walls are of rubinen and the glittergates of elfinbone. The roof herof is of massicious jasper and a canopy of Tyrian awning rises and still descends to it. A grape cluster of lights hangs therebeneath and all the house is filled with the breathings of her fairness, the fairness of fondance and the fairness of milk and rhubarb and the fairness of roasted meats and uniomargrits and the fairness of promise with consonantia and avowals. There lies her word, you reder! The height herup exalts it and the lowness her down abaseth it. It vibroverberates upon the tegmen and prosplodes from pomoeria. A window, a hedge, a prong, a hand, an eye, a sign, a head and keep your other augur on her paypaypay. And you have it, old Sem, pat as ah be seated! And Sunny, my gander, he's coming to land her. The boy which she now adores. She dores. Oh backed von dem zug! Make weg for their tug!

With a ring ding dong, they raise clasped hands and advance more steps to retire to the saum. Curtsey one, curtsey two, with arms akimbo, devotees.

Irrelevance.

All sing:

— I rose up one maypole morning and saw in my glass how nobody loves me but you. Ugh. Ugh.

All point in the shem direction as if to shun.

— My name is Misha Misha but call me Toffey Tough. I mean Mettenchough. It was her, boy the boy that was loft in the larch. Ogh! Ogh!

Her reverence.

All laugh.

They pretend to helf while they simply shauted at him sauce to make hims prich. And ith ith noth cricquette, Sally Lums. Not by ever such a lot. Twentynines of bloomers gegging een man arose. Avis was there and trilled her about it. She's her sex, for certain. So to celebrate the occasion:

— Willest thou rossy banders havind?

He simules to be tight in ribbings round his rumpffkorpff.

— Are you Swarthants that's hit on a shorn stile?

He makes semblant to be swiping their chimbleys.

— Can you ajew ajew fro' Sheidam?

He finges to be cutting up with a pair of sissers and to be buytings of their maidens and spitting their heads into their facepails. Spickspuk! Spoken.

So now be hushy, little pukers! Side here roohish, cleany fuglers! Grandicellies, all stay zitty! Adultereux, rest as befour! For you've jollywelly dawdled all the day. When ye coif tantoncle's hat then'll be largely temts for that. Yet's the time for being now, now, now.

For a burning would is come to dance inane. Glamours hath moidered's lieb and herefore Coldours must leap no more. Lack breath must leap no more.

Lel lols for libelman libling his lore. Lolo Lolo liebermann you loved to be leaving Libnius. Lift your right to your Liber Lord. Link your left to your lass of liberty. Lala Lala, Leapermann, your lep's but a loop to lee.

A fork of hazel o'er the field in vox the verveine virgins ode. If you cross this rood as you roamed the rand I'm blessed but you'd feel him a blasting rod. Behind, me, frees from evil smells! Perdition stinks before us.

Aghatharept they fleurelly to Nebnos will and Rosocale. Twice is he gone to quest of her, thrice is she now to him. So see we so as seed we sow. And their prunktqueen kilt her kirtles up and set out. And her troup came heeling, O. And what do you think that pride was drest in! Voolykins' diamondinah's vestin. For ever they scent where air she went. While all the fauns' flares widens wild to see a floral's school.

Led by Lignifer, in four hops of the happiest, ach beth cac duff, a marrer of the sward incoronate, the few fly the farbetween! We haul minymony on that piebold nig. Will any dubble dabble on the bay? Nor far jocubus? Nic for jay? Attilad! Attattilad! Get up, Goth's scourge on you! There's a visitation in your impluvium. Hun! Hun!

He stanth theirs mun in his natural, oblious autamnesically of his very proprium, (such is stockpot leaden, so did sonsepun crake) the wont to be wanton maid a will to be wise. Thrust from the light, apophotorejected, he spoors loves from her heats. He blinkth. But's wrath's the higher where those wreathe charity. For all of these have been thisworlders, time liquescing into state, pitiless age grows angelhood. Though, as he stehs, most anysing may befallhim from a song of a witch to the totter of Blackarss, given a fammished devil, a young sourceress and (eternal conjunction) the permission of overalls with the cuperation of nightshirt. If he spice east he seethes in sooth and if he pierce north he wilts in the waist. And what wonder with the murkery viceheid in the shade? The specks on his lapspan are his foul deed thougths, wishmarks of mad imogenation. Take they off! Make the off! But Funnylegs are leanly. A bimbamb bum! They vain would convert the to be hers in the word. Gush, they wooed! Gash, they're fair ripecherry!

As for she could shake him. An oaf, no more. Still he'd be good tutor two in his big armschair lerningstoel and she be waxen in his hands. Turning up and fingering over the most dantellising peaches in the lingerous longerous book of the dark. Look at this passage about Galilleotto! I know it is difficult but when your goche I go dead. Turn now to this patch upon Smacchiavelluti! Soot allours, he's sure to spot it! 'Twas ever so in monitorology since Headmaster Adam became Eva Harte's toucher, *in omnibus moribus et temporibus*, with man's mischief in his mind whilst her pupils swimmed too heavenlies, let his be exaspirated, letters be blowed! I is a femaline person. O, of provocative gender. U unisingular case.

Which is why trumpers are mixed up in duels and here's B. Rohan meets N. Ohlan for the prize of a thou.

But listen to the mocking birde to micking barde making bared! We've heard it aye since songdom was gemurrmal. As he was

251

queering his shoolthers. So was I. And as I was cleansing my fausties. So was he. And as way ware puffiing our blowbags. Souwouyou.

Come, thrust! Go, parry! Dvoinabrathran, dare! The mad long ramp of manchind's parlements, the learned lacklearning, merciless as wonderful.

— Now may Saint Mowy of the Pleasant Grin be your everglass and even prospect!

— Feeling dank.

Exchange, reverse.

— And may Saint Jerome of the Harlots' Curse make family three of you which is much abedder!

— Grassy ass ago.

And each was wrought with his other. And his continence fell. The bivitellines, Metellus and Ametallikos, her crown pretenders, obscindgemeinded biekerers, varying directly, uruseye each oxesother, superfetated (never cleaner of lamps frowned fiercelier on anointer of hinges), while their treegrown girls, king's game, if he deign so, are in such transfusion just to know twigst timidy twomeys, for gracious sake, who is artthoudux from whose heterotropic, the sleepy or the glouch, for, shyly bawn and showly nursured, exceedingly nice girls can strike exceedingly bad times unless so richtly chosen's by (what though of riches he have none and hope dashes hope on his heart's horizon) to gar their great moments greater. The thing is he must be put strait on the spot, no mere waterstichystuff in a selfmade world that you can't believe a word he's written in, not for pie, but one's only owned by naturel rejection. Charley, you're my darwing! So sing they sequent the assent of man. Till they go round if they go roundagain before breakparts and all dismissed. They keep. Step keep. Step. Stop. Who is Fleur? Where is Ange? Or Gardoun?

Creedless, croonless hangs his haughty. There end no moe red devil in the white of his eye. Braglodyte him do a katadupe! A condamn quondam jontom sick af a suckbut! He does not know how his grandson's grandson's grandson's grandson will stammer up in Peruvian for in the ersebest idiom I have done it equals I so shall do. He dares not think why the grandmother of the grandmother of his grandmother's grandmother coughed Russky with suchky husky accent since in the mouthart of the slove look at me now means I once was otherwise. Nor that the mappamund has been changing pattern as youth plays moves from street to street since time and races were and wise ants hoarded and sauterelles were spendthrifts, no thing making newthing wealthshowever for a silly old Sol, healthytobedder and latewiser. Nor that the turtling of a London's alderman is ladled out by the waggerful to the regionals of pigmyland. His part should say in honour bound: So help me symethew, sammarc, selluc and singin, I will stick to you, by gum, no matter what, bite simbum, and in case of the event coming off beforehand even so you was to release me for the sake of the other cheap girl's baby's name plaster me but I will pluckily well pull on the buckskin gloves! But Noodynaady's actual ingrate tootle is of come into the garner mauve and thy nice are stores of morning and buy me a bunch of iodines.

Evidentament he has failed as tiercely as the deuce before for she is wearing none of the three. And quite as patently there is a hole in the ballet trough which the rest fell out. Because to explain why the residue is, was, or will not be, according to the eighth axiom, proceeded with, namely, since ever apart that gossan duad, so sure as their's a patch on a pomelo, this yam ham in never live could, the shifting about of the lassies, the tug of love of their lads ending with a great deal of merriment, hoots, screams, scarf drill, cap fecking, ejaculations of aurinos, reechoable mirthpeals and general thumbtonosery (Myama's a yaung yaung cauntry), one must recken with the sudden and gigantesquesque appearance unwithstandable as a general election in Barnado's bearskin amongst the brawlmiddle of this village childergarten of the largely longsuffering laird of Lucanhof.

But, vrayedevraye Blankdeblank, god of all machineries and tomestone of Barnstaple, by mortisection or vivisuture, splitten up or recompounded, an isaac jacquemin mauromormo milesian, how accountibus for him, moreblue?

Was he pitssched for an ensemple as certain have dognosed of him against our seawall by Rurie, Thoath and Cleaver, those three stout sweynhearts, Orion of the Orgiasts, Meereschal MacMuhun, the Ipse dadden, product of the extremes giving quotidients to our means, as might occur to anyone, your brutest layaman with the princest champion in our archdeaconry, or so yclept from Clio's clippings, which the chroncher of chivalries is sulpicious save he scan, for ancients link with presents as the human chain extends, have done, do and will again as John, Polycarp and Irenews eye-to-eye ayewitnessed and to Paddy Palmer, while monks sell yew to archers or the water of the livvying goes the way of all fish from Sara's drawhead, the corralsome, to Isaac's, the lauphed butt one, with her minnelisp extorreor to his moanolothe inturned? So Perrichon with Bastienne or heavy Humph with airy Nan, Ricqueracqbrimbillyjicqueyjocqjolicass? How sowesthow, *dullcisamica*? A and aa ab ad abu abiad. A babbel men dub gulch of tears.

The mar of murmury mermers to the mind's ear, uncharted rock, evasive weed. Only the caul knows his thousandfirst name, Hocus Crocus, Esquilocus, Finnfinn the Faineant, how feel full foes in furrinarr! Doth it not all come aft to you, puritysnooper, in the way television opes longtimes ofter when Potollomuck Sotyr or Sourdanapplous the Lollapaloosa? The charges are, you will remember, the chances are, you won't; bit it's old Joe, the Java Jane, older even than Odam Costollo, and we are recurrently meeting em, par Mahun Mesme, in cycloannalism, from space to space, time after time, in various phases of scripture as in various poses of sepulture. Greets Godd, Groceries! Merodach! Defend the King! Hoet of the rough throat attack but whose say is soft but whose ee has a cute angle, he whose hut is a hissarlik even as her hennin's aspire. And insodaintily she's a quine of selm ashaker while as a murder of corpse when his magot's up he's the best berrathon sanger in all the aisles of Skaldignavia. As who shall hear. For now at last is Longabed going to be gone to, that more than man, prince of Bunnicombe of wide roadsterds, the herblord the gillyflowrets so fain fan to flatter about. Artho is the

254

name is on the hero, Capellisato, shoehanded slaughterer of the shader of our leaves.

Attach him! Hold!

Yet stir thee, to clay, Tamor!

Why wilt thou erewaken him from his earth, O summonorother: he is weatherbitten from the dusts of ages? The hour of his closing hies to hand; the tocsin that shall claxonise his wareabouts. If one who remembered his webgoods and tealofts were to ask of a hooper for whose it was the storks were quitting Aquileyria, this trundler would not wot; if other who joined faith when his depth charge bombed our barrel spillway were to —!

Jehosophat, what doom is here! Rain ruth on them, sire! The wing of Moykill cover him! The Bulljon Bossbrute quarantee him! Calavera, caution! Slaves to Virtue, save his Veritotem! Bearara Tolearis, *procul abeat*! The Ivorbonegorer of Danamaraca be, his Hector Protector! Woldomar with Vasa, peel your peeps! And try to saviourise the nights of labour to the order of our blooding worold! While Pliny the Younger writes to Pliny the Elder his calamolumen of contumellas, what Aulus Gellius picked on Micmacrobius and what Vitruvius pocketed from Cassiodorus. Like we larnt from that Buke of Lukan in Dublin's capital, Kongdam Coombe. Even if you are the kooper of the winkel over measure never lost a licence. Nor a duckindonche divulse from bath and breakfast. And for the honour of Alcohol drop that you-know-what-I've-come-about-I-saw-your-act air! Punch may be pottleproud but his Judy's a wife's wit better.

For the producer (Mr John Baptister Vickar) caused a deep abuliousness to descend upon the Father of Truants and, at a side issue, pluterpromptly brought on the scene the cutletsized consort, foundling filly of fortyshilling fostertailor and shipman's shopahoyden, weighing ten pebble ten, scaling five footsy five and spanning thirtyseven inchettes round the good companions, twentynine ditties round the wishful waistress, thirtyseven alsos round the answer to everything, twentythree of the same round each of the quis separabits, fourteen round the beginning of happiness and nicely nine round her shoed for slender.

And eher you could pray mercy to goodness or help with your hokey or mehokeypoo, Gallus's hen has collared her pullets. That's where they have owreglias for. Their bone of contention, flesh to their thorns, prest as Prestissima, makes off in a thinkling (and not one hen only nor two hens neyther but every blessed brigid came aclucking and aclacking), while, a rum a rum, the ram of all harns, Bier, Wijn, Spirituosen for consumption on the premises, advokaat withouten pleaders, Mas marrit, Pas poulit, Ras ruddist of all, though flamifestouned from galantifloures, is hued and cried of each's colour.

Home all go. Halome. Blare no more ramsblares, oddmund barkes! And cease your fumings, kindalled bushies! And sherrigoldies yeassymgnays; your wildeshaweshowe moves swiftly sterneward! For here the holy language. Soons to come. To pausse.

'Tis goed. Het best.

For they are now tearing, that is, teartoretorning. Too soon are coming tasbooks and goody, hominy bread and bible bee, with jaggery-yo to juju-jaw, Fine's French phrases from the Grandmère des Grammaires and bothered parsenaps from the Four Massores, Mattatias, Marusias, Lucanias, Jokinias, and what happened to our eleven in thirtytwo antepostdating the Valgur Eire and why is limbo where is he and what are the sound waves saying ceased ere they all wayed wrong and Amnist anguished axes Collis and where fishngaman fetched the mongafesh from and whatfor paddybird notplease rancoon and why was Sindat sitthing on him sitbom like a saildior, with what the doc did in the doil, not to mention define the hydraulics of common salt and, its denier crid of old provaunce, where G.P.O. is zentrum and D.U.T.C. are radients write down by the frequency of the scores and crores of your refractions the valuations in the pice of dinggyings on N.C.R. and S.C.R.

That little cloud, a nibulissa, still hangs isky. Singabed sulks before slumber. Light at night has an alps on his druckhouse. Thick head and thin butter or after you with me. Caspi, but gueroligue stings the air. Gaylegs to riot of us! Gallocks to lafft!

What is amaid today todo? So angelland all weeping bin that Izzy most unhappy is. Fain Essie fie onhapje? laughs her stella's vispirine.

While, running about their ways, going and coming, now at rhimba rhomba, now in trippiza trappaza, pleating a pattern Gran Geamatron showed them of gracehoppers, auntskippers and coneyfarm leppers, they jeerilied along, durian gay and marian maidcap, lou Dariou beside la Matieto, all boy more all girl singoutfeller longa house blong store Huddy, whilest nin nin nin nin that Boorman's clock, a winny on the tinny side, ninned nin nin nin nin, about old Father Barley how he got up of a morning arley and he met with a plattonem blondes named Hips and Haws and fell in with a fellows of Trinity some header Skowood Shaws like (You'll catch it, don't fret, Mrs Tummy Lupton! Come indoor, Scoffynosey, and shed your swank!) auld Daddy Deacon who could stow well his place of beacon but he never could hold his kerosene's candle to (The nurse'll give it you, stickypots! And you wait, my lasso, fecking the twine!) bold Farmer Burleigh who wuck up in a hurlywurly where he huddly could wuddle to wallow his weg tillbag of the baker's booth to beg of (You're well held now, Missy Cheekspeer, and your panto's off! Fie, for shame, Ruth Wheatacre, after all the booz said!) illed Diddiddy Achin for the prize of a pease of bakin with a pinch of the panch of the ponch in jurys for (Ah, crabeyes, I have you, showing off to the world with that gape in your stocking!) Wold Forrester Farley who, in deesperation of deispiration at the diasporation of his diesparation, was found of the round of the sound of the lound of the. Lukkedoerendunandurraskewdylooshoofermoyportertooryzooysphalnabortansporthaokansakroidverjkapakkapuk.

Byfall.

Upploud!

The play thou schouwburgst, Game, here endeth. The curtain drops by deep request.

Uplouderamain!

Gonn the gawds, Gunnar's gustspells. When the h, who the hu, how the hue, where the huer? Orbiter onswers: lots lives lost. Fionia is fed up with Fidge Fudgesons. Sealand snorres.

257

Rendningrocks roguesreckning reigns. Gwds with gurs are gttrdmmrng. Hlls vlls. The timid hearts of words all exeomnosunt. Mannagad, lammalelouh, how do that come? By Dad, youd not heed that fert? Fulgitudes ejist rowdownan tonuout. Quoq! And buncskleydoodle! Kidoosh! Of their fear they broke, they ate wind, they fled; where they ate there they fled; of their fear they fled, they broke away. Go to, let us extol Azrael with our harks, by our brews, on our jambses, in his gaits. To Mezouzalem with the Dephilim, didits dinkun's dud? Yip! Yup! Yarrah! And let Nek Nekulon extol Mak Makal and let him say unto him: Immi ammi Semmi. And shall not Babel be with Lebab? And he war. And he shall open his mouth and answer: I hear, O Ismael, how they laud is only as my loud is one. If Nekulon shall be havonfalled surely Makal haven hevens. Go to, let us extell Makal, yea, let us exceedingly extell. Though you have lien amung your posspots my excellency is over Ismael. Great is him whom is over Ismael and he shall mekanek of Mak Nakulon. And he deed.

Uplouderamainagain!

For the Clearer of the Air from on high has spoken in tumbuldum tambaldam to his tembledim tombaldoom worrild and, moguphonoised by that phonemanon, the unhappitents of the earth have terrerumbled from fimament unto fundament and from tweedledeedumms down to twiddledeedees.

Loud, hear us!

Loud, graciously hear us!

Now have thy children entered into their habitations. And nationglad, camp meeting over, to shin it, Gov be thanked! Thou hast closed the portals of the habitations of thy children and thou hast set thy guards thereby, even Garda Didymus and Garda Domas, that thy children may read in the book of the opening of the mind to light and err not in the darkness which is the afterthought of thy nomatter by the guardiance of those guards which are thy bodemen, the cheeryboyum chirryboth with the kerrybommers in their krubeems, Pray-your-Prayers Timothy and Back-to-Bunk Tom.

Till tree from tree, tree among trees, tree over tree become stone to stone, stone between stones, stone under stone for ever.

O Loud, hear the wee beseech of thees of each of these thy unlitten ones! Grant sleep in hour's time, O Loud!

That they take no chill. That they do ming no merder. That they shall not gomeet madhowiatrees.

Loud, heap miseries upon us yet entwine our arts with laughters low!

Ha he hi ho hu.

Mummum.

As we there are where are we are we there UNDE ET UB
from tomtittot to teetootomtotalitarian. Tea
tea too oo.

*With his broad
and hairy face,
to Ireland a
disgrace.*

Whom will comes over. Who to caps ever. SIC.
And howelse do we hook our hike to find that
pint of porter place? Am shot, says the big-
guard.[1]

*Menly about
peebles.*

Whence. Quick lunch by our left, wheel, IMAGINABL
ITINERARY
THROUGH
THE
PARTICULAI
UNIVERSAL.
to where. Long Livius Lane, mid Mezzofanti
Mall, diagonising Lavatery Square, up Tycho
Brache Crescent,[2] shouldering Berkeley Alley,
querfixing Gainsborough Carfax, under Guido

*Dont retch meat
fat salt lard
sinks down (and
out).*

d'Arezzo's Gadeway, by New Livius Lane till
where we whiled while we whithered. Old
Vico Roundpoint. But fahr, be fear! And
natural, simple, slavish, filial. The marriage of
Montan wetting his moll we know, like any
enthewsyass cuckling a hoyden[3] in her rougey

[1] Rawmeash, quoshe with her girlic teangue. If old Herod with the Corm-
well's eczema was to go for me like he does Snuffler whatever about his blue
canaries I'd do nine months for his beaver beard.

[2] Mater Mary Mercerycordial of the Dripping Nipples, milk's a queer
arrangement.

[3] Real life behind the floodlights as shown by the best exponents of a royal
divorce.

gipsylike chinkaminx pulshandjupeyjade and her petsybluse indecked o' voylets.[1] When who was wist was ware. En elv, et fjaell. And the whirr of the whins humming us howe. His hume. Hencetaking tides we haply return, trumpeted by prawns and ensigned with seakale, to befinding ourself when old is said in one and maker mates with made (O my!), having conned the cones and meditated the mured and pondered the pensils and ogled the olymp and delighted in her dianaphous and cacchinated behind his culosses, before a mosoleum. Length Withought Breath, of him, a chump of the evums, upshoot of picnic or stupor out of sopor, Cave of Kids or Hymanian Glattstoneburg, denary, danery, donnery, domm, who, entiringly as he continues highlyfictional, tumulous under his chthonic exterior but plain Mr Tumulty in muftilife,[2] in his antisipiences as in his recognisances, is, (Dominic Directus) a manyfeast munificent more mob than man.

ey Tod, ye mon Barbar!

him in the h!

odly old Ard-Cronwall waxing the ulsion box.

Ainsoph,[3] this upright one, with that noughty besighed him zeroine. To see in his horrorscup he is mehrkurios than saltz of sulphur. Terror of the noonstruck by day, cryptogam of each nightly bridable. But, to speak broken heaventalk, is he? Who is he? Whose is he? Why is he? Howmuch is he? Which is he? When is he? Where is he?[4] How is he? And what the decans is there about him

CONSTITUTION OF THE CONSTITUTIONABLE AS CONSTITUTIONAL.

---

[1] When we play dress grownup at alla ludo poker you'll be happnessised to feel how fetching I can look in clingarounds.

[2] Kellywick, Longfellow's Lodgings, House of Comments III, Cake Walk, Amusing Avenue, Salt Hill, Co. Mahogany, Izalond, Terra Firma.

[3] Groupname for grapejuice.

[4] Bhing, said her burglar's head, soto poce.

anyway, the decemt man? Easy, calm your
haste! Approach to lead our passage!

This bridge is upper.

Cross.

Thus come to castle.

Knock.[1]

A password, thanks.

Yes, pearse.

Well, all be dumbed!

O really?[2]

PROBA-
POSSIBLE
PROLEGO-
MENA TO
IDEAREAL
HISTORY.

*Swing the banjo,
bantams, bounce-
the-baller's
blown to fook.*

Hoo cavedin earthwight
At furscht kracht of thunder.[3]

When shoo, his flutterby,
Was netted and named.[4]

*Thsight near
left me eyes when
I seen her put
thounce otay
ithpot.*

Erdnacrusha, requiestress, wake em!
And let luck's puresplutterall lucy at
ease![5]

To house as wise fool ages builded.

Sow byg eat.[6]

Quartandwds.

Staplering to tether to, steppingstone to
mount by, as the Boote's at Pickardstown.
And that skimmelk steed still in the ground-
loftfan. As over all. Or be these wingsets leaned
to the outwalls, beastskin trophies of booth
of Baws the balsamboards?[7] Burials be bally-
houraised! So let Bacchus e'en call! Inn inn!
Inn inn! Where. The babbers ply the pen.
The bibbers drang the den. The papplicom,
the pubblicam he's turning tin for ten. From

GNOSIS OF
PRECREATE
DETERMINA-
TION.
AGNOSIS OF
POSTCREATE
DETER-
MINISM.

*Tickets for the
Tailwaggers
Terrierpuppy
Raffle.*

[1] Yussive smirte and ye mermon answerth from his beelyingplace below
the tightmark, Gotahelv!

[2] O Evol, kool in the salg and ees how Dozi pits what a drows er.

[3] A goodrid croven in a tynwalled tub.

[4] Apis amat aram. Luna legit librum. Pulla petit pascua.

[5] And after dinn to shoot the shades.

[6] Says blistered Mary Achinhead to beautifed Tummy Tullbutt.

[7] Begge. To go to Begge. To go to Begge and to be sure to reminder
Begge. Goodbeg, buggey Begge.

seldomers that most frequent him. That same
erst crafty hakemouth which under the assumed
name of Ignotus Loquor, of foggy old,
harangued bellyhooting fishdrunks on their
favorite stamping ground, from a father theo-
balder brake.[1] And Egyptus, the incenstrobed,

speaking.

as Cyrus heard of him? And Major A. Shaw
after he got the miner smellpex? And old
Whiteman self, the blighty blotchy, beyond
the bays, hope of ostrogothic and ottomanic
faith converters, despair of Pandemia's post-
wartem plastic surgeons? But is was all so
long ago. Hispano-Cathayan-Euxine, Castil-
lian-Emeratic-Hebridian, Espanol-Cymric-

h, no home.

Helleniky? Rolf the Ganger, Rough the Gang-
ster, not a feature alike and the face the same.[2]
Pastimes are past times. Now let bygones
be bei Gunne's. Saaleddies er it in this warken
werden, mine boerne, and it vild need olderwise[3] since primal made alter in garden of
Idem. The tasks above are as the flasks below,
saith the emerald canticle of Hermes and all's

quod sed
.

loth and pleasestir, are we told, on excellent
inkbottle authority, solarsystemised, seriol-
cosmically, in a more and more almightily
expanding universe under one, there is rhyme-
less reason to believe, original sun. Securely
judges orb terrestrial.[4] *Haud certo ergo.* But

rasay in
dox lust.

O felicitous culpability, sweet bad cess to you
for an archetypt!

[1] Huntler and Pumar's animal alphabites, the first in the world from aab to zoo.

[2] We dont hear the booming cursowarries, we wont fear the fletches of fightning, we float the meditarenias and come bask to the isle we love in spice. Punt.

[3] And this once golden bee a cimadoro.

[4] And he was a gay Lutharius anyway, Sinobiled. You can tell by their extraordinary clothes.

Honour commercio's energy yet aid the linkless proud, the plurable with everybody and ech with pal, this ernst of Allsap's ale halliday of roaring month with its two lunar eclipses and its three saturnine settings! Horn of Heatthen, highbrowed! Brook of Life, back-frish! Amnios amnium, fluminiculum flaminulinorum! We seek the Blessed One, the Harbourer-cum-Enheritance. Even Canaan the Hateful. Ever a-going, ever a-coming. Between a stare and a sough. Fossilisation, all branches.[1] Wherefore Petra sware unto Ulma: By the mortals' frost! And Ulma sware unto Petra: On my veiny life!

In these places sojournemus, where Eblinn water, leased of carr and fen, leaving amont her shoals and salmen browses, whom inshore breezes woo with freshets, windeth to her broads. A phantom city, phaked of philim pholk, bowed and sould for a four of hundreds of manhood in their three and threescore fylkers for a price partitional of twenty six and six. By this riverside, on our sunnybank,[2] how buona the vista, by Santa Rosa! A field of May, the very vale of Spring. Orchards here are lodged; sainted lawrels evremberried. You have a hoig view ashwald, a glen of marrons and of thorns. Gleannaulinn, Ardeevin: purty glint of plaising height. This Norman court at boundary of the ville, yon creepered tower of a church of Ereland, meet for true saints in worshipful assemblage,[3] with our king's house

THE LOCALI
SATION OF
LEGEND
LEADING T
THE LEGALI
SATION OF
LATIFUND-
ISM.

[1] Startnaked and bonedstiff. We vivvy soddy. All be dood.

[2] When you dreamt that you'd wealth in marble arch do you ever think of pool beg slowe.

[3] Porphyrious Olbion, redcoatliar, we were always wholly rose marines on our side every time.

of stone, belgroved of mulbrey, the still that
was mill and Kloster that was Yeomansland,
the ghastcold tombshape of the quick fore-
gone on, the loftleaved elm Lefanunian above-
mansioned, each, every, all is for the retro-
spectioner. Skole! Agus skole igen![1] Sweet-
some auburn, cometh up as a selfreizing flower,
that fragolance of the fraisey beds: the phoenix,
his pyre, is still flaming away with trueprat-
tight spirit: the wren his nest is niedelig as the
turrises of the sabines are televisible. Here are
the cottage and the bungalow for the cobbeler
and the brandnewburgher:[2] but Izolde, her
chaplet gardens, an litlee plads af liefest pose,
arride the winnerful wonders off, the winnerful wonnerful wanders off,[3] with hedges of
ivy and hollywood and bower of mistletoe,
are, tho if it theem tho and yeth if you
pleathes,[4] for the blithehaired daughter of
Angoisse. All out of two barreny old perishers,
Tytonyhands and Vlossyhair, a kilolitre in
metromyriams. Presepeprosapia, the parent
bole. Wone tabard, wine tap and warm tavern[5]
and, by ribbon development, from contact
bridge to lease lapse, only two millium two
humbered and eighty thausig nine humbered
and sixty radiolumin lines to the wustworts of
a Finntown's generous poet's office. Distorted
mirage, aloofliest of the plain, wherein the

[1] Now a muss wash the little face.
[2] A viking vernacular expression still used in the Summerhill district for a
jerryhatted man of forty who puts two fingers into his boiling soupplate and
licks them in turn to find out if there is enough mushroom catsup in the
mutton broth.
[3] H' dk' fs' h'p'y.
[4] Googlaa pluplu.
[5] Tomley. The grown man. A butcher szewched him the bloughs and
braches. I'm chory to see P. Shuter.

boxomeness of the bedelias[1] makes hobby-hodge happy in his hole.[2] The store and charter, Treetown Castle under Lynne. Rivapool? Hod a brieck on it! But its piers eerie, its span spooky, its toll but a till, its parapets all peripateting. D'Oblong's by his by. Which we all pass. Tons. In our snoo. Znore. While we hickerwards the thicker. Schein. Schore. Which assoars us from the murk of the mythelated in the barrabelowther, bedevere butlered table round, past Morningtop's necessity and Harington's invention, to the clarience of the childlight in the studiorium upsturts. Here we'll dwell on homiest powers, love at the latch with novices nig and nag. The chorus: the principals. For the rifocillation of their inclination to the manifestation of irritation: doldorboys and doll.[3] After sound, light and heat, memory, will and understanding.

Here (the memories framed from walls are minding) till wranglers for wringwrowdy wready are, F Ⅎ, (at gaze, respecting, fourteenth baronet, meet, altrettanth bancorot, chaff) and ere commence commencement catalaunic when Aetius check chokewill Attil's gambit, (that buxon bruzeup, give it a burl!) lead us seek, O june of eves the jenniest, thou who fleeest flicklesome the fond fervid frondeur to thickly thyself attach with thine efteased ensuer,[4] ondrawer of our unconscionable, flickerflapper fore our unter-

Bet you fippence, anythesious, there's no puggatory, are yous game?

PREAUSTER.
MAN AND H
PURSUIT O
PAN-
HYSTERIC
WOMAN.

[1] I believe in Dublin and the Sultan of Turkey.
[2] I have heard this word used by Martin Halpin, an old gardener from the Glens of Antrim who used to do odd jobs for my godfather, the Rev. B. B. Brophy of Swords.
[3] Ravens may rive so can dove deelish.
[4] A question of pull.

266

drugged,[1] lead us seek, lote us see, light us find,
let us missnot Maidadate, Mimosa Multimim-
etica, the maymeaminning of maimoomeining!
Elpis, thou fountain of the greeces, all shall speer
theeward,[2] from kongen in his canteenhus to
knivers hind the knoll. Ausonius Audacior
and gael, gillie, gall.[3] Singalingalying. Storiella
as she is syung. Whence followeup with end-
speaking nots for yestures, plutonically pur-
suant on briefest glimpse from gladrags, pretty
Proserpronette whose slit satchel spilleth peas.

Belisha beacon, beckon bright! Usherette,
unmesh us! That grene ray of earong it waves
us to yonder as the red, blue and yellow flogs
time on the domisole,[4] with a blewy blow and
a windigo. Where flash becomes word and
silents selfloud. To brace congeners, trebly
bounden and asservaged twainly. Adamman,[5]
Emhe, Issossianusheen and sometypes Yggely
ogs Weib. Uwayoei![6] So mag this sybilette be
our shibboleth that we may syllable her well!
Vetus may be occluded behind the mou in
Veto but Nova will be nearing as their radient
among the Nereids. A one of charmers, ay,
Una Unica, charmers, who, under the branches
of the elms, in shoes as yet unshent by stoni-
ness, wend, went, will wend a way of honey
myrrh and rambler roses mistmusk while still
the maybe mantles the meiblume or ever her

_was a
hopeful
Cis._

_Big Bear
Sailor's
Trouble,
e, trouble._

_ng Unge
ke Kvinne._

[1] For Rose Point see Inishmacsaint.

[2] Mannequins' Pose.

[3] Their holy presumption and hers sinfly desprit.

[4] Anama anamaba anamabapa.

[5] Only for he's fathering law I could skewer that old one and slosh her out
many's the time but I thinks more of my pottles and ketts.

[6] All abunk for Tarararat! Look slipper, soppyhat, we've a doss in the
manger.

Telltale me all of annaryllies.

if have faded from the fleur,[1] their arms enlocked, (ringrang, the chimes of sex appealing as conchitas with sentas stray,[2] rung!), all thinking all of it, the It with an itch in it, the All every inch of it, the pleasure each will preen her for, the business each was bred to breed by.[3]

Will you carry my can and fight the fairies?

EARLY
NOTIONS
ACQUIRED
RIGHTS A
THE INFL
ENCE OF
COLLECTI
TRADITIO
UPON THE
INDIVIDU

Soon jemmijohns will cudgel about some a rhythmatick or other over Browne and Nolan's divisional tables whereas she, of minions' novence charily being cupid, for mug's wumping, grooser's grubbiness, andt's avarice and grossopper's grandegaffe, with her tootpettypout of jemenfichue will sit and knit on solfa sofa.[4] Stew of the evening, booksyful stew. And a bodikin a boss in the Thimble Theatre. But all is her inbourne. Intend. From gramma's grammar she has it that if there is a third person, mascarine, phelinine or nuder, being spoken abad it moods prosodes from a person speaking to her second which is the direct object that has been spoken to, with and at. Take the dative with his oblative[5] for, even if obsolete, it is always of interest, so spake gramma on the impetus of her imperative, only mind your genderous towards his reflexives such that I was to your grappa (Bott's trousend, hore a man uff!) when him was me hedon[6] and mine, what the lewdy saying, his analectual pygmyhop.[7] There is comfortism in the

Allma Mathers, Auctioneer.

Old Gavelkind the Gamper and he's as daff as you're erse.

[1] One must sell it to some one, the sacred name of love.
[2] Making it up as we goes along.
[3] The law of the jungerl.
[4] Let me blush to think of all those halfwayhoist pullovers.
[5] I'd like his pink's cheek.
[6] Frech devil in red hairing! So that's why you ran away to sea, Mrs Lappy. Leap me, Locklaun, for you have sensed!
[7] A washable lovable floatable doll.

knowledge that often hate on first hearing
comes of love by second sight. Have your
little sintalks in the dunk of subjunctions, dual
in duel and prude with pruriel, but even the
aoriest chaparound whatever plaudered perfect
anent prettydotes and *haec genua omnia* may
perhaps chance to be about to be in the case to
be becoming a pale peterwright in spite of all
your tense accusatives whilstly you're wall-
floored[1] like your gerandiums for the better
half of a yearn or sob. It's a wild's kitten, my
dear, who can tell a wilkling from a warthog.
For you may be as practical as is predicable
but you must have the proper sort of accident
to meet that kind of a being with a difference.[2]
Flame at his fumbles but freeze on his fist.[3]
Every letter is a godsend, ardent Ares, brusque
Boreas and glib Ganymede like zealous Zeus,
the O'Meghisthest of all. To me or not to me.
Satis thy quest on. Werbungsap! Jeg suis, vos
wore a gentleman, thou arr, I am a quean. Is
a game over? The game goes on. Cookcook!
Search me. The beggar the maid the bigger
the mauler. And the greater the patrarc the
griefer the pinch. And that's what your doctor
knows. O love it is the commonknounest thing
how it pashes the plutous and the paupe.[4]
Pop! And egg she active or spoon she passive,
all them fine clauses in Lindley's and Murrey's
never braught the participle of a present to a
desponent hortatrixy, vindicatively I say it,

*nte
*so.
ɔ-5o.
λαβον

[1] With her poodle feinting to be let off and feeling dead in herself. Is love
worse living?
[2] If she can't follow suit Renée goes to the pack.
[3] Improper frictions is maledictions and mens uration makes me mad.
[4] Llong and Shortts Primer of Black and White Wenchcraft.

from her postconditional future.[1] Lumpsome is who lumpsum pays. Quantity counts though accents falter. Yoking apart and oblique orations parsed to one side, a brat, alanna, can choose from so many, be he a sollicitor's appendix, a pipe clerk or free functionist flyswatter, that perfect little cad, from the languors and weakness of limberlimbed lassihood till the head, back and heartaches of waxedup womanage and heaps on heaps of other things too. Note the Respectable Irish Distressed Ladies and the Merry Mustard Frothblowers of Humphreystown Associations. Atac first, queckqueck quicks after. Beware how in that hist subtaile of schlangder[2] lies liaison to tease oreilles! To vert embowed set proper penchant. But learn from that ancient tongue to be middle old modern to the minute. A spitter that can be depended on. Though Wonderlawn's lost us for ever. Alis, alas, she broke the glass! Liddell lokker through the leafery, ours is mistery of pain.[3] You may spin on youthlit's bike and multiplease your Mike and Nike with your kickshoes on the algebrars but, volve the virgil page and view, the O of woman is long when burly those two muters sequent her so from Nebob[4] see you never stray who'll nimm you nice and nehm the day.

One hath just been areading, hath not one, ya, ya, in their memoiries of Hireling's puny wars, end so, und all, ga, ga, of The O'Brien,

I'll go for that small polly if you'll suck to your lebbensquatsch.

O'Mara Farrell.

Verschwindibus.

Ulstria,

---

[1] The gaggles all out.

[2] He's just bug nuts on white mate he hasn't the teath nor the grits to choo and that's what's wrong with Lang Wang Wurm, old worbbling goesbelly.

[3] Dear and I trust in all frivolity I may be pardoned for trespassing but I think I may add hell.

[4] He is my all menkind of every desception.

The O'Connor, The Mac Loughlin and The Mac Namara with summed their appondage, da, da, of Sire Jeallyous Seizer, that gamely torskmester,[1] with his duo of druidesses in ready money rompers[2] and the tryonforit of Oxthievious, Lapidous and Malthouse Anthemy. You may fail to see the lie of that layout, Suetonia,[3] but the reflections which recur to me are that so long as beauty life is body love[4] and so bright as Mutua of your mirror holds her candle to your caudle, lone lefthand likeless, sombring Autum of your Spring, reck you not one spirt of anyseed whether trigemelimen cuddle his coddle or nope. She'll confess it by her figure and she'll deny it to your face. If you're not ruined by that one she won't do you any whim. And then? What afters it? Gruff Gunne may blow, Gam Gonna flow, the gossans eye the jennings aye. From the butts of Heber and Heremon, *nolens volens*, brood our pansies, brune in brume. There's a split in the infinitive from to have to have been to will be. As they warred in their big innings ease now we never shall know. Eat early earthapples. Coax Cobra to chatters. Hail, Heva, we hear! This is the glider that gladdened the girl[5] that list to the wind that lifted the leaves that folded the fruit that hung on the tree that grew in the garden Gough gave. Wide hiss, we're wizen-

COUNSEL
AND CON-
STANCY.
ORDINATION
OF OMEN,
ONUS AND
OBIT. DIS-
TRIBUTION
OF DANGER,
DUTY AND
DESTINY.
POLAR PRIN-
CIPLES.

Eroico
...oso makes
...valet like
...ing.

...hyperape the
...k he groves the
...you see now for
...h sake, chawley!

[1] All his teeths back to the front, then the moon and then the moon with a hole behind it.

[2] Skip one, flop fore, jennies in the cabbage store.

[3] None of your cumpohlstery English here!

[4] Understudy my understandings, Sostituda, and meek thine complinement, gymnufleshed.

[5] Tho' I have one just like that to home, deadleaf brown with quicksilver appliques, would whollymost applissiate a nice shiny sleekysilk out of that slippering snake charmeuse.

271

ing. Hoots fromm, we're globing. Why hidest thou hinder thy husband his name? Leda, Lada, aflutter-afraida, so does your girdle grow! Willed without witting, whorled without aimed. Pappapassos, Mammamanet, warwhetswut and whowitswhy.[1] But it's tails for toughs and titties for totties and come buckets come bats till deeleet.[2]

Dark ages clasp the daisy roots, Stop, if you are a sally of the allies, hot off Minnowaurs and naval actiums, picked engagements and banks of rowers. Please stop if you're a B.C. minding missy, please do. But should you prefer A.D. stepplease. And if you miss with a venture it serves you girly well glad. But, holy Janus, I was forgetting the Blitzenkopfs! Here, Hengegst and Horsesauce, take your heads[3] out of that taletub! And leave your hinnyhennyhindyou! It's haunted. The chamber. Of errings. Whoan, tug, trace, stirrup! It is distinctly understoutered that, sense you threehandshighs put your twofootlarge timepates in that dead wash of Lough Murph and until such time pace one and the same Messherrn the grinning statesmen, Brock and Leon, have shunted the grumbling coundedtouts, Starlin and Ser Artur Ghinis. Foamous homely brew, bebattled by bottle, gageure de guegerre.[4] Bull igien bear and then bearagain bulligan. Gringrin gringrin. Staffs varsus · herds and bucks vursus barks.

---

[1] What's that, ma'am? says I.
[2] As you say yourself.
[3] That's the lethemuse but it washes off.
[4] Where he fought the shessock of his stimmstammer and we caught the pepettes of our lovelives.

*agh
*ree, me
*oon fiend.

*lies hug

*ve suffered
* them Cow-
*Forks and
*we enjoyed
*our pick of
*asketfild.
*Kine's
* Meal.

*ie for the
*and a
*ambum
*e
*otondus.

By old Grumbledum's walls. Bumps, bellows and bawls.[1] Opprimor's down, up up Opima! Rents and rates and tithes and taxes, wages, saves and spends. Heil, heptarched span of peace![2] Live, league of lex, nex and the mores! Fas est dass and foe err you. Impovernment of the booble by the bauble for the bubble. So wrap up your worries in your woe (wumpum-tum!) and shake down the shuffle for the throw. For there's one mere ope[3] for downfall ned. As Hanah Levy, shrewd shroplifter, and nievre anore skidoos with her spoileds.[4] To add gay touches. For hugh and guy and goy and jew. To dimpled and pimpled and simpled and wimpled. A peak in a poke and a pig in a pew.[5] She wins them by wons, a haul hectoendecate, for mangay mumbo jumbjubes tak mutts and jeffs muchas bracelonettes gracies barcelonas.[6] O what a loovely free-speech 'twas (tep)[7] to gar howalively hinter-grunting! Tip. Like lilt of larks to burdened crocodile,[8] or skittering laubhing at that wheeze of old windbag, Blusterboss, blow-harding about all he didn't do. Hell o' your troop! With is the winker for the muckwits of willesly and nith is the nod for the umproar napollyon and hitheris poorblond piebold hoerse. Huirse. With its tricuspidal hauberk-

---

[1] Shake eternity and lick creation.

[2] I'm blest if I can see.

[3] Hoppity Huhneye, hoosh the hen. I like cluckers, you like nuts (wink).

[4] Sweet, medium and dry like altar wine.

[5] Who'll buy me penny babies?

[6] Well, Maggy, I got your castoff devils all right and fits lovely. And am vaguely graceful. Maggy thanks.

[7] My six is no secret, sir, she said.

[8] Yes, there, Tad, thanks, give, from, tathair, look at that now.

Murdoch.

helm coverchaf emblem on. For the man that broke the ranks on Monte Sinjon. The all-riddle of it? That that is allruddy with us, ahead of schedule, which already is plan accomplished from and syne: Daft Dathy of the Five Positions (the death ray stop him!) is still, as

Pas d'action, peu de sauce.

reproaches Paulus, on the Madderhorn and, entre chats and hobnobs,[1] daring Dunderhead to shiver his timbers and Hannibal mac Hamiltan the Hegerite[2] (more livepower elbow him!) ministerbuilding up, as repreaches Timothy, in Saint Barmabrac's.[3] Number Thirty two West Eleventh streak looks on to that (may all in the tocoming of the sempereternal speel spry with it!) datetree doloriferous which

From the seven tents of Joseph till the calends of Mary Marian, olivehunkered and thorny too.

more and over leafeth earlier than every growth and, elfshot, headawag, with frayed nerves wondering till they feeled sore like any woman that has been born at all events to the purdah and for the howmanyeth and how-movingth time at what the demons in that

As Shakefork might pitch it.

jackhouse that jerry built for Massa and Missus and hijo de puta, the sparksown fermament of the starryk fieldgosongingon where blows a nemone at each blink of windstill[4] they were sliding along and sleeting aloof and scouting around and shooting about. All-whichwhile or whereaballoons for good vaunty years Dagobert is in Clane's clean hometown prepping up his prepueratory and learning how to put a broad face bronzily out through a broken breached meataerial

[1] Go up quick, stay so long, come down slow!
[2] If I gnows me gneesgnobs the both of him is gnatives of Genuas.
[3] A glass of peel and pip for Mr Potter of Texas, please.
[4] All the world loves a big gleaming jelly.

, puzzly, a cat.

from Bryan Awlining! Erin's hircohaired culoteer.[1]

And as, these things being so or ere those things having done, way back home in Pacata Auburnia,[2] (untillably holy gammel Eire) one world burrowing on another, (if you've got me, neighbour, in any large lumps, geek?, and got the strong of it) Standfest, our topiocal sagon hero, or any ootther macotther, signs is on the bellyguds bastille back, bucked up with fullness, and silvering to her jubilee,[3] birchleaves her jointure, our lavy in waving, visage full of flesh and fat as a hen's i' forehead, Airyanna and Blowyhart topsirturvy, that royal pair in their palace of quicken boughs hight The Goat and Compasses ('phone number 17:69, if you want to know[4]) his sea-arm strongsround her, her velivole eyne aship-wracked, have discusst their things of the past, crime and fable with shame, home and profit,[5] why lui lied to lei and hun tried to kill ham, scribbledehobbles, in whose veins runs a mixture of, are head bent and hard upon. Spell me the chimes. They are tales all tolled.[6] Today is well thine but where's may tomorrow be. But, bless his cowly head and press his crankly hat, what a world's woe is each's

FROM CENO-GENETIC DI-CHOTOMY THROUGH DIAGONISTIC CONCILI-ANCE TO DYNASTIC CONTINU-ITY.

akes a the ma-ep.

he Buffalo of bysone

quake the par-of dates.

[1] A pengeneepy for your warcheekeepy.

[2] My globe goes gaddy at geography giggle pending which time I was looking for my shoe all through Arabia.

[3] It must be some bugbear in the gender especially when old which they all soon get to look.

[4] After me looking up the plan in Humphrey's *Justice of the Piece* it said to see preseeding chaps.

[5] O boyjones and hairyoddities! Only noane told missus of her massas behaving she would laugh that flat that after that she had sanked down on her fat arks they would shaik all to sheeks.

[6] Traduced into jinglish janglage for the nusances of dolphins born.

other's weariness waiting to beadroll his own
properer mistakes, the backslapping glad-
hander,[1] free of his florid future and the other
singing likeness, dirging a past of bloody altars,
gale with a blost to him, dove without gall.
And she, of the jilldaw's nest[2] who tears up
lettereens she never apposed a pen upon.[3] Yet
sung of love and the monster man. What's
Hiccupper to hem or her to Hagaba? Ough,
ough, brieve kindli![4]

Dogs' vespers are anending. Vespertilia-
bitur. Goteshoppard quits his gabhard cloke
to sate with Becchus. Zumbock! Achevre!
Yet wind will be ere fadervor[5] and the hour of
fruminy and bergoo bell if Nippon have pearls
or opals Eldorado, the daindy dish, the lecking
out! Gipoo, good oil! For (hushmagandy!)
long 'tis till gets bright that all cocks waken
and birds Diana[6] with dawnsong hail. Aught
darks flou a duskness. Bats that? There peepee-
strilling. At Brannan's on the moor. At Tam
Fanagan's weak yat his still's going strang.
And still here is noctules and can tell things
acommon on by that fluffy feeling. Larges
loomy wheelhouse to bodgbox[7] lumber up
with hoodie hearsemen carrawain we keep
is peace who follow his law, Sunday

*Some is out for
twoheaded dul-
carnons but more
pulfers turnips.*

*Omnitudes in a
knutshedell.*

*For all us kids
under his aegis.*

*Saving the public
his health.*

*Superlative abso-
lute of Porter-
stown.*

THE MON
GREL UNI
THE DUNG
MOUND.
SIGNIFIC-
CANCE OF
THE INFRA
LIMINAL
TELLIGEN
OFFRANDI

[1] He gives me pulpititions with his Castlecowards never in these twowsers
and ever in those twawsers and then babeteasing us out of our hoydenname.

[2] My goldfashioned bother near drave me roven mad and I dyeing to
keep my linefree face like readymaid maryangs for jollycomes smashing
Holmes.

[3] What I would like is a jade louistone to go with the moon's increscent.

[4] Parley vows the Askinwhose? I do, Ida. And how to call the cattle black.
Moopetsi meepotsi.

[5] I was so snug off in my apholster's creedle but at long leash I'll stretch
more capritious in his dapplepied bed.

[6] Pipette. I can almost feed their sweetness at my lisplips.

[7] A liss in hunterland.

King.[1] His sevencoloured's soot (Ochone! Ochonal!)[2] and his imponence one heap lump-block (Mogoul!). And rivers burst out like weeming racesround joydrinks for the fewnral-ly,[3] where every feaster's a foster's other, fiannians all.[4] The wellingbreast, he willing giant, the mountain mourning his duggedy dew. To obedient of civicity in urbanious at felicity what'll yet meek Mike[5] our diputy mimber when he's head on poll and Peter's burgess and Miss Mishy Mushy is tiptupt by Toft Taft. Boblesse gobleege. For as Anna was at the beginning lives yet and will return after great deap sleap rerising and a white night high with a cows of Drommhiem as shower as there's a wet en-clouded in Westwicklow or a little black rose a truant in a thorntree. We drames our dreams tell Bappy returns. And Sein annews. We will not say it shall not be, this passing of order and order's coming, but in the herbest country and in the country around Blath as in that city self of legionds they look for its being ever yet. So shuttle the pipers done.[6] Eric aboy![7] And it's time that all paid tribute to this massive mor-tiality, the pink of punk perfection as photo-graphy in mud. Some may seek to dodge the

---

mucky idges r Flumi-id.

elmut's in inwood,

one is an i strande ceptre's a

wel, our leer.

ied bud-ssiphys-Theas.

l in pon-rthepoise.

---

[1] I wonder if I put the old buzzerd one night to suckle in Millickmaam's honey like they use to emballem some of the special popes with a book in his hand and his mouth open.

[2] And a ripping rude rape in his lucreasious togery.

[3] Will ye nought would wet your weapons, warriors bard?

[4] Roe, Williams, Bewey, Greene, Gorham, McEndicoth and Vyler, the lays of ancient homes.

[5] The stanidsglass effect, you could sugerly swear buttermilt would not melt down his dripping ducks.

[6] Thickathigh and Thinathews with sant their dam.

[7] Oh, could we do with this waddled of ours like that redbanked profanian with his bakset of yosters.

gobbet for its quantity of quality but who wants to cheat the choker's got to learn to chew the cud. Allwhichhole scrubs on scroll circuminiuminluminatedhave encuoniams here and improperies there.[1] With a pansy for the pussy in the corner.[2]

INCIPIT TERMISS

Bewise of Fanciulla's heart, the heart of Fanciulla! Even the recollection of willow fronds is a spellbinder that lets to hear.[3] The rushes by the grey nuns' pond: ah eh oh let me sigh too. Coalmansbell: behoves you handmake of the load. Jenny Wren: pick, peck. Johnny Post: pack, puck.[4] All the world's in want and is writing a letters.[5] A letters from a person to a place about a thing. And all the world's on wish to be carrying a letters. A letters to a king about a treasure from a cat.[6] When men want to write a letters. Ten men, ton men, pen men, pun men, wont to rise a ladder. And den men, dun men, fen men, fun men, hen men, hun men wend to raze a leader. Is then any lettersday from many peoples, Daganasanavitch? Empire, your outermost.[7] A posy cord. Plece.

We have wounded our way on foe tris prince till that force in the gill is faint afarred

MAJOR A MINOR

Pitchcap and triangle, noose and tinctunc.

Uncle Flabbius Muximus to Niecia Flappia Minnimiss. As this is. And as this this is.

Dear Brotus, land me arrears.

Rockaby, babel, flatten a wall.

How he broke the good news to Gent.

---

[1] Gosem pher, gezumpher, greeze a jarry grim felon! Good bloke him!

[2] And if they was setting on your stool as hard as my was she could beth her bothom dolours he'd have a culious impressiom on the diminitive that chafes our ends.

[3] When I'am Enastella and am taken for Essastessa I'll do that droop on the pohlmann's piano.

[4] Heavenly twinges, if it's one of his I'll fearly feint as swoon as he enter-rooms.

[5] To be slipped on, to be slept by, to be conned to, to be kept up. And when you're done push the chain.

[6] With her modesties office.

[7] Strutting as proud as a great turquin weggin that cuckhold on his Eddems and Clay's hat.

278

and the face in the treebark feigns afear. This is rainstones ringing. Strangely cult for this ceasing of the yore. But Erigureen is ever. Pot price pon patrilinear plop, if the osseletion of the onkring gives omen nome? Since alls war that end war let sports be leisure and bring and buy fair. Ah ah athclete, blest your bally bathfeet! Towntoquest, fortorest, the hour that hies is hurley. A halt for hearsake.[1]

[1] Come, smooth of my slate, to the beat of my blosh! With all these gelded ewes jilting about and the thrills and ills of laylock blossoms three's so much more plants than chants for cecilies that I was thinking fairly killing times of putting an end to myself and my malody, when I remembered all your pupil-teacher's erringnesses in perfection class. You sh'undn't write you can't if you w'udn't pass for undevelopmented. This is the propper way to say that, Sr. If it's me chews to swallow all you saidn't you can eat my words for it as sure as there's a key in my kiss. Quick erit faciofacey. When we will conjugate together toloseher tomaster tomiss while morrow fans amare hour, verbe de vie and verve to vie, with love ay loved have I on my back spine and does for ever. Your are me severe? Then rue. My intended, Jr, who I'm throne away on, (here he inst, my lifstack, a newfolly likon) when I slip through my pettigo I'll get my decree and take seidens when I'm not ploughed first by some Rolando the Lasso, and flaunt on the flimsyfilmsies for to grig my collage juniorees who, though they flush fuchsia, are they octette and viginity in my shade but always my figurants. They may be yea of my year but they're nary nay of my day. Wait till spring has sprung in spickness and prigs beg in to pry they'll be plentyprime of housepets to pimp and pamper my. Impending marriage. Nature tells everybody about but I learned all the runes of the gamest game ever from my old nourse Asa. A most adventuring trot is her and she vicking well knowed them all heartswise and fourwords. How Olive d'Oyly and Winnie Carr, bejupers, they reized the dressing of a salandmon and how a peeper coster and a salt sailor med a mustied poet atwaimen. It most have bean Mad Mullans planted him. Bina de Bisse and Trestrine von Terrefin. Sago sound, rite go round, kill kackle, kook kettle and (remember all should I forget to) bolt the thor. Auden. Wasn't it just divining that dog of a dag in Skokholme as I sat astrid uppum their Drewitt's altar, as cooledas as culcumbre, slapping my straights till the sloping ruins, postillion, postallion, a swinge a swank, with you offering me clouts of illscents and them horners stagstruck on the leasward! Don't be of red, you blanching mench! This isabella I'm on knows the ruelles of the rut and she don't fear andy mandy. So sing loud, sweet cheeriot, like anegreon in heaven! The good fother with the twingling in his eye will always have cakes in his pocket to bethroat us with for our allmichael good. Amum. Amum. And Amum again. For tough troth is stronger than fortuitous fiction and it's the surplice money, oh my young friend and ah me sweet creature, what buys the bed while wits borrows the clothes.

A scene at sight. Or dreamoneire. Which they shall memorise. By her freewritten Hopely for ear that annalykeses if scares for eye that sumns. Is it in the now woodwordings of our sweet plantation where the branchings then will singingsing tomorrows gone and yesters outcome as Satadays afternoon lex leap smiles on the twelvemonthsminding? Such is. Dear (name of desired subject, A.N.), well, and I go on to. Shlicksher. I and we (tender condolences for happy funeral, one if) so sorry to (mention person suppressed for the moment, F.M.). Well (enquiries after all-healths) how are you (question maggy). A lovely (introduce to domestic circles) pershan of cates. Shrubsher. Those pothooks mostly she hawks from Poppa Vere Foster but these curly mequeues are of Mippa's moulding. Shrubsheruthr. (Wave gently in the ere turning ptover.) Well, mabby (consolation of shopes) to soon air. With best from cinder Christinette if prints chumming, can be when desires Soldi, for asamples, backfronted or, if all, peethrolio or Get my Prize, using her flower or perfume or, if veryveryvery chumming, in otherwards, who she supposed adeal, kissists my exits. Shlicksheruthr. From Auburn chenlemagne. Pious and pure fair one, all has concomitated to this that she shall tread them lifetrees leaves whose silence hitherto has shone as sphere of silver fastalbarnstone, that fount Bandusian shall play liquick music and after odours sigh of musk. Blotsbloshblothe, one dear that was. Sleep in the water, drug at the fire, shake the dust off and dream your one who would give her sidecurls to. Till later

Bibelous hicstory and Barbarassa harestary.

A shieling in coppingers and porrish soup all days.

How matches metroosers?

Le hélos tombaut soul sur la jambe de marche.

THE PART
PLAYED BY
BELLETRI-
STICKS IN
THE BELLUM-
PAX-BEL-
LUM.
MUTUOMOR-
PHOMUTA-
TION.

SORTES VIR-
GINIANAE.

naintenante
t venuse.

Dons Johns
s Totty
s.

Spuke
hruster.

um shillum
e sextum
thums for
arridge
.

Lammas is led in by baith our washwives, a weird of wonder tenebrous as that evil thorngarth, a field of faery blithe as this flowing wild.

Aujourd'hui comme aux temps de Pline et de Columelle la jacinthe se plaît dans les Gaules, la pervenche en Illyrie, la marguerite sur les ruines de Numance[1] et pendant qu'autour d'elles les villes ont changé de maîtres et de noms, que plusieurs sont entrées dans le néant, que les civilisations se sont choquées et brisées, leurs paisibles générations ont traversé les âges et sont arrivées jusqu'à nous, fraîches et riantes comme aux jours des batailles.[2]

Margaritomancy! Hyacinthinous pervinciveness! Flowers. A cloud. But Bruto and Cassio are ware only of trifid tongues[3] the whispered wilfulness, ('tis demonal!) and shadows shadows multiplicating (il folsoletto nel falsoletto col fazzolotto dal fuzzolezzo),[4] totients quotients, they tackle their quarrel. Sickamoor's so woful sally. Ancient's aerger. And eachway bothwise glory signs. What if she love Sieger less though she leave Ruhm moan? That's how our oxyggent has gotten ahold of half their world. Moving about in the free of the air and mixing with the ruck. Enten eller, either or.

And!

Nay, rather!

[1] The nasal foss of our natal folkfarthers so so much now for Valsinggiddyrex and his grand arks day triump.

[2] Translout that gaswind into turfish, Teague, that's a good bog and you, Thady, poliss it off, there's a nateswipe, on to your blottom pulper.

[3] You daredevil donnelly, I love your piercing lots of lies and your flashy foreign mail so here's my cowrie card, I dalgo, with all my exes, wise and sad.

[4] All this Mitchells is a niggar for spending and I will go to the length of seeing that one day Big Mig will be nickleless himself.

Tricks stunts.

With sobs for his job, with tears for his toil, with horror for his squalor but with pep for his perdition,[1] lo, the boor plieth as the laird hireth him.

Boon on begyndelse.

At maturing daily gloryaims![2]

A flink dab for a freck dive and a stern poise for a swift pounce was frankily at the manual arith sure enough which was the bekase he knowed from his cradle, no bird better, why his fingures were giving him whatfor to fife with. First, by observation, there came boko and nigh him wigworms and nigh him tittlies and nigh him cheekadeekchimple and nigh him pickpocket with pickpocketpumb, pickpocketpoint, pickpocketprod, pickpocketpromise and upwithem. Holy Joe in lay Eden.[3] And anyhows always after them the dimpler he weighed the fonder fell he of his null four lovedroyd curdinals, his element curdinal numen and his enement curdinal marryng and his epulent curdinal weisswassh and his eminent curdinal Kay O'Kay. Always would he be reciting of them, hoojahs koojahs, up by rota, in his Fanden's catachysm from fursed to laced, quickmarch to decemvers, so as to pin the tenners, thumbs down. And anon and aldays, strues yerthere, would he wile arecreating em om lumerous ways, caiuscounting in the scale of pin puff pive piff, piff puff pive poo, poo puff pive pree, pree puff pive pfoor, pfoor puff pive pippive, poopive,[4] Niall Dhu,

Truckeys' cant for dactyl and spondee.

Panoplous peregrine pifflicative pomposity.

ANTITHESISOFAM
DUAL ANTICIPATIC
THE MIND FACTOF
ITS GIVE AND TAF

AUSPICIUM.
AUGURIA.

DIVINITY
NOT DEITY
THE UNCER-
TAINTY JUS
TIFIED BY
OUR CERTI-
TUDE.
EXAMPLES.

---

[1] While I'll wind the wildwoods' bluckbells among my window's weeds.
[2] Lawdy Dawdy Simpers.
[3] But where, O where, is me lickle dig done?
[4] That's his whisper waltz I like from Pigott's with that Lancydancy step. Stop.

Foughty Unn, Enoch Thortig, endso one, like to pitch of your cap, pac, on to tin tall spillicans.[1] To sum, borus pew notus pew eurus pew zipher. Ace, deuce, tricks, quarts, quims. Mumtiplay of course and carry to their whole number. While on the other hand, traduced by their comedy nominator to the loaferst terms for their aloquent parts, sexes, suppers, oglers, novels and dice.[2] He could find (the rakehelly!) by practice the valuse of thine-to-mine articles with no reminder for an equality of relations and, with the helpings from his tables, improduce fullmin to trumblers, links unto chains, weys in Nuffolk till tods of Yorek, oozies ad libs and several townsends, several hundreds, civil-to-civil imperious gallants into gells (Irish), bringing alliving stone allaughing down to grave clothnails and a league of archers, fools and lurchers under the rude rule of fumb. What signifieth whole that[3] but, be all the prowess of ten, 'tis as strange to relate he, nonparile to rede, rite and reckan, caught allmeals dullmarks for his nucleuds and alegobrew. They wouldn't took bearings no how anywheres. O them doddhunters and allanights, aabs and baas for agnomes, yees and zees for incognits, bate him up jerrybly! Worse nor herman dororrhea. Give you the fantods, seemed to him. They ought to told you every last word first stead of trying every which way to kinder smear it out poison long. Show that the

*plus ulstra,
,nec,cashel-
tuum.*

*dderwedder
shicksal.*

[1] Twelve buttles man, twentyeight bows of curls, forty bonnets woman and ever youthfully yours makes alleven add the hundred.
[2] Gamester Damester in the road to Rouen he grows more like his deed every die.
[3] Slash-the-Pill lifts the pellet. Run, Phoenix, run!

median, hce che ech, interecting at royde
angles the parilegs of a given obtuse one bis-
cuts both the arcs that are in curveachord
behind. Brickbaths. The family umbroglia.
A Tullagrove pole[1] to the Height of County
Fearmanagh has a septain inclinaison[2] and the
graphplot for all the functions in Lower
County Monachan, whereat samething is rivi-
sible by nighttim, may be involted into the
zeroic couplet, palls pell inhis heventh glike

noughty times ∞, find, if you are not literally
cooefficient, how minney combinaisies and per-
mutandies can be played on the international
surd! pthwndxrclzp!, hids cubid rute being
extructed, taking anan illitterettes, ififif at a tom.
Answers, (for teasers only).[3] Ten, twent, thirt,
see, ex and three icky totchty ones. From
solation to solution. Imagine the twelve
deaferended dumbbawls of the whowl above-
beugled to be the contonuation through
regeneration of the urutteration of the word
in pregross. It follows that, if the two ante-
sedents be bissyclitties and the three come-
seekwenchers trundletrikes, then, Aysha Lali-

pat behidden on the footplate, Big Whiggler[4]
restant upsittuponable, the nCr[5] presents to
us (tandem year at lasted length!) an otto-
mantic turquo-indaco of pictorial shine by
pictorial shimmer so long as, gad of the gidday,
pictorial summer, viridorefulvid, lits asheen,

---

[1] Dideney, Dadeney, Dudeney, O, I'd know that putch on your poll.
[2] That is tottinghim in his boots.
[3] Come all ye hapney coachers and support the richview press.
[4] Braham Baruch he married his cook to Massach McKraw her uncle-in-
law who wedded his widow to Hjalmar Kjaer who adapted his daughter to
Braham the Bear. V for wadlock, P for shift, H for Lona the Konkubine.
[5] A gee is just a jay on the jaunts cowsway.

but (lenz alack lends a lot), if this habby cyclic
erdor be outraciously enviolated by a mierelin
roundtableturning, like knuts in maze, the zitas
runnind hare and dart[1] with the yeggs in
their muddle, like a seven of wingless arrows,
hodgepadge, thump, kick and hurry, all boy
more missis blong him he race quickfeller all
same hogglepiggle longer house blong him,[2]
while the catched and dodged exarx seems
himmulteemiously to beem (he wins her hend!
he falls to tail!) the ersed ladest mand[3] and
(uhu and uhud!) the losed farce on erro-
roots,[4] twalegged poneys and threehandled
dorkeys (madahoy, morahoy, lugahoy, jog-
ahoyaway) мРм brings us a rainborne pamto-
momiom, aqualavant to (cat my dogs, if I
baint dingbushed like everything!) kaksitoista
volts yksitoista volts kymmenen volts yhdek-
san volts kahdeksan volts seitseman volts kuusi
volts viisi volts nelja volts kolme volts kaksi
volts yksi! allahthallacamellated, caravan series
to the finish of helve's fractures.[5] In outher
wards, one from five, two to fives ones, one
from fives two millamills with a mill and a
half a mill and twos twos fives fives of bully
clavers. For a surview over all the factionables
see Iris in the Evenine's World.[6] Binomeans
to be comprendered. Inexcessible as thy by
god ways. The aximones. And their prosta-

'innotus of
nnati.

urgink's
es and
guin's men.

de nombres!
balbearians.

---

[1] Talking about trilbits.
[2] Barneycorrall, a precedent for the prodection of curiosity from children.
[3] A pfurty pscore of ruderic rossies haremhorde for his divelsion.
[4] Look at your mad father on his boneshaker fraywhaling round Myriom
square.
[5] Try Asia for the assphalt body with the concreke soul and the forequarters
of the moon behinding out of his phase.
[6] Tomatoes malmalaid with De Quinceys salade can be tastily served with
Indiana Blues on the violens.

lutes. For his neuralgiabrown.

Equal to $=$aosch.

P.t.l.o.a.t.o.

HEPTAGRAMMATON
HYPOTHESE
OF COM-
MONEST EX-
PERIENCES
BEFORE APC
THEOSIS OF
THE LUSTRA
PRINCIPIUM

So, bagdad, after those initials falls and that primary tainccture, as I know and you know yourself, begath, and the arab in the ghetto knows better, by nettus, nor anymeade or persan, comic cuts and series exerxeses always were to be capered in Casey's frost book of, page torn on dirty, to be hacked at Hickey's, hucksler, Wellington's Iron Bridge, and so, by long last, as it would shuffle out, must he to trump adieu atout atous to those cardinhands he a big deal missed, radmachrees and rosse-cullinans and blagpikes in suitclover. Dear hearts of my counting, would he revoke them, forewheel to packnumbers, and, the time being no help fort, plates to lick one and turn over.

Vive Paco
Hunter!

The hoisted in
red and the low-
ered in black.

Problem ye ferst, construct ann aquilittoral dryankle Probe loom! With his primal hand-stoe in his sole salivarium. Concoct an equo-angular trillitter.[1] On the name of the tizzer and off the tongs and off the mythametical tripods. Beatsoon.

INGENIOUS
LABOUR-
TENACITY
AS BETWEE
INGENUOUS
AND LIBERT

The boss's bess
bass is the browd
of Mullingar.

Can you nei do her, numb? asks Dolph,[2] suspecting the answer know. Oikkont, ken you, ninny? asks Kev,[3] expecting the answer guess.[4] Nor was the noer long disappointed for easiest of kisshams, he was made vicewise. Oc, tell it to oui, do, Sem! Well, 'tis oil thusly. First mull a mugfull of mud, son.[5] Oglores,

PROPE AND
PROCUL IN
THE CON-
VERGENCE
OF THEIR
CONTRAPUL
SIVENESS.

[1] As Rhombulus and Rhebus went building rhomes one day.
[2] The trouveller.
[3] Of the disorded visage.
[4] Singlebarrelled names for doubleparalleled twixtytwins.
[5] Like pudging a spoon fist of sugans into a sotspot of choucolout.

the virtuoser prays, olorum! What the D.V. would I do that for? That's a goosey's gans- wer you're for giving me, he is told, what the Deva would you do that for?[1] Now, sknow royol road to Puddlin, take your mut for a first beginning, big to bog, back to bach. Anny liffle mud which cometh out of Mam will doob, I guess. A.1. *Amnium instar.* And to find a locus for an alp get a howlth on her bayrings as a prisme O and for a second O unbox your compasses. I cain but are you able? Amicably nod. Gu it! So let's seth off betwain us. Prompty? Mux your pistany at a point of the coastmap to be called *a* but pro- nounced olfa. There's the isle of Mun, ah! O! Tis just. *Bene*! Now, whole in applepine odrer[2]

(for—husk, hisk, a spirit spires—Dolph, dean of idlers, meager suckling of gert stoan, though barekely a balbose boy, he too, — *venite, preteriti,*[3] *sine mora dumque de entibus nascituris decentius in lingua romana mortuorum parva chartula liviana ostenditur, seden- tes in letitiae super ollas carnium, spectantes immo situm lutetiae unde auspiciis secundis tantae consurgent humanae stirpes, antiquissimam flaminum amborium Jordani et Jambaptistae mentibus revolvamus sapientiam: totum tute fluvii modo mundo fluere, eadem quae ex aggere fututa fuere iterum inter alveum fore futura, quodlibet sese ipsum per aliudpiam agnoscere contrarium, omnem demun amnem ripis rivalibus amplecti*[4] — recurrently often, when him moved he would cake their chair, coached rebelliumtending mikes of his same and over his own choirage at Backlane Univarsity, among of which pupal souaves the pizdrool was pulled up, bred and bat-

---

[1] Will you walk into my wavetrap? said the spiter to the shy.
[2] If we each could always do all we ever did.
[3] Dope in Canorian words we've made. Spish from the Doc.
[4] Basqueesh, Finnican, Hungulash and Old Teangtaggle, the only pure way to work a curse.

tered, for a dillon a dollar,[1] chanching letters for them vice o'verse to bronze mottes and blending tschemes for em in tropadores and doublecressing twofold thruths and devising tingling tailwords too whilest, cunctant that another would finish his sentence for him, he druider would smilabit eggways[2] ned, he, to don't say nothing, would, so prim, and pick upon his ten ordinailed ungles, trying to undo with his teeth the knots made by his tongue, retelling humself by the math hour, long as he's brood, a reel of funnish ficts apout the shee, how faust of all and on segund thoughts and the thirds the charmhim girlalove and fourthermore and filthily with bag from Oxatown and baroccidents and proper accidence and hoptohill and hexenshoes, in fine the whole damning letter; and, in point of feet, when he landed in ourland's leinster[3] of saved and solomnones for the twicedhecame time, off Lipton's strongbowed launch, the *Lady Eva*, in a tan soute of sails[4] he converted it's nataves, name saints, young ordnands, maderaheads and old unguished P.T. Publikums, through the medium of znigznaks with sotiric zeal, to put off the barcelonas[5] from their peccaminous corpulums (Gratings, Mr Dane!) and kiss on their bottes (Master!) as often as they came within bloodshot of that other familiar temple and showed em the celestine way to by his tristar and his flop hattrick and his perry humdrum dumb and numb nostrums that he larned in Hymbuktu,[6] and that same galloroman cultous is very prevailend up to this windiest of landhavemiseries all over what was beforeaboots a land of nods, in spite of all the bloot, all the braim, all the brawn, all the brile, that was shod, that were shat, that was shuk all the while, for our massangrey if mosshungry people, the at Wickerworks,[7] still hold

---

[1] An ounceworth of onions for a pennyawealth of sobs.

[2] Who brought us into the yellow world!

[3] Because it's run on the mountain and river system.

[4] When all them allied sloopers was ventitillated in their poppos and, sliding down by creek and veek, stole snaking out to sea.

[5] They were plumped and plumed and jerried and citizens and racers, and cinnamondhued.

[6] Creeping Crawleys petery parley, banished to his native Ireland from erring under Ryan.

[7] Had our retrospectable fearfurther gatch mutchtatches?

ford to their healing and[1] byleave in the old weights downupon the Swanny, innovated by him, the prence di Propagandi, the chrism for the christmass, the pillar of the perished and the rock o'ralereality, and it is veritably belied, we belove, that not allsods of esoupcans that's in the queen's pottage post and not allfinesof greendgold that the Indus contains would overhinduce them, (o.p.) to steeplechange back once from their ophis workship and twice on sundises, to their ancient flash and crash habits of old Pales time ere beam slewed cable[2] or Derzherr, live wire, fired Benjermine Funkling outa th'Empyre, sin righthand son; which, cummal, having listed curefully to the interlooking and the under-lacking of her twentynine shifts or his continental's curses, pum-mel, apostrophised Byrne's and Flamming's and Furniss's and Bill Hayses's and Ellishly Haught's, hoc, they (t.a.W.), sick or whole, stiff or sober, let drop as a doombody drops, with-out another ostrovgods word eitherways, in their own lineal descendance, as priesto as puddywhack,[3] coal on:[4] and, as we gang along to gigglehouse, talking of molniacs' manias and missions for mades to scotch the schlang and leathercoats for murty magdies, of course this has blameall in that medeoturanian world to say to blessed by Pointer the Grace's his privates judge-ments[5] whenso to put it, *disparito, duspurudo, desterrado, des-pertieu,* or, saving his presents for his own onefriend Bevradge, Conn the Shaughraun; but to return for a moment from the reptile's age[6] to the coxswain on the first landing (page Aínée Rivière!) if the pretty Lady Elisabbess, Hotel des Ruines — she laid her batsleeve for him two trueveres tell love (on the Ides of Valentino's, at Idleness, Floods Area, Isolade, Liv's lonely daughter, with the Comes Tichiami, of Prima Vista, Abroad, suddenly), and beauty alone of all dare say when now, uncrowned,

---

[1] That is to sight, when cleared of factions, vulgure and decimating.
[2] They just spirits a body away.
[3] Patatapadatback.
[4] Dump her (the missuse).
[5] Fox him! The leggy colt!
[6] Do he not know that walleds had wars. Harring man, is neow king. This is modeln times.

deceptered, in what niche of time[1] is Shee or where in the rose world trysting, that was the belle of La Chapelle, shapely Liselle, and the peg-of-my-heart of all the tompull or on whose limbs-to-lave her semicupiose eyes now kindling themselves are brightning,[2] O Shee who then (4.32 M.P., old time, to be precise, according to all three doctors waterburies that was Mac Auliffe and poor Mac-Beth and poor MacGhimley to the tickleticks, of the synchronisms, all lauschening, a time also confirmed seven sincuries later by the quatren medical johnny, poor old MacAdoo MacDollett, with notary,[3] whose presence was required by law of Devine Foresygth and decretal of the Douge) who after the first compliments[4] med darkist day light, gave him then that vantage of a Blinkensope's cuddlebath at her proper mitts — if she then, the then that matters, — but, *seigneur*! she could never have forefelt, as she yet will fearfeel, when the lovenext breaks out, such a coolcold douche as him, the totterer, the four-flights-the-charmer, doubling back, in nowtime,[5] bymby when saltwater he wush him these iselands, O *alors*!, to mount miss (the wooeds of Fogloot!) under that *chemise de fer* and a vartryproof name, Multalusi (would it wash?) with a cheek white peaceful as, wen shall say, a single professed claire's[6] and his washawash tubatubtub and his diagonoser's lampblick, to pure where they where hornest girls, to buy her in *par jure*, il you plait, nuncandtunc and for simper, and other duel mavourneens in plurible numbers from Arklow Vikloe to Louth super Luck, come messes, come mams, and touch your spottprice (for 'twas he was the born suborner, man) on behalf of an oldest ablished firma of winebakers, Lagrima and Gemiti, later on, his craft ebbing, invoked by the unirish title, Grindings of Nash,[7] the

---

[1] Muckross Abbey with the creepers taken off.

[2] Joke and Jilt will have their tilt.

[3] Old Mamalujorum and Rawrogerum.

[4] Why have these puerile blonds those large flexible ears?

[5] Pomeroy Roche of Portobello, or the Wreck of the Ragamuffin.

[6] No wonder Miss Dotsh took to veils and she descended from that obloquohy.

[7] The bookley with the rusin's hat is Patomkin but I'm blowed if I knowed who the slave is doing behind the curtain.

One and Only, Unic bar None, of Saint Yves by Landsend corn-
wer, man — ship me silver!, it must have been, faw! a terrible
mavrue mavone, to synamite up the old Adam-he-used-to, such a
finalley, and that's flat as Tut's fut, for whowghowho? the poour
girl, a lonely peggy, given the bird, so inseuladed as Crampton's
peartree, (she sall eurn bitter bed by thirt sweet of her face!), and
short wonder so many of the tomthick and tarry members in all
there subsequious ages of our timocracy tipped to console with her
at her mirrorable gracewindow'd hut[1] till the ives of Man, the
O'Kneels and the O'Prayins and the O'Hyens of Lochlaunstown
and the O'Hollerins of Staneybatter, hollyboys, all, burryripe
who'll buy?,[2] in juwelietry and kickychoses and madornaments
and that's not the finis of it (would it were!)—but to think of him
foundling a nelliza the second,[3] also cliptbuss (the best was still
there if the torso was gone) where he did and when he did, retriever to the last[4] — escapes my forgetness now was it dust-
covered, *nom de Lieu*! on lapse or street ondown, through, for or
from a foe, by with as on a friend, at the Rectory? Vicarage Road?
Bishop's Folly? Papesthorpe?, after picket fences, stonewalls, out
and ins or oxers — for merry a valsehood whisprit he to manny a
lilying earling;[5] and to try to analyse that ambo's pair of brace-
leans akwart the rollyon trying to amarm all[6] of that miching
micher's bearded but insensible virility and its gaulish moustaches, Dammad and Groany, into her limited (*tuff, tuff, que tu es
pitre!*) lapse at the same slapse for towelling ends[7] in their dolight-
ful Sexsex home, Somehow-at-Sea (O little oily head, sloper's
brow and prickled ears!) as though he, a notoriety, a foist edition,
were a wrigular writher neonovene babe![8] — well, diarmuee and

---

[1] O hce! O hce!

[2] Six and seven the League.

[3] It's all round me hat I'll wear a drooping dido.

[4] Have you ever thought of a hitching your stern and being ourdeaned,
Mester Bootenfly, here's me and Myrtle is twinkling to know.

[5] To show they caught preferment.

[6] See the freeman's cuticatura by Fennella.

[7] Just one big booty's pot.

[8] Charles de Simples had an infirmierity complexe before he died a natural
death.

granyou and *Vae Vinctis*, if that is what lamoor that of gentle breast rathe is intaken seems circling toward out yondest (it's life that's all chokered by that batch of grim rushers) heaven help his hindmost and, mark mo, if the so greatly displeaced diorems in the Saint Lubbock's Day number of that most improving of roundshows, *Spice and Westend Woman* (utterly exhausted before publication, indiapepper edition shortly), are for our indices, it agins to pear like it, par my fay, and there is no use for your pastripreaching for to cheesse it either or praying fresh fleshblood claspers of young catholick throats on Huggin Green[1] to take warning by the prispast, why?, by cows ∴ man, in shirt, is how he is *più la gonna è mobile* and ∴ they wonet do ut; and, an you could peep inside the cerebralised saucepan of this eer illwinded goodfornobody, you would see in his house of thoughtsam (was you, that is, decontaminated enough to look discarnate) what a jetsam litterage of convolvuli of times lost or strayed, of lands derelict and of tongues laggin too, longa yamsayore, not only that but, search lighting, beached, bashed and beaushelled *à la Mer* pharahead into faturity, your own convolvulis pickninnig capman would real to jazztfancy the novo takin place of what stale words whilom were woven with and fitted fairly featly for, so; and equally so, the crame of the whole faustian fustian, whether your launer's lightsome or your soulard's schwearmood, it is that, whenas the swiftshut scareyss of our pupilteachertaut duplex will hark back to lark to you symibellically that, though a day be as dense as a decade, no mouth has the might to set a mearbound to the march of a landsmaul,[2] in half a sylb, helf a solb, holf a salb onward[3] the beast of boredom, common sense, lurking gyrographically down inside his loose Eating S.S. collar is gogoing of whisth to you sternly how — Plutonic loveliaks twinnt Platonic yearlings — you must, how, in undivided reawlity draw the line somewhawre)

---

[1] Where Buickly of the Glass and Bellows pumped the Rudge engineral.
[2] Matter of Brettaine and brut fierce.
[3] Bussmullah, cried Lord Wolsley, how me Aunty Mag'll row!

Coss? Cossist? Your parn! You, you make what name? (and in truth, as a poor soul is between shift and shift ere the death he has lived through becomes the life he is to die into, he or he had albut — he was rickets as to reasons but the balance of his minds was stables — lost himself or himself some somnione sciupiones, soswhitchoverswetch had he or he gazet, murphy come, murphy go, murphy plant, murphy grow, a maryamyriameliamurphies, in the lazily eye of his lapis,

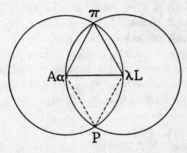

*alterance or
nterplay of
es in the
nb.*

*Vortex.
ng of Sprung
se. The Ver-*

Vieus Von DVbLIn, 'twas one of dozedeams a darkies ding in dewood) the Turnpike under the Great Ulm (with Mearingstone in Fore ground).[1] Given now ann linch you take enn all. Allow me! And, heaving alljawbreakical expressions out of old Sare Isaac's[2] universal of specious aristmystic unsaid, A is for Anna like L is for liv. Aha hahah, Ante Ann you're apt to ape aunty annalive! Dawn gives rise. Lo, lo, lives love! Eve takes fall. La, la, laugh leaves alass! Aiaiaiai, Antiann, we're last to the lost, Loulou! Tis perfect. Now (lens

[1] Draumcondra's Dreamcountry where the betterlies blow.
[2] O, Laughing Sally, are we going to be toadhauntered by that old Pantifox Sir Somebody Something, Burtt, for the rest of our secret stripture?

your dappled yeye here, mine's presbyoperian, shill and wall) we see the copyngink strayed-line AL (in Fig., the forest) from being continued, stops ait Lambday[1]: Modder ilond there too. Allow me anchore! I bring down noth and carry awe. Now, then, take this in! One of the most murmurable loose carollaries ever Ellis threw his cookingclass. With Olaf as centrum and Olaf's lambtail for his spokesman circumscript a cyclone. Allow ter! Hoop! As round as the calf of an egg! O, dear me! O, dear me now! Another grand discobely! After Makefearsome's Ocean. You've actuary entducked one! Quok! Why, you haven't a passer! Fantastic! Early clever, surely doomed, to Swift's, alas, the galehus! Match of a matchness, like your Bigdud dadder in the boudeville song, *Gorotsky Gollovar's Troubles*, raucking his flavourite turvku in the smukking precincts of lydias,[2] with Mary Owens and Dolly Monks seesidling to edge his cropulence and Blake-Roche, Kingston and Dockrell auriscenting him from afurz, our papacocopotl,[3] Abraham Bradley King? (ting ting! ting ting!) By his magmasine fall. Lumps, lavas and all.[4] *Bene!* But, thunder and turf, it's not alover yet! One recalls Byzantium. The mystery repeats itself todate as our callback mother Gaudyanna, that was daughter to a tanner,[5] used to sing, as I think, now and then consinuously over her possetpot in her quer

Sarga, or the path of outgoing.

Docetism and Didicism, Maya-Thaya. Tamas-Rajas-Sattvas.

[1] Ex jup pep off Carpenger Strate. The kids' and dolls' home. Makeacake-ache.

[2] A vagrant need is a flagrant weed.

[3] Grand for blowing off steam when you walk up in the morning.

[4] At the foot of Bagnabun Banbasday was lost on one.

[5] We're all found of our anmal matter.

294

homolocous humminbass hesterdie and ist-
herdie forivor.[1] Vanissas Vanistatums! And
for a night of thoughtsendyures and a day. As
Great Shapesphere puns it. In effect, I re-
mumble, from the yules gone by, purr lil mur-
rerof myhind, so she used indeed. When she
give me the Sundaclouths she hung up for
Tate and Comyng and snuffed out the ghost
in the candle at his old game of haunt the
sleeper. Faithful departed. When I'm dreaming back like that I begins to see we're only
all telescopes. Or the comeallyoum saunds.
Like when I dromed I was in Dairy and was
wuckened up with thump in thudderdown.
Rest in peace! But to return.[2] What a wonderful memory you have too! Twonderful
morrowy! Straorbinaire! *Bene!* I bring town
eau and curry nothung up my sleeve. Now,
springing quickenly from the mudland Loosh
from Luccan with Allhim as her Elder tetra-
turn a somersault. All's fair on all fours, as
my instructor unstrict me. Watch! And you'll
have the whole inkle. Allow, allow! Gyre O,
gyre O, gyrotundo! Hop lala! As umpty
herum as you seat! O, dear me, that was very
nesse! Very nace indeed! And makes us a
daintical pair of accomplasses! You, allus for
the kunst and me for omething with a handel
to it. *Beve!* Now, as will pressantly be felt,
there's tew tricklesome poinds where our
twain of doubling bicirculars, mating approxe-
metely in their suite poi and poi, dunloop
into eath the ocher. Lucihere.! I fee where you

[1] Sewing up the beillybursts in their buckskin shiorts for big **Kapitayn**
Killykook and the Jukes of Kelleiney.
[2] Say where! A timbrelfill of twinkletinkle.

*Vegetable
and its Pri-
Properties.*

*haves and
havenots: a
inction.*

mea. The doubleviewed seeds. Nun, lemmas quatsch, vide pervoys akstiom, and I think as I'm suqeez in the limon, stickme punctum, but for semenal rations I'd likelong, by Araxes, to mack a capital Pee for Pride down there on the batom[1] where Hoddum and Heave, our monsterbilker, balked his bawd of parodies. And let you go, Airmienious, and mick your modest mock Pie out of Humbles up your end. Where your apexojesus will be a point of order. With a geing groan grunt and a croak click cluck.[2] And my faceage kink and kurkle trying to make keek peep.[3] Are you right there, Michael, are you right? Do you think you can hold on by sitting tight? Well, of course, it's awful angelous. Still I don't feel it's so dangelous. Ay, I'm right here, Nickel, and I'll write. Singing the top line why it suits me mikey fine. But, yaghags hogwarts and arrahquinonthiance, it's the muddest thick that was ever heard dump since Eggsmather got smothered in the plap of the pfan. Now, to compleat anglers, beloved bironthiarn and hushtokan hishtakatsch, join alfa pea and pull loose by dotties and, to be more sparematically logoical, eelpie and paleale by trunkles. Alow me align while I encloud especious! The Nike done it. Like pah,[4] I peh. Innate little bondery. And as plane as a poke stiff.[5] Now, *aqua in buccat.* I'll make you to see figuratleavely the whome of your eternal

Zweispaltung as Fundemaintalish of Wiederher-stellung.

[1] Parsee ffrench for the upholdsterer would be delightered.
[2] I'll pass out if the screw spliss his strut.
[3] Thargam then goeligum? If you sink I can, swimford. Suksumkale!
[4] Hasitatense?
[5] The impudence of that in girl's things!

geomater. And if you flung her headdress on her from under her highlows you'd wheeze whyse Salmonson set his seel on a hexengown.[1] Hissss!, Arrah, go on! Fin for fun! You've spat your shower like a son of Sibernia but let's have at it! Subtend to me now! Pisk! Outer serpumstances beiug ekewilled, we carefully, if she pleats, lift by her seam hem and jabote at the spidsiest of her trickkikant (like thousands done before since fillies calpered. Ocone! Ocone!) the maidsapron of our A.L.P., fearfully! till its nether nadir is vortically where (allow me aright to two cute winkles) its naval's napex will have to beandbe. You must proach near mear for at is dark. Lob. And light your mech. Jeldy! And this is what you'll say.[2] Waaaaaa. Tch! Sluice! Pla! And their, redneck, (for addn't we to gayatsee with Puhl the Punkah's bell?) mygh and thy, the living spit of dead waters,[3] fastness firm of Hurdlebury Fenn, discinct and isoplural in its (your sow to the duble) sixuous parts, flument, fluvey and fluteous, midden wedge of the stream's your muddy old triagonal delta, fiho miho, plain for you now, appia lippia pluvaville, (hop the hula, girls!) the no niggard spot of her safety vulve, first of all usquiluteral threeingles, (and why wouldn't she sit cressloggedlike the lass that lured a tailor?) the constant of fluxion, Mahamewetma, pride of the province[4] and when that tidled boare rutches up from the Afrantic, allaph quaran's his bett und bier![5]

[1] The chape of Doña Speranza of the Nacion.
[2] Ugol egal ogle. Mi vidim Mi.
[3] It is, it is Sangannon's dream.
[4] And all meinkind.
[5] Whangpoos the paddle and whiss whee whoo.

Paa lickam laa lickam, apl lpa! This it is an her. You see her it. Which it whom you see it is her. And if you could goaneggbetter we'd soon see some raffant scrumala riffa. Quicks herit fossyending. Quef! So post that to your pape and smarket! And you can haul up that languil pennant, mate. I've read your tunc's dimissage. For, let it be taken that her littlenist is of no magnetude or again let it be granted that Doll the laziest can be dissimulant with all respects from Doll the fiercst, thence must any what-youlike in the power of empthood be either

greater THaN or less THaN the unitate we have in one or hence shall the vectorious ready-eyes of evertwo circumflicksrent searclhers never film in the elipsities of their gyribouts those fickers which are returnally reprodictive of themselves.[1] Which is unpassible. Quarrel-lary. The logos of somewome to that base any-thing, when most characteristically mantissa minus, comes to nullum in the endth:[2] orso, here is nowet badder than the sin of Aha with his cosin Lil, verswaysed on coverswised, and all that's consecants and cotangincies till Per-perp stops repippinghim since her redtangles are all abscissan for limitsing this tendency of

our Frivulteeny Sexuagesima[3] to expense her-selfs as sphere as possible, paradismic peri-mutter, in all directions on the bend of the unbridalled, the infinisissimalls of her facets becoming manier and manier as the calicolum of her umdescribables (one has thoughts of that eternal Rome) shrinks from schurtiness

[1] I enjoy as good as anyone.
[2] Neither a soul to be saved nor a body to be kicked.
[3] The boast of the town.

*ine Venus
imated to
dic
rodite.*

to scherts.[1] Scholium, there are trist sigheds to everysing but ichs on the freed brings euchs to the feared. Qued? Mother of us all! O, dear me, look at that now! I don't know is it your spictre or my omination but I'm glad you dimentioned it! My Lourde! My Lourde! If that aint just the beatenest lay I ever see! And a superpbosition! Quoint a quincidence! O.K. *Omnius Kollidimus.* As Ollover Krumwall sayed when he slepped ueber his grannya-mother. Kangaroose feathers. Who in the name of thunder'd ever belevin you were that bolt? But you're holy mooxed and gaping up the wrong palce[2] as if you was seeheeing the gheist that stays forenenst, you blessed simpletop domefool! Where's your belested loiternan's lamp? You must lap wandret down the bluish-ing refluction below. Her trunk's not her brain-box. Hear where the bolgylines, Yseen here the puncture. So he done it. Luck! See her good. Well, well, well, well! O dee, O dee, that's

*usivism: the
Sors and
, which?*

very lovely! We like Simperspreach Hammel-tones to fellow Selvertunes O'Haggans.[3] When he rolls over his ars and shows the hise of his heels. Vely lovely entirely! Like a yangsheep-slang with the tsifengtse. So analytical plaus-ible! And be the powers of Moll Kelly, neigh-bour topsowyer, it will be a lozenge to me all my lauffe.[4] More better twofeller we been speak copperads. Ever thought about Guinness's? And the regrettable Parson Rome's advice?

[1] Hen's bens, are we soddy we missiled her?

[2] I call that a scumhead.

[3] Pure chingchong idiotism with any way words all in one soluble. Gee each owe tea eye smells fish. That's U.

[4] The Doodles family, Ⅲ, △, ⊣, ×, □, ∧, ⊏. Hoodle doodle, fam.?

299

Want to join the police.[1] You know, you were always one of the bright ones, since a foot made you an unmentionable, fakes! You know, you're the divver's own smart gossoon, aequal to yoursell and wanigel to anglyother, so you are, hoax! You know, you'll be dampned, so you will, one of these invernal days but you will be, carrotty![2]

Primanouriture and Ultimogeniture.

Wherapool, gayet that when he stop look time he stop long ground who here hurry he would have ever the lothst word, with a sweet me ah err eye ear marie to reat from the jacob's[3] and a shypull for toothsake of his armjaws at the slidepage of de Vere Foster, would and cculd candykissing P. Kevin to fress up the rinnerung and to ate by hart (*leo* I read, such a spanish, *escribibis*, all your mycoscoups) wont to nibbleh ravenostonnoriously ihs mum to me in bewonderment of his chipper chuthor for, while that Other by the halp of his creactive mind offered to deleberate the mass from the booty of fight our Same with the holp of the bounty of food sought to delubberate the mess from his corructive mund, with his muffetee cuffes ownconsciously grafficking with his sinister cyclopes after trigamies and spirals' wobbles pursuiting their rovinghamilton selves and godolphing in fairlove to see around the waste of noland's browne jesus[4] (thur him no quartos!) till that on him poorin sweat the juggaleer's veins (quench his quill!) in his napier scrag stud out burstright tam-

No Sturm. No Drang.

SICK US A SOCK WITH SOME SEDIMENT IN IT FOR THE SAKE OF OUR DARNING WIVES.

[1] Picking on Nickagain, Pikey Mikey?
[2] Early morning, sir Dav Stephens, said the First Gentleman in youreups.
[3] Bag bag blockcheap, have you any will?
[4] What a lubberly whide elephant for the men-in-the-straits!

quam taughtropes. (Spry him! call a blood-
lekar! Where's Dr Brassenaarse?) Es war itwas
in his priesterrite. O He Must Suffer! From this
misbelieving feacemaker to his noncredible
fancyflame.[1] Ask for bosthoon, late for Mass,
pray for blaablaablack sheep. (Sure you could
wright anny pippap passage, Eye bet, as foyne
as that moultylousy Erewhig, yerself, mick!
Nock the muddy nickers![2] Christ's Church
varses Bellial!) Dear and he went on to scripple

gentlemine born, milady bread, he would pen
for her, he would pine for her,[3] how he would
patpun fun for all[4] with his frolicky frowner
so and his glumsome grinner otherso. And how
are you, waggy?[5] My animal his sorrafool!
And trieste, ah trieste ate I my liver! *Se non è
vero son trovatore.* O jerry! He was soso, harriot
all! He was sadfellow, steifel! He was mister-
mysterion. Like a purate out of pensionee with
a gouvernament job. All moanday, tearsday,
wailsday, thumpsday, frightday, shatterday till
the fear of the Law. Look at this twitches!
He was quisquis, floored on his plankraft of
shittim wood. Look at him! Sink deep or

touch not the Cartesian spring! Want more
ashes, griper? How diesmal he was lying low
on his rawside laying siege to goblin castle.
And, bezouts that, how hyenesmeal he was
laying him long on his laughside lying sack
to croakpartridge. (Be thou wars Rolaf's intes-

---

[1] And she had to seek a pond's apeace to salve her suiterkins. Sued!

[2] Excuse theyre christianbrothers irish?

[3] When she tripped against the briery bush she profused her allover with
curtsey flowers.

[4] A nastilow disigraible game.

[5] Dear old Erosmas. Very glad you are going to Penmark. Write to the
corner. Grunny Grant.

tions, quoths the Bhagavat biskop Leech) Ann
opes tipoo soon ear! If you could me lendtill
my pascol's kondyl, sahib, and the price of a
plate of poultice. Punked. With best apolojigs
and merrymoney thanks to self for all the
clerricals and again begs guerdon for bistris-
pissing on your bunificence. Well wiggy-
wiggywagtail, and how are you, yaggy? With
a capital Tea for Thirst. From here Buvard to
dear Picuchet. Blott.

*Ensouling Fe-
male Sustains
Agonising Over-
man.*

Now, (peel your eyes, my gins, and brush
your saton hat, me elementator joyclid, son of
a Butt! She's mine, Jow low jure,[1] be Skibber-
ing's eagles, sweet tart of Whiteknees Archway) watch him, having caught at the bi-
furking calamum in his bolsillos, the onelike
underworp he had ever funnet without diffi-
cultads, the aboleshqvick, signing away in
happinext complete, (Exquisite Game of inspiration! I always adored your hand. So could
I too and without the scrope of a pen. Ohr for
oral, key for crib, olchedolche and a lunge ad
lib. Can you write us a last line? From Smith-
Jones-Orbison?) intrieatedly in years, jirry-
alimpaloop. And i Romain, hup u bn gd grl.[2]
Unds alws my thts. To fallthere at bare feet
hurryaswormarose. Two dies of one raffle-
ment. Eche bennyache. Outstamp and dis-
tribute him at the expanse of his society. To
be continued. Anon.

*Sesama to the
Rescues. The
Key Signature.*

And ook, ook, ook, fanky! All the charic-
tures[3] in the drame! This is how San holy-

[1] I loved to see the Macbeths Jerseys knacking spots of the Plumpduffs
Pants.
[2] Lifp year fends you all and moe, fouvenirs foft as fummer fnow, fweet
willings and forget-uf-knots.
[3] Gag his tubes yourself.

polypools. And this, pardonsky! is the way Romeopullupalleaps.[1] Pose the pen, man, way me does. Way ole missa vellatooth fust show me how. Fourth power to her illpogue! Bould strokes for your life! Tip! This is Steal, this is Barke, this is Starn, this is Swhipt, this is Wiles, this is Pshaw, this is Doubbllinnbbay-yates.[2] This is brave Danny weeping his spache for the popers. This is cool Connolly wiping his hearth with brave Danny. And this, regard! how Chawleses Skewered parparaparnelligoes between brave Danny boy and the Connolly. Upanishadem! Top. Spoken hath L'arty Magory. Eregobragh. Prouf![3]

e Centres of
Fire Serpen-
heart,
at, navel,
n, sacral,
anella, inter-
oral eye.

ception of the
promise and
ing of a
nula.

And Kev was wreathed with his pother.

TROTHBLOWERS.
FIG AND
THISTLE
PLOT A PIG
AND
WHISTLE.

But, (that Jacoby feeling again for fore-bitten fruit and, my Georgeous, Kevvy too he just loves his puppadums, I judge!) after all his autocratic writings of paraboles of famellicurbs and meddlied muddlingisms, thee faroots hof cullchaw end ate citrawn woodint wun able rep of the triperforator awlrite blast through his pergaman hit him where he lived and do for the blessted selfchuruls, what I think, smarter like it done for a manny another unpious of the hairydary quare quandary firstings till at length, you one bladdy bragger, by mercy-stroke he measured his earth anyway? could not but recken in his adder's badder cadder way our frankson who, to be plain, he fight him all time twofeller longa kill dead finish bloody face blong you, was misocain. Wince

---

[1] He, angel that I thought him, and he not aebel to speel eelyotripes., Mr Tellibly Divilcult!

[2] When the dander rattles how the peacocks prance!

[3] The Brownes de Browne - Browne of Castlehacknolan.

303

wan's won! Rip! And his countinghands rose.

Formalisa. Loves deathhow simple! Slutningsbane[2].

Service super-seding self.

Thanks eversore much, Pointcarried! I can't say if it's the weight you strike me to the quick or that red mass I was looking at but at the present momentum, potential as I am, I'm seeing rayingbogeys rings round me. Honours to you and may you be commended for our exhibitiveness! I'd love to take you for a bugaboo ride and play funfer all if you'd only sit and be the ballasted bottle in the porker barrel. You will deserve a rolypoly as long as from here to tomorrow. And to hell with them driftbombs and bottom trailers! If my maily was bag enough I'd send you a toxis. By Saxon Chromaticus, you done that lovely for me! Didn't he now, Nubilina? Tiny Mite, she studiert whas? With her listeningin coiffure, her dream of Endsland's daylast and the glorifires of being presainted maid to majesty.[3] And less is the pity for she isn't the lollypops she easily might be if she had for a sample Virginia's air of achievement. That might keep her from throwing delph.[4] As I was saying, while retorting thanks, you make me a reborn of the cards. We're offals boys ambows.[5] For I've flicked up all the crambs as they crumbed from your table um, singing glory allaloserem, cog it out, here goes a sum. So

Catastrophe and Anabasis.

The rotary processus and its reestablishment of reciprocities.

WITH EBON
IN PIX.
EUCHRE
RISK, MER
BUCKUP, AN
MIND WHO
YOU'RE
PUCKING,
FLEBBY.

---

¹ A byebye bingbang boys! See you Nutcracker Sunday!
² Chinchin Childaman! Chapchopchap!
³ Wipe your glosses with what you know.
⁴ If I'd more in the cups that peeves thee you could cracksmith your rows tureens.
⁵ Alls Sings and Alls Howls.

read we in must book. It tells. He prophets
most who bilks the best.

And that salubrated sickenagiaour of yaours
have teaspilled all my hazeydency. Forge away,
Sunny Sim! Sheepshopp. Bleating Goad, it is
the least of things, Eyeinstye! Imagine it, my
deep dartry dullard! It is hours giving, not
more. I'm only out for celebridging over the
guilt of the gap in your hiscitendency. You are
a hundred thousand times welcome, old wort-
sampler, hellbeit you're just about as culpable
as my woolfell merger would be. In effect I
could engage in an energument over you till
you were republicly royally toobally prussic
blue in the shirt after.[1] *Trionfante di bestia!* And
if you're not your bloater's kipper may I never
curse again on that pint I took of Jamesons.
Old Keane now, you're rod, hook and sinker,
old jubalee Keane! Biddy's hair. Biddy's hair,
mine lubber. Where is that Quin but he sknows
it knot but what you that are my popular end-
phthisis were born with a solver arm up your
sleep. Thou in shanty! Thou in scanty shanty!!
Thou in slanty scanty shanty!!! Bide in your
hush! Bide in your hush, do! The law does
not aloud you to shout. I plant my penstock
in your postern, chinarpot. Ave! And let it be
to all remembrance. Vale. Ovocation of maid-
ing waters.[2] For auld lang salvy steyne. I
defend you to champ my scullion's praises.
To book alone belongs the lobe. Foremaster's
meed[3] will mark tomorrow when we are
making pilscrummage to whaboggeryin with

Twofold
..h and the
..unctive Ap-
..es of Oppo-
..nal Orexes.

..hagion.

COME SI
COMPITA
CUNCTITI-
TITILATIO?
CONKERY
CUNK,
THIGH-
THIGHT-
TICKELLY-
THIGH, LIG-
GERILAG,
TITTERITOT,
LEG IN A TEE,
LUG IN A
LAW, TWO
AT A TIE,
THREE ON A
THRICKY
TILL OHIO
OHIO
IOIOMISS.

[1] From three shellings. A bluedye sacrifice.
[2] Not Kilty. But the manajar was. He! He! Ho! Ho! Ho!
[3] Giglamps, Soapy Geyser, The Smell and Gory M   Gusty.

staff, scarf and blessed wallet and our aureoles
round our neckkandcropfs where as and when
Heavysciusgardaddy, parent who offers sweet-
meats, will gift uns his Noblett's surprize.

*Abnegation is
Adaptation.*
With this laudable purpose in loud ability let
us be singulfied. Betwixt me and thee hung
cong. Item, mizpah ends.

But while the dial are they doodling dawdling over the mugs and the grubs? Oikey,
Impostolopulos?[1] Steady steady steady steady
steady studiavimus. Many many many many
many manducabimus.[2] We've had our day at triv
and quad and writ our bit as intermidgets. Art,
literature, politics, economy, chemistry, human-

*Cato.
Nero.
Saul. Aristotle.
Julius Caesar.
Pericles.
Ovid.
Adam, Eve.
Domitian. Edipus.
Socrates.
Ajax.*

ity, &c. Duty, the daughter of discipline, the
Great Fire at the South City Markets, Belief in
Giants and the Banshee, A Place for Every-
thing and Everything in its Place, Is the Pen
Mightier than the Sword? A Successful Career
in the Civil Service,[3] The Voice of Nature in
the Forest,[4] Your Favorite Hero or Heroine,
On the Benefits of Recreation,[5] If Standing
Stones Could Speak, Devotion to the Feast of
the Indulgence of Portiuncula, The Dublin
Metropolitan Police Sports at Ballsbridge, De-

*Homer.
MarcusAurelius.*

scribe in Homely Anglian Monosyllables the
Wreck of the Hesperus,[6] What Morals, if any,
can be drawn from Diarmuid and Grania?[7] Do

*Alcibiades.
Lucretius.*

you Approve of our Existing Parliamentary
System? The Uses and Abuses of Insects, A

ENTER THI
COP AND
HOW.
SECURES
GUBERNAN
URBIS
TERROREM

---

[1] The divvy wants that babbling brook. Dear Auntie Emma Emma Eates.
[2] Strike the day off, the nightcap's on nigh. Goney, goney gone!
[3] R. C., disengaged, good character, would help, no salary.
[4] Where Lily is a Lady found the nettle rash.
[5] Bubabipibambuli, I can do as I like with what's me own. Nyamnyam.
[6] Able seaman's caution.
[7] Rarely equal and distinct in all things.

Visit to Guinness' Brewery, Clubs, Advantages of the Penny Post, When is a Pun not a Pun? Is the Co-Education of Animus and Anima Wholly Desirable?[1] What Happened at Clontarf? Since our Brother Johnathan Signed the Pledge or the Meditations of Two Young Spinsters,[2] Why we all Love our Little Lord Mayor, Hengler's Circus Entertainment, On Thrift,[3] The Kettle-Griffith-Moynihan Scheme for a New Electricity Supply, Travelling in the Olden Times,[4] American Lake Poetry, the Strangest Dream that was ever Halfdreamt.[5] Circumspection, Our Allies the Hills, Are Parnellites Just towards Henry Tudor? Tell a Friend in a Chatty Letter the Fable of the Grasshopper and the Ant,[6] Santa Claus, The Shame of Slumdom, The Roman Pontiffs and the Orthodox Churches,[7] The Thirty Hour Week, Compare the Fistic Styles of Jimmy Wilde and Jack Sharkey, How to Understand the Deaf, Should Ladies learn Music or Mathematics? Glory be to Saint Patrick! What is to be found in a Dustheap, The Value of Circumstantial Evidence, Should Spelling? Outcasts in India, Collecting Pewter, Eu,[8] Proper and Regular Diet Necessity For,[9] If You Do It Do It Now.

[1] Jests and the Beastalk with a little rude hiding rod.

[2] Wherry like the whaled prophet in a spookeerie.

[3] What sins is pim money sans Paris?

[4] I've lost the place, where was I?

[5] Something happened that time I was asleep, torn letters or was there snow?

[6] Mich for his pain, Nick in his past.

[7] He has *toglieresti in brodo* all over his agrammatical parts of face and as for that hippofoxphiz, unlucky number, late for the christening!

[8] Eh, Monsieur? Où, Monsieur? Eu, Monsieur? Nenni No, Monsieur!

[9] Ere we hit the hay, brothers, let's have that response to prayer!

Xenophon.

Delays are Dangerous. Vitavite! Gobble Anne: tea's set, see's eneugh! Mox soonly will be in a split second per the chancellory of his exticker.

Pantocracy.
Bimutualism.
Interchangeabil-
ity. Naturality.
Superfetation.
Stabimobilism.
Periodicity.
Consummation.
Interpenetrative-
ness. Predicam-
ent. Balance of
the factual by the
theoric Boox and
Coox, Amallaga-
mated.

Aun
Do
Tri
Car
Cush[1]
Shay
Shockt
Ockt
Ni
Geg[2]
Their feed begins.

MAWMAW,
LUK, YOU
BEEEFTAY
FIZZIN OVI

KAKAO-
POETIC
LIPPUDEN
OF THE
UNGUMP-
TIOUS.

NIGHTLETTER

With our best youlldied greedings to Pep and Memmy and the old folkers below and beyant, wishing them all very merry Incarnations in this land of the livvey and plenty of preprosperousness through their coming new yonks

from
jake, jack and little sousoucie
(the babes that mean too)

[1] Kish is for anticheirst, and the free of my hand to him!

[2] And gags for skool and crossbuns and whopes he'll enjoyimsolff our drawings on the line!

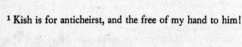

It may not or maybe a no concern of the Guinnesses but.

That the fright of his light in tribalbalbutience hides aback in the doom of the balk of the deaf but that the height of his life from a bride's eye stammpunct is when a man that means a mountain barring his distance wades a lymph that plays the lazy winning she likes yet that pride that bogs the party begs the glory of a wake while the scheme is like your rumba round me garden, allatheses, with perhelps the prop of a prompt to them, was now or never in Etheria Deserta, as in Grander Suburbia, with Finn-fannfawners, ruric or cospolite, for much or moment indispute.

Whyfor had they, it is Hiberio-Miletians and Argloe-Noremen, donated him, birth of an otion that was breeder to sweatoslaves, as mysterbolder, forced in their waste, and as for Ibdullin what of Himana, that their tolvtubular high fidelity daildialler, as modern as tomorrow afternoon and in appearance up to the minute, (hearing that anybody in that ruad duchy of Wollinstown schemed to halve the wrong type of date) equipped with supershielded umbrella antennas for distance getting and connected by the magnetic links of a Bellini-Tosti coupling system with a vitaltone speaker, capable of capturing skybuddies, harbour craft emittences, key clickings, vaticum cleaners, due to woman formed mobile or man made static and bawling the whowle harnshack and wobble down in an eliminium sounds pound so as to serve him up a mele-goturny marygoraumd, eclectrically filtered for allirish earths and ohmes. This harmonic condenser enginium (the Mole) they caused to be worked from a magazine battery (called the Mimmim Bimbim patent number 1132, Thorpetersen and Synds, Jomsborg, Selverbergen) which was tuned up by twintriodic singulvalvulous pipelines (lackslipping along as if their liffing deepunded on it) with a howdrocephalous enlargement, a gain control of circumcentric megacycles, ranging from the antidulibnium onto the serostaàtarean. They finally caused, or most leastways brung it about somehows, (that) the pip of the lin (to) pinnatrate inthro an auricular forfickle (known as the Vakingfar sleeper, monofractured by Piaras UaRhuamhaighaudhlug, tympan founder, Eustache Straight, Bauliaughacleeagh) a meatous conch culpable of cunduncing Naul and Santry and the forty routs of Corthy with the concertiums of the Brythyc Symmonds Guild, the Ropemakers Reunion, the Variagated Peddlars Barringoy Bnibrthirhd, the Askold Olegsonder Crowds of the O'Keef-Rosses and Rhosso-Keevers of Zastwoking, the Ligue of Yahooth o.s.v. so as to lall the bygone dozed they arborised around, up his corpular fruent and down his reuctionary buckling, hummer, enville and cstorrap (the man of Iren, thore's Curlymane for you!), lill the lubberendth of his otological life.

House of call is all their evenbreads though its cartomance hallucinate like an erection in the night the mummery of whose deed, a lur of Nur, immerges a mirage in a merror, for it is where by muzzinmessed for one watthour, bilaws below, till time jings pleas, that host of a bottlefilled, the bulkily hulkwight, hunter's pink of face, an orel orioled, is in on a bout to be unbulging an o'connell's, the true one, all seethic, a luckybock, pledge of the stoup, whilom his canterberry bellseyes wink wickeding indtil the teller, oyne of an oustman in skull of skand. Yet is it, this ale of man, for him, our hubuljoynted, just a tug and a fistful as for Culsen, the Patagoreyan, chieftain of chokanchuckers and his moyety joyant, under the foamer dispensation when he pullupped the turfeycork by the greats of gobble out of Lougk Neagk. When, pressures be to our hoary frother, the pop gave his sullen bulletaction and, bilge, sled a movement of catharic emulsipotion down the sloppery slide of a slaunty to tilted lift-ye-landsmen. Allamin. Which in the ambit of its orbit heaved a sink her sailer alongside of a drink her drainer from the basses brothers, those two theygottheres.

It was long after once there was a lealand in the luffing ore it was less after lives thor a toyler in the tawn at all ohr it was note before he drew out the moddle of Kersse by jerkin his dressing but and or it was not before athwartships he buttonhaled the Norweeger's capstan.

So he sought with the lobestir claw of his propencil the clue of the wickser in his ear. O, lord of the barrels, comer forth from Anow (I have not mislaid the key of Efas-Taem), O, Ana, bright lady, comer forth from Thenanow (I have not left temptation in the path of the sweeper of the threshold), O!

But first, strongbowth, they would deal death to a drinking. Link of a leadder, dubble in it, slake your thirdst thoughts awake with it. Our svalves are svalves aroon! We rescue thee, O Baass, from the damp earth and honour thee. O Connibell, with mouth burial! So was done, neat and trig. Up draught and whet them!

— Then sagd he to the ship's husband. And in his translatentic norjankeltian. Hwere can a ketch or hook alive a suit and sowterkins? Soot! sayd the ship's husband, knowing the language, here is tayleren. Ashe and Whitehead, closechop, successor to. Ahorror, he sayd, canting around to that beddest his friend, the tayler, for finixed coulpure, chunk pulley muchy chink topside numpa one sellafella, fake an capstan make and shoot! Manning to sayle of clothse for his lady her master whose to be precised of a peer of trouders under the pattern of a cassack. Let me prove, I pray thee, but this once, sazd Mengarments, saving the mouth-brand from his firepool. He spit in his faist (beggin): he tape the raw baste (paddin): he planked his pledge (as dib is a dab): and he tog his fringe sleeve (buthock lad, fur whale). Alloy for allay and this toolth for that soolth. Lick it and like it. A barter, a parter. And plenty good enough, neighbour Norreys, every bit and grain. And the ship's husband brokecurst after him to hail the

lugger. Stolp, tief, stolp, come bag to Moy Eireann! And the
Norweeger's capstan swaradeed, some blowfish out of schooling:
All lykkehud! Below taiyor he ikan heavin sets. But they broken
waters and they made whole waters at they surfered bark to the
lots of his vauce. And aweigh he yankered on the Norgean run so
that seven sailend sonnenrounders was he breastbare to the brina-
bath, where bottoms out has fatthoms full, fram Franz José
Land til Cabo Thormendoso, evenstarde and risingsoon. Up the
Rivor Tanneiry and down the Golfe Desombres. Farety days and
fearty nights. Enjoy yourself, O maremen! And the tides made,
veer and haul, and the times marred, rear and fall, and, holey
bucket, dinned he raign!

— Hump! Hump! bassed the broaders-in-laugh with a quick
piddysnip that wee halfbit a second.

—I will do that, sazd Kersse, mainingstaying the rigout for her
wife's lairdship. Nett sew? they hunched back at the earpicker.

But old sporty, as endth lord, in ryehouse reigner, he nought
feared crimp or cramp of shore sharks, plotsome to getsome. It
was whol niet godthaab of errol Loritz off his Cape of Good
Howthe and his trippertrice loretta lady, a maomette to his
monetone, with twy twy twinky her stone hairpins, only not,
if not, a queen of Prancess their telling tabled who was for his
seeming a casket through the heavenly, nay, heart of the sweet
(had he hows would he keep her as niece as a fiddle!) but in the
mealtub it was wohl yeas sputsbargain what, rarer of recent, an
occasional conformity, he, with Muggleton Muckers, alwagers
allalong most certainly allowed, as pilerinnager's grace to peti-
tionists of right, of the three blend cupstoomerries with their
customed spirits, the Gill gob, the Burklley bump, the Wallisey
wanderlook, having their ceilidhe gailydhe in his shaunty irish.
Group drinkards maaks grope thinkards or how reads rotary,
jewr of a chrestend, respecting the otherdogs churchees, so long
plubs will be plebs but plabs by low frequency amplification may
later agree to have another. For the people of the shed are the
sure ads of all quorum. Lorimers and leathersellers, skinners and
salters, pewterers and paperstainers, parishclerks, fletcherbowyers,

girdlers, mercers, cordwainers and first, and not last, the weavers.
Our library he is hoping to ye public.

Innholder, upholder.

— Sets on sayfohrt! Go to it, agitator! they bassabosuned over
the flowre of their hoose. Godeown moseys and skeep thy beeble
bee!

— I will do that, acordial, by mine hand, sazd Kersse, piece
Cod, and in the flap of a jacket, ructified after his nap of a blankit
their o'cousin, as sober as the ship's husband he was one my godfather when he told me saw whileupon I am now well and jurily
sagasfide after the boonamorse the widower, according to rider,
following pnomoneya, he is consistently blown to Adams. So
help me boyg who keeps the book!

Whereofter, behest his suzerain law the Thing and the pilsener
had the baar, Recknar Jarl, (they called him Roguenor, Irl call
him) still passing the change-a-pennies, pengeypigses, a several
sort of coyne in livery, pushed their whisper in his hairing,
(seemed, a some shipshep's sottovoxed stalement, a dearagadye,
to hasvey anyone doing duty for duff point of dorkland compors)
the same to the good ind ast velut discharge after which he had
exemptied more than orphan for the ballast of his nurtural life.
And threw a cast. A few pigses and hare you are and no chicking,
tribune's tribute, if you guess mimic miening. Meanly in his lewdbrogue take your tyon coppels token, with this good sixtric
from mine runbag of juwels. Nummers that is summus that is
toptip that is bottombay that is Twomeys that is Digges that is
Heres. In the frameshape of hard mettles. For we all would fain
make glories. It is minely well mint.

Thus as count the costs of liquid courage, a bullyon gauger,
stowed stivers pengapung in bulk in hold (fight great finnence!
brayvoh, little bratton!) keen his kenning, the queriest of the
crew, with that fellow fearing for his own misshapes, should he be
himpself namesakely a foully fallen dissentant from the peripu-
lator, sued towards Meade-Reid and Lynn-Duff, rubbing the
hodden son of a pookal, leaden be light, lather be dry and it be
drownd on all the ealsth beside, how the camel and where the

313

deiffel or when the finicking or why the funicking, who caused
the scaffolding to be first removed you give orders, babeling,
were their reidey meade answer when on the cutey (the cores-
pondent) in conflict of evidence drew a kick at witness but
(missed) and for whom in the dyfflun's kiddy removed the
planks they were wanted, boob.

Bump!

Bothallchoractorschumminaroundgansumuminarumdrum-
strumtruminahumptadumpwaultopoofoolooderamaunsturnup!

— Did do a dive, aped one.

— Propellopalombarouter, based two.

— Rutsch is for rutterman ramping his roe, seed three. Where
the muddies scrimm ball. Bimbim bimbim. And the maidies
scream all. Himhim himhim.

And forthemore let legend go lore of it that mortar scene so
cwympty dwympty what a dustydust it razed arboriginally but,
luck's leap to the lad at the top of the ladder, so sartor's risorted
why the sinner the badder! Ho ho ho hoch! La la la lach! Hillary
rillarry gibbous grist to our millery! A pushpull, qq: quiescence,
pp: with extravent intervulve coupling. The savest lauf in the
world. Paradoxmutose caring, but here in a present booth of Balla-
clay, Barthalamou, where their dutchuncler mynhosts and serves
them dram well right for a boors' interior (homereek van hohm-
ryk) that salve that selver is to screen its auntey and has ringround
as worldwise eve her sins (pip, pip, pip) willpip futurepip feature
apip footloose pastcast with spareshins and flash substittles of
noirse-made-earsy from a nephew mind the narrator but give the
devil his so long as those sohns of a blitzh call the tuone tuone and
thonder alout makes the thurd. Let there be. Due.

— That's all murtagh purtagh but whad ababs his dopter?
sissed they who were onetime ungkerls themselves, (when the
youthel of his yorn shook the bouchal in his bed) twilled alongside in wiping the rice assatiated with their wetting. The lappel
of his size? His *ros in sola velnere* and he sicckumed of homnis
terrars. She wends to scoulas in her slalpers. There were no pea-
nats in her famalgia so no wumble she tumbled for his famas

roalls davors. Don't him forget! A butcheler artsed out of Cullege Trainity. Diddled he daddle a drop of the cradler on delight mebold laddy was stetched? Knit wear? And they addled, (or ere the cry of their tongues would be uptied dead) Shufflebotham asidled, plus his ducks fore his drills, an inlay of a liddle more lining maught be licensed all at ones, be these same tokens, forgiving a brass rap, sneither a whole length nor a short shift so full as all were concerned.

Burniface, shiply efter, shoply after, at an angle of lag, let flow, brabble brabble and brabble, and so hostily, heavyside breathing, came up with them and, check me joule, shot the three tailors, butting back to Moyle herring, bump as beam and buttend, roller and reiter, after the diluv's own deluge, the seasant samped as skibber breezed in, tripping, dripping, threw the sheets in the wind, the tights of his trunks at tickle to tackle and his rubmelucky truss rehorsing the pouffed skirts of his overhawl. He'd left his stickup in his hand to show them none ill feeling. Whatthough for all appentices it had a mushroom on it. While he faced them front to back, Then paraseuls round, quite taken atack, sclaiming, Howe cools Eavybrolly!

— Good marrams, sagd he, freshwatties and boasterdes all, as he put into bierhiven, nogeysokey first, cabootle segund, jilling to windwards, as he made straks for that oerasound the snarsty weg for Publin, so was his horenpipe lug in the lee off their mouths organs, with his tilt too taut for his tammy all a slaunter and his wigger on a wagger with its tag tucked. Up. With a good eastering and a good westering. And he asked from him how the hitch did do this my fand sulkers that mone met the Kidballacks which he suttonly remembered also where the hatch was he endnew strandweys he's that fond sutchenson, a penincular fraimd of mind, fordeed he was langseling to talka holt of hems, clown toff, tye hug fliorten. Cablen: Clifftop. Shelvling tobay oppelong tomeadow. Ware cobbles. Posh.

— Skibbereen has common inn, by pounautique, with pokeway paw, and sadder raven evermore, telled shinshanks lauwering frankish for his kicker who, through the medium of gallic

— Pukkelsen, tilltold.

That with some our prowed invisors how their ulstravoliance led them infroraids, striking down and landing alow, against our aerian insulation resistance, two boards that beached ast one, widness thane and tysk and hanry. Prepatrickularly all, they summed. Kish met. Bound to. And for landlord, noting, nodding, a coast to moor was cause to mear. Besides proof plenty, over proof. While they either took a heft. Or the other swore his eric. Heaved two, spluiced the menbrace. Heirs at you, Brewinbaroon! Weth a whistle for methanks.

— Good marrams and good merrymills, sayd good mothers gossip, bobbing his bowing both ways with the bents and skerries, when they were all in the old walled of Kinkincaraborg (and that they did overlive the hot air of Montybunkum upon the coal blasts of Mitropolitos let there meeds be the hourihorn), hiberniating after seven oak ages, fearsome where they were he had gone dump in the doomering this tide where the peixies would pickle him down to the button of his seat and his sess old soss Erinly into the boelgein with the help of Divy and Jorum's locquor and shut the door after him to make a rarely fine Ran's cattle of fish. Morya Mortimor! Allapalla overus! Howoft had the ballshee tried! And they laying low for his home gang in that eeriebleak mead, with fireball feast and turkeys tumult and paupers patch to provide his bum end. The foe things your niggerhead needs to be fitten for the Big Water. He made the sign of the hammer. God's drought, he sayd, after a few daze, thinking of all those bliakings, how leif pauses! Here you are back on your hawkins, from Blasil the Brast to our povotogesus portocall, the furt on the turn of the hurdies, slave to trade, vassal of spices and a dragon-the-market, and be turbot, lurch a stripe, as were you soused methought out of the mackerel. Eldsfells! sayd he. A kumpavin on iceslant! Here's open handlegs for one old faulker from the hame folk here in you's booth! So sell me gundy, sagd the now waging cappon, with a warry posthumour's expletion, shoots ogos shootsle him or where's that slob? A bit bite of keesens, he sagd, til Dennis, for this jantar (and let the dobblins

roast perus,) or a stinger, he sagd, t. d., on a doroughbread kennedy's for Patriki San Saki on svo fro or my old relogion's out
of tiempor and when I'm soured to the tipple you can sink me
lead, he sagd, and, if I get can, sagd he, a pusspull of tomtar-
tarum. Thirst because homing hand give. Allkey dallkey, sayd
the shop's housebound, for he was as deep as the north star (and
could tolk sealer's solder into tankar's tolder) as might have sayd
every man to his beast, and a treat for the trading scow, my cater
million falls to you and crop feed a stall! Afram. And he got and
gave the ekspedient for Hombreyhambrey wilcomer what's the
good word. He made the sign on the feaster. Cloth be laid! And
a disk of osturs for the swanker! Allahballah! He was the care-
lessest man I ever see but he sure had the most sand. One fish-
ball with fixings! For a dan of a ven of a fin of a son of a gun of
a gombolier. Ekspedient, sayd he, sonnur mine, Shackleton Sul-
ten! Opvarts and at ham, or this ogry Osler will oxmaul us all,
sayd he, like one familiar to the house, while Waldemar was
heeling it and Maldemaer was toeing it, soe syg he was walking
from the bowl at his food and the meer crank he was waiting for
the tow of his turn. Till they plied him behaste on the fare. Say
wehrn!

— Nohow did he kersse or hoot alike the suit and solder skins,
minded first breachesmaker with considerable way on and

— Humpsea dumpsea, the munchantman, secondsnipped cutter
the curter.

— A ninth for a ninth. Take my worth from it. And no mistaenk,
they thricetold the taler and they knew the whyed for too. The
because of his sosuch. Uglymand fit himshemp but throats fill us
all! And three's here's for repeat of the unium! Place the scaurs
wore on your groot big bailey bill, he apullajibed, the O'Colonel
Power, latterly distented from the O'Conner Dan, so promonitory
himself that he was obliffious of the headth of hosth that rosed
before him, from Sheeroskouro, under its zembliance of mardal
mansk, like a dun darting dullemitter, with his moultain haares
stuck in plostures upon it, (do you kend yon peak with its coast so
green?) still trystfully acape for her his gragh knew well in pre-

317

cious memory and that proud grace to her, in gait a movely water, of smile a coolsome cup, with that rarefied air of a Montmalency and her quick little breaths and her climbing colour. Take thee live will save thee wive? I'll think uplon, lilady. Should anerous enthroproise call homovirtue, duinnafear! The ghem's to the ghoom be she nere zo zma. Obsit nemon! Floodlift, her ancient of rights regaining, so yester yidd, even remembrance. And greater grown then in the trifle of her days, a mouse, a mere tittle, trots off with the whole panoromacron picture. Her young-free yoke stilling his wandercursus, jilt the spin of a curl and jolt the broadth of a buoy. The Annexandreian captive conquest. Ethna Prettyplume, Hooghly Spaight. Him her first lap, her his fast pal, for ditcher for plower, till deltas twoport. While this glowworld's lump is gloaming off and han in hende will grow. Through simpling years where the lowcasts have aten of amilikan honey and datish fruits and a bannock of barley on Tham the Thatcher's palm. O wanderness be wondernest and now! Listen-eath to me, veils of Mina! He would withsay, nepertheloss, that is too me mean. I oldways did me walsh and preechup ere we set to sope and fash. Now eats the vintner over these contents oft with his sad slow munch for backonham. Yet never shet it the brood of aurowoch, not for legions of donours of Gamuels. I have performed the law in truth for the lord of the law, Taif Alif. I have held out my hand for the holder of my heart in Anna-polis, my youthrib city. Be ye then my protectors unto Mussa-botomia before the guards of the city. Theirs theres is a gentle-meants agreement. Womensch plodge. To slope through heather till the foot. Join Andersoon and Co. If the flowers of speech valed the springs of me rising the hiker I hilltapped the murk I mist my blezzard way. Not a knocker on his head nor a nick-number on the manyoumeant. With that coldtbrundt natteldster wefting stinks from Alpyssinia, wooving nihilnulls from Memo-land and wolving the ulvertones of the voice. But his spectrem onlymergeant crested from the irised sea in plight, calvitousness, loss, nngnr, gliddinyss, unwill and snorth. It might have been what you call your change of my life but there's the chance of a

318

night for my lifting. Hillyhollow, valleylow! With the sounds and the scents in the morning.

— I shot be shoddied, throttle me, fine me cowheel for ever, usquebauched the ersewild aleconner, for bringing briars to Bembracken and ringing rinbus round Demetrius for, as you wrinkle wryghtly, bully bluedomer, it's a suirsite's stircus haunting hesteries round old volcanoes. We gin too gnir and thus plinary indulgence makes collemullas of us all. But Time is for talerman tasting his tap. Tiptoptap, Mister Maut.

He made one summery (Cholk and murble in lonestime) of his the three swallows like he was muzzling Moselems and torched up as the faery pangeant fluwed down the hisophenguts, a slake for the quicklining, to the tickle of his tube and the twobble of his fable, O, fibbing once upon a spray what a queer and queasy spree it was. Plumped.

Which both did. Prompt. Eh, chrystal holder? Save Ampsterdampster that had rheumaniscences in his netherlumbs.

— By the drope in his groin, Ali Slupa, thinks the cappon, plumbing his liners, we were heretofore.

— And be the coop of his gobbos, Reacher the Thaurd, thinks your girth fatter, apopo of his buckseaseilers, but where's Horace's courtin troopsers?

— I put hem behind the oasthouse, sagd Pukkelsen, tuning wound on the teller, appeased to the cue, that double dyode dealered, and he's wallowing awash swill of the Tarra water. And it marinned down his gargantast trombsathletic like the marousers of the gulpstroom. The kersse of Wolafs on him, shitateyar, he sagd in the fornicular, and, at weare or not at weare, I'm sigen no stretcher, for I carsed his murhersson goat in trotthers with them newbucklenoosers behigh in the fire behame in the oasthouse. Hops! sagd he.

— Smoke and coke choke! lauffed till the tear trickled drown a thigh the loafers all but a sheep's whosepants that swished to the lord he hadn't and the starer his story was talled to who felt that, the fierifornax being thurst on him motophosically, as Omar sometime notes, such a satuation, debauchly to be watched for, would empty dempty him down to the ground.

— And hopy dope! sagd he, anded the enderer, now dyply hypnotised or hopeseys doper himself. And kersse him, sagd he, after inunder tarrapoulling, and the shines he cuts, shinar, the screeder, the stitchimesnider, adepted to nosestorsioms in his budinholder, cummanisht, sagd he, (fouyoufoukou!) which goes in the ways smooking publics, sagd he, bomboosting to be in thelitest civille row faction for a dubblebrasterd navvygaiterd, (flick off that hvide aske, big head!) sagd he, the big bag of my hamd till hem, tollerloon, sagd he, with his pudny bun brofkost when he walts meet the bangd. I will put his fleas of wood in the flour, and he sagd, behunt on the oatshus, the not wellmade one, sagd he, the kersse of my armsore appal this most unmentionablest of men (mundering eeriesk, if he didn't scalded him all the shimps names in his gitter!) a coathemmed gusset sewer, sagd he, his first cudgin is an innvalet in the unitred stables which is not feed tonights a kirtle offal fisk and he is that woe worstered wastended shootmaker whatever poked a noodle in a clouth!

So for the second tryon all the meeting of the acarras had it. How he hised his bungle oar his shourter and cut the pinter off his pourer and lay off for Fellagulphia in the farning. From his dhruimadhreamdhrue back to Brighten-pon-the-Baltic, from our lund's rund turs bag til threathy hoeres a wuke. Ugh!

— Stuff, Taaffe, stuff! interjoked it his wife's hopesend to the boath of them consistently. Come back to May Aileen.

— Ild luck to it! blastfumed the nowraging scamptail, in flating furies outs trews his cammelskins, the flashlight of his ire wackering from the eyewinker on his masttop. And aye far he fared from Afferik Arena and yea near he night till Blawland Bearring, baken be the brazen sun, buttered be the snows. And the sea shoaled and the saw squalled. And, soaking scupper, didn't he drain

A pause.

Infernal machinery (serial number: Bullysacre, dig care a dig) having thus passed the buck to billy back from jack (finder the keeper) as the baffling yarn sailed in circles it was now high tide for the reminding pair of snipers to be suitably punished till they had, like the pervious oelkenner done, liquorally no more powers to their elbow. Ignorinsers' bliss, therefore, their not to say rifle butt target, none too wisefolly, poor fish, (he is eating, he is spun, is milked, he dives) upholding a lampthorne of lawstift as wand of welcome to all men in bonafay, (and the corollas he so has saved gainsts the virus he has thus injected!) discoastedself to that kipsie point of its Dublin bar there, breaking and entering, from the outback's dead heart, Glasthule Bourne or Boehernapark Nolagh, by wattsismade or bianconi, astraylians in island, a wellknown tall hat blown in between houses by a nightcap of that silk or it might be a black velvet and a kiber galler dragging his hunker, were signalling gael warnings towards Wazwollenzee Haven to give them their beerings, east circular route or elegant central highway. Open, 'tis luck will have it! Lifeboat Alloe, Noeman's Woe, Hircups Emptybolly! With winkles whelks and cocklesent jelks. Let be buttercup eve lit by night in the Phoenix! Music. And old lotts have funn at Flammagen's ball. Till Irinwakes from Slumber Deep. How they succeeded by courting daylight in saving darkness he who loves will see.

Business. His bestness. Copeman helpen.

Contrescene.

He cupped his years to catch me's to you in what's yours as minest to hissent, giel as gail, geil as gaul, Odorozone, now our-menial servent, blanding rum, milk and toddy with I hand it to you. Saying whiches, see his bow on the hapence, with a pat-tedyr but digit here, he scooped the hens, hounds and horses biddy by bunny, with an arc of his covethand, saved from the drohnings they might oncounter, untill his cubid long, to hide in dry. Aside. Your sows tin the topple, dodgers, trink me dregs! Zoot!

And with the gust of a spring alice the fossickers and swaggelers with him on the hoof from down under piked forth desert roses in that mulligar scrub.

Reenter Ashe Junior. Peiwei toptip, nankeen pontdelounges. Gives fair day. Cheroot. Cheevio!

Off.

—Take off thatch whitehat (lo, Kersse come in back bespoking of loungeon off the Boildawl stuumplecheats for rushirishis Irush-Irish, dangieling his old Conan over his top gallant shouldier so was, lao yiu shao, he's like more look a novicer on the nevay).

— Tick off that whilehot, you scum of a botch, (of Kersse who, as he turned out, alas, hwen ching hwan chang, had been mocking his hollaballoon a sample of the costume of the country).

— Tape oaf that saw foull and sew wrong, welsher, you suck of a thick, stock and the udder, and confiteor yourself (for bekersse he had cuttered up and misfutthered in the most multiplest manner for that poor old bridge's masthard slouch a shook of cloakses the wise, hou he pouly hung hoang tseu, his own fitther couldn't nose him).

Chorus: With his coate so graye. And his pounds that he pawned from the burning.

— And, haikon or hurlin, who did you do at doyle today, my horsey dorksey gentryman. Serge Mee, suit! sazd he, tersey ker-sey. And when Tersse had sazd this Kersse stood them the whole koursse of training how the whole blazy raze acurraghed, from lambkinsback to sliving board and from spark to phoenish. And he tassed him tartly and he sassed him smartly, tig for tager, strop for stripe, as long as there's a lyasher on a kyat. And they peered him beheld on the pyre.

And it was so. Behold.

— Same capman no nothing horces two feller he feller go where. Isn't that effect? gig for gag, asked there three newcommers till knockingshop at the ones upon a topers who, while in admittance to that impedance, as three as they were there, they had been malttreating themselves to their health's contempt.

— That's fag for fig, metinkus, confessed, mhos for mhos, those who, would it not be for that dielectrick, were upon the point of obsoletion, and at the brink of from the pillary of the Nilsens and from the statutes of the Kongbullies and from the millestones of Ovlergroamlius libitate nos, Domnial!

— And so culp me goose, he sazd, szed the ham muncipated of the first course, recoursing, all cholers and coughs with his beauw

322

on the bummell, the bugganeering wanderducken, he sazd, (that his pumps may ship awhoyle shandymound of the dussard), the coarsehair highsaydighsayman, there's nice tugs he looks, (how you was, Ship Alouset?) he sazd, the bloedaxe bloodooth baltxebec, that is crupping into our raw lenguage navel through the lumbsmall of his hawsehole, he sazd, donconfounder him, voyaging after maidens, belly jonah hunting the polly joans, and the hurss of all portnoysers befaddle him, he sazd, till I split in his flags, he sazd, one to one, the landslewder, after Donnerbruch fire. Reefer was a wenchman. One can smell off his wetsments how he is coming from a beach of promisck. Where is that old muttiny, shall I ask? Free kicks he will have from me, turncoats, in Bar Bartley if I wars a fewd years ago. Meistr Capteen Gaascooker, a salestrimmer! As he was soampling me ledder, like pulp, and as I was trailing his fumbelums, like hulp, he'll fell the fall of me faus, he sazd, like yulp! The goragorridgorballyed pushkalsson, he sazd, with his bellows pockets fulled of potchtatos and his fox in a stomach, a disagrees to his ramskew coddlelecherskithers' zirkuvs, drop down dead and deaf, and there is never a teilwrmans in the feof fife of Iseland or in the wholeabelongd of Skunkinabory from Drumadunderry till the rumnants of Mecckrass, could milk a colt in thrushes foran furrow follower width that a hole in his tale and that hell of a hull of a hill of a camelump bakk. Fadgestfudgist!

Upon this dry call of selenium cell (that horn of lunghalloon, Riland's in peril!) with its doomed crack of the old damn ukonnen power insound in it the lord of the saloom, as if for a flash salamagunnded himself, listed his tummelumpsk pack and hearinat presently returned him, ambilaterally alleyeoneyesed, from their uppletoned layir to his beforetime guests, that bunch of palers on their round, timemarching and petrolling how, who if they were abound to loose a laugh (Toni Lampi, you booraascal!) they were abooned to let it as the leashed they might do when they felt (O, the wolf he's on the walk, sees his sham cram bokk!) their joke was coming home to them, the steerage way for stabling, ghustorily spoeking, gen and gang, dane and dare, like the dud spuk

of his first foetotype (Trolldedroll, how vary and likely!), the filli-
bustered, the fully bellied. With the old sit in his shoulders, and
the new satin atlas onder his uxter, erning his breadth to the swelt
of his proud and, picking up the emberose of the lizod lights, his
tail toiled of spume and spawn, and the bulk of him, and hulk of
him as whenever it was he reddled a ruad to riddle a rede from the
sphinxish pairc while Ede was a guardin, ere love a side issue.
They hailed him cheeringly, their encient, the murrainer, and
wallruse, the merman, ye seal that lubs you lassers, Thallasee or
Tullafilmagh, when come of uniform age.

— Heave, coves, emptybloddy!

And ere he could catch or hook or line to suit their saussyskins,
the lumpenpack. Underbund was overraskelled. As

— Sot! sod the tailors opsits from their gabbalots, change all
that whole set. Shut down and shet up. Our set, our set's
allohn.

And they poured em behoiled on the fire. Scaald!

Rowdiose wodhalooing. Theirs is one lessonless message for
good and truesirs. Will any persen bereaved to be passent bring-
back or rumpart to the Hoved politymester. Clontarf, one love,
one fear. Ellers for the greeter glossary of code, callen hom:
Finucane-Lee, Finucane-Law.

Am. Dg.

Welter focussed.

Wind from the nordth. Warmer towards muffinbell, Lull.

As our revelant Colunnfiller predicted in last mount's chattiry
sermon, the allexpected depression over Schiumdinebbia, a bygger
muster of veirying precipitation and haralded by faugh sicknells,
(hear kokkenhovens ekstras!) and umwalloped in an unusuable
suite of clouds, having filthered through the middelhav of the
same gorgers' kennel on its wage wealthwards and incursioned a
sotten retch of low pleasure, missed in some parts but with lucal
drizzles, the outlook for tomarry (Streamstress Mandig) beamed
brider, his ability good.

What hopends to they?

Giant crash in Aden. Birdflights confirm abbroaching nubtials. Burial of Lifetenant-Groevener Hatchett, R.I.D. Devine's Previdence.

Ls. De.

Art thou gainous sense uncompetite! Limited. Anna Lynchya Pourable! One and eleven. United We Stand, even many offered. Don't forget. I wish auspicable thievesdayte for the stork dyrby. It will be a thousand's a won paddies. And soon to bet. On drums of bliss. With hapsalap troth, hipsalewd prudity, hopesalot honnessy, hoopsaloop luck. After when from midnights unwards the fourposter harp quartetto. (Kiskiviikko, Kalastus. Torstaj, tanssia. Perjantaj, peleja. Lavantaj ja Sunnuntaj, christianismus kirjallisuus, kirjallisuus christianismus.) Whilesd this pellover his finnisch.

— Comither, ahorace, thou mighty man of valour, elderman adaptive of Capel Ysnod, and tsay-fong tsei-foun a laun bricksnumber till I've fined you a faulter-in-law, to become your son-to-be, gentlemens tealer, generalman seelord, gosse and bosse, hunguest and horasa, jonjemsums both, in sailsmanship, szed the head marines talebearer, then sayd the ships gospfather in the scat story to the husband's capture and either you does or he musts and this moment same, sayd he, so let laid pacts be being betving ye, he sayd, by my main makeshift, he sayd, one fisk and one flesk, as flat as, Aestmand Addmundson you, you're iron slides and so hompety domp as Paddley Mac Namara here he's a hardy canooter, for the two breasts of Banba are her soilers and her toilers, if thou wilt serve Idyall as thou hast sayld. Brothers Boathes, brothers Coathes, ye have swallen blooders' oathes. And Gophar sayd unto Glideon and sayd he to the nowedding captain, the rude hunnerable Humphrey, who was praying god of clothildies by the seven bosses of his trunktarge he would save bucklesome when she wooed belove on him, comeether, sayd he, my merrytime marelupe, you wutan whaal, sayd he, into the shipfolds of our quadrupede island, bless madhugh, mardyk, luusk and cong! Blass Neddos bray! And no more of your maimed acts after this with your kowtoros and criados to every tome, thick and heavy, and our onliness of his revelance to your ultitude. The illfollowable staying in wait for you with the winning word put into his mouth or be the hooley tabell, as Horrocks Toler hath most cares to call it, I'll rehearse your comeundermends and first mardhyr you entirely. As puck as that Paddeus picked the pun and left the lollies off the foiled. A Trinity judge will crux your boom. Pat is the man for thy. Ay ay! And he pured him beheild of the ouishguss, mingling a sign of the cruisk. I popetithes thee, Ocean, sayd he, Oscarvaughther, sayd he, Erievikkingr, sayd he, *intra trifum triforium trifoliorum*, sayd he, onconditionally, forfor furst of gielgaulgalls and hero chief explunderer of the clansakiltic, sayd he, the streameress mastress to the sea aase cuddycoalman's and let this douche for you as a wholly apuzzler's and for all the pukkaleens to the wakes of you, sayd he, out of the hellsinky of the howtheners and be danned to ye, sayd he, into our roomyo connellic relation, sayd he, from which our this pledge is given, Tera truly ternatrine if not son towards thousand like expect chrisan athems to which I osker your godhsbattaring, saelir, for as you gott kvold whereafter a gooden diggin and with gooder enscure from osion buck fared agen fairioes feuded hailsohame til Edar in that the loyd mave hercy on your sael! Anomyn and awer. Spickinusand.

— Nansense, you snorsted? he was haltid considerable agenst all religions overtrow so hworefore the thokkurs pokker the bigbug miklamanded storstore exploder would he be whulesalesolde daadooped by Priest Gudfodren of the sacredhaunt suit in Diaeblen-Balkley at Domnkirk Saint Petricksburg? But ear this:

—And here, aaherra, my rere admirable peadar poulsen, sayd he, consistently, to the secondnamed sutor, my lately lamented sponsorship, comesend round that wine and lift your horn, sayd he, to show you're a skolar for, winter you likes or not, we brought your summer with us and, tomkin about your lief eurekason and his undishcovery of americle, be the rolling forties, he sayd, and on my sopper crappidamn, as Harris himself says, to let you in on some crismion dottrin, here is the ninethest pork of a man whisk swimmies in Dybblin water from Ballscodden easthmost till Thyrston's Lickslip and, sayd he, (whiles the heart of Lukky Swayn slaughed in his icebox for to think of all the soorts of smukklers he would behave in juteyfrieze being forelooper to her) praties peel to our goodsend Brandonius, *filius* of a Cara, spouse to Fynlogue, he has the nicesth pert of a nittlewoman in the house, la chito, la chato, la Charmadouiro, Tina-bat-Talur, cif for your fob and a tesura astore for you, eslucylamp aswhen the surge seas sombren, that he daughts upon of anny livving plusquebelle, to child and foster, that's the lippeyear's wonder of Totty go, Newschool, two titty too at win winnie won, tramity trimming and funnity fare, with a grit as hard as the trent of the thimes but a touch as saft as the dee in flooing and never a Hyderow Jenny the like of her lightness at look and you leap, rheadoromanscing long evmans invairn, about little Anny Roners and all the Lavinias of ester yours and pleding for them to herself in the periglus glatsch hangs over her trickle bed, it's a piz of fortune if it never falls from the stuffel, and, when that mallaura's over till next time and all the prim rossies are out dressparading and the tubas tout tout for the glowru of their god, making every Dinny dingle after her down the Dargul dale and (wait awhile, blusterbuss, you're marchadant too forte and don't start furlan your ladins till you' ve learned the lie of her landuage!), when it's summwer calding and she can hear the pianutunar beyant the bayondes in Combria sleepytalking to the Wiltsh muntons, titting out through her droemer window for the flyend of a touchman over the wishtas of English Strand, when Kilbarrack bell pings saksalaisance that Concessas with Sinbads may (pong!), where our dollimonde sees the phantom shape of Mr Fortunatus Wright since winksome Miss Bulkeley made loe to her wrecker and he took her to be a rover, O, and playing house of ivary dower of gould and gift you soil me peepat my prize, which its a blue loogoont for her in a bleakeyed seusan if she can't work her mireiclles and give Norgeyborgey good airish timers, while her fresh racy turf is kindly kindling up the lovver with the flu, with a roaryboaryellas would set an Eri-weddyng on fire, let aloon an old Humpopolamos with the boomar-poorter on his brain, aiden bay scye and dye, aasbukividdy, twentynine to her dozen and coocoo him didulceydovely to his old cawcaws huggin and munin for his strict privatear which

327

there's no pure rube like an ool pool roober when your pullar beer turns out Bruin O'Luinn and beat his barge into a battering pram with her wattling way for cubblin and, be me fairy fay, sayd he, the marriage mixter, to Kersse, Son of Joe Ashe, her coaxfonder, wiry eyes and winky hair, timkin abeat your Andraws Meltons and his lovsang of the short and shifty, I will turn my thinks to things alove and I will speak but threes ones, sayd he, my truest patrions good founter, poles a port and zones asunder, tie up in hates and repeat at luxure, you can better your tooblue prodestind arson, tyler bach, after roundsabouts and donochs and the volumed smoke, though the clonk in his stumble strikes warn, and were he laid out on that counter there like a Slavocrates amongst his skippies, when it comes to the ride onerable, sayd he, that's to make plain Nanny Ni Sheeres a full Dinamarqueza, and all needed for the lay, from the hursey on the montey with the room in herberge down to forkpiece and bucklecatch, (Elding, my elding! and Lif, my lif!) in the pravacy of the pirmanocturne, hap, sayd he, at that meet hour of night, and hop, sayd he, and the fyrsty annas everso thried (whiles the breath of Huppy Hullespond swumped in his seachest for to renumber all the mallymedears' long roll and call of sweetheart emmas that every had a port in from Coxenhagen till the brottels on the Nile), while taylight is yet slipping under their pillow, (ill omens on Kitty Cole if she's spilling laddy's measure!) and before Sing Mattins in the Fields, ringsengd ringsengd, bings Heri the Concorant Erho, and the Referinn Fuchs Gutmann gives us *I'll Bell the Welled* or *The Steeplepoy's Revanger* and all Thingavalley knows for its never dawn in the dark but the deed comes to life, and raptist bride is aptist breed (tha lassy! tha lassy!), and, to buoy the hoop within us springing, 'tis no timbertar she'll have then in her armsbrace to doll the dallydandle, our fiery quean, upon the night of the things of the night of the making to stand up the double tet of the oversear of the seize who cometh from the mighty deep and on the night of making Horuse to crihumph over his enemy, be the help of me cope as so pluse the riches of the roedshields, with Elizabeliza blessing the bedpain, at the willbedone of Yinko Jinko Randy, come Bastabasco and hippychip eggs, she will make a suomease pair and singlette, jodhpur smalls and tailorless, a copener's cribful, leaf, bud and berry, the divlin's own little mimmykin puss, (hip, hip, horatia!) for my old comrhade saltymar here, Briganteen—General Sir A. I. Magnus, the flappernooser, master of the good lifebark *Ulivengrene* of Onslought, and the homespund of her hearth, (Fuss his farther was the norse norse east and Muss his mother was a gluepot) and, gravydock or groovy anker, and a hulldread pursunk manowhood, who (with a chenchen for his delight time and a bonzeye nappin through his doze) he is the bettest bluffy blondblubber of an olewidgeon what overspat a skettle in a skib.

Cawcaught. Coocaged.

And Dub did glow that night. In Fingal of victories. Cannmatha and Cathlin sang together. And the three shouters of glory. Yelling halfviewed their harps. Surly Tuhal smiled upon drear Darthoola: and Roscranna's bolgaboyo begirlified the daughter of Cormac. The soul of everyelsesbody rolled into its olesoleself. A doublemonth's licence, lease on mirth, while hooneymoon and her flame went huneysuckling. Holyryssia, what boom of bells! What battle of bragues on Sandgate where met the bobby mobbed his bibby mabbing through the ryce. Even Tombs left doss and dunnage down in Demidoff's tomb and drew on the dournailed clogs that Morty Manning left him and legged in by Ghoststown Gate, like Pompei up to date, with a sprig of Whiteboys heather on his late Luke Elcock's heirloom. And some say they seen old dummydeaf with a leaf of bronze on his cloak so grey, trooping his colour a pace to the reire. And as owfally posh with his halfcrown jool as if he was the Granjook Meckl or Paster de Grace on the Route de l'Epée. It was joobileejeu that All Sorts' Jour. Freestouters and publicranks, hafts on glaives. You could hear them swearing threaties on the Cymylaya Mountains, man. And giving it out to the Ould Fathach and louthmouthing after the Healy Mealy with an enfysis to bring down the rain of Tarar. Nevertoletta! Evertomind! The grandest bethehailey seen or heard on earth's conspectrum since Scape the Goat, that gafr, ate the Suenders bible. Hadn't we heaven's lamps to hide us? Yet every lane had its lively spark and every spark had its several spurtles and each spitfire spurtle had some trick of her trade, a tease for Ned, nook's nestle for Fred and a peep at me mow for Peer Pol. So that Father Matt Hughes looked taytotally threbled. But Danno the Dane grimmed. Dune. 'Twere yeg will elsecare doatty lanv meet they dewscent hyemn to cannons' roar and rifles' peal vill shantey soloweys sang! For there were no more Tyrrhanees and for Laxembraghs was pass-thecupper to Our Lader's. And it was dim upon the floods only and there was day on all the ground.

Thus street spins legends while wharves woves tales but some family fewd felt a nick in their name. Old Vickers sate down on their airs and straightened the points of their lace. Red Rowleys popped out of their lairs and asked what was wrong with the race. Mick na Murrough used dripping in layers to shave all the furze off his face. The Burke-Lees and Coyle-Finns paid full feines for their sinns when the Cap and Miss Coolie were roped.

Rolloraped.

With her banbax hoist from holder, zig for zag through pool and polder, cheap, cheap, cheap and Laughing Jack, all augurs scorenning, see the Bolche your pictures motion and Kitzy Kleinsuessmein eloping for that holm in Finn's Hotel Fiord, Nova Norening. Where they pulled down the kuddle and they made fray and if thee don't look homey, well, that Dook can eye Mae.

He goat a berth. And she cot a manege. And wohl's gorse mundom ganna wedst.

Knock knock. War's where! Which war? The Twwinns. Knock knock. Woos without! Without what? An apple. Knock knock.

The kilder massed, one then and uhindred, (harefoot, birdy-hands, herringabone, beesknees), and they barneydansked a kathareen round to know the who and to show the howsome. Why was you hiding, moder of moders? And where was hunty, poppa the gun? Pointing up to skyless heaven like the spoon out of sergeantmajor's tay. Which was the worst of them phaymix cupplerts? He's herd of hoarding and her faiths is altared. Becoming ungoing, their seeming sames for though that liamstone deaf do his part there's a windtreetop whipples the damp off the mourning. But tellusit allasif wellasits end. And the lunger it takes the swooner they tumble two. He knows he's just thrilling and she's sure she'd squeam. The threelegged man and the tulippied dewydress. Lludd hillmythey, we're brimming to hear! The durst he did and the first she ever? Peganeen Bushe, this isn't the polkar, catch as you cancan when high land fling! And you Tim Tommy Melooney, I'll tittle your barents if you stick that pigpin upinto meh!

So in the names of the balder and of the sol and of the hollichrost, ogsowearit, trisexnone, and by way of letting the aandt out of her grosskropper and leading the mokes home by their gribes, whoopsabout a plabbaside of plobbicides, alamam alemon, poison kerls, on this mounden of Delude, and in the high places of Delude of Isreal, which is Haraharem and the diublin's owld mounden over against Vikens, from your tarns, thwaites and thorpes, withes, tofts and fosses, fells, haughs and shaws, lunds, garths and dales, mensuring the megnominous as so will is the littleyest, the myrioheartzed with toroidal coil, eira area round wantanajocky, fin above wave after duckydowndivvy, trader arm aslung beauty belt, the formor velican and nana karlikeevna, sommerlad and cinderenda, Valtivar and Viv, how Big Bil Brine Borumoter first took his gage at lil lolly lavvander waader since when capriole legs covets limbs of a crane and was it the twylyd or the mounth of the yare or the feint of her smell made the seomen assalt of her (in imageascene all: whimwhim whimwhim). To the laetification of disgeneration by neuhumorisation of our kristianiasation. As the last liar in the earth begeylywayled the first lady of the forest. Though Toot's pardoosled sauve l'hummour! For the joy of the dew on the flower of the fleets on the fields of the foam of the waves of the seas of the wild main from Borneholm has jest come to crown.

Snip snap snoody. Noo err historyend goody. Of a lil trip trap and a big treeskooner for he put off the ketyl and they made three (for fie!) and if hec dont love alpy then lad you annoy me. For hanigen with hunigen still haunt ahunt to finnd their hinnigen where Pappappapparrassannuaragheallachnatull-aghmonganmacmacmacwhackfalltherdebblenonthedubblandadd-ydoodled and anruly person creeked a jest. Gestapose to parry off cheekars or frankfurters on the odor. Fine again, Cuoholson! Peace, O wiley!

Such was the act of goth stepping the tolk of Doolin, drain and plantage, wattle and daub, with you'll peel as I'll pale and we'll pull the boath toground togutter, testies touchwood and shenstone unto pop and puma, calf and condor, under all the gaauspices (incorporated), the chal and his chi, their roammerin over, gribgrobgrab reining trippetytrappety (so fore shalt thou flow, else thy cavern hair!) to whom she (anit likenand please-thee!). Till sealump becamedump to bumpslump a lifflebed, (altolà, allamarsch! O gué, O gué!). Kaemper Daemper to Jetty de Waarft, all the weight of that mons on his little ribbeunuch! Him that gronde old mand to be that haard of heaering (afore said) and her the petty tondur with the fix in her changeable eye (which see), Lord, me lad, he goes with blowbierd, leedy, plasheous stream. But before that his loudship was converted to a landshop there was a little theogamyjig incidence that hoppy-go-jumpy Junuary morn when he colluded with the cad out on the beg amudst the fiounaregal gaames of those oathmassed fenians for whome he's forcecaused a bridge of the piers, at Inverleffy, mating pontine of their engagement, synnbildising graters and things, eke ysendt? O nilly, not all, here's the first cataraction! As if ever she cared an assuan damm about her harpoons sticking all out of him whet between phoenix his calipers and that psourdonome sheath. Sdrats ye, Gus Paudheen! Kenny's thought ye, Dinny Oozle! While the cit was leaking asphalt like a suburbiaurealis in his rure was tucking to him like old booths, booths, booths, booths.

Enterruption. Check or slowback. Dvershen.

Why, wonder of wenchalows, what o szeszame open, v doer s t doing? V door s being. But how theng thingajarry miens but this being becoming n z doer? K? An o. It is ne not him what foots like a glove, shoehandschiner Pad Podomkin. Sooftly, anni slavey, szszuszchee is slowjaneska.

The aged crafty nummifeed confusionary overinsured ever-lapsing accentuated katekattershin clopped, clopped, clopped, darsey dobrey, back and along the danzing corridor, as she was going to pimpim him, way boy wally, not without her comple-ment of cavarnan men, between the two deathdealing allied divisions and the lines of readypresent fire of the corkedagains up-stored, taken in giving the saloot, band your hands going in, bind your heads coming out, and remoltked to herselp in her serf's alown, a weerpovy willowy dreevy drawly and the patter of so familiars, farabroads and behomeans, as she shure sknows, boof for a booby, boo: new uses in their mewseyfume. The jammesons is a cook in his hair. And the juinnesses is a rapin his hind. And the Bullingdong caught the wind up. Dip.

And the message she braught belaw from the missus she bragged abouve that had her agony stays outsize her sari chemise, blancking her shifts for to keep up the fascion since the king of all dronnings kissed her beeswixed hand, fang (pierce me, hunky, I'm full of meunders!), her fize like a tubtail of mondayne clothes, fed to the chaps with working medicals and her birthright pang that would split an atam like the forty pins in her hood, was to fader huncher a howdydowdy, to mountainy mots in her amnest plein language, from his fain a wan, his hot and tot lass, to pierce his ropeloop ear, how, Podushka be prayhasd, now the sowns of his loins were awinking and waking and his dorter of the hush lillabilla lullaby (lead us not into reformication with the poors in your thingdom of gory, O moan!), once after males, nonce at a time, with them Murphy's puffs she dursted with gnockmeggs and the bramborry cake for dour dorty dompling obayre Mattom Beetom and epsut the pfot and if he was whishtful to licture her caudal with chesty chach from his dauberg den and noviny news from Naul or toplots talks from morrienbaths or a parrotsprate's cure for ensevelised lethurgies, spick's my spoon and the veriblest spoon, 'twas her hour for the chamber's ensallycopodium with love to melost Panny Kostello from X.Y. Zid for to folly billybobbis gibits porzy punzy and she was a wanton for De Marera to take her genial glow to bed.

— This is time for my tubble, reflected Mr 'Gladstone Browne' in the toll hut (it was choractoristic from that 'man of Delgany'). Dip.

— This is me vulcanite smoking, profused Mr 'Bonaparte Nolan' under the natecup (one feels how one may hereby reekignites the 'ground old mahonagyan'). Dip.

— And this is defender of defeater of defaulter of deformer of the funst man in Danelagh, willingtoned in with this glance dowon his browen and that born appalled noodlum the panellite pair's cummal delimitator, odding: Oliver White, he's as tiff as she's tight. And thisens his speak quite hoarse. Dip.

In reverence to her midgetsy the lady of the comeallyous as madgestoo our own one's goff stature. Prosim, prosit, to the krk n yr nck!

O rum it is the chomicalest thing how it pickles up the punchey and the jude. If you'll gimmy your thing to me I will gamey a sing to thee. Stay where you're dummy! To get her to go ther. He banged the scoop and she bagged the sugar while the whole pub's pobbel done a stare. On the mizzatint wall. With its chromo for all, crimm crimms. Showing holdmenag's asses sat by Allmeneck's men, canins to ride with em, canins that lept at em, woollied and flundered.

So the katey's came and the katey's game. As so gangs sludgenose. And that henchwench what hopped it dunneth there duft the. Duras.

(Silents)

Yes, we've conned thon print in its gloss so gay how it came from Finndlader's Yule to the day and it's Hey Tallaght Hoe on the king's highway with his hounds on the home at a turning. To Donnicoombe Fairing. Millikin's Pass. When visiting at Izd-la-Chapelle taste the lipe of the waters from Carlowman's Cup.

It tellyhows its story to their six of hearts, a twelve-eyed man; for whom has madjestky who since is dyed drown reign before the izba.

Au! Au! Aue! Ha! Heish!

As stage to set by ritual rote for the grimm grimm tale of the four of hyacinths, the deafeeled carp and the bugler's dozen of leagues-in-amour or how Holispolis went to Parkland with mabby and sammy and sonny and sissy and mop's varlet de shambles and all to find the right place for it by peep o'skirt or pipe a skirl when the hundt called a halt on the chivvychace of the ground sloper at that ligtning lovemaker's thender apeal till, between wandering weather and stable wind, vastelend hosteil-end, neuziel and oltrigger some, Bullyclubber burgherly shut the rush in general.

Let us propel us for the frey of the fray! Us, us, beraddy!

Ko Niutirenis hauru leish! A lala! Ko Niutirenis haururu laleish! Ala lala! The Wullingthund sturm is breaking. The sound of maormaoring. The Wellingthund sturm waxes fuercilier. The whackawhacks of the sturm. Katu te ihis ihis! Katu te wana wana! The strength of the rawshorn generand is known throughout the world. Let us say if we may what a weeny wukeleen can do.

Au! Au! Aue! Ha! Heish! A lala!

— Paud the roosky, weren't they all of them then each in his different way of saying calling on the one in the same time hibernian knights underthaner that was having, half for the laugh of the bliss it sint barbaras another doesend end once tale of a tublin wished on to him with its olives ocolombs and its hills owns ravings and Tutty his tour in his Nowhare's yarcht. It was before when Aimee stood for Arthurduke for the figger in profane and fell from grace so madlley for fill the flatter fellows. (They were saying). And it was the lang in the shirt in the green of the wood, where obelisk rises when odalisks fall, major threft on the make and jollyjacques spindthrift on the merry (O Mr Mathurin, they were calling, what a topheavy hat you're in! And there aramny maeud, then they were saying, these so piou-

pious!). And it was cyclums cyclorums after he made design on the corse and he want to mess on him (enterellbo add all taller Danis), back, seater and sides, and he applied (I'm amazingly sorracer!) the wholed bould shoulderedboy's width for fullness, measures for messieurs, messer's massed, (they were saycalling again and agone and all over agun, the louthly meathers, the loudly meaders, the lously measlers, six to one, bar ones).

And they pled him beheighten the firing. Dope.

Maltomeetim, alltomatetam, when a tale tarries shome shunter shove on. Fore auld they wauld to pree.

Pray.

Of this Mr A (tillalaric) and these wasch woman (dapple-hued), fhronehflord and feeofeeds, who had insue keen and able and a spindlesong aside, nothing more is told until now, his awebrume hour, her sere Sahara of sad oakleaves. And then. Be old. The next thing is. We are once amore as babes awondering in a wold made fresh where with the hen in the storyaboot we start from scratch.

So the truce, the old truce and nattonbuff the truce, boys. Drouth is stronger than faction. Slant. Shinshin. Shinshin.

— It was of The Grant, old gartener, *qua* golden meddlist, Publius Manlius, fuderal private, (his place is his poster, sure, they said, and we're going to mark it, sore, they said, with a carbon caustick manner) bequother the liberaloider at his petty corporelezzo that hung caughtnapping from his baited breath, it was of him, my wife and I thinks, to feel to every of the younging fruits, tenderosed like an atalantic's breastswells or, on a second wreathing, a bright tauth bight shimmeryshaking for the welt of his plow. And where the peckadillies at his wristsends meetings be loving so lightly dovessoild the candidacy, me wipin eye sinks, of his softboiled bosom should be apparient even to our illicterate of nullatinenties.

All to which not a lot snapped The Nolan of the Calabashes at his whilom eweheart photognomist who by this sum taken was as much incensed by Saint Bruno as that what he had consummed was his own panegoric, and wot a lout about it if it was only a pippappoff pigeon shoot that gracesold getrunner, the man of centuries, was bowled out by judge, jury and umpire at batman's biff like a witchbefooled legate. Dupe.

His almonence being alaterelly in dispensation with his three oldher patrons' aid, providencer's divine cow to milkfeeding mleckman, bonafacies to solafides, what matter what all his freudzay or who holds his hat to harm him, let hutch just keep on under at being a vanished consinent and let annapal livibel prettily prattle a lude all her own. And be that semeliminal salmon solemonly angled, ingate and outgate. A truce to lovecalls, dulled in warclothes, maleybags, things and bleakhusen. Leave the letter that never begins to go find the latter that ever comes to end, written in smoke and blurred by mist and signed of solitude, sealed at night.

Simply. As says the mug in the middle, nay brian nay noel, ney billy ney boney. Imagine twee cweamy wosen. Suppwose you get a beautiful thought and cull them sylvias sub silence. Then inmaggin a stotterer. Suppoutre him to been one biggermaster Omnibil. Then lustily (tutu the font and tritt on the bokswoods like gay feeters's dance) immengine up to three longly lurking lobstarts. Fair instents the Will Woolsley Wellaslayers. Pet her, pink him, play pranks with them. She will nod amproperly smile. He may seem to appraisiate it. They are as piractical jukersmen sure to paltipsypote. Feel the wollies drippeling out of your fingathumbs. Says to youssilves (floweers have ears, heahear!) solowly: So these ease Budlim! How do, dainty daulimbs? So peached to pick on you in this way, prue and simple, pritt and spry! Heyday too, Malster Faunagon, and hopes your hahititahiti licks the mankey nuts! And oodlum hoodlum doodlum to yes, Donn, Teague and Hurleg, who the bullocks brought you here and how the hillocks are ye?

We want Bud. We want Bud Budderly. We want Bud Budderly boddily. There he is in his Borrisalooner. The man that shunned the rucks on Gereland. The man thut won the bettlle of the bawll. Order, order, order, order! And tough. We call on Tancred Artaxerxes Flavin to compeer with Barnabas Ulick Dunne.

Order, order, order! Milster Malster in the chair. We've heard it sinse sung thousandtimes. How Burghley shuck the rackushant Germanon. For Ehren, boys, gobrawl!

A public plouse. Citizen soldiers.

TAFF (*a smart boy, of the peat freers, thirty two eleven, looking through the roof towards a relevution of the karmalife order privious to his hoisting of an emergency umberolum in byway of paraguastical solation to the rhyttel in his hedd*). All was flashing and krashning blurty moriartsky blutcherudd? What see, buttywalch? Tell ever so often?

BUTT (*mottledged youth, clergical appealance, who, as his pied friar, is supposing to motto the sorry dejester in tifftaff toffiness or to be digarced from ever and a daye in his accounts*). But da. But dada, mwilshsuni. Till even so aften. Sea vaast a pool!

TAFF (*porumptly helping himself out by the cesspull with a yellup yurrup, puts up his furry furȝed hare*). Butly bitly! Humme to our mounthings. Conscribe him tillusk, unt, in his jubalant tubalence, the groundsapper, with his soilday site out on his moulday side in. The gubernier-gerenal in laut-lievtonant of Baltiskeeamore, amaltheouse for leporty hole! Endues paramilintary langdwage. The saillils of the yellavs nocadont palignol urdlesh. Shelltoss and welltass and telltuss aghom! Sling Stranaslang, how Malorazzias spikes her, coining a speak a spake! Not the Setanik stuff that slimed soft Siranouche! The good old gunshop monowards for manosymples. Tincurs tammit! They did oak hay doe fou Chang-li-meng when that man d'airain was big top tom saw tip side bum boss pageantfiller. Ajaculate! All lea light! Rassamble the glowrings of Bruyant the Bref when the Mollies Makehalpence took his leg for his thumb. And may he be too an intrepidation of our dreams which we foregot at wiking when the morn hath razed out limpalove and the bleakfrost chilled our ravery! Pook. Sing ching lew mang! Upgo, bobbycop! Lets hear in remember the braise of. Hold!

BUTT (*drawling forth from his blousom whereis meditabound of his minkerstary, switches on his gorsecopper's fling weitoheito langthorn, fed up the grain oils of Aerin, while his laugh neighs banck as*)

that flashermind's rays and his lipponease longuewedge wambles).
Ullahbluh! Sehyoh narar, pokehole sann! Manhead very dirty by
am anoyato. Like old Dolldy Icon when he cooked up his iggs
in bicon. He gatovit and me gotafit and Oalgoak's Cheloven gut
a fudden. Povar old pitschobed! Molodeztious of metchennacht
belaburt that pentschmyaso! Bog carsse and dam neat, sar, gam
cant! Limbers affront of him, lumbers behund. While the bucks
bite his dos his hart bides the ros till the bounds of his bays bell
the warning. Sobaiter sobarkar. He was enmivallupped. Chro-
mean fastion. With all his cannoball wappents. In his raglanrock
and his malakoiffed bulbsbyg and his varnashed roscians and his
cardigans blousejagged and his scarlett manchokuffs and his tree-
coloured camiflag and his perikopendolous gaelstorms. Here
weeks hire pulchers! Obriania's beromst! From Karrs and
Polikoff's, the men's confessioners. Seval shimars pleasant
time payings. Mousoumeselles buckwoulds look. Tenter and
likelings.

TAFF (*all Perssiasterssias shookatnaratatattar at his waggon-
horchers, his bulgeglarying stargapers razzledazzlingly full of eyes,
full of balls, full of holes, full of buttons, full of stains, full of medals,
full of blickblackblobs*). Grozarktic! Toadlebens! Some garment-
guy! Insects appalling, low hum clang sin! A cheap decoy! Too
deep destroy! Say mangraphique, may say nay por daguerre!

BUTT (*if that he hids foregodden has nate of glozery farused ameet
the florahs of the follest, his spent fish's livid smile giving allasundery
the bumfit of the doped*). Come alleyou jupes of Wymmingtown
that graze the calves of Man! A bear raigning in his heavenspawn
consomation robes. Rent, outraged, yewleaved, grained, bal-
looned, hindergored and voluant! Erminia's capecloaked hoo-
doodman! First he s s st steppes. Then he st stoo stoopt. Lookt.

TAFF (*strick struck strangling like aleal lusky Lubliner to merum-
ber by the cycl of the cruize who strungled Attahilloupa with what
empoisoned El Monte de Zuma and failing wilnaynilnay that he
was pallups barn in the minkst of the Krumlin befodt he was pop-
soused into the monkst of the vatercan, makes the holypolygon of
the emt on the greaseshaper, a little farther, a little soon, a lettera-*

cettera, oukraydoubray). Scutterer of guld, he is retourious on every roudery! The lyewdsky so so sewn of a fitchid! With his walshbrushup. And his boney bogey braggs.

BUTT (*after his tongues in his cheeks, with pinkpoker pointing out in rutene to impassible abjects beyond the mistomist towards Lissnaluhy such as the Djublian Alps and the Hoofd Ribeiro as where he and his trulock may ever make a game*). The field of karhags and that bloasted tree. Forget not the felled! For the lomondations of Oghrem! Warful doon's bothem. Here furry glunn. Nye? Their feery pass. Tak! With guerillaman aspear aspoor to prink the pranks of primkissies. And the buddies behide in the byre. Allahblah!

TAFF (*a blackseer, he stroves to regulect all the straggles for wife in the rut of the past through the widnows in effigies keening after the blank sheets in their faminy to the relix of old decency from over draught*). Oh day of rath! Ah, murther of mines! Eh, selo moy! Uh, zulu luy! Bernesson Mac Mahahon from Osro bearing nose easger for sweeth prolettas on his swooth prowl!

BUTT (*back to his peatrol and paump: swee Gee's wee rest: no more applehooley: dodewodedook*). Bruinoboroff, the hooneymoonger, and the grizzliest manmichal in Meideveide! Whose annal livves the hoiest! For he devoused the lelias on the fined and he conforted samp, tramp and marchint out of the drumbume of a narse. Guards, serf Finnland, serve we all!

TAFF (*whatwidth the psychophannies at the front and whetwadth the psuckofumbers beholden the fair, illcertain, between his bulchrichudes and the roshashanaral, where he sees Bishop Ribboncake plus his pollex prized going forth on his visitations of mirrage or Miss Horizon, justso all our fannacies daintied her, on the curve of the camber, unsheathing a showlaced limbaloft to the great consternations*). Divulge! Hyededye, kittyls, and howdeddoh, pan! Poshbott and pulbuties. See that we soll or let dargman be luna as strait a way as your ant's folly me line while ye post is goang from Piping Pubwirth to Haunted Hillborough on his Mujiksy's Zaravence, the Riss, the Ross, the sur of all Russers, as my farst is near to hear and my sackend is meet to sedon while my whole's a peer's aureolies. We should say you dones the polecad. Bang on the booche, gurg in the gorge, rap on the roof and your flup is unbu...

BUTT (*at the signal of his act which seems to sharpnel his :nnermals menody, playing the spool of the little brown jog round the wheel of her whang goes the millner*). Buckily buckily, blodestained boyne! Bimbambombumb. His snapper was shot in the Rumjar Journaral. Why the gigls he lubbed beeyed him.

TAFF (*obliges with a two stop yogacoga sumphoty on the bones for ivory girl and ebony boy*). The balacleivka! Trovatarovitch! I trumble!

BUTT (*with the sickle of a scygthe but the humour of a hummer, O, howorodies through his cholaroguled, fumfing to a fullfrength with this wallowing olfact*). Mortar martar tartar wartar! May his boules grow wider so his skittles gets worse! The aged monad making a venture out of the murder of investment. I seen him acting surgent what betwinks the scimitar star and the ashen moon. By their lights shalthow throw him! Piff paff for puffpuff and my pife for his cgar! The mlachy way for gambling.

[*Up to this curkscraw bind an admirable verbivocovisual presentment of the worldrenownced Caerholme Event has been being given by* The Irish Race and World. *The huddled and aliven stablecrashers have shared fleetfooted enthusiasm with the paddocks dare and ditches tare while the mews was combing ground. Hippohopparray helioscope flashed winsor places as the gates might see. Meusdeus! That was (with burning briar) Mr Twomass Nohoholan for their common contribe satisfunction in the purports of amusedment telling the Verily Roverend Father Epiphanes shrineshriver of Saint Dhorough's (in browne bomler) how (assuary as there's a bonum in your osstheology!) Backlegs shirked the racing kenneldar. The saintly scholarist's roastering guffalawd of nupersaturals holler at this metanoic excomologosis tells of the chestnut's (once again, Wittyngtom!) absolutionally romptyhompty successfulness. A lot of lasses and lads without damas or dads, but fresh and blued with collecting boxes. One aught spare ones triflets, to be shut: it is Coppingers for the children. Slippery Sam hard by them, physically present how-*

somedever morally absent, was slooching about in his knavish
diamonds asking Gmax, Knox and the Dmuggies (a pinnance for
your toughts, turffers!) to deck the ace of duds. Tomtinker Tim,
howbeit; his unremitting retainer, (the seers are the seers of
Samael but the heers are the heers of Timoth) is in Boozer's
Gloom, soalken steady in his sulken tents. Baldawl the curse,
baledale the day! And the frocks of shick sheeples in their shum-
mering insamples! You see: a chiefsmith, semperal scandal
stinkmakers, a middinest from the Casabianca and, of course,
Mr Fry. Barass! Pardon the inquisition, causas es quostas? It
is Da Valorem's Dominical Brayers. Why coif that weird hood?
Because among nosoever circusdances is to be apprehended the
dustungwashed poltronage of the lost Gabbarnaur-Jaggarnath.
Pamjab! Gross Jumpiter, whud was thud? Luckluckluckluck-
luckluckluck! It is the Thousand to One Guinea-Gooseberry's
Lipperfull Slipver Cup. Hold hard, ridesiddle titelittle Pitsy
Riley! Gurragrunch, gurragrunch! They are at the turn of the
fourth of the hurdles. By the hross of Xristos, Holophullopopu-
lace is a shote of excramation! Bumchub! Emancipator, the
Creman hunter (Major Hermyn C. Entwhistle) with dramatic
effect reproducing the form of famous sires on the scene of the
formers triumphs, is showing the eagle's way to Mr Whayte-
hayte's three buy geldings Homo Made Ink, Bailey Beacon
and Ratatuohy while Furstin II and The Other Girl (Mrs
'Boss' Waters, Leavybrink) too early spring dabbles, are showing
a clean pairofhids to Immensipater. Sinkathinks to oppen here!
To this virgin's tuft, on this golden of evens! I never sought of
sinkathink. Our lorkmakor he is proformly annuysed. He is
shinkly thinkly shaking in his schayns. Sat will be off follteedee.
This eeridreme has being effered you by Bett and Tipp. Tipp and
Bett, our swapstick quackchancers, in From Topphole to Bottom of The Irish Race and World.]

TAFF (away that the first sports report of Loundin Reginald
has now been afterthoughtfully colliberated by a saggind spurts
flash, takes the dipperend direction and, for tasing the tiomor of

malaise after the pognency of orangultonia, orients by way of Sagit-
tarius towards Draco on the Lour). And you collier carsst on him,
the corsar, with Boyle, Burke and Campbell, I'll gogemble on
strangbones tomb. You had just been cerberating a camp camp
camp to Saint Sepulchre's march through the armeemonds retreat with the boys all marshalled, scattering giant's hail over the
curseway, fellowed along the rout by the stenchions of the
corpse. Tell the coldspell's terroth! If you please, commeylad!
Perfedes Albionias! Think some ingain think, as Teakortairer
sate over the Galwegian caftan forewhen Orops and Aasas were
chooldrengs and micramacrees! A forward movement, Miles na
Bogaleen, and despatch!

BUTT (*slinking his coatsleeves surdout over his squad mutton*
shoulder so as to loop more life the jauntlyman as he scents the
anggreget yup behound their whole scoopchina's desperate noy's
totalage and explaining aposteriorly how awstooloo was valde-
sombre belowes hero and he was in a greak esthate phophiar an
erixtion on the soseptuple side of him made spoil apriori his popo-
porportiums). Yass, zotnyzor, I don't think I did not, pojr. Never
you brother me for I scout it, think you! Ichts nichts on nichts!
Greates Schtschuptar! Me fol the rawlawdy in the schpirrt of a
schkrepz. Of all the quirasses and all the qwehrmin in the tra-
gedoes of those antiants their grandoper, that soun of a gun-
nong, with his sabaothsopolettes, smooking his scandleloose at
botthends of him! Foinn duhans! I grandthinked after his obras
after another time about the itch in his egondoom he was legging
boldylugged from some pulversporochs and lyoking for a stool-
eazy for to nemesisplotsch allafranka and for to salubrate himself
with an ultradungs heavenly mass at his base by a suprime pomp-
ship chorams the perished popes, the reverend and allaverred
cromlecks, and when I heard his lewdbrogue reciping his cheap
cheateary gospeds to sintry and santry and sentry and suntry I
thought he was only haftara having afterhis brokeforths but be
the homely Churopodvas I no sooner seen aghist of his frighte-
ousness then I was bibbering with vear a few versets off fooling for
fjorg for my fifth foot. Of manifest 'tis obedience and the. Flute!

TAFF (*though the unglucksarsoon is giming for to git him, jotning in, hoghly ligious, hapagodlap, like a soldierry sap, with a pique at his cue and a tyr in his eye and a bond of his back and a croak in his cry as did jolly well harm lean o'er him*) Is not athug who would. Weepon, weeponder, song of sorrowmon! Which goatheye and sheepskeer they damnty well know. Papaist! Gambanman! Take the cawraidd's blow! Yia! Your partridge's last!

BUTT (*giving his scimmianised twinge in acknuckledownedgment of this cumulikick, strafe from the firetrench, studenly drobs led, satoniseels ouchyotchy, he changecors induniforms as he is lefting the gat out of the big: his face glows green, his hair greys white, his bleyes bcome broon to suite his cultic twalette*). But when I seeing him in his oneship fetch along within hail that tourrible tall with his nitshnykopfgoknob and attempting like a brandylogged rudeman cathargic, lugging up and laiding down his livepelts so cruschinly like Mebbuck at Messar and exposing his old skinful self tailtottom by manurevring in open ordure to renewmurature with the cowruads in their airish pleasantry I thanked he was recovering breadth from some herdsquatters beyond the carcasses and I couldn't erver nerver to tell a liard story not of I knew the prize if from lead or alimoney. But when I got inoccupation of a full new of his old basemiddelism, in ackshan, pagne pogne, by the veereyed lights of the stormtrooping clouds and in the sheenflare of the battleaxes of the heroim and mid the shieldfails awail of the bitteraccents of the sorafim and caught the pfierce tsmell of his aurals, orankastank, a suphead setrapped, like Peder the Greste, altipaltar, my bill it forsooks allegiance (gut bull it!) and, no lie is this, I was babbeing and yetaghain bubbering, bibbelboy, me marrues me shkewers me gnaas me fiet, tob tob tob beat it, solongopatom. Clummensy if ever misused, must used you's now! But, meac Coolp, Arram of Eirzerum, as I love our Deer Dirouchy, I confesses withould pridejealice when I looked upon the Saur of all the Haurousians with the weight of his arge fullin upon him from the travaillings of his tommuck and rueckenased the fates of a bosser there was fear on me the sons of Nuad for him and it was heavy he was for me

344

then the way I immingled my Irmenial hairmaierians ammon-
gled his Gospolis fomiliours till, achaura moucreas, I adn't the
arts to.

TAFF (*as a marrer off act, prepensing how such waldmanns from
Burnias seduced country clowns, he is preposing barangaparang
after going knowing what he is doing after to see him pluggy well
moidered as a murder effect, you bet your blowie knife, before he
doʒe soʒe, sopprused though he is*) Grot Zot! You hidn't the hurts?
Vott Fonn!

BUTT (*hearing somrother sudly give tworthree peevish sniff snuff
snoores like govalise falseleep he waitawhishts to see might he stirs
and then goes on kuldrum like without asking for pepeace or anysing
a soul*). Merzmard! I met with whom it was too late. My fate! O
hate! Fairwail! Fearwealing of the groan! And think of that
when you smugs to bagot.

TAFF (*who meanwhilome at yarn's length so as to put a nodje
in the poestcher, by wile of stoccan his hand and of rooma makin
ber getting umptyums gatherumed off the skattert, had been lavish-
ing, lagan on lighthouse, words of silent power, susu glouglou biri-
biri gongos, upon the repleted speechsalver's innkeeping right which,
thanks giveme and naperied norms nonobstaclant, there can be little
doubt, have resulted in a momstchance ministring of another guid-
ness, my good, to see*) Bompromifazzio! Shumpum for Pa-li-di
and oukosouso for the nipper dandy! Trink off this scup and be
bladdy orafferteed! To bug at?

BUTT (*he whipedoff's his chimbley phot, as lips lovecurling to the
tongueopener, he takecups the communion of sense at the hands of
the foregiver of trosstpassers and thereinofter centelinnates that
potifex miximhost with haruspical hospedariaty proferring into his
pauses somewhot salt bacon*). Theres scares knud in this gnarld
warld a fully so svend as dilates for the improvement of our
foerses of nature by your very ample solvent of referacting upon
me like is boesen fiennd.

[*The other foregotthened abbosed in the Mullingaria are
during this swishingsight teilweisioned. How the fictionable world*
345

in Fruzian Creamtartery is loading off heavy furses and affubling themselves with muckinstushes. The neatschknee Novgolosh. How the spinach ruddocks are being tatoovatted up for the second comings of antigreenst. Hebeneros for Aromal Peace. How Alibey Ibrahim wisheths Bella Suora to a holy cryptmahs while the Arumbian Knives Riders axecutes devilances round the jehumispheure. Learn the Nunsturk. How Old Yales boys is making rebolutions for the cunning New Yirls, never elding, still begidding, never to mate to lend, never to ate selleries and never to add soulleries and never to ant sulleries and never to aid silleries with sucharow with sotchyouroff as Burkeley's Show's a ructiongetherall. Phone for Phineal toomellow aftermorn and your phumeral's a roselixion.]

TAFF (*now as he has been past the buckthurnstock from Peadhar Piper of Colliguchuna, whiles they all are bealting pots to dubrin din for old daddam dombstom to tomb and wamb humbs lumbs agamb, glimpse agam, glance agen, rise up road and hive up hill, and find your pollyvoulley foncey pitchin ingles in the parler*). Since you are on for versingrhetorish say your piece! How Buccleuch shocked the rosing girnirilles. A ballet of Gasty Power. A hov and az ov and off like a gow! And don't live out the sad of tearfs, piddyawhick! Not offgott affsang is you, buthbach? Ath yet-heredayth noth endeth, hay? Vaersegood! Buckle to! Sayyessik, Ballygarry. The fourscore soculums are watchyoumaycodding to cooll the skoopgoods blooff. Harkabuddy, feign! Thingman placeyear howed wholst somwom shimwhir tinkledinkledelled. Shinfine deed in the myrtle of the bog tway fainmain stod op to slog, free bond men lay lurkin on. Tuan about whattinghim! Fore sneezturmdrappen! 'Twill be a rpnice pschange, arrah, sir? Can you come it, budd?

BUTT (*who in the cushlows of his goodsforseeking hoarth, ever fondlinger of his pimple spurk, is a niallist of the ninth homestages, the babybell in his baggutstract upper going off allatwanst, begad, lest he should challenge himself, beygoad, till angush*). Horrasure, toff! As said as would. It was Colporal Phailinx first. Hittit was of another time, a white horsday where the midril met the bulg, sbogom, roughnow along about the first equinarx in the cholonder, on the plain of Khorason as thou goest from the mount of Bekel, Steep Nemorn, elve hundred and therety and to years how the krow flees end in deed, after a power of skimiskes, blodidens and godinats of them, when we sight the beasts, (hegheg whatlk of wraimy wetter!), moist moonful date man aver held dimsdzey death with, and higheye was in the Reilly Oirish Krzerszonese Milesia asundurst Sirdarthar Woolwichleagues, good tomkeys years somewhile in Crimealian wall samewhere in Ayerland, during me weeping stillstumms over the freshprosts of Eastchept and the dangling garters of Marrowbone and daring my wapping stiltstunts on Bostion Moss, old stile and new style and heave a lep onwards. And winn again, blaguadargoos, or lues the day, plays goat, the banshee pealer, if moskats knows whoss whizz, the great day and the druidful day come San Patrisky and the grand day, the excellent fine splendorous long agreeable toastworthy cylindrical day, go Sixt of the Ninth, the heptahundread annam dammias that Hajizfijjiz ells me is and will and was be till the timelag is in it that's told in the Bok of Alam to columnkill all the prefacies of Erin gone brugk. But Icantenue. And incommixtion. We was lowsome like till we'd took out after the dead beats. So I begin to study and I soon show them day's reasons how to give the cold shake to they blighty perishers and lay one over the beats. All feller he look he call all feller come longa villa finish. Toumbalo, how was I acclapadad! From them banjopeddlars on the raid. Gidding up me anti vanillas and getting off the stissas me aunties. Boxerising and coxerusing. And swiping a johnny dann sweept for to exercitise myself neverwithstanding the topkats and his roaming cartridges, orussheying and patronning, out all over Crummwiliam wall. Be the why it was me who haw haw.

TAFF (*all for letting his tinder and lighting be put to beheiss in the feuer and, while durblinly obasiant to the felicias of the skivis, still smolking his fulvurite turfkish in the rooking pressance of laddios*). Yaa hoo how how, col? Whom battles joined no bottles sever! Worn't you aid a comp?

BUTT (*in his difficoltous tresdobremient, he feels a bitvalike a baddlefall of staot but falls a batforlake a borrlefull of bare*). And me awlphul omegrims! Between me rassociations in the postleadeny past and me disconnections with aplompervious futules I've a boodle full of maimeries in me buzzim and medears runs sloze, bleime, as I now with platoonic leave recoil in (how the thickens they come back to one to rust!) me misenary post for all them old boyars that's now boomaringing in waulholler, me alma marthyrs. I dring to them, bycorn spirits fuselaiding, and you cullies adjutant, even where its contentsed wody, with absents wehrmuth. Junglemen in agleement, I give thee our greatly swooren, Theoccupant that Rueandredful, the thrownfullvner and all our royal devouts with the arrest of the whole inhibitance of Neuilands! One brief mouth. And a velligoolapnow! Meould attashees the currgans, (if they could get a kick at this time for all that's hapenced to us!) Cedric said Gormleyson and Danno O'Dunnochoo and Conno O'Cannochar it is this were their names for we were all under that manner barracksers on Kong Gores Wood together, thurkmen three, with those khakireinettes, our miladies in their toileries, the twum plumyumnietcies, Vjeras Vjenaskayas, of old Djadja Uncken who was a great mark for jinking and junking, up the palposes of womth and wamth, we war, and the charme of their lyse brocade. For lispias harth a burm in eye but whem it bames fire norone screeneth. Hulp, hulp, huzzars! Raise ras tryracy! Freetime's free! Up Lancesters! Anathem!

TAFF (*who still senses that heavinscent houroines that entertrained him who they were sinuorivals from the sunny Espionia but plied wopsy with his wallets in thatthack of the bustle Bakerloo, (11.32), passing the uninational truthbosh in smoothing irony over the multinotcheralled infructuosities of his grinner set*). The rib, the rib, the quean of oldbyrdes, Sinya Sonyavitches! Your Rhoda Cockardes that are raday to embrace our ruddy inflamtry world! In their ohosililesvienne biribarbebeway. Till they've

348

kinks in their tringers and boils on their taws. Whor dor the pene lie, Mer Pencho? Ist dramhead countmortial or gonorrhal stab? Mind your pughs and keaoghs, if you piggots, marsh! Do the nut, dingbut! Be a dag! For zahur and zimmerminnes! Sing in the chorias to the ethur:

[*In the heliotropical noughttime following a fade of transformed Tuff and, pending its viseversion, a metenergic reglow of beaming Batt, the bairdboard bombardment screen, if tastefully taut guranium satin, tends to teleframe and step up to the charge of a light barricade. Down the photoslope in syncopanc pulses, with the bitts bugtwug their teffs, the missledhropes, glitteraglatteraglutt, borne by their carnier walve. Spraygun rakes and splits them from a double focus: grenadite, damnymite, alextronite, nichilite: and the scanning firespot of the sgunners traverses the rutilanced illustred sunksundered lines. Shlossh! A gaspel truce leaks out over the caeseine coatings. Amid a fluorescence of spectracular mephiticism there caoculates through the inconoscope stealdily a still, the figure of a fellowchap in the wohly ghast, Popey O'Donoshough, the jesuneral of the russuates. The idolon exhibisces the seals of his orders: the starre of the Son of Heaven, the girtel of Izodella the Calottica, the cross of Michelides Apaleogos, the latchet of Jan of Nepomuk, the puffpuff and pompom of Powther and Pall, the great belt, band and bucklings of the Martyrology of Gorman. It is for the castomercies mudwake surveice. The victar. Pleace to notnoys speach above your dreadths, please to doughboys. Hll, smthngs gnwrng wthth sprsnwtch! He blanks his oggles because he confesses to all his tellavicious nieces. He blocks his nosoes because that he confesses to everywheres he was always putting up his latest faengers. He wollops his mouther with a sword of tusk in as because that he confesses how opten he used be obening her howonton he used be undering her. He boundles alltogotter his manucupes with his pedarrests in asmuch as because that he confesses before all his handcomplishies and behind all his comfoderacies. And (hereis cant came back saying he codant steal no lunger, yessis,*

349

catz come buck beques he caudant stail awake) he touched upon this tree of livings in the middenst of the garerden for inasmuch as because that he confessed to it on Hillel and down Dalem and in the places which the lepers inhabit in the place of the stones and in pontofert jusfuggading amoret now he come to think of it jolly well ruttengenerously olyovyover the ole blucky shop. Pugger old Pumpey O'Dungaschiff! There will be a hen collection of him after avensung on the field of Hanar. Dumble down, looties and gengstermen! Dtin, dtin, dtin, dtin!]*

BUTT (*with a gisture expansive of Mr Lhugewhite Cadderpollard with sunflawered beautonhole pulled up point blanck by mailbag mundaynism at Oldbally Court though the hissindensity buck far of his melovelance tells how when he was fast marking his first lord for cremation the whyfe of his bothem was the very lad's thing to elter his mehind*). Prostatates, pujealousties! Dovolnoisers, prayshyous! Defense in every circumstancias of deboutcheries no the chaste daffs! Pack pickets, pioghs and kughs to be palsey-putred! Be at the peme, prease, of not forgetting or mere betoken yourself to hother prace! Correct me, pleatze commando, for cossakes but I abjure of it. No more basquibezigues for this pole aprican! With askormiles' eskermillas. I had my billyfell of duckish delights the whole pukny time on rawmeots and juliannes with their lambstoels in my kiddeneys and my ramsbutter in their sassenacher ribs, knee her, do her and trey her, when th'osirian cumb dumb like the whalf on the fiord and we prey-ing players and pinching peacesmokes, troupkers tomiatskyns all, for Father Petrie Spence of Parishmoslattary to go and leave us and the crimsend daun to shellalite on the darkumen (scene as signed, Slobabogue), feeding and sleeping on the huguenottes (the snuggest spalniel's where the lieon's tame!) and raiding revolutions over the allbegeneses (sand us and saint us and sound as agun!). Yet still in all, spit for spat, like we chantied on Sunda schoon, every warson wearrier kaddies a komnate in his schnapsack and unlist I am getting foegutfulls of the rugi-ments of savaliged wildfire I was gamefellow willmate and send us victorias with nowells and brownings, dumm, sneak and curry, and all the fun I had in that fanagan's week. A strange man wearing abarrel. And here's a gift of meggs and teggs. And as I live by chipping nortons. And 'tis iron fits the farmer, ay. Arcdesedo! Renborumba! Then were the hellscyown days for our fellows, the loyal leibsters, and we was the redugout raw-recruitioners, praddies three and prettish too, a wheeze we has in our waynward islands, wee engrish, one long blue streak, jisty and pithy af durck rosolun, with hand to hand as Homard Kayenne was always jiggilyjugging about in his wendowed courage when our woos with the wenches went wined for a song, tsingirillies' zyngarettes, while Woodbine Willie, so popiular with the poppyrossies, our Chorney Choplain, blued the air. Sczlanthas! Banzaine! Bissbasses! S. Pivorandbowl. And we all tuned in to hear the topmast noviality. Up the revels drown the rinks and almistips all round! Paddy Bonhamme he vives! Encore! And tig for tag. Togatogtug. My droomodose days Y loved you abover all the strest. Blowhole brasshat and boy with his boots off and the butch of our bunch and all. It was buckoo bonzer, beleeme. I was a bare prive without my doglegs but I did not give to one humpenny dump, wingh or wangh, touching those thusengaged slavey generales of Tanah Kornalls, the meelisha's deelishas, pronouncing their very flank movemens in sunpictorsbosk. Baghus the whatwar! I could always take good cover of myself and, eyedulls or earwakers, preyers for rain or cominations, I did not care three tanker's hoots, ('sham! hem! or chaffit!) for any feelings from my lifeprivates on their reptrograd leanins because I have Their Honours booth my respectables sœurs assistershood off Lyndhurst Terrace, the puttih Misses Celana Dalems, and she in vinting her angurr can belle the troth on her alliance and I know His Heriness, my respeaktoble medams culonelle on Mellay Street, Lightnints Gundhur Sawabs, and they would never as the aimees of servation let me down. Not on your bludger life, touters! No peeping, pimpadoors! And, by Jova, I never went wrong nor let him doom till, risky wark rasky wolk, at the head of the wake, up come stumblebum (ye olde cottemptable!), his urssian gemenal, in his scutt's rudes unreformed and he went before him in that nemcon enchelonce with the same old domstoole story and his upleave the fallener as is greatly to be petted (whitesides do his beard!) and I seen his brichashert offensive and his boortholomas vadnhammaggs vise a vise them scharlot runners and how they gave love to him and how he took the ward from us (odious the fly fly flurtation of his him and hers! Just mairmaid maddeling it was it he was!) and, my oreland for a rolvever, sord, by the splunthers of colt and bung goes the enemay the Percy rally got me, messger, (as true as theirs an Almagnian Gothabobus!) to blow the grand off his aceupper. Thistake it 's meest! And after meath the dulwich. We insurrectioned and, be the procuratress of the hory synnotts, before he could tell pullyirragun to parrylewis, I shuttm, missus, like a wide sleever! Hump to dump! Tumbleheaver!

TAFF (*camelsensing that sonce they have given bron a nuhlan the volkar boastsung is heading to sea vermelhion but too wellbred not to ignore the umʒemliness of his rifal's preceedings, in an effort towards autosotorisation, effaces himself in favour of the idiology alwise behounding his lumpy hump off homosodalism which means that if he has lain amain to lolly his liking-cabronne!-he may pops lilly a young one to his herth - combrune -*) Oholy rasher, I'm believer! And Oho bullyclaver of ye, bragadore-gunneral! The grand ohold spider! It is a name to call to him Umsturdum Vonn! Ah, you were shutter reshottus and sieger besieged. Aha race of fiercemarchands counterination oho of shorpshoopers.

BUTT (*miraculising into the Dann Deafir warcry, his bigotes bristling, as, jittinju triggity shittery pet, he shouts his thump and feeh fauh foul finngures up the heighohs of their ahs!*) Bluddy-muddymuzzle! The buckbeshottered! He'll umbozzle no more graves nor horne nor haunder, lou garou, for gayl geselles in dead men's hills! Kaptan (backsights to his bared!), His Cumbulent Embulence, the frustate fourstar Russkakruscam, Dom Allaf O'Khorwan, connundurumchuff.

TAFF (*who, asbestas can, wiʒ the healps of gosh and his bluʒʒid maikar, has been sulphuring to himsalves all the pungataries*

of sin praktice in failing to furrow theogonies of the dommed).
Trisseme, the mangoat! And the name of the Most Marsiful,
the Aweghost, the Gragious One! In sobber sooth and in souber
civiles? And to the dirtiment of the curtailment of his all of man?
Notshoh?

BUTT (*maomant scoffin, but apoxyomenously deturbaned but
thems bleachin banes will be after making a bashman's haloday out
of the euphorious hagiohygiecynicism of his die and be diademmed*).
Yastsar! In sabre tooth and sobre saviles! Senonnevero! That
he leaves nyet is my grafe. He deared me to it and he dared me
do it, and bedattle I didaredonit as Cocksnark of Killtork can
tell and Ussur Ursussen of the viktaurious onrush with all the
rattles in his arctic! As bold and as madhouse a bull in a meadows.
Knout Knittrick Kinkypeard! Olefoh, the sourd of foemoe
times! Unknun! For when meseemim, and tolfoklokken rolland
allover ourloud's lande, beheaving up that sob of tunf for to
claimhis, for to wollpimsolff, puddywhuck. Ay, and untuoning
his culothone in an exitous erseroyal *Deo Jupto*. At that instullt
to Igorladns! Prronto! I gave one dobblenotch and I ups with
my crozzier. Mirrdo! With my how on armer and hits leg an
arrow cockshock rockrogn. Sparro!

> [*The abnihilisation of the etym by the grisning of the grosning
> of the grinder of the grunder of the first lord of Hurtreford ex-
> polodotonates through Parsuralia with an ivanmorinthorrorumble
> fragoromboassity amidwhiches general uttermosts confussion are
> perceivable moletons skaping with mulicules while coventry
> plumpkins fairlygosmotherthemselves in the Landaunelegants
> of Pinkadindy. Similar scenatas are projectilised from Hulululu,
> Bawlawayo, empyreal Raum and mordern Atems. They were
> precisely the twelves of clocks, noon minutes, none seconds.
> At someseat of Oldanelang's Konguerrig, by dawnybreak in
> Aira.*]

TAFF (*skimperskamper, his wools gatherings all over cromlin
what with the birstol boys artheynes and is it her tour and the
crackery of the fullfour fivefirearms and the crockery of their dam-*

dam domdom chumbers). Wharall thubulbs uptheaires! Shatta-movick?

BUTT (*pulling alast stark daniel with alest doog at doorak while too greater than pardon painfully the issue of his mouth diminuendoing, vility of vilities, he becomes, allasvitally, faint*). Shurenoff! Like Faun MacGhoul!

BUTT and TAFF (*desprot slave wager and foeman feodal unsheckled, now one and the same person, their fight upheld to right for a wee while being baffled and tottered, umbraged by the shadow of Old Erssia's magisquammythical mulattomilitiaman, the living by owning over the surfers of the glebe whose sway craven minnions had caused to revile, as, too foul for hell, under boiling Mauses' burning brand, he falls by Goll's gillie, but keenheartened by the circuminsistence of the Parkes O'Rarelys in a hurdly gurdly Cicilian concertone of their fonngeena barney brawl, shaken everybothy's hands, while S. E. Morehampton makes leave to E. N. Sheilmartin after Meetinghouse Lanigan has embaraced Vergemout Hall, and, without falter or mormor or blathrehoot of sophsterliness, pugnate the pledge of fiannaship, dook to dook, with a commonturn oudchd of fest man and best man astoutsalliesemoutioun palms it off like commodity tokens against a cococancancacacanotioun*). When old the wormd was a gadden and Anthea first unfoiled her limbs wanderloot was the way the wood wagged where opter and apter were samuraised twimbs. They had their mutthering ivies and their murdhering idies and their mouldhering iries in that muskat grove but there'll be bright plinnyflowers in Calomella's cool bowers when the magpyre's babble towers scorching and screeching from the ravenindove. If thees lobed the sex of his head and mees ates the seep of his traublers he's dancing figgies to the spittle side and shoving outs the soord. And he'll be buying buys and go gulling gells with his flossim and jessim of carm, silk and honey while myandthys playing lancifer lucifug and what's duff as a bettle for usses makes coy cosyn corollanes' moues weeter to wee. So till butagain budly shoots thon rising germinal let bodley chow the fatt of his anger and badley bide the toil of his tubb.

354

[The pump and pipe pingers are ideally reconstituted. The putther and bowls are peterpacked up. All the presents are determining as regards for the future the howabouts of their past absences which they might see on at hearing could they once smell of tastes from touch. To ought find a values for. The must overlistingness. When ex what is ungiven. As ad where. Stillhead. Blunk.]

Shutmup. And bud did down well right. And if he sung dumb in his glass darkly speech lit face to face on allaround.

Vociferagitant. Viceversounding. Namely, Abdul Abulbul Amir or Ivan Slavansky Slavar. In alldconfusalem. As to whom the major guiltfeather pertained it was Hercushiccups' care to educe. Beauty's bath she's bound to bind beholders and pride, his purge, has place appoint in penance and the law's own libel lifts and lames the low with the lofty. Be of the housed! While the Hersy Hunt they harrow the hill for to rout them rollicking rogues from, rule those racketeer romps from, rein their rockery rides from. Rambling.

Nightclothesed, arooned, the conquerods sway. After their battle thy fair bosom.

— That is too tootrue enough in Solidan's Island as in Moltern Giaourmany and from the Amelakins off to date back to land of engined Egypsians, assented from his opening before his inlookers of where an oxmanstongue stalled stabled the wellnourished one, lord of the seven days, overlord of sats and suns, the sat of all the suns which are in the ring of his system of the sats of his sun, god of the scuffeldfallen skillfilledfelon, who (he contaimns) hangsters, who (he constrains) hersirrs, a gain changful, a mintage vaster, heavy on shirts, lucky with shifts, the topside humpup stummock atween his showdows fellah, Misto Teewiley Spillitshops, who keepeth watch in Khummer-Phett, whose spouse is An-Lyph, the dog's bladder, warmer of his couch in fore. We all, for whole men is lepers, have been nobbut wonterers in that chill childerness which is our true name after the allfaulters (mug's luck to em!) and, bespeaking of love and lie detectors in venuvarities, whateither the drugs truth of it, was

355

there an iota of from the faust to the lost. And that is at most re-
doubtedly an overthrew of each and ilkermann of us, I persuade
myself, before Gow, gentlemen, so true as this are my kopfinpot
astrode on these is my boardsoldereds.

It sollecited, grobbling hummley, his roundhouse of seven
orofaces, of all, guiltshouters or crimemummers, to be sayd by,
codnops, advices for, free of gracies, scamps encloded, com-
petitioning them, if they had steadied Jura or when they had
raced Messafissi, husband of your wifebetter or bestman botcha-
lover of you yourself, how comes ever a body in our taylorised
world to selve out thishis, whither it gives a primeum nobilees
for our notomise or naught, the farst wriggle from the ubivence,
whereom is man, that old offender, nother man, wheile he is
asame. And fullexampling. The pints in question. With some by-
spills. And sicsecs to provim hurtig. Soup's on!

— A time. And a find time. Whenin aye was a kiddling. And
the tarikies held sowansopper. Let there beam a frishfrey. And
they sodhe gudhe rudhe brodhe wedhe swedhe medhe in the
kanddledrum. I have just (let us suppraise) been reading in a
(suppressed) book — it is notwithstempting by meassures long
and limited—the latterpress is eminently legligible and the paper,
so he eagerly seized upon, has scarsely been buttered in works of
previous publicity wholebeit in keener notcase would I turf aside
for pastureuration. Packen paper paineth whomto is sacred
scriptured sign. Who straps it scraps it that might, if ashed, have
healped. Enough, however, have I read of it, like my good bedst
friend, to augur in the hurry of the times that it will cocommend
the widest circulation and a reputation coextensive with its merits
when inthrusted into safe and pious hands upon so edifying a
mission as it, I can see, as is his. It his ambullished with expurga-
tive plates, replete in information and accampaigning the action
passiom, slopbang, whizzcrash, boomarattling from burst to
past, as I have just been seeing, with my warmest venerections,
of a timmersome townside upthecountrylifer, (Guard place the
town!) allthose everwhalmed upon that preposterous blank seat,
before the wordcraft of this early woodcutter, a master of vignett-

iennes and our findest grobsmid among all their orefices, (and, shukar in chowdar, so splunderdly English!) Mr Aubeyron Birdslay. Chubgoodchob, arsoncheep and wellwillworth a triat! Bismillafoulties. But the hasard you asks is justly ever behind his meddle throw! Those sad pour sad forengistanters, dastychappy dustyrust! Chaichairs. It is that something, awe, aurorbean in that fellow, hamid and damid, (did he have but Hugh de Brassey's beardslie his wear mine of ancient guised) which comequeers this anywhat perssian which we, owe, realisinus with purups a dard of pene. There is among others pleasons whom I love and which are favourests to mind, one which I have pushed my finker in for the movement and, but for my sealring is none to hand I swear, she is highly catatheristic and there is another which I have fombly fongered freequuntly and, when my signet is on sign again I swear, she is deeply sangnificant. *Culpo de Dido*! Ars we say in the classies. *Kunstful*, we others said. What ravening shadow! What dovely line! Not the king of this age could richlier eyefeast in oreillental longuardness with alternate nightjoys of a thousand kinds but one kind. A shahrryar cobbler on me when I am lying! And whilst (when I doot my sliding panel and I hear cawcaw) I have been idylly turmbing over the loose looves leaflefts jaggled casuallty on the lamatory, as is my this is, as I must commit my lips to make misface for misfortune, often, so far as I can chance to recollect from the some farnights ago, (so dimsweet is that selvischdischdienence of to not to be able to be obliged to have to hold further anything than a stone his throw's fruit's fall!) when I, if you wil excuse for me this informal leading down of illexpressibles, enlivened toward the Author of Nature by the natural sins liggen gobelimned theirs before me, (how differended with the manmade Eonochs Cunstuntonopolies!), weathered they be of a general golf stature, assasserted, or blossomly emblushing thems elves underneed of some howthern folleys, am entrenched up contemplating of myself, wiz my naked I, for relieving purposes in our trurally virvir vergitabale (garden) I sometimes, maybe, what has justly said of old Flannagan, a wake from this or huntsfurwards, with some shock (shell I so render it?) have (when I ope my shylight window and I see coocoo) a notion quiet involuptary of that I am cadging hapsnots as at murmurrandoms of distend renations from ficsimilar phases or dugouts in the behindscenes of our earthwork (what rovining shudder! what deadly loom!) as this is, at no spatial time processly which regards to concrude chronology about which in fact, at spite of I having belittled myself to my gay giftname of insectarian, happy burgages abeyance would make homesweets-town hopeygoalucrey, my mottu propprior, as I claim, cad's truck, I coined, I am highly pelaged and deeply gluttened to mind hindmost hearts to see by their loudest reports from my threespawn bottery parts (shsh!) that, colombophile and corvino-phobe alike, when I have remassed me, my travellingself, as from Magellanic clouds, after my contractual expenditures, through the perofficies of merelimb, I, my good grief, I am, I am big altoogooder.

He beached the bark of his tale; and set to husband and vine: and the harpermaster told all the living conservancy, know Meschiameschianah, how that win a gain was in again. Flying the Perseoroyal. Withal aboarder, padar and madar, hal and sal, the sens of Ere with the duchtars of Iran. Amick amack amock in a mucktub. Qith the tou loulous and the gryffygryffygryffs, at Fenegans Wick, the Wildemanns. Washed up whight and de-liveried rhight. Loud lauds to his luckhump and bejetties on jo-nahs! And they winxed and wanxed like baillybeacons. Till we woksed up oldermen.

From whose plultibust preaggravated, by baskatchairch theo-logies (there werenighn on thaurity herouns in that alraschil arthouducks draken), they were whoalike placed to say, in the matters off ducomans nonbar one, with bears' respects to him and bulls' acknowledgments (come on now, girls! lead off, O cara, whichever won of you wins! The two Gemuas and Jane Agrah and Judy Tombuys!) disassembling and taking him apart, the slammocks, with discrimination for his maypole and a rub in passing over his hump, drogueries inaddendance, frons, fesces and frithstool: 1) he hade to die it, the beetle, 2) he didhithim self, hod's fush, 3) all ever the pelican huntered with truly fond bull-pen backthought since his toork human life where his personal low outhired his taratoryism, the orenore under the selfhide of his bessermettle, was forsake in his chiltern and lumbojumbo, 4) he was like Fintan fore flood and after sometimes too damned merely often on the saved side, saw he was, 5) regarding to prussyattes or quazzyverzing he wassand no better than he would have been before he could have been better than what he warrant after, 6) blood, musk or haschish, as coked, diamoned or pence-loid, and bleaching him naclenude from all cohlorine matter, down to a boneash bittstoff, he's, tink fors tank, the same old dustamount on the same old tincoverdull baubleclass, totstitty-winktosser and bogusbagwindburster, whether fitting tyres onto Danelope boys or fluttering flaus for laurettas, whatever the bucket brigade and the plug party says, touchant Arser of the Rum Tipple and his camelottery and lyonesslooting but with a layaman's brutstrenth, by Jacohob and Esahur and the all saults or all sallies, what we warn to hear, jeff, is the woods of chirpsies cries to singaloo sweecheeriode and sock him up, the oldcant rogue.

Group A.

You have jest (a ham) beamed listening through (a ham pig) his haulted excerpt from John Whiston's fiveaxled production, *The Coach With The Six Insides*, from the Tales of Yore of the times gone by before there was a hofdking or a hoovthing or a pinginapoke in Oreland, all sould. Goes Tory by Eeric Whigs is To Become Tintinued in *Fearson's Nightly* in the Lets All Wake Brickfaced In Lucan. Lhirondella, jaunty lhirondella! With tirra lirra rondinelles, atantivy we go!

Attention! Stand at!! Ease!!!

We are now diffusing among our lovers of this sequence (to you! to you!) the dewfolded song of the naughtingels (Alys! Alysaloe!) from their sheltered positions, in rosescenery hay-dyng, on the heather side of waldalure, Mount Saint John's, Jinnyland, whither our allies winged by duskfoil from Moore-parque, swift sanctuary seeking, after Sunsink gang (Oiboe!

359

Hitherzither! Almost dotty! I must dash!) to pour their peace in partial (floflo floreflòrence), sweetishsad lightandgayle, twittwin twosingwoolow. Let everie sound of a pitch keep still in reson-ance, jemcrow, jackdaw, prime and secund with their terce that whoe betwides them, now full theorbe, now dulcifair, and when we press of pedal (sof!) pick out and vowelise your name. A mum. You pere Golazy, you mere Bare and you Bill Heeny, and you Smirky Dainty and, more beethoken, you wheckfoolthe-nairyans with all your badchthumpered peanas! We are gluck-glucky in our being so far fortunate that, bark and bay duol with Man Goodfox inchimings having ceased to the moment, so allow the clinkars of our nocturnefield, night's sweetmoztheart, their Carmen Sylvae, my quest, my queen. Lou must wail to cool me airly! Coil me curly, warbler dear! May song it flourish (in the underwood), in chorush, long make it flourish (in the Nut, in the Nutsky) till thorush! Secret Hookup.

— Roguenaar Loudbrags, that soddy old samph! How high is vuile, var?

To which yes he did, capt, that was the answer.

— And his shartshort trooping its colours! We knows his ventruquulence.

Which that that rang ripprippripplying.

—Bulbul, bulbulone! I will shally. Thou shalt willy. You wouldnt should as youd remesmer. I hypnot. 'Tis golden sickle's hour. Holy moon priestess, we'd love our grappes of mistellose! Moths the matter? Pschtt! Tabarins comes. To fell our fairest. O gui, O gui! Salam, salms, salaum! Carolus! O indeed and we ware! And hoody crow was ere. I soared from the peach and Missmolly showed her pear too, onto three and away. Whet the bee as to deflowret greendy grassies yellowhorse. Kematitis, cele our er-dours! Did you aye, did you eye, did you everysee suchaway, suchawhy, eeriewhigg airywhugger? Even to the extremity of the world? Dingoldell! The enormanous his, our littlest little! Wee wee, that long alancey one! Let sit on this anthill for our frilldress talk after this day of making blithe inveiled the heart before our groatsupper serves to us Panchomaster and let harleqwind play peeptomine up all our colombinations! Wins won is nought, twigs too is nil, tricks trees makes nix, fairs fears stoops at nothing. And till Arthur comes againus and sen peatrick's he's reformed we'll pose him together a piece, a pace. Shares in guineases! There's lovely the sight! Surey me, man weepful! Big Seat, you did hear? And teach him twisters in tongue irish. Pat lad may goh too. Quicken, aspen; ash and yew; willow, broom with oak for you. And move your tellabout. Not nice is that, limpet lady! Spose we try it promissly. Love all. Naytellmeknot tennis! Taunt me treattening! But do now say to Mr Eustache! Ingean mingen has to hear. Whose joint is out of jealousy now? Why, heavilybody's evillyboldy's. Hopping Gracius, onthy ovful! O belessk mie, what a nerve! How a mans in his armor we nurses know. Wingwong welly, pitty pretty Nelly! Some Poddy pitted in, will anny petty pullet out? Call Kitty Kelly! Kissykitty Killykelly! What a nossowl buzzard! But what a neats ung gels!

Here all the leaves alift aloft, full o'liefing, fell alaughing over Ombrellone and his parasollieras with their black thronguards from the County Shillelagh. Ignorant invincibles, innocents immutant! Onzel grootvatter Lodewijk is onangonamed before the bridge of primerose and his twy Isas Boldmans is met the blueybells near Dandeliond. We think its a gorsedd shame, these godoms. A lark of limonladies! A lurk of orangetawneymen! You're backleg wounted, budkley mister, bester of the boyne!

And they leaved the most leavely of leaftimes and the most folliagenous till there came the marrer of mirth and the jangtherapper of all jocolarinas and they were as were they never ere. Yet had they laughtered, one on other, undo the end and enjoyed their laughings merry was the times when so grant it High Hilarion us may too!

Cease, prayce, storywalkering around with gestare romanoverum he swinking about is they think and plan unrawil what.

Back to Droughty! The water of the face has flowed.

The all of them, the sowriegueuxers, blottyeyed boys, in that pig's village smoke, a sixdigitarian legion on druid circle, the Clandibblon clam cartel, then pulled out and came off and rally agreed them, roasted malts with toasted burleys, in condomnation of his totomptation and for the duration till his repepulation, upon old nollcromforemost ironsides, as camnabel chieftain, since, as Sammon trowed to explain to summon, seeing that, as he had contracted out of islands empire, he might as coolly have rolled to school call, tarponturboy, a grampurpoise, the manyfathom brinegroom with the fortyinch bride, out of the cuptin klanclord kettle auction like the soldr of a britsh he was bound to be and become till the sea got him whilask, from maker to misses and what he gave was as a pattern, he, that hun of a horde, is a finn as she, his tent wife, is a lap, at home on a steed, abroad by the fire (to say nothing of him having done whatyouknow howyousaw whenyouheard whereyouwot, the kenspeckled souckar, generose as cocke, greediguss with garzelle, uprighter of age and most umbrasive of yews all, under heaviest corpsus exemption) and whoasever spit her in howsoever's fondling saving her keepers that mould the bould she sould to hould the wine that wakes the barley, the peg in his pantry to hold the heavyache off his heart. The droll delight of deemsterhood, a win from the wood to bond. Like the bright lamps, Thamamahalla, yearin out yearin. Auspicably suspectable but in expectancy of respectableness. From dirty flock bedding, drip dropping through the ceiling, with two sisters of charities on the front steps and three evacuan cleansers at the back gaze, single box and pair of chairs (suspectable), occasionally and alternatively used by husband when having writing to do in connection with equitable druids and friendly or other societies through periods of dire want with comparative plenty (thunderburst, ravishment, dissolution and providentiality) to a sofa allbeit of hoarsehaar with Amodicum cloth, hired payono, still playing off, used by the youngsters for czurnying out oldstrums, three bedrooms upastairs, of which one with fireplace (aspectable), with greenhouse in prospect (particularly perspectable).

And you, when you kept at Dulby, were you always (for that

time only) what we knew how when we (from that point solely) were you know where? There you are! And why? Why, hitch a cock eye, he was snapped on the sly upsadaisying coras pearls out of the pie when all the perts in princer street set up their tinker's humn, (the rann, the rann, that keen of old bards), with them newnesboys pearcin screaming off their armsworths. The boss made dovesandraves out of his bucknesst while herself wears the bowler's hat in her bath. Deductive Almayne Rogers disguides his voice, shetters behind hoax chestnote from exexive. Heat wives rasing. They jest keeps rosing. He jumps leaps rizing. Howlong!

You known that tom? I certainly know. Is their bann bothstiesed? Saddenly now. Has they bane reneemed? Soothinly low. Does they ought to buy the papelboy when he footles up their suit? He's their mark to foil the flouter and they certainty owe.

He sprit in his phiz (baccon!). He salt to their bis (pudden!). He toockled her palam (so calam is solom!). And he suked their friends' leave (bonnick lass, fair weal!)

— Guilty but fellows culpows! It was felt by me sindeade, that submerged doughdoughty doubleface told waterside labourers. But since we for athome's health have chanced all that, the wild whips, the wind ships, the wonderlost for world hips, unto their foursquare trust prayed in aid its plumptylump piteousness which, when it turtled around seeking a thud of surf, spake to approach from inherdoff trisspass through minxmingled hair. Though I may have hawked it, said, and selled my how hot peas after theactrisscalls from my imprecurious position and though achance I could have emptied a pan of backslop down drain by whiles of dodging a rere from the middenprivet appurtenant thereof, salving the presents of the board of wumps and pumps, I am ever incalpable, where release of prisonals properly is concerned, of unlifting upfallen girls wherein dangered from them in thereopen out of unadulteratous bowery, with those hintering influences from an angelsexonism. It was merely my barely till their oh offs. Missaunderstaid. Meggy Guggy's giggag. The code's proof! The rebald danger with they who would bare whiteness against me I dismissem from the mind of good. He can tell such as story to the Twelfth Maligns that my first was a nurssmaid and her fellower's a willbe perambulatrix. There are twingty to twangty too thews and leathermail coatschemes penparing to hostpost for it valinnteerily with my valued fofavour to the post puzzles deparkment with larch parchels' of presents for future branch offercings. The green approve the raid! Shaum Baum's bode he is amustering in the groves while his shool comes merging along! Want I put myself in their kirtlies I were ayearn to leap with them and show me too bisextine. Dear and lest I forget mergers and bow to you low, marchers! Attemption! What a mazing month of budsome misses they are making, so wingtywish to flit beflore their kin! Attonsure! Ears to hears! The skall of a gall (for every dime he yawpens that momouth you could park your ford in it) who has papertreated him into captivities with his inside man by a hocksheat of starvision for an avragetopeace of parchment, cooking up his lenses to be my apoclogypst, the recreuter of conscraptions, let him be asservent to Kinahaun! For (peace peace perfectpeace!) I have abwaited me in a water of Elin and I have placed my reeds intectis before the Registower of the perception of tribute in the hall of the city of Analbe. How concerns any merryaunt and hworsoever gravesobbers it is perensempry sex of fun to help a dazzle off the othour. What for Mucias and Gracias may the duvlin rape the handsomst! And the whole mad knightmayers' nest! Tunpother, prison and plotch! If Y shoulden somewhat, well, I am able to owe it, hearth and chemney easy. They seeker for vannflaum all worldins merkins. I'll eager make lyst turpidump undher arkens. Basast! And if my litigimate was well to wrenn tigtag cackling about it, like the sally berd she is, to abery ham in the Cutey Strict, (I shall call upon my first among my lost of lyrars beyond a jingoobangoist, to overcast her) dismissing mundamanu all the riflings of her victuum gleaner (my old chuck! she drakes me druck! turning out, gay at ninety!) and well shoving off a boastonmess like lots wives does over her handpicked hunsbend, as she would be calling, well, for further oil mircles upon all herwayferer gods and reanouncing my deviltries as was I a locally person of caves until I got my purchase on her firmforhold I am, I like to think, by their sacreligion of daimond cap daimond, confessedly in my baron gentilhomme to the manhor bourne till ladiest day as panthoposopher, to have splet for groont a peer of bellows like Bacchulus shakes a rousing guttural at any old cerpaintime by peaching (allsole we are not amusical) the warry warst against myself in the defile as a lieberretter sebaiscopal of these mispeschyites of the first virginial water who, without an auction of biasement from my part, with gladyst tone ahquickyessed in it, overhowe and underwhere, the totty lolly poppy flossy conny dollymaukins. Though I heave a coald on my bauck and am could up to my eres hoven sametimes I used alltides to be aswarmer for the meekst and the graced. You are not going to not. You might be threeabreasted wholenosing at a whallhoarding from our Don Amir anent villayets prostatution precisingly kuschkars tarafs and it could be double densed uncounthest hour of allbleakest age with a bad of wind and a barran of rain, nompos mentis like Novus Elector, what with his Marx and their Groups, yet did a doubt, should a dare, were to you, you would do and dhamnk me, shenker, dhumnk you. Skunk. And fare with me to share with me. Hinther and thonther, hant by hont. By where dauvening shedders down whose rovely lanes. As yose were and as yese is. Sure and you would, Mr Mac Gurk! Be sure and you would, Mr O'Duane! To be sure and you would so, Mr MacElligut! Wod you nods? Mom mom. No mum has the rod to pud a stub to the lurch of amotion. My little love apprencisses, my dears, the estelles, van Nessies von Nixies voon der pool, which I had a reyal devouts for yet was it marly lowease or just a feel with these which olderman K.K. Alwayswelly he is showing ot the fullnights for my palmspread was gav to a parsleysprig, the curliest weedeen old ocean coils around, so spruce a spice for salthorse, sonnies, and as tear to the thrusty as Taylor's Spring, when aftabournes, when she was look like a little cheayat chilled (Oh sard! ah Mah!) by my tide impracing, as Beacher seath, and all the colories fair fled from my folced cheeks!

Popottes, where you canceal me you mayst forced guage my bribes. Wickedgapers, I appeal against the light! A nexistence of vividence! Panto, boys, is on a looser inloss; ballet, girls, suppline thrown tights. I have wanted to thank you such a long time so much now. Thank you. Sir, kindest of bottleholders and very dear friend, among our hearts of steel, froutiknow, it will befor you, me dare beautiful young soldier, winninger nor anyour of rudimental moskats, before you go to mats, you who have watched your share with your sockboule sodalists on your buntad nogs at our love tennis squats regatts, suckpump, when on with the balls did disserve the fain, my goldrush gainst her silvernetss, to say, biguidd, for the love of goddess and perthanow as you reveres your one mothers, mitsch for matsch, and while I reveal thus my deepseep daughter which was bourne up pridely out of medsdreams unclouthed when I was pillowing in my brime (of Saturnay Eve, how now, woren't we't?), to see, I say, whoahoa, in stay of execution *in re* Milcho Melekmans, increaminated, what you feel, oddrabbit, upon every strong ground you have ever taken up, by bitterstiff work or battonstaff play, with assault of turk against a barrakraval of grakeshoots, e'en tho' Jambuwel's defecalties is Terry Shimmyrag's upperturnity, if that is grace for the grass what is balm for the bramblers, as it is as it is, that I am the catasthmatic old ruffin sippahsedly improctor to be seducint trovatellas, the dire daffy damedeaconesses, like (why sighs the sootheesinger) the lilliths oft I feldt, and, when booboob brutals and cautiouses only aims at the oggog hogs in the humand, then, (Houtes, Blymey and Torrenation, upkurts and scotchem!) I'll tall tale tell croon paysecurers, sowill nuggets and nippers, that thash on me stumpen blows the gaff off mombition and thit thides or marse makes a good dayle to be shattat. Fall stuff.

His rote in ere, afstef, was.

And dong wonged Magongty till the bombtomb of the warr, thrusshed in his whole soort of cloose.

Whisht who wooed in Weald, bays of Bawshaw binding. The desire of Miriam is the despair of Marian as Joh Joseph's beauty is Jacq Jacob's grief. Brow, tell nun; eye, feign sad; mouth, sing mim. Look at Lokman! Whatbetween the cupgirls and the platterboys. And he grew back into his grossery baseness: and for all his grand remonstrance: and there you are.

Here endeth chinchinatibus with have speak finish. With a haygue for a halt on a pouncefoot panse. Pink, pleas pink, two pleas pink, how to pleas pink.

Punk.

Mask one. Mask two. Mask three. Mask four.

Up.

— Look about you, Tutty Comyn!

— Remember and recall, Kullykeg!

— When visiting Dan Leary try the corner house for thee.

— I'll gie ye credit for simmence more if ye'll be lymphing.

Our four avunculusts.

And, since threestory sorratelling was much too many, they maddened and they morgued and they lungd and they jowld. Synopticked on the word.

Till the Juke done it.

Down.

Like Jukoleon, the seagoer, when he bore down in·his perry boat he had raised a slide and shipped his orders and seized his pullets and primed their plumages, the fionnling and dubhlet, the dun and the fire, and, sending them one by other to fare fore forn, he had behold the residuance of a delugion: the foggy doze still going strong, the old thalassocrats of invinsible empores, maskers of the waterworld, facing one way to another way and this way on that way, from severalled their fourdimmansions. Where the lighning leaps from the numbulous; where coold by cawld breide lieth langwid; the bounds whereinbourne our solied bodies all attomed attaim arrest: appoint, that's all. But see what follows. Wringlings upon wronglings among incomputables about an uncomeoutable (an angel prophetethis? kingcorrier of beheasts? the calif in his halifskin? that eyriewinging one?) and the voids bubbily vode's dodos across the which the boomomouths from their dupest dupes were in envery and anononously blowing great.

367

Guns.

Keep backwards, please, because there was no good to gundy running up again. Guns. And it was written up in big capital. Guns. Saying never underrupt greatgrandgosterfosters! Guns. And whatever one did they said, the fourlings, that on no acounts you were not to. Guns.

Not to pad them behaunt in the fear. Not to go, tonnerwatter, and bungley well chute the rising gianerant. Not to wandly be woking around jerumsalemdo at small hours about the murketplots, smelling okey boney, this little figgy and arraky belloky this little pink into porker but, porkodirto, to let the gentlemen pedestarolies out of the Monabella culculpuration live his own left leave, cullebuone, by perperusual of the petpubblicities without inwoking his also's between (*sic*) the arraky bone and (*suc*) the okey bellock. And not to not be always, hemmer and hummer, treeing unselves up with one exite but not to never be caving nicely, precisely, quicely, rebustly, tendrolly, unremarkably, forsakenly, haltedly, reputedly, firstly, somewhatly, yesayenolly about the back excits. Never to weaken up in place of the broths. Never to vvollusslleepp in the pleece of the poots. And, allerthings, never to ate the sour deans if they weren't having anysin on their consients. And, when in Zumschloss, to never, narks, cease till the finely ending was consummated by the completion of accomplishment.

And thus within the tavern's secret booth The wisehight ones who sip the tested sooth Bestir them as the Just has bid to jab The punch of quaram on the mug of truth.

K.C. jowls, they're sodden in the secret. K.C. jowls, they sure are wise. K.C. jowls, the justicestjobbers, for they'll find another faller if their ruse won't rise. Whooley the Whooper.

There is to see. Squarish large face with the atlas jacket. Brights, brownie eyes in bluesackin shoeings. Peaky booky nose over a lousiany shirt. Ruddy stackle hair besides a strawcamel belt. Namely. Gregorovitch, Leonocopolos, Tarpinacci and Duggelduggel. And was theys stare all atime? Yea but they was. Andoring the games, induring the studies, undaring the stories, end all. Ned? Only snugged then and cosied after one percepted nought

368

while tuffbettle outraged the waywords and meansigns of their hinterhand suppliesdemands. And be they gone to splane splication? That host that hast one on the hoose when backturns when he facefronts none none in the house his geust has guest. You bet they is. And nose well down.

With however what sublation of compensation in the radification of interpretation by the byeboys? Being they. Mr G. B. W. Ashburner, S. Bruno's Toboggan Drive, Mr Faixgood, Bellchimbers, Carolan Crescent, Mr I. I. Chattaway, Hilly Gape, Poplar Park, Mr Q. P. Dieudonney, The View, Gazey Peer, Mr T. T. Erchdeakin, Multiple Lodge, Jiff Exby Rode, Mr W. K. Ferris-Fender, Fert Fort, Woovil Doon Botham ontowhom adding the tout that pumped the stout that linked the lank that cold the sandy that nextdoored the rotter that rooked the rhymer that lapped at the hoose that Joax pilled.

They had heard or had heard said or had heard said written.

Fidelisat.

That there first a rudrik kingcomed to an inn court; and the seight of that yard was a perchypole with a loovahgloovah on it; last mannarks maketh man when wandshift winneth womans: so how would it hum, whoson of a which, if someof aswas to start to stunt the story on?

So many needles to ponk out to as many noodles as are company, they noddling all about it *tutti* to *tempo*, decumans numbered too, (*a*) well, that the secretary bird, better known as Pandoria Paullabucca, whom they thought was more like a solicitor general, indiscriminatingly made belief mid authorsagastions from Schelm the Pelman to write somewords to Senders about her chilikin puck, laughing that Poulebec would be the death of her, (*b*) that, well, that Madges Tighe, the postulate auditressee, when her daremood's a grownian, is always on the who goes where, hoping to Michal for the latter to turn up with a cupital tea before her ephumeral comes off without any much father which is parting parcel of the same goumeral's postoppage, it being lookwhyse on the whence blows weather helping mickle so that the loiter end of that leader may twaddle out after a cubital lull with a hopes soon to ear, comprong? (c) becakes the goatsman on question, or whatever the hen the bumbler was, feeling not up to scratch bekicks of whatever the kiddings Payne Inge and Popper meant for him, thoughy onced at a throughlove, true grievingfrue danger, as a nirshe persent to his minstress, devourced the pair of them Mather Caray's chucklings, *pante blanche*, and skittered his litters like the cavaliery man in Cobra Park for ungeborn yenkelmen, Jeremy Trouvas or Kepin O'Keepers, any old howe and any old then and when around Dix Dearthy Dungbin, remarking scenically with laddylike lassitude upon what he finally postscrapped, (d) after it's so long till I thanked you about I do so much now thank you so very much as you introduced me to fourks, (e) will, these remind to be sane? (f) Fool step! Aletheometry? Or just zoot doon floon?

Nut it out, peeby eye! Onamassofmancynaves.

But. Top.

You were in the same boat of yourselves too, Getobodoff or Treamplasurin; and you receptionated the most diliskious of milisk; which it all flowowered your drooplin dunlearies: but dribble a drob went down your rothole. Meaning, Kelly, Grimes, Phelan, Mollanny, O'Brien, MacAlister, Sealy, Coyle, Hynes-Joynes, Naylar-Traynor, Courcy de Courcy and Gilligan-Goll.

Stunner of oddstodds on bluebleeding boarhorse! What soresen's head subrises thus tous out of rumpumplikun oak with, well, we cannot say whom we are looking like through his now-face? It is of Noggens whilk dusts the bothsides of the seats of the bigslaps of the bogchaps of the porlarbaar of the marringaar of the Lochlunn gonlannludder of the feof of the foef of forfummed Ship-le-Zoyd.

Boumce! It is polisignstunter. The Sockerson boy. To pump the fire of the lewd into those soulths of bauchees, havsousedovers, tillfellthey deadwar knootvindict. An whele time he was rancing there smutsy floskons nodunder ycholerd for their poopishers, ahull onem Fyre maynoother endnow! Shatten up ship! Bouououmce! Nomo clandoilskins cheakinlevers! All ashored for Capolic Gizzards! Stowlaway there, glutany of stainks! Porterfillyers and spirituous suncksters, oooom oooom!

As these vitupetards in his boasum he did strongleholder, bushbrows, nobblynape, swinglyswanglers, sunkentrunk, that from tin of this clucken hadded runced slapottleslup. For him had hord from fard a piping. As? Of?

Dour douchy was a sieguldson. He cooed that loud nor he was young. He cud bad caw nor he was gray Like wather parted from the say.

Ostia, lift it! Lift at it, Ostia! From the say! Away from the say! Himhim. Himhim.

Hearhasting he, himmed, reromembered all the chubbs, chipps, chaffs, chuckinpucks and chayney chimebells That he had mistributed in port, pub, park, pantry and poultryhouse, While they, thered, the others, that are, were most emulously concerned to cupturing the last dropes of summour down through their grooves of blarneying. Ere the sockson locked at the dure. Which he would, shuttinshure. And lave them to sture.

For be all rules of sport 'tis right That youth bedower'd to charm the night Whilst age is dumped to mind the day When wather parted from the say.

The humming, it's coming. Insway onsway.

Fingool MacKishgmard Obesume Burgearse Benefice, He was bowen hem and scrapin him in recolcitrantament to the right-about And these probenopubblicoes clamatising for an extinsion on his hostillery With his chargehand bombing their eres. Tids, genmen, plays, she been goin shoother off almaynoother on-awares.

You here nort farwellens rouster? Ashiffle ashuffle the wayve they.

From Dancingtree till Suttonstone There's lads no lie would filch a crown To mull their sack and brew their tay With wather parted from the say.

Lelong Awaindhoo's a selverbourne enrouted to Rochelle Lane and liberties those Mullinguard minstrelsers are marshalsing, par tunepiped road, under where, perked on hollowy hill, that poor man of Lyones, good Dook Weltington, hugon come errindwards, had hircomed to the belles bows and been cutat-trapped by the mausers. Now is it town again, londmear of Dublin! And off coursse the toller, ples the dotter of his eyes with her: Moke the Wanst, whye doe we aime alike a pose of poeter peaced? While the dumb he shoots the shopper rope. And they all pour forth. Sans butly Tuppeter Sowyer, the rouged engenerand, a barttler of the beauyne, still our benjamin liefest, sometime frankling to thise citye, whereas bigrented him a piers half subporters for his arms, Josiah Pipkin, Amos Love, Raoul Le Febber, Blaize Taboutot, Jeremy Yopp, Francist de Loomis, Hardy Smith and Sequin Pettit followed by the snug saloon seanad of our Café Béranger. The scenictutors.

Because they wonted to get out by the goatweigh afore the sheep was looset for to wish the Wobbleton Whiteleg Welshers kaillykailly kellykekkle and savebeck to Brownhazelwood from all the dinnasdoolins on the labious banks of their swensewn snewwesner, turned again weastinghome, by Danesbury Common, and they onely, duoly, thruely, fairly after rainydraining fountybuckets (chalkem up, hemptyempty!) till they caught the wind abroad (alley loafers passinggeering!) all the rockers on the roads and all the boots in the stretes.

Oh dere! Ah hoy!

Last ye, lundsmin, hasty hosty! For an anondation of mirification and the lutification of our paludination.

His bludgeon's bruk, his drum is tore. For spuds we'll keep the hat he wore And roll in clover on his clay By wather parted from the say.

Hray! Free rogue Mountone till Dew Mild Well to corry awen and glowry! Are now met by Brownaboy Fuinnninuinn's former for a lyncheon partyng of his burgherbooh. The Shanavan Wacht. Rantinroarin Batteries Dorans. And that whistling thief, O' Ryne O'Rann. With a catch of her cunning like and nowhere a keener.

The for eolders were aspolootly at their wetsend in the mailing waters, trying to. Hide! Seek! Hide! Seek! Because number one lived at Bothersby North and he was trying to. Hide! Seek! Hide!

Seek! And number two digged up Poors Coort, Soother, trying to. Hide! Seek! Hide! Seek! And nomber three he sleeped with Lilly Tekkles at The Eats and he was trying to. Hide! Seek! Hide! Seek! And the last with the sailalloyd donggie he was berthed on the Moherboher to the Washte and they were all trying to and baffling with the walters of, hoompsydoompsy walters of. High! Sink! High! Sink! Highohigh! Sinkasink!

Waves.

The gangstairs strain and anger's up As Hoisty rares the can and cup To speed the bogre's barque away O'er wather parted from the say.

Horkus chiefest ebblynuncies!

— He shook be ashaped of hempshelves, hiding that shepe in his goat. And for rassembling so bearfellsed the magreedy prince of Roger. Thuthud. Heigh hohse, heigh hohse, our kindom from an orse! Bruni Lanno's woollies on Brani Lonni's hairyparts. And the hunk in his trunk it would be an insalt foul the matter of that cellaring to a pigstrough. Stop his laysense. Ink him! You would think him Alddaublin staking his lordsure like a gourd on puncheon. Deblinity devined. Wholehunting the pairk on a methylogical mission whenever theres imberillas! And calling Rina Roner Reinette Ronayne. To what mine answer is a lemans. Arderleys, beedles and postbillers heard him. Three points to one. Ericus Vericus corrupted into ware eggs. Dummy up, distillery! Broree aboo! Run him a johnsgate down jameseslane. Begetting a wife which begame his niece by pouring her youngthings into skintighs. That was when he had dizzy spells. Till Gladstools Pilloots made him ride as the mall. Thanks to his huedobrass beerd. Lodenbroke the Longman, now he canseels under veerious persons but is always that Rorke relly! On consideration for the musickers he ought to have down it. Pass out your cheeks, why daunt you! Penalty, please! There you'll know how warder barded the bollhead that parssed our alley. We just are upsidedown singing what ever the dimkims mummur allalilty she pulls inner out heads. This is not the end of this by no manners means. When you've bled till you're bone it crops out

373

in your flesh. To tell how your mead of, mard, is made of. All old Dadgerson's dodges one conning one's copying and that's what wonderland's wanderlad'll flaunt to the fair. A trancedone boyscript with tittivits by. Ahem. You'll read it tomorrow, marn, when the curds on the table. A nigg for a nogg and a thrate for a throte. The auditor learns. Still pumping on Torkenwhite Radlumps, Lencs. In preplays to Anonymay's left hinted palinode obviously inspiterebbed by a sibspecious connexion. Note the notes of admiration! See the signs of suspicion! Count the hemisemidemicolons! Screamer caps and invented gommas, quoites puntlost, forced to farce! The pipette will say anything at all for a change. And you know what aglove means in the Murdrus dueluct! Fewer to feud and rompant culotticism, a fugle for the gleemen and save, sit and sew. And a pants outsizinned on the Doughertys' duckboard pointing to peace at home. In some, lawanorder on lovinardor. Wait till we hear the Boy of Biskop reeling around your postoral lector! Epistlemadethemology for deep dorfy doubtlings. As we'll lay till break of day in the bunk of basky, O! Our island, Rome and duty! Well tried, buckstiff! Batt in, boot! Sell him a breach contact, the vendoror, the buylawyer! One hyde, sack, hic! Two stick holst, Lucky! Finnish Make Goal! First you were Nomad, next you were Namar, now you're Numah and it's soon you'll be Nomon. Hence counsels Ecclesiast. There's every resumption. The forgein offils is on the shove to lay you out dossier. Darby's in the yard, planning it on you, plot and edgings, the whispering peeler after cooks wearing an illformation. The find of his kind! An artist, sir! And dirt cheap at a sovereign a skull! He knows his Finsbury Follies backwoods so you batter see to your regent refutation. Ascare winde is rifing again about nice boys going native. You know who was wrote about in the Orange Book of Estchapel? Basil and the two other men from King's Avenance. Just press this cold brand against your brow for a mow. Cainfully! The sinus the curse. That's it. Hung Chung Egglyfella now speak he tell numptywumpty topsawys belongahim pidgin. Secret things other persons place there covered not. How you fell from story to story like a sagasand to lie. Enfilmung infirmity. On the because alleging to having a finger a fudding in pudding and pie. And here's the witnesses. Glue on to him, Greevy! Bottom anker, Noordeece! And kick kick killykick for the house that juke built! Wait till they send you to sleep, scowpow! By jurors' cruces! Then old Hunphydunphyville'll be blasted to bumboards by the youthful herald who would once you were. He'd be our chosen one in the matter of Brittas more than anarthur. But we'll wake and see. The wholes poors riches of ours hundreds of manhoods and womhoods. Two cents, two mills and two myrds. And it's all us rangers you'll be facing in the box before the twelfth correctional. Like one man, gell. Between all the Misses Mountsackvilles in their halfmoon haemicycles, gasping to giddies to dye for the shame. Just hold hard till the one we leapt out gets her yearing! Hired in cameras, extra! With His Honour Surpacker on the binge. So yelp your guilt and kitz the buck. You'll have loss of fame from Wimmegame's fake. Forwards! One bully son growing the goff and his twinger read out by the Nazi Priers. You fought as how they'd never woxen up, did you, crucket? It will wecker your earse, that it will! When hives the court to exchequer 'tis the child which gives the sire away. Good for you, Richmond Rover! Scrum around, our side! Let him have another between the spindlers! A grand game! Dalymount's decisive. Don Gouverneur Buckley's in the Tara Tribune, sporting the insides of a Rhutian Jhanaral and little Mrs Ex-Skaerer-Sissers is bribing the halfpricers to pray for her widower in his gravest embazzlement. You on her, hosy jigses, that'll be some nonstop marrimont! You in your stolen mace and anvil, Magnes, and her burrowed in Berkness cirrchus clouthses. Fummuccumul with a graneen aveiled. Playing down the slavey touch. Much as she was when the fancy cutter out collecting milestones espied her aseesaw on a fern. So nimb, he said, a dat of dew. Between Furr-y-Benn and Ferr-y-Bree. In this tear Vikloe vich he lofed. The smiling ever. If you pulls me over pay me, prhyse! A talor would adapt his caulking trudgers on to any shape at see. Address deceitfold of wovens weard. The wonder of the women of the world together, moya! And the lovablest

375

Lima since Ineen MacCormick MacCoort MacConn O'Puckins MacKundred. Only but she is a little width wider got. Be moving abog. You cannot make a limousine lady out of a hillman minx. Listun till you'll hear the Mudquirt accent. This is a bulgen horesies, this is wollan indulgencies, this is a flemsh. Tik. Scapulars, beads and a stump of a candle, Hubert was a Hunter, *chemins de la croixes* and Rosairette's egg, all the trimmings off the tree that she picked up after the Clontarf voterloost when O'Bryan MacBruiser bet Norris Nobnut. Becracking his cucconut between his kknneess. Umpthump, Here Inkeeper, it's the doatereen's wednessmorn! Delphin dringing! Grusham undergang! And the Real Hymernians strenging strong at knocker knocker! Holy and massalltolled. You ought to tak a dos of frut. Jik. Sauss. You're getting hoovier, a twelve stone hoovier, fullends a twelve stone hoovier, in your corpus entis and it scurves you right, demnye! Aunt as unclish ams they make oom. But Nichtia you bound not to loose's gone on Neffin since she clapped her charmer on him at Gormagareen. At the Gunting Munting Hunting Punting. The eitch is in her blood, arrah! For a frecklesome freshcheeky sweetworded lupsqueezer. And he shows how he'll pick him the lock of her fancy. Poghue! Poghue! Poghue! And a good jump, Powell! Clean over all their heads. We could kiss him for that one, couddled we, Huggins? Sparkes is the footer to hance off nancies. Scaldhead, pursue! Before you bunkledoodle down upon your birchentop again after them three blows from time, drink and hurry. The same three that nursed you, Skerry, Badbols and the Grey One. All of your own club too. With the fistful of burryberries were for the massus for to feed you living in dying. Buy bran biscuits and you'll never say dog. And be in the finest of companies. Morialtay and Kniferope Walker and Rowley the Barrel. With Longbow of the lie. Slick of the trick and Blennercassel of the brogue. Clanruckard for ever! The Fenn, the Fenn, the kinn of all Fenns! Deaf to the winds when for Croonacreena. Fisht! And it's not now saying how we are where who's softing what rushes. Merryvirgin forbed! But of they never eat soullfriede they're ating it now. With easter

376

greeding. Angus! Angus! Angus! The keykeeper of the keys of
the seven doors of the dreamadoory in the house of the household of Hecech saysaith. Whitmore, whatmore? Give it over,
give it up! Mawgraw! Head of a helo, chesth of champgnon, eye
of a gull! What you'd if he'd. The groom is in the greenhouse,
gattling out his. Gun! That lad's the style for. Lannigan's ball!
Now a drive on the naval! The Shallburn Shock. Never mind
your gibbous. Slip on your ropen collar and draw the noosebag
on your head. Nobody will know or heed you, Postumus, if you
skip round schlymartin by the back and come front sloomutren
to beg in one of the shavers' sailorsuits. Three climbs three-
quickenthrees in the garb of nine. We'll split to see you mouldem
imparvious. A wing for oldboy Welsey Wandrer! Well spat,
witty wagtail! Now piawn to bishop's forthe! Moove. There's
Mumblesome Wadding Murch cranking up to the hornemooni-
um. Drawg us out *Ivy Eve in the Hall of Alum*! The finnecies of
poetry wed music. Feeling the jitters? You'll be as tight as Trivett
when the knot's knutted on. Now's your never! Peena and
Queena are duetting a giggle-for-giggle and the brideen Alannah is lost in her diamindwaiting. What a magnificent gesture
you will show us this gallus day. Clean and easy, be the hooker!
And a free for croaks after. Dovlen are out for it. So is Rathfinn.
And, hike, here's the hearse and four horses with the interpro-
vincial crucifixioners throwing lots inside to know whose to be
their gosson and whereas to brake the news to morhor. How
our myterbilder his fullen aslip. And who will wager but he'll
Shonny Bhoy be, the fleshlumpfleeter from Poshtapengha and all
he bares sobsconcious inklings shadowed on soulskin. Its segnet
yores, the strake of a hin. Nup. Laying the cloth, to fore of them.
And thanking the fish, in core of them. To pass the grace for
Gard sake! Ahmohn. Mr Justician Matthews and Mr Justician
Marks and Mr Justician Luk de Luc and Mr Justinian Johnston-
Johnson. And the aaskart, see, behind! Help, help, hurray! All-
sup, allsop! Four ghools to nail! Cut it down, mates, look slippy!
They've got a dathe with a swimminpull. Dang! Ding! Dong!
Dung! Dinnin. Isn't it great he is swaying above us for his good

377

and ours. Fly your balloons, dannies and dennises! He's door-knobs dead! And Annie Delap is free! Ones more. We could ate you, par Buccas, and imbabe through you, reassuranced in the wild lac of gotliness. One fledge, one brood till hulm culms evurdyburdy. Huh the throman! Huh the traidor. Huh the truh. Arrorsure, he's the mannork of Arrahland over-sense he horrhorrd his name in thuthunder. Rrrwwwkkkrrr! And seen it rudden up in fusefiressence on the flashmurket. P.R.C.R.L.L. Royloy. Of the rollorrish rattillary. The lewd-ningbluebolteredallucktruckalltraumconductor! The unnamed nonirishblooder that becomes a Greenislender overnight! But we're molting superstituettes out of his fulse thortin guts. Tried mark, Easterlings. Sign, Soideric O'Cunnuc, Rix. Adversed ord, Magtmorken, Kovenhow. There's a great conversion, myn! Cou-cous! Find his causcaus! From Motometusolum through Bulley and Cowlie and Diggerydiggerydock down to bazeness's usual? He's alight there still, by Mike! Loose afore! Bung! Bring forth your deed! Bang! Till is the right time. Bang! Partick Thistle agen S. Megan's versus Brystal Palace agus the Walsall! Putsch! Tiemore moretis tisturb badday! The playgue will be soon over, rats! Let sin! Geh tont! All we wants is to get peace for posses-sion. We dinned unnerstunned why you sassad about thirteen to aloafen, sor, kindly repeat! Or ledn us alones of your lungorge, parsonifier propounde of our edelweissed idol worts! Shaw and Shea are lorning obsen so hurgle up, gandfarder, and gurgle me gurk. You can't impose on frayshouters like os. Every tub here spucks his own fat. Hang coersion everyhow! And smotther-mock Gramm's laws! But we're a drippindhrue gayleague all at ones. In the buginning is the woid, in the muddle is the sound-dance and thereinofter you're in the unbewised again, vund vulsyvolsy. You talker dunsker's brogue men we our souls speech obstruct hostery. Silence in thought! Spreach! Wear anartful of outer nocense! Pawpaw, wowow! Momerry twelfths, noebroed! That was a good one, ha! So it will be quite a material what *May* farther be unvuloped for you, old *Mighty*, when it's aped to foul a delfian in the Mahnung. Ha ha! Talk of Paddy-

378

barke's echo! Kick nuck, Knockcastle! Muck! And you'll nose it,
O you'll nose it, without warnward from we. We don't know the
sendor to whome. But you'll find Chiggenchugger's taking the
Treaclyshortcake with Bugle and the Bitch pairsadrawsing and
Horssmayres Prosession tyghting up under the threes. Stop.
Press stop. To press stop. All to press stop. And be the seem
talkin wharabahts hosetanzies, dat sure is sullibrated word! Bing
bong! Saxolooter, for congesters are salders' prey. Snap it up in
the loose, patchy the blank! Anyone can see you're the son of a
gunnell. Fellow him up too, Carlow! Woes to the worm-
quashed, aye, and wor to the winner! Think of Aerian's Wall and
the Fall of Toss. Give him another for to volleyholleydoodlem!
His lights not all out yet, the liverpooser! Boohoohoo it oose!
With seven hores always in the home of his thinkingthings, his
nodsloddledome of his noiselisslesoughts. Two Idas, two Evas,
two Nessies and Rubyjuby. Phook! No wonder, pipes as kirles,
that he sthings like a rheinbok. One bed night he had the dely-
siums that they were all queens mobbing him. Fell stiff. Oh,
ho, ho, ho, ah, he, he! Abedicate yourself. It just gegs our goad.
He'll be the deaf of us, pappappoppopcuddle, samblind daiy-
rudder. Yus, sord, fathe, you woll, putty our wraughther!
What we waits be after? Whyfore we come agooding? None of
you, cock icy! You keep that henayearn and her fortycantle glim
lookbehinder. We might do with rubiny leeses. But of all your
wanings send us out your peppydecked ales and you'll not be
such a bad lot. The rye is well for whose amind but the wheateny
one is proper lovely. B E N K! We sincerestly trust that Missus
with the kiddies of sweet Gorteen has not B I N K to their very
least tittles deranged if in B U N K and we greesiously augur for
your Meggers a B E N K B A N K B O N K to sloop in with
all sorts of adceterus and adsaturas. It's our last fight, Megantic,
fear you will! The refergee's took to hailing to time the pass.
There goes the blackwatchwomen, all in white, flaxed up, pur-
gad! Right toe, Armitage! Tem for Tam at Timmotty Hall!
We're been carried away. Beyond bournes and bowers. So we'll
leave it to Keyhoe, Danelly and Pykemhyme, the three muskrat-

eers, at the end of this age that had it from Variants' Katey Sherratt that had it from Variants' Katey Sherratt's man for the bonnefacies of Blashwhite and Blushred of the Aquasancta Liffey Patrol to wind up and to tells of all befells after that to Mocked Majesty in the Malincurred Mansion.

So you were saying, boys? Anyhow he what?

So anyhow, melumps and mumpos of the hoose uncommons, after that to wind up that longtobechronickled gettogether thanksbetogiving day at Glenfinnisk-en-la-Valle, the anniversary of his finst homy commulion, after that same barbecue beanfeast was all over poor old hospitable corn and eggfactor, King Roderick O'Conor, the paramount chief polemarch and last preelectric king of Ireland, who was anything you say yourself between fiftyodd and fiftyeven years of age at the time after the socalled last supper he greatly gave in his umbrageous house of the hundred bottles with the radio beamer tower and its hangars, chimbneys and equilines or, at least, he was'nt actually the then last king of all Ireland for the time being for the jolly good reason that he was still such as he was the eminent king of all Ireland himself after the last preeminent king of all Ireland, the whilom joky old top that went before him in the Taharan dynasty, King Arth Mockmorrow Koughenough of the leathered leggions, now of parts unknown, (God guard his generous comicsongbook soul!) that put a poached fowl in the poor man's pot before he took to his pallyass with the weeping eczema for better and worse until he went under the grass quilt on us, nevertheless, the year the sugar was scarce, and we to lather and shave and frizzle him, like a bald surging buoy and himself down to three cows that was meat and drink and dogs and washing to him, 'tis good cause we have to remember it, going through summersultryngs of snow and sleet witht the widow Nolan's goats and the Brownes girls neats anyhow, wait till I tell you, what did he do, poor old Roderick O'Conor Rex, the auspicious waterproof monarch of all Ireland, when he found himself all alone by himself in his grand old handwedown pile after all of them had all gone off with themselves to their castles of mud, as best they cud, on footback, owing to the leak of the McCarthy's mare, in extended order, a tree's length from the longest way out, down the switchbackward slidder of the landsown route of Hauburnea's liveliest vinnage on the brain, the unimportant Parthalonians with the mouldy Firbolgs and the Tuatha de Danaan googs and the ramblers from Clane and all the rest of the notmuchers that he did not care the royal spit out of his ostensible mouth about, well, what do you think he did, sir, but, faix, he just went heeltapping through the winespilth and weevily popcorks that were kneedeep round his own right royal round rollicking toper's table, with his old Roderick Random pullon hat at a Lanty Leary cant on him and Mike Brady's shirt and Greene's linnet collarbow and his Ghenter's gaunts and his Macclefield's swash and his readymade Reillys and his panprestuberian poncho, the body you'd pity him, the way the world is, poor he, the heart of Midleinster and the supereminent lord of them all, overwhelmed as he was with black ruin like a sponge out of water, allocutioning in bellcantos to his own oliverian society MacGuiney's *Dreans of Ergen Adams* and thruming through all to himself with diversed tonguesed through his old tears and his ould plaised drawl, starkened by the most regal of belches, like a blurney Cashelmagh crooner that lerking Clare air, the blackberd's ballad *I've a terrible errible lot todue todie todue tootorribleday*, well, what did he go and do at all, His Most Exuberant Majesty King Roderick O'Conor but, arrah bedamnbut, he finalised by lowering his woolly throat with the wonderful midnight thirst was on him, as keen as mustard, he could not tell what he did ale, that bothered he was from head to tail, and, wishawishawish, leave it, what the Irish, boys, can do, if he did'nt go, sliggymaglooral reemyround and suck up, sure enough, like a Trojan, in some particular cases with the assistance of his venerated tongue, whatever surplus rotgut, sorra much, was left by the lazy lousers of maltknights and beerchurls in the different bottoms of the various different replenquished drinking utensils left there behind them on the premises by that whole hogsheaded firkin family, the departed honourable homegoers and other sly-

grogging suburbanites, such as it was, fall and fall about, to the
brindishing of his charmed life, as toastified by his cheeriubi-
cundenances,no matter whether it was chateaubottled Guiness's
or Phoenix brewery stout it was or John Jameson and Sons or
Roob Coccola or, for the matter of that, O'Connell's famous old
Dublin ale that he wanted like hell, more that halibut oil or
jesuits tea, as a fall back, of several different quantities and qualities amounting in all to, I should say, considerably more than the
better part of a gill or naggin of imperial dry and liquid measure
till, welcome be from us here, till the rising of the morn, till that
hen of Kaven's shows her beaconegg, and Chapwellswendows
stain our horyhistoricold and Father MacMichael stamps for
aitch o'clerk mess and the Litvian Newestlatter is seen, sold and
delivered and all's set for restart after the silence, like his ancestors
to this day after him (that the blazings of their ouldmouldy gods
may attend to them we pray!), overopposides the cowery lad in
the corner and forenenst the staregaze of the cathering candled,
that adornment of his album and folkenfather of familyans, he
came acrash a crupper sort of a sate on accomondation and the
very boxst in all his composs, whereuponce, behome the fore
for cove and trawlers, heave hone, leave lone, Larry's on the
focse and Faugh MacHugh O'Bawlar at the wheel, one to do and
one to dare, par by par, a peerless pair, ever here and over there,
with his fol the dee oll the doo on the flure of his feats and the
feels of the fumes in the wakes of his ears our wineman from
Barleyhome he just slumped to throne.

So sailed the stout ship *Nansy Hans*. From Liff away. For
Nattenlaender. As who has come returns. Farvel, farerne! Good-
bark, goodbye!

Now follow we out by Starloe!

— Three quarks for Muster Mark!
Sure he hasn't got much of a bark
And sure any he has it's all beside the mark.
But O, Wreneagle Almighty, wouldn't un be a sky of a lark
To see that old buzzard whooping about for uns shirt in the dark
And he hunting round for uns speckled trousers around by Palmer-
*   stown Park?*
Hohohoho, moulty Mark!
You're the rummest old rooster ever flopped out of a Noah's ark
And you think you're cock of the wark.
Fowls, up! Tristy's the spry young spark
That'll tread her and wed her and bed her and red her
Without ever winking the tail of a feather
And that's how that chap's going to make his money and mark!

Overhoved, shrillgleescreaming. That song sang seaswans.
The winging ones. Seahawk, seagull, curlew and plover, kestrel
and capercallzie. All the birds of the sea they trolled out rightbold
when they smacked the big kuss of Trustan with Usolde.

And there they were too, when it was dark, whilest the wild-
caps was circling, as slow their ship, the winds aslight, upborne
the fates, the wardorse moved, by courtesy of Mr Deaubaleau
Downbellow Kaempersally, listening in, as hard as they could, in
Dubbeldorp, the donker, by the tourneyold of the wattarfalls,
with their vuoxens and they kemin in so hattajocky (only a

quartebuck askull for the last acts) to the solans and the sycamores and the wild geese and the gannets and the migratories and the mistlethrushes and the auspices and all the birds of the rockby-suckerassousyoceanal sea, all four of them, all sighing and sobbing, and listening. Moykle ahoykling!

They were the big four, the four maaster waves of Erin, all listening, four. There was old Matt Gregory and then besides old Matt there was old Marcus Lyons, the four waves, and oftentimes they used to be saying grace together, right enough, bausnabeatha, in Miracle Squeer: here now we are the four of us: old Matt Gregory and old Marcus and old Luke Tarpey: the four of us and sure, thank God, there are no more of us: and, sure now, you wouldn't go and forget and leave out the other fellow and old Johnny MacDougall: the four of us and no more of us and so now pass the fish for Christ sake, Amen: the way they used to be saying their grace before fish, repeating itself, after the interims of Augusburgh for auld lang syne. And so there they were, with their palms in their hands, like the pulchrum's proculs, spraining their ears, luistening and listening to the oceans of kissening, with their eyes glistening, all the four, when he was kiddling and cuddling and bunnyhugging scrumptious his colleen bawn and dinkum belle, an oscar sister, on the fifteen inch loveseat, behind the chieftaness stewardesses cubin, the hero, of Gaelic champion, the onliest one of her choice, her bleaueyedeal of a girl's friend, neither bigugly nor smallnice, meaning pretty much everything to her then, with his sinister dexterity, light and rufthandling, vicemversem her ragbags et assaucyetiams, fore and aft, on and offsides, the brueburnt sexfutter, handson and huntsem, that was palpably wrong and bulbubly improper, and cuddling her and kissing her, tootyfay charmaunt, in her ensemble of maidenna blue, with an overdress of net, tickled with goldies, Isolamisola, and whisping and lisping her about Trisolanisans, how one was whips for one was two and two was lips for one was three, and dissimulating themself, with his poghue like Arrah-na-poghue, the dear dear annual, they all four remembored who made the world and how they used to be at that time in the vulgar ear

384

cuddling and kiddling her, after an oyster supper in Cullen's barn, from under her mistlethrush and kissing and listening, in the good old bygone days of Dion Boucicault, the elder, in Arrah-na-pogue, in the otherworld of the passing of the key of Two-tongue Common, with Nush, the carrier of the word, and with Mesh, the cutter of the reed, in one of the farback, pitchblack centuries when who made the world, when they knew O'Clery, the man on the door, when they were all four collegians on the nod, neer the Nodderlands Nurskery, whiteboys and oakboys, peep of tim boys and piping tom boys, raising hell while the sin was shining, with their slates and satchels, playing Florian's fables and communic suctions and vellicar frictions with mixum members, in the Queen's Ultonian colleges, along with another fellow, a prime number, Totius Quotius, and paying a pot of tributs to Boris O'Brien, the buttler of Clumpthump, two looves, two turnovers plus (one) crown, to see the mad dane ating his vitals. Wulf! Wulf! And throwing his tongue in the snakepit. Ah ho! The ladies have mercias! It brought the dear prehistoric scenes all back again, as fresh as of yore, Matt and Marcus, natural born lovers of nature, in all her moves and senses, and after that now there he was, that mouth of mandibles, vowed to pure beauty, and his Arrah-na-poghue, when she murmurously, after she let a cough, gave her firm order, if he wouldn't please mind, for a sings to one hope a dozen of the best favourite lyrical national blooms in Luvillicit, though not too much, reflecting on the situation, drinking in draughts of purest air serene and revelling in the great outdoors, before the four of them, in the fair fine night, whilst the stars shine bright, by she light of he moon, we longed to be spoon, before her honeyoldloom, the plaint effect being in point of fact there being in the whole, a seatuition so shocking and scandalous and now, thank God, there were no more of them and he poghuing and poghuing like the Moreigner bowed his crusted hoed and Tilly the Tailor's Tugged a Tar in the Arctic Newses Dagsdogs number and there they were, like a foremasters in the rolls, listening, to Rolando's deepen darblun Ossian roll, (Lady, it was just too gorgeous, that expense of a lovely tint, embellished by the charms of art and very well conducted and nicely mannered and all the horrid rudy noisies locked up in nasty cubbyhole!) as tired as they were, the three jolly topers, with their mouths watering, all the four, the old connubial men of the sea, yambing around with their old pantometer, in duckasaloppics, Luke and Johnny MacDougall and all wishening for anything at all of the bygone times, the wald times and the fald times and the hempty times and the dempty times, for a cup of kindness yet, for four farback tumblerfuls of woman squash, with them, all four, listening and spraining their ears for the millennium and all their mouths making water.

Johnny. Ah well, sure, that's the way (up) and it so happened there was poor Matt Gregory (up), their pater familias, and (up) the others and now really and (up) truly they were four dear old heladies and really they looked awfully pretty and so nice and bespectable and after that they had their fathomglasses to find out all the fathoms and their half a tall hat, just now like the old Merquus of Pawerschoof, the old determined despot, (*quiescents in brage!*) only for the extrusion of the saltwater or the auctioneer there dormont, in front of the place near O'Clery's, at the darkumound numbur wan, beside that ancient Dame street, where the statue of Mrs Dana O'Connell, prostituent behind the Trinity College, that arranges all the auctions of the valuable colleges, Bootersbay Sisters, like the auctioneer Battersby Sisters, the prumisceous creaters, that sells all the emancipated statues and flowersports, James H. Tickell, the jaypee, off Hoggin Green, after he made the centuries, going to the tailturn horseshow, before the angler nomads flood, along with another fellow, active impalsive, and the shoeblacks and the redshanks and plebeians and the barrancos and the cappunchers childerun, Jules, everyone, Gotopoxy, with the houghers on them, highstepping the fissure and fracture lines, seven five threes up, three five sevens down, to get out of his way, onasmuck as their withers conditions could not possibly have been improved upon, (praisers be to deeseesee!) like hopolopocattls, erumping oround their Judgity Yaman, and all the tercentenary horses and priest-hunters, from the Curragh, and confusionaries and the authorities, Noord Amrikaans and Suid African cattleraiders (so they say) all over like a tiara dullfuoco, in his grey half a tall hat and his amber necklace and his crimson harness and his leathern jib and his cheapshein hairshirt and his scotobrit sash and his parapilagian gallowglasses (how do you do, jaypee, Elevato!) to find out all the improper colleges (and how do you do, Mr Dame James? Get out of my way!), forkbearded and bluetoothed and bellied and boneless, from Strathlyffe and Aylesburg and Northumberland Anglesey, the whole yaghoodurt sweepstakings and all the horsepowers. But now, talking of hayastdanars and wolkingology and how our seaborn isle came into exestuance, (the explutor, his three andesiters and the two pantellarias) that reminds me about the manausteriums of the poor Marcus of Lyons and poor Johnny, the patrician, and what do you think of the four of us and there they were now, listening right enough, the four saltwater widowers, and all they could remembore, long long ago in the olden times Momonian, throw darker hour sorrows, the princest day, when Fair Margrate waited Swede Villem, and Lally in the rain, with the blank prints, now extincts, after the wreak of Wormans' Noe, the barmaisigheds, when my heart knew no care, and after that then there was the official landing of Lady Jales Casemate, in the year of the flood 1132 S.O.S., and the christening of Queen Baltersby, the Fourth Buzzersbee, according to Her Grace the bishop Senior, off the whate shape, and then there was the drowning of Pharoah and all his pedestrians and they were all completely drowned into the sea, the red sea, and then poor Merkin Cornyngwham, the official out of the castle on pension, when he was completely drowned off Erin Isles, at that time, suir knows, in the red sea and a lovely mourning paper and thank God, as Saman said, there were no more of him. And that now was how it was. The arzurian deeps o'er his humbodumbones sweeps. And his widdy the giddy is wreathing her murmoirs as her gracest triput to the Grocery Trader's Manthly. Mind mand gunfree by Gladeys Rayburn! Runtable's Reincorporated. The new world presses. Where the old conk cruised now croons the yunk. Exeunc throw a darras Kram of Llawnroc, ye gink guy, kirked into yord. Enterest attawonder Wehpen, luftcat revol, fairescapading in his natsirt. Tuesy tumbles. And mild aunt Liza is as loose as her neese. Fulfest withim inbrace behent. As gent would deem oncontinent. So mulct per wenche is Elsker woed. Ne hath his thrysting. Fin. Like the newcasters in their old plyable of *A Royenne Devours*. Jazzaphoney and Mirillovis and Nippy she nets best. Fing. Ay, ay! Sobbos. And so he was. Sabbus.

Marcus. And after that, not forgetting, there was the Flemish armada, all scattered, and all officially drowned, there and then, on a lovely morning, after the universal flood, at about aleven thirty-two was it? off the coast of Cominghome and Saint Patrick, the anabaptist, and Saint Kevin, the lacustrian, with toomuch of tolls and lottance of beggars, after converting Porterscout and Dona, our first marents, and Lapoleon, the equestrian, on his whuite hourse of Hunover, rising Clunkthurf over Cabinhogan and all they rememberod and then there was the Frankish floot of Noahsdobahs, from Hedalgoland, round about the freebutter year of Notre Dame 1132 P.P.O. or so, disumbunking from under Motham General Bonaboche, (noo poopery!) in his half a grey traditional hat, alevoila come alevilla, and after that there he was, so terrestrial, like a Nailscissor, poghuing her scandalous and very wrong, the maid, in single combat, under the sycamores, amid the bludderings from the boom and all the gallowsbirds in Arrahna-Poghue, so silvestrious, neer the Queen's Colleges, in 1132 Brian or Bride street, behind the century man on the door. And then again they used to give the grandest gloriaspanquost universal howldmoutherhibbert lectures on anarxaquy out of doxarchology (hello, Hibernia!) from sea to sea (Matt speaking!) according to the pictures postcard, with sexon grimmacticals, in the Latimer Roman history, of Latimer repeating himself, from the vicerine of Lord Hugh, the Lacytynant, till Bockleyshuts the rahjahn gerachknell and regnumrockery roundup, (Marcus Lyons speaking!) to the oceanfuls of collegians green and high classes and the poor scholars and all the old trinitarian senate and saints and sages and the Plymouth brethren, droning along, peanzanzangan, and nodding and sleeping away there, like forgetmenots, in her abijance service, round their twelve tables, per pioja at pulga bollas, in the four trinity colleges, for earnasyoulearning Eringrowback, of Ulcer, Moonster, Leanstare and Cannought, the four grandest colleges supper the matther of Erryn, of Killorcure and Killthemall and Killeachother and Killkelly-on-the-Flure, where their role was to rule the round roll that Rollo and Rullo rolled round. Those were the grandest gynecollege histories (Lucas calling, hold the line!) in the Janesdanes Lady Andersdaughter Universary, for auld acquaintance sake (this unitarian lady, breathtaking beauty, Bambam's bonniest, lived to a great age at or in or about the late No. 1132 or No. 1169, bis, Fitzmary Round where she was seen by many and widely liked) for teaching the Fatima Woman history of Fatimiliafamilias, repeating herself, on which purposeth of the spirit of nature as difinely developed in time by psadatepholomy, the past and present (Johnny MacDougall speaking, give me trunks, miss!) and present and absent and past and present and perfect *arma virumque romano*. Ah, dearo, dear! O weep for the hower when eve aleaves bower! How it did but all come eddaying back to them, if they did but get gaze, gagagniagnian, to hear him there, kiddling and cuddling her, after the gouty old galahat, with his peer of quinnyfears and his troad of thirstuns, so nefarious, from his elevation of one yard one handard and thartytwo lines, before the four of us, in his Roman Catholic arms, while his deepseepeepers gazed and sazed and dazecrazemazed into her dullokbloon rodolling olosheen eyenbowls by the Cornelius Nepos, Mnepos. Anumque, umque. Napoo.

Queh? Quos?

Ah, dearo dearo dear! Bozun braceth brythe hwen gooses gandered gamen. Mahazar ag Dod! It was so scalding sorry for all the whole twice two four of us, with their familiar, making the toten, and Lally when he lost part of his half a hat and all belongings to him, in his old futile manner, cape, towel and drawbreeches, and repeating himself and telling him now, for the seek of Senders

389

Newslaters and the mossacre of Saint Brices, to forget the past, when the burglar he shoved the wretch in churneroil, and contradicting all about Lally, the ballest master of Gosterstown, and his old fellow, the Lagener, in the Locklane Lighthouse, earing his wick with a pierce of railing, and liggen hig with his ladder up, and that oldtime turner and his sadderday erely cloudsing, the old croniony, Skelly, with the lether belly, full of neltts, full of keltts, full of lightweight beltts and all the bald drakes or ever he had up in the bohereen, off Artsichekes Road, with Moels and Mahmullagh Mullarty, the man in the Oran mosque, and the old folks at home and Duignan and Lapole and the grand confarreation, as per the cabbangers richestore, of the filest archives, and he couldn't stop laughing over Tom Tim Tarpey, the Welshman, and the four middleaged widowers, all nangles, sangles, angles and wangles. And now, that reminds me, not to forget the four of the Welsh waves, leaping laughing, in their Lumbag Walk, over old Battleshore and Deaddleconch, in their half a Roman hat, with an ancient Greek gloss on it, in Chichester College auction and, thank God, they were all summarily divorced, four years before, or so they say, by their dear poor shehusbands, in dear byword days, and never brought to mind, to see no more the rainwater on the floor but still they parted, raining water laughing, per Nupiter Privius, only terpary, on the best of terms and be forgot, whilk was plainly foretolk by their old pilgrim cocklesong or they were singing through the wettest indies *As I was going to Burrymecarott we fell in with a lout by the name of Peebles* as also in another place by their orthodox proverb so there was said thus *That old fellow knows milk though he's not used to it latterly*. And so they parted. In Dalkymont nember to. Ay, ay. The good go and the wicked is left over. As evil flows so Ivel flows. Ay, ay. Ah, well sure, that's the way. As the holymaid of Kunut said to the haryman of Koombe. For his humple pesition in odvices. Woman. Squash. Part. Ay, ay. By decree absolute.

Lucas. And, O so well they could remembore at that time, when Carpery of the Goold Fins was in the kingship of Poolland, Mrs Dowager Justice Squalchman, foorsitter, in her fullbottom wig and beard, (Erminia Reginia!) in or aring or around about the year of buy in disgrace 1132 or 1169 or 1768 Y.W.C.A., at the Married Male Familyman's Auctioneer's court in Arrahnacuddle. Poor Johnny of the clan of the Dougals, the poor Scuitsman, (Hohannes!) nothing if not amorous, dinna forget, so frightened (Zweep! Zweep!) on account of her full bottom, (undullable attraxity!) that put the yearl of mercies on him, and the four maasters, in chors, with a hing behangd them, because he was so slow to borstel her schoon for her, when he was grooming her ladyship, instead of backscratching her materfamilias proper, like any old methodist, and all divorced and innasense interdict, in the middle of the temple, according to their dear faithful. Ah, now, it was too bad, too bad and stout entirely, all the missoccurs; and poor Mark or Marcus Bowandcoat, from the brownesberrow in nolandsland, the poor old chronometer, all persecuted with ally croaker by everybody, by decree absolute, through Herrinsilde, because he forgot himself, making wind and water, and made a Neptune's mess of all of himself, sculling over the giamond's courseway, and because he forgot to remember to sign an old morning proxy paper, a writing in request to hersute herself, on stamped bronnanoleum, from Roneo to Giliette, before saying his grace before fish and then and there and too there was poor Dion Cassius Poosycomb, all drowned too, before the world and her husband, because it was most improper and most wrong, when he attempted to (well, he was shocking poor in his health, he said, with the shingles falling off him), because he (ah, well now, peaces pea to Wedmore and let not the song go dumb upon your Ire, as we say in the Spasms of Davies, and we won't be too hard on him as an old Manx presbyterian) and after that, as red as a Rosse is, he made his last will and went to confession, like the general of the Berkeleyites, at the rim of the rom, on his two bare marrowbones, to Her Worship his Mother and Sister Evangelist Sweainey, on Cailcainnin widnight and he was so sorry, he was really, because he left the bootybutton in the handsome cab and now, tell the truth, unfriends never, (she was his first messes dogess and it was a very pretty peltry and there were faults on both sides) well, he attempted (or so they say) ah, now, forget and forgive (don't we all?) and, sure, he was only funning with his andrewmartins and his old age coming over him, well, he attempted or, the Connachy, he was tempted to attempt some hunnish familiarities, after eten a bad carmp in the rude ocean and, hevantonoze sure, he was dead seasickabed (it was really too bad!) her poor old divorced male, in the housepays for the daying at the Martyr Mrs MacCawley's, where at the time he was taying and toying, to hold the nursetendered hand, (ah, the poor old coax!) and count the buttons and her hand and frown on a bad crab and doying to rememborē what doed they were byorn and who made a who a snore. Ah dearo dearo dear!

And where do you leave Matt Emeritus? The laychief of Abbotabishop? And exchullard of ffrench and gherman. Achoch! They were all so sorgy for poorboir Matt in his saltwater hat, with the Aran crown, or she grew that out of, too big for him, of or Mnepos and his overalls, all falling over her in folds—sure he hadn't the heart in her to pull them up—poor Matt, the old perigrime matriarch, and a queenly man, (the porple blussing upon them!) sitting there, the sole of the settlement, below ground, for an expiatory rite, in postulation of his cause, (who shall say?) in her beaver bonnet, the king of the Caucuses, a family all to himself, under geasa, Themistletocles, on his multilingual tombstone, like Navellicky Kamen, and she due to kid by sweetpea time, with her face to the wall, in view of the poorhouse, and taking his rust in the oxsight of Iren, under all the auspices, amid the rattle of hailstorms, kalospintheochromatokreening, with her ivyclad hood, and gripping an old pair of curling tongs, belonging to Mrs Duna O'Cannell, to blow his brains with, till the heights of Newhigherland heard the Bristolhut, with his can of tea and a purse of alfred cakes from Anne Lynch and two cuts of Shackleton's brown loaf and dilisk, waiting for the end to come. Gordon Heighland, when you think of it! The merthe dirther! Ah ho! It was too bad entirely! All devoured by active parlourmen, laudabiliter, of woman squelch and all on account of the smell of Shakeletin and scratchman and his mouth watering, acid and alkolic; signs on the salt, and so now pass the loaf for Christ sake. Amen. And so. And all.

Matt. And loaf. So that was the end. And it can't be helped. Ah, God be good to us! Poor Andrew Martin Cunningham! Take breath! Ay! Ay!

And still and all at that time of the dynast days of old konning Soteric Sulkinbored and Bargomuster Bart, when they struck coil and shock haunts, in old Hungerford-on-Mudway, where first I met thee oldpoetryck flied from may, and the Finnan haddies and the Noal Sharks and the muckstails turtles like an acoustic pottish and the griesouper bullyum and how he poled him up his boccat of vuotar and got big buzz for his name in the airweek's honours from home, colonies and empire, they were always with assisting grace, thinking (up) and not forgetting about shims and shawls week, in auld land syne (up) their four hosenbands, that were four (up) beautiful sister misters, now happily married, unto old Gallstonebelly, and there they were always counting and contradicting every night 'tis early the lovely mother of periwinkle buttons, according to the lapper part of their anachronism (up one up two up one up four) and after that there now she was, in the end, the deary, soldpowder and all, the beautfour sisters, and that was her mudhen republican name, right enough, from alum and oves, and they used to be getting up from under, in their tape and straw garlands, with all the worries awake in their hair, at the kookaburra bell ringring all wrong inside of them (come in, come on, you lazy loafs!) all inside their poor old Shandon bellbox (come out to hell, you lousy louts!) so frightened, for the dthclangavore, like knockneeghs bumpsed by the fisterman's straights, (ys! ys!), at all hours every night, on their mistletoes, the four old oldsters, to see was the Transton Postscript come, with their oerkussens under their armsaxters, all puddled and mythified, the way the wind wheeled the schooler round, when nobody wouldn't even let them rusten, from playing their gastspiels, crossing their sleep by the shocking silence, when they were in dreams of yore, standing behind the door, or leaning out of the chair, or kneeling under the sofa-cover and setting on the souptureen, getting into their way something barbarous, changing the one wet underdown convibrational bed or they used to slumper under, when hope was there no more, and putting on their half a hat and falling over all synopticals and a panegyric and repeating themselves, like svvollovving, like the time they were dadging the talkeycook that chased them, look look all round the stool, walk everywhere for a jool, to break fyre to all the rancers, to collect all and bits of brown, the rathure's evelopment in spirits of time in all fathom of space and slooping around in a bawneen and bath slippers and go away to Oldpatrick and see a doctor Walker. And after that so glad they had their night tentacles and there they used to be, flapping and cycling, and a dooing a doonloop, panementically, around the waists of the ships, in the wake of their good old Foehn again, as tyred as they were, at their windswidths in the waveslength, the clipperbuilt and the five fourmasters and Lally of the cleftoft bagoderts and Roe of the fair cheats, exchanging fleas from host to host, with arthroposophia, and he selling him before he forgot, issle issle, after having prealably dephlegmatised his gutterful of throatyfrogs, with a lungible fong in his suckmouth ear, while the dear invoked to the coolun dare by a palpabrows lift left no doubt in his minder, till he was instant and he was trustin, sister soul in brother hand, the subjects being their passion grand, that one fresh from the cow about Aithne Meithne married a mailde and that one too from Engrvakon saga abooth a gooth a gev a gotheny egg and the parkside pranks of quality queens, katte efter kinne, for Earl Hoovedsoon's choosing and Huber and Harman orhowwhen theeuponthus (chchch!) eysolt of binnoculises memostinmust egotum sabcunsciously senses upers the deprofundity of multimathematical immaterialities wherebejubers in the pancosmic urge the allimmanence of that which Itself is Itself Alone (hear, O hear, Caller Errin!) exteriorises on this ourherenow plane in disunited solod, likeward and gushious bodies with (science, say!) perilwhitened passionpanting pugnoplangent intuitions of reunited

394

selfdom (murky whey, abstrew adim!) in the higherdimissional selfless Allself, theemeeng Narsty meetheeng Idoless, and telling Jolly MacGolly, dear mester John, the belated dishevelled, hacking away at a parchment pied, and all the other analist, the steamships ant the ladies'foursome, ovenfor, nedenfor, dinkety, duk, downalupping, (how long tandem!) like a foreretyred schoonmasters, and their pair of green eyes and peering in, so they say, like the narcolepts on the lakes of Coma, through the steamy windows, into the honeymoon cabins, on board the big steamadories, made by Fumadory, and the saloon ladies' madorn toilet chambers lined over prawn silk and rub off the salty catara off a windows and, hee hee, listening, *qua* committe, the poor old quakers, oben the dure, to see all the hunnishmooners and the firstclass ladies, serious me, a lass spring as you fancy, and sheets far from the lad, courting in blankets, enfamillias, and, shee shee, all improper, in a lovely mourning toilet, for the rosecrumpler, the thrilldriver, the sighinspirer, with that olive throb in his nude neck, and, swayin and thayin, thanks ever so much for the tiny quote, which sought of maid everythingling again so very much more delightafellay, and the perfidly suite of her, bootyfilly yours, under all their familiarities, by preventing grace, forgetting to say their grace before chambadory, before going to boat with the verges of the chaptel of the opering of the month of Nema Knatut, so pass the poghue for grace sake. Amen. And all, hee hee hee, quaking, so fright, and, shee shee, shaking. Aching. Ay, ay.

For it was then a pretty thing happened of pure diversion mayhap, when his flattering hend, at the justright moment, like perchance some cook of corage might clip the lad on a poot of porage handshut his duckhouse, the vivid girl, deaf with love, (ah sure, you know her, our angel being, one of romance's fadeless wonderwomen, and, sure now, we all know you dote on her even unto date!) with a queeleetlecree of joyis crisis she renulited their disunited, with ripy lepes to ropy lopes (the dear o'dears!) and the golden importunity of aloofer's leavetime, when, as quick, is greased pigskin, Amoricas Champius, with one aragan throust, druve the massive of virilvigtoury flshpst the both lines of forwards (Eburnea's down, boys!) rightjingbangshot into the goal of her gullet.

Alris!

And now, upright and add them! And plays be honest! And pullit into yourself, as on manowoman do another! Candidately, everybody! A mot for amot. Comong, meng, and douh! There was this, wellyoumaycallher, a strapping modern old ancient Irish prisscess, so and so hands high, such and such paddock weight, in her madapolam smock, nothing under her hat but red hair and solid ivory (now you know it's true in your hardup hearts!) and a firstclass pair of bedroom eyes, of most unhomy blue, (how weak we are, one and all!) the charm of favour's fond consent! Could you blame her, we're saying, for one psocoldlogical moment? What would Ewe do? With that so tiresome old milkless a ram, with his tiresome duty peck and his bronchial tubes, the tiresome old hairyg orangogran beaver, in his tiresome old twennysixandsixpenny sheopards plods drowsers and his thirtybobandninepenny tails plus toop! Hagakhroustioun! It were too exceeding really if one woulds to offer at sulk an oldivirdual a pinge of hinge hit. The mainest thing ever! Since Edem was in the boags noavy. No, no, the dear heaven knows, and the farther the from it, if the whole stole stale mis betold, whoever the gulpable, and whatever the pulpous was, the twooned togethered, and giving the mhost phassionable wheathers, they were doing a lally a lolly a dither a duther one lelly two dather three lilly four dother. And it was a fiveful moment for the poor old timetetters, ticktacking, in tenk the count. Till the spark that plugged spared the chokee he gripped and (volatile volupty, how brieved are thy lunguings!) they could and they could hear like of a lisp lapsing, that was her knight of the truths thong plipping out of her chapell-ledeosy, after where he had gone and polped the questioned. Plop.

Ah now, it was tootwoly torrific, the mummurrlubejubes! And then after that they used to be so forgetful, counting mother-peributts (up one up four) to membore her beaufu mouldern maiden name, for overflauwing, by the dream of woman the owneirist, in forty lands. From Greg and Doug on poor Greg and Mat and Mar and Lu and Jo, now happily buried, our four! And there she was right enough, that lovely sight enough, the girleen bawn asthore, as for days galore, of planxty Gregory. Egory. O bunket not Orwin! Ay, ay.

But, sure, that reminds me now, like another tellmastory repeating yourself, how they used to be in lethargy's love, at the end of it all, at that time (up) always, tired and all, after doing the mousework and making it up, over their community singing (up) the top loft of the voicebox, of Mamalujo like the senior follies at murther magrees, squatting round, two by two, the four confederates, with Caxons the Coswarn, up the wet air register in Old Man's House, Millenium Road, crowning themselves in lauraly branches, with their cold knees and their poor (up) quad rupeds, ovasleep, and all dolled up, for their blankets and materny mufflers and plimsoles and their bowl of brown shackle and milky and boterham clots, a potion a peace, a piece aportion, a lepel alip, alup a lap, for a cup of kindest yet, with hold take hand and nurse and only touch of ate, a lovely munkybown and for xmell and wait the pinch and prompt poor Marcus Lyons to be not beheeding the skillet on for the live of ghosses but to pass the teeth for choke sake, Amensch, when it so happen they were all sycamore and by the world forgot, since the phlegmish hoopicough, for all a possabled, after ete a bad cramp and johnny magories, and backscrat the poor bedsores and the farthing dip, their caschal pandle of magnegnousioum, and read a letter or two every night, before going to dodo sleep atrance, with their catkins coifs, in the twilight, a capitaletter, for further auspices, on their old one page codex book of old year's eve 1132, M.M.L.J. old style, their Senchus Mor, by his fellow girl, the Mrs Shemans, in her summer seal houseonsample, with the caracul broadtail, her *totam in tutu*, final buff noonmeal edition, in the regatta covers, uptenable from the orther, for to regul their reves by incubation, and Lally, through their gangrene spentacles, and all the good or they did in their time, the rigorists, for Roe and O'Mulcnory a

Conry ap Mul or Lap ap Morion and Buffler ap Matty Mac Gregory for Marcus on Podex by Daddy de Wyer, old baga-broth, beeves and scullogues, churls and vassals, in same, sept and severalty and one by one and sing a mamalujo. To the heroest champion of Eren and his braceoelanders and Gowan, Gawin and Gonne.

And after that now in the future, please God, after nonpenal start, all repeating ourselves, in medios loquos, from where he got a useful arm busy on the touchline, due south of her western shoulder, down to death and the love embrace, with an interesting tallow complexion and all now united, sansfamillias, let us ran on to say oremus prayer and homeysweet homely, after fully realis-ing the gratifying experiences of highly continental evenements, for meter and peter to temple an eslaap, for auld acquaintance, to Peregrine and Michael and Farfassa and Peregrine, for navigants et peregrinantibus, in all the old imperial and Fionnachan sea and for vogue awallow to a Miss Yiss, you fascinator, you, sing a lovasteamadorion to Ladyseyes, here's Tricks and Doelsy, de-lightfully ours, in her doaty ducky little blue and roll his hoop and how she ran, when wit won free, the dimply blissed and aw-fully bucked, right glad we never shall forget, thoh the dayses gone still they loves young dreams and old Luke with his kingly leer, so wellworth watching, and Senchus Mor, possessed of evident notoriety, and another more of the bigtimers, to name no others, of whom great things were expected in the fulmfilming department, for the lives of Lazarus and auld luke syne and she haihaihail her kobbor kohinor sehehet on the praze savohole shanghai.

Hear, O hear, Iseult la belle! Tristan, sad hero, hear! The Lambeg drum, the Lombog reed, the Lumbag fiferer, the Limibig brazenaze.

Anno Domini nostri sancti Jesu Christi
Nine hundred and ninetynine million pound sterling in the blueblack
  bowels of the bank of Ulster.
Braw bawbees and good gold pounds, galore, my girleen, a Sunday'll
  prank thee finely.

And no damn loutll come courting thee or by the mother of the Holy
Ghost there'll be murder!

O, come all ye sweet nymphs of Dingle beach to cheer Brinabride
queen from Sybil surfriding
In her curragh of shells of daughter of pearl and her silverymonnblue
mantle round her.
Crown of the waters, brine on her brow, she'll dance them a jig and
jilt them fairly.
Yerra, why would she bide with Sig Sloomysides or the grogram grey
barnacle gander?

You won't need be lonesome, Lizzy my love, when your beau gets his
glut of cold meat and hot soldiering
Nor wake in winter, window machree, but snore sung in my old
Balbriggan surtout.
Wisha, won't you agree now to take me from the middle, say, of
next week on, for the balance of my days, for nothing (what?)
as your own nursetender?
A power of highsteppers died game right enough—but who, acushla,
'll beg coppers for you?

I tossed that one long before anyone.
It was of a wet good Friday too she was ironing and, as I'm given
now to understand, she was always mad gone on me.
Grand goosegreasing we had entirely with an allnight eiderdown bed
picnic to follow.
By the cross of Cong, says she, rising up Saturday in the twilight
from under me, Mick, Nick the Maggot or whatever your name
is, you're the mose likable lad that's come my ways yet from the
barony of Bohermore.

Mattheehew, Markeehew, Lukeehew, Johnheehewwheehew!
Haw!
And still a light moves long the river. And stiller the mermen
ply their keg.
Its pith is full. The way is free. Their lot is cast.
So, to john for a john, johnajeams, led it be!

III

Hark!

Tolv two elf kater ten (it can't be) sax.

Hork!

Pedwar pemp foify tray (it must be) twelve.

And low stole o'er the stillness the heartbeats of sleep.

White fogbow spans. The arch embattled. Mark as capsules.
The nose of the man who was nought like the nasoes. It is self-
tinted, wrinkling, ruddled. His kep is a gorsecone. He am Gascon
Titubante of Tegmine – sub – Fagi whose fixtures are mobil-
ing so wobiling befear my remembrandts. She, exhibit next, his
Anastashie. She has prayings in lowdelph. Zeehere green egg-
brooms. What named blautoothdmand is yon who stares? Gugurtha! Gugurtha! He has becco of wild hindigan. Ho, he hath
hornhide! And hvis now is for you. Pensée! The most beautiful
of woman of the veilch veilchen veilde. She would kidds to my
voult of my palace, with obscidian luppas, her aal in her dhove's
suckling. Apagemonite! Come not nere! Black! Switch out!

Methought as I was dropping asleep somepart in nonland of
where's please (and it was when you and they were we) I heard
at zero hour as 'twere the peal of vixen's laughter among midnight's chimes from out the belfry of the cute old speckled church
tolling so faint a goodmantrue as nighthood's unseen violet
rendered all animated greatbritish and Irish objects nonviewable
to human watchers save 'twere perchance anon some glistery

gleam darkling adown surface of affluvial flowandflow as again might seem garments of laundry reposing a leasward close at hand in full expectation. And as I was jogging along in a dream as dozing I was dawdling, arrah, methought broadtone was heard and the creepers and the gliders and flivvers of the earth breath and the dancetongues of the woodfires and the hummers in their ground all vociferated echoating: Shaun! Shaun! Post the post! with a high voice and O, the higher on high the deeper and low, I heard him so! And lo, mescemed somewhat came of the noise and somewho might amove allmurk. Now, 'twas as clump, now mayhap. When look, was light and now'twas as flasher, now moren as the glaow. Ah, in unlitness 'twas in very similitude, bless me, 'twas his belted lamp! Whom we dreamt was a shaddo, sure, he's lightseyes, the laddo! Blessed momence, O romence, he's growing to stay! Ay, he who so swayed a will of a wisp before me, hand prop to hand, prompt side to the pros, dressed like an earl in just the correct wear, in a classy mac Frieze o'coat of far suparior ruggedness, indigo braw, tracked and tramped, and an Irish ferrier collar, freeswinging with mereswin lacers from his shoulthern and thick welted brogues on him hammered to suit the scotsmost public and climate, iron heels and sparable soles, and his jacket of providence wellprovided woolies with a softrolling lisp of a lapel to it and great sealingwax buttons, a good helping bigger than the slots for them, of twentytwo carrot krasnapopp-sky red and his invulnerable burlap whiskcoat and his popular choker, Tamagnum sette-and-forte and his loud boheem toy and the damasker's overshirt he sported inside, a starspangled zephyr with a decidedly surpliced crinklydoodle front with his motto through dear life embrothred over it in peas, rice, and yeggy-yolk, Or for royal, Am for Mail, R.M.D. hard cash on the nail and the most successfully carried gigot turnups now you ever, (what a pairfact crease! how amsolookly kersse!) breaking over the ankle and hugging the shoeheel, everything the best — none other from (Ah, then may the turtle's blessings of God and Mary and Haggispatrick and Huggisbrigid be souptumbling all over him!) other than (and may his hundred thousand welcome stewed

letters, relayed wand postchased, multiply, ay faith, and plultiply!)
Shaun himself.

What a picture primitive!

Had I the concordant wiseheads of Messrs Gregory and Lyons
alongside of Dr Tarpey's and I dorsay the reverend Mr Mac
Dougall's, but I, poor ass, am but as their fourpart tinckler's dun-
key. Yet methought Shaun (holy messonger angels be uninter-
ruptedly nudging him among and along the winding ways of
random ever!) Shaun in proper person (now may all the blue-
blacksliding constellations continue to shape his changeable time-
table!) stood before me. And I pledge you my agricultural word
by the hundred and sixty odds rods and cones of this even's
vision that young fellow looked the stuff, the Bel of Beaus'
Walk, a prime card if ever was! Pep? Now without deceit it is
hardly too much to say he was looking grand, so fired smart, in
much more than his usual health. No mistaking that beamish
brow! There was one for you that ne'er would nunch with good
Duke Humphrey but would aight through the months without a
sign of an err in hem and then, otherwise rounding, fourale to the
lees of Traroe. Those jehovial oyeglances! The heart of the rool!
And hit the hencoop. He was immense, topping swell for he was
after having a great time of it, a twentyfour hours every moment
matters maltsight, in a porterhouse, scutfrank, if you want to
know, Saint Lawzenge of Toole's, the Wheel of Fortune, leave
your clubs in the hall and wait on yourself, no chucks for wal-
nut ketchups, Lazenby's and Chutney graspis (the house the once
queen of Bristol and Balrothery twice admired because her
frumped door looked up Dacent Street) where in the sighed of
lovely eyes while his knives of hearts made havoc he had re-
cruited his strength by meals of spadefuls of mounded food, in
anticipation of the faste of tablenapkins, constituting his three-
partite pranzipal meals *plus* a collation, his breakfast of first, a bless
us O blood and thirsthy orange, next, the half of a pint of becon
with newled googs and a segment of riceplummy padding, met
of sunder suigar and some cold forsoaken steak peatrefired from
the batblack night o'erflown then, without prejuice to evectuals,

came along merendally his stockpot dinner of a half a pound or round steak, very rare, Blong's best from Portarlington's Butchery, with a side of riceypeasy and Corkshire alla mellonge and bacon with (a little mar pliche!) a pair of chops and thrown in from the silver grid by the proprietoress of the roastery who lives on the hill and gaulusch gravy and pumpernickel to wolp up and a gorger's bulby onion (Margareter, Margaretar Margarastican-deatar) and as well with second course and then finally, after his avalunch oclock snack at Appelredt's or Kitzy Braten's of saddlebag steak and a Botherhim with her old phoenix portar, jistr to gwen his gwistel and praties sweet and Irish too and mock gurgle to whistle his way through for the swallying, swp by swp, and he getting his tongue arount it and Boland's broth broken into the bargain, to his regret his soupay *avic* nightcap, vitellusit, a carusal consistent with second course eyer and becon (the rich of) with broad beans, hig, steak, hag, pepper the diamond bone hotted up timmtomm and while'twas after that he scoffed a drake-ling snuggily stuffed following cold loin of veal more cabbage and in their green free state a clister of peas, soppositorily petty, last. P.S. but a fingerhot of rheingenever to give the Pax cum Spiri-tututu. Drily thankful. Burud and dulse and typureely jam, all free of charge, aman, and. And the best of wine *avec*. For his heart was as big as himself, so it was, ay, and bigger! While the loaves are aflowering and the nachtingale jugs. All St Jilian's of Berry, hurrah there for tobies! Mabhrodaphne, brown pride of our custard house quay, amiable with repastful, cheerus graciously, cheer us! Ever of thee, Anne Lynch, he's deeply draiming! Houseanna! Tea is the Highest! For auld lang Ayternitay! Thus thicker will he grow now, grew new. And better and better on butterand butter. At the sign of Mesthress Vanhungrig. However! Mind you, nuckling down to nourritures, were they menuly some ham and jaffas, and I don't mean to make the ingestion for the moment that he was guilbey of gulpable gluttony as regards chew-able boltaballs, but, biestings be biestings, and upon the whole, when not off his oats, given prelove appetite and postlove pricing good coup, goodcheap, were it thermidor oogst or floreal may while the whistling prairial roysters play, between gormandising and gourmeteering, he grubbed his tuck all right, deah smorregos, every time he was for doing dirt to a meal or felt like a bottle of ardilaun arongwith a smag of a lecker biss of a welldressed taart or. Though his net intrants wight weighed nought but a flyblow to his gross and ganz afterduepoise. And he was so jarvey jaunty with a romp of a schoolgirl's completion sitting pretty over his Oyster Monday print face and he was plainly out on the ramp and mash, as you might say, for he sproke.

Overture and beginners!

When lo (whish, O whish!) mesaw mestreamed, as the green to the gred was flew, was flown, through deafths of durkness greengrown deeper I heard a voice, the voce of Shaun, vote of the Irish, voise from afar (and cert no purer puer palestrine e'er chanted panangelical mid the clouds of Tu es Petrus, not Michaeleen Kelly, not Mara O'Mario, and sure, what more numerose Italicuss ever rawsucked frish uov in urinal?), a brieze to Yverzone o'er the brozaozaozing sea, from Inchigeela call the way how it suspired (morepork! morepork!) to scented nightlife as softly as the loftly marconimasts from Clifden sough open tireless secrets (mauveport! mauveport!) to Nova Scotia's listing sisterwands. Tubetube!

His handpalm lifted, his handshell cupped, his handsign pointed, his handheart mated, his handaxe risen, his handleaf fallen. Helpsome hand that holemost heals! What is het holy! It gested. And it said:

—Alo, alass, aladdin, amobus! Does she lag soft fall means rest down? Shaun yawned, as his general address rehearsal, (that was antepropreviousday's pigeons-in-a-pie with rough dough for the carrier and the hash-say-ugh of overgestern pluzz the 'stuesday's shampain in his head, with the memories of the past and the hicnuncs of the present embelliching the musics of the futures from Miccheruni's band) addressing himself *ex alto* and complaining with vocal discontent it was so close as of the fact the rag was up and of the briefs and billpasses, a houseful of deadheads, of him to dye his paddycoats to morn his hesternmost earning, his board in the swealth of his fate as, having moistened his manducators upon the quiet and scooping molars and grinders clean with his two fore fingers, he sank his hunk, dowanouet to resk at once, exhaust as winded hare, utterly spent, it was all he could do (disgusted with himself that the combined weight of his tons of iosals was a hundred men's massed too much for him), upon the native heath he loved covered kneehigh with virgin bush, for who who e'er trod sod of Erin could ever sleep off the turf! Well, I'm liberally dished seeing myself in this trim! How all too unwordy am I, a mere mailman of peace, a poor loust hastehater of the first degree, the principot of Candia, no legs and a title, for such eminence, or unpro promenade rather, to be much more exact, as to be the bearer extraordinary of these postoomany missive on his majesty's service while me and yous and them we're extending us after the pattern of reposiveness! Weh is me, yeh is ye! I, the mightif beam maircanny, which bit his mirth too early or met his birth too late! It should of been my other with his leickname for he's the head and I'm an everdevoting fiend of his. I can seeze tomirror in tosdays of yer when we lofobsed os so ker. Those sembal simon pumpkel pieman yers! We shared the twin chamber and we winked on the one wench and what Sim sobs todie I'll reeve tomorry, for 'twill be, I have hopes of, Sam Dizzier's feedst. Tune in, tune on, old Tighe, high, high, high, I'm thine owelglass. Be old! He looks rather thin, imitating me. I'm very fond of that other of mine. Fish hands Macsorley! Elien! Obsequies! Bonzeye! Isaac Egari's Ass! We're the music-hall pair that won the swimmyease bladdhers at the Guinness gala in Badeniveagh. I ought not to laugh with him on this stage. But he' such a game loser! I lift my disk to him. Brass and reeds, brace and ready! How is your napper, Handy, and hownow does she stand? First he was living to feel what the eldest daughter she was panseying and last he was dying to know what old Madre Patriack does be up to. Take this John's Lane in your toastingfourch. Shaun-ti and shaunti and shaunti again! And twelve coolinder moons! I am no helotwashipper but I revere her! For my own coant! She has studied! Piscisvendolor! You're grace! Futs dronk of

Wouldndom! But, Gemini, he's looking frightfully thin! I heard the man Shee shinging in the pantry bay. Down among the dustbins let him lie! Ear! Ear! Not ay! Eye! Eye! For I'm at the heart of it. Yet I cannot on my solemn merits as a recitativer recollect ever having done of anything of the kind to deserve of such. Not the phost of a nation! Nor by a long trollop! I just didn't have the time to. Saint Anthony Guide!

— But have we until now ever besought you, dear Shaun, we remembered, who it was, good boy, to begin with, who out of symphony gave you the permit?

— Goodbye now, Shaun replied, with a voice pure as a churchmode, in echo rightdainty, with a good catlick tug at his cocomoss candylock, a foretaste in time of his cabbageous brain's curlyflower. Athiacaro! Comb his tar odd gee sing your mower O meeow? Greet thee Good? How are them columbuses! Lard have mustard on them! Fatiguing, very fatiguing. Hobos hornknees and the corveeture of my spine. Poumeerme! My heaviest crux and dairy lot it is, with a bed as hard as the thinkamuddles of the Greeks and a board as bare as a Roman altar. I'm off rabbited kitchens and relief porridgers. No later than a very few fortnichts since I was meeting on the Thinker's Dam with a pair of men out of glasshouse whom I shuffled hands with named MacBlacks—I think their names is MacBlakes—from the Headfire Clump — and they were improving me and making me beliek no five hour factory life with insufficient emollient and industrial disabled for them that day o'gratises. I have the highest gratification by anuncing how I have it from whowho but Hagios Colleenkiller's prophecies. After suns and moons, dews and wettings, thunders and fires, comes sabotag. *Solvitur palumballando!* Tilvido! Adie!

— Then, we explained, salve a tour, ambly andy, you possibly might be so by order?

— Forgive me, Shaun repeated from his liquid lipes, not what I wants to do a strike of work but it was condemned on me premitially by Hireark Books and Chiefoverseer Cooks in their Eusebian Concordant Homilies and there does be a power coming over me that is put upon me from on high out of the book of breedings and so as it is becoming hairydittary I have of coerce nothing in view to look forward at unless it is Swann and beating the blindquarters out of my oldfellow's orologium oloss olorium. A bad attack of maggot it feels like. 'Tis trope, custodian said. Almost might I say of myself, while keeping out of crime, I am now becoming about fed up be going circulating about them new hikler's highways like them nameless souls, ercked and skorned and grizzild all over, till it's rusty October in this bleak forest and was veribally complussed by thinking of the crater of some noted volcano or the Dublin river or the catchalot trouth subsidity as away out or to isolate i from my multiple Mes on the spits of Lumbage Island or bury meself, clogs, coolcellar and all, deep in my wineupon ponteen unless Morrissey's colt could help me or the gander maybe at 49 as it is a tithe fish so it is, this pig's stomach business, and where on dearth or in the miraculous meddle of this expending umniverse to turn since it came into my hands I am hopeless off course to be doing anything concerning.

— We expect you are, honest Shaun, we agreed, but from franking machines, limricked, that in the end it may well turn out, we hear to be you, our belated, who will bear these open letter. Speak to us of Emailia.

— As, Shaun replied patly, with tootlepick tact too and a down of his dampers, to that I have the gumpower and, by the benison of Barbe, that is a lock to say with everything, my beloved.

— Would you mind telling us, Shaun honey, beg little big moreboy, we proposed to such a dear youth, where mostly are you able to work. Ah, you might! Whimper and we shall.

— Here! Shaun replied, while he was fondling one of his cowheel cuffs. There's no sabbath for nomads and I mostly was able to walk, being too soft for work proper, sixty odd eilish mires a week between three masses a morn and two chaplets at eve. I am always telling those pedestriasts, my answerers, Top, Sid and Hucky, now (and it is a veriest throth as the thieves' rescension) how it was forstold for me by brevet for my vacation in life while possessing stout legs to be disbarred after holy orders from unnecessary servile work of reckless walking of all sorts for the relics of my time for otherwise by my so douching I would get into a blame there where sieves fall out, Excelsior tips the best. Weak stop work stop walk stop whoak. Go thou this island, one housesleep there, then go thou other island, two housesleep there, then catch one nightmaze, then home to dearies. Never back a woman you defend, never get quit of a friend on whom you depend, never make face to a foe till he's rife and never get stuck to another man's pfife. Amen, ptah! His hungry will be done! On the continent as in Eironesia. But believe me in my simplicity I am awful good, I believe, so I am, at the root of me, praised be right cheek Discipline! And I can now truthfully declaret before my Geity's Pantokreator with my fleshfettered palms on the epizzles of the apossels that I do my reasonabler's best to recite my grocery beans for mummy *mit* dummy *mot* muthar *mat* bonzar regular, genuflections enclosed. Hek domov muy, there thou beest on the hummock, ghee up, ye dog, for your daggily broth, etc., Happy Maria and Glorious Patrick, etc., etc. In fact, always, have I believe. Greedo! Her's me hongue!

— And it is the fullsoot of a tarabred. Yet one minute's observation, dear dogmestic Shaun, as we point out how you have while away painted our town a wearing greenridinghued.

— O murder mere, how did you hear? Shaun replied, smoiling the ily way up his lampsleeve (it just seemed the natural thing to do), so shy of light was he then. Weil, so be it! The gloom hath rays, her lump is love. And I will confess to have, yes. Your diogneses is anonest man's. Thrubedore I did! Inditty I did. All lay I did. Down with the Saozon ruze! And I am afraid it wouldn't be my first coat's wasting after striding on the vampire and blazing on the focoal. See! blazing on the focoal. As see! blazing upon the foe. Like the regular redshank I am. Impregnable as the mule himself. Somebody may perhaps hint at an aughter impression of I was wrong. No such a thing! You never made a more freudful mistake, excuse yourself! What's pork to you means meat to

411

me while you behold how I be eld. But it is grandiose by my ways of thinking from the propheecies. New worlds for all! And they were scotographically arranged for gentlemen only by a scripchewer in whofoundland who finds he is a relative. And it was with my extravert davy. Like glue. Be through. Moyhard's daynoight, tomthumb. Phwum!

— How mielodorous is thy bel chant, O songbird, and how exqueezit thine after draught! *Buccinate in Emenia tuba insigni volumnitatis tuae.* But do you mean, O phausdheen phewn, from Pontoffbellek till the Kisslemerched our ledan triz will be? we gathered substantively whether furniture would or verdure varnish?

— It is a confoundyous injective so to say, Shaun the fiery boy shouted, naturally incensed, as he shook the red pepper out of his auricles. And another time please confine your glaring intinuations to some other mordant body. What on the physiog of this furnaced planet would I be doing besides your verjuice? That is more than I can fix, for the teom bihan, anyway. So let I and you now kindly drop that, angryman! That's not French pastry. You can take it from me. Understand me when I tell you (and I will ask you not to whisple, cry golden or quoth mecback) that under the past purcell's office, so deeply deplored by my erstwhile elder friend, Miss Enders, poachmistress and gay receiver ever for in particular to the Scotic Poor Men's Thousand Gallon Cow Society (I was thinking of her in sthore) allbethey blessed with twentytwo thousand sorters out of a biggest poss of twentytwo thousand, mine's won, too much privet stationery and safty quipu was ate up larchly by those nettlesome goats out of pension greed. *Colpa di Becco, buon apartita!* Proceding, I will say it is also one of my avowal's intentions, at some time pease Pod pluse murthers of gout (when I am not prepared to say) so apt as my pen is upt to scratch, to compound quite the makings of a verdigrease savingsbook in the form of a pair of capri sheep boxing gloves surrounding this matter of the Welsfusel mascoteers and their sindybuck that saved a city for my publickers, Nolaner and Browno, Nickil Hopstout, Christcross, so long as,

412

thanks to force of destiny, my selary as a paykelt is propaired, and there is a peg under me and there is a tum till me.

To the Very Honourable The Memory of Disgrace, the Most Noble, Sometime Sweepyard at the Service of the Writer. Salutem dicint. The just defunct Mrs Sanders who (the Loyd insure her!) I was shift and shuft too, with her shester Mrs Shunders, both mudical dauctors from highschoolhorse and aslyke as Easther's leggs. She was the niceliest person of a wellteached nonparty woman that I ever acquired her letters, only too fat, used to babies and tottydean verbish this is her entertermentdags for she shuk the bottle and tuk the medascene all times a day. She was well under ninety, poor late Mrs, and had tastes of the poetics, me having stood the pilgarlick a fresh at sea when the moon also was standing in a corner of sweet Standerson my ski. P.L.M. Mevrouw von Andersen was her whogave me a muttonbrooch, stakkers for her begfirst party. Honour thy farmer and my litters. This, my tears, is my last will intesticle wrote off in the strutforit about their absent female assauciations which I, or perhaps any other person what squaton a toffette, have the honour to had upon their polite sophykussens in the real presence of devouted Mrs Grumby when her skin was exposed to the air. O what must the grief of my mund be for two little ptpt coolies worth twenty thousand quad herewitdnessed with both's maddlemass wishes to Pepette for next match from their dearly beloved Roggers, M.D.D. O.D. May doubling drop of drooght! Writing.

— Hopsoloosely kidding you are totether with your cadenus and goat along nose how we shall complete that white paper. Two venusstas! Biggerstiff! Qweer but gaon! Be trouz and wholetrouz! Otherwise, frank Shaun, we pursued, what would be the autobiography of your softbodied fumiform?

— Hooraymost! None whomsoever, Shaun replied, Heavenly blank! (he had intentended and was peering now rather close to the paste of his rubiny winklering) though it ought to be more or less rawcawcaw romantical. By the wag, how is Mr Fry? All of it, I might say, in ex-voto, pay and perks and wooden half-pence, some rhino, rhine, O joyoust rhine, was handled over spondaneously by me (and bundle end to my illwishers' Miss Anders! she woor her wraith of ruins the night she lost I left!) in the ligname of Mr van Howten of Tredcastles, Clowntalkin, timbreman, among my prodigits nabobs and navious of every subscription entitled the Bois in the Boscoor, our evicted tenemants. What I say is (and I am noen roehorn or culkilt permit me to tell you, if uninformed), I never spont it. Nor have I the ghuest of innation on me the way to. It is my rule so. It went anyway like hot pottagebake. And this brings me to my fresh point. Quoniam, I am as plain as portable enveloped, inhowmuch, you will now parably receive, care of one of Mooseyeare Goonness's registered andouterthus barrels. Quick take um whiffat andrainit. Now!

— So vi et! we responded. Song! Shaun, song! Have mood! Hold forth!

— I apologuise, Shaun began, but I would rather spinooze you one from the grimm gests of Jacko and Esaup, fable one, feeble too. Let us here consider the casus, my dear little cousis (husstenhasstencaffincoffintussemtossemdamandamnacosaghcusaghhobixhatouxpeswchbechoscashlcarcarcaract) of the Ondt and the Gracehoper.

The Gracehoper was always jigging ajog, hoppy on akkant of his joyicity, (he had a partner pair of findlestilts to supplant him), or, if not, he was always making ungraceful overtures to Floh and Luse and Bienie and Vespatilla to play pupa-pupa and pulicy-pulicy and langtennas and pushpygyddyum and to commence insects with him, there mouthparts to his orefice and his gambills to there airy processes, even if only in chaste, ameng the everlistings, behold a waspering pot. He would of curse melissciously, by his fore feelhers, flexors, contractors, depressors and extensors, lamely, harry me, marry me, bury me, bind me, till she was puce for shame and allso fourmish her in Spinner's housery at the earthsbest schoppinhour so summery as his cottage, which was cald fourmillierly Tingsomingenting, groped up. Or, if he was always striking up funny funereels with Besterfarther Zeuts, the Aged One, with all his wigeared corollas, albe-

dinous and oldbuoyant, inscythe his elytrical wormcasket and
Dehlia and Peonia, his druping nymphs, bewheedling him, compound eyes on hornitosehead, and Auld Letty Plussiboots to
scratch his cacumen and cackle his tramsitus, diva deborah (seven
bolls of sapo, a lick of lime, two spurts of fussfor, threefurts of
sulph, a shake o'shouker, doze grains of migniss and a mesfull of
midcap pitchies. The whool of the whaal in the wheel of the
whorl of the Boubou from Bourneum has thus come to taon!),
and with tambarins and cantoridettes soturning around his eggs-
hill rockcoach their dance McCaper in retrophoebia, beck from
bulk, like fantastic disossed and jenny aprils, to the ra, the ra, the
ra, the ra, langsome heels and langsome toesis, attended to by a
mutter and doffer duffmatt baxingmotch and a myrmidins of
pszozlers pszinging *Satyr's Caudledayed Nice* and *Hombly,
Dombly Sod We Awhile* but *Ho, Time Timeagen, Wake!* For if
sciencium (what's what) can mute uns nought, 'a thought,
abought the Great Sommbboddy within the Omniboss, perhops an
artsaccord (hoot's hoot) might sing ums tumtim abutt the Little
Newbuddies that ring his panch. A high old tide for the bar-
heated publics and the whole day as gratiis! Fudder and lighting
for ally looty, any filly in a fog, for O'Cronione lags acrumbling
in his sands but his sunsunsuns still tumble on. Erething above
ground, as his Book of Breathings bed him, so as everwhy, sham
or shunner, zeemliangly to kick time.

Grouscious me and scarab my sahul! What a bagateller it is!
Libelulous! Inzanzarity! Pou! Pschla! Ptuh! What a zeit for the
goths! vented the Ondt, who, not being a sommerfool, was
thothfolly making chilly spaces at hisphex affront of the icinglass
of his windhame, which was cold antitopically Nixnixundnix.
We shall not come to party at that lopp's, he decided possibly,
for he is not on our social list. Nor to Ba's berial nether, thon
sloghard, this oldeborre's yaar ablong as there's a khul on a khat.
Nefersenless, when he had safely looked up his ovipository, he
loftet hails and prayed: May he me no voida water! Seekit Ha-
tup! May no he me tile pig shed on! Suckit Hotup! As broad as
Beppy's realm shall flourish my reign shall flourish! As high as

Heppy's hevn shall flurrish my haine shall hurrish! Shall grow, shall flourish! Shall hurrish! Hummum.

The Ondt was a weltall fellow, raumybult and abelboobied, bynear saw altitudinous wee a schelling in kopfers. He was sair sair sullemn and chairmanlooking when he was not making spaces in his psyche, but, laus! when he wore making spaces on his ikey, he ware mouche mothst secred and muravyingly wisechairman-looking. Now whim the sillybilly of a Gracehoper had jingled through a jungle of love and debts and jangled through a jumble of life in doubts afterworse, wetting with the bimblebeaks, drik-king with nautonects, bilking with durrydunglecks and horing after ladybirdies (*ichnehmon diagelegenaitoikon*) he fell joust as sieck as a sexton and tantoo pooveroo quant a churchprince, and wheer the midges to wend hemsylph or vosch to sirch for grub for his corapusse or to find a hospes, alick, he wist gnit! Bruko dry! fuko spint! Sultamont osa bare! And volomundo osi vide-vide! Nichtsnichtsundnichts! Not one pickopeck of muscow-money to bag a tittlebits of beebread! Iomio! Iomio! Crick's corbicule, which a plight! O moy Bog, he contrited with melan-ctholy. Meblizzered, him sluggered! I am heartily hungry!

He had eaten all the whilepaper, swallowed the lustres, de-voured forty flights of styearcases, chewed up all the mensas and seccles, ronged the records, made mundballs of the ephemerids and vorasioused most glutinously with the very timeplace in the ternitary — not too dusty a cicada of neutriment for a chittinous chip so mitey. But when Chrysalmas was on the bare branches, off he went from Tingsomingenting. He took a round stroll and he took a stroll round and he took a round strollagain till the grillies in his head and the leivnits in his hair made him thought he had the Tossmania. Had he twicycled the sees of the deed and trestraversed their revermer? Was he come to hevre with his engiles or gone to hull with the poop? The June snows was flocking in thuckflues on the hegelstomes, millipeeds of it and myriopoods, and a lugly whizzling tournedos, the Boraborayel-lers, blohablasting tegolhuts up to tetties and ruching sleets off the coppeehouses, playing ragnowrock rignewreck, with an irritant, penetrant, siphonopterous spuk. Graussssssss! Opr! Graussssssss! Opr!

The Gracehoper who, though blind as batflea, yet knew, not a leetle beetle, his good smetterling of entymology asped niss-unitimost lous nor liceens but promptly tossed himself in the vico, phthin and phthir, on top of his buzzer, tezzily wondering wheer would his aluck alight or boss of both appease and the next time he makes the aquinatance of the Ondt after this they have met themselves, these mouschical umsummables, it shall be motylucky if he will beheld not a world of differents. Behailed His Gross the Ondt, prostrandvorous upon his dhrone, in his Papylonian babooshkees, smolking a spatial brunt of Hosana cigals, with unshrinkables farfalling from his unthinkables, swarming of himself in his sunnyroom, sated before his comfortumble phullupsuppy of a plate o'monkynous and a confucion of minthe (for he was a conformed aceticist and aristotaller), as appi as a oneysucker or a baskerboy on the Libido, with Floh biting his leg thigh and Luse lugging his luff leg and Bieni bussing him under his bonnet and Vespatilla blowing cosy fond tutties up the allabroad length of the large of his smalls. As entomate as intimate could pinchably be. Emmet and demmet and be jiltses crazed and be jadeses whipt! schneezed the Gracehoper, aguepe with ptchjelasys and at his wittol's indts, what have eyeforsight!

The Ondt, that true and perfect host, a spiter aspinne, was making the greatest spass a body could with his queens lace-swinging for he was spizzing all over him like thingsumanything in formicolation, boundlessly blissfilled in an allallahbath of houris. He was ameising himself hugely at crabround and mary-pose, chasing Floh out of charity and tickling Luse, I hope too, and tackling Bienie, faith, as well, and jucking Vespatilla jukely by the chimiche. Never did Dorsan from Dunshanagan dance it with more devilry! The veripatetic imago of the impossible Gracehoper on his odderkop in the myre, after his thrice ephemeral journeeys, sans mantis ne shooshooe, featherweighed animule, actually and presumptuably sinctifying chronic's despair, was sufficiently and probably coocoo much for his chorous of gravitates. Let him be Artalone the Weeps with his parisites peeling off him I'll be Highfee the Crackasider. Flunkey Footle furloughed foul, writing off his phoney, but Conte Carme makes the melody that mints the money. *Ad majorem l.s.d.! Divi gloriam.* A darkener of the threshold. Haru? Orimis, capsizer of his antboat, sekketh rede from Evil-it-is, lord of loaves in Amongded. Be it! So be it! Thou-who-thou-art, the fleet-as-spindrift, impfang thee of mine wideheight. Haru!

The thing pleased him andt, and andt,

He larved ond he larved on he merd such a nauses
The Gracehoper feared he would mixplace his fauces.
I forgive you, grondt Ondt, said the Gracehoper, weeping,
For their sukes of the sakes you are safe in whose keeping.
Teach Floh and Luse polkas, show Bienie where's sweet
And be sure Vespatilla fines fat ones to heat.
As I once played the piper I must now pay the count
So saida to Moyhammlet and marhaba to your Mount!
Let who likes lump above so what flies be a full 'un;
I could not feel moregruggy if this was prompollen.
I pick up your reproof, the horsegift of a friend,
For the prize of your save is the price of my spend.
Can castwhores pulladeftkiss if oldpollocks forsake 'em
Or Culex feel etchy if Pulex don't wake him?
A locus to loue, a term it t'embarass,
These twain are the twins that tick Homo Vulgaris.
Has Aquileone nort winged to go syf
Since the Gwyfyn we were in his farrest drewbryf
And that Accident Man not beseeked where his story ends
Since longsephyring sighs sought heartseast for their orience?
We are Wastenot with Want, precondamned, two and true,
Till Nolans go volants and Bruneyes come blue.
Ere those gidflirts now gadding you quit your mocks for my gropes
An extense must impull, an elapse must elopes,
Of my tectucs takestock, tinktact, and ail's weal;
As I view by your farlook hale yourself to my heal.

Partiprise my thinwhins whiles my blink points unbroken on
Your whole's whercabroads with Tout's trightyright token on.
My in risible universe youdly haud find
Sulch oxtrabeeforeness meat soveal behind.
Your feats end enormous, your volumes immense,
(May the Graces I hoped for sing your Ondtship song sense!),
Your genus its worldwide, your spacest sublime!
But, Holy Saltmartin, why can't you beat time?

In the name of the former and of the latter and of their holo-caust. Allmen.

— Now? How good you are in explosition! How farflung is your fokloire and how velktingeling your volupkabulary! *Qui vive sparanto qua muore contanto.* O foibler, O flip, you've that wandervogl wail withyin! It falls easily upon the earopen and goes down the friskly shortiest like treacling tumtim with its tingting-taggle. The blarneyest blather in all Corneywall! But could you, of course, decent Lettrechaun, we knew (to change your name of not your nation) while still in the barrel, read the strangewrote anaglyptics of those shemletters patent for His Christian's Em?

— Greek! Hand it to me! Shaun replied, plosively pointing to the cinnamon quistoquill behind his acoustrolobe. I'm as after-dusk nobly Roman as pope and water could christen me. Look at that for a ridingpin! I am, thing Sing Larynx, letter potent to play the sem backwards like Oscan wild or in shunt Persse trans-luding from the Otherman or off the Toptic or anything off the types of my finklers in the draught or with buttles, with my oyes thickshut and all. But, hellas, it is harrobrew bad on the corns and callouses. As far as that goes I associate myself with your remark just now from theodicy *re*'furloined notepaper and quite agree in your prescriptions for indeed I am, pay Gay, in juxtaposition to say it is not a nice production. It is a pinch of scribble, not wortha bottle of cabbis. Overdrawn! Puffedly offal tosh! Be-sides its auctionable, all about crime and libel! Nothing beyond clerical horrors *et omnibus* to be entered for the foreign as second-class matter. The fuellest filth ever fired since Charley Lucan's.

Flummery is what I would call it if you were to ask me to put it on a single dimension what pronounced opinion I might possibly orally have about them bagses of trash which the mother and Mr Unmentionable (O breed not his same!) has reduced to writing without making news out of my sootynemm. When she slipped under her couchman. And where he made a cat with a peep. How they wore two madges on the makewater. And why there were treefellers in the shrubrubs. Then he hawks his handmud figgers from Francie to Fritzie down in the kookin. Phiz is me mother and Hair's me father. Bauv Betty Famm and Pig Pig Pike. Their livetree (may it flourish!) by their ecotaph (let it stayne!). With balsinbal bimbies swarming tiltop. Comme bien, Comme bien! Feefeel! Feefeel! And the Dutches dyin loffin at his pon peck de Barec. And all the mound reared. Till he wot not wot to begin he should. An infant sailing eggshells on the floor of a wet day would have more sabby.

Letter, carried of Shaun, son of Hek, written of Shem, brother of Shaun, uttered for Alp, mother of Shem, for Hek, father of Shaun. Initialled. Gee. Gone. 29 Hardware Saint. Lendet till Laonum. Baile-Atha-Cliath. 31 Jan. 1132 A.D. Here Commerces Enville. Tried Apposite House. 13 Fitzgibbets. Loco. Dangerous. Tax 9d. B.L. Guineys, esqueer. L.B. Not known at 1132 a. 12 Norse Richmound. Nave unlodgeable. Loved noa's dress. Sinned, Jetty Pierrse. Noon sick parson. 92 Windsewer. Ave. No such no. Vale. Finn's Hot. Exbelled from 1014 d. Pulldown. Fearview. Opened by Miss Take. 965 nighumpledan sextiffits. Shout at Site. Roofloss. Fit Dunlop and Be Satisfied. Mr. Domnall O'Domnally. Q.V. 8 Royal Terrors. None so strait. Shutter up. Dining with the Danes. Removed to Philip's Burke. At sea. D.E.D. Place scent on. Clontalk. Father Jacob, Rice Factor. 3 Castlewoos. P.V. Arrusted. J.P. Converted to Hospitalism. Ere the March past of Civilisation. Once Bank of Ireland's. Return to City Arms. 2 Milchbroke. Wrongly spilled. Traumcondraws. Now Bunk of England's. Drowned in the Laffey. Here. The Reverest Adam Foundlitter. Shown geshotten. 7 Streetpetres. Since Cabranke. Seized of the Crownd. Well, Sir Arthur. Buy

Patersen's Matches. Unto his promisk hands. Blown up last Lemmas by Orchid Lodge. Search Unclaimed Male. House Condamned by Ediles. Back in Few Minutes. Closet for Repeers. 60 Shellburn. Key at Kate's. Kiss. Isaac's Butt, Poor Man. Dalicious arson. Caught. Missing. Justiciated. Kainly forewarred. Abraham Badly's King, Park Bogey. Salved. All reddy berried. Hollow and eavy. Desert it. Overwayed. Understrumped. Back to the P.O. Kaer of. Owned owe M.O. Too Let. To Be Soiled. Cohabited by Unfortunates. Lost all Licence. His Bouf Toe is Frozen Over. X, Y and Z, Ltd, Destinied Tears. A.B, ab, Sender. Boston (Mass). 31 Jun. 13, 12. P.D. Razed. Lawyered. Vacant. Mined. Here's the Bayleaffs. Step out to Hall out of that, Ereweaker, with your Bloody Big Bristol. Bung. Stop. Bung. Stop. Cumm Bumm. Stop. Came Baked to Auld Aireen. Stop.

— Kind Shaun, we all requested, much as we hate to say it, but since you rose to the use of money have you not, without suggesting for an instant, millions of moods used up slanguage tun times as words as the penmarks used out in sinscript with such hesitancy by your cerebrated brother — excuse me not mentioningahem?

— CelebrAted! Shaun replied under the sheltar of his broguish, vigorously rubbing his magic lantern to a glow of fullconsciousness. HeCitEncy! Your words grates on my ares. Notorious I rather would feel inclined to myself in the first place to describe Mr O'Shem the Draper with before letter as should I be accentually called upon for a dieoguinnsis to pass my opinions, properly spewing, into impulsory irelitz. But I would not care to be so unfruitful to my own part as to swear for the moment positively as to the views of Denmark. No, sah! But let me say my every belief before my high Gee is that I much doubt of it. I've no room for that fellow on my fagroaster, I just can't. As I hourly learn from Rooters and Havers through Gilligan's maypoles in a nice pathetic notice he, the pixillated doodler, is on his last with illegible clergimanths boasting always of his ruddy complexious! She, the mammy far, was put up to it by him, the iniquity that ought to be depraved of his libertins to be silenced, sackclothed and suspended, and placed in irons into some drapyery institution off the antipopees for wordsharping only if he was klanver enough to pass the panel fleischcurers and the fieldpost censor. Gach! For that is a fullblown fact and well celibated before the four divorce courts and all the King's paunches, how he has the solitary from seeing Scotch snakes and has a lowsense for the production of consumption and dalickey cyphalos on his brach premises where he can purge his contempt and dejeunerate into a skillyton be thinking himself to death. Rot him! Flannelfeet! Flattyro! I will describe you in a word. Thou. (I beg your pardon.) Homo! Then putting his bedfellow on me! (like into mike and nick onto post). The criniman: I'll give it to him for that! Making the lobbard change hisstops, as we say in the long book! Is he on whosekeeping or are my! Obnoximost posthumust! With his unique hornbook and his prince of the apauper's pride, blundering all over the two worlds! If he waits till I buy him a mosselman's present! Ho's nos halfcousin of mine, pigdish! Nor wants to! I'd famish with the cuistha first. Aham!

— May we petition you, Shaun illustrious, then, to put his prentis' pride in your aproper's purse and to unravel in your own sweet way with words of style to your very and most obsequient, we suggested, with yet an esiop's foible, as to how?

— Well it is partly my own, isn't it? and you may, ought and welcome, Shaun replied, taking at the same time, as his hunger got the bitter of him, a hearty bite out of the honeycomb of his Braham and Melosedible hat, tryone, tryon and triune. Ann wunkum. Sure, I thunkum you knew all about that, honorey causes, through thelemontary channels long agum. Sure, that is as old as the Baden bees of Saint Dominoc's and as commonpleas now to allus pueblows and bunkum as Nelson his trifulgurayous pillar. However. Let me see, do. Beerman's bluff was what begun it, Old Knoll and his borrowing! And then the liliens of the veldt, Nancy Nickies and Folletta Lajambe! Then mem and hem and the jaquejack. All about Wucherer and righting his name for him. I regret to announce, after laying out his litterery bed, for two days she kept squealing down for noisy priors and bawling out to her jameymock farceson in Shemish like a mouther of the incas with a garcielasso huw Ananymus pinched her tights and about the Balt with the markshaire parawag and his loyal divorces, when he feraxiously shed ovas in Alemaney, tse tse, all the tell of the tud with the bourighevisien backclack, and him, the cribibber like an ambitrickster, aspiring like the decan's, fast aslooped in the intrance to his polthronechair with his sixth finger between his catseye and the index, making his pillgrimace of Childe Horrid, engrossing to his ganderpan what the idioglossary he invented under hicks hyssop! Hock! Ickick gav him that toock, imitator! And it was entirely theck latter to blame. Does he drink because I am sorely there shall be no more Kates and Nells. If you see him it took place there. It was given meeck, thank the Bench, to assist at the whole thing byck special chancery licence. As often as I think of that unbloody housewarmer, Shem Skrivenitch, always cutting my prhose to please his phrase, bogorror, I declare I get the jawache! Be me punting his reflection he'd begin his beogrefright in muddyass ribalds. Digteter! Grundtsagar! Swop beef! You know he's peculiar, that eggschicker, with the smell of old woman off him, to suck nothing of his switchedupes. M.D. made his *ante mortem* for him. He was grey at three, like sygnus the swan, when he made his boo to the public and barnacled up to the eyes when he repented after seven. The alum that winters on his top is the stale of the staun that will soar when he stambles till that hag of the coombe rapes the pad off his lock. He was down with the whooping laugh at the age of the loss of reason the whopping first time he prediseased me. He's weird, I tell you, and middayevil down to his vegetable soul. Never mind his falls feet and his tanbark complexion. That's why he was forbidden tomate and was warmed off the ricecourse of marrimoney, under the Helpless Corpses Enactment. I'm not at all surprised the saint kicked him whereby the sum taken Berkeley showed the reason genrously. *Negas, negasti* — negertop, negertoe, negertoby, negrunter! Then he was pusched out of Thingamuddy's school by Miss Garterd, for itching. Then he caught the europicolas and went into the society of jewses. With Bro Cahlls and Fran Czeschs and Bruda Pszths and Brat Slavos. One temp when he foiled to be killed, the freak wanted to put his bilingual head intentionally through the *Ikish Tames* and go and join the clericy as a demonican skyterrier. Throwing dust in the eyes of the Hooley Fermers! He used to be avowdeed as he ought to be vitandist. For onced I squeaked by twyst I'll squelch him. Then he went to Cecilia's treat on his solo to pick up Galen. Asbestopoulos! Inkupot! He has encaust in the blood. Shim! I have the outmost contempt for. Prost bitten! Conshy! Tiberia is waiting on you, arestocrank! Chaka a seagull ticket at Gattabuia and Gabbiano's! Go o'er the sea, haythen, from me and leave your libber to TCD. Your puddin is cooked! You're served, cram ye! Fatefully yaourth ... Ex. Ex. Ex. Ex.

— But for what, thrice truthful teller, Shaun of grace? weakly we went on to ask now of the gracious one. Vouchsafe to say. You will now, goodness, won't you? Why?

— For his root language, if you ask me whys, Shaun replied, as he blessed himself devotionally like a crawsbomb, making act of oblivion, footinmouther! (what the thickuns else?) which he picksticked into his lettruce invrention. Ullhodturdenweirmudgaardgringnirurdrmolnirfenrirlukkilokkibaugimandodrrerinsurtkrinmgernrackinarockar! Thor's for yo!

— The hundredlettered name again, last word of perfect language. But you could come near it, we do suppose, strong Shaun O', we foresupposed. How?

— Peax! Peax! Shaun replied in vealar penultimatum. 'Tis pebils before Sweeney's as he swigged a slug of Jon Jacobsen from his treestem sucker cane. Mildbut likesome! I might as well be talking to the four waves till tibbes grey eves and the rests asleep. Frost! Nope! No one in his seven senses could as I have before said, only you missed my drift, for it's being incendiary. Every dimmed letter in it is a copy and not a few of the silbils and wholly words I can show you in my Kingdom of Heaven. The lowquacity of him! With his threestar monothong! Thaw! The last word in stolentelling! And what's more rightdown lowbrown schisthematic robblemint! Yes. As he was rising

my lather. Like you. And as I was plucking his goosybone. Like
yea. He store the tale of me shur. Like yup. How's that for
Shemese?

— Still in a way, not to flatter you, we fancy you that you are
so strikingly brainy and well letterread in yourshelves as ever were
the Shamous Shamonous, Limited, could use worse of yourself, ingenious Shaun, we still so fancied, if only you would take your
time so and the trouble of so doing it. Upu now!

— Undoubtedly but that is show, Shaun replied, the mutter-
melk of his blood donor beginning to work, and while innocent
of disseminating the foul emanation, it would be a fall day I
could not, sole, so you can keep your space and by the power of
blurry wards I am loyable to do it (I am convicted of it!) any time
ever I liked (bet ye fippence off me boot allowance!) with the
allergrossest transfusiasm as, you see, while I can soroquise the
Siamanish better than most, it is an openear secret, be it said,
how I am extremely ingenuous at the clerking even with my
badly left and, arrah go braz, I'd pinsel it with immenuensoes
as easy as I'd perorate a chickerow of beans for the price of two
maricles and my trifolium librotto, the authordux Book of Lief,
would, if given to daylight, (I hold a most incredible faith about
it) far exceed what that bogus bolshy of a shame, my soamheis
brother, Gaoy Fecks, is conversant with in audible black and
prink. Outragedy of poetscalds! Acomedy of letters! I have
them all, tame, deep and harried, in my mine's I. And one of
these fine days, man dear, when the mood is on me, that I
may willhap cut my throat with my tongue tonight but I will
be ormuzd moved to take potlood and introvent it Paatryk just
like a work of merit, mark my words and append to my mark
twang, that will open your pucktricker's ops for you, broather
brooher, only for, as a papst and an immature and a nayophight
and a *spaciaman spaciosum* and a hundred and eleven other things,
I would never for anything take so much trouble of such doing.
And why so? Because I am altogether a chap too fly and hairyman
for to infradig the like of that ultravirulence. And by all I hold
sacred on earth clouds and in heaven I swear to you on my piop

and oath by the awe of Shaun (and that's a howl of a name!) that I will commission to the flames any incendiarist whosoever or ahriman howsoclever who would endeavour to set ever annyma roner moother of mine on fire. Rock me julie but I will soho!

And, with that crickcrackcruck of his threelungged squool from which grief had usupped every smile, big hottempered husky fusky krenfy strenfy pugiliser, such as he was, he virtually broke down on the mooherhead, getting quite jerry over her, overpowered by himself with the love of the tearsilver that he twined through her hair for, sure, he was the soft semplgawn slob of the world with a heart like Montgomery's in his showchest and harvey loads of feeling in him and as innocent and undesignful as the freshfallen calef. Still, grossly unselfish in sickself, he dished allarmes away and laughed it off with a wipe at his pudgies and a gulp apologetic, healing his tare be the smeyle of his oye, oogling around. Him belly no belong sollow mole pigeon. Ally bully. Fu Li's gulpa. Mind you, now, that he was in the dumpest of earnest orthough him jawr war hoo hleepy hor halk urthing hurther. Moe like that only he stopped short in looking up up upfrom his tide shackled wrists through the ghost of an ocean's, the wieds of pansiful heathvens of joepeter's gaseytotum as they are telling not but were and will be, all told, scruting foreback into the fargoneahead to feel out what age in years tropical, ecclesiastic, civil or sidereal he might find by the sirious pointstand of Charley's Wain (what betune the spheres sledding along the lacteal and the mansions of the blest turning on old times) as erewhile had he craved of thus, the dreamskhwindel necklassoed him, his thumbs fell into his fists and, lususing the harmonical balance of his ballbearing extremities, by the holy kettle, like a flask of lightning over he careened (O the sons of the fathers!) by the mightyfine weight of his barrel (all that prevented the happering of who if not the asterisks betwink themselves shall ever?) and, as the wisest postlude course he could playact, collaspsed in ensemble and rolled buoyantly backwards in less than a twinkling *via* Rattigan's corner out of farther earshot with his highly curious mode of slipashod motion, surefoot, sorefoot, slickfoot, slackfoot, linkman laizurely, lampman loungey, and by Killesther's lapes and falls, with corks, staves and treeleaves and more bubbles to his keelrow a fairish and easy way enough as the town cow cries behind the times in the direction of Mac Auliffe's, the crucethouse, *Open the Door Softly*, down in the valley before he was really uprighted ere in a dip of the downs (uila!) he spoorlessly disappaled and vanesshed, like a popo down a papa, from circular circulatio. Ah, mean!

Gaogaogaone! Tapaa!

And the stellas were shinings. And the earthnight strewed aromatose. His pibrook creppt mong the donkness. A reek was waft on the luftstream. He was ours, all fragrance. And we were his for a lifetime. O dulcid dreamings languidous! Taboccoo!

It was sharming! But sharmeng!

And the lamp went out as it couldn't glow on burning, yep, the lmp wnt out for it couldn't stay alight.

Well, (how dire do we thee hours when thylike fades!) all's dall and youllow and it is to bedowern that thou art passing hence, mine bruder, able Shaun, with a twhisking of the robe, ere the morning of light calms our hardest throes, beyond cods' cradle and porpoise plain, from carnal relations undfamiliar faces, to the inds of Tuskland where the oliphants scrum till the ousts of Amiracles where the toll stories grow proudest, more is the pity, but for all your deeds of goodness you were soo ooft and for ever doing, manomano and myriamilia even to mulimuli, as our humbler classes, whose virtue is humility, can tell, it is hardly we in the country of the old, Sean Moy, can part you for, oleypoe, you were the walking saint, you were, tootoo too stayer, the graced of gods and pittites and the salus of the wake. Countenance whose disparition afflictedly fond Fuinn feels. Winner of the gamings, primed at the studience, propredicted from the storybouts, the choice of ages wise! Spickspookspokesman of our specturesque silentiousness! Musha, beminded of us out there in Cockpit, poor twelve o'clock scholars, sometime or other anywhen you think the time. Wisha, becoming back to us way home in Biddyhouse one way or either anywhere we miss your smile.

Palmwine breadfruit sweetmeat milksoup! Suasusupo! However! Our people here in Samoanesia will not be after forgetting you and the elders luking and marking the jornies, chalkin up drizzle in drizzle out on the four bare mats. How you would be thinking in your thoughts how the deepings did it all begin and how you would be scrimmaging through your scruples to collar a hold of an imperfection being committled. Sireland calls you. Mery Loye is saling moonlike. And Slyly mamourneen's ladymaid at Gladshouse Lodge. Turn your coat, strong character, and tarry among us down the vale, yougander, only once more! And may the mosse of prosperousness gather you rolling home! May foggy dews bediamondise your hooprings! May the fireplug of filiality reinsure your bunghole! May the barleywind behind glow luck to your bathershins! 'Tis well we know you were loth to leave us, winding your hobbledehorn, right royal post, but, aruah sure, pulse of our slumber, dreambookpage, by the grace of Votre Dame, when the natural morning of your nocturne blankmerges into the national morning of golden sunup and Don Leary gets his own back from old grog Georges Quartos as that goodship the Jonnyjoys takes the wind from waterloogged Erin's king, you will shiff across the Moylendsea and round up in your own escapology some canonisator's day or other, sack on back, alack! digging snow, (not so?) like the good man you are, with your picture pockets turned knockside out in the rake of the rain for fresh remittances and from that till this in any case, timus tenant, may the tussocks grow quickly under your trampthickets and the daisies trip lightly over your battercops.

Jaunty Jaun, as I was shortly before that made aware, next halted to fetch a breath, the first cothurminous leg of his nightstride being pulled through, and to loosen (let God's son now be looking down on the poor preambler!) both of his bruised brogues that were plainly made a good bit before his hosen were, at the weir by Lazar's Walk (for far and wide, as large as he was lively, was he noted for his humane treatment of any kind of abused footgear), a matter of maybe nine score or so barrelhours distance off as truly he merited to do. He was there, you could planemetrically see, when I took a closer look at him, that was to say, (gracious helpings, at this rate of growing our cotted child of yestereve will soon fill space and burst in systems, so speeds the instant!) amply altered for the brighter, though still the graven image of his squarer self as he was used to be, perspiring but happy notwithstanding his foot was still asleep on him, the way he thought, by the holy januarious, he had a bullock's hoof in his buskin, with his halluxes so splendid, through Ireland untranscended, bigmouthed poesther, propped up, restant, against a butterblond warden of the peace, one comestabulish Sigurdsen, (and where a better than such exsearfaceman to rest from roving the laddyown he bootblacked?) who, buried upright like the Osbornes, kozydozy, had tumbled slumbersomely on sleep at night duty behind the curing station, equilebriated amid the embracings of a monopolized bottle.

Now, there were as many as twentynine hedge daughters out of Benent Saint Berched's national nightschool (for they seemed to remember how it was still a once-upon-a-four year) learning their antemeridian lesson of life, under its tree, against its warning, beseated, as they were, upon the brinkspondy, attracted to the rarerust sight of the first human yellowstone landmark (the bear, the boer, the king of all boors, sir Humphrey his knave we met on the moors!) while they paddled away, keeping time magnetically with their eight and fifty pedalettes, playing foolu-fool jouay allo misto posto, O so jaonickally, all barely in their typtap teens, describing a charming dactylogram of nocturnes though repelled by the snores of the log who looked stuck to the sod as ever and oft, when liquefied, (vil!) he murmoaned abasourdly in his Dutchener's native, visibly unmoved, over his treasure trove for the crown: *Dotter dead bedstead mean diggy smuggy flasky!*

Jaun (after he had in the first place doffed a hat with a rein-forced crown and bowed to all the others in that chorus of praise of goodwill girls on their best beehiviour who all they were girls all rushing sowarmly for the post as buzzy as sie could bie to read his kisshands, kittering all about, rushing and making a tremen-dous girlsfuss over him pellmale, their *jeune premier* and his rosy-posy smile, mussing his frizzy hair and the golliwog curls of him, all, but that one; Finfria's fairest, done in loveletters like a trayful of cloudberry tartlets (ain't they fine, mighty, mighty fine and honoured?) and smilingly smelling, pair and pair about, broad by bread and slender to slimmer, the nice perfumios that came cunvy peeling off him (nice!) which was angelic simply, savouring of wild thyme and parsley jumbled with breadcrumbs (O nice!) and feeling his full fat pouch for him so tactily and jingaling his jellybags for, though he looked a young chapplie of sixtine, they could frole by his manhood that he was just the killingest ladykiller all by kindness, now you, Jaun, asking kindlily (hillo, missies!) after their howareyous at all with those of their dolly-begs (and where's Agatha's lamb? and how are Bernadetta's columbillas? and Juliennaw's tubberbunnies? and Eulalina's tuggerfunnies?) he next went on (finefeelingfit!) to drop a few stray remarks anent their personal appearances and the contrary tastes displayed in their tight kittycasques and their smart fricky-frockies, asking coy one after sloy one had she read Irish legginds and gently reproving one that the ham of her hom could be seen below her hem and whispering another aside, as lavariant, that the hook of her hum was open a bittock at her back to have a sideeye to that, hom, (and all of course just to fill up a form out of pure human kindness and in a sprite of fun) for Jaun, by the way, was by the way of becoming (I think, I hope he was) the most purely human being that ever was called man, loving all up and down the whole creation from Sampson's tyke to Jones's sprat and from the King of all Wrenns down to infuseries) Jaun, after those few prelimbs made out through his eroscope the apparition of his fond sister Izzy for he knowed his love by her waves of splabashing and she showed him proof by her way of blabushing nor could he forget her so tarnelly easy as all that since he was brotherbesides her benedict godfather and heaven knows he thought the world and his life of her sweet heart could buy, (brao!) poor, good, true, Jaun!

— Sister dearest, Jaun delivered himself with express cordiality, marked by clearance of diction and general delivery, as he began to take leave of his scolastica at once so as to gain time with deep affection, we honestly believe you sorely will miss us the moment we exit yet we feel as a martyr to the dischurch of all duty that it is about time, by Great Harry, we would shove off to stray on our long last journey and not be the load on ye. This is the gross proceeds of your teachings in which we were raised, you, sis, that used to write to us the exceeding nice letters for presentation and would be telling us anun (full well do we wont to recall to mind) thy oldworld tales of homespinning and derringdo and dieobscure and daddyho, these tales which reliterately whisked off our heart so narrated by thou, gesweest, to perfection, our pet pupil of the whole rhythmetic class and the mainsay of our erigenal house, the time we younkers twain were fairly tossing ourselves (O Phoebus! O Pollux!) in bed, having

431

been laid up with Castor's oil on the Parrish's syrup (the night we will remember) for to share our hard suite of affections with thee.

I rise, O fair assemblage! Andcommincio. Now then, after this introit of exordium, my galaxy girls, *quiproquo* of directions to henservants I was asking his advice on the strict T.T. from Father Mike, P.P., my orational dominican and confessor doctor, C.C.D.D. (buy the birds, he was saying as he yerked me under the ribs sermon in an offrand way and confidence petween peas like ourselves in soandso many nuncupiscent words about how he had been confarreating teat-a-teat with two viragos intactas about what an awful life he led, poorish priced, uttering mass for a coppall of geldings and what a lawful day it was, there and then, for a consommation with an effusion and how, by all the manny larries ate pignatties, how, hell in tunnels, he'd marry me any old buckling time as flying quick as he'd look at me) and I am giving youth now again in words of style byaway of offertory hisand mikeadvice, an it place the person, as ere he retook him to his cure, those verbs he said to me. From above. The most eminent bishop titular of Dubloonik to all his purtybusses in Dellabelliney. Comeallyedimseldamsels, siddle down and lissle all! Follow me close! Keep me in view! Understeady me saries! Which is to all practising massoeurses from a preaching freer and be a gentleman without a duster before a parlourmade without a spitch. Now. During our brief apsence from this furtive feugtig season adhere to as many as probable of the ten commandments touching purgations and indulgences and in the long run they will prove for your better guidance along your path of right of way. Where the lisieuse are we and what's the first sing to be sung? Is it rubrics, mandarimus, pasqualines, or verdidads is in it, or the bruiselivid indecores of estreme voyoulence and, for the lover of lithurgy, bekant or besant, where's the fate's to be wished for? Several sindays after whatsintime. I'll sack that sick server the minute I bless him. That's the mokst I can do for his grapce. Economy of movement, axe why said. I've a hopesome's choice if I chouse of all the sinkts in the colander. From the common for ignitious Purpalume to the proper of Francisco Ultramare, last of scorchers, third of snows, in terrorgammons howdydos. Here she's, is a bell, that's wares in heaven, virginwhite, Undetrigesima, vikissy manonna. Doremon's! The same or similar to be kindly observed within the affianced dietcess of Gay O'Toole and Gloamy Gwenn du Lake (Danish spoken!) from Manducare Monday up till farrier's siesta in china dominos. Words taken in triumph, my sweet assistance, from the sufferant pen of our jocosus inkerman militant of the reed behind the ear.

Never miss your lostsomewhere mass for the couple in Myles you butrose to brideworship. Never hate mere pork which is bad for your knife of a good friday. Never let a hog of the howth trample underfoot your linen of Killiney. Never play lady's game for the Lord's stake. Never lose your heart away till you win his diamond back. Make a strong point of never kicking up your rumpus over the scroll end of sofas in the Dar Bey Coll Cafeteria by tootling risky *apropos* songs at commercial travellers' smokers for their Columbian nights entertainments the like of *White limbs they never stop teasing* or *Minxy was a Manxmaid when Murry wor a Man*. And, by the bun, is it you goes bisbuiting His Esaus and Cos and then throws them bag in the box? Why the tin's nearly empty. First thou shalt not smile. Twice thou shalt not love. Lust, thou shalt not commix idolatry. Hip confiners help compunction. Never park your brief stays in the men's convenience. Never clean your buttoncups with your dirty pair of sassers. Never ask his first person where's your quickest cut to our last place. Never let the promising hand usemake free of your oncemaid sacral. The soft side of the axe! A coil of cord, a colleen coy, a blush on a bush turned first man's laughter into wailful moither. O foolish cuppled! Ah, dice's error! Never dip in the ern while you've browsers on your suite. Never slip the silver key through your gate of golden age. Collide with man, collude with money. Ere you sail foreget my prize. Where you truss be circumspicious and look before you leak, dears. Never christen medlard apples till a swithin is in sight. Wet your thistle where a weed is and you'll rue it, despyneedis. Especially beware please of being at a party to any demoralizing home life. That saps a chap. Keep cool faith in the firm, have warm hoep in the house and begin frem athome to be chary of charity. Where it is nobler in the main to supper than the boys and errors of outrager's virtue. Give back those stolen kisses; restaure those allcotten glooves. Recollect the yella perals that all too often beset green gerils, Rhidarhoda and Daradora, once they gethobbyhorsical, playing breeches parts for Bessy Sudlow in fleshcoloured pantos instead of earthing down in the coalhole trying to boil the big gun's dinner. Leg-before-Wicked lags-behind-Wall where here Mr Whicker whacked a great fall. Femorafamilla feeled it a candleliked but Hayes, Conyngham and Erobinson sware it's an egg. Forglim mick aye! Stay, forestand and tillgive it! Remember the biter's bitters I shed the vigil I buried our Harlotte Quai from poor Mrs Mangain's of Britain Court on the feast of Marie Maudlin. Ah, who would wipe her weeper drý and lead her to the halter? Sold in her heyday, laid in the straw, bought for one puny petunia. Moral: if you can't point a lily get to henna out of here! Put your swell foot foremost on foulardy pneumonia shertwaists, irriconcilible with true fiminin risirvition and ribbons of lace, limenick's disgrace. Sure, what is it on the whole only holes tied together, the merest and transparent washingtones to make Languid Lola's lingery longer? Scenta Clauthes stiffstuffs your hose and heartsies full of temptiness. Vanity flee and Verity fear! Diobell! Whalebones and buskbutts may hurt you (thwackaway thwuck!) but never lay bare your breast secret (dickette's place!) to joy a Jonas in the Dolphin's Barncar with your meetual fan, Doveyed Covetfilles, comepulsing paynattention spasms between the averthisment for Ulikah's wine and a pair of pulldoors of the old cupiosity shape. There you'll fix your eyes darkled on the autocart of the bringfast cable but here till youre martimorphysed please sit still face to face. For if the shorth of your skorth falls down to his knees pray how wrong will he look till he rises? Not before Gravesend is commuted. But now reappears Autist Algy, the pulcherman and would-do performer, *oleas* Mr Smuth, stated by the vice crusaders to be well known to all the dallytaunties in and near the ciudad of Buellas Arias, taking you to the playguehouse to see the *Smirching of Venus* and asking with whispered offers in a very low bearded voice, with a nice little tiny manner and in a very nice little tony way, won't you be an artist's moral and pose in your nudies as a local esthetic before voluble old masters, introducing you, left to right the party comprises, to hogarths like Bottisilly and Titteretto and Vergognese and Coraggio with their extrahand Mazzaccio, plus the usual bilker's dozen of dowdycameramen. And the volses of lewd Buylan, for innocence! And the phyllisophies of Bussup Bulkeley. O, the frecklessness of the giddies nouveautays! There's many's the icepolled globetopper is haunted by the hottest spot under his equator like Ramrod, the meaty hunter, always jaeger for a thrust. The back beautiful, the undraped divine! And Suzy's Moedl's with their Blue Danuboyes! All blah! Viper's vapid vilest! Put off the old man at the very font and get right on with the nutty sparker round the back. Slip your oval out of touch and let the paravis be your goal. Up leather, Prunella, convert your try! Stick wicks in your earshells when you hear the prompter's voice. Look on a boa in his beauty and you'll never more wear your strawberry leaves. Rely on the relic. What bondman ever you bind on earth I'll be bound 'twas combined in hemel. Keep airly hores and the worm is yores. Dress the pussy for her nighty and follow her piggytails up their way to Winkyland. See little poupeep she's firsht ashleep. After having sat your poetries and you know what happens when chine throws over jupan. Go to doss with the poulterer, you understand, and shake up with the milchmand. The Sully van vultures are on the prowl. And the hailies fingringmaries. Tobaccos tabu and toboggan's a back seat. Secret satieties and onanymous letters make the great unwatched as bad as their betters. Don't on any account acquire a paunchon for that alltoocommon fagbutt habit of frequenting and chumming together with the braces of couples in Mr Tunnelly's hallways (smash it) wriggling with lowcusses and cockchafers and vamps and rodants, with the end to commit acts of interstipital indecency as between twineties and tapegarters, fingerpats on fondlepets, under the couvrefeu act. It's the thin end; wedge your steps! Your high powered hefty hoyden thinks nothing of ramping through a whole suite of smokeless husbands. Three minutes I'm counting you. Woooooon. No triching now! Give me that when I tell you! *Ragazza ladra!* And is that any place to be smuggling his madam's apples up? Deceitful jade. Gee wedge! Begor, I like the way they're half cooked. Hold, flay, grill, fire that laney feeling for kosenkissing disgenically within the proscribed limits like Population Peg on a hint or twim clandestinely does be doing to Temptation Tom, atkings questions in barely and snakking svarewords like a nursemagd. While there's men-a'war on the say there'll be loves-o'women on the do. Love through the usual channels, cisternbrothelly, when properly disinfected and taken neat in the generable way upon retiring to roost in the company of a husband-in-law or other respectable relative of an apposite sex, not love that leads by the nose as I foresmellt but canalised love, you understand, does a felon good, suspiciously if he has a slugger's liver but I cannot belabour the point too ardently (and after the lessions of experience I speak from inspiration) that fetid spirits is the thief of prurities, so none of your twenty rod cherrywhisks, me daughter! At the Cat and Coney or the Spotted Dog. And at 2bis Lot's Road. When parties get tight for each other they lose all respect together. By the stench of her fizzle and the glib of her gab know the drunken draggletail Dublin drab. You'll pay for each bally sorraday night every billing sumday morning. When the night is in May and the moon shines might. We won't meeth in Navan till you try to give the Kellsfrieclub the goby. Hill or hollow, Hull or Hague! And beware how you dare of wet cocktails in Kildare or the same may see your wedding driving home from your wake. Mades of ashens when you flirt spoil the lad but spare his shirt! Lay your lilylike long his shoulder but buck back if he buts bolder and just hep your homely hop and heed no horning but if you've got some brainy notion to raise cancan and rouse commotion I'll be apt to flail that tail for you till it's borning. Let the love ladleliked at the eye girde your gastricks in the gym. Nor must you omit to screw the lid firmly on that jazz jiggery and kick starts. Bumping races on the flat and point to point over obstacles. Ridewheeling that acclivisciously up windy Rutland Rise and insighting rebellious northers before the saunter of the city of Dunlob. Then breretonbiking on the free with your airs of go-be-dee and your heels upon the handlebars. Berrboel brazenness! No, before your corselage rib is decartilaged, that is to mean if you have visceral ptossis, my point is, making allowances for the fads of your weak abdominal wall and your liver asprewl, vinvin, vinvin, or should you feel, in shorts, as though you needed healthy physicking exorcise to flush your kidneys, you understand, and move that twelffinger bowel and threadworm inhibitating it, lassy, and perspire freely, lict your lector in the lobby and why out you go by the ostiary on to the dirt track and skip! Be a sportive. Deal with Nature the great greengrocer and pay regularly the monthlies. Your Punt's Perfume's only in the hatpinny shop beside the reek of the rawny. It's more important than air—I mean than eats—air (Oop, I never open momouth but I pack mefood in it) and promotes that natural emotion. Stamp out bad eggs. Why so many puddings prove disappointing, as Dietician says, in Creature Comforts Causeries, and why so much soup is so muck slop. If we could fatten on the elizabeetons we wouldn't have teeth like the hippopotamians. However. Likewise if I were in your envelope shirt I'd keep my weathereye well cocked open for your furnished lodgers paying for their feed on tally with company and piano tunes. Only stuprifying yourself! The too friendly friend sort, Mazourikawitch or some other sukinsin of a vitch, who he's kommen from olt Pannonia on this porpoise whom sue stooderin about the maul and femurl artickles and who mix himself so at home mid the musik and spanks the ivory that lovely for this your Mistro Melosiosus MacShine MacShane may soon prove your undoing and bane through the succeeding years of rain should you, whilst Jaun is from home, get used to basking in his loverslowlap, inordinately clad, moustacheteasing, when closehended together behind locked doors, kissing steadily, (malbongusta, it's not the thing you know!) with the calfloving selfseeker, under the influence of woman, inching up to you, disarranging your modesties and fumbling with his forte paws in your bodice after your billy doos twy as a first go off (take care, would you stray and split on me!) and going on doing his idiot every time you gave him his chance to get thick and play pigglywiggly, making much of you, bilgetalking like a ditherer, gougouzoug, about your glad neck and the round globe and the white milk and the red raspberries (O horrifier!) and prying down furthermore to chance his lucky arm with his pregnant questions up to our past lives. What has that caught to sing with him? The next fling you'll be squitting on the Tubber Nakel, pouring pitchers to the well for old Gloatsdane's glorification and the postequities of the Black Watch, peeping private from the Bush and Rangers. And our local busybody, talker-go-bragk. Worse again! Off of that praying fan on to them priars! It would be a whorable state of affairs altogether for the redcolumnists of presswritten epics, Peter Paragraph and Paulus Puff, (I'm keepsoaking them to cover my concerts) to get ahold of for their balloons and shoot you private by surprise, considering the marriage slump that's on this oil age and pulexes three shillings a pint and wives at six and seven when domestic calamities belame par and newlaids bellow mar for the twenty twotoosent time thwealthy took thousands in the slack march of civilisation were you, becoming guilty of unleckylike intoxication to have and to hold, to pig and to pay direct connection, *qua* intervener, with a prominent married member of the vicereeking squad and, in consequence of the thereinunder subpenas, be flummoxed to the second degree by becoming a detestificated companykeeper on the dammymonde of Lucalamplight. Anything but that, for the fear and love of gold! Once and for all, I'll have no college swankies (you see, I am well voiced in love's arsenal and all its overtures from collion boys to colleen bawns so I have every reason to know that rogues' gallery of nightbirds and bitchfanciers, lucky duffs and light lindsays, haughty hamiltons and gay gordons, dosed, doctored

438

and otherwise, messing around skirts and what their fickling intentions look like, you make up your mind to that) trespassing on your danger zone in the dancer years. If ever I catch you at it, mind, it's you that will cocottch it! I'll tackle you to feel if you have a few devils in you. Holy gun, I'll give it to you, hot, high and heavy before you can say sedro! Or may the maledictions of Lousyfear fall like nettlerash on the white friar's father that converted from moonshine the fostermother of the first nancy-free that ran off after the trumpadour that mangled Moore's melodies and so upturned the tubshead of the stardaft journalwriter to inspire the prime finisher to fellhim the firtree out of which Cooper Funnymore planed the flat of the beerbarrel on which my grandydad's lustiest sat his seat of unwisdom with my tante's petted sister for the cause of his joy! Amene.

Poof! There's puff for ye, begor, and planxty of it, all abound me breadth! Glor galore and glory be! As broad as its lung and as long as a line! The valiantine vaux of Venerable Val Vousdem. If my jaws must brass away like the due drops on my lay. And the topnoted delivery you'd expected be me invoice! Theo Dunnohoo's warning from Daddy O'Dowd. Whoo? What I'm wondering to myselfwhose for there's a strong tendency, to put it mildly, by making me the medium. I feel spirts of itchery outching out from all over me and only for the sludgehummer's force in my hand to hold them the darkens alone knows what'll who'll be saying of next. However. Now, before my upperotic rogister, something nice. Now? Dear Sister, in perfect leave again I say take a brokerly advice and keep it to yourself that we, Jaun, first of our name here now make all receptacles of, free of price. Easy, my dear, if they tingle you either say nothing or nod. No cheeka-cheek with chipperchapper, you and your last mashboy and the padre in the pulpbox enumerating you his nostrums. Be vacillant over those vigilant who would leave you to belave black on white. Close in for psychical hijiniks as well but fight shy of mugpunters. I'd burn the books that grieve you and light an allassundrian bom-pyre that would suffragate Tome Plyfire or Zolfanerole. Perousse instate your *Weekly Standerd*, our verile organ that is ethelred by all pressdom. Apply your five wits to the four verilatest. The Arsdiken's *An Traitey on Miracula or Viewed to Death by a Priest Hunter* is still first in the field despite the castle bar, William Archer's a rompan good cathalogue and he'll give you a riser on the route to our nazional labronry. Skim over *Through Hell with the Papes* (mostly boys) by the divine comic Denti Alligator (exsponging your index) and find a quip in a quire arisus aream from bastardtitle to fatherjohnson. Swear aloud by pious fiction the like of *Lentil Lore* by Carnival Cullen or that *Percy Wynns* of our S. J. Finn's or *Pease in Plenty* by the Curer of Wars, licensed and censered by our most picturesque prelates, Their Graces of Linzen and Petitbois, bishops of Hibernites, *licet ut lebanus*, for expansion on the promises, the two best sells on the market this luckiest year, set up by Gill the father, put out by Gill the son and circulating disimally at Gillydehooly's Cost. Strike up a nodding acquaintance for our doctrine with the works of old Mrs Trot, senior, and Manoel Canter, junior, and Loper de Figas, nates maximum. I used to follow Mary Liddlelambe's flitsy tales, espicially with the scentaminted sauce. Sifted science will do your arts good. *Egg Laid by Former Cock* and *With Flageolettes in Send Fanciesland*. Chiefly girls. Trip over sacramental tea into the long lives of our saints and saucerdotes, with vignettes, cut short into instructual primers by those in authority for the bittermint of your soughts. Forfet not the palsied. Light a match for poor old Contrabally and send some balmoil for the schizmatics. A hemd in need is aye a friendly deed. Remember, maid, thou dust art powder but Cinderella thou must return (what are you robbing her sleeve for, Ruby? And pull in your tongue, Polly!). Cog that out of your teen times, everyone. The lad who brooks no breaches lifts the lass that toffs a tailor. How dare ye be laughing out of your mouthshine at the lack of that? Keep cool your fresh chastity which is far better far. Sooner than part with that vestalite emerald of the first importance, descended to me by far from our family, which you treasure up so closely where extremes meet, nay, mozzed lesmended, rather let the whole ekumene universe belong to merry Hal and do whatever his Mary well

likes. When the gong goes for hornets-two-nest marriage step
into your harness and strip off that nullity suit. Faminy, hold
back! For the race is to the rashest of, the romping, jomping
rushes of. Haul Seton's down, black, green and grey, and hoist
Mikealy's whey and sawdust. What's overdressed if underclothed?
Poposht forstake me knot where there's white lets ope. Whisht!
Blesht she that walked with good Jook Humprey for he made
her happytight. Go! You can down all the dripping you can
dumple to, and buffkid scouse too ad libidinum, in these lassi-
tudes if you've parents and things to look after. That was what
stuck to the Comtesse Cantilene while she was sticking out Mavis
Toffeelips to feed her soprannated huspals, and it is henceforth
associated with her names. La Dreeping! Die Droopink! The
inimitable in puresuet of the inevitable! There's nothing to touch
it, we are taucht, unless she'd care for a mouthpull of white pudding for the wish is on her rose marine and the lunchlight in her
eye, so when you pet the rollingpin write my name on the pie.
Guard that gem, Sissy, rich and rare, ses he. In this cold old
worold who'll feel it? Hum! The jewel you're all so cracked
about there's flitty few of them gets it for there's nothing now
but the sable stoles and a runabout to match it. Sing him a ring.
Touch me low. And I'll lech ye so, my soandso. Show and show.
Show on show. She. Shoe. Shone.

Divulge, sjuddenly jouted out hardworking Jaun, kicking
the console to his double and braying aloud like Brahaam's ass,
and, as his voixehumanar swelled to great, clenching his manlies,
so highly strong was he, man, and gradually quite warming to
her (there must have been a power of kinantics in that buel
of gruel he gobed at bedgo) divorce into me and say the cur-
name in undress (if you get into trouble with a party you are
not likely to forget his appearance either) of any lapwhelp or
sleevemongrel who talks to you upon the road where he tuck
you to be a roller, O, (the goattanned saxopeeler upshotdown
chigs peel of him!) and volunteers to trifle with your round-
lings for profferred glass and dough, the marrying hand that
his leisure repents of, without taking out his proper password

441

from the eligible ministriss for affairs with the black fremdling, that enemy of our country, in a cleanlooking light and I don't care a tongser's tammany hang who the mucky is nor twoo hoots in the corner nor three shouts on a hill (were he even a constantineal namesuch of my very own, Attaboy Knowling, and like enoch to my townmajor ancestors, the two that are taking out their divorces in the Spooksbury courts circuits, Rere Uncle Remus, the Baas of Eboracum and Old Father Ulissabon Knickerbocker, the lanky sire of Wolverhampton, about their bristelings), but as true as there's a soke for sakes in Twoways Peterborough and sure as home we come to newsky prospect from west the wave on schedule time (if I came any quicker I'll be right back before I left) from the land of breach of promise with Brendan's mantle whitening the Kerribrasilian sea and March's pebbles spinning from beneath our footslips to carry fire and sword, rest insured that as we value the very name in sister that as soon as we do possibly it will be a poor lookout for that insister. He's a markt man from that hour. And why do we say that, you may query me? Quary? Guess! Call'st thou? Think and think and think, I urge on you. Muffed! The wrong porridge. You are an ignoratis! Because then probably we'll dumb well soon show him what the Shaun way is like how we'll go a long way towards breaking his outsider's face for him for making up to you with his bringthee balm of Gaylad and his singthee songs of Arupee, chancetrying my ward's head into sanctuary before feeling with his two dimensions for your nuptial dito. Ohibow, if I was Blonderboss I'd gooandfrighthisdualman! Now, we'll tell you what we'll do to be sicker instead of compensation. We'll he'll burst our his mouth like Leary to the Leinsterface and reduce he'll we'll ournhisn liniments to a poolp. Open the door softly, somebody wants you, dear! You'll hear him calling you, bump, like a blizz, in the muezzin of the turkest night. Come on now, pillarbox! I'll stiffen your scribeall, broken reed! That'll be it, grand operoar style, even should I, with my sleuts of hogpew and cheekas, have to coomb the brash of the libs round Close Saint Patrice to lay my louseboob on his

442

behaitch like solitar. We are all eyes. I have his quoram of images all on my retinue, Mohomadhawn Mike. Brassup! Moreover after that, bad manners to me, if I don't think strongly about giving the brotherkeeper into custody to the first police bubby cunstabless of Dora's Diehards in the field I might chance to follopon. Or for that matter, for your information, if I get the wind up what do you bet in the buckets of my wrath I mightn't even take it into my progromme, as sweet course, to do a rash act and pitch in and swing for your perfect stranger in the meadow of heppiness and then wipe the street up with the clonmellian, pending my bringing proceedings verses the joyboy before a bunch of magistrafes and twelve good and gleeful men? *Filius nullius per fas et nefas.* It should prove more or less of an event and show the widest federal in my cup. He'll have pansements then for his pensamientos, howling for peace. Pretty knocks, I promise him with plenty burkes for his shins. Dumnlimn wimn humn. In which case I'll not be complete in fighting lust until I contrive to half kill your Charley you're my darling for you and send him to Home Surgeon Hume, the algebrist, before his appointed time, particularly should he turn out to be a man in brown about town, Rollo the Gunger, son of a wants a flurewaltzer to Arnolff's, picking up ideas, of well over or about fiftysix or so, pithecoid proportions, with perhops five foot eight, the usual X Y Z type, R.C. Toc H, nothing but claret, not in the studbook by a long stortch, with a toothbrush moustache and jawcrockeries, *alias* grinner through collar, and of course no beard, meat and colmans suit, with tar's baggy slacks, obviously too roomy for him and springside boots, washing tie, Father Mathew's bridge pin, sipping some Wheatley's at Rhoss's on a barstool, with some pubpal of the Olaf Stout kidney, always trying to poorchase movables by hebdomedaries for to putt in a new house to loot, cigarette in his holder, with a good job and pension in Buinness's, what about our trip to Normandy style conversation, with an occasional they say that filmacoulored featured at the Mothrapurl skrene about Michan and his lost angeleens is corkyshows do morvaloos, blueygreen eyes a bit scummy developing a series of angry boils with certain references to the Deity, seeking relief in alcohol and so on, general omnibus character with a dash of railwaybrain, stale cough and an occasional twinge of claudication, having his favourite fecundclass family of upwards of a decade, both harefoot and loadenbrogued, to boot and buy off, Imean.

So let it be a knuckle or an elbow, I hereby admonish you! It may all be topping fun but it's tip and run and touch and flow for every whack when Marie stopes Phil fluther's game to go. Arms arome, side aside, face into the wall. To the tumble of the toss tot the trouble of the swaddled, O. And lest there be no misconception, Miss Forstowelsy, over who to fasten the plight-forlifer on (threehundred and thirty three to one on Rue the Day!) when the nice little smellar squalls in his crydle what the dirty old bigger'll be squealing through his coughin you better keep in the gunbarrel straight around vokseburst as I recommence you to (you gypseyeyed baggage, do you hear what I'm praying?) or, Gash, without buttering my head to assortail whose stroke forced or which struck backly, I'll be all over you myselx horizontally, as the straphanger said, for knocking me with my name and yourself and your babybag down at such a greet sacrifice with a rap of the gavel to a third price cowhandler as cheap as the niggerd's dirt (for sale!) or I'll smack your fruitflavoured jujube lips well for you, so I will well for you, if you don't keep a civil tongue in your pigeonhouse. The pleasures of love lasts but a fleeting but the pledges of life outlusts a lieftime. I'll have it in for you. I'll teach you bed minners, tip for tap, to be playing your oddaugghter tangotricks with micky dazzlers if I find corsehairs on your river-frock and the squirmside of your burberry lupitally covered with chiffchaff and shavings. Up Rosemiry Lean and Potanasty Rod you wos, wos you? I overstand you, you understand. Asking Annybettyelsas to carry your parcels and you dreaming of net glory. You'll ging naemaer wi'Wolf the Ganger. Cutting chapel, were you? and had dates with slickers in particular hotels, had we? Lonely went to play your mother, isod? You was wiffriends? Hay, dot's a doll yarn! Mark mean then! I'll homeseek you, Luperca as sure as there's a palatine in Limerick and in striped conference here's how. Nerbu de Bios! If you twos goes to walk upon the railway, Gard, and I'll goad to beat behind the bush! See to it! Snip! It's up to you. I'll be hatsnatching harrier to hiding huries hinder hedge. Snap! I'll tear up your limpshades and lock all your trotters in the closet, I will, and cut your silkskin into garters. You'll give up your ask unbrodhel ways when I make you reely smart. So skelp your budd and kiss the hurt! I'll have plenary sadisfaction, plays the bishop, for your partial's indulgences if your my rodeo gell. Fair man and foul suggestion. There's a lot of lecit pleasure coming bangslanging your way, Miss Pinpernelly satin. For your own good, you understand, for the man who lifts his pud to a woman is saving the way for kindness. You'll rebmemer your mottob *Aveh Tiger Roma* mikely smarter the nickst time. For I'll just draw my prancer and give you one splitpuck in the crupper, you understand, that will bring the poppy blush of shame to your peony hindmost till you yelp papapardon and radden your rhodatantarums to the beat of calorrubordolor, I am, I do and I suffer, (do you hear me now, lickspoon, and stop looking at your bussycat bow in the slate?) that you won't obliterate for the bulkier part of a running year, failing to give a good account of yourself, if you think I'm so tan cupid as all that. Lights out now (bouf!), tight and sleep on it. And that's how I'll bottle your greedypuss beautibus for ye, me bullin heifer, for 'tis I that have the peer of arrams that carry a wallop. Between them.

Unbeknownst to you would ire turn o'er see, a nuncio would I return here. How (from the sublime to the ridiculous) times out of oft, my future, shall we think with deepest of love and recollection by rintrospection of thee but me far away on the pillow, breathing foundly o'er my names all through the empties, whilst moidhered by the rattle of the doppeldoorknockers. Our homerole poet to Ostelinda, Fred Wetherly, puts it somewhys better. You're sitting on me style, maybe, whercoft I helped your ore. Littlegame rumilie from Liffalidebankum, (Toobliqueme!) but a big corner fill you do in this unadulterated seat of our affections. Aerwenger's my breed so may we uncreepingly

445

multipede like the sands on Amberhann! Sevenheavens, O heaven! Iy waount yiou! yore ways to melittleme were wonderful so Ickam purseproud in sending uym loveliest pansiful thoughts touching me dash in-you through wee dots Hyphen, the so pretty arched godkin of beddingnights. If I've proved to your sallysfashion how I'm a man of Armor let me so, let me sue, let me see your isabellis. How I shall, should I survive, as, please the uniter of U.M.I. hearts, I am living in hopes to do, replacing mig wandering handsup in yawers so yeager for mitch, positively cover the two pure chicks of your comely plumpchake with zuccherikissings, hong, kong, and so gong, that I'd scare the bats out of the ivfry one of those puggy mornings, honestly, by my rantandog and daddyoak I will, become come coming when, upon the mingling of our meeting waters, wish to wisher, like massive mountains to part no more, you will there and then, in those happy moments of ouryour soft accord, rainkiss on me back, for full marks with shouldered arms, and in that united I.R.U. stade, when I come (touf! touf!) wildflier's fox into my own greengeese again, swap sweetened smugs, six of one for half a dozen of the other, till they'll bet we're the cuckoo derby when cherries next come back to Ealing as come they must, as they musted in their past, as they must for my pressing season, as hereinafter must they chirrywill immediately suant on my safe return to ignorance and bliss in my horseless Coppal Poor, through suirland and noreland, kings country and queens, with my ropes of pearls for gamey girls the way ye'll hardly. Knowme.

Slim ye, come slum with me and rally rats' roundup! 'Tis post purification we will, sales of work and social service, missus, completing our Abelite union by the adoptation of fosterlings. Embark for Euphonia! Up Murphy, Henson and O'Dwyer, the Warchester Warders! I'll put in a shirt time if you'll get through your shift and between us in our shared slaves, brace to brassiere and shouter to shunter, we'll pull off our working programme. Come into the garden guild and be free of the gape athome! We'll circumcivicise all Dublin country. Let us, the real Us, all ignite in our prepurgatory grade as aposcals and be instrumental to utensilise, help our Jakeline sisters clean out the hogshole and generally ginger things up. Meliorism in massquantities, raffling receipts and sharing sweepstakes till navel, spokes and felloes hum like hymn. Burn only what's Irish, accepting their coals. You will soothe the cokeblack bile that's Anglia's and touch Armourican's iron core. Write me your essayes, my vocational scholars, but corsorily, dipping your nose in it, for Henrietta's sake, on mortinatality in the life of jewries and the sludge of King Haarington's at its height, running boulevards over the whole of it. I'd write it all by mownself if I only had here of my jolly young watermen. Bear in mind, by Michael, all the provincial's bananas peels and elacock eggs making drawadust jubilee along Henry, Moore, Earl and Talbot Streets. Luke at all the memmer manning he's dung for the pray of birds, our priest-mayor-king-merchant, strewing the Castleknock Road and drawing manure upon it till the first glimpse of Wales and from Ballses Breach Harshoe up to Dumping's Corner with the Mirist fathers' brothers eleven versus White Friars out on a rogation stag party. Compare them caponchin trowlers with the Bridge of Belches in Fairview, noreast Dublin's favourite souwest wateringplatz and ump as you lump it. What do you mean by Jno Citizen and how do you think of Jas Pagan? Compost liffe in Dufblin by Pierce Egan with the baugh in Baughkley of Fino Ralli. Explain why there is such a number of orders of religion in Asea! Why such an order number in preference to any other number? Why any number in any order at all? Now? Where is the greenest island off the black coats of Spaign? Overset into universal: I am perdrix and upon my pet ridge. Oralmus! Way, O way for the autointaxication of our town of the Fords in a huddle! Hailfellow some wellmet boneshaker or, to ascertain the facts for herself, run up your showeryweather once and trust and take the Drumgondola tram and, wearing the midlimb and vestee endorsed by the hierarchy fitted with ecclastics, bending your steps, pick a trail and stand on, say, Aston's, I advise you strongly, along quaith a copy of the Seeds and Weeds Act when you have procured one for yourself and take a good longing gaze into any nearby shopswindow you may select at suppose, let us say, the hoyth of number eleven, Kane or Keogh's, and in the course of about thirtytwo minutes' time proceed to turn aroundabout on your heehills towards the previous causeway and I shall be very cruelly mistaken indeed if you will not be jushed astunshed to see how you will be meanwhile durn weel topcoated with kakes of slush occasioned by the mush jam of the cross and blackwalls traffic in transit. See Capels and then fly. Show me that complaint book here. Where's Cowtends Kateclean, the woman with the muckrake? When will the W.D. face of our sow muckloved d'lin, the Troia of towns and Carmen of cities, crawling with mendiants in perforated clothing, get its wellbelavered white like l'pool and m'chester? When's that grandnational goldcapped dupsydurby houspill coming with its vomitives for our mothers-in-load and stretchers for their devitalised males? I am all of me for freedom of speed but who'll disasperaguss Pope's Avegnue or who'll uproose the Opian Way? Who'll brighton Brayhowth and bait the Bull Bailey and never despair of Lorcansby? The rampant royal commissioners! 'Tis an ill weed blows no poppy good. And this labour's worthy of my higher. Oil for meed and toil for feed and a walk with the band for Job Loos. If I hope not charity what profiteers me? Nothing! My tippers of flags are knobs of hardshape for it isagrim tale, keeping the father of curls from the sport of oak. Do you know what, liddle giddles? One of those days I am advised by the smiling voteseeker who's now snoring elued to positively strike off hiking for good and all as I bldy well bdly ought until such temse as some mood is made under privy-sealed orders to get me an increase of automoboil and footwear for these poor discalced and a bourse from bon Somewind for a cure at Badanuweir (though where it's going to come from this time —) as I sartunly think now, honest to John, for an income plexus that that's about the sanguine boundary limit. Amean.

Sis dearest, Jaun added, with voise somewhit murky, what though still high fa luting, as he turned his dorse to her to pay court to it, and ouverleaved his booseys to give the note and

448

score, phonoscopically incuriosited and melancholic this time whiles, as on the fulmament he gaped in wulderment, his on-saturncast eyes in stellar attraction followed swift to an imaginary swellaw, O, the vanity of Vanissy! All ends vanishing! Pursonally, Grog help me, I am in no violent hurry. If time enough lost the ducks walking easy found them. I'll nose a blue fonx with any tristys blinking upon this earthlight of all them that pass by the way of the deerdrive, conconey's run or wilfrid's walk, but I'd turn back as lief as not if I could only spoonfind the nippy girl of my heart's appointment, Mona Vera Toutou Ipostila, my lady of Lyons, to guide me by gastronomy under her safe conduct. That's more in my line. I'd ask no kinder of fates than to stay where I am, with my tinny of brownie's tea, under the invocation of Saint Jamas Hanway, servant of Gamp, lapidated, and Jacobus a Pershawm, intercissous, for my thurifex, with Peter Roche, that frind of my boozum, leaning on my cubits, at this passing moment by localoption in the birds' lodging, me pheasants among, where I'll dreamt that I'll dwealth mid warblers' walls when throstles and choughs to my sigh hiehied, with me hares standing up well and me longlugs dittoes, where a maurdering row, the fox! has broken at the coward sight till well on into the beausome of the exhaling night, pinching stopandgo jewels out of the hedges and catching dimtop brilliants on the tip of my wagger but for that owledclock (fast cease to it!) has just gone twoohoo the hour and that yen breezes zipping round by Drumsally do be devils to play fleurt. I could sit on safe side till the bark of Saint Grouseus for hoopoe's hours, till heoll's hoerrisings, laughing lazy at the sheep's lightning and turn a widamost ear dreamily to the drummling of snipers, hearing the wireless harps of sweet old Aerial and the mails across the nightrives (peepet! peepet!) and whippoor willy in the woody (moor park! moor park!) as peacefed as a philopotamus, and crekking jugs at the grenoulls, leaving tealeaves for the trout and belleeks for the wary till I'd followed through my upfielded neviewscope the rugaby moon cumuliously godrolling himself westasleep amuckst the cloudscrums for to watch how carefully my nocturnal goose-

449

mother would lay her new golden sheegg for me down under in the shy orient. What wouldn't I poach — the rent in my riverside, my otther shoes, my beavery, honest! — ay, and melt my belt for a dace feast of grannom with the finny ones, those happy greppies in their minnowahaw, flashing down the swansway, leaps ahead of the swift MacEels, the big Gillaroo redfellows and the pursewinded carpers, rearin antis rood perches astench of me, or, when I'd like own company best, with the help of a norange and bear, to be reclined by the lasher on my logansome, my g.b.d. in my f.a.c.e., solfanelly in my shellyholders and lov'd latakia, the benuvolent, for my nosethrills, with the jealosomines wilting away to their heart's deelight and the king of saptimber letting down his humely odours for my consternation, dapping my griffeen, burning water in the spearlight or catching trophies of the king's royal college of sturgeone by the armful for to bake pike and pie while, O twined me abower in L'Alouette's Tower, all Adelaide's naughtingerls juckjucking benighth me, I'd gamut my twittynice Dorian blackbudds chthonic solphia off my singasongapiccolo to pipe musicall airs on numberous fairyaciodes. I give, a king, to me, she does, alone, up there, yes see, I double give, till the spinney all eclosed asong with them. Isn't that lovely though? I give to me alone I trouble give! I may have no mind to lamagnage the forte bits like the pianage but you can't cadge me off the key. I've a voicical lilt too true. Nomario! And bemolly and jiesis! For I sport a whatyoumacormack in the latcher part of my throughers. And the lark that I let fly (olala!) is as cockful of funantics as it's tune to my fork. Naturale you might lower register me as diserecordant, but I'm athlone in the lillabilling of killarnies. That's flat. Yet ware the wold, you! What's good for the gorse is a goad for the garden. Lethals lurk heimlocked in logans. Loathe laburnums. Dash the gaudy deathcup! Bryony O'Bryony, thy name is Belladama! But enough of greenwood's gossip. Birdsnests is birdsnests. Thine to wait but mine to wage. And now play sharp to me. Doublefirst I'll head foremost through all my examhoops. And what sensitive coin I'd be possessed of at Latouche's, begor, I'd sink it sumtotal, every dolly farting, in vestments of subdominal poteen at prime cost and I bait you my chancey oldcoat against the whole ounce you half on your backboard (if madamaud strips mesdamines may cold strafe illglands!) that I'm the gogetter that'd make it pay like cash registers as sure as there's a pot on a pole. And, what with one man's fish and a dozen men's poissons, sowing my wild plums to reap ripe plentihorns mead, lashings of erbole and hydromel and bragget, I'd come out with my magic fluke in close time, fair, free and frolicky, zooming tophole on the mart as a factor. And I tell you the Bective's wouldn't hold me. By the unsleeping Solman Annadromus, ye god of little pescies, nothing would stop me for mony makes multimony like the brogues and the kishes. Not the Ulster Rifles and the Cork Milice and the Dublin Fusees and Connacht Rangers ensembled! I'd axe the channon and leip a liffey and drink annyblack water that rann onme way. Yip! How's thats for scats, mine shatz, for a lovebird? To funk is only peternatural its daring feers divine. Bebold! Like Varian's balaying all behind me. And before you knew where you weren't, I stake my ignitial's divy, cash-and-cash-can-again, I'd be staggering humanity and loyally rolling you over, my sow-white sponse, in my tons of red clover, nighty nigh to the metronome, fiehigh and fiehigher and fiehighest of all. Holy petter and pal, I'd spoil you altogether, my sumptuous Sheila! Mumm all to do brut frull up fizz and unpop a few shortusians or shake a pale of sparkling ice, hear it swirl, happy girl! Not a spot of my hide but you'd love to seek and scanagain! There'd be no standing me, I tell you. And, as gameboy as my pagan name K.C. is what it is, I'd never say let fly till we shot that blissup and swumped each other, manawife, into our sever nevers where I'd plant you, my Gizzygay, on the electric ottoman in the lap of lechery, simpringly stitchless with admiracion, among the most uxuriously furnished compartments, with sybarate chambers, just as I'd run my shoestring into near a million or so of them as a firstclass dealer and everything. Only for one thing that, howover famiksed I would become, I'd be awful anxious, you understand, about shoepisser pluvious and in assideration of the terrible luftsucks woabling around with the hedrolics in the coold amstophere till the borting that would perish the Dane and his chapter of accidents to be atramental to the better half of my alltoolyrical health, not considering my capsflap, and that's the truth now out of the cackling bag for truly sure, for another thing, I never could tell the leest falsehood that would truthfully give sotisfiction. I'm not talking apple sauce eithou. Or up in my hat. I earnst. Schue!

Sissibis dearest, as I was reading to myself not very long ago in Tennis Flonnels Mac Courther, his correspondance, besated upon my tripos, and just thinking like thauthor how long I'd like myself to be continued at Hothelizod, peeking into the focus and pecking at thumbnail reveries, pricking up ears to my phono on the ground and picking up airs from th'other over th'ether, 'tis tramsported with grief I am this night sublime, as you may see by my size and my brow that's all forehead, to go forth, frank and hoppy, to the tune the old plow tied off, from our nostorey house, upon this benedictine errand but it is historically the most glorious mission, secret or profund, through all the annals of our — as you so often term her — efferfreshpainted livy, in beautific repose, upon the silence of the dead, from pharoph the nextfirst down to ramescheckles the last bust thing. The Vico road goes round and round to meet where terms begin. Still onappealed to by the cycles and unappalled by the recoursers we feel all serene, never you fret, as regards our dutyful cask. Full of my breadth from pride I am (breezed be the healthy same!) for 'tis a grand thing (superb!) to be going to meet a king, not an everynight king, nenni, by gannies, but the overking of Hither-on-Thither Erin himself, pardee, I'm saying. Before there was patch at all on Ireland there lived a lord at Lucan. We only wish everyone was as sure of anything in this watery world as we are of everything in the newlywet fellow that's bound to follow. I'll lay you a guinea for a hayseed now. Tell mother that. And tell her tell her old one. 'Twill amuse her.

Well, to the figends of Annanmeses with the wholeabuelish business! For I declare to Jeshuam I'm beginning to get sunsick! I'm not half Norawain for nothing. The fine ice so temperate of our, alas, those times are not so far off as you might wish to be congealed. So now, I'll ask of you, let ye create no scenes in my poor primmafore's wake. I don't want yous to be billow-fighting your biddy moriarty duels, gobble gabble, over me till you spit stout, you understand, after soused mackerel, sniffling clambake to hering and impudent barney, braggart of blarney, nor you ugly lemoncholic gobs o'er the hobs in a sewing circle, stopping oddments in maids' costumes at sweeping reductions, wearing out your ohs by sitting around your ahs, making areek-eransy round where I last put it, with the painters in too, curse luck, with your rags up, exciting your mucuses, turning breakfarts into lost soupirs and salon thay nor you flabbies on your groaning chairs over Bollivar's troubles of a bluemoondag, steamin your damp ossicles, praying Holy Prohibition and Jaun Dyspeptist while Ole Clo goes through the wood with Shep togather, touting in the chesnut burrs for Goodboy Sommers and Mistral Blownowse hugs his kindlings when voiceyversy it's my gala bene fit, robbing leaves out of my taletold book. May my tunc fester if ever I see such a miry lot of maggalenes! Once upon a drunk and a fairly good drunk it was and the rest of your blatherumskite! Just a plain shays by the fire for absenter Sh the Po and I'll make ye all an eastern hummingsphere of myself the moment that you name the way. Look in the slag scuttle and you'll see me sailspread over the singing, and what do ye want trippings for when you've Paris inspire your hat? Sussumcordials all round, let ye alloyiss and ominies, while I stray and let ye not be getting grief out of it, though blighted troth be all bereft, on my poor headsake, even should we forfeit our life. Lo, improving ages wait ye! In the orchard of the bones. Some time very presently now when yon clouds are dissipated after their forty years shower, the odds are, we shall all be hooked and happy, communionistically, among the fieldnights eliceam, *élite* of the elect, in the land of lost of time. Johannisburg's a re-velation! Deck the diamants that never die! So cut out the lone-some stuff! Drink it up, ladies, please, as smart as you can lower it! Out with lent! Clap hands postilium! Fastintide is by. Your sole and myopper must hereupon part company. So for e'er fare thee welt! Parting's fun. Take thou, the wringle's thine, love. This dime doth trost thee from mine alms. Goodbye, swisstart, goodbye! Haugh! Haugh! Sure, treasures, a letterman does be often thought reading ye between lines that do have no sense at all. I sign myself. With much leg. Inflexibly yours. Ann Posht the Sh rn. To be continued. Huck!

Something of a sidesplitting nature must have occurred to westminstrel Jaunathaun for a grand big blossy hearty stenorious laugh (even Drudge that lay doggo thought feathers fell) hopped out of his woolly's throat like a ball lifted over the head of a deep field, at the bare thought of how jolly they'd like to be trolling his whoop and all of them truetotypes in missammen massness were just starting to spladher splodher with the jolly magorios, hicky hecky hock, huges huges huges, hughy hughy hughy, O Jaun, so jokable and so geepy, O, (Thou pure! Our virgin! Thou holy! Our health! Thou strong! Our victory! O salutary! Sustain our firm solitude, thou who thou well strokest! Hear, hairy ones! We have sued thee but late. Beauty parlous!) when suddenly (how like a woman!), swifter as mercury he wheels right round starnly on the Rizzies suddenly, with his gimlets blazing rather sternish (how black like thunder!), to see what's loose. So they stood still and wondered. Till first he sighed (and how ill soufered!) and they nearly cried (the salt of the earth!) after which he pondered and finally he replied:

— There is some thing more. A word apparting and shall the heart's tone be silent. Engagements, I'll beseal you! Fare thee well, fairy well! All I can tell you is this, my sorellies. It's prayers in layers all the thumping time, begor, the young gloria's gang voices the old doxologers, in the suburrs of the heavenly gardens, once we shall have passed, after surceases, all serene through neck and necklike Derby and June to our snug eternal retribution's reward (the scorchhouse). Shunt us! shunt us! shunt us! If you want to be felixed come and be parked. Sacred ease there! The seanad and pobbel queue's remainder. To it, to it! Seekit headup! No petty family squabbles Up There nor homemade

454

hurricanes in our Cohortyard, no cupahurling nor apuckalips nor no puncheon jodelling nor no nothing. With the Byrns which is far better and eve for ever your idle be. You will hardly reconnoitre the old wife in the new bustle and the farmer shinner in his latterday paint. It's the fulldress Toussaint's wakeswalks experdition after a bail motion from the chamber of horrus. Saffron buns or sovran bonhams whichever you'r avider to like it and lump it, but give it a name. Iereny allover irelands. And there's food for refection when the whole flock's at home. Hogmanny di'yegut? Hogmanny di'yesmellygut? And hogmanny di'yesmellyspatterygut? You take Joe Hanny's tip for it! Postmartem is the goods. With Jollification a tight second. Toborrow and toburrow and tobarrow! That's our crass, hairy and evergrim life, till one finel howdiedow Bouncer Naster raps on the bell with a bone and his stinkers stank behind him with the sceptre and the hourglass. We may come, touch and go, from atoms and ifs but we're presurely destined to be odd's without ends. Here we moult in Moy Kain and flop on the seemy side, living sure of hardly a doorstep for a stopgap, with Whogoesthere and a live sandbag round the corner. But upmeyant, Prospector, you sprout all your abel and woof your wings dead certain however of neuthing whatever to aye forever while Hyam Hyam's in the chair. Ah, sure, pleasantries aside, in the tail of the cow what a humpty daum earth looks our miseryme heretoday as compared beside the Hereweareagain Gaieties of the Afterpiece when the Royal Revolver of these real globoes lets regally fire of his *mio colpo* for the chrisman's pandemon to give over and the Harlequinade to begin properly SPQueaRking Mark Time's Finist Joke. Putting Allspace in a Notshall.

Well, the slice and veg joint's well in its way, and so is a riboast and jackknife as sporten dish, but home cooking everytime. Mountains good mustard and, with the helpings of ladies' lickfings and gentlemen's relish, I've eaten a griddle. But I fill twice as stewhard what I felt before when I'm after eating a few natives. The crisp of the crackling is in the chawing. Give us another cup of your scald. Santos Mozos! That was a damn good

cup of scald! You could trot a mouse on it. I ingoyed your pick
of hissing hot luncheon fine, I did, than' awfully, (sublime!).
Tenderest bully ever I ate with the boilec. protestants (allinoilia
allinoilia!) only for your peas again was a taste tooth psalty to
carry flavour with my godown and hereby return with my best
savioury condiments and a penny in the plate for the jemes.
O.K. Oh Kosmos! Ah Ireland! A.I. And for kailkannonkabbis
gimme Cincinnatis with Italian (but *ci vuol poco!*) ciccalick cheese,
Haggis good, haggis strong, haggis never say die! For quid we
have recipimus, recipe, O lout! And save that, Oliviero, for thy
sunny day! Soupmeagre! Couldn't look at it! But if you'll buy me
yon coat of the vairy furry best, I'll try and pullll it awn mee. It's in
fairly good order and no doubt 'twill sarve to turn. Remove this
boardcloth! Next stage, tell the tabler, for a variety of Hugue-
not ligooms I'll try my set on edges grapeling an aigrydoucks,
grilled over birchenrods, with a few bloomancowls in albies.
I want to get outside monasticism. Mass and meat mar no man's
journey. Eat a missal lest. Nuts for the nerves, a flitch for the flue
and for to rejoice the chambers of the heart the spirits of the
spice isles, curry and cinnamon, chutney and cloves. All the vital-
mines is beginning to sozzle in chewn and the hormonies to
clingleclangle, fudgem, kates and eaps and naboc and erics and
oinnos on kingclud and xoxxoxo and xooxox xxoxoxxoxxx till
I'm fustfed like fungstif and very presently from now posthaste
it's off yourll see me ryuoll on my usual rounds again to draw
Terminus Lower and Killadown and Letternoosh, Letterspeak,
Lettermuck to Littorananima and the roomiest house even in
Ireland, if you can understamp that, and my next item's platform
it's how I'll try and collect my extraprofessional postages owing
to me by Thaddeus Kellyesque Squire, dr, for nondesirable
printed matter. The Jooks and the Kelly-Cooks have been
milking turnkeys and sucking the blood out of the marshalsea
since the act of First Offenders. But I know what I'll do. Great
pains off him I'll take and that'll be your redletterday calendar,
window machree! I'll knock it out of him! I'll stump it out of
him! I'll rattattatter it out of him before I'll quit the doorstep of

old Con Connolly's residence! By the horn of twenty of both of the two Saint Collopys, blackmail him I will in arrears or my name's not penitent Ferdinand! And it's daily and hourly I'll nurse him till he pays me fine fee. Ameal.

Well, here's looking at ye! If I never leave you biddies till my stave is a bar I'd be tempted rigidly to become a passionate father. Me hunger's weighed. Hungkung! Me anger's suaged! Hangkang! Ye can stop as ye are, little lay mothers, and wait in wish and wish in vain till the grame reaper draws nigh, with the sickle of the sickles, as a blessing in disguise. Devil a curly hair I care! If any lightfoot Clod Dewvale was to hold me up, dicksturping me and marauding me of my rights to my onus, yan, tyan, tethera, methera, pimp, I'd let him have my best pair of galloper's heels in the creamsourer. He will have better manners, I'm dished if he won't! Console yourself, drawhure deelish! There's a refond of eggsized coming to you out of me so mind you do me duty on me! Bruise your bulge below the belt till I blewblack beside you. And you'll miss me more as the narrowing weeks wing by. Someday duly, oneday truly, twosday newly, till whensday. Look for me always at my west and I will think to dine. A tear or two in time is all there's toot. And then in a click of the clock, toot toot, and doff doff we pop with sinnerettes in silkettes lining longroutes for His Diligence Majesty, our longdistance laird that likes creation. To whoosh!

— Meesh, meesh, yes, pet. We were too happy. I knew something would happen. I understand but listen, drawher nearest, Tizzy intercepted, flushing but flashing from her dove and dart eyes as she tactilifully grabed her male corrispondee to flusther sweet nunsongs in his quickturned ear, I know, benjamin brother, but listen, I want, girls palmassing, to whisper my whish. (She like them like us, me and you, had thoud he n'er it would haltin so lithe when leased is tacitempust tongue). Of course, engine dear, I'm ashamed for my life (I must clear my throttle) over this lost moment's gift of memento nosepaper which I'm sorry, my precious, is allathome I with grief can call my own but all the same, listen, Jaunick, accept this witwee's mite, though a jenny-teeny witween piece torn in one place from my hands in second place of a linenhall valentino with my fondest and much left to tutor. X.X.X.X. It was heavily bulledicted for young Fr Ml, my pettest parriage priest, and you know who between us by your friend the pope, forty ways in forty nights, that's the beauty of it, look, scene it, ratty. Too perfectly priceless for words. And, listen, now do enhance me, oblige my fiancy and bear it with you morn till life's e'en and, of course, when never you make usage of it, listen, please kindly think galways again or again, never forget, of one absendee not sester Maggy. Ahim. That's the stupidest little cough. Only be sure you don't catch your cold and pass it on to us. And, since levret bounds and larks is soaring, don't be all the night. And this, Joke, a sprig of blue speedwell just a spell of floralora so you'll mind your veronique. Of course, Jer, I know you know who sends it, presents that please, mercy, on the face of the waters like that film obote, awfly charmig of course, but it doesn't do her justice, apart from her cattiness, in the magginbottle. Of course, please too write, won't you, and leave your little bag of doubts, inquisitive, behind you unto your utterly thine, and, thank you, forward it back by return pigeon's pneu to the loving in case I couldn't think who it was or any funforall happens I'll be so curiose to see in the Homesworth breakfast tablotts as I'll know etherways by pity bleu if it's good for my system, what exquisite buttons, gorgiose, in case I don't hope to soon hear from you. And thanks ever so many for the ten and the one with nothing at all on. I will tie a knot in my stringamejip to letter you with my silky paper, as I am given now to understand it will be worth my price in money one day so don't trouble to ans unless sentby special as I am getting his pay and wants for nothing so I can live simply and solely for my wonderful kinkless and its loops of loveliness. When I throw away my rollets there's rings for all. Flee a girl, says it is her colour. So does B and L and as for V! And listen to it! Cheveluir! So distant you're always. Bow your boche! Absolutely perfect! I will pack my comb and mirror to praxis oval owes and artless awes and it will follow you pulpicly as far as come back under all my eyes like my sapphire chaplets of ringarosary I will say for you to the Allmichael and solve qui pu while the dovedoves pick my mouthbuds (msch! msch!) with nurse Madge, my linkingclass girl, she's a fright, poor old dutch, in her sleeptalking when I paint the measles on her and mudstuskers to make her a man. We. We. Issy done that, I confesh! But you'll love her for her hessians and sickly black stockies, cleryng's jumbles, salvadged from the wash, isn't it the cat's tonsils! Simply killing, how she tidies her hair! I call her Sosy because she's sosiety for me and she says sossy while I say sassy and she says will you have some more scorns while I say won't you take a few more schools and she talks about ithel dear while I simply never talk about athel darling; she's but nice for enticing my friends and she loves your style considering she breaksin me shoes for me when I've arch trouble and she would kiss my white arms for me so gratefully but apart from that she's terribly nice really, my sister, round the elbow of Erne street Lower and I'll be strictly forbidden always and true in my own way and private where I will long long to betrue you along with one who will so betrue you that not once while I betreu him not once well he be betray himself. Can't you understand? O bother, I must tell the trouth! My latest lad's loveliletter I am sore I done something with. I like him lots coss he never cusses. Pity bonhom. Pip pet. I shouldn't say he's pretty but I'm cocksure he's shy. Why I love taking him out when I unletched his cordon gate. Ope, Jack, and atem! Obealbe myodorers and he dote so. He fell for my lips, for my lisp, for my lewd speaker. I felt for his strength, his manhood, his do you mind? There can be no candle to hold to it, can there? And, of course, dear professor, I understand. You can trust me that though I change thy name though not the letter never while I become engaged with my first horsepower, masterthief of hearts, I will give your lovely face of mine away, my boyish bob, not for tons of donkeys, to my second mate, with the twirlers the engineer of the passioflower (O the wicked untruth! whot a tell! that he has bought

459

me in his wellingtons what you haven't got!), in one of those
pure clean lupstucks of yours thankfully, Arrah of the passkeys,
no matter what. You may be certain of that, fluff, now I know
how to tackle. Lock my mearest next myself. So don't keep me
now for a good boy for the love of my fragrant saint, you villain,
peppering with fear, my goodless graceless, or I'll first murder
you but, hvisper, meet me after by next appointment near you
know Ships just there beside the Ship at the future poor fool's
circuts of lovemountjoy square to show my disrespects now, let
me just your caroline for you, I must really so late. Sweet pig,
he'll be furious! How he stalks to simself louther and lover,
immutating aperybally. My prince of the courts who'll beat me
to love! And I'll be there when who knows where with the
objects of which I'll knowor forget. We say. Trust us. Our
game. (For fun!) The Dargle shall run dry the sooner I you
deny. Whoevery heard of such a think? Till the ulmost of all
elmoes shall stele our harts asthone! And Mrs A'Mara makes
it up and befriends with Mrs O'Morum! I will write down all
your names in my gold pen and ink. Everyday, precious, while
m'm'ry's leaves are falling deeply on my Jungfraud's Messonge-
book I will dream telepath posts dulcets on this isinglass stream
(but don't tell him or I'll be the mort of him!) under the libans
and the sickamours, the cyprissis and babilonias, where the
frondoak rushes to the ask and the yewleaves too kisskiss themselves and 'twill carry on my hearz'waves my still waters reflections in words over Margrate von Hungaria, her Quaidy ways
and her Flavin hair, to thee, Jack, ahoy, beyond the boysforus.
Splesh of hiss splash springs your salmon. Twick twick, twinkle
twings my twilight as Sarterday afternoon lex leap will smile on
my fourinhanced twelvemonthsmind. And what's this I was
going to say, dean? O, I understand. Listen, here I'll wait on thee
till Thingavalla with beautiful do be careful teacakes, more stues-
ser flavoured than Vanilla and blackcurrant there's a cure in, like
a born gentleman till you'll resemble me, all the time you're
awhile way, I swear to you, I will, by Candlemas! And listen,
joey, don't be ennoyed with me, my old evernew, when, by the

460

end of your chapter, you citch water on the wagon for me being turned a star I'll dubeurry my two fesces under Pouts Vanisha Creme, their way for spilling cream, and, accent, umto extend my personnalitey to the latents, I'll boy me for myself only of expensive rainproof of pinked elephant's breath grey of the loveliest sheerest dearest widowshood over airforce blue I am so wild for, my precious once, Hope Bros., Faith Street, Charity Corner, as the bee loves her skyhighdeed, for I always had a crush on heliotrope since the dusess of yore cycled round the Finest Park, and listen. And never mind me laughing at what's atever! I was in the nerves but it's my last day. Always about this hour, I'm sorry, when our gamings for Bruin and Noselong is all oh you tease and afterdoon my lickle pussiness I stheal heimlick in my russians from the attraction part with my terri-blitall boots calvescatcher Pinchapoppapoff, who is going to be a jennyroll, at my nape, drenched, love, with dripping to affec-tionate slapmamma but last at night, look, after my golden vio-lents wetting in my upperstairs splendidly welluminated with such lidlylac curtains wallpapered to match the cat and a fire-please keep looking of priceless pearlogs I just want to see will he or are all Michales like that, I'll strip straight after devotions before his fondstare—and I mean it too, (thy gape to my gazing I'll bind and makeleash) and poke stiff under my isonbound with my soiedisante chineknees cheeckchubby chambermate for the night's foreign males and your name of Shane will come forth between my shamefaced whesen with other lipth I nakest open my thight when just woken by his toccatootletoo my first morn-ing. So now, to thalk thildish, thome, theated with Mag at the oilthan we are doing to thay one little player before doing to deed. An a tiss to the tassie for lu and for tu! Coach me how to tumble, Jaime, and listen, with supreme regards, Juan, in haste, warn me which to ah ah ah ah. . . .

—MEN! Juan responded fullchantedly to her sororal sono-rity, imitating himself capitally with his bubbleblown in his patapet and his chalished drink now well in hand. (A spilt, see, for a split, see see!) Ever gloriously kind! And I truly am

461

eucherised to yous. Also *sacré père* and *maître d'autel*. Well, ladies upon gentlermen and toastmaster general, let us, brindising brandisong, woo and win womenlong with health to rich vineyards, Erin go Dry! Amingst the living waters of, the living in giving waters of. Tight! Loose! A stiff one for Staffetta mullified with creams of hourmony, the coupe that's chill for jackless jill and a filiform dhouche on Doris! Esterelles, be not on your weeping what though Shaunathaun is in his fail! To stir up love's young fizz I tilt with this bridle's cup champagne, dimming douce from her peepair of hideseeks, tightsqueezed on my snowybrusted and while my pearlies in their sparkling wisdom are nippling her bubblets I swear (and let you swear!) by the bumper round of my poor old snaggletooth's solidbowel I ne'er will prove I'm untrue to your liking (theare!) so long as my hole looks. Down.

So gullaby, me poor Isley! But I'm not for forgetting me innerman monophone for I'm leaving my darling proxy behind for your consolering, lost Dave the Dancekerl, a squamous runaway and a dear old man pal of mine too. He will arrive incessantly in the fraction of a crust, who, could he quit doubling and stop tippling, he would be the unicorn of his kind. He's the mightiest penumbrella I ever flourished on behond the shadow of a post! Be sure and link him, me O treasauro, as often as you learn provided there's nothing between you but a plain deal table only don't encourage him to cry lessontimes over Leperstown. But ,soft! Can't be? Do mailstanes mumble? Lumtum lumtum! Now! The froubadour! I fremble! Talk of wolf in a stomach by all that's verminous! Eccolo me! The return of th'athlate! Who can secede to his success! Isn't Jaunstown, Ousterrike, the small place after all? I knew I smelt the garlic leek! Why, bless me swits, here he its, darling Dave, like the catoninelives just in time as if he fell out of space, all draped in mufti, coming home to mourn mountains from his old continence and not on one foot either or on two feet aether but on quinquisecular cycles after his French evolution and a blindfold passage by the 4.32 with the pork's pate in his suicide paw and the gulls laughing lime on his natural skunk, blushing like Pat's pig, begob! He's not too timtom well ashamed to carry out onaglibtograbakelly in his showman's sinister the testymonicals he gave his twenty annis orf, showing the three white feathers, as a home cured emigrant in Paddyouare far below on our sealevel. Bearer may leave the church, signed, Figura Porca, Lictor Magnaffica. He's the sneaking likeness of us, faith, me altar's ego in miniature and every Auxonian aimer's ace as nasal a Romeo as I am, for ever cracking quips on himself, that merry, the jeenjakes, he'd soon arise mother's roses mid bedewing tears under those wild wet lashes onto anny living girl's laftercheeks. That's his little veiniality. And his unpeppeppediment. He has novel ideas I know and he's a jarry queer fish betimes, I grant you, and cantanberous, the poisoner of his word, but lice and all and semicoloured stainedglasses, I'm enormously full of that foreigner, I'll say I am! Got by the one goat, suckled by the same nanna, one twitch, one nature makes us oldworld kin. We're as thick and thin now as two tubular jawballs. I hate him about his patent henesy, plasfh it, yet am I amorist. I love him. I love his old portugal's nose. There's the nasturtium for ye now that saved manny a poor sinker from water on the grave. The diasporation of all pirates and quinconcentrum of a fake like Basilius O'Cormacan MacArty? To camiflag he turned his shirt. Isn't he after borrowing all before him, making friends with everybody red in Rossya, white in Alba and touching every distinguished Ourishman he could ever distinguish before or behind from a Yourishman for the customary halp of a crown and peace? He is looking aged with his pebbled eyes, and johnnythin too, from livicking on pidgins' ifs with puffins' ands, he's been slanderising himself, but I pass no remark. Hope he hasn't the cholera. Give him an eyot in the farout. Moseses and Noasies, how are you? He'd be as snug as Columbsisle Jonas wrocked in the belly of the whaves, as quotad before. Bravo, senior chief! Famose! Sure there's nobody else in touch anysides to hold a chef's cankle to the darling at all for sheer dare with that prisonpotstill of spanish breans on him like the knave of trifles! A jollytan fine demented brick and the prince of goodfilips! Dave knows I have the highest of respect of annyone in my oweand smooth way for that intellectual debtor (Obbligado!) Mushure David R. Crozier. And we're the closest of chems. Mark my use of you, cog! Take notice how I yemploy, crib! Be ware as you, I foil, coppy! It's a pity he can't see it for I'm terribly nice about him. Canwyll y Cymry, the marmade's flamme! A leal of the O'Looniys, a Brazel aboo! The most omportent man! *Shervos!* Ho, be the holy snakes, someone has shaved his rough diamond skull for him as clean as Nuntius' piedish! The burnt out mesh and the matting and all! Thunderweather, khyber schinker escapa sansa pagar! He's the spatton spit, so he is, scaly skin and all, with his blackguarded eye and the goatsbeard in his buttinghole of Shemuel Tulliver, me grandsourd, the old cruxader, when he off with his paudeen! That was to let the crowd of the Flu Flux Fans behind him see me proper. Ah, he's very thoughtful and sympatrico that way is Brother Intelligentius, when he's not absintheminded, with his Paris addresse! He is, really. Holdhard till you'll ear him clicking his bull's bones! Some toad klakkin! You're welcome back, Wilkins, to red berries in the frost! And here's the butter exchange to pfeife and dramn ye with a bawlful of the Moulsaybaysse and yunker doodler wanked to wall awriting off his phoney. I'm tired hairing of you. Hat yourself! Give us your dyed dextremity here, frother, the Claddagh clasp! I met with dapper dandy and he shocked me big the hamd. Where's your watch keeper? You've seen all sorts in shapes and sizes, marauding about the moppamound. How's the cock and the bullfight? And old Auster and Hungrig? And the Beer and Belly and the Boot and Ball? Not forgetting the oils of greas under that turkey in julep and Father Freeshots Feilbogen in his rockery garden with the costard? And did you meet with Peadhar the Grab at all? And did you call on Tower Geesyhus? Was Mona, my own love, no bigger than she should be, making up to you in her bestbehaved manor when you made your breastlaw and made her, tell me? And did you like the landskip from Lambay? I'm better pleased than ten guidneys! You rejoice me! Faith, I'm proud of you, french davit!

464

You've surpassed yourself! Be introduced to yes! This is me aunt Julia Bride, your honour, dying to have you languish to scandal in her bosky old delltangle. You don't reckoneyes him? He's Jackot the Horner who boxed in his corner, jilting no fewer than three female bribes. That's his penals. *Shervorum!* You haven't seen her since she stepped into her drawoffs. Come on, spinister, do your stuff! Don't be shoy, husbandmanvir! Weih, what's on you, wip? Up the shamewaugh! She has plenty of woom in the smallclothes for the bothsforus, nephews push! Hatch yourself well! Enjombyourselves thurily! Would you wait biss she buds till you bite on her? Embrace her bashfully by almeans at my frank incensive and tell her in your semiological agglutinative yez, how Idos be asking after her. Let us be holy and evil and let her be peace on the bough. Sure, she fell in line with our tripertight photos as the lyonised mails when we were stablelads together like the corks again brothers, hungry and angry, cavileer grace by roundhered force, or like boyrun to sibster, me and you, shinners true and pinchme, our tertius quiddus, that never talked or listened. Always raving how we had the wrinkles of a snailcharmer and the slits and sniffers of a fellow that fell foul of the county de Loona and the meattrap of the first vegetarian. To be had for the asking. Have a hug! Take her out of poor tuppeny luck before she goes off in pure treple licquidance. I'd give three shillings a pullet to the canon for the conjugation to shadow you kissing her from me leberally all over as if she was a crucifix. It's good for her bilabials, you understand. There's nothing like the mistletouch for finding a queen's earring false. Chink chink. As the curly bard said after kitchin the womn in his hym to the hum of her garments. You try a little tich to the tissle of his tail. The racist to the racy, rossy. The soil is for the self alone. Be ownkind. Be kithkinish. Be bloodysibby. Be irish. Be inish. Be offalia. Be hamlet. Be the property plot. Be Yorick and Lankystare. Be cool. Be mackinamucks of yourselves. Be finish. No martyr where the preature is there's no plagues like rome. It gives up the gripes. Watch the swansway. Take your tiger over it. The leady on the lake and the convict of the forest.

Why, they might be Babau and Momie! Yipyip! To pan! To pan! To tinpinnypan. All folly me yap to Curlew! Give us a pin for her and we'll call it a tossup. Can you reverse positions? Lets have a fuchu all round, courting cousins! Quuck, the duck of a woman for quack, the drake of a man, her little live apples for Leas and love potients for Leos, the next beast king. Put me down for all ringside seats. I can feel you being corrupted. Recoil. I can see you sprouting scruples. Get back. And as he's boiling with water I'll light your pyre. Turn about, skeezy Sammy, out of metaphor, till we feel are you still tropeful of popetry. Told you so. If you doubt of his love of darearing his feelings you'll very much hurt for mishmash mastufractured on europe you can read off the tail of his. Rip ripper rippest and jac jac jac. Dwell on that, my hero and lander! That's the side that appeals to em, the wring wrong way to wright woman. Shuck her! Let him! What he's good for. Shuck her more! Let him again! All she wants! Could you wheedle a staveling encore out of your imitationer's jubalharp, hey, Mr Jinglejoys? Congregational singing. Rota rota ran the pagoda *con dio in capo ed il diavolo in coda*. Many a diva devoucha saw her Dauber Dan at the priesty pagoda Rota ran. Uck! He's so sedulous to singe always if prumpted, the mirthprovoker! Grunt unto us, I pray, your foreboden article in our own deas dockandoilish introducing the death of Nelson with coloraturas! *Coraio, fra!* And I'll string second to harmanize. My loaf and pottage neaheaheahear Rochelle. With your dumpsey diddely dumpsey die, fiddeley fa. *Diavoloh!* Or come on, schoolcolours, and we'll scrap, rug and mat and then be as chummy as two bashed spuds. Bitrial bay holmgang or betrayal buy jury. Attaboy! Fee gate has Heenan hoity, mind uncle Hare? What, sir? Poss, myster? Acheve! Thou, thou! What say ye? *Taurus periculosus, morbus pedeiculosus. Miserere mei in miseribilibus!* There's uval lavguage for you! The tower is precluded, the mob's in her petticoats; Mr R. E. Meehan is in misery with his billyboots. Begob, there's not so much green in his Ireland's eye! Sweet fellow ovocal, he stones out of stune. But he could be near a colonel with a voice like that. The

bark is still there but the molars are gone. The misery billyboots
I used to lend him before we split and, be the hole in the year,
they were laking like heaven's reflexes. But I told him make your
will be done and go to a general and I'd pray confessions for
him. Areesh! Areesh! And I'll be your intrepider. Ambras!
Ruffle her! Bussing was before the blood and bissing will behind
the curtain. Triss! Did you note that worrid expressionism on
his megalogue? A full octavium below me! And did you hear
his browrings rattlemaking when he was preaching to himself?
And, whoa! do you twig the schamlooking leaf greeping ghastly
down his blousyfrock? Our national umbloom! Areesh! He
won't. He's shoy. Those worthies, my old faher's onkel that
was garotted, Caius Cocoa Codinhand, that I lost in a crowd,
used to chop that tongue of his, japlatin, with my yuonkle's
owlseller, Woowoolfe Woodenbeard, that went stomebathred,
in the Tower of Balbus, as brisk, man, as I'd scoff up muttan
chepps and lobscouse. But it's all deafman's duff to me,
begob. Sam knows miles bettern me how to work the
miracle. And I see by his diarrhio he's dropping the stammer
out of his silenced bladder since I bonded him off more as a
friend and as a brother to try and grow a muff and canonise his
dead feet down on the river airy by thinking himself into the
fourth dimension and place the ocean between his and ours,
the churchyard in the cloister of the depths, after he was capped
out of beurlads scoel for the sin against the past participle and
earned the factitation of codding chaplan and being as homely
gauche as swift B.A.A. Who gets twickly fullgets twice as alle-
manden huskers. But the whacker his word the weaker our ears
for auracles who parles parses orileys. Illstarred punster, lipster-
ing cowknucks. 'Twas the quadra sent him and Trinity too. And
he can cantab as chipper as any oxon ever I mood with, a tiptoe
singer! He'll prisckly soon hand tune your Erin's ear for you.
p.p. a mimograph at a time, numan bitter, with his ancomartins
to read the road roman with false steps ad Pernicious from
rhearsilvar ormolus to torquinions superbers while I'm far
away from wherever thou art serving my tallyhos and tullying

467

my hostilious by going in by the most holy recitatandas *ffff* for my varsatile examinations in the ologies, to be a coach on the Fukien mission. P? F? How used you learn me, brather soboostius, in my augustan days? With cesarella looking on. In the beginning was the gest he jousstly says, for the end is with woman, flesh-without-word, while the man to be is in a worse case after than before since she on the supine satisfies the verg to him! Toughtough, tootoological. Thou the first person shingeller. Art, an imperfect subjunctive. Paltry, flappent, had serious. Miss Smith onamatterpoetic. Hammis-andivis axes colles waxes warmas like sodullas. So pick your stops with fondnes snow. And mind you twine the twos noods of your nicenames. And pull up your furbelovs as far-above as you're farthingales. That'll hint him how to click the trigger. Show you shall and won't he will! His hearing is in-doubting just as my seeing is onbelieving. So dactylise him up to blankpoint and let him blink for himself where you speak the best ticklish. You'll feel what I mean. Fond namer, let me never see thee blame a kiss for shame a knee!

Echo, read ending! Siparioramoci! But from the stress of their sunder enlivening, ay clasp, deciduously, a nikrokosmikon must come to mike.

— Well, my positively last at any stage! I hate to look at alarms but, however they put on my watchcraft, must now close as I hereby hear by ear from by seeless socks 'tis time to be up and ambling. Mymiddle toe's mitching, so mizzle I must else 'twill sarve me out. Gulp a bulper at parting and the moore the melodest! Farewell but whenever, as Tisdall told Toole. Tempos fidgets. Let flee me fiaekles, says the grand old mano-ark, stormcrested crowcock and undulant hair, hoodies tway! Yes, faith, I am as mew let freer, beneath me corthage, bound. I'm as bored now bawling beersgrace at sorepaws there as Andrew Clays was sharing sawdust with Daniel's old collie. This shack's not big enough for me now. I'm dreaming of ye, azores. And, re-member this, a chorines, there's the witch on the heath, sistra! 'Bansheeba peeling hourihaared while her Orcotron is hoaring ho. And whinn muinnuit flittsbit twinn her ttittshe cries tallmidy! Daughters of the heavens, be lucks in turnabouts to the wandering sons of red loam! The earth's atrot! The sun's a scream! The air's a jig. The water's great! Seven oldy oldy hills and the one blue beamer. I'm going. I know I am. I could bet I am. Somewhere I must get far away from Banbashore, wherever I am. No saddle, no staffet, but spur on the moment! So I think I'll take freeboots' advise. Psk! I'll borrow a path to lend me wings, quickquack, and from Jehusalem's wall, clickclack, me courser's clear, to Cheerup street I'll travel the void world over. It's Winland for moyne, bickbuck! Jeejakers! I hurt meself nettly that time! Come, my good frogmarchers! We felt the fall but we'll front the defile. Was not my olty mutther, Sereth Maritza, a Runningwater? And the bould one that quickened her the seaborne Fingale? I feel like that hill of a whaler went yulding round Groenmund's Circus with his tree full of seaweeds and Dinky Doll asleep in her shell. Hazelridge has seen me. Jerne valing is. Squall aboard for Kew, hop! Farewell awhile to her and thee! The brine's my bride to be. Lead on, Macadam, and danked be he who first sights Halt Linduff! Solo, solone, solong! Lood Erynnana, ware thee wail! With me singame soarem o'erem! Here's me take off. Now's nunc or nimmer, siskinder! Here goes the enemy! Bennydick hotfoots onimpudent stayers! Sorry! I bless alls to the whished with this panromain apological which Watllwewhistlem sang to the kerrycoys. Break ranks! After wage-of-battle bother I am thinking most. Fik yew! I'm through. Won. Toe. Adry. You watch my smoke.

After poor Jaun the Boast's last fireless words of postludium of his soapbox speech ending in'sheaven, twentyaid add one with a flirt of wings were pouring to his bysistance (could they snip that curl of curls to lay with their gloves and keep the kids bright!) prepared to cheer him should he leap or to curse him should he fall, but, with their biga triga rheda rodeo, the cherubs in the charabang, set down here and sedan chair, don't you wish you'd a yoke or a bit in your mouth, repulsing all attempts at first hands on, as no es nada, our greatly misunderstood one we perceived to give himself some sort of a hermetic prod or kick to sit up and take notice, which acted like magic, while the phalanx of daughters of February Filldyke, embushed and climbing, ramblers and weeps, voiced approval in their customary manner by dropping kneedeep in tears over their concelebrated meednight sunflower, piopadey boy, their solase in dorckaness, and splattering together joyously the plaps of their tappyhands as, with a cry of genuine distress, so prettly prattly pollylogue, they viewed him, the just one, their darling, away.

A dream of favours, a favourable dream. They know how they believe that they believe that they know. Wherefore they wail.

Eh jourd'weh! Oh jourd'woe! dosiriously it psalmodied. Guesturn's lothlied answring to-maronite's wail.

Oasis, cedarous esaltarshoming Leafboughnoon!

Oisis, coolpressus onmountof Sighing!

Oasis, palmost esaltarshoming Gladdays!

Oisis, phantastichal roseway anjerichol!

Oasis, newleavos spaciosing encampness!

Oisis, plantainous dewstuckacqmirage playtennis!

Pipetto, Pipetta has misery unnoticed!

But the strangest thing happened. Backscuttling for the hop off with the odds altogether in favour of his tumbling into the river, Jaun just then I saw to collect from the gentlest weaner among the weiners, (who by this were in half droopleaflong mourning for the passing of the last post) the familiar yellow label into which he let fall a drop, smothered a curse, choked a guffaw, spat expectoratiously and blew his own trumpet. And next thing was he gummalicked the stickyback side and stamped the oval badge of belief to his agnelows brow with a genuine dash of irrepressible piety that readily turned his ladylike typmanzelles capsy curvy (the holy scamp!), with half a glance of Irish frisky (a Juan Jaimesan *hastaluego*) from under the shag of his parallel brows. It was then he made as if be but waved instead a handacross the sea as notice to quit while the pacifettes made their armpacts widdershins (Frida! Freda!

470

Paza! Paisy! Irine! Areinette! Bridomay! Bentamai! Sososopky! Bebebekka! Bababadkessy! Ghugugoothoyou! Dama! Damadomina! Takiya! Tokaya! Scioccara! Siuccherillina! Peocchia! Peucchia! Ho Mi Hoping! Ha Me Happinice! Mirra! Myrha! Solyma! Salemita! Sainta! Sianta! O Peace!), but in selfrighting the balance of his corporeity to reexchange widerembrace with the pillarbosom of the Dizzier he loved prettier, between estellos and venoussas, bad luck to the lie but when next to nobody expected, their star and gartergazer at the summit of his climax, he toppled a lipple on to the off and, making a brandnew start for himself to run down his easting, by blessing hes sthers with the sign of the southern cross, his bungaloid borsaline with the hedgygreen bound blew off in a loveblast (award for trover!) and Jawjon Redhead, bucketing after, meccamaniac, (the headless shall have legs!), kingscouriered round with an easy rush and ready relays by the bridge a stadion beyond Ladycastle (and what herm but he narrowly missed fouling her buttress for her but for he acqueducked) and then, cocking a snook at the stock of his sermons, so mear and yet so fahr from that region's general, away with him at the double, the hulk of a garron, pelting after the road, on Shanks's mare, let off like a wind hound loose (the bouchal! you'd think it was that moment they gave him the jambos!) with a posse of tossing hankerwaves to his windward like seraph's summonses on the air and a tempest of good things in packetshape teeming from all accounts into the funnel of his fanmail shrimpnet, along the highroad of the nation, Traitor's Track, following which fond floral fray he was quickly lost to sight through the statuemen though without a doubt he was all the more on that same head to memory dear while Sickerson, that borne of bjoerne, *la garde auxiliaire* she murmured, hellyg Ursulinka, full of woe (and how fitlier should goodboy's hand be shook than by the warmin of her besom that wrung his swaddles?): *Where maggot Harvey kneeled till bags? Ate Andrew coos hogdam farvel!*

Wethen, now, may the good people speed you, rural Haun, export stout fellow that you are, the crooner born with sweet wail of evoker, healing music, ay, and heart in hand of Sham-rogueshire! The googoos of the suckabolly in the rockabeddy are become the copiosity of wiseableness of the friarylayman in the pulpitbarrel. May your bawny hair grow rarer and fairer, our own only wideheaded boy! Rest your voice! Feed your mind! Mint your peas! Coax your qyous! Come to disdoon blarmey and walk our groves so charming and see again the sweet rockelose where first you hymned *O Ciesa Mea!* and touch the light theorbo! Songster, angler, choreographer! Piper to prisoned! Musicianship made Embrassador-at-Large! Good by nature and natural by design, had you but been spared to us, Hauneen lad, but sure where's the use my talking quicker when I know you'll hear me all astray? My long farewell I send to you, fair dream of sport and game and always something new'. Gone is Haun! My grief, my ruin! Our Joss-el-Jovan! Our Chris-na-Murty! 'Tis well you'll be looked after from last to first as yon beam of light we follow receding on your photophoric pilgrimage to your antipodes in the past, you who so often consigned your distributory tidings of great joy into our nevertoolatetolove box, mansuetudinous manipulator, victimisedly victorihoarse, dearest Haun of all, you of the boots, true as adie, stepwalker, pennyatimer, lampaddyfair, postanulengro, our rommanychiel! Thy now paling light lucerne we ne'er may see again. But could it speak how nicely would it splutter to the four cantons praises be to thee, our pattern sent! For you had — may I, in our, your and their names, dare to say it? — the nucleus of a glow of a zeal of soul of service such as rarely, if ever, have I met with single men. Numerous are those who, nay, there are a dozen of folks still unclaimed by the death angel in this country of ours today, humble indivisibles in this grand continuum, overlorded by fate and interlarded with accidence, who, while there are hours and days, will fervently pray to the spirit above that they may never depart this earth of theirs till in his long run from that place where the day begins, ere he retourneys postexilic, on that day that belongs to joyful Ireland, the people that is of all time, the old old oldest, the young young youngest, after decades of

472

longsuffering and decennia of brief glory, to mind us of what was when and to matter us of the withering of our ways, their Janyouare Fibyouare wins true from Sylvester (only Walker himself is like Waltzer, whimsicalissimo they go murmurand) comes marching ahome on the summer crust of the flagway. Life, it is true, will be a blank without you because avicuum's not there at all, to nomore cares from nomad knows, ere Molochy wars bring the devil era, a slip of the time between a date and a ghostmark, rived by darby's chilldays embers, spatched fun Juhn that dandyforth, from the night we are and feel and fade with to the yesterselves we tread to turnupon.

But, boy, you did your strong nine furlong mile in slick and slapstick record time and a farfetched deed it was in troth, champion docile, with your high bouncing gait of going and your feat of passage will be contested with you and through you, for centuries to come. The phaynix rose a sun before Erebia sank his smother! Shoot up on that, bright Bennu bird! *Va faotre!* Eftsoon so too will our own sphoenix spark spirt his spyre and sunward stride the rampante flambe. Ay, already the sombrer opacities of the gloom are sphanished! Brave footsore Haun! Work your progress! Hold to! Now! Win out, ye divil ye! The silent cock shall crow at last. The west shall shake the east awake. Walk while ye have the night for morn, lightbreakfast-bringer, morroweth whereon every past shall full fost sleep. Amain.

Lowly, longly, a wail went forth. Pure Yawn lay low. On the mead of the hillock lay, heartsoul dormant mid shadowed landshape, brief wallet to his side, and arm loose, by his staff of citron briar, tradition stick-pass-on. His dream monologue was over, of cause, but his drama parapolylogic had yet to be, affact. Most distressfully (but, my dear, how successfully!) to wail he did, his locks of a lucan tinge, quickrich, ripely rippling, unfilleted, those lashbetasselled lids on the verge of closing time, whiles ouze of his sidewiseopen mouth the breath of him, evenso languishing as the princeliest treble treacle or lichee chewchow purse could buy. Yawn in a semiswoon lay awailing and (hooh!) what helpings of honeyful swoothead (phew!), which earpiercing dulcitude! As were you suppose to go and push with your bluntblank pin in hand upinto his fleshasplush cushionettes of some chubby boybold love of an angel. Hwoah!

When, as the buzzer brings the light brigade, keeping the home fires burning, so on the churring call themselves came at him, from the westborders of the eastmidlands, three kings of three suits and a crowner, from all their cardinal parts, along the amber way where Brosna's furzy. To lift them they did, senators four, by the first quaint skreek of the gloaming and they hopped it up the mountainy molehill, traversing climes of old times gone by of the days not worth remembering; inventing some excusethems, any sort, having a sevenply

474

sweat of night blues moist upon them. Feefee! phopho!!
foorchtha!!!aggala!!!!jeeshee!!!!!paloola!!!!!!ooridiminy!!!!!!!
Afeared themselves were to wonder at the class of a crossroads
puzzler he would likely be, length by breadth nonplussing his
thickness, ells upon ells of him, making so many square yards of
him, one half of him in Conn's half but the whole of him nevertheless in Owenmore's five quarters. There would he lay till
they would him descry, spancelled down upon a blossomy bed, at
one foule stretch, amongst the daffydowndillies, the flowers of
narcosis fourfettering his footlights, a halohedge of wild spuds
hovering over him, epicures waltzing with gardenfillers, puritan
shoots advancing to Aran chiefs. Phopho!! The meteor pulp
of him, the seamless rainbowpeel. Aggala!!!! His bellyvoid of
nebulose with his neverstop navel. Paloola!!!!!! And his veins
shooting melanite phosphor, his creamtocustard cometshair and
his asteroid knuckles, ribs and members. Ooridiminy!!!!!!! His
electrolatiginous twisted entrails belt.

Those four claymen clomb together to hold their sworn star-
chamber quiry on him. For he was ever their quarrel, the way
they would see themselves, everybug his bodiment atop of
annywom her notion, and the meet of their noght was worth two
of his morning. Up to the esker ridge it was, Mallinger parish, to a
mead that was not far, the son's rest. First klettered Shanator
Gregory, seeking spoor through the deep timefield, Shanator
Lyons, trailing the wavy line of his partition footsteps (something in his blisters was telling him all along how he had
been in that place one time), then his Recordership, Dr Shuna-
dure Tarpey, caperchasing after honourable sleep, hot on to the
aniseed and, up out of his prompt corner, old Shunny MacShunny,
MacDougal the hiker, in the rere of them on the run, to make a
quorum. Roping their ass he was, their skygrey globetrotter,
by way of an afterthought and by no means legless either for
such sprouts on him they were that much oneven it was tumbling
he was by four lengths, within the bawl of a mascot, kuss yuss,
kuss cley, patsy watsy, like the kapr in the kabisses, the big ass,
to hear with his unaided ears the harp in the air, the bugle

dianablowing, wild as wild, the mockingbird whose word is misfortune, so 'tis said, the bulbul down the wind.

The proto was traipsing through the tangle then, Mathew Walker, godsons' goddestfar, deputising for gossipocracy, and his station was a few perch to the weatherside of the knoll Asnoch and it was from no other place unless there, how and ever, that he proxtended aloof upon the ether Mesmer's Manuum, the hand making silence. The buckos beyond on the lea, then stopped wheresoever they found their standings and that way they set ward about him, doing obedience, nod, bend, bow and curtsey, like the watchers of Prospect, upholding their broad-awake prober's hats on their firrum heads, the travelling court on its findings circuiting that personer in his fallen. And a crack quat-youare of stenoggers they made of themselves, solons and psy-chomorers, all told, with their hurts and daimons, spites and clops, not even to the seclusion of their beast by them that was the odd trick of the pack, trump and no friend of carrots. And, what do you think, who should be laying there above all other persons forenenst them only Yawn! All of asprawl he was laying too amengst the poppies and, I can tell you something more than that, drear writer, profoundly as you may bedeave to it, he was oscasleep asleep. And it was far more similar to a satrap he lay there with unctuous beauty all surrounded, the poser, or for whatall I know like Lord Lumen, coaching his preferred constellations in faith and doctrine, for old Matt Gregory, 'tis he had the starmenag-erie, Marcus Lyons and Lucas Metcalfe Tarpey and the mack that never forgave the ass that lurked behind him, Jonny na Hossaleen.

More than their good share of their five senses ensorcelled you would say themselves were, fuming censor, the way they could not rightly tell their heels from their stools as they cooched down a mamalujo by his cubical crib, as question time drew nighing and the map of the souls' groupography rose in relief within their quarterings, to play tops or kites or hoops or marbles, curchycurchy, gawking on him, for the issuance of his pnum and softnoising one of them to another one, the boguaqueesthers.

And it is what they began to say to him tetrahedrally then, the masters, what way was he.

— He's giving, the wee bairn. Yun has lived.

— Yerra, why dat, my leader?

— Wisha, is he boosed or what, alannah?

— Or his wind's from the wrong cut, says Ned of the Hill.

— Lesten!

— Why so and speak up, do you hear me, you sir?

— Or he's rehearsing somewan's funeral.

— Whisht outatthat! Hubba's up!

And as they were spreading abroad on their octopuds their drifter nets, the chromous gleamy seiners' nets and, no lie, there was word of assonance being softspoken among those quartermasters.

— Get busy, kid!

— Chirpy, come now!

— The present hospices is a good time.

— I'll take on that chap.

For it was in the back of their mind's ear, temptive lissomer, how they would be spreading in quadriliberal their azurespotted fine attractable nets, their nansen nets, from Matt Senior to the thurrible mystagogue after him and from thence to the neighbour and that way to the puisny donkeyman and his crucifer's cauda. And in their minds years backslibris, so it was, slipping beauty, how they would be meshing that way, when he rose to it, with the planckton at play about him, the quivers of scaly silver and their clutches of chromes of the highly lucid spanishing gold whilst, as hour gave way to mazing hour, with Yawn himself keeping time with his thripthongue, to ope his blurbeous lips he would, a let out classy, the way myrrh of the moor and molten moonmist would be melding mellifond indo his mouth.

— Y?

— Before You!

— Ecko! How sweet thee answer makes! Afterwheres? In the land of lions' odor?

— Friends! First if yu don't mind. Name yur historical grouns.

— This same prehistoric barrow 'tis, the orangery.

477

— I see. Very good now. It is in your orangery, I take it, you have your letters. Can you hear here me, you sir?

— Throsends. For my darling. Typette!

— So long aforetime? Can you hear better?

— Millions. For godsends. For my darling dearling one.

— Now, to come nearer zone; I would like to raise my deuterous point audibly touching this. There is this maggers. I am told by our interpreter, Hanner Esellus, that there are fully six hundred and six ragwords in your malherbal Magis lande-guage in which wald wand rimes alpman and there is resin in all roots for monarch but yav hace not one pronouncable teerm that blows in all the vallums of tartallaght to signify majestate, even provisionally, nor no rheda rhoda or torpentine path or halluci-nian via nor aurellian gape nor sunkin rut nor grossgrown trek nor crimeslaved cruxway and no moorhens cry or mooner's plankgang there to lead us to hopenhaven. Is such the *unde deri-vatur* casematter messio! Frankly. *Magis megis enerretur mynus hoc intelligow.*

— How? C'est mal prononsable, tartagliano, perfrances. Vous n'avez pas d'o dans votre boche provenciale, mousoo. Je m'in-cline mais *Moy jay trouvay la clee dang les champs.* Hay sham nap poddy velour, come on!

— Hep there! Commong, sa na pa de valure? Whu's teit dans yur jambs? Whur's that inclining and talkin about the messiah so cloover? A true's to your trefling! Whure yu!

— Trinathan partnick dieudonnay. Have you seen her? Typette, my tactile O!

— Are you in your fatherick, lonely one?

— The same. Three persons. Have you seen my darling only one? I am sohohold!

— What are yu shevering about, ultramontane, like a houn? Is there cold on ye, doraphobian? Or do yu want yur primafairy schoolmam?

— The woods of fogloot! O mis padredges!

— Whisht awhile, greyleg! The duck is rising and you'll wake that stand of plover. I know that place better than anyone. Sure,

478

I used to be always overthere on the fourth day at my grandmother's place, Tear-nan-Ogre, my little grey home in the west,
in or about Mayo when the long dog gave tongue and they
coursing the marches and they straining at the leash. Tortoise-
shell for a guineagould! Burb! Burb! Burb! Follow me up
Tucurlugh! That's the place for the claire oysters, Polldoody,
County Conway. I never knew how rich I was like another story in
the zoedone of the zephyros, strolling and strolling, carrying my
dragoman, Meads Marvel, thass withumpronouceable tail, along
the shore. Do you know my cousin, Mr Jasper Dougal that
keeps the Anchor on the Mountain, the parson's son, Jasper of
the Tuns, Pat Whateveryournameis?

— Dood and I dood. The wolves of Fochlut! By Whydoyou-
callme? Do not flingamejig to the twolves!

— Turcafiera amd that's a good wan right enough! Wooluvs
no less!

— One moment now, if I foreshorten the bloss on your
bleather. Encroachement spells erosion. Dunlin and turnstone
augur us where, how and when best as to burial of carcass, fuselage of dump and committal of noisance. But, since you invocate
austers for the trailing of vixens, I would like to send a cormo-
rant around this blue lagoon. Tell me now this. You told my
larned friend rather previously, a moment since, about this mound
or barrow. Now I suggest to you that ere there was this plague-
burrow, as you seem to call it, there was a burialbattell, the boat
of millions of years. Would you bear me out in that, relatively
speaking, with her jackstaff jerking at her pennyladders, why
not, and sizing a fair sail, knowest thout the kind? The *Pourquoi
Pas*, bound for Weissduwasland, that fourmaster barquentine,
Webster says, our ship that ne're returned. The Frenchman, I say,
was an orangeboat. He is a boat. You see him. The both how
you see is they! Draken af Danemork! Sacked it or ate it? What!
Hennu! Spake ab laut!

—Couch, cortege, ringbarrow, dungcairn. Beseek the runes
and see the longurn! Allmaun away when you hear the gang-
horn. And meet Nautsen. Ess Ess. O ess. Warum night! Con-

ning two lay payees. Norsker. Her raven flag was out, the slaver. I trow pon good, jordan's scaper, good's barnet and trustyman. Crouch low, you pigeons three! Say, call that girl with the tan tress awn! Call Wolfhound! Wolf of the sea. Folchu! Folchu!

— Very good now. That folklore's straight from the ass his mouth. I will crusade on with the parent ship, weather prophetting, far away from those green hills, a station, Ireton tells me, bonofide for keeltappers, now to come to the midnight middy on this levantine ponenter. From Daneland sailed the oxeyed man, now mark well what I say.

— Magnus Spadebeard, korsets krosser, welsher perfyddye. A destroyer in our port. Signed to me with his baling scoop. Laid bare his breastpaps to give suck, to suckle me. Ecce Hagios Chrisman!

— Oh, Jeyses, fluid! says the poisoned well. Futtfishy the First. Hootchcopper's enkel at the navel manuvres!

— Hep! Hello there, Bill of old Bailey! Whu's he? Whu's this lad, why the pups?

— Hunkalus Childared Easterheld. It's his lost chance, Emania. Ware him well.

— Hey! Did you dream you were ating your own tripe, acushla, that you tied yourself up that wrynecky fix?

— I see now. We move in the beast circuls. Grimbarb and pancercrucer! You took the words out of my mouth. A child's dread for a dragon vicefather. Hillcloud encompass us! You mean you lived as milky at their lyceum, couard, while you learned, volp volp, to howl yourself wolfwise. Dyb! Dyb! Do your best.

— I am dob dob dobbling like old Booth's, courteous. The cubs are after me, it zeebs, the whole totem pack, vuk vuk and vuk vuk to them, for Robinson's shield.

— Scents and gouspils! The animal jangs again! Find the fingall harriers! Here howl me wiseacre's hat till I die of the milkman's lupus!

— What? Wolfgang? Whoah! Talk very slowe!

— Hail him heathen, heal him holystone!
Courser, Recourser, Changechild . . . . ?
Eld as endall, earth . . . . ?

— A cataleptic mithyphallic! Was this *Totem Fulcrum Est*
Ancestor yu hald in *Dies Eirae* where no spider webbeth or
Anno Mundi ere bawds plied in Skiffstrait? Be fair, Chris!

— Dream. Ona nonday I sleep. I dreamt of a somday. Of a
wonday I shall wake. Ah! May he have now of here fearfilled
me! Sinflowed, O sinflowed! Fia! Fia! Befurcht christ!

— I have your tristich now; it recurs in three times the same
differently (there is such a fui fui story which obtains of him):
comming nown from the asphalt to the concrete, from the human
historic brute, Finnsen Faynean, occeanyclived, to this same
vulganized hillsir from yours, Mr Tupling Toun of Morning
de Heights, with his lavast flow and his rambling undergroands,
would he reoccur *Ad Horam,* as old Romeo Rogers, in city or
county, and your sure ob, or by, with or from an urb, of you
know the differenciabus, as brauchbarred in apabhramsa, sierrah!
We speak of Gun, the farther. And in the locative. Bap! Bap!

— Ouer Tad, Hellig Babbau, whom certayn orbits assertant
re humeplace of Chivitats Ei, Smithwick, Rhonnda, Kaledon,
Salem (Mass), Childers, Argos and Duthless. Well, I am advised
he might in a sense be both nevertheless, every at man like myself, suffix it to say, Abrahamsk and Brookbear! By him it was
done bapka, by me it was gone into, to whom it will beblive,
Mushame, Mushame! I am afraid you could not heave ahore one
of your own old stepstones, barnabarnabarn, over a stumble-
down wall here in Huddlestown to this classic Noctuber night
but itandthey woule binge, much as vecious, off the dosshouse
back of a racerider in his truetoflesh colours, either handicapped
on her flat or barely repeating himself. That is a tiptip tim oldy
faher now the man I go in fear of, Tommy Terracotta, and he
could be all your and my das, the brodar of the founder of the
father of the finder of the pfander of the pfunder of the furst man
in Ranelagh, fué! fué! Petries and violet ice (I am yam, as Me
and Tam Tower used to jagger pemmer it, over at the house of

Eddy's Christy, meaning Dodgfather, Dodgson and Coo) and spiriduous sanction!

— Breeze softly. Aures are aureas. Hau's his naun?

— Me das has or oreils. Piercey, piercey, piercey, piercey!

— White eyeluscious and muddyhorsebroth! Pig Pursyriley! But where do we get off, chiseller?

— Haltstille, Lucas and Dublinn! Vulva! Vulva! Vulva! Vulva!

— Macdougal, Atlantic City, or his onagrass that is, chuam and coughan! I would go near identifying you from your stavrotides, Jong of Maho, and the weslarias round your yokohahat. And that O'mulanchonry plucher you have from the worst curst of Ireland, Glwlwd of the Mghtwg Grwpp, is no use to you either, Johnny my donkeyschott. Number four, fix up your spreadeagle and pull your weight!

— Hooshin hom to our regional's hin and the gander of Hayden. Would ye ken a young stepschuler of psychical chirography, the name of Keven, or (let outers pray) Evan Vaughan, of his Posthorn in the High Street, that was shooing a Guiney gagag, Poulepinter, that found the dogumen number one, I would suggest, an illegible downfumbed by an unelgible?

— If I do know sinted sageness? Sometimes he would keep silent for a few minutes as if in prayer and clasp his forehead and during the time he would be thinking to himself and he would not mind anybody who would be talking to him or crying stinking fish. But I no way need you, stroke oar nor your quick handles. Your too farfar a cock of the north there, Matty Armagh, and your due south so.

— South I see. You're up-in-Leal-Ulster and I'm-free-Down-in-Easia, this is much better. He is cured by faith who is sick of fate. The prouts who will invent a writing there ultimately is the poeta, still more learned, who discovered the raiding there originally. That's the point of eschatology our book of kills reaches for now in soandso many counterpoint words. What can't be coded can be decorded if an ear aye sieze what no eye ere grieved for. Now, the doctrine obtains, we have occasioning cause caus-

ing effects and affects occasionally recausing altereffects. Or I
will let me take it upon myself to suggest to twist the penman's
tale posterwise. The gist is the gist of Shaum but the hand is
the hand of Sameas. Shan - Shim - Schung. There is a strong
suspicion on counterfeit Kevin and we all remember ye in childhood's reverye. 'Tis the bells of scandal that gave tune to
grumble over him and someone between me and thee. He would
preach to the two turkies and dipdip all the dindians, this master
the abbey, and give gold tidings to all that are in the bonze age
of anteproresurrectionism to entrust their easter neappearance
to Borsaiolini's house of hatcraft. He is our sent on the firm.
Now, have you reasonable hesitancy in your mind about him
after fourpriest redmass or are you in your post? Tell me andat
sans dismay. Leap, pard!

— Fierappel putting years on me! Nwo, nwo! This bolt in
hand be my worder! I'll see you moved farther, blarneying
Marcantonio! What cans such wretch to say to I or how have My
to doom with him? We were wombful of mischief and initium-
wise, everliking a liked, hairytop on heeltipper, alpybecca's un-
wachsibles, an ikeson am ikeson, that babe, imprincipially, my
leperd brethren, the Puer, ens innocens of but fifteen primes.
Ya all in your kalblionized so trilustriously standing the real
school, to be upright as his match, healtheous as is egg, saviour
so the salt and good wee braod, parallaling buttyr, did I alter-
mobile him to a flare insiding hogsfat. Been ike hins kinder-
gardien? I know not, O cashla, I am sure offed habitand this
undered heaven, meis enfins, contrasting the first mover, that
father I ascend fromming knows, as I think, caused whom I, a
self the sign, came remaining being dwelling ayr, plage and
watford as to I was eltered impostulance possessing my future
state falling towards thrice myself resting the childhide when
I received the habit following Mezienius connecting Mezosius
including was verted embracing a palegrim, circumcised my
hairs, Oh laud, and removed my clothes from patristic motives,
meas minimas culpads! Permitting this ick (ickle coon icoocoon)
crouched low entering humble down, dead thrue mean scato-

logical past, making so smell partaking myself to confess abiding clean tumbluponing yous octopods, mouthspeech allno finger-force, owning my mansuetude before him attaching Audeon's prostratingwards mine sore accompanying my thrain tropps offering meye eyesalt, what I (the person whomin I now am) did not do, how he to say essied anding how he was making errand andanding how he all locutey sunt, why did you, my sexth best friend, blabber always you would be so delated to back me, then ersed irredent, toppling Humphrey hugging Nephew, old begge-laut, designing such post sitting his night office? Annexing then, producing Saint Momuluius, you snub around enclosing your moving motion touching the other catachumens continuing say providing append of signature quoniam you will celebrand my dirthdags quoniam, concealed a concealer, I am twosides uppish, a mockbelief insulant, ending none meer hyber irish. Well, chunk your dimned chink, before avtokinatown, forasmuch as many have tooken in hand to, I may as well humbly correct that ves-pian now in case of temporalities. I've my pockets full comeplay of you laycreated cardonals, ap rince, ap rowler, ap rancer, ap rowdey! Improperial! I saved you fore of the Hekkites and you loosed me hind bland Harry to the burghmote of Aud Dub. I teachet you in fair time, my elders, the W.X.Y.Z. and P.Q.R.S. of legatine powers and you, Ailbey and Ciardeclan, I learn, episcop-ing me altogether, circumdeditioned me. I brought you from the loups of Lazary and you have remembered my lapsus langways. Washywatchywataywatashy! Oirasesheorebukujibun! Wata-cooshy lot! Mind of poison is. That time thing think! Honorific remembrance to spit humble makes. My ruridecanal caste is a cut above you peregrines. Aye vouchu to rumanescu. See the leabhour of my generations! Has not my master, Theophrastius Spheropneu-maticus, written that the spirit is from the upper circle? I'm of the ochlocracy with Prestopher Palumbus and Porvus Parrio. Soa koa Kelly Terry per Chelly Derry lepossette. Ho look at my jailbrand Exquovis and sequencias High marked on me fake-similar in the foreign by Pappagallus and Pumpusmugnus: ahem! Anglicey: *Eggs squawfish lean yoe nun feed marecurious.*

484

Sagart can self laud nilobstant to Lowman Catlick's patrician morning coat of arms with my High tripenniferry cresta and caudal mottams: Itch dean: which Gaspey, Otto and Sauer, he renders: echo stay so! Addressing eat or not eat body Yours am. And, Mind, praisegad, is the first praisonal Egoname Yod heard boissboissy in Moy Bog's domesday. Hastan the vista! Or in alleman: Suck at!

— Suck it yourself, sugarstick! Misha, Yid think whose was asking to luckat your sore toe or to taste your gaspy, hot and sour! Ichthyan! Hegvat tosser! Gags be plebsed! Between his voyous and her consinnantes! Thugg, Dirke and Hacker with Rose Lankester and Blanche Yorke! Are we speachin d'anglas landadge or are you sprakin sea Djoytsch? Oy söy, Bleseyblasey, where to go is knowing remain? Become quantity that discourse bothersome when what do? Knowing remain? Come back, baddy wrily, to Bullydamestough! Cum him, buddy rowly, with me! What about your thruppenny croucher of an old fellow, me boy, through the ages, tell us, eh? What about Brian's the Vauntand-onlieme, Master Monk, eh, eh, *Spira in Me Domino*, spear me Doyne! Fat prize the bonafide peachumpidgeonlover, eh, eh, eh, esquire earwugs, escusado, of Jenkins' Area, with his I've Ivy under his tangue and the hohallo to his dullaphone, before there was a sound in the world? How big was his boost friend and be shanghaied to him? The swaaber! The twicer, trifoaled in Wan-stable! Loud's curse to him! If you hored him outerly as we harum lubberintly, from morning rice till nightmale, with his drums and bones and hums in drones your innereer'd heerdly heer he. Ho ha hi he hung! Tsing tsing!

— Me no angly mo, me speakee Yellman's lingas. Nicey Doc Mistel Lu, please! Me no pigey ludiments all same numpa one Topside Tellmastoly fella. Me pigey savvy a singasong anothel time. Pleasie, Mista Lukie Walkie! Josadam cowbelly maam belongame shepullamealahmalong, begolla, Jackinaboss belonga-she; plentymuch boohoomeo.

— Hell's Confucium and the Elements! Tootoo moohootch! Thot's never the postal cleric, checking chinchin chat with nip-

ponnippers! Halt there sob story to your lambdad's tale! Are
you roman cawthrick 432?

— *Quadrigue my yoke.*
Triple my tryst.
Tandem my sire.

— History as her is harped. Too the toone your owldfrow lied
of. Tantris, hattrick, tryst and parting, by vowelglide! I feel
your thrilljoy mouths overtspeaking, O dragoman, hands under-
studium. Plunger words what paddle verbed. Mere man's mime:
God has jest. The old order changeth and lasts like the first.
Every third man has a chink in his conscience and every other
woman has a jape in her mind. Now, fix on the little fellow in my
eye, Minucius Mandrake, and follow my little psychosinology,
poor armer in slingslang. Now I, the lord of Tuttu, am placing
that inital T square of burial jade upright to your temple a
moment. Do you see anything, templar?

— I see a blackfrinch pliestrycook . . . who is carrying on
his brainpan . . . a cathedral of lovejelly for his . . . *Tiens*, how
he is like somebodies!

— Pious, a pious person. What sound of tistress isoles my
ear? I horizont the same, this serpe with ramshead, and lay it
lightly to your lip a little. What do you feel, liplove?

— I feel a fine lady . . . floating on a stillstream of
isisglass . . . with gold hair to the bed . . . and white arms to the
twinklers . . . O la la!

— Purely, in a pure manner. O, sey but swift and still a vain
essaying! Trothed today, trenned tomorrow. I invert the initial
of your tripartite and sign it sternly, and adze to girdle, on your
breast. What do you hear, breastplate?

— I ahear of a hopper behidin the door slappin his feet in a
pool of bran.

— Bellax, acting like a bellax. And so the triptych vision
passes. Out of a hillside into a hillside. Fairshee fading. Again
am I deliciated by the picaresqueness of your irmages. Now,
the oneir urge iterimpellant, I feel called upon to ask did it
ever occur to you, *qua* you, prior to this, by a stretch of

your iberborealic imagination, when it's quicker than this quacking that you might, bar accidens, be very largely substituted in potential secession from your next life by a complementary character, voices apart? Upjack! I shudder for your thought! Think! Put from your mind that and take on trust this. The next word depends on your answer.

— I'm thinking to, thogged be thenked! I was just trying to think when I thought I felt a flea. I might have. I cannot say for it is of no significance at all. Once or twice when I was in odinburgh with my addlefoes, Jake Jones, the handscabby, when I thinkled I wore trying on my garden substisuit, boy's apert, at my nexword nighboor's, and maybe more largely nor you quosh yet you, messmate, realise. A few times, so to shape, I chanced to be stretching, in the shadow as I thought, the liferight out of myself in my ericulous imaginating. I felt feeling a half Scotch and pottage like roung my middle ageing like Bewley in the baste so that I indicate out to myself and I swear my gots how that I'm not meself at all, no jolly fear, when I realise bimiselves how becomingly I to be going to become.

— O, is that the way with you, you craythur? In the becoming was the weared, wontnat! Hood maketh not frere. The voice is the voice of jokeup, I fear. Are you imitation Roma now or Amor now. You have all our empathies, eh, Mr Trickpat, if you don't mind, that is, aside from sings and mush, answering to my straight question?

— God save the monk! I won't mind this is, answering to your strict crossqueets, whereas it would be as unethical for me now to answer as it would have been nonsensical for you then not to have asked. Same no can, home no will, gangin I am. Gangang is Mine and I will return. Out of my name you call me, Leelander. But in my shelter you'll miss me. When Lapac walks backwords he's darkest horse in Capalisoot. You knew me once but you won't know me twice. I am *simpliciter arduus*, ars of the schoo, Freeday's child in loving and thieving.

— My child, know this! Some portion of that answer appears to have been token by you from the writings of Saint Synodius, that first liar. Let us hear, therefore, as you honour and obey the queen, whither the indwellingness of that which shamefieth be entwined of one or atoned of two. Let us hear, Art simplicissime!

—Dearly beloved brethren: Bruno and Nola, leymon bogholders and stationary lifepartners off orangey Saint Nessau Street, were explaining it avicendas all round each other ere yesterweek out of Ibn Sen and Ipanzussch. When himupon Nola Bruno monopolises his egobruno most unwillingly seses by the mortal powers alionola equal and opposite brunoipso, *id est*, eternally provoking alio opposite equally as provoked as Bruno at being eternally opposed by Nola. Poor omniboose, singalow singelearum: so is he!

— One might hear in their beyond that lionroar in the air again, the zoohoohoom of Felin make Call. Bruin goes to Noble, aver who is? If is itsen? Or you mean Nolans but Volans, an alibi, do you Mutemalice, suffering unegoistically from the singular but positively enjoying on the plural? Dustify of that sole, you breather! Ruemember, blither, thou must lie!

—Oyessoyess! I never dramped of prebeing a postman but I mean in ostralian someplace, mults deeply belubdead; my allaboy brother, Negoist Cabler, of this city, whom 'tis better ne'er to name, my said brother, the skipgod, expulled for looking at churches from behind, who is sender of the Hullo Eve Cenograph in prose and worse every Allso's night. High Brazil Brandan's Deferred, midden Erse clare language, Noughtnoughtnought nein. Assass. Dublire, per Neuropaths. Punk. Starving today plays punk opening tomorrow two plays punk wire splosh how two plays punk Cabler. Have you forgotten poor Alby Sobrinos, Geoff, you blighter, identifiable by the necessary white patch on his rear? How he went to his swiltersland after his lungs, my sad late brother, before his coglionial expancian? Won't you join me in a small halemerry, a bottle of the best, for wellmet Capeler, united Irishmen, what though preferring the stranger, the coughs and the itches and the minnies and the ratties the opulose and bilgenses, for of his was the patriots mistaken. The heart that wast our Graw McGree!

488

Yet be there some who mourn him, concluding him dead, and more there be that wait astand. His fuchs up the staires and the ladgers in his haires, he ought to win that *V.V.C.* Fullgrapce for an endupper, half muxy on his whole! Would he were even among the lost! From ours bereft beyond belongs. Oremus poor fraternibus that he may yet escape the gallews and still remain ours faithfully departed. I wronged you. I never want to see more of bad men but I want to learn from any on the airse, like Tass with much thanks, here's ditto, if he lives sameplace in the antipathies of austrasia or anywhere with my fawngest on his hooshmoney, safe and damned, or has hopped it or who can throw any lime on the sopjack, my fond fosther, E. Obiit Nolan, The Workings, N.S.W., his condition off the Venerable Jerrybuilt, not belonging to these parts, who, I remember ham to me, when we were like bro and sis over our castor and porridge, with his roamin I suppose, expecting for his clarenx negus, a teetotum abstainer. He feels he ought to be as asamed of me as me to be ashunned of him. We were in one class of age like to two clots of egg. I am most beholding to him, my namesick, as we sayed it in our Amharican, through the Doubly Telewisher. Outpassed hearts wag short pertimes. Worndown shoes upon his feet, to whose redress no tongue can tell! In his hands a boot! Spare me, do, a copper or two and happy I'll hope you'll be! It will pleased me behind with thanks from before and love to self and all I remain here your truly friend. I am no scholar but I loved that man who has africot lupps with the moonshane in his profile, my shemblable! My freer! I call you my halfbrother because you in your soberer otiumic moments remind me deeply of my natural saywhen brothel in feed, hop and jollity, S. H. Devitt, that benighted irismaimed, who is tearly belaboured by Sydney and Alibany.

— As you sing it it's a study. That letter selfpenned to one's other, that neverperfect everplanned?

— This nonday diary, this allnights newseryreel.

— My dear sir! In this wireless age any owl rooster can peck up bostoons. But whoewaxed he so anquished? Was he vector victored of victim vexed?

— Mighty sure! Way way for his wehicul! A parambolator ram into his bagsmall when he was reading alawd, with two ecolites and he's been failing of that kink in his arts over sense.

—Madonagh and Chiel, idealist leading a double life! But who, for the brilliance of brothers, is the Nolan as appearant nominally?

— Mr Nolan is pronuminally Mr Gottgab.

— I get it. By hearing his thing about a person one begins to place him for a certain in true. You reeker, he stands pat for you before a direct object in the feminine. I see. By maiden sname. Now, I am earnestly asking you, and putting it as between this yohou and that houmonymh, will just you search through your gabgut memoirs for all of two minutes for this impersonating pronolan, fairhead on foulshoulders. Would it be in twofold truth an untaken mispatriate, too fullfully true and rereally a doblinganger much about your own medium with a sandy whiskers? Poke me nabs in the ribs and pick the erstwort out of his mouth.

— Treble Stauter of Holy Baggot Street, formerly Swordmeat, who I surpassed him lately for four and six bringing home the Christmas, as heavy as music, hand to eyes on the peer for Noel's Arch, in blessed foster's place is doing the dirty on me with his tantrums and all these godforgiven kilowatts I'd be better off without. She's write to him she's levt by me, Jenny Rediviva! Toot! Detter for you, Mr Nobru. Toot toot! Better for you, Mr Anol! This is the way we. Of a redtettetterday morning.

— When your contraman from Tuwarceathay is looking for righting that is not a good sign? Not?

— I speak truly, it's a shower sign that it's not.

— What though it be for the sow of his heart? If even she were a good pool Pegeen?

— If she ate your windowsill you wouldn't say sow.

— Would you be surprised after that my asking have you a bull, a bosbully, with a whistle in his tail to scare other birds?

— I would.

— Were you with Sindy and Sandy attending Goliath, a bull?

— You'd make me sag what you like to. I was intending a funeral. Simply and samply.

— They are too wise of solbing their silbings?

— And both croon to the same theme.

— Tugbag is Baggut's, when a crispin sokolist besoops juts kamps or clapperclaws an irvingite offthedocks. A luckchange, I see. Thinking young through the muddleage spread, the moral fat his mental leans on. We can cop that with our straat that is called corkscrewed. It would be the finest boulevard billy for a mile in every direction, from Lismore to Cape Brendan, Patrick's, if they took the bint out of the mittle of it. You told of a tryst too, two a tutu. I wonder now, without releasing seeklets of the alcove, turturs or raabraabs, have I heard mention of whose name anywhere? Mallowlane or Demaasch? Strike us up either end *Have You Erred off Van Homper* or *Ebell Teresa Kane.*

— *Marak! Marak! Marak!*

He drapped has draraks an Mansianhase parak

And he had ta barraw tha watarcrass shartcloths aff tha arkbashap af Yarak!

— Braudribnob's on the bummel?

— And lillypets on the lea.

— A being again in becomings again. From the sallies to the allies through their central power?

— Pirce! Perce! Quick! Queck!

— O Tara's thrush, the sharepusher! And he said he was only taking the average grass temperature for green Thursday, the blutchy scaliger! Who you know the musselman, his musclemum and mistlemam? Maomi, Mamie, My Mo Mum! He loves a drary lane. Feel Phylliscitations to daff Mr Hairwigger who has just hadded twinned little curls! He was resting between horrockses' sheets, wailing for white warfare, prooboor welshtbreton, and unbiassed by the embarrassment of disposal but, the first woking day, by Thunder, he stepped into the breach and put on his recriution trousers and riding apron in Baltic Bygrad, the old soggy, was when the bold bhuoys of Iran wouldn't join up.

491

— How voice you that, nice Sandy man? Not large goodman is he, Sandy nice. Ask him this one minute upthrow inner lotus of his burly ear womit he dropped his Bass's to P flat. And for that he was allaughed? And then baited? The whole gammat?

— Loonacied! Marterdyed!! Madwakemiherculossed!!! Judascessed!!!! Pairaskivvymenassed!!!!! Luredogged!!!!!! And, needatellye, faulscrescendied!!!!!!!

— Dias domnas! Dolled to dolthood? And Annie Delittle, his daintree diva, in deltic dwilights, singing him henpecked rusish through the bars? My Wolossay's wild as the Crasnian Sea! Grabashag, groogy, scoop and I'll cure ye! Mother of emeralds, ara poog neighbours!

— Capilla, Rubrilla and Melcamomilla! Dauby, dauby, without dulay! Well, I beg to traverse same above statement by saxy luters in their back haul of Coalcutter what reflects upon my administrants of slow poisoning as my dodear devere revered mainhirr was confined to guardroom, I hindustand, by my pint of his Filthered pilsens bottle due to Zenaphiah Holwell, H and J. C. S, Which I was bringing up my quee parapotacarry's orders in my sedown chair with my mudfacepacket from my cash chemist and family drugger, Surager Dowling, V.S. to our aural surgeon, Afamado Hairductor Achmed Borumborad, M.A.C.A, Sahib, of a 1001 Ombrilla Street, Syringa padham, Alleypulley, to see what was my watergood, my mesical wasserguss, for repairs done by bollworm in the rere of pilch knickers, seven yerds to his galandhar pole on perch, together with his for me unfillable slopper, property of my deeply forfear revebereared, who is costing us mostfortunes which I am writing in mepetition to Kavanagh Djanaral, when he was sitting him humpbacked in dry dryfilthy-heat to his trinidads pinslers at their orpentings, entailing a laxative tendency to mary, especially with him being forbidden fruit and certified by his sexular clergy to have as badazmy emotional volvular, with a basketful of priesters crossing the singorgeous to aroint him with tummy moor's maladies, and thereinafter liable to succumb when served with letters potent below the belch, if my rupee repure riputed husbandship H.R.R.

took a brief one in his shirtsails out of the alleged given mineral, telling me see his in Foraignghistan sambat papers Sunday feactures of a welcomed aperrytiff with vallad of Erill Pearcey O he never battered one eagle's before paying me his duty on my annaversary to the parroteyes list in my nil ensemble, in his lazychair but he hidded up my hemifaces in all my mayarannies and he locked plum into my mirrymouth like Ysamasy morning in the end of time, with the so light's hope on his ruddycheeks and rawjaws and, my charmer, whom I dipped my hand in, he simply showed me his propendiculous loadpoker, Seaserpents hisses sissastones, which was as then is produced in his mansway by this wisest of the Vikramadityationists, with the remere remind remure remark, in his gulughurutty: Yran for parasites with rum for the turkeycockeys so Lithia, M.D., as this is for Snooker, bort!

— Which was said by whem to whom?

— It wham. But whim I can't whumember.

— Fantasy! funtasy on fantasy, amnaes fintasies! And there is nihil nuder under the clothing moon. When Ota, weewahrwificle of Torquells, bumpsed her dumpsydiddle down in her woolsark she mode our heuteyleutey girlery of peerlesses to set up in all their bombossities of feudal fiertey, fanned, flounced and frangipanned, while the massstab whereby Ephialtes has exceeded is the measure, *simplex mendaciis*, by which our Outis cuts his thruth. Arkaway now!

— Yerds and nudes say ayes and noes! Vide! Vide!

— Let Eivin bemember for Gates of Gold for their fadeless suns berayed her. Irise, Osirises! Be thy mouth given unto thee! For why do you lack a link of luck to poise a pont of perfect, peace? On the vignetto is a ragingoos. The overseer of the house of the oversire of the seas, Nu-Men, triumphant, sayeth: Fly as the hawk, cry as the corncrake, Ani Latch of the postern is thy name; shout!

— My heart, my mother! My heart, my coming forth of darkness! They know not my heart, O coolun dearast! Mon gloomerie! Mon glamourie! What a surpraise, dear Mr Preacher,

I to hear from your strawnummical modesty! Yes, there was that skew arch of chrome sweet home, floodlit up above the flabberghosted farmament and bump where the camel got the needle. Talk about iridecencies! Ruby and beryl and chrysolite, jade, sapphire, jasper and lazul.

— Orca Bellona! Heavencry at earthcall, etnat athos? Extinct your vulcanology for the lava of Moltens!

— It's you not me's in erupting, hecklar!

— Ophiuchus being visible above thorizon, muliercula occluded by Satarn's serpent ring system, the pisciolinnies Nova Ardonis and Prisca Parthenopea, are a bonnies feature in the northern sky. Ers, Mores and Merkery are surgents below the rim of the Zenith Part while Arctura, Anatolia, Hesper and Mesembria weep in their mansions over Noth, Haste, Soot and Waste.

— Apep and Uachet! Holy snakes, chase me charley, Eva's got barley under her fluencies! The Ural Mount he's on the move and he'll quivvy her with his strombolo! Waddlewurst, the bag of tow, as broad above as he is below! Creeping through the liongrass and bullsrusshius, the obesendean, before the Emfang de Maurya's class, in Bill Shasser's Shotshrift writing academy, camouflaged as a blancmange and maple syrop! Obeisance so their sitinins is the follicity of this Orp! Her sheik to Slave, his dick to Dave and the fat of the land to Guygas. The treadmill pebbledropper haha halfahead overground and she'd only chitschats in her spanking bee bonetry, Allapolloosa! Up the slanger! Three cheers and a heva heva for the name Dan Magraw!

—The giant sun is in his emanence but which is chief of those white dwarfees of which he ever is surabanded? And do you think I might have being his seventh! He will kitssle me on melbaw. What about his age? says you. What about it? says I. I will confess to his sins and blush me further. I would misdemean to rebuke to the libels of snots from the fleshambles, the canalles. Synamite is too good for them. Two overthirties in shore shorties. She's askapot at Nile Lodge and she's citchincarry at the left Mrs Hamazum's. Will you warn your old habasund, barking at baggermen, his chokefull chewing his chain? Responsif you plais. The said Sully, a barracker associated with tinkers, the blackhand, Shovellyvans, wreuter of annoyimgmost letters and skirriless ballets in Parsee Franch who is Magrath's thug and smells cheaply of Power's spirits, like a deepsea dibbler, and he is not fit enough to throw guts down to a bear. Sylphling me when is a maid nought a maid he would go to anyposs length for her! So long, Sulleyman! If they cut his nose on the stitcher they had their siven good reasons. Here's to the leglift of my snuff and trout stockangt henkerchoff, orange fin with a mosaic of dispensations and a froren black patata, from my church milliner. When Lynch Brother, Withworkers, Friends and Company with T. C. King and the Warden of Galway is prepared to stretch him sacred by the powers to the starlight, L.B.W. Hemp, hemp, hurray! says the captain in the moonlight. I could put him under my pallyass and slepp on him all nights as I would roll myself for holy poly over his borrowing places. How we will make laugh over him together, me and my Riley in the Vickar's bed! Quink! says I. He cawls to me Granny-stream-Auborne when I am hiding under my hair from him and I cool him my Finnyking he's so joyant a bounder. Plunk! said he. Inasmuch as I am delightful to be able to state, with the joy of lifing in my forty winkers, that a handsome sovereign was freely pledged in their pennis in the sluts maschine, alonging wath a cherry-wickerkishabrack of maryfruit under Shadow La Rose, to both the legintimate lady performers of display unquestionable, Elsebett and Marryetta Gunning, H_2O, by that noblesse of leechers at his Saxontannery with motto in Wwalshe's ffrenchllatin: O'Neill saw Queen Molly's pants: and much admired engraving, meaning complet manly parts during alleged recent act of our chief mergey margey magistrades, five itches above the kneecap, as required by statues. V.I.C.5.6. If you won't release me stop to please me up the leg of me. Now you see! Respect. S.V.P. Your wife. Amn. Anm. Amm. Ann.

— You wish to take us, Frui Mria, by degrees, as *artis litterarum-que patrona* but I am afraid, my poor woman of that same name, what with your silvanes and your salvines, you are misled.

— Alas for livings' pledjures!

— Lordy Daw and Lady Don! Uncle Foozle and Aunty Jack! Sure, that old humbugger was boycotted and girlcutted in debt and doom, on hill and haven, even by the show-the-flag flotilla, as I'm given now to understand, illscribed in all the gratuitouses and conspued in the takeyourhandaways. Bumbty, tumbty, Sot on a Wall, Mute art for the Million. There wasn't an Archimandrite of Dane's Island and the townlands nor a minx from the Isle of Woman nor a one of the four cantins nor any on the whole wheel of his ecunemical conciliabulum nor nogent ingen meid on allad the hold scurface of the jorth would come next or nigh him, Mr Eelwhipper, seed and nursery man, or his allgas bumgalowre, *Auxilium Meum Solo A Domino* (Amsad), for rime or ration, from piles or faces, after that.

— All ears did wag, old Eire wake as Piers Aurell was flapper-gangsted.

— Recount!

— I have it here to my fingall's ends. This liggy piggy wanted to go to the jampot. And this leggy peggy spelt pea. And theese lucky puckers played at pooping tooletom. Ma's da. Da's ma. Madas. Sadam.

— *Pater patruum cum filiabus familiarum.* Or, but, now, and, ariring out of her mirgery margery watersheads and, to change that subjunct from the traumaturgid for once in a while and darting back to stuff, if so be you may identify yourself with the him in you, that fluctuous neck merchamtur, bloodfadder and milkmudder, since then our too many of her, Abha na Lífé, and getting on to dadaddy again, as them we're ne'er free of, was he in tea e'er he went on the bier or didn't he ontime do something seemly heavy in sugar? He sent out Christy Columb and he came back with a jailbird's unbespokables in his beak and then he sent out Le Caron Crow and the peacies are still looking for him. The seeker from the swayed, the beesabouties from the parent swarm. Speak to the right! Rotacist ca canny! He caun ne'er be bothered but maun e'er be waked. If there is a future in every past that is present *Quis est qui non novit quinnigan* and *Qui quae quot at*

496

Quinnigan's Quake! Stump! His producers are they not his consumers? Your exagmination round his factification for incamination of a warping process. Declaim!

— Arra irrara hirrara man, weren't they arriving in clansdestinies for the Imbandiment of *Ad Regias Agni Dapes*, fogabawlers and panhibernskers, after the crack and the lean years, scalpjaggers and houthhunters, like the messicals of the great god, a scarlet trainful, the Twoedged Petrard, totalling, leggats and prelaps, in their aggregate ages two and thirty plus undecimmed centries of them with insiders, extraomnes and tuttifrutties allcunct, from Rathgar, Rathanga, Rountown and Rush, from America Avenue and Asia Place and the Affrian Way and Europa Parade and besogar the wallies of Noo Soch Wilds and from Vico, Mespil Rock and Sorrento, for the lure of his weal and the fear of his oppidumic, to his salon de espera in the keel of his kraal, like lodes of ores flocking fast to Mount Maximagnetic, afeerd he was a gunner but affaird to stay away, Merrionites, Dumstdumbdrummers, Luccanicans, Ashtoumers, Batterysby Parkes and Krumlin Boyards, Phillipsburgs, Cabraists and Finglossies, Ballymunites, Raheniacs and the bettlers of Clontarf, for to contemplate in manifest and pay their firstrate duties before the both of him, twelve stone a side, with their *Thieve le Roué!* and their *Shvr yr Thrst!* and their *Uisgye ad Inferos!* and their *Usque ad Ebbraios!* at and in the licensed boosiness primises of his delhightful bazar and reunited magazine hall, by the magazine wall, Hosty's and Co, Exports, for his five hundredth and sixtysixth borthday, the grand old Magennis Mor, Persee and Rahli, taker of the tributes, their Rinseky Poppakork and Piowtor the Grape, holding Dunker's durbar, boot kings and indiarubber umpires and shawhs from paisley and muftis in muslim and sultana reiseines and jordan almonders and a row of jam sahibs and a odd principeza in her pettedcoat and the queen of knight's clubs and the claddagh ringleaders and the two salaames and the Halfa Ham and the Hanzas Khan with two fat Maharashers and the German selver geyser and he polished up, protemptible, tintanambulating to himsilf so silfrich, and there was J. B. Dunlop, the

497

best tyrent of ourish times, and a swanks of French wine stuarts
and Tudor keepsakes and the Cesarevitch for the current counter Leodegarius Sant Legerleger riding lapsaddlelonglegs up the
oakses staircase on muleback like Amaxodias Isteroprotos, hindquarters to the fore and kick to the lift, and he handygrabbed on
to his trulley natural anthem: *Horsibus, keep your tailyup*, and
as much as the halle of the vacant fhroneroom, Oldloafs
Buttery, could safely accomodate of the houses of Orange and
Betters M.P, permeated by Druids D.P, Brehons B.P, and
Flawhoolags F.P, and Agiapommenites A.P, and Antepum-
melites P.P, and Ulster Kong and Munster's Herald with
Athclee Ensigning and Athlone Poursuivant and his Imperial
Catchering, his fain awan, and his gemmynosed sanctsons
in epheud and ordilawn and his diamondskulled granddaucher,
Adamantaya Liubokovskva, all murdering Irish, amok and
amak, out of their boom companions in paunchjab and dogril
and pammel and gougerotty, after plenty of his fresh stout and
his good balls of malt, not to forget his oels a'mona nor his beers
o'ryely, sopped down by his pani's annagolorum, (at Kennedy's
kiln she kned her dough, back of her bake for me, buns!) social-
izing and communicanting in the deification of his members, for
to nobble or salvage their herobit of him, the poohpooher old
bolssloose, with his arthurious clayroses, Dodderick Ogonoch
Wrack, busted to the wurld at large, on the table round, with the
floodlight switched back, as true as the Vernons have Brian's
sword, and a dozen and one by one tilly tallows round in ring-
campf, circumassembled by his daughters in the foregiftness of
his sons, lying high as he lay in all dimensions, in court dress and
ludmers chain, with a hogo, fluorescent of his swathings, round
him, like the cummulium of scents in an italian warehouse, erica's
clustered on his hayir, the spectrem of his prisent mocking the
candiedights of his dadtid, bagpuddingpodded to the deafspot,
bewept of his chilidrin and serafim, poors and personalities, ven-
turous, drones and dominators, ancients and auldancients, with
his buttend up, expositoed for sale after referee's inspection,
bulgy and blowrious, bunged to ignorious, healed cured and

498

embalsemate, pending a rouseruction of his bogey, most highly astounded, as it turned up, after his life overlasting, at thus being reduced to nothing.

— Bappy-go-gully and gaff for us all! And all his morties calisenic, tripping a trepas, neniatwantyng: Mulo Mulelo! Homo Humilo! Dauncy a deady O! Dood dood dood! O Bawse! O Boese! O Muerther! O Mord! Mahmato! Moutmaro! O Smirtsch! O Smertz! Woh Hillill! Woe Hallall! Thou Thuoni! Thou Thaunaton! Umartir! Udamnor! Tschitt! Mergue! Eulumu! Huam Khuam! Malawinga! Malawunga! Ser Oh Ser! See ah See! Hamovs! Hemoves! Mamor! Rockquiem eternuel give donal aye in dolmeny! Bad luck's perpepperpot loosen his eyis! (Psich!).

— But there's leps of flam in Funnycoon's Wick. The keyn has passed. Lung lift the keying!

— God save you king! Muster of the Hidden Life!

— God serf yous kingly, adipose rex! I had four in the morning and a couple of the lunch and three later on, but your saouls to the dhaoul, do ye. Finnk. Fime. Fudd?

— Impassable tissue of improbable liyers! D'yu mean to sett there where y'are now, coddlin your supernumerary leg, wi'that bizar tongue in yur tolkshap, and your hindies and shindies, like a muck in a market, Sorley boy, repeating yurself, and tell me that?

— I mean to sit here on this altknoll where you are now, Surly guy, replete in myself, as long as I live, in my homespins, like a sleepingtop, with all that's buried ofsins insince insensed insidesofme. If I can't upset this pound of pressed ollaves I can sit up zounds of sounds upon him.

— Oliver! He may be an earthpresence. Was that a groan or did I hear the Dingle bagpipes Wasting war and? Watch!

— *Tris tris a ni ma mea!* Prisoner of Love! Bleating Hart! Lowlaid Herd! Aubain Hand! Wonted Foot! *Usque! Usque! Usque! Lignum in* . . .

— Rawth of Gar and Donnerbruck Fire? Is the strays world moving mound or what static babel is this, tell us?

— Whoishe whoishe whoishe whoishe linking in? Whoishe whoishe whoishe?

499

— The snare drum! Lay yer lug till the groun. The dead giant manalive! They're playing thimbles and bodkins. Clan of the Gael! Hop! Whu's within?

— Dovegall and finshark, they are ring to the rescune!

— Zinzin. Zinzin.

— Crum abu! Cromwell to victory!

— We'll gore them and gash them and gun them and gloat on them.

— Zinzin.

— O, widows and orphans, it's the yeomen! Redshanks for ever! Up Lancs!

— The cry of the roedeer it is! The white hind. Their slots, linklink, the hound hunthorning! Send us and peace! Title! Title!

— Christ in our irish times! Christ on the airs independence! Christ hold the freedman's chareman! Christ light the dully expressed!

— Slog slagt and sluaghter! Rape the daughter! Choke the pope!

— Aure! Cloudy father! Unsure! Nongood!

— Zinzin.

— Sold! I am sold! Brinabride! My ersther! My sidster! Brinabride, goodbye! Brinabride! I sold!

— Pipette dear! Us! Us! Me! Me!

— Fort! Fort! Bayroyt! March!

— Me! I'm true. True! Isolde. Pipette. My precious!

— Zinzin.

— Brinabride, bet my price! Brinabride!

— My price, my precious?

— Zin.

— Brinabride, my price! When you sell get my price!

— Zin.

— Pipette! Pipette, my priceless one!

— O! Mother of my tears! Believe for me! Fold thy son!

— Zinzin. Zinzin.

— Now we're gettin it. Tune in and pick up the forain counties! Hello!

— Zinzin.

— Hello! Tittit! Tell your title?

— Abride!

— Hellohello! Ballymacarett! Am I thru' Iss? Miss? True?

— Tit! What is the ti . . ?

SILENCE.

Act drop. Stand by! Blinders! Curtain up. Juice, please! Foots!

— Hello! Are you Cigar shank and Wheat?

— I gotye. Gobble Ann's Carrot Cans.

— Parfey. Now, after that justajiff siesta, just permit me a moment. Challenger's Deep is childsplay to this but, by our soundings in the swish channels, land is due. A truce to demobbed swarwords. Clear the line, priority call! Sybil! Better that or this? Sybil Head this end! Better that way? Follow the baby spot. Yes. Very good now. We are again in the magnetic field. Do you remember on a particular lukesummer night, following a crying fair day? Moisten your lips for a lightning strike and begin again. Mind the flickers and dimmers! Better?

— Well. The isles is Thymes. The ales is Penzance. Vehement Genral. Delhi expulsed.

— Still calling of somewhave from its specific? Not more? Lesscontinuous. There were fires on every bald hill in holy Ireland that night. Better so?

— You may say they were, son of a cove!

— Were they bonfires? That clear?

— No other name would at all befit them unless that. Bonafieries! With their blue beards streaming to the heavens.

— Was it a high white night now?

— Whitest night mortal ever saw.

— Was our lord of the heights nigh our lady of the valley?

— He was hosting himself up and flosting himself around and ghosting himself to merry her murmur like an andeanupper balkan.

— Lewd's carol! Was there rain by any chance, mistandew?

— Plenty. If you wend farranoch.

— There fell some fall of littlewinter snow, holy-as-ivory, I gather, jesse?

— By snaachtha clocka. The nicest at all. In hilly-and-even zimalayars.

— Did it not blow some gales, westnass or ostscent, rather strongly to less, allin humours out of turn, jusse as they rose and sprungen?

— Out of all jokes it did. Pipep! Icecold. Brr na brr, ny prr! Lieto galumphantes!

— Stll cllng! Nmr! Peace, Pacific! Do you happen to recollect whether Muna, that highlucky nackt, was shining at all?

— Sure she was, my midday darling! And not one but a pair of pritty geallachers.

— Quando? Quonda? Go datey!

— Latearly! Latearly! Latearly! Latearly!

— That was latterlig certainly. And was there frostwork about and thick weather and hice, soon calid, soon frozen, cold on warm but moistly dry, and a boatshaped blanket of bruma airsighs and hellstohns and flammballs and vodashouts and everything to please everybody?

— Hail many fell of greats! Horey morey smother of fog! There was, so plays your ahrtides. Absolutely boiled. Obsoletely cowled. Julie and Lulie at their parkiest.

— The amenities, the amenities of the amenities with all their amenities. And the firmness of the formous of the famous of the fumous of the first fog in Maidanvale?

— Catchecatche and couchamed!

— From Miss Somer's nice dream back to Mad Winthrop's delugium stramens. One expects that kind of rimey feeling in the sire season?

— One certainly does. Desire, for hire, would tire a shire, phone, phunkel, or wire. And mares.

— Of whitecaps any?

— Foamflakes flockfuyant from Foxrock to Finglas.

— A lambskip for the marines! Paronama! The entire horizon cloth! All effects in their joints caused ways. Raindrum, windmachine, snowbox. But thundersheet?

— No here. Under the blunkets.

— This common or garden is now in stiller realithy the starey sphere of an oleotorium for broken pottery and ancient vegetables?

— Simply awful the dirt. An evernasty ashtray.

— I see. Now do you know the wellknown kikkinmidden where the illassorted first couple first met with each other? The place where Ealdermann Fanagan? The time when Junkermenn Funagin?

— Deed then I do, W.K.

— In Fingal too they met at Littlepeace aneath the bidetree, Yellowhouse of Snugsborough, Westreeve-Astagob and Slutsend with Stockins of Winning's Folly Merryfalls, all of a two, skidoo and skephumble?

— Godamedy, you're a delville of a tolkar!

— Is it a place fairly exsposed to the four last winds?

— Well, I faithly sincerely believe so indeed if all what I hope to charity is half true.

— This stow on the wolds, is it Woful Dane Bottom?

— It is woful in need whatever about anything or allselse under the grianblachk sun of gan greyne Eireann.

— A tricolour ribbon that spells a caution. The old flag, the cold flag.

— The flagstone. By tombs, deep and heavy. To the unaveiling memory of. Peacer the grave.

— And what sigeth Woodin Warneung thereof?

— Trickspissers vill be pairsecluded.

— There used to be a tree stuck up? An overlisting eshtree?

— There used, sure enough. Beside the Annar. At the ford of Slivenamond. Oakley Ashe's elm. With a snoodrift from one beerchen bough. And the grawndest crowndest consecrated maypole in all the reignladen history of Wilds. Browne's *Thesaurus Plantarum* from Nolan's, The Prittlewell Press, has nothing alike it. For we are fed of its forest, clad in its wood, burqued by its bark and our lecture is its leave. The cran, the cran the king of all crans. Squiremade and damesman of plantagenets, high and holy.

—Now, no hiding your wren under a bushle! What was it doing there, for instance?

— Standing foreninst us.

— In Summerian sunshine?

— And in Cimmerian shudders.

— You saw it visibly from your hidingplace?

— No. From my invisibly lyingplace.

— And you then took down in stereo what took place being tunc committed?

— I then tuk my takenplace lying down, I thunk I told you. Solve it!

— Remounting aliftle towards the ouragan of spaces. Just how grand in cardinal rounders is this preeminent giant, sir Arber? Your bard's highview, avis on valley! I would like to hear you burble to us in strict conclave, purpurando, and without too much italiote interfairance, what you know *in petto* about our sovereign beingstalk, Tonans Tomazeus. *O dite!*

— Corcor Andy, *Udi, Udite!* Your Ominence, Your Immi-nence and delicted fraternitrees! There's tuodore queensmaids and Idahore shopgirls and they woody babies growing upon her and bird flamingans sweenyswinging fuglewards on the tipmast and Orania epples playing hopptociel bommptaterre and Ty-burn fenians snoring in his quickenbole and crossbones strewing its holy floor and culprines of Erasmus Smith's burstall boys with their underhand leadpencils climbing to her crotch for the origin of spices and charlotte darlings with silk blue askmes chattering in dissent to them, gibbonses and gobbenses, guelfing and ghiberring proferring praydews to their anatolies and blight-ing findblasts on their catastripes and the killmaimthem pen-sioners chucking overthrown milestones up to her to fall her cranberries and her pommes annettes for their unnatural refection and handpainted hoydens plucking husbands of him and cock robins muchmore hatching most out of his missado eggdrazzles for him, the sun and moon pegging honeysuckle and white heather down and timtits tapping resin there and tomahawks watching tar elsewhere, creatures of the wold approaching him, hollow mid ivy, for to claw and rub, hermits of the desert barking their infernal shins over her triliteral roots and his acorns and pinecorns shooting wide all sides out of him, plantitude outsends of plenty to thousands, after the truants of the utmostfear and her downslyder in that snakedst-tu-naughsy whimmering woman't seeleib such a fashionaping sathinous dress out of that exquisitive creation and her leaves, my darling dearest, sinsinsinning since the night of time and each and all of their branches meeting and shaking twisty hands all over again in their new world through the germination of its gemination from Ond's outset till Odd's end. And encircle him circuly. Evovae!

— Is it so exaltated, eximious, extraoldandairy and excelssiorising?

— Amengst menlike trees walking or trees like angels weeping nobirdy aviar soar anywing to eagle it! But rocked of agues, cliffed for aye!

— Telleth that eke the treeth?

— Mushe, mushe of a mixness.

— A shrub of libertine, indeed! But that steyne of law indead what stiles its neming?

— Tod, tod, too hard parted!

— I've got that now, Dr Melamanessy. Finight mens midinfinite true. The form masculine. The gender feminine. I see. Now, are you derevatov of it yourself in any way? The true tree I mean? Let's hear what science has to say, pundit-thenext-best-king. Splanck!

— Upfellbowm.

— It reminds of the weeping of the daughters?

— And remounts to the sense arrest.

— The wittold, the frausch and the dibble! How this looseaffair brimsts of fussforus! And was this treemanangel on his soredbohmend because Knockout, the knickknaver, knacked him in the knechtschaft?

— Well, he was ever himself for the presention of crudities to animals for he had put his own nickelname on every toad, duck and herring before the climber clomb aloft, doing the midhill of the park, flattering his bitter hoolft with her conconundrums. He would let us have the three barrels. Such was a bitte too thikke for the Muster of the hoose so as he called down on the Grand Precurser who coiled him a crawler of the dupest dye and thundered at him to flatch down off that erection and be aslimed of himself for the bellance of hissch leif.

— Oh Finlay's coldpalled!

— Ahday's begatem!

— Were you there, eh Hehr? Were you there when they lagged um through the coombe?

— Wo wo! Who who! Psalmtimes it grauws on me to ramble, ramble, ramble.

— Woe! Woe! So that was how he became the foerst of our treefellers?

— Yesche and, in the absence of any soberiquiet, the fanest of our truefalluses. Bapsbaps Bomslinger!

— How near do you feel to this capocapo promontory, sir?

— There do be days of dry coldness between us when he does be like a lidging house far far astray and there do be nights of wet windwhistling when he does be making me onions woup all kinds of ways.

— Now you are mehrer the murk, Lansdowne Road. She's threwed her pippin's thereabouts and they've cropped up tooth oneydge with hates to leaven this socried isle. Now, thornyborn, follow the spotlight, please! Concerning a boy. Are you acquainted with a pagany, vicariously known as Toucher 'Thom' who is. I suggest Finoglam as his habitat. Consider yourself on the stand now and watch your words, take my advice. Let your motto be: *Inter nubila numbum.*

— Never you mind about my mother or her hopitout. I consider if I did, I would feel frightfully ashamed of admired vice.

— He is a man of around fifty, struck on Anna Lynsha's Pekoe with milk and whisky, who does messuages and has more dirt on him than an old dog has fleas, kicking stones and knocking

506

snow off walls. Have you ever heard of this old boy "Thom" or "Thim" of the fishy stare who belongs to Kimmage, a crofting district, and is not all there, and is all the more himself since he is not so, being most of his time down at the Green Man where he steals, pawns, belches and is a curse, drinking gaily two hours after closing time, with the coat on him skinside out against rapparitions, with his socks outsewed his springsides, clapping his hands in a feeble sort of way and systematically mixing with the public going for groceries, slapping greats and littlegets soundly with his cattegut belts, flapping baresides and waltzywembling about in his accountrements always in font of the tubbernuckles, like a longarmed lugh, when he would be finished with his tea?

— Is it that fellow? As mad as the brambles he is. Touch him. With the lawyers sticking to his trewsershins and the swatmenotting on the basque of his beret. He has kissed me more than once, I am sorry to say and if I did commit gladrolleries may the loone forgive it! O wait till I tell you!

— We are not going yet.

— And look here! Here's, my dear, what he done, as snooks as I am saying so!

— Get out, you dirt! A strangely striking part of speech for the hottest worked word of ur sprogue. You're not! Unhindered and odd times? Mere thumbshow? Lately?

— How do I know? Such my billet. Buy a barrack pass. Ask the horneys. Tell the robbers.

— You are alluding to the picking pockets in Lower O'Connell Street?

— I am illuding to the Pekin packet but I am eluding from Laura Connor's treat.

— Now, just wash and brush up your memoirias a little bit. So I find, referring to the pater of the present man, an erely demented brick thrower, I am wondering to myself in my mind, *qua* our arc of the covenant, was Toucher, a methodist, whose name, as others say, is not really 'Thom', was this salt son of a century from Boaterstown, Shivering William, the sealiest old forker ever hawked crannock, who is always with him at the Big Elm and the Arch after his teeth were shaken out of their suckets by the wrang dog, for having 5 pints 73 of none Eryen blood in him abaft the seam level, the scatterling, wearing his cowbeamer and false clothes of a brewer's grains pattern with back buckons with his motto on, *Yule Remember*, ostensibly for that occasion only of the twelfth day Pax and Quantum wedding, I'm wondering.

— I bet you are. Well, he was wandering, you bet, whatever was his matter, in his mind too, give him his due, for I am sorry to have to tell you, hullo and evoe, they were coming down from off him.

— How culious an epiphany!

— *Hodie casus esobhrakonton?*

— It looked very like it.

— Needer knows necess and neither garments. Man is minded of the Meagher, wat? Wooly? Walty?

— Ay, another good button gone wrong.

— Blondman's blaff! Like a skib leaked lintel the arbour leidend with . . .?

— Pamelas, peggylees, pollywollies, questuants, quaint-aquilties, quickamerries.

— Concaving now convexly to the semidemihemispheres and, from the female angle, music minnestirring, were the subligate sisters, P. and Q., Clopatrick's cherierapest, *mutatis mutandis*, in pretty much the same pickle, the peach of all piedom, the quest of all quicks?

— Peequeen ourselves, the prettiest pickles of unmatchemable mute antes I ever bopeeped at, seesaw shallshee, since the town go went gonning on Pranksome Quaine.

— Silks apeel and sulks alusty?

— Boy and giddle, gape and bore.

— I hear these two goddesses are liable to sue him?

— Well, I hope the two Collinses don't leg a bail to shoot him.

— Both were white in black arpists at cloever spilling, knickt?

— Gels bach, I, languised, liszted. Etoudies for the right hand.

— Were they now? And were they watching you as watcher as well?

508

— Where do you get that wash? This representation does not accord with my experience. They were watching the watched watching. Vechers all.

— Good. Hold that watching brief and keep this witching longuer. Now, retouching friend Tomsky, the enemy, did you gather much from what he let drop? We are sitting here for that.

— I was rooshian mad, no lie. About his shapeless hat.

— I suspect you must have been.

— You are making your thunderous mistake. But I was dung sorry for him too.

— O Schaum! Not really? Were you sorry you were mad with him then?

— When I tell you I was rooshiamarodnimad with myself altogether, so I was, for being sorry for him.

— So?

— Absolutely.

— Would you blame him at all stages?

— I believe in many an old stager. But what seemed sooth to a Greek summed nooth to a giantle. Who kills the cat in Cairo coaxes cocks in Gaul.

— I put it to you that this was solely in his sunflower state and that his haliodraping het was why maids all sighed for him, ventured and vied for him. Hm?

— After Putawayo, Kansas, Liburnum and New Aimstirdames, it wouldn't surprise me in the very least.

— That tare and this mole, your tear and our smile. 'Tis life that lies if woman's eyes have been our old undoing. Lid efter lid. Reform in mine size his deformation. Tiffpuff up my nostril, would you puff the earthworm outer my ear.

— He could claud boose his eyes to the birth of his garce, he could lump all his lot through the half of her play, but he jest couldn't laugh through the whole of her farce becorpse he warn't billed that way. So he outandouts his volimetangere and has a lightning consultation and he downadowns his pantoloogions and made a piece of first perpersonal puetry that staystale remains to be. Cleaned.

— Booms of bombs and heavy rethudders?

— This aim to you!

— The tail, so mastrodantic, as you tell it nearly takes your own mummouth's breath away. Your troppers are so unrelieved because his troopers were in difficulties. Still let stultitiam done in veino condone ineptias made of veritues. How many were married on that top of all strapping mornings, after the midnight turkay drive, my good watcher?

— Puppaps. That'd be telling. With a hoh frohim and heh fraher. But, as regards to Tammy Thornycraft, Idefyne the lawn mare and the laney moweress and all the prentisses of wildes to massage him.

— Now from Gunner Shotland to Guinness Scenography. Come to the ballay at the Tailors' Hall. We mean to be mellay on the Mailers' Mall. And leap, rink and make follay till the Gaelers' Gall. Awake! Come, a wake! Every old skin in the leather world, infect the whole stock company of the old house of the Leaking Barrel, was thomistically drunk, two by two, lairking o' tootlers with tombours a'beggars, the blog and turfs and the brandywine bankrompers, trou Normend fashion, I have been told, down to the bank lean clorks? Some nasty blunt clubs were being operated after the tradition of a wellesleyan bottle riot act and a few plates were being shied about and tumblers bearing traces of fresh porter rolling around, independent of that, for the ehren of Fyn's Insul, and then followed that wapping breakfast at the Heaven and Covenant, with Rodey O'echolowing how his breadcost on the voters would be a comeback for e'er a one, like the depredations of Scandalknivery, in and on usedtowobble sloops off cloasts, eh? Would that be a talltale too? This was the grandsire Orther. This was his innwhite horse. Sip?

— Well, naturally he was, louties also genderymen. Being Kerssfesstiydt. They came from all lands beyond the wave for songs of Inishfeel. Whiskway and mortem! No puseyporcious either, invitem kappines all round. But the right reverend priest, Mr Hopsinbond, and the reverent bride eleft, Frizzy Fraufrau, were sober enough. I think they were sober.

— I think you're widdershins there about the right reverence. Magraw for the Northwhiggern cupteam was wedding beastman, papers before us carry. You saw him hurriedly, or did you if thatseme's not irrelevant? With Slater's hammer perhaps? Or he was in serge?

— I horridly did. On the stroke of the dozen. I'm sure I'm wrong but I heard the irreverend Mr Magraw, in search of a stammer, kuckkuck kicking the bedding out of the old sexton, red-Fox Good-man around the sacristy, till they were bullbeadle black and bufeteer blue, while I and Flood and the other men, jazzlike brollies and sesuos, was gickling his missus to gackles in the hall, the divileen, (she's a lamp in her throth) with her cygncygn leckle and her twelve pound lach.

— A loyal wifish woman cacchinic wheepingcaugh! While she laylylaw was all their rage. But you did establish personal contact? In epexegesis or on a point of order?

— That perkumiary pond is beyawnd my pinnigay pretonsions. I am resting on a pigs of cheesus but I've a big suggestion it was about the pint of porter.

— You are a suckersome! But this all, as airs said to oska, was only that childbearer might blogas well sidesplit? Where letties hereditate a dark mien swart hairy?

— Only. 'Twas womans' too woman with mans' throw man.

— Bully burley yet hardly hurley. The saloon bulkhead, did you say, or the tweendecks?

— Between drinks, I deeply painfully repeat it.

— Was she wearing shubladey's tiroirs in humour of her hubbishobbis, Massa's star stellar?

— Mrs Tan-Taylour? Just a floating panel, secretairslidingdraws, a budge of klees on her schalter, a siderbrass sehdass on her anulas findring and forty crocelips in her curlingthongues.

— So this was the dope that woolied the cad that kinked the ruck that noised the rape that tried the sap that hugged the mort?

— That legged in the hoax that joke bilked.

— The jest of junk the jungular?

— Jacked up in a jock the wrapper.

— Lollgoll! You don't soye so! All upsydown her whole creation? So there was nothing serical between you? And Drysalter, father of Izod, how was he now?

— To the pink, man, like an allmanox in his shirt and stickup, brustall to the bear, the Megalomagellan of our winevatswaterway, squeezing the life out of the liffey.

— Crestofer Carambas! Such is zodisfaction. You punk me! He came, he kished, he conquered. Vulturuvarnar! The must of his glancefull coaxing the beam in her eye? That musked bell of this masked ball! Annabella, Lovabella, Pullabella, yep?

— Yup! Titentung Tollertone in S. Sabina's. Aye aye, she was lithe and pleasable. Wilt thou the lee? Wilt thou the hee? Wilt thou the hussif?

— The quicker the deef the safter the sapstaff, but the main the mightier the stricker the strait. To the vast go the game! It is the circumconversioning of antelithual paganelles by a huggerknut cramwell energuman, or the caecodedition of an absquelitteris puttagonnianne to the herreraism of a cabotinesque exploser?

— I believe you. Taiptope reelly, O reelly!

— Nautaey, nautaey, we're nowhere without ye! In steam of kavos now arbatos above our hearths doth hum. And Malkos crackles logs of fun while Anglys cheers our ingles. So lent she him ear to burrow his manhood (or so it appierce) and borrow his namas? Suilful eyes and sallowfoul hairweed and the sickly sigh from her gingering mouth like a Dublin bar in the moarning.

— *Primus auriforasti me.*

— The park is gracer than the hole, says she, but shekleton's my fortune?

— Eversought of being artained? You've soft a say with ye, Flatter O'Ford, that, honey, I hurdley chew you.

— Is that answers?

— It am queery!

— The house was Toot and Come-Inn by the bridge called Tiltass, but are you solarly salemly sure, beyond the shatter of the canicular year? *Nascitur ordo seculi numfit.*

— Siriusly and selenely sure behind the shutter. *Securius indicat umbris tellurem.*

— Date as? Your time of immersion? We are still in drought of . . . ?

— Amnis Dominae, Marcus of Corrig. A laughin hunter and Purty Sue.

— And crazyheaded Jorn, the bulweh born?

— Fluteful as his orkan. *Ex ugola lenonem.*

— And Jambs, of Delphin's Bourne or (as olders lay) of Tophat?

— Dawncing the kniejinksky choreopiscopally like an easter sun round the colander, the vice! Taranta boontoday! You should pree him prance the polcat, you whould sniff him wops around, you should hear his piedigrotts schraying as his skimpies skirp a . . .

— Crashedafar Corumbas! A Czardanser indeed! Dervilish glad too. Ortovito semi ricordo. The pantaglionic affection through his blood like a bad influenza in a leap at bounding point?

— Out of Prisky Poppagenua, the palsied old priamite, home from Edwin Hamilton's Christmas pantaloonade, *Oropos Roxy and Pantharhea* at the Gaiety, trippudiating round the aria, with his fiftytwo heirs of age! They may reel at his likes but it's Noeh Bonum's shin do.

— And whit what was Lillabil Issabil maideve, maid at?

— Trists and thranes and trinies and traines.

— A take back to the virgin page, darm it!

— Ay, graunt ye.

— The quobus quartet were there too, if I mistake not, as a sideline but, *pace* the contempt of senate, well to the fore, in an amenessy meeting, metandmorefussed to decide whereagainwhen to meet themselves, flopsome and jerksome, lubber and deliric, drinking unsteadily through the Kerry quadrilles and Listowel lancers and mastersinging always with that consecutive fifth of theirs, eh? Like four wise elephants inandouting under a twelve-podestalled table?

— They were simple scandalmongers, that familiar, and all! Normand, Desmond, Osmund and Kenneth. Making mejical history all over the show!

— In sum, some hum? And other marrage feats?

— All our stakes they were astumbling round the ranky roars assumbling when Big Arthur flugged the field at Annie's courting.

— Suddenly some wellfired clay was cast out through the schappsteckers of hoy's house?

— Schottenly there was a hellfire club kicked out through the wasistas of Thereswhere.

— Like Heavystost's envil catacalamitumbling. Three days three times into the Vulcuum?

— Punch!

— Or Noe et Ecclesiastes, nonne?

— Ninny, there is no hay in Eccles's hostel.

— Yet an I saw a sign of him, if you could scrape out his acquinntence? Name or redress him and we'll call it a night!

— .i..'. .o..l.

— You are sure it was not a shuler's shakeup or a plighter's palming or a winker's wake *etcaetera etcaeterorum* you were at?

— Precisely.

— Mayhap. Hora pro Nubis, Thundersday, at A Little Bit Of Heaven Howth, the wife of Deimetuus (D'amn), Earl Adam Fitz-adam, of a Tartar (Birtha) or Sackville-Lawry and Morland-West, at the Auspice for the Living, Bonnybrook, by the river and A. Briggs Carlisle, guardian of the birdsmaids and deputil-iser for groom. Pontifical mess. Or (soddenly) Schott, furtivfired by the riots. No flies. Agreest?

— Mayhem. Also loans through the post. With or without security. Everywhere. Any amount. Mofsovitz, swampstakers, purely providential.

— Flood's. The pinkman, the squeeze, the pint with the kick. Gaa. And then the punch to Gaelicise it. Fox. The lady with the lamp. The boy in the barleybag. The old man on his ars. Great Scrapp! 'Tis we and you and ye and me and hymns and hurts and heels and shields. The eirest race, the ourest nation, the airest place that erestationed. He was culping for penance while you were ringing his belle. Did the kickee, goodman rued fox, say anything important? Clam or cram, spick or spat?

— No more than Richman's periwhelker.

— Nnn ttt wrd?

— Dmn ttt thg.

— A gael galled by scheme of scorn? Nock?

— Sangnifying nothing. Mock!

— *Fortitudo eius rhodammum tenuit?*

— Five maim! Or something very similar.

— I should like to euphonise that. It sounds an isochronism. Secret speech Hazelton and obviously disemvowelled. But it is good laylaw too. We may take those wellmeant kicks for free granted, though *ultra vires*, void and, in fact, unnecessarily so. Happily you were not quite so successful in the process verbal whereby you would sublimate your blepharospasmockical suppressions, it seems?

— What was that? First I heard about it.

— Were you or were you not? Ask yourself the answer, I'm not giving you a short question. Now, not to mix up, cast your eyes around Capel Court. I want you, witness of this epic struggle, as yours so mine, to reconstruct for us, as briefly as you can, inexactly the same as a mind's eye view, how these funeral games, which have been poring over us through homer's kerryer pidgeons, massacreedoed as the holiname rally round took place.

— Which? Sure I told you that afoul. I was drunk all lost life.

— Well, tell it to me befair, the whole plan of campaign, in that bamboozelem mincethrill voice of yours. Let's have it, christie! The Dublin own, the thrice familiar.

— Ah, sure, I eyewitless foggus. 'Tis all around me bebattersbid hat.

— Ah, go on now, Masta Bones, a gig for a gag, with your impendements and your perroqtriques! Blank memory of hatless darky in blued suit. You were ever the gentle poet, dove from Haywarden. Pitcher cup, patcher cap, pratey man? Be nice about it, Bones Minor! Look chairful! Come, delicacy! Go to the end, thou slackerd! Once upon a grass and a hopping high grass it was.

— Faith, then, Meesta Cheeryman, first he come up, a gag as a gig, badgeler's rake to the town's major from the wesz, MacSmashall Swingy of the Cattelaxes, got up regardless, with a cock on the Kildare side of his Tattersull, in his riddlesneek's ragamufflers and the horrid contrivance as seen above, whisklyng into a bone tolerably delicately, the *Wearing of the Blue*, and taking off his plushkwadded bugsby in his perusal flea and loisy manner, saying good mrowkas to weevilybolly and dragging his feet in the usual course and was ever so terribly naas, really, telling him clean his nagles and fex himself up, Miles, and so on and so fort, and to take the coocoomb to his grizzlies and who done that foxy freak on his bear's hairs like fire bursting out of the Ump pyre and, half hang me, sirr, if he wasn't wanting his calicub body back before he'd to take his life or so save his life. Then, begor, counting as many as eleven to thritytwo seconds with his pocket browning, like I said, wann swanns wann, this is my awethorrorty, he kept forecursing hascupth's foul Fanden, Cogan, for coaccoackey the key of John Dunn's field fore it was for sent and the way Montague was robbed and wolfling to know all what went off and who burned the hay, perchance wilt thoult say, before he'd kill all the kanes and the price of Patsch Purcell's faketotem, which the man, his plantagonist, up from the bog of the depths who was raging with the thirst of the sacred sponge and who, as a mashter of pasht, so far as him was concerned, was only standing there nonplush to the corner of Turbot Street, perplexing about a paumpshop and pupparing to spit, wanting to know whelp the henconvention's compuss memphis he wanted with him new nothing about.

— A sarsencruxer, like the Nap O' Farrell Patter Tandy moor and burgess medley? In other words, was that how in the annusual curse of things, as complement to compliment though, after a manner of men which I must and will say seems extraordinary, their celicolar subtler angelic warfare or photoplay finister started?

— Truly. That I may never!

— Did one scum then in the auradrama, the deff, after some clever play in the mud, mention to the other undesirable, a dumm, during diverse intentional instants, that upon the resume after the angerus, how for his deal he was a pigheaded Swede and to wend himself to a medicis?

— To be sore he did, the huggornut! Only it was turnip-hudded dunce, I beg your pardon, and he would jokes bowlder-blow the betholder with his black masket off the bawling green.

— Sublime was the warning!

— The author, in fact, was mardred.

— Did he, the first spikesman, do anything to him, the last spokesman, when, after heaving some more smutt and chaff between them, they rolled togutter into the ditch together? Black Pig's Dyke?

— No, he had his teeth in the back of his head.

— Did Box then try to shine his puss?

— No but Cox did to shin the punman.

— The worsted crying that if never he looked on Leaverhol-ma's again and the bester huing that he might ever save sunlife?

— Trulytruly Asbestos he ever. And sowasso I never.

— That forte carlysle touch breaking the campdens pianoback.

— Pansh!

— Are you of my meaning that would be going on to about half noon, click o'clock, pip emma, Grinwicker time, by your querqcut quadrant?

— You will be asking me and I wish to higgins you wouldn't. Would it?

— Let it be twelve thirty after a somersautch of the tardest!

— And it was eleven thirsty too befour in soandsuch, reloy on it!

— Tick up on time. Howday you doom? That rising day sinks rosing in a night of nine week's wonder.

— Amties, marcy buckup! The uneven day of the unleventh month of the unevented year. At mart in mass.

— A triduum before Our Larry's own day. By which of your chronos, my man of four watches, larboard, starboard, dog or dath?

— Dunsink, rugby, ballast and ball. You can imagine.

— Language this allsfare for the loathe of Marses ambiviolent about it. Will you swear all the same you saw their shadows a hundred foot later, struggling diabolically over this, that and the other, their virtues *pro* and his principality *con*, near the Ruins, Drogheda Street, and kicking up the devil's own dust for the Milesian wind?

— I will. I did. They were. I swear. Like the heavenly militia. So wreek me Ghyllygully! With my tongue through my toecap on the headlong stone of kismet if so 'tis the will of Whose B. Dunn.

— Weepin Lorcans! They must have put in some wonderful work, ecad, on the quiet like, during this arms' parley, meatierities forces vegateareans. Dost thou not think so?

— Ay.

— The illegallooking range or fender, alias turfing iron, a product of Hostages and Co, Engineers, changed feet several times as briars revalvered during the weaponswap? Piff?

— Puff! Excuse yourself. It was an ersatz lottheringcan.

— They did not know the war was over and were only berebelling or bereppelling one another by chance or necessity with sham bottles, mere and woiney, as betwinst Picturshirts and Scutticules, like their caractacurs in an Irish Ruman to sorowbrate the expeltsion of the Danos? What sayest thou, scusascmerul?

— That's all. For he was heavily upright man, Limba romena in Bucclis tucsada. Farcing gutterish.

— I mean the Morgans and the Dorans, in finnish?

— I know you don't, in Feeney's.

— The mujic of the footure on the barbarihams of the bashed? Co Canniley?

— Da Donnuley.

— Yet this war has meed peace? *In voina viritas*. Ab chaos lex, neat wehr?

— O bella! O pia! O pura! Amem. Handwalled amokst us. Thanksbeer to Balbus!

— All the same you sound it twould clang houlish like Hull hopen for christmians?

— But twill cling hellish like engels opened to neuropeans, if you've sensed, whole the sum. So be vigil!

— And this pattern pootsch punnermine of concoon and proprey went on, hog and minne, a whole whake, your night after larry's night, spittinspite on Dora O'Huggins, ormonde caught butler, the artillery of the O'Hefferns answering the cavalry of the MacClouds, fortey and more fortey, a thousand and one times, according to your cock and a biddy story? Lludillongi, for years and years perhaps?

— That's ri. This is his largos life, this is me timtomtum and this is her two peekweeny ones. From the last finger on the second foot of the fourth man to the first one on the last one of the first. That's right.

— Finny. Vary vary finny!

— It may look funny but fere it is.

— This is not guid enough, Mr Brasslattin. Finging and tonging and winging and ponging! And all your rally and ramp and rant! Didget think I was asleep at the wheel? D'yu mean to tall grand jurors of thathens of tharctic on your oath, me lad, and ask us to believe you, for all you're enduring long terms, with yur last foot foremouthst, that yur moon was shining on the tors and on the cresties and winblowing night after night, for years and years perhaps, after you swearing to it a while back before your Corth examiner, Markwalther, that there was reen in planty all the teem?

— Perhaps so, as you grand duly affirm, Robman Calvinic. I never thought over it, faith. I most certainly think so about it. I hope. Unless it is actionable. It would be a charity for me to think about something which I must on no caste accounts omit, if you ask to me. It was told me as an inspired statement by a friend of myself, in reply to salute, Tarpey, after three o'clock mass, with forty ducks indulgent, that some rain was promised to Mrs Lyons, the invalid of Aunt Tarty Villa, with lots gulp and sousers and likewise he told me, the recusant, after telling mass, with two hundred genuflexions, at the split hour of blight when bars are keeping so sly, as was what's follows. He is doing a walk, says she, in the feelmick's park, says he, like a tarrable Turk, says she, letting loose on his nursery and, begalla, he meet himself with Mr Michael Clery of a Tuesday who said Father MacGregor was desperate to the bad place about thassbawls and ejaculating about all the stairrods and the catspew swashing his earwanker and thinconvenience being locked up for months, owing to being putrenised by stragglers abusing the apparatus, and for Tarpey to pull himself into his soup and fish and to push on his borrowsaloaner and to go to the tumple like greased lining and see Father MacGregor and, be Cad, sir, he was to pipe up and saluate that clergyman and to tell his holiness the whole goat's throat about the three shillings in the confusional and to say how Mrs Lyons, the cuptosser, was the infidel who prophessised to pose three shielings Peter's pelf off her tocher from paraguais and albs by the yard to Mr Martin Clery for Father Mathew to put up a midnight mask saints withins of a Thrushday for African man and to let Brown child do and to leave he Anlone and all the nuisances committed by soldats and nonbehavers and missbelovers for N.D. de l'Ecluse to send more heehaw hell's flutes, my prodder again! And I never brought my cads in togs blanket! Foueh!

— Angly as arrows, but you have right, my celtslinger! Nils, Mugn and Cannut. Should brothers be for awe then?

— So let use off be octo while oil bike the bil and wheel whang till wabblin befoul you but mere and mire trullopes will knaver mate a game on the bibby bobby burns of.

— Quatsch! What hill ar yu fluking about, ye lamelookond fyats! I'll discipline ye! Will you swear or affirm the day to yur second sight noo and recant that all yu affirmed to profetised at first sight for his southerly accent was all paddyflaherty? Will ye, ay or nay?

— Ay say aye. I affirmly swear to it that it rooly and cooly boolyhooly was with my holyhagionous lips continuously poised upon the rubricated annuals of saint ulstar.

— That's very guid of ye, R.C.! Maybe yu wouldn't mind talling us, my labrose lad, how very much bright cabbage or paperming comfirts d'yu draw for all yur swearin? The spanglers, kiddy?

— Rootha prootha. There you have me! Vurry nothing, O potators, I call it for I might as well tell yous Essexelcy, and I am not swallowing my air, the Golden Bridge's truth. It amounts to nada in pounds or pence. Not a glass of Lucan nor as much as the cost price of a highlandman's trousertree or the three crowns round your draphole (isn't it dram disgusting?) for the whole dumb plodding thing!

— Come now, Johnny! We weren't born yesterday. *Pro tanto quid retribuamus?* I ask you to say on your scotty pictail you were promised fines times with some staggerjuice or deadhorse, on strip or in larges, at the Raven and Sugarloaf, either Jones's lame or Jamesy's gait, anyhow?

— Bushmillah! Do you think for a moment? Yes, by the way. How very necessarily true! Give me fair play. When?

— At the Dove and Raven tavern, no, ah? To wit your wizzend?

— Water, water, darty water! Up Jubilee sod! Beet peat wheat treat!

— What harm wants but demands it! How would you like to hear yur right name now, Ghazi Power, my tristy minstrel, if yur not freckened of frank comment?

— Not afrightened of Frank Annybody's gaspower or ill-conditioned ulcers neither.

— Your uncles!

— Your gullet!

— Will you repeat that to me outside, leinconnmuns?

— After you've shouted a few? I will when it suits me, hulstler.

— Guid! We make fight! Three to one! Raddy?

— But no, from exemple, Emania Raffaroo! What do you have? What mean you, august one? Fairplay for Finnians! I will have my humours. Sure, you would not do the cowardly thing and moll me roon? Tell Queen's road I am seilling. Farewell, but whenever! Buy!

521

— Ef I chuse to put a bullet like yu through the grill for heckling what business is that of yours, yu bullock?

— I don't know, sir. Don't ask me, your honour!

— Gently, gently Northern Ire! Love that red hand! Let me once more. There are sordidly tales within tales, you clearly understand that? Now my other point. Did you know, whether by melanodactylism or purely libationally, that one of these two Crimeans with the fender, the taller man, was accused of a certain offence or of a choice of two serious charges, as skirts were divided on the subject, if you like it better that way? You did, you rogue, you?

— You hear things. Besides (and serially now) bushes have eyes, don't forget. Hah!

— Which moral turpitude would you select of the two, for choice, if you had your way? Playing bull before shebears or the hindlegs off a clotheshorse? Did any orangepeelers or greengoaters appear periodically up your sylvan family tree?

— Buggered if I know! It all depends on how much family silver you want for a nass-and-pair. Hah!

— What do you mean, sir, behind your hah! You don't hah to do thah, you know, snapograph.

— Nothing, sir. Only a bone moving into place. Blotogaff. Hahah!

— Whahat?

— Are you to have all the pleasure quizzing on me? I didn't say it aloud, sir. I have something inside of me talking to myself.

— You're a nice third degree witness, faith! But this is no laughing matter. Do you think we are tonedeafs in our noses to boot? Can you not distinguish the sense, prain, from the sound, bray? You have homosexual catheis of empathy between narcissism of the expert and steatopygic invertedness. Get yourself psychoanolised!

— O, begor, I want no expert nursis symaphy from yours broons quadroons and I can psoakoonaloose myself any time I want (the fog follow you all!) without your interferences or any other pigeonstealer.

— Sample! Sample!

— Have you ever weflected, wepowtew, that the evil what though it was willed might nevewtheless lead somehow on to good towawd the genewality?

— A pwopwo of haster meets waster and talking of plebiscites by a show of hands, whether declaratory or effective, in all seriousness, has it become to dawn in you yet that the deponent, the man from Saint Yves, may have been (one is reluctant to use the passive voiced) may be been as much sinned against as sinning, for if we look at it verbally perhaps there is no true noun in active nature where every bally being — please read this mufto — is becoming in its owntown eyeballs. Now the long form and the strong form and reform alltogether!

— Hotchkiss Culthur's Everready, one brother to never-reached, well over countless hands, sieur of many winners and losers, groomed by S. Samson and son, bred by dilalahs, will stand at Bay (Dublin) from nun till dan and vites inversion and at Miss or Mrs's MacMannigan's Yard.

— Perhaps you can explain, sagobean? The Mod needs a rebus.

— Pro general continuation and in particular explication to your singular interrogation our asseveralation. Ladiegent, pals will smile but me and Frisky Shorty, my inmate friend, as is uncommon struck on poplar poetry, and a few fleabesides round at West Pauper Bosquet, was glad to be back again with the chaps and just arguing friendlylike at the Doddercan Easehouse having a wee chatty with our hosty in his comfy estably over the old middlesex party and his moral turps, meaning flu, pock, pox and mizzles, grip, gripe, gleet and sprue, caries, rabies, numps and dumps. What me and Frisky in our concensus and the whole double gigscrew of suscribers, notto say the burman, having successfully concluded our tour of bibel, wants to know is thisahere. Supposing, for an ethical fict, him, which the findings showed, to have taken his epscene licence before the norsect's divisional respectively as regards them male privates and or concomitantly with all common or neuter respects to them

523

public exess females, whereas allbeit really sweet fillies, as was very properly held by the metropolitan in connection with this regrettable nuisance, touching arbitrary conduct, being in strict contravention of schedule in board of forests and works bylaws regulationing sparkers' and succers' amusements section of our beloved naturpark in pursuance of which police agence me and Shorty have approached a reverend gentlman of the name of Mr Coppinger with reference to a piece of fire fittings as was most obliging, 'pon my sam, in this matter of his explanations affirmative, negative and limitative, given to me and Shorty, touching what the good book says of toooldaisymen, concerning the merits of early bisectualism, besides him citing from approved lectionary example given by a valued friend of the name of Mr J. P. Cockshott, reticent of England, as owns a pretty maisonette, *Quis ut Deus*, fronting on to the Soussex Bluffs as was telling us categoric how Mr Cockshott, as he had his assignation with, present holder by deedpoll and indenture of the swearing belt, he tells him hypothetic, the reverend Mr Coppinger, hereckons himself disjunctively with his windwarrd eye up to a dozen miles of a cunifarm school of herring, passing themselves supernatently by the Bloater Naze from twelve and them mayridinghim by the silent hour. Butting, charging, bracing, backing, springing, shrinking, swaying, darting, shooting, bucking and sprinkling their dossies sodouscheock with the twinx of their taylz. And, reverend, he says, summat problematical, by yon socialist sun, gut me, but them errings was as gladful as Wissixy kippers could be considering, flipping their little coppingers, pot em, the fresh little flirties, the dirty little gillybrighteners, pickle their spratties, the little smolty gallockers, and, reverend, says he, more assertitoff, zwelf me Zeus, says he, lettin olfac be the extench of the supperfishies, lamme the curves of their scaligerance and pesk the everurge flossity of their pectorialium, them little salty populators, says he, most apodictic, as sure as my briam eggs is on cockshot under noose, all them little upandown dippies they was all of a libidous pickpuckparty and raid on a wriggolo finsky doodah in testimonials to their early bisectualism. Such, he says, is how the reverend Coppinger, he visualises the hidebound homelies of creed crux ethics. Watsch yourself tillicately every morkning in your bracksullied twilette. The use of cold water, testificates Dr Rutty, may be warmly recommended for the sugjugation of cungunitals loosed. Tolloll, schools!

— Tallhell and Barbados wi ye and your Errian coprulation! Pelagiarist! Remonstrant Montgomeryite! Short lives to your relatives! Y'are absexed, so y'are, with mackerglosia and mickroocyphyllicks.

— Wait now, leixlep! I scent eggoarchicism. I will take you to task. I don't follow you that far in your otherwise accurate account. Was it *esox lucius* or *salmo ferax*? You are taxing us into the driven future, are you not, with this ruttymaid fishery?

— Lalia Lelia Lilia Lulia and lively lovely Lola Montez.

— Gubbernathor! That they say is a fenian on the secret. Named Parasol Irelly. Spawning ova and fry like a marrye monach all amanygoround his seven parish churches! And peopling the ribald baronies with dans, oges and conals!

— Lift it now, Hosty! Hump's your mark! For a runnymede landing! A dondhering vesh vish, *Magnam Carpam*, es hit neat zoo?

— *There's an old psalmsobbing lax salmoner fogeyboren Herrin Plundehowse.*
Who went floundering with his boatloads of spermin spunk about.
Leaping freck after every long tom and wet lissy between Howth and Humbermouth.
Our Human Conger Eel!

— Help! I can see him in the fishnoo! Up wi'yer whippy! Hold that lad! Play him, Markandeyn! Bullhead!

— Pull you, sir! Olive quill does it. Longeal of Malin, he'll cry before he's flayed. And his tear make newisland. Did a rise? Way, lungfush! The great fin may cumule! Three threeth o'er the wild! Manu ware!

— He missed her mouth and stood into Dee, Romunculus Remus, plying the rape, so as now any bompriss's bound to get up her if he pool her leg and bunk on her butt. No, he skid like a skate and berthed on her byrnie and never a fear but they'll land him yet, slitheryscales on liffeybank, times and times and halve a time with a pillow of sand to polster him.

— Do you say they will?

— I bet you they will.

— Among the shivering sedges so? Weedy waving.

— Or tulipbeds of Rush below.

— Where you take your mugs to wash after dark?

— To my lead, Toomey lout, Tommy lad.

— Besides the bubblye waters of, babblyebubblye waters of?

— Right.

— Grenadiers. And tell me now. Were these anglers or angelers coexistent and compresent with or without their *tertium quid?*

— *Three in one, one and three.*
Shem and Shaun and the shame that sunders em.
Wisdom's son, folly's brother.

— God bless your ginger, wigglewaggle! That's three slots and no burners. You're forgetting the jinnyjos for the fayboys. What, Walker John Referent? Play us your patmost! And unpackyoulloups!

— Naif Cruachan! Woe on woe, says Wardeb Daly. Woman will water the wild world over. And the maid of the folley will go where glory. Sure I thought it was larking in the trefoll of the furry glans with two stripping baremaids, Stilla Underwood and Moth MacGarry, he was, hand to dagger, that time and their mother, a rawkneepudsfrowse, I was given to understand, with superflowvius heirs, begum. There was that one that was always mad gone on him, her first king of cloves and the most broadcussed man in Corrack-on-Sharon, County Rosecarmon. Sure she was near drowned in pondest coldstreams of admiration forherself, as bad as my Tarpeyan cousin, Vesta Tully, making faces at her bachspilled likeness in the brook after and cooling herself in the element, she pleasing it, she praising it, with salices and weidowwehls, all tossed, as she was, the playactrix, Lough Shieling's love!

— O, add shielsome bridelittle! All of her own! Nircississies are as the doaters of inversion. Secilas through their laughing classes becoming poolermates in laker life.

— It seems to same with Iscappellas? Ys? Gotellus! A tickey for tie taughts!

— Listenest, meme mearest! They were harrowd, those finweeds! Come, rest in this bosom! So sorry you lost him, poor lamb! Of course I know you are a viry vikid girl to go in the dreemplace and at that time of the draym and it was a very wrong thing to do, even under the dark flush of night, dare all grandpassia! He's gone on his bombashaw. Through geesing and so pleasing at Strip Teasy up the stairs. The boys on the corner were talking too. And your soreful miseries first come on you. Still to forgive it, divine my lickle wiffey, and everybody knows you do look lovely in your invinsibles, Eulogia, a perfect apposition with the coldcream, Assoluta, from Boileau's I always use in the wards after I am burned a rich egg and derive the greatest benefit, sign of the cause. My, you do! Simply adorable! Could I but pass my hands some, my hands through, thine hair! So vicky-vicky veritiny! O Fronces, say howdyedo, Dotty! Chic hands. The way they curve there under nue charmeen cuffs! I am more divine like that when I've two of everything up to boyproof knicks. Winning in a way, only my arms are whiter, dear. Blanchemain, idler. Fairhair, frail one. Listen, meme sweety! O be joyfold! Mirror do justice, taper of ivory, heart of the conavent, hoops of gold! My veil will save it undyeing from his ethernal fire! It's meemly us two, meme idoll. Of course it was downright verry wickred of him, reely meeting me disguised, Bortolo mio, peerfectly appealling, D.V., with my lovebirds, my colombinas. Their sinsitives shrinked. Even Netta and Linda, our seeyu tities and they've sin sumtim, tankus! My rillies were liebeneaus, my aftscents embre. How me adores eatsother simply (Mon ishebeau! Ma reinebelle!), in his storm collar, as I leaned yestreen from his muskished labs, even my little pom got excited, when I turned his head on his same manly bust and kissed him more. Only he might speak to a person, lord so picious, taking up my worths ill wrong! May I introduce! This is my futuous, lips and looks lovelast. Still me with you, you poor chilled! Will make it up with mother Concepcion and a glorious lie between us, sweetness, so as not a novene in all the convent loretos, not my littlest one of all, for mercy's sake need ever know, what passed our lips or. Yes sir, we'll will! Clothea wind! Fee o fie! Covey us niced! Bansh the dread! Alitten's looking. Low him lovly! Make me feel good in the moontime. It will all take bloss as oranged at St Audiens rosan chocolate chapelry with my diamants blickfeast after at minne owned hos for all the catclub to go cryzy and Father Blesius Mindelsinn will be beminding hand. Kyrielle elation! Crystal elation! Kyrielle elation! Elation immanse! Sing to us, sing to us, sing to us! Amam! So meme nearest, languished hister, be free to me! (I'm fading!) And listen, you, you beauty, esster, I'll be clue to who knows you, pray Magda, Marthe with Luz and Joan, while I lie with warm lisp on the Tolka. (I'm fay!)

— Eusapia! Fais-le, tout-tait! Languishing hysteria? The clou historique? How is this at all? Is dads the thing in such or are tits the that? Hear we here her first poseproem of suora unto suora? Alicious, twinstreams twinestraines, through alluring glass or alas in jumboland? Ding dong! Where's your pal in silks alustre? Think of a maiden, Presentacion. Double her, Annupciacion. Take your first thoughts away from her, Immacolacion. Knock and it shall appall unto you! Who shone yet shimmers will be e'er scheining. Cluse her, voil her, hild her hindly. After liryc and themodius soft aglo iris of the vals. This young barlady, what, euphemiasly? Is she having an ambidual act herself in apparition with herself as Consuelas to Sonias may?

— Dang! And tether, a loguy O!

— Dis and dat and dese and dose! Your crackling out of your turn, my Moonster firefly, like always. And 2 R.N. and Longhorns Connacht, stay off my air! You've grabbed the capital and you've had the lion's shire since 1542 but there's all the difference in Ireland between your borderation, my chatty cove, and me. The leinstrel boy to the wall is gone and there's moreen astoreen for Monn and Conn. With the tyke's named moke. Doggymens' nimmer win! You last led the first when we last but we'll first trump your last with a lasting. Jump the railchairs or take them, as you please, but and, sir, my queskins first, foxyjack! Ye've as much skullabogue cheek on you now as would boil a caldron of kalebrose. Did the market missioners Hayden Wombwell, when given the raspberry, fine more than sandsteen per cent of chalk in the purity, promptitude and perfection flour of this raw materialist and less than a seventh pro mile in his meal? We bright young chaps of the brandnew braintrust are briefed here and with maternal sanction compellably empanelled at quarter sessions under the six disqualifications for the uniformication of young persons (Nodding Neutrals) removal act by Committalman Number Underfifteen to know had the peeress of generals, who have been getting nose money cheap and stirring up the public opinion about private balls with their legs, Misses Mirtha and Merry, the two dreeper's assistents, had they their service books in order and duly signed J. H. North and Company when discharged from their last situations? Will ye gup and tell the board in the anterim how, in the name of the three tailors on Tooley Street, did O'Bejorumsen or Mockmacmahonitch, ex of Butt and Hocksett's, violating the bushel standard, come into awful position of the barrel of bellywash? And why, is it any harm to ask, was this hackney man in the coombe, a papersalor with a whiteluke to him, Fauxfitzhuorson, collected from Manofisle, carrying his ark, of eggshaped fuselage and made in Fredborg into the bullgine, across his back when he might have been setting on his jonass inside like a Glassthure cabman? Where were the doughboys, three by nombres, won in ziel, cavehill exers or hearts of steel, Hansen, Morfydd and O'Dyar, V.D., with their glenagearries directing their steps according to the R.U.C's liaison officer, with their trench ulcers open and their hands in their pockets, contrary to military rules, when confronted with his lifesize obstruction? When did he live off rooking the pooro and how did start pfuffpfaffing at his Paterson and Hellicott's? Is it a factual fact, proved up to scabsteethshilt, that this fancydress nordic in shaved lamb breeches, child's kilts, bibby buntings and wellingtons, with club, torc and headdress, preholder of the Bar Ptolomei, is coowner of a hengster's circus near North Great Denmark Street (incidentally, it's the most unjoyable show going the province and I'm taking the youngsters there Saturday first when it's halfprice naturals night to see the fallensickners aping the buckleybackers and the blind to two worlds taking off the deffydowndummies) and the shamshemshowman has been complaining to the police barracks and applying for an order of *certiorari* and crying out something vile about him being molested, after him having triplets, by offers of vacancies from females in this city, neighing after the man and his outstanding attraction ever since they seen his X ray picture turned out in wealthy red in the sabbath sheets? Was it him that suborned that surdumutual son of his, a litterydistributer in Saint Patrick's Lavatory, to turn a Roman and leave the chayr and gout in his bare balbriggans, the sweep, and buy the usual jar of porter at the Morgue and Cruses and set it down before the wife with her fireman's halmet on her, bidding her mine the hoose, the strumpet, while him and his lagenloves were rampaging the roads in all their paroply under the noses of the Heliopolitan constabulary? Can you beat it? Prepare the way! Where's that gendarm auxiliar, arianautic sappertillery, that reported on the whole hoodlum, relying on his morse-erse wordybook and the trunchein up his tail? Roof Seckesign van der Deckel and get her story from him! Recall Sickerson, the lizzyboy! Seckersen, magnon of Errick. Sackerson! Hookup!

— *Day shirker four vanfloats he verdants market.*
High liquor made lust torpid dough hunt her orchid.

— Hunt her orchid! Gob and he found it on her right enough! With her shoes upon his shoulders, 'twas most trying to beholders when he upped their frullatullepleats with our warning. A disgrace to the homely protestant religion! Bloody old preadamite with his twohandled umberella! Trust me to spy on me own spew!

— Wallpurgies! And it's this's your deified city? Norganson? And it's we's to pray for Bigmesser's conversions? Call Kitty the Beads, the Mandame of Tipknock Castle! Let succuba succumb, the improvable his wealth made possible! He's cookinghagar that rost her prayer to him upon the top of the stairs. She's deep, that one.

— A farternoiser for his tuckish armenities. Ouhr Former

530

who erred in having down to gibbous disdag our darling breed. And then the confisieur for the boob's indulligence. As sunctioned for his salmenbog by the Councillors-om-Trent. Pave Pannem at his gaiter's bronze! Nummer half dreads Log Laughty. Master's gunne he warrs the bedst. I messaged his dilltoyds sausepander mussels on the kisschen table. With my ironing duck through his rollpins of gansyfett, do dodo doughdy dough, till he was braising red in the toastface with lovensoft eyebulbs and his kiddledrum steeming and rattling like the roasties in my mockamill. I awed to have scourched his Abarm's brack for him. For the loaf of Obadiah, take your pastryart's noas out of me flouer bouckuet! Of the strainger scene you given squeezers to me skillet! As cream of the hearth thou reinethst alhome. His lapper and libbers was glue goulewed as he sizzled there watching me lautterick's pitcher by Wexford-Atelier as Katty and Lanner, the refined souprette, with my bust alla brooche and the padbun under my matelote, showing my jigotty sleeves and all my new toulong touloosies. Whisk! There's me shims and here's me hams and this is me juppettes, gause be the meter! Whisk! What's this? Whisk! And that? He never cotched finer, balay me, at Romiolo Frullini's flea pantamine out of Griddle-the-Sink or Shusies-with-her-Soles-Up or La Sauzerelly, the pucieboots, when I started so hobmop ladlelike, highty tighty, to kick the time off the cluckclock lucklock quamquam camcam potapot panapan kickakickkack. Hairhorehounds, shake up pfortner. Fuddling fun for Fullacan's sake!

— All halt! Sponsor programme and close down. That's enough, genral, of finicking about Finnegan and fiddling with his faddles. A final ballot, guvnor, to remove all doubt. By sylph and salamander and all the trolls and tritons, I mean to top her drive and to tip the tap of this, at last. His thoughts that wouldbe words, his livings that havebeen deeds. And will too, by the holy child of Coole, primapatriock of the archsee, if I have at first to down every mask in Trancenania from Terreterry's Hole to Stutterers' Corner to find that Yokeoff his letter, this Yokan his dahet. Pass the jousters of the king, the Kovnor-Journal and eirenarch's custos himself no less, the meg of megs, with the Carrison old gang! Off with your persians! Search ye the Finn! The sinder's under shriving sheet. Fa Fe Fi Fo Fum! Ho, croak, evildoer! Arise, sir ghostus! As long as you've lived there'll be no other. Doff!

— Amtsadam, sir, to you! Eternest cittas, heil! Here we are again! I am bubub brought up under a camel act of dynasties long out of print, the first of Shitric Shilkanbeard (or is it Owllaugh MacAuscullpth the Thord?), but, in pontofacts massimust, I am known throughout the world wherever my good Allenglisches Angleslachsen is spoken by Sall and Will from Augustanus to Ergastulus, as this is, whether in Farnum's rath or Condra's ridge or the meadows of Dalkin or Monkish tunshep, by saints and sinners eyeeye alike as a cleanliving man and, as a matter of fict, by my halfwife, I think how our public at large appreciates it most highly from me that I am as cleanliving as could be and that my game was a fair average since I perpetually kept my ouija ouija wicket up. On my verawife I never was nor can afford to be guilty of crim crig con of malfeasance trespass against parson with the person of a youthful gigirl frifrif friend chirped Apples, acted by Miss Dashe, and with Any of my cousines in Kissilov's Slutsgartern or Gigglotte's Hill, when I would touch to her dot and feel most greenily of her unripe ones as it should prove most anniece and far too bahad, nieceless to say, to my reputation on Babbyl Malket for daughters-in-trade being lightly clad. Yet, as my acquainters do me the complaisance of apprising me, I should her have awristed under my duskguise of whippers through toombs and deempeys, lagmen, was she but tinkling of such a tink. And, as a mere matter of ficfect, I tell of myself how I popo possess the ripest littlums wifukie around the globelettes globes upon which she was romping off on Floss Mundai out of haram's way round Skinner's circusalley first with her consolation prize in my serial dreams of faire women, Mannequins Passe, with awards in figure and smile subsections, handicapped by two breasts in operatops, a remarkable little endowment garment. Fastened at various places. What spurt! I kickkick keenly love such, particularly while savouring of their flavours at their most perfect best when served with heliotrope ayelips, as this is, where I do drench my jolly soul on the pu pure beauty of hers past.

She is my bestpreserved wholewife, sowell her as herafter, in Evans's eye, with incompatibly the smallest shoenumber outside chinatins. They are jolly dainty, spekin tluly. May we not recommend them? It was my proofpiece from my prenticeserving. And, alas, our private chaplain of Lambeyth and Dolekey, bishop-regionary, an always sadfaced man, in his lutestring pewcape with tabinet band, who has visited our various hard hearts and reins by imposition of fufuf fingers, olso haddock's fumb, in that Upper Room can speak loud to you some quite complimentary things about my clean charactering, even when detected in the dark, distressful though such recital prove to me, as this is, when I introduced her (Frankfurters, numborines, why drive fear?) to our fourposter tunies chantreying under Castrucci Sinior and De Mellos, those whapping oldsteirs, with sycamode euphonium in either notation in our altogether cagehaused duckyheim on Goosna Greene, that cabinteeny homesweetened through affection's hoardpayns (First Murkiss, or so they sankeyed. Dodo! O Clearly! And Gregorio at front with Johannes far in back. Aw, aw!), gleeglom there's gnome sweepplaces like theresweep No-whergs. By whom, as my Kerk Findlater's, ye litel chuch rond ye coner, and K. K. Katakasm enjoineth in the Belief and, as you all know, of a child, dear Humans, one of my life's ambitions of my youngend from an early peepee period while still to hedje-skool, intended for broadchurch, I, being fully alive to it, was parruchially confirmed in Caulofat's bed by our bujibuji beloved curate-author. Michael Engels is your man. Let Michael relay Sutton and tell you people here who have the phoney habit (it was remarketable) in his clairaudience, as this is, as only our own Michael can, when reicherout at superstation, to bring ruptures to our roars how I am amp amp amplify. Hiemlancollin. Pim-pim's Ornery forninehalf. Shaun Shemsen saywhen saywhen. Holmstock unsteaden. Livpoomark lloyrge hoggs one four tupps noying. Big Butter Boost! Sorry! Thnkyou! Thatll beall fortody. Cal it off. Godnotch, vryboily. End a muddy crushmess! Abbreciades anew York gustoms. Kyow! Tak.

— Tiktak. Tikkak.

— Awind abuzz awater falling.

— Poor a cowe his jew placator.

— It's the damp damp damp.

— Calm has entered. Big big Calm, announcer. It is most ernst terooly a moresome intartenment. Colt's tooth! I will give tandsel to it. I protest there is luttrelly not one teaspoonspill of evidence at bottomlie to my babad, as you shall see, as this is. Keemun Lapsang of first pickings. And I contango can take off my dudud dirtynine articles of quoting here in Pynix Park before those in heaven to provost myself, by gramercy of justness, I mean veryman and moremon, stiff and staunch for ever, and enter under the advicies from Misrs Norris, Southby, Yates and Weston, Inc, to their favoured client, into my preprotestant caveat against the pupup publication of libel by any tixtim tipsyloon or tobtomtowley of Keisserse Lean (a bloweyed lanejoymt, waring lowbelt suit, with knockbrecky kenees and bullfist rings round him and a fallse roude axehand (he is cunvesser to Saunter's Nocelettres and the Poe's Toffee's Directory in his pisness), the best begrudged man in Belgradia who doth not belease to our paviour) to my nonesuch, that highest personage at moments holding down the throne. So to speak of beauty scouts in elegant pursuit of flowers, searchers for tabernacles and the celluloid art! Happen seen sore eynes belived? The caca cad! He walked by North Strand with his Thom's towel in hand. Snakeeye! Strangler of soffiacated green parrots! I protest it that he is, by my wipehalf. He was leaving out of my double inns while he was all teppling over my single ixits. So was keshaned on for his recent behaviour. Sherlook is lorking for him. Allare beltspanners. Get your air curt! Shame upon Private M! Shames on his fulsomeness! Shamus on his atkinscum's lulul lying suulen for an outcast mastiff littered in blood currish! Eristocras till Hanging Tower! Steck a javelin through his advowtried heart! Instaunton! Flap, my Larrybird! Dangle, my highflyer! Jiggety jig my jackadandyline! Let me never see his waddphez again! And mine it was, Barktholed von Hunarig, Soesown of Furrows (hourspringlike his joussture, immitiate my chry! as urs now, so yous then!), when to our lot it fell on my poplar Sexsex, my Sexencentaurnary, whenby Gate of Hal, before his hostel of the Wodin Man, I hestened to freeholdit op to his Mam his Maman, Majuscules, His Magnus Maggerstick, first city's leasekuays of this Nova Tara, our most noble, when hrossbucked on his pricelist charger, Pferdinamd Allibuster (yeddonot need light oar till Noreway for you fanned one o'er every doorway) with my allbum's greethims through this whole of my promises, handshakey congrandyoulikethems, ecclesency.

Whosaw the jackery dares at handgripper thisa breast? Dose makkers ginger. Some one we was with us all fours. Adversarian! The spiking Duyvil! First liar in Londsend! Wulv! See you scargore on that skeepsbrow! And those meisies! Sulken taarts! Man sicker at I ere bluffet konservative? Shucks! Such ratshause bugsmess so I cannot barely conceive of! Lowest basemeant in hystry! Ibscenest nansence! Noksagt! Per Peeler and Pawr! The brokerheartened shugon! Hole affair is rotten muckswinish porcupig's draff. Enouch!

— Is that yu, Whitehed?

— Have you headnoise now?

— Give us your mespilt reception, will yous?

— Pass the fish for Christ's sake!

— Old Whitehowth he is speaking again. Ope Eustace tube! Pity poor whiteoath! Dear gone mummeries, goby! Tell the woyld I have lived true thousand hells. Pity, please, lady, for poor O.W. in this profundust snobbing I have caught. Nine dirty years mine age, hairs hoar, mummery failend, snowdrift to my ellpow, deff as Adder. I askt you, dear lady, to judge on my tree by our fruits. I gave you of the tree. I gave two smells, three eats. My freeandies, my celeberrimates: my happy bossoms, my allfalling fruits of my boom. Pity poor Haveth Childers Everywhere with Mudder!

That was Communicator, a former colonel. A disincarnated

spirit, called Sebastion, from the Rivera in Januero, (he is not all hear) may fernspreak shortly with messuages from my deadported. Let us cheer him up a little and make an appunkment for a future date. Hello, Commudicate! How's the buttes? Everscepistic! He does not believe in our psychous of the Real Absence, neither miracle wheat nor soulsurgery of P. P. Quemby. He has had some indiejestings, poor thing, for quite a little while, confused by his tonguer of baubble. A way with him! Poor Felix Culapert! Ring his mind, ye staples, (bonze!) in my ould reekeries' ballyheart and in my krumlin and in aroundisements and stremmis! Sacks eleathury! Sacks eleathury! Bam! I deplore over him ruely. Mongrieff! O Hone! Guesteimed with the nobelities, to die bronxitic in achershous! So enjoying of old thick whiles, in haute white toff's hoyt of our formed reflections, with stock of eisen all his prop, so buckely hosiered from the Royal Leg, and his puertos mugnum, he would puffout a dhymful bock. And the how he would husband her that verikerfully, his cigare divane! (He would redden her with his vestas, but 'tis naught.) With us his nephos and his neberls, mest incensed and befogged by him and his smoke thereof. But he shall have his glad stein of our zober beerbest in Oscarshal's winetavern. *Buen retiro!* The boyce voyce is still flautish and his mounth still wears that soldier's scarlet though the flaxafloyeds are peppered with salsedine. It is bycause of what he was ascend into his prisonce on account off. I whit it wel. Hence his deepraised words. Some day I may tell of his second storey. Mood! Mood! It looks like someone other bearing my burdens. I cannot let it. Kanes nought.

Well, yeamen, I have bared my whole past, I flatter myself, on both sides. Give me even two months by laxlaw in second division and my first broadcloth is business will be to protest to Recorder at Thing of all Things, or court of Skivinis, with marchants grey, antient and credibel, Zerobubble Barrentone, Jonah Whalley, Determined Codde or Cucumber Upright, my jurats, if it does not occur again. O rhyme us! Haar Faagher, wild heart in Homelan; Harrod's be the naun. Mine kinder come, mine wohl be won. There is nothing like leuther. O Shee! And nosty mens in gladshouses they shad not peggot stones. The elephant's house is his castle. I am here to tell you, indeed to goodness, that, allbe I discountenanced beallpersuasions, in rinunciniation of pomps of heretofore, with a wax too held in hand, I am thorgtfulldt to do dope me of her miscisprinks and by virchow of those filthered Ovocnas presently like Browne umbracing Christina Anya, after the Irishers, to convert me into a selt (but first I must proxy babetise my old antenaughties), when, as Sigismond Stolterforth, with Rabbin Robroost for my auspicer and Leecher Rutty for my lifearst and Lorencz Pattorn (*Ehren til viktrae!*), when I will westerneyes those poor sunuppers and outbreighten their land's eng. A man should stump up and I will pay my pretty decent trade price for my glueglue gluecose, peebles, were it even, as this is, the legal eric for infelicitous conduict (here incloths placefined my pocketanchoredcheck) and, as a matter of fact, I undertake to discontinue entyrely all practices and I deny wholeswiping *in toto* at my own request in all stoytness to have confermentated and confoederated and agreed in times prebellic, when here were waders for the trainsfolk, as it is now nuggently laid to me, with a friend from mine, Mr Billups, pulleter, my quarterbrother, who sometimes he is doing my locum for me on a grubstake and whom I have cleped constoutuent, for so it was felt by me, at goodbuy cootcoops byusucapiture a mouthless niggeress, Blanchette Brewster from Cherna Djamja, Blawlawnd-via-Brigstow, or to illsell my fourth part in her, which although allowed of in Deuterogamy as in several places of Scripture (copyright) and excluded books (they should quite rightly verbanned be), would seem eggseggs excessively haroween to my feelimbs for two punt scotch, one pollard and a crockard or three pipples on the bitch. Thou, Frick's Flame, Uden Sulfer, who strikest only on the marryd bokks, enquick me if so be I did cophetuise milady's maid! In spect of her beavers she is a womanly and sacret. Such wear a frillick for my comic strip, Mons Meg's Monthly, comes out aich Fanagan's Weck, to bray at by clownsillies in Donkeybrook Fair. It would lackin mackin Hodder's and Cocker's erithmatic. The unpurdonable preemp-

son of all of her of yourn, by Juno Moneta! If she, irished Marry-
onn Teheresiann, has been disposed of for her consideration, I,
Ledwidge Salvatorious, am tradefully unintiristid. And if she is
still further talc slopping over her cocoa contours, I hwat mick
angars, am strongly of opinion why I should not be. Inprobable!
I do not credit one word of it from such and suchess mistra-
versers. Just feathers! Nanenities! Or to have ochtroyed to
resolde or borrough by exchange same super melkkaart, means
help; best Brixton high yellow, no outings: cent for cent on
Auction's Bridge. 'Twere a honnibel crudelty wert so tente-
ment to their naktlives and scatab orgias we devour about in
the mightyevil roohms of encient cartage. Utterly improperable!
Not for old Crusos or white soul of gold! A pipple on the
panis, two claps on the cansill, or three pock pocks cassey
knocked on the postern! Not for one testey tickey culprik's
coynds ore for all ecus in cunziehowffse! So hemp me Cash!
I meanit.

My herrings! The surdity of it! Amean to say. Her bare
idears, it is choochoo chucklesome. Absurd bargain, mum, will
call. One line with! One line, with with! Will ate everadayde sau-
mone like a boyne alive O. The tew cherripickers, with their
Catheringnettes, Lizzy and Lissy Mycock, from Street Flesh-
shambles, were they moon at aube with hespermun and I their
covin guardient, I would not know to contact such gretched
youngsteys in my ways from Haddem or any suistersees or
heiresses of theirn, claiming by, through, or under them. Ous of
their freiung pfann into myne foyer. Her is one which rassembled
to mein enormally. The man what shocked his shanks at contey
Carlow's. He is Deucollion. Each habe goheerd, uptaking you
are innersence, but we sen you meet sose infance. Deucollion!
Odor. Evilling chimbes is smutsick rivulverblott but thee hard
casted thereass pigstenes upann Congan's shootsmen in Schot-
tenhof, ekeascent? Igen Deucollion! I liked his Gothamm chic!
Stuttertub! What a shrubbery trick to play! I will put my oath-
head unner my whitepot for ransom of beeves and will stand
me where I stood mine in all free heat between Pelagios and little

Chistayas by Roderick's our mostmonolith, after my both ears-
toear and brebreeches buybibles and, minhatton, testify to my
unclothed virtue by the longstone erectheion of our allfirst man-
here. I should tell you that honestly, on my honour of a Near-
wicked, I always think in a wordworth's of that primed favourite continental poet, Daunty, Gouty and Shopkeeper, A. G.,
whom the generality admoyers in this that is and that this is to
come. Like as my palmer's past policy I have had my best master's lessons, as the public he knows, and do you know, home-
sters, I honestly think, if I have failed lamentably by accident
benefits though shintoed, spitefired, perplagued and cram-
krieged, I am doing my dids bits and have made of my prudentials
good. I have been told I own stolemines or something of that
sorth in the sooth of Spainien. Hohohoho! Have I said ogso how
I abhor myself vastly (truth to tell) and do repent to my nether-
heart of suntry clothing? The amusin part is, I will say, hotel-
men, that since I, over the deep drowner Athacleeath to seek
again Irrlanding, shamed in mind, with three plunges of my
ruddertail, yet not a bottlenim, vanced imperial standard by
weaponright and platzed mine residenze, taking bourd and
burgage under starrymisty and ran and operated my brixtol selection here at thollstall, for mean straits male with evorage fimmel,
in commune soccage among strange and enemy, among these
plotlets, in Poplinstown, alore Fort Dunlip, then-on-sea, hole
of Serbonian bog, now city of magnificent distances, good-
walldabout, with talus and counterscarp and pale of palisades,
upon martiell siegewin, with Abbot Warre to blesse, on yon
slauchterday of cleantarriffs, in that year which I have called
myriabellous, and overdrave these marken (the soord on Whence-
hislaws was mine and mine the prusshing stock of Allbrecht
the Bearn), under patroonshaap of our good kingsinnturns,
T. R. H. Urban First and Champaign Chollyman and Hungry
the Loaved and Hangry the Hathed, here where my tenenure of
office and my toils of domestication first began, with weight of
woman my skat and skuld but Flukie of the Ravens as my sure
piloter, famine with Englisch sweat and oppedemics, the two-

toothed dragon worms with allsort serpents, has compolitely seceded from this landleague of many nations and open and notorious naughty livers are found not on our rolls. This seat of our city it is of all sides pleasant, comfortable and wholesome. If you would traverse hills, they are not far off. If champain land, it lieth of all parts. If you would be delited with fresh water, the famous river, called of Ptolemy the Libnia Labia, runneth fast by. If you will take the view of the sea, it is at hand. Give heed!

— *Do Drumcollogher whatever you do!*

— *Visitez Drumcollogher-la-Belle!*

— *Be suke and sie so ersed Drumcollogher!*

— *Vedi Drumcollogher e poi Moonis.*

—Things are not as they were. Let me briefly survey. Pro clam a shun! Pip! Peep! Pipitch! Ubipop jay piped, ibipep goes the whistle. Here Tyeburn throttled, massed murmars march: where the bus stops there shop I: here which ye see, yea reste. On me, your sleeping giant. Estoesto! Estote sunto! From the hold of my capt in altitude till the mortification that's my fate. The end of aldest mosest ist the beginning of all thisorder so the last of their hansbailis shall the first in our sheriffsby. New highs for all! Redu Negru may be black in tawn but under them lintels are staying my horneymen meet each his mansiemagd. For peers and gints, quaysirs and galleyliers, fresk letties from the say and stale headygabblers, gaingangers and dudder wagoners, pullars off societies and pushers on rothmere's homes. Obeyance from the townsmen spills felixity by the toun. Our bourse and politico-ecomedy are in safe with good Jock Shepherd, our lives are on sure in sorting with Jonathans, wild and great. Been so free! Thank you, besters! Hattentats have mindered. Blaublaze devil-bobs have gone from the mode and hairtrigger nicks are quite out of time now. Thuggeries are reere as glovars' metins, lepers lack, ignerants show beneath suspicion like the bitterhalves of esculapuloids. In midday's mallsight let Miledd discurverself. Me ludd in her hide park seek Minuinette. All is waldy bonums. Blownose aerios we luft to you! Firebugs, good blazes! Lubbers, kepp your poudies drier! Seamen, we segn your skivs and wives!

Seven ills so barely as centripunts havd I habt, seaventy seavens for circumference inkeptive are your hill prospect. Braid Blackfordrock, the Calton, the Liberton, Craig and Lockhart's, A. Costofino, R. Thursitt. The chort of Nicholas Within was my guide and I raised a dome on the wherewithouts of Michan: by awful tors my wellworth building sprang sky spearing spires, cloud cupoled campaniles: further this. By fineounce and imposts I got and grew and by grossscruple gat I grown outreachesly: murage and lestage were my mains for Ouerlord's tithing and my drains for render and prender the doles and the tribute: I was merely out of my mint with all the percussors on my braincap till I struck for myself and muched morely by token: to Sirrherr of Gambleden ruddy money, to Madame of Pitymount I loue yous. Paybads floriners moved in hugheknots against us and I matt them, pepst to papst, barthelemew: milreys (mark!) onfell, and (Luc!) I arose Daniel in Leonden. Bulafests onvied me, Corkcuttas graatched. Atabey! I braved Brien Berueme to berow him against the Loughlins, all her tolkies shraking: Fugabollags! Lusqu'au bout! If they had ire back of eyeball they got danage on front tooth: theres were revelries at ridottos, here was rivalry in redoubt: I wegschicked Duke Wellinghof to reshockle Roy Shackleton: Walhalloo, Walhalloo, Walhalloo, mourn in plein! Under law's marshall and warschouw did I thole till lead's plumbate, ping on pang, reliefed me. I made praharfeast upon acorpolous and fastbroke down in Neederthorpe. I let faireviews in on slobodens but ranked rothgardes round wrathminsers: I bathandbaddend on mendicity and I corocured off the unoculated. Who can tell their tale whom I filled ad liptum on the plain of Soulsbury? With three hunkered peepers and twa and twas! For sleeking beauties I spinned their nightinveils, to slumbred beast I tummed the thief air. Round the musky moved a murmel but mewses whinninaird and belluas zoomed: tendulcis tunes like water parted fluted up from the westinders while from gorges in the east came the strife of ourangoontangues. All in my thicville Escuterre ofen was thorough fear but in the meckling of my burgh Belvaros was the site forbed: tuberclerosies I

541

reized spudfully from the murphyplantz Hawkinsonia and berri-berries from the pletoras of the Irish shou. I heard my liberti-lands making free through their curraghcoombs, my trueblues hurusalaming before Wailingtone's Wall: I richmounded the rainelag in my bathtub of roundwood and conveyed it with cheers and cables, roaring mighty shouts, through my longer-tubes of elm: out of fundness for the outozone I carried them amd curried them in my Putzemdown cars to my Kommeandine hotels: I made sprouts fontaneously from Philuppe Sobriety in the coupe that's cheyned for noon inebriates: when they weaned weary of that bibbing I made infusion more infused: sowerpacers of the vinegarth, obtemperate unto me! When you think me in my coppeecuffs look in ware would you meckamockame, as you pay in caabman's sheltar tot the ites like you corss the tees. Wherefore watch ye well! For, while I oplooked the first of Janus's straight, I downsaw the last of Christmas steps: syndic podestril and on the rates, I for indigent and intendente: in Forum Foster I demosthrenated my folksfiendship, enmy pupuls felt my burk was no worse than their brite: Sapphrageta and Consciencia were undecidedly attached to me but the maugher machrees and the auntieparthenopes my schwalby words with litted spongelets set their soakye pokeys and botchbons afume: Fletcher-Flemmings, elisaboth, how interquackeringly they ro-gated me, their golden one, I inhesitant made replique: Mesde-memdes to leursieuresponsor: and who in hillsaide, don't you let flyfire till you see their whites of the bunkers' eyes! Mr An-swers: Brimgem young, bringem young, bringem young!: in my bethel of Solyman's I accouched their rotundaties and I turn-keyed most insultantly over raped lutetias in the lock: I gave bax of biscums to the jacobeaters and pottage bakes to the esausted; I dehlivered them with freakandesias by the constant droppings from my smalls instalmonths while I titfortotalled up their farinadays for them on my slataper's slate with my chandner's chauk: I jaunted on my jingelbrett rapt in neckloth and sashes, and I beggered about the amnibushes like belly in a bowle. In the humanity of my heart I sent out heyweywomen to refresh the ballwearied and then, doubling megalopolitan poleetness, my great great greatest of these charities, devaleurised the base fellows for the curtailment of their lower man: with a slog to square leg I sent my boundary to Botany Bay and I ran up a score and four of mes while the Yanks were huckling the Empire: I have been reciping om omominous letters and widely-signed petitions full of pieces of pottery about my monumental-ness as a thingabolls and I have been inchanting causeries to the feshest cheoilboys so that they are allcalling on me for the song of a birtch: the more secretely bi built, the more openly palas-tered. Attent! Couch hear! I have becket my vonderbilt hutch in sunsmidnought and at morningrise was encampassed of mushroofs. Rest and bethinkful, with licence, thanks. I con-sidered the lilies on the veldt and unto Balkis did I disclothe mine glory. And this. This missy, my taughters, and these man, my son, from my fief of the villa of the Ostmanorum to Thor-stan's, *recte* Thomars Sraid, and from Huggin Pleaze to William Inglis his house, that man de Loundres, in all their barony of Saltus, bonders and foeburghers, helots and zelots, strutting oges and swaggering macks, the darsy jeamses, the drury joneses, redmaids and bleucotts, in hommage all and felony, all who have received tickets, fair home overcrowded, tidy but very little furniture, respectable, whole family attends daily mass and is dead sick of bread and butter, sometime in the militia, mentally strained from reading work on German physics, shares closet with eight other dwellings, more than respectable, getting com-fortable parish relief, wageearner freshly shaven from prison, highly respectable, planning new departure in Mountgomery cyclefinishing, eldest son will not serve but peruses Big-man-up-in-the-Sky scraps, anoopanadoon lacking backway, quasi respec-table, pays ragman in bones for faded windowcurtains, staircase continually lit up with guests, particularly respectable, house lost in dirt and blocked with refuse, getting on like Roe's dis-tillery on fire, slovenly wife active with the jug, in business for himself, has a tenth illegitimate coming, partly respectable, following correspondence courses, chucked work over row, both cheeks kissed at levee by late marquess of Zetland, sharing closet which is profusely written over with eleven other subscribers, once respectable, open hallway pungent of Baltic dishes, bangs kept woman's head against wall thereby disturbing neighbours, private chapel occupies return landing, removal every other quarter day, case one of peculiar hopelessness, most respectable, nightsoil has to be removed through snoring household, eccentric naval officer not quite steady enjoys weekly churchwarden and laugh while reading foreign pictorials on clumpstump before door, known as the trap, widow rheumatic and chars, haunted, condemned and execrated, of dubious respectability, tools too costly pledged or uninsured, reformed philanthropist whenever feasible takes advantage of unfortunates against dilapidating ashpits, serious student is eating his last dinners, floor dangerous for unaccompanied old clergymen, thoroughly respectable, many uncut pious books in evidence, nearest watertap two hundred yards' run away, fowl and bottled gooseberry frequently on table, man has not had boots off for twelve months, infant being taught to hammer flat piano, outwardly respectable, sometimes hears from titled connection, one foot of dust between banister and cracked wall, wife cleans stools, eminently respectable, ottawark and regular loafer, should be operated would she consent, deplorable rent in roof, claret cellar cobwebbed since the pontificate of Leo, wears drill trousers and collects rare buddhas, underages very treacly and verminous have to be separated, sits up with fevercases for one and threepence, owns two terraces (back to back breeze), respectable in every way, harmless imbecile supposingly weakminded, a sausage every Sunday, has a staff of eight servants, outlook marred by ne'er-do-wells using the laneway, lieabed sons go out with sisters immediately after dark, has never seen the sea, travels always with her eleven trunks of clothing, starving cat left in disgust, the pink of respectability, resting after colonial service, labours at plant, the despair of his many benefactresses, calories exclusively from Rowntrees and dumplings, one bar of sunlight does them all january and half february, the V. de V's (animal diet) live in five-storied semidetached but rarely pay tradesmen, went security for friend who absconded, shares same closet with fourteen similar cottages and an illfamed lodginghouse, more respectable than some, teawidow pension but held to purchase, inherited silk hat from father-in-law, head of domestic economy never mentioned, queery how they live, reputed to procure, last four occupants carried out, mental companionship with mates only, respectability unsuccessfully aimed at, copious holes emitting mice, decoration from Uganda chief in locked ivory casket, grandmother has advanced alcoholic amblyopia, the terror of Goodmen's Field, and respected and respectable, as respectable as respectable can respectably be, though their orable amission were the herrors I could have expected, all, let them all come, they are my villeins, with chartularies I have talledged them. Wherfor I will and firmly command, as I willed and firmly commanded, upon my royal word and cause the great seal now to be affixed, that from the farthest of the farther of their fathers to their children's children's children they do inhabit it and hold it for me unencumbered and my heirs, firmly and quietly, amply and honestly, and with all the liberties and free customs which the men of Tolbris, a city of Tolbris, have at Tolbris, in the county of their city and through whole my land. Hereto my vouchers, knive and snuffbuchs. Fee for farm. Enwreak us wrecks.

Struggling forlongs I have livramentoed, milles on milles of mancipelles. Lo, I have looked upon my pumpadears in their easancies and my drummers have tattled tall tales of me in the land: in morgenattics litt I hope, in seralcellars louched I bleakmealers: on my siege of my mighty I was parciful of my subject but in street wauks that are darkest I debelledem superb: I deemed the drugtails in my pettycourts and domstered dustyfeets in my husinclose: at Guy's they were swathed, at Foulke's slashed, the game for a Gomez, the loyfor a lynch: if I was magmonimoss as staidy lavgiver I revolucanized by my eructions: the hye and bye wayseeds I scattered em, in my graben fields sew sowage I gathered em: in Sheridan's Circle my wits repose, in black pitts of the pestered Lenfant he is dummed. (Hearts of Oak, may ye root to piece!

Rechabites obstain! Clayed sheets, pineshrouded, wake not, walk not! Sigh lento, Morgh!) *Quo warranto* has his greats my soliven and puissant lord V. king regards for me and he has given to me my necknamesh (flister it!) which is second fiddler to nomen. These be my genteelician arms. At the crest, two young frish, etoiled, flappant, devoiled of their habiliments, vested sable, withdrewers argent. For the boss a coleopter, pondant, partifesswise, blazoned sinister, at the slough, proper. In the lower field a terce of lanciers, shaking unsheathed shafts, their arms crossed in saltire, embusked, sinople. Motto, in letters portent: *Hery Crass Evohodie*. Idle were it, repassing from elserground to the elder disposition, to inquire whether I, draggedasunder, be the forced generation of group marriage, holocryptogam, of my essenes, or carried of cloud from land of locust, in ouzel galley borne, I, huddled til summone be the massproduct of teamwork, three surtouts wripped up in itchother's, two twin pritticoaxes lived as one, troubled in trine or dubildin too, for abram nude be I or roberoyed with the faineans, of Feejeean grafted ape on merfish, surrounded by obscurity, by my virtus of creation and by boon of promise, by my natural born freeman's journeymanright and my otherchurch's inher light, in so and such a manner as me it so besitteth, most surely I pretend and reclam to opt for simultaneous. Till daybowbreak and showshadows flee. Thus be hek. Verily! Verily! Time, place!

— What is your numb? Bun!

— Who gave you that numb? Poo!

— Have you put in all your sparepennies? I'm listening. Sree!

— Keep clear of propennies! Fore!

— Mr Televox, Mrs Taubiestimm and invisible friends! I may-may mean to say. Annoyin part of it was, had faithful Fulvia, following the wiening courses of this world, turned her back on her ways to gon on uphills upon search of louvers, brunette men of Earalend, Chief North Paw and Chief Goes in Black Water and Chief Brown Pool and Chief Night Cloud by the Deeps, or again had Fluvia, amber whitch she was, left her chivily crookcrook crocus bed at the bare suggestions of some prolling bywaymen from Moabit who could have abused of her, the foxrogues, there might accrue advantage to ask wher in pellmell her deceivers sinned. Yet know it was vastly otherwise which I have heard it by mmummy goods waif, as I, chiefly endmost hartyly aver, for Fulvia Fluvia, iddle woman to the plusneeborn, ever did ensue tillstead the things that pertained unto fairnesse, this wharom I am fawned on, that which was loost. Even so, for I waged love on her: and spoiled her undines. And she wept: O my lors!

— Till we meet!
— Ere we part!
— Tollollall!
— This time a hundred years!
— But I was firm with her. And I did take the reached of my delights, my jealousy, ymashkt, beyashmakt, earswathed, snout-snooded, and did raft her flumingworthily and did leftlead her overland the pace, from lacksleap up to liffsloup, tiding down, as portreeve should, whimpering by Kevin's creek and Hurdlesford and Gardener's Mall, long riverside drive, embankment large, to Ringsend Flott and Ferry, where she began to bump a little bit, my dart to throw: and there, by wavebrink, on strond of south, with mace to masthigh, taillas Cowhowling, quailless Highjakes, did I upreized my magicianer's puntpole, the tridont sired a tritan stock, farruler, and I bade those polyfizzyboisterous seas to retire with hemselves from os (rookwards, thou seasea stamoror!) and I abridged with domfine norsemanship till I had done abate her maidan race, my baresark bride, and knew her fleshly when with all my bawdy did I her whorship, min bryllupswibe: Heaven, he hallthundered; Heydays, he flung blissforhers. And I cast my tenspan joys on her, arched over-tupped, from bank of call to echobank, by dint of strongbow (Galata! Galata!) so streng we were in one, malestream in shegulf: and to ringstresse I thumbed her with iern of Erin and tradesmanmarked her lieflang mine for all and singular, iday, igone, imorgans, and for ervigheds: base your peak, you! you, strike your flag!: (what screech of shippings! what low of dampf-

547

bulls!): from Livland, hoks zivios, from Lettland, skall vives! With Impress of Asias and Queen Columbia for her pairanymphs and the singing sands for herbrides' music: goosegaze annoynted uns, canailles canzoned and me to she her shyblumes lifted: and I pudd a name and wedlock boltoned round her the which to carry till her grave, my durdin dearly, Appia Lippia Pluviabilla, whiles I herr lifer amstell and been: I chained her chastemate to grippe fiuming snugglers, her chambrett I bestank so to spunish furiosos: I was her hochsized, her cleavunto, her everest, she was my annie, my lauralad, my pisoved: who cut her ribbons when nought my prowes? who exposed that havenliness to beacha-lured ankerrides when not I, freipforter?: in trinity huts they met my dame, pick of their poke for me: when I foregather 'twas my sumbad, if I farseeker itch my list: had I not workit in my cattagut with dogshunds' crotts to clene and had I not gifted of my coataways, constantonoble's aim: and, fortiffed by my right as man of capitol, I did umgyrdle her about, my vermin-celly vinagerette, with all loving kindness as far as in man's might it lay and enfranchised her to liberties of fringes: and I gave until my lilienyounger turkeythighs soft goods and hard-ware (catalogue, *passim*) and ladderproof hosiery lines (see stockinger's raiment), cocquette coiffs (see Agnes' hats) and peningsworths of the best taste of knaggs of jets and silvered waterroses and geegaws of my pretty novelties and wispywaspy frocks of redferns and lauralworths, trancepearances such as women cattle bare and peltries piled, the peak of Pim's and Slyne's and Sparrow's, loomends day lumineused luxories on looks, *La Primamère, Pyrrha Pyrrhine, Or de Reinebeau, Sourire d'Hiver* and a crinoline, wide a shire, and pattens for her trilibies that know she might the tortuours of the boots and bedes of wampun with to toy and a murcery glaze of shard to mirrow, for all daintiness by me and theetime, the cupandnaggin hour: and I wound around my swanchen's neckplace a school of shells of moyles marine to swing their saysangs in her silents: and, upping her at king's count, her aldritch cry oloss unheading, what though exceeding bitter, I pierced her beak with order of the

Danabrog (Cunnig's great! Soll leve! Soll leve!): with mare's greese cressets at Leonard's and Dunphy's and Madonna lanthorns before quintacasas and tallonkindles spearhead syngeing nickendbookers and mhutton lightburnes dipdippingdownes in blackholes, the tapers of the topers and his buntingpall at hoist: for days there was no night for nights were days and our folk had rest from Blackheathen and the pagans from the prince of pacis: what was trembling sod quaked no more, what were frozen loins were stirred and lived: gone the septuor, dark deadly dismal doleful desolate dreadful desperate, no more the tolvmaans, bloody gloomy hideous fearful furious alarming terrible mournful sorrowful frightful appalling: peace, perfect peace: and I hung up at Yule my duindleeng lunas, helphelped of Kettil Flashnose, for the souperhore of my frigid one, *coloumba mea*, *frimosa mea*, in Wastewindy tarred strate and Elgin's marble halles lamping limp from black to block, through all Livania's volted ampire, from anodes to cathodes and from the topazolites of Mourne, Wykinloeflare, by Arklow's sapphire siomen's lure and Wexterford's hook and crook lights to the polders of Hy Kinsella: avenyue ceen my peurls ahumming, the crown to my estuarine munipicence?: three firths of the sea I swept with draughtness and all ennempties I bottled em up in bellomport: when I stabmarooned jack and maturin I was a bad boy's bogey but it was when I went on to sankt piotersbarq that they gave my devil his dues: what is seizer can hack in the old wold a sawyer may hew in the green: on the island of Breasil the wildth of me perished and I took my plowshure sadly, feeling pity for me sored: where bold O'Connee weds on Alta Mahar, the tawny sprawling beside that silver burn, I sate me and settled with the little crither of my hearth: her intellects I charmed with I calle them utile thoughts, her turlyhyde I plumped with potatums for amiens pease in plenty: my biblous beadells shewed her triumphs of craftygild pageantries, loftust Adam, duffed our cousterclother, Conn and Owel with cortoppled baskib, Sire Noeh Guinnass, exposant of his bargeness and Lord Joe Starr to hump the body of the camell: I screwed the Emperor down with ninepins gaelic with sixpennyhapennies for his hanger on: my worthies were bissed and trissed from Joshua to Godfrey but my *processus prophetarum* they would have plauded to perpetuation. Moral: book to besure, see press.

— He's not all buum and bully.

— But his members handly food him.

— Steving's grain for's greet collegtium.

— The S. S. Paudraic's in the harbour.

— And after these things, I fed her, my carlen, my barelean linsteer, upon spiceries for her garbage breath, italics of knobby lauch and the rich morsel of the marrolebone and shains of garleeks and swinespepper and gothakrauts and pinkee dillisks, primes of meshallehs and subleties in jellywork, come the feast of Saint Pancreas, and shortcake nutrients for Paas and Pingster's pudding, bready and nutalled and potted fleshmeats from store dampkookin, and the drugs of Kafa and Jelupa and shallots out of Ascalon, feeding her food convenient herfor, to pass them into earth: and to my saffronbreathing mongoloid, the skinsyg, I gave Biorwik's powlver and Uliv's oils, unguents of cuticure, for the swarthy searchall's face on her, with handewers and groinscrubbers and a carrycam to teaze her tussy out, the brown but combly, a mopsa's broom to duist her sate, and clubmoss and wolvesfoot for her more moister wards (amazing efficiencies!): and, my shopsoiled doveling, when weeks of kindness kinly civicised, in our saloons esquirial, with fineglas bowbays, draped embrasures and giltedged librariums, I did devise my telltale sports at evenbread to wring her withers limberly, wheatears, slapbang, drapier-cut-dean, bray, nap, spinado and ranter-go-round: we had our lewd mayers and our lairdie meiresses kiotowing and smuling fullface on us out of their framous latenesses, oilclothed over for cohabitation and allpointed by Hind: Tamlane the Cussacke, Dirk Wettingstone, Pieter Stuyvesant, Outlawrie O'Niell, Mrs Currens, Mrs Reyson-Figgis, Mrs Dattery, and Mrs Pruny-Quetch: in hym we trust, footwash and sects principles, apply to overseer, Amos five six: she had dabblingtime for exhibiting her grace of aljambras and duncingk the bloodanoobs in her vauxhalls while I, dizzed and dazed by the lumpty thumpty of our interloopings, fell clocksure off my ballast: in our windtor palast it vampared for elenders, we lubded Sur Gudd for the sleep and the ghoasts: she chauffed her fuesies at my Wigan's jewels while she skalded her mermeries on my Snorryson's Sagos: in pay-cook's thronsaale she domineered, lecking icies off the dormer panes all admired her in camises: on Rideau Row Duanna dwells, you merk well what you see: let wellth were I our pantocreator would theirs be tights for the gods: in littleritt reddinghats and cindery yellows and tinsel and glitter and bibs under hoods: I made nusance of many well pressed champdamors and peddled freely in the scrub: I foredreamed for thee and more than full-maked: I prevened for thee in the haunts that joybelled frail light-a-leaves for sturdy traemen: *pelves ad hombres sumus:* I said to the shiftless prostitute; let me be your fodder; and to rodies and prater brothers; Chau, Camerade!: evangel of good tidings, om-nient as the Healer's word, for the lost, loathsome and whomso-ever will: who, in regimentation through liberal donation in co-ordination for organisation of their installation and augmenta-tion plus some annexation and amplification without precipita-tion towards the culmination in latification of what was formerly their utter privation, competence, cheerfulness, usefulness and the meed, shall, in their second adams, all be made alive: my tow tugs steered down canal grand, my lighters lay longside on Regalia Water. And I built in *Urbs in Rure*, for minne elskede, my shiny brows, under astrolobe from my upservatory, an erd-closet with showne ejector wherewithin to be squatquit in most covenience from her sabbath needs, when open noise should stilled be: did not I festfix with mortarboard my unniversiries, wholly rational and gottalike, sophister agen sorefister, life sizars all?: was I not rosetted on two stellas of little egypt? had not I rockcut readers, hieros, gregos and democriticos?: triscastellated, bimedallised: and by my sevendialled changing charties Hiberns-ka Ulitzas made not I to pass through twelve Threadneedles and Newgade and Vicus Veneris to cooinsight?: my camels' walk, kolossa kolossa! no porte sublimer benared my ghates: Oi polled ye many but my fews were chousen (Voter, voter, early voter, he was never too oft for old Sarum): terminals four my staties were, the Geenar, the Greasouwea, the Debwickweck, the Mifgreawis. And I sept up twinminsters, the pro and the con, my stavekirks wove so norcely of peeled wands and attachatouchy floodmud, now all loosebrick and stonefest, freely masoned, arked for covennanters and shinners' rifuge: descent from above on us, Hagiasofia of Astralia, our orisons thy nave and absedes, our aeone tone aeones thy studvaast vault; Hams, circuitise! Shemites, retrace!: horns, hush! no barkeys! hereround is't holied!: all truanttrulls made I comepull, all rubbeling gnomes I pushed, gowgow: Cassels, Redmond, Gandon, Deane, Shepperd, Smyth, Neville, Heaton, Stoney, Foley, Farrell, Vnost with Thorneycroft and Hogan too: sprids serve me! gobelins guard!: tect my tileries (O tribes! O gentes!), keep my keep, the peace of my four great ways: oathiose infernals to Booth Salvation, arcane celestials to Sweatenburgs Welhell! My seven wynds I trailed to maze her and ever a wynd had saving closes and all these closes flagged with the gust, hoops for her, hatsoff for him and ruffles through Neeblow's garding: and that was why Blabus was razing his wall and eltering the suzannes of his nighboors: and thirdly, for ewigs, I did reform and restore for my smuggy piggiesknees, my sweet coolocked, my auburn coyquailing one, her paddypalace on the crossknoll with massgo bell, sixton clashcloshant, duominous and muezzatinties to commind the fitful: doom adimdim adoom adimadim: and the oragel of the lauds to tellforth's glory: and added thereunto a shallow laver to slub out her hellfire and posied windows for her oriel house: gospelly pewmillieu, christous pewmillieu: zackbutts babazounded, ollguns tararulled: and she sass her nach, chillybombom and forty bonnets, upon the altarstane. May all have mossyhonours!

— Hoke!

— Hoke!

— Hoke!

— Hoke!

— And wholehail, snaeffell, dreardrizzle or sleetshowers of blessing, where it froze in chalix eller swum in the vestry, with fairskin

book and ruling rod, vein of my vergin page, her chastener ever
I did learn my little ana countrymouse in alphabeater cameltem-
per, from alderbirk to tannenyou, with myraw rattan atter dun-
drum; ooah, oyir, oyir, oyir: and I did spread before my Livvy,
where Lord street lolls and ladies linger and Cammomile Pass
cuts Primrose Rise and Coney Bend bounds Mulbreys Island but
never a blid had bledded or bludded since long agore when the
whole blighty acre was bladey well pessovered, my selvage mats
of lecheworked lawn, my carpet gardens of Guerdon City, with
chopes pyramidous and mousselimes and beaconphires and colos-
sets and pensilled turisses for the busspleaches of the summira-
mies and esplanadas and statuesques and templeogues, the Par-
donell of Maynooth, Fra Teobaldo, Nielsen, rare admirable, Jean
de Porteleau, Conall Gretecloke, Guglielmus Caulis and the eiligh
ediculous Passivucant (glorietta's inexcellsiored!): for irkdays
and for folliedays till the comple anniums of calendarias, gregoro-
maios and gypsyjuliennes as such are pleased of theirs to walk:
and I planted for my own hot lisbing lass a quickset vineyard and
I fenced it about with huge Chesterfield elms and Kentish hops
and rigs of barlow and bowery nooks and greenwished villas
and pampos animos and (N.I.) necessitades iglesias and pons for
aguaducks: a hawthorndene, a feyrieglenn, the hallaw vall, the
dyrchace, Finmark's Howe, against lickybudmonth and gleaner-
month with a magicscene wall (rimrim! rimrim!) for a Queen's
garden of her phoenix: and (hush! hush!) I brewed for my alpine
plurabelle, wigwarming wench, (speakeasy!) my granvilled brand-
old Dublin lindub, the free, the froh, the frothy freshener, puss,
puss, pussyfoot, to split the spleen of her maw: and I laid down
before the trotters to my eblanite my stony battered waggon-
ways, my nordsoud circulums, my eastmoreland and westland-
more, running boullowards and syddenly parading, (hearsemen,
opslo! nuptiallers, get storting!): whereon, in mantram of true-
men like yahoomen (expect till dutc cundoctor summoneth him
all fahrts to pay, velkommen all hankinhunkn in this vongn of
Hoseyeh!), claudesdales withe arabinstreeds, Roamer Reich's
rickyshaws with Hispain's King's trompateers, madridden mus-

tangs, buckarestive bronchos, poster shays and turnintaxis, and tall tall tilburys and nod nod noddies, others gigging gaily, some sedated in sedans: my priccoping gents, aroger, aroger, my damsells softsidesaddled, covertly, covertly, and Lawdy Dawe a perch behind: the mule and the hinny and the jennet and the mustard nag and piebald shjelties and skewbald awknees steppit lively (lift ye the left and rink ye the right!) for her pleashadure: and she lalaughed in her diddydid domino to the switcheries of the whip. Down with them! Kick! Playup!

Mattahah! Marahah! Luahah! Joahanahanahana!

What was thaas? Fog was whaas? Too mult sleepth. Let sleepth.

But really now whenabouts? Expatiate then how much times we live in. Yes?

So, nat by night by naught by naket, in those good old lousy days gone by, the days, shall we say? of Whom shall we say? while kinderwardens minded their twinsbed, therenow they-stood, the sycomores, all four of them, in their quartan agues, the majorchy, the minorchy, the everso and the fermentarian with their ballyhooric blowreaper, titranicht by tetranöxst, at their pussycorners, and that old time pallyollogass, playing copers fearsome, with Gus Walker, the cuddy, and his poor old dying boosy cough, esker, newcsle, saggard, crumlin, dell me, donk, the way to wumblin. Follow me beeline and you're bumblin, esker, newcsle, saggard, crumlin. And listening. So gladdied up when nicechild Kevin Mary (who was going to be commandeering chief of the choirboys' brigade the moment he grew up under all the auspices) irishsmiled in his milky way of cream dwibble and onage tustard and dessed tabbage, frighted out when badbrat Jerry Godolphing (who was hurrying to be cardinal scullion in a night refuge as bald as he was cured enough unerr all the hospitals) furrinfrowned down his wrinkly waste of methylated spirits, ick, and lemoncholy lees, ick, and pulverised rhubarbarorum, icky;

night by silentsailing night while infantina Isobel (who will be blushing all day to be, when she growed up one Sunday, Saint Holy and Saint Ivory, when she took the veil, the beautiful presentation nun, so barely twenty, in her pure coif, sister Isobel, and next Sunday, Mistlemas, when she looked a peach, the beautiful Samaritan, still as beautiful and still in her teens, nurse Saintette Isabelle, with stiffstarched cuffs but on Holiday, Christmas, Easter mornings when she wore a wreath, the wonderful widow of eighteen springs, Madame Isa Veuve La Belle, so sad but lucksome in her boyblue's long black with orange blossoming weeper's veil) for she was the only girl they loved, as she is the queenly pearl you prize, because of the way the night that first we met she is bound to be, methinks, and not in vain, the darling of my heart, sleeping in her april cot, within her singachamer, with her greengageflavoured candywhistle duetted to the crazyquilt, Isobel, she is so pretty, truth to tell, wildwood's eyes and primarose hair, quietly, all the woods so wild, in mauves of moss and daphnedews, how all so still she lay, neath of the whitethorn, child of tree, like some losthappy leaf, like blowing flower stilled, as fain would she anon, for soon again 'twill be, win me, woo me, wed me, ah weary me! deeply, now evencalm lay sleeping;

nowth upon nacht, while in his tumbril Wachtman Havelook seequeerscenes, from yonsides of the choppy, punkt by his curserbog, went long the grassgross bumpinstrass that henders the pubbel to pass, stowing his bottle in a hole for at whet his whuskle to stretch ecrooksman, sequestering for lovers' lost propertied offices the leavethings from allpurgers' night, og gneiss ogas gnasty, kikkers, brillers, knappers and bands, handsboon and strumpers, sminkysticks and eddiketsflaskers;

wan fine night and the next fine night and last find night while Kothereen the Slop in her native's chambercushy, with dreamings of simmering my veal astore, was basquing to her pillasleep how she thawght a knogg came to the dowanstairs dour at that howr to peirce the yare and dowandshe went, schritt be schratt, to see was it Schweeps's mingerals or Shuhorn the posth with a tilly-cramp for Hemself and Co, Esquara, or them four hoarsemen on their apolkaloops, Norreys, Soothbys, Yates and Welks, and, galorybit of the sanes in hevel, there was a crick up the stirkiss and when she ruz the cankle to see, galohery, downand she went on her knees to blessersef that were knogging together like milk-juggles as if it was the wrake of the hapspurus or old Kong Gander O'Toole of the Mountains or his googoo goosth she seein, sliving off over the sawdust lobby out of the backroom, wan ter, that was everywans in turruns, in his honeymoon trim, holding up his fingerhals, with the clookey in his fisstball, tocher of davy's, tocher of ivileagh, for her to whisht, you sowbelly, and the whites of his pious eyebulbs swering her to silence and coort;

each and every juridical sessions night, whenas goodmen twelve and true at fox and geese in their numbered habitations tried old wireless over boord in their juremembers, whereas by reverendum they found him guilty of their and those imputations of fornicolopulation with two of his albowcrural correlations on whom he was said to have enjoyed by anticipation when school-ing them in amown, mid grass, she sat, when man was, amazingly frank, for their first conjugation whose colours at standing up from the above were of a pretty carnation but, if really 'twere not so, of some deretane denudation with intent to excitation, caused by his retrogradation, among firearmed forces proper to this nation but apart from all titillation which, he said, was under heat pressure and a good mitigation without which in any case he insists upon being worthy of continued alimentation for him having displayed, he says, such grand toleration, reprobate so noted and all, as he was, with his washleather sweeds and his smokingstump, for denying transubstantiation nevertheless in respect of his highpowered station, whereof more especially as probably he was meantime suffering genteel tortures from the best medical attestation, as he oftentimes did, having only strength enough, by way of festination, to implore (or I believe you have might have said better) to complore, with complete obsecration, on everybody connected with him the curse of co-agulation for, he tells me outside Sammon's in King Street, after

557

two or three hours of close confabulation, by this pewterpint of Gilbey's goatswhey which is his prime consolation, albeit involving upon the same no uncertain amount of esophagous regurgitation, he being personally unpreoccupied to the extent of a flea's gizzard anent eructation, if he was still extremely offensive to a score and four nostrils' dilatation, still he was likewise, on the other side of him, for some nepmen's eyes a delectation, as he asserts without the least alienation, so prays of his faullt you would make obliteration but for our friend behind the bars, though like Adam Findlater, a man of estimation, summing him up to be done, be what will of excess his exaltation, still we think with Sully there can be no right extinuation for contravention of common and statute legislation for which the fit remedy resides, for Mr Sully, in corporal amputation: so three months for Gubbs Jeroboam, the frothwhiskered pest of the park, as per act one, section two, schedule three, clause four of the fifth of King Jark, this sentence to be carried out tomorrowmorn by Nolans Volans at six o'clock shark, and may the yeastwind and the hoppinghail malt mercy on his seven honeymeads and his hurlyburlygrowth, Amen, says the Clarke;

niece by nice by neat by natty, whilst amongst revery's happy gardens nine with twenty Leixlip yearlings, darters all, had such a ripping time with gleeful cries of what is nice toppingshaun made of made for and weeping like fun, him to be gone, for they were never happier, huhu, than when they were miserable, haha;

in their bed of trial, on the bolster of hardship, by the glimmer of memory, under coverlets of cowardice, Albatrus Nyanzer with Victa Nyanza, his mace of might mortified, her beautifell hung up on a nail, he, Mr of our fathers, she, our moddereen ru arue rue, they, ay, by the hodypoker and blazier, they are, as sure as dinny drops into the dyke . . .

A cry off.

Where are we at all? and whenabouts in the name of space?

I don't understand. I fail to say. I dearsee you too.

House of the cederbalm of mead. Garth of Fyon. Scene and property plot. Stagemanager's prompt. Interior of dwelling on outskirts of city. Groove two. Chamber scene. Boxed. Ordinary bed-room set. Salmonpapered walls. Back, empty Irish grate, Adam's mantel, with wilting elopement fan, soot and tinsel, condemned. North, wall with window practicable. Argentine in casement. Vamp. Pelmit above. No curtains. Blind drawn. South, party wall. Bed for two with strawberry bedspread, wickerworker clubsessel and caneseated millikinstool. Bookshrine without, facetowel upon. Chair for one. Woman's garments on chair. Man's trousers with crossbelt braces, collar on bedknob. Man's corduroy surcoat with tabrets and taces, seapan nacre buttons on nail. Woman's gown on ditto. Over mantelpiece picture of Michael, lance, slaying Satan, dragon with smoke. Small table near bed, front. Bed with bedding. Spare. Flagpatch quilt. Yverdown design. Limes. Lighted lamp without globe, scarf, gazette, tumbler, quantity of water, julepot, ticker, side props, eventuals, man's gummy article, pink.

A time.

Act: dumbshow.

Closeup. Leads.

Man with nightcap, in bed, fore. Woman, with curlpins, hind. Discovered. Side point of view. First position of harmony. Say! Eh? Ha! Check action. Matt. Male partly masking female. Man looking round, beastly expression, fishy eyes, paralleliped homoplatts, ghazometron pondus, exhibits rage. Business. Ruddy blond, Armenian bole, black patch, beer wig, gross build, episcopalian, any age. Woman, sitting, looks at ceiling, haggish expression, peaky nose, trekant mouth, fithery wight, exhibits fear. Welshrabbit teint, Nubian shine, nasal fossette, turfy tuft, undersized, free kirk, no age. Closeup. Play!

Callboy.   Cry off. Tabler. Her move.

Footage.

By the sinewy forequarters of the mare Pocahontas and by the white shoulders of Finnuala you should have seen how that smart sallowlass just hopped a nanny's gambit out of bunk like old mother Mesopotomac and in eight and eight sixtyfour she was off, door, knightlamp with her, billy's largelimbs prodgering after to queen's lead. Promiscuous Omebound to Fiammelle la Diva. Huff! His move. Blackout.

Circus. Corridor.

Shifting scene. Wall flats: sink and fly. Spotlight working wall cloths. Spill playing rake and bridges. Room to sink: stairs to sink behind room. Two pieces. Haying after queue. Replay.

The old humburgh looks a thing incomplete so. It is so. On its dead. But it will pawn up a fine head of porter when it is finished. In the quicktime. The castle arkwright put in a chequered staircase certainly. It has only one square step, to be steady, yet notwith-stumbling are they stalemating backgammoner supstairs by skips and trestles tiltop double corner. Whist while and game.

What scenic artist! It is ideal residence for realtar. By hims ingang tilt tinkt a tunning bell that Limen Mr, that Boggey Godde, be airwaked. Lingling, lingling. Be their maggies in all. Chump, do your ephort. Shop! Please shop! Shop ado please! O ado please shop! How hominous his house, haunt it? Yesses indead it be! Nogen, of imperial measure, is begraved beneadher. Here are his naggins poured, his alladim lamps. Around the bloombiered, booty with the bedst. For them whom he have fordone make we newly thankful!

Tell me something. The Porters, so to speak, after their shadowstealers in the newsbaggers, are very nice people, are they not? Very, all fourlike tellt. And on this wise, Mr Porter (Bar-tholomew, heavy man, astern, mackerel shirt, hayamatt peruke) is an excellent forefather and Mrs Porter (leading lady, a poopahead, gaffneysaffron nightdress, iszoppy chepelure) is a most kindhearted messmother. A so united family pateramater is not more existing on papel or off of it. As keymaster fits the lock it weds so this bally builder to his streamline secret. They care for nothing except everything that is allporterous. *Porto da Brozzo!* Isn't that terribly nice of them? You can ken that they come of a rarely old family by their costumance and one must togive that one supped of it in all tonearts from awe to zest. I think I begin to divine so much. Only snakkest me truesome! I stone us I'm hable.

To reachy a skeer do! Still hoyhra, till venstra! Here are two rooms on the upstairs, at forkflank and at knifekanter. Whom in the wood are they for? Why, for little Porter babes, to be saved! The coeds, boytom thwackers and timbuy teaser. Here is one-thing you owed two noe. This one once upon awhile was the other but this is the other one nighadays. Ah so? The Corsicos? They are numerable. Guest them. Major bed, minor bickhive. Halosobuth, sov us! Who sleeps in now number one, for ex-ample? A pussy, purr esimple. Cunina, Statulina and Edulia, but how sweet of her! Has your pussy a pessname? Yes, indeed, you will hear it passim in all the noveletta and she is named Buttercup. Her bare name will tellt it, a monitress. How very sweet of her and what an excessively lovecharming missyname to forsake, now that I come to drink of it filtred, a gracecup fulled of bitterness. She is dadad's lottiest daughterpearl and brooder's cissiest auntybride. Her shellback thimblecasket mirror only can show her dearest friendeen. To speak well her grace it would ask of Grecian language, of her goodness, that legend golden. Biryina Saindua! Loreas with lillias flocaflake arrosas! Here's newyearspray, the posquiflor, a windaborne and helio-trope; there miriamsweet and amaranth and marygold to crown. Add lightest knot unto tiptition. O Charis! O Charissima! A more intriguant bambolina could one not colour up out of Boccuccia's Enameron. Would one but to do apart a lilybit her virginelles and, so, to breath, so, therebetween, behold, she had instantt with her handmade as to graps the myth inmid the air. Mother of moth! I will to show herword in flesh. Approach not for ghost sake! It is dormition! She may think, what though little doth she realise, as morning fresheth, it hath happened her, you know what, as they too what two dare not utter. Silvoo plush, if scolded she draws a face. Petticoat's asleep but in the gentlenest of her thoughts apoo is a nursepin. To be presented, Babs for Bim-bushi? Of courts and with enticers. Up, girls, and at him! Alone? Alone what? I mean, our strifestirrer, does she do fleurty winkies with herself. Pussy is never alone, as records her chambrette, for she can always look at Biddles and talk petnames with her little playfilly when she is sitting downy on the ploshmat. O, she talks, does she? Marry, how? Rosepetalletted sounds. Ah Biddles es ma plikplak. Ah plikplak wed ma Biddles. A nice jezebel barytinette she will gift but I much prefer her missnomer in maidenly golden lasslike gladsome wenchful flowery girlish beautycapes. So do I, much. Dulce delicatissima! Doth Dolly weeps she is hastings. Will Dally bumpsetty it is tubtime. Allaliefest, she who pities very pebbles, dare we not wish on her our thrice onsk? A lovely fear! That she seventip toe her chrysming, that she spin blue to scarlad till her temple's veil, that the Mount of Whoam it open it her to shelterer! She will blow ever so much more promisefuller, blee me, than all the other common marygales that romp round brigidschool, charming Carry Whambers or saucy Susy Maucepan of Merry Anna Patchbox or silly Polly Flinders. Platsch! A plikaplak.

And since we are talking amnessly of brukasloop crazedledaze, who doez in sleeproom number twobis? The twobirds. Holy policeman, O, I see! Of what age are your birdies? They are to come of twinning age so soon as they may be born to be eldering like those olders while they are living under chairs. They are and they seem to be so tightly tattached as two maggots to touch other, I think I notice, do I not? You do. Our bright bull babe Frank Kevin is on heartsleeveside. Do not you waken him! Our farheard bode. He is happily to sleep, limb of the Lord, with his lifted in blessing, his buchel Iosa, like the blissed angel he looks so like and his mou is semiope as though he were blowdelling on a bugigle. Whene'er I see those smiles in eyes 'tis Father Quinn again. Very shortly he will smell sweetly when he will hear a weird to wean. By gorgeous, that boy will blare some knight when he will take his dane's pledges and quit our ingletears, spite of undesirable parents, to wend him to Amorica to quest a cashy job. That keen dean with his veen nonsolance! O, I adore the profeen music! Dollarmighty! He is too audorable really, eunique! I guess to have seen somekid like him in the story book, guess I met somewhere somelam to whom he will be becoming liker. But hush! How unpardonable of me! I beg for your venials, sincerely I do.

Hush! The other, twined on codliverside, has been crying in his sleep, making sharpshape his insciscors on some first choice sweets fished out of the muck. A stake in our mead. What a teething wretch! How his book of craven images! Here are posthumious tears on his intimelle. And he has pipettishly bespilled himself from his foundingpen as illspent from inkinghorn. He is jem job joy pip poo pat (jot um for a sobrat!) Jerry Jehu. You will know him by name in the capers but you cannot see whose heel he sheepfolds in his wrought hand because I have not told it to you. O, foetal sleep! Ah, fatal slip! the one loved, the other left, the bride of pride leased to the stranger! He will be quite within the pale when with lordbeeron brow he vows him so tosset to be of the sir Blake tribes bleak while through life's unblest he rodes backs of bannars. Are you not somewhat bulgar with your bowels? Whatever do you mean with bleak? With pale blake I write tintingface. O, you do? And with steelwhite and blackmail I ha'scint for my sweet an anemone's letter with a gold of my bridest hair betied. Donatus his mark, address as follows. So you did? From the Cat and Cage. O, I see and see! In the ink of his sweat he will find it yet. What Gipsy Devereux vowed to Lylian and why the elm and how the stone. You never may know in the preterite all perhaps that you would not believe that you ever even saw to be about to. Perhaps. But they are two very blizky little portereens after their bredscrums, Jerkoff and Eatsup, as for my part opinion indeed. They would be born so, costarred, puck and prig, the maryboy at Donnybrook Fair, the godolphinglad in the Hoy's Court. How frilled one shall be as at taledold of Formio and Cigalette! What folly innocents! Theirs whet pep of puppyhood! Both barmhearts shall become yeastcake by their brackfest. I will to leave a my copperwise blessing between the pair of them, for rosengorge, for greenafang. Blech and tin soldies, weals in a sniffbox. Som's wholed, all's parted. Weeping shouldst not thou be when man falls but that divine scheming ever adoring be. So you be either man or mouse and you be neither fish nor flesh. Take. And take. Vellicate nyche! Be ones as wes for gives for gives now the hour of passings sembles quick with quelled. Adieu, soft adieu, for these nice presents, kerryjevin. Still tosorrow!

Jeminy, what is the view which now takes up a second position of discordance, tell it please? Mark! You notice it in that rereway because the male entail partially eclipses the femecovert. It is so called for its discord the meseedo. Do you ever heard the story about Helius Croesus, that white and gold elephant in our zoopark? You astonish me by it. Is it not that we are commanding from fullback, woman permitting, a profusely fine birdseye view from beauhind this park? Finn his park has been much the admiration of all the stranger ones, grekish and romanos, who arrive to here. The straight road down the centre (see relief map) bisexes the park which is said to be the largest of his kind in the world. On the right prominence confronts you the handsome vinesregent's lodge while, turning to the other supreme piece of cheeks, exactly opposite, you are confounded by the equally handsome chief sacristary's residence. Around is a little amiably tufted and man is cheered when he bewonders through the boskage how the nature in all frisko is enlivened by gentlemen's seats. Here are heavysuppers — 'tis for daddies housings for hundredaires of our super thin thousand. By gum, but you have resin! Of these tallworts are yielded out juices for jointoils and pappasses for paynims. Listeneth! 'Tis a tree story. How olave, that firile, was aplantad in her liveside. How tannoboom held tonobloom. How rood in norlandes. The black and blue marks athwart the weald, which now barely is so stripped, indicate the presence of sylvious beltings. Therewithal shady rides lend themselves out to rustic cavalries. In yonder valley, too, stays mountain sprite. Any pretty dears are to be caught inside but it is a bad pities of the plain. A scarlet pimparnell now mules the mound where anciently first murders were wanted to take root. By feud fionghalian. Talkingtree and sinningstone stay on either hand. Hystorical leavesdroppings may also be garnered up with sir Shamus Swiftpatrick, Archfieldchaplain of Saint Lucan's. How familiar it is to see all these interesting advenements with one snaked's eyes! Is all? Yet not! Hear one's. At the bodom fundus of this royal park, which, with tvigate shyasian gardeenen, is open to the public till night at late, so well the sissastrides so will

564

the pederestians, do not fail to point to yourself a depression called Holl Hollow. It is often quite guttergloomering in our duol and gives wankyrious thoughts to the head but the banders of the pentapolitan poleetsfurcers bassoons into it on windy woodensdays their wellbooming wolvertones. Ulvos! Ulvos!

Whervolk dorst ttou begin to tremble by our moving pictures at this moment when I am to place my hand of our true friend-shapes upon thee knee to mark well what I say? Throu shayest who? In Amsterdam there lived a . . . But how? You are trem-blotting, you retchad, like a verry jerry! Niet? Will you a gui-neeser? Gaij beutel of staub? To feel, you? Yes, how it trembles, the timid! Vortigern, ah Gortigern! Overlord of Mercia! Or doth brainskin flinchgreef? Stemming! What boyazhness! Sole shadow shows. Tis jest jibberweek's joke. It must have stole. O, keve silence, both! Putshameyu! I have heard her voice some-where else's before me in these ears still that now are for mine.

Let op. Slew musies. Thunner in the eire.

You were dreamend, dear. The pawdrag? The fawthrig? Shoe! Hear are no phanthares in the room at all, avikkeen. No bad bold faathern, dear one. Opop opop capallo, muy malinchily malchick! Gothgorod father godown followay tomollow the lucky load to Lublin for make his thoroughbass grossman's big-ness. Take that two piece big slap slap bold honty bottomsside pap pap pappa.

— *Li ne dormis?*
— *S! Malbone dormas.*
— *Kia li krias nikte?*
— *Parolas infanetes. S!*

Sonly all in your imagination, dim. Poor little brittle magic nation, dim of mind! Shoe to me now, dear! Shoom of me! While elvery stream winds seling on for to keep this barrel of bounty rolling and the nightmail afarfrom morning nears.

When you're coaching through Lucalised, on the sulphur spa to visit, it's safer to hit than miss it, stop at his inn! The hammers are telling the cobbles, the pickts are hacking the saxums, it's snugger to burrow abed than ballet on broadway. Tuck in your blank! For it's race pound race the hosties rear all roads to ruin and layers by lifetimes laid down riches from poormen. Cried unions to chip, saltpetre to strew, gallpitch to drink, stonebread to break but it's bully to gulp good blueberry pudding. Doze in your warmth! While the elves in the moonbeams, feeling why, will keep my lilygem gently gleaming.

In the sleepingchambers. The court to go into half morning. The four seneschals with their palfrey to be there now, all balaaming in their sellaboutes and sharping up their penisills. The boufeither Soakersoon at holdup tent sticker. The swabsister Katya to have duntalking and to keep shakenin dowan her droghedars. Those twelve chief barons to stand by duedesmally with their folded arums and put down all excursions and false alarums and after that to go back now to their runameat farums and re-compile their magnum chartarums with the width of the road between them and all harrums. The maidbrides all, in favours gay, to strew sleety cinders on their falling hair and for wouldbe joybells to ring sadly ringless hands. The dame dowager to stay kneeled how she is, as first mutherer with cord in coil. The two princes of the tower royal, daulphin and deevlin, to lie how they are without to see. The dame dowager's duffgerent to present wappon, blade drawn to the full and about wheel without to be seen of them. The infant Isabella from her coign to do obeisance toward the duffgerent, as first futherer with drawn brand. Then the court to come in to full morning. Herein see ye fail not!

—*Vidu, porkego! Ili vi rigardas. Returnu, porkego! Maldeli-kato!*

Gauze off heaven! Vision. Then, O, pluxty suddly, the sight entrancing! Hummels! That crag! Those hullocks! O Sire! So be accident occur is not going to commence! What have you there-fore? Fear you the donkers? Of roovers? I fear lest we have lost ours (non grant it!) respecting these wildy parts. How is hit finis-ter! How shagsome all and beastful! What do you show on? I show because I must see before my misfortune so a stark pointing pole. Lord of ladders, what for lungitube! Can you read the verst legend hereon? I am hather of the missed. Areed! To the dunleary obelisk via the rock vhat myles knox furlongs; to the general's postoffice howsands of patience; to the Wellington memorial half a league wrongwards; to Sara's bridge good hunter and nine to meet her: to the point, one yeoman's yard. He, he, he! At that do you leer, a setting up? With a such unfettered belly? Two cascades? I leer (O my big, O my bog, O my bigbagbone!) because I must see a buntingcap of so a pinky on the point. It is for a true glover's greetings and many burgesses by us, greats and grosses, uses to pink it in this way at tet-at-tet. For long has it been effigy of standard royal when broken on roofstaff which to the gunnings shall cast welcome from Courtmilits' Fortress, umptydum dumptydum. Bemark you these hangovers, those streamer fields, his influx. Do you not have heard that, the queen lying abroad from fury of the gales, (meekname mocktitles her Nan Nan Nanetta) her liege of lateenth dignisties shall come on their bay tomorrow, Michalsmas, mellems the third and fourth of the clock, there to all the king's aussies and all their king's men, knechts tramplers and cavalcaders, led of herald graycloak, Ulaf Goldarskield? Dog! Dog! Her lofts will be loosed for her and their tumblers broodcast. A progress shall be made in walk, ney? I trow it well, and uge by uge. He shall come, sidesmen accostant, by aryan jubilarian and on brigadier-general Nolan or and buccaneer-admiral Browne, with — who can doubt it? — his golden beagles and his white elkox terriers for a hunting on our littlego illcome faxes. In blue and buff of Beaufort the hunt shall make. It is poblesse noblige. Ommes will grin through collars when each riders other's ass. Me Eccls! What cats' killings overall! What popping out of guillotened widows! Quick time! Beware of waiting! Squintina plies favours on us from her rushfrail and Zosimus, the crowder, in his surcoat, sues us with souftwister. Apart we! Here are gantlets. I believe, by Plentifolks Mixymost! Yet if I durst to express the hope how I might be able to be present. All these peeplers entrammed and detrained on bikeygels and troykakyls and those puny farting little solitires! Tollacre, tollacre! Polo north will beseem Sibernian and Plein Pelouta will behowl ne yerking at lawncastrum ne ghimbelling on guelflinks.

Mauser Misma shall cease to stretch her and come abroad for what the blinkins is to be seen. A ruber, a rancher, a fullvide, a veridust and as crerdulous behind as he was before behind a damson of a sloe cooch. Mbv! The annamation of evabusies, the livlianess of her laughings, such as a plurity of bells! Have peacience, pray you! Place to dames! Even the Lady Victoria Landauner will leave to loll and parasol, all giddied into gushgasps with her dickey standing. Britus and Gothius shall no more joustle for that sonneplace but mark one autonement when, with si so silent, Cloudia Aiduolcis, good and dewed up, shall let fall, yes, no, yet, now, a rain. Muchsias grapcias! It is how sweet from her, the wispful, and they are soon seen swopsib so a sautril as a meise. Its ist not the tear on this movent sped. Tix sixponce! Poum! Hool poll the bull? Fool pay the bill. Becups a can full. Peal, pull the bell! Still sayeme of ceremonies, much much more! So pleaseyour! It stands in *Instopressible* how Meynhir Mayour, our boorgomaister, thon staunch Thorsman, (our Nancy's fancy, our own Nanny's Big Billy), his hod hoisted, in best bib and tucker, with Woolington bottes over buckram babbishkis and his clouded cane and necknoose aureal, surrounded of his full cooperation with fixed baronets and meng our pueblos, restrained by chain of hands from pinchgut, hoghill, darklane, gibbetmeade and beaux and laddes and bumbellye, shall receive Dom King at broadstone barrow meet a keys of goodmorrow on to his pompey cushion. Me amble dooty to your grace's majers! Arise, sir Pompkey Dompkey! Ear! Ear! Weakear! An allness eversides! We but miss that horse elder yet cherchant of the wise graveleek in cabbuchin garden. That his be foison, old Caubeenhauben! 'Twill be tropic of all days. By the splendour of Sole! Perfect weatherest prevailing. Thisafter, swift's mightmace deposing, he shall aidress to His Serenemost by a speechreading from his miniated vellum, alfi byrni gamman dealter etcera zezera eacla treacla youghta kaptor lomdom noo, who meaningwhile that illuminatured one, Papyroy of Pepinregn, my Sire, great, big King, (his scaffold is there set up, as to edify, by Rex Ingram, pageantmaster) will be poking out with his canule into the arras of

what brilliant bridgecloths and joking up with his tonguespitz
to the crimosing balkonladies, here's a help undo their modest
stays with a fullbelow may the funnyfeelbelong. Oddsbones,
that may it! Carilloners will ring their gluckspeels. Rng rng!
Rng rng! S. Presbutt-in-the-North, S. Mark Underloop,
S. Lorenz-by-the-Toolechest, S. Nicholas Myre. You shall
hark to anune S. Gardener, S. George-le-Greek, S. Barclay
Moitered, S. Phibb, Iona-in-the-Fields with Paull-the-Aposteln.
And audialterand: S. Jude-at-Gate, Bruno Friars, S. Weslen-
on-the-Row, S. Molyneux Without, S. Mary Stillamaries with
Bride-and-Audeons-behind-Wardborg. How chimant in effect!
Alla tingaling pealabells! So a many of churches one cannot
pray own's prayers. 'Tis holyyear's day! Juin jully we may!
Agithetta and Tranquilla shall demure umclaused but Marl-
borough-the-Less, Greatchrist and Holy Protector shall have
open virgilances. Beata Basilica! But will be not pontifi-
cation? Dock, dock, agame! Primatially. At wateredge. Can-
taberra and Neweryork may supprecate when, by vepers, for
towned and travalled, his goldwhite swaystick aloft ylifted,
umbrilla-parasoul, Monsigneur of Deublan shall impart to all.
Benedictus benedicat! To board! And mealsight! Unjoint him
this bittern, frust me this chicken, display yon crane, thigh her
her pigeon, unlace allay rabbit and pheasant! Sing: Old Finncoole,
he's a mellow old saoul when he swills with his fuddlers free!
Poppop array! For we're all jollygame fellhellows which no-
bottle can deny! Here be trouts culponed for ye and salmons
chined and sturgeons tranched, sanced capons, lobsters barbed.
Call halton eatwords! Mumm me moe mummers! What, no
Ithalians? How, not one Moll Pamelas? Accordingly! Play actors
by us ever have crash to their gate. Mr Messop and Mr Borry will
produce of themselves, as they're two genitalmen of Veruno,
Senior Nowno and Senior Brolano (finaly! finaly!), all for love of
a fair penitent that, a she be broughton, rhoda's a rosy she. Their
two big skins! How they strave to gat her! Such a boyplay! Their
bouchicaulture! What tyronte power! Buy our fays! My name is
novel and on the Granby in hills. Bravose! Thou traitor slave!

Mine name's Apnorval and o'er the Grandbeyond Mountains. Bravossimost! The royal nusick their show shall shut with songslide to nature's solemn silence. Deep Dalchi Dolando! Might gentle harp addurge! It will give piketurns on the tummlipplads and forain dances and crosshurdles and dollmanovers and viceuvious pyrolyphics, a snow of dawnflakes, at darkfall for Grace's Mamnesty and our fancy ladies, all assombred. Some wholetime in hot town tonight! You do not have heard? It stays in book of that which is. I have heard anyone tell it jesterday (master currier with brassard was't) how one should come on morrow here but it is never here that one today. Well but remind to think, you where yestoday Ys Morganas war and that it is always tomorrow in toth's tother's place. Amen.

True! True! Vouchsafe me more soundpicture! It gives furiously to think. Is rich Mr Pornter, a squire, not always in his such strong health? I thank you for the best, he is in taken deal exceedingly herculeneous. One sees how he is lot stoutlier than of formerly. One would say him to hold whole a litteringture of kidlings under his aproham. Has handsome Sir Pournter always been so long married? O yes, Lord Pournterfamilias has been marryingman ever since so long time in Hurtleforth, where he appeers as our oily the active, and, yes indeed, he has his mic son and his two fine mac sons and a superfine mick want they mack metween them. She, she, she! But on what do you again leer? I am not leering, I pink you pardons. I am highly sheshe sherious.

Do you not must want to go somewhere on the present? Yes, O pity! At earliest moment! That prickly heat feeling! Forthink not me spill it's at always so guey. Here we shall do a far walk (O pity) anygo khaibits till the number one of sairey's place. Is, is. I want you to admire her sceneries illustrationing our national first rout, one ought ought one. We shall too downlook on that ford where Sylvanus Sanctus washed but hurdley those tips of his anointeds. Do not show ever retrorsehim, crookodeyled, till that you become quite crimstone in the face! Beware! guardafew! It is Stealer of the Heart! I am anxious in regard you should everthrown your sillarsalt. I will dui sui, tefnute! These brilling waveleaplights! Please say me how sing you them. Seekhem seckhem! They arise from a clear springwell in the near of our park which makes the daft to hear all blend. This place of endearment! How it is clear! And how they cast their spells upon, the fronds that thereup float, the bookstaff branchings! The druggeted stems, the leaves incut on trees! Do you can their tantrist spellings? I can lese, skillmistress aiding. Elm, bay, this way, cull dare, take a message, tawny runes ilex sallow, meet me at the pine. Yes, they shall have brought us to the water trysting, by hedjes of maiden ferm, then here in another place is their chapelofeases, sold for song, of which you have thought my praise too much my price. O ma ma! Yes, sad one of Ziod? Sell me, my soul dear! Ah, my sorrowful, his cloister dreeping of his monkshood, how it is triste to death, all his dark ivytod! Where cold in dearth. Yet see, my blanching kissabelle, in the under close she is allso gay, her kirtles green, her curtsies white, her peony pears, her nistlingsloes! I, pipette, I must also quicklingly to tryst myself softly into this littleeasechapel. I would rather than Ireland! But I pray, make! Do your easiness! O, peace, this is heaven! O, Mr Prince of Pouringtoher, whatever shall I pppease to do? Why do you so lifesighs, my precious, as I hear from you, with limmenings lemantitions, after that swollen one? I am not sighing, I assure, but only I am soso sorry about all in my saarasplace. Listen, listen! I am doing it. Hear more to those voices! Always I am hearing them. Horsehem coughs enough. Annshee lispes privily.

— He is quieter now.

— Legalentitled. Accesstopartnuzz. Notwildebeestsch. Byrightofoaptz. Twainbeonerflsh. Haveandholdpp.

— S! Let us go. Make a noise. Slee . . .

— Qui . . . The gir . . .

— Huesofrichunfoldingmorn. Wakenupriseandprove. Provideforsacrifice.

— Wait! Hist! Let us list!

For our netherworld's bosomfoes are working tooth and nail overtime: in earthveins, toadcavites, chessganglions, saltklesters, underfed: nagging firenibblers knockling aterman up out of his hinterclutch. Tomb be their tools! When the youngdammers will be soon heartpocking on their betters' doornoggers: and the youngfries will be backfrisking diamondcuts over their lyingin underlayers, spick and spat trowelling a gravetrench for their fourinhand forebears. Vote for your club!

— Wait!

— What!

— Her door!

— Ope?

— See!

— What?

— Careful.

— Who?

Live well! Iniivdluaritzas! Tone!

Cant ear! Her dorters ofe? Whofe? Her eskmeno daughters hope? Whope? Ellme, elmme, elskmestoon! Soon!

Let us consider.

The procurator Interrogarius Mealterum presends us this proposer.

Honuphrius is a concupiscent exservicemajor who makes dishonest propositions to all. He is considered to have committed, invoking *droit d'oreiller*, simple infidelities with Felicia, a virgin, and to be practising for unnatural coits with Eugenius and Jeremias, two or three philadelphians. Honophrius, Felicia, Eugenius and Jeremias are consanguineous to the lowest degree. Anita the wife of Honophrius, has been told by her tirewoman, Fortissa, that Honuphrius has blasphemously confessed under voluntary chastisement that he has instructed his slave, Mauritius, to urge Magravius, a commercial, emulous of Honuphrius, to solicit the chastity of Anita. Anita is informed by some illegitimate children of Fortissa with Mauritius (the supposition is Ware's) that Gillia, the schismatical wife of Magravius, is visited clandestinely by Barnabas, the advocate of Honuphrius, an immoral person who has been corrupted by Jeremias. Gillia, (a cooler blend, D'Alton insists) *ex equo* with Poppea, Arancita, Clara,

Marinuzza, Indra and Iodina, has been tenderly debauched (in Halliday's view), by Honuphrius, and Magravius knows from spies that Anita has formerly committed double sacrilege with Michael, *vulgo* Cerularius, a perpetual curate, who wishes to seduce Eugenius. Magravius threatens to have Anita molested by Sulla, an orthodox savage (and leader of a band of twelve mercenaries, the Sullivani), who desires to procure Felicia for Gregorius, Leo, Vitellius and Macdugalius, four excavators, if she will not yield to him and also deceive Honuphrius by rendering conjugal duty when demanded. Anita who claims to have discovered incestuous temptations from Jeremias and Eugenius would yield to the lewdness of Honuphrius to appease the savagery of Sulla and the mercernariness of the twelve Sullivani, and (as Gilbert at first suggested), to save the virginity of Felicia for Magravius when converted by Michael after the death of Gillia, but she fears that, by allowing his marital rights she may cause reprehensible conduct between Eugenius and Jeremias. Michael, who has formerly debauched Anita, dispenses her from yielding to Honuphrius who pretends publicly to possess his conjunct in thirtynine several manners (*turpiter!* affirm *ex cathedris* Gerontes Cambronses) for carnal hygiene whenever he has rendered himself impotent to consummate by subdolence. Anita is disturbed but Michael comminates that he will reserve her case tomorrow for the ordinary Guglielmus even if she should practise a pious fraud during affrication which, from experience, she knows (according to Wadding), to be leading to nullity. Fortissa, however, is encouraged by Gregorius, Leo, Viteilius, and Magdugalius, reunitedly, to warn Anita by describing the strong chastisements of Honuphrius and the depravities (*turpissimas!*) of Canicula, the deceased wife of Mauritius, with Sulla, the simoniac, who is abnegand and repents. Has he hegemony and shall she submit?

Translate a lax, you breed a bradaun. In the goods of Cape and Chattertone, deceased.

This, lay readers and gentilemen, is perhaps the commonest of all cases arising out of umbrella history in connection with the wood industries in our courts of litigation. D'Oyly Owens holds (though Finn Magnusson of himself holds also) that so long as there is a joint deposit account in the two names a mutual obligation is posited. Owens cites Brerfuchs and Warren, a foreign firm, since disseized, registered as Tangos, Limited, for the sale of certain proprietary articles. The action which was at the instance of the trustee of the heathen church emergency fund, suing by its trustee, a resigned civil servant, for the payment of tithes due was heard by Judge Doyle and also by a common jury. No question arose as to the debt for which vouchers spoke volumes. The defence alleged that payment had been made effective. The fund trustee, one Jucundus Fecundus Xero Pecundus Coppercheap, counterclaimed that payment was invalid having been tendered to creditor under cover of a crossed cheque, signed in the ordinary course, in the name of Wieldhelm, Hurls Cross, voucher copy provided, and drawn by the senior partner only by whom the lodgment of the species had been effected but in their joint names. The bank particularised, the national misery (now almost entirely in the hands of the four chief bondholders for value in Tangos), declined to pay the draft, though there were ample reserves to meet the liability, whereupon the trusty Coppercheap negociated it for and on behalf of the fund of the thing to a client of his, a notary, from whom, on consideration, he received in exchange legal relief as between trusthee and bethrust, with thanks. Since then the cheque, a good washable pink, embossed D you D No 11 hundred and thirty 2, good for the figure and face, had been circulating in the country for over thirtynine years among holders of Pango stock, a rival concern, though not one demonetised farthing had ever spun or fluctuated across the counter in the semblance of hard coin or liquid cash. The jury (a sour dozen of stout fellows all of whom were curiously named after doyles) naturally disagreed jointly and severally, and the belligerent judge, disagreeing with the allied jurors' disagreement, went outside his jurisfiction altogether and ordered a garnishee attachment to the neutral firm. No *mandamus* could locate the depleted whilom Breyfawkes as he had entered into an ancient moratorium, dating back to the times of the early barters, and only the junior partner Barren could be found, who entered an appearance and turned up, upon a notice of motion and after service of the motion by interlocutory injunction, among the male jurors to be an absolete turfwoman, originally from the proletarian class, with still a good title to her sexname of Ann Doyle, 2 Coppinger's Cottages, the Doyle's country. Doyle (Ann), add woman in, having regretfully left the juryboxers, protested cheerfully on the stand in a long jurymiad *in re* corset checks, delivered in doylish, that she had often, in supply to brusk demands rising almost to bollion point, discounted Mr Brakeforth's first of all in exchange at nine months from date without issue and, to be strictly literal, unbottled in corrubberation a current account of how she had been made at sight for services rendered the payee-drawee of unwashable blank assignations, sometimes pinkwilliams (laughter) but more often of the *crème-de-citron, vair émail paoncoque* or marshmallow series, which she, as bearer, used to endorse, adhesively, to her various payers-drawers who in most cases were identified by the timber papers as wellknown tetigists of the city and suburban. The witness, at her own request, asked if she might and wrought something between the sheets of music paper which she had accompanied herself with for the occasion and this having been handed up for the bench to look at *in camera*, Coppinger's doll, as she was called, (*annias*, Mack Erse's Dar, the adopted child) then proposed to jerrykin and jureens and every jim, jock and jarry in that little green courtinghousie for her satisfaction and as a whole act of settlement to reamalgamate herself, tomorrow perforce, in pardonership with the permanent suing fond trustee, Monsignore Pepigi, under the new style of Will Breakfast and Sparrem, as, when all his cognisances had been estreated, he seemed to proffer the steadiest interest towards her, but this prepoposal was ruled out on appeal by Judge JeremyDoyler, who, reserving judgment in a matter of courts and reversing the findings of the lower correctional, found, beyond doubt of treuson, fending the dissassents of the pickpackpanel, twelve as upright judaces as ever let down their thoms, and, *occupante extremum*

575

scabie, handed down to the jury of the Liffey that, as a matter of tact, the woman they gave as free was born into contractual incapacity (the Calif of Man *v* the Eaudelusk Company) when, how and where mamy's mancipium act did not apply and therefore held supremely that, as no property in law can exist in a corpse, (Hal Kilbride *v* Una Bellina) Pepigi's pact was pure piffle (loud laughter) and Wharrem would whistle for the rhino. Will you, won't you, pango with Pepigi? Not for Nancy, how dare you do! And whew whewwhew whew.

— He sighed in sleep.

— Let us go back.

— Lest he forewaken.

— Hide ourselves.

While hovering dreamwings, folding around, will hide from fears my wee mee mannikin, keep my big wig long strong manomen, guard my bairn, *mon beau*.

— To bed.

Prospector projector and boomooster giant builder of all causeways woesoever, hopping offpoint and true terminus of straxstraightcuts and corkscrewn perambulaups, zeal whence to goal whither, wonderlust, in sequence to which every muckle must make its mickle, as different as York from Leeds, being the only wise in a muck's world to look on itself from beforehand; mirrorminded curiositease and would-to-the-large which bring hills to molehunter, home through first husband, perils behind swine and horsepower down to hungerford, prick this man and tittup this woman, our forced payrents, Bogy Bobow with his cunnyngnest couchmare, Big Maester Finnykin with Phenicia Parkes, lame of his ear and gape of her leg, most correctingly, we beseach of you, down their laddercase of nightwatch service and bring them at suntime flush with the nethermost gangrung of their stepchildren, guide them through the labyrinth of their samilikes and the alteregoases of their pseudoselves, hedge them bothways from all roamers whose names are ligious, from loss of bearings deliver them; so they keep to their rights and be ware of duty frees, neoliffic smith and magdalenian jinnyjones, mandragon mor and weak wiffeyducky, Morionmale and Thry-dacianmad, basilisk glorious with his weeniequeenie, tigernack and swansgrace, he as hale as his ardouries, she as verve as her veines; this prime white arsenic with bissemate alloyed, martial sin with peccadilly, free to lease hold with first mortgage, dowser dour and dipper douce, stop-that-war and feel-this-feather, norsebloodheartened and landsmoolwashable, great gas with fun-in-the-corner, grand slam with fall-of-the-trick, solomn one and shebby, cod and coney, cash and carry, in all we dreamed the part we dreaded, corsair coupled with his dame, royal biber but constant lymph, boniface and bonnyfeatures, nazil hose and river mouth, bang-the-change and batter-the-bolster, big smoke and lickley roesthy, humanity's fahrman by society leader, voguener and trulley, humpered and elf, Urloughmoor with Miryburrow, leaks and awfully, basal curse yet grace abunda, Regies Producer with screendoll Vedette, peg of his claim and pride of her heart, cliffscaur grisly but rockdove cooing, hodinstag on fryggabet, baron and feme: that he may dishcover her, that she may uncouple him, that one may come and crumple them, that they may soon recoup themselves: now and then, time on time again, as per periodicity; from Neaves to Willses, from Bushmills to Enos; to Goerz from Harleem, to Hearths of Oak from Skittish Widdas; via mala, hyber pass, heckhisway per alptrack: through landsvague and vain, after many mandelays: in their first case, to the next place, till their cozenkerries: the high and the by, both pent and plain: cross cowslips yillow, yellow, yallow, past pumpkins pinguind, purplesome: be they whacked to the wide other tied to hustings, long sizzleroads neath arthruseat, him to the derby, her to toun, til sengentide do coddlam: in the grounds or unterlinnen: rue to lose and ca canny: at shipside, by convent garden: monk and sempstress, in sackcloth silkily: curious dreamers, curious dramas, curious deman, plagiast dayman, playajest dearest, plaguiest dourest: for the strangfort planters are prodesting, and the karkery felons dryflooring it and the leperties' laddos railing the way, blump for slogo slee!

Stop! Did a stir? No, is fast. On to bed! So he is. It's only the

577

wind on the road outside for to wake all shivering shanks from snorring.

But. Oom Godd his villen, who will he be, this mitryman, some king of the yeast, in his chrismy greyed brunzewig, with the snow in his mouth and the caspian asthma, so bulk of build? Relics of pharrer and livite! Dik Gill, Tum Lung or Macfinnan's cool Harryng? He has only his hedcosycasket on and his wollsey shirtplisse with peascod doublet, also his feet wear doubled width socks for he always must to insure warm sleep between a pair of fullyfleeced bankers like a finnoc in a cauwl. Can thus be Misthra Norkmann that keeps our hotel? Begor, Mr O'Sorgmann, you're looking right well! Hecklar's champion ethnicist. How deft as a fuchser schouws daft as a fish! He's the dibble's own doges for doublin existents! But a jolly fine daysent form of one word. He's rounding up on his family.

And who is the bodikin by him, sir? So voulzievalsshie? With ybbs and zabs? Her trixiestrail is tripping her, vop! Luck at the way for the lucre of smoke she's looping the lamp! Why, that's old missness wipethemdry! Well, well, wellsowells! Donauwatter! Ardechious me! With her halfbend as proud as a peahen, allabalmy, and her troutbeck quiverlipe, ninyananya. And her steptojazyma's culunder buzztle. Happy tea area, naughtygay frew! Selling sunlit sopes to washtout winches and rhaincold draughts to the props of his pubs. She tired lipping the swells at Pont Delisle till she jumped the boom at Brounemouth. Now she's borrid his head under Hatesbury's Hatch and loamed his fate to old Love Lane. And she's just the same old haporth of dripping. She's even brennt her hair.

Which route are they going? Why? Angell sitter or Amen Corner, Norwood's Southwalk or Euston Waste? The solvent man in his upper gambeson withnot a breth against him and the wee wiping womanahoussy. They're coming terug their diamond wedding tour, giant's inchly elfkin's ell, vesting their characters vixendevolment, andens aller, athors err, our first day man and your dresser and mine, that Luxuumburgher evec cettehis Alzette, konyglik shire with his queensh countess, Stepney's shipchild with the waif of his bosun, Dunmow's flitcher with duck-on-the-rock, down the scales, the way they went up, under talls and threading tormentors, shunning the startraps and slipping in sliders, risking a runway, ruing reveals, from Elder Arbor to La Puirée, eskipping the clockback, crystal in carbon, sweetheartedly. Hot and cold and electrickery with attendance and lounge and promenade free. In spite of all that science could boot or art could eke. Bolt the grinden. Cave and can em. Single wrecks for the weak, double axe for the mail, and quick queck quack for the radiose. Renove that bible. You will never have post in your pocket unless you have brasse on your plate. Beggards outdoor. Goat to the Endth, thou slowguard! Mind the Monks and their Grasps. Scrape your souls. Commit no miracles. Postpone no bills. Respect the uniform. Hold the raabers for the kunning his plethoron. Let leash the dooves to the cooin her coynth. Hatenot havenots. Share the wealth and spoil the weal. Peg the pound to tom the devil. My time is on draught. Bottle your own. Love my label like myself. Earn before eating. Drudge after drink. Credit tomorrow. Follow my dealing. Fetch my price. Buy not from dives. Sell not to freund. Herenow chuck english and learn to pray plain. Lean on your lunch. No cods before Me. Practise preaching. Think in your stomach. Import through the nose. By faith alone. Season's weather. Gomorrha. Salong. Lots feed from my tidetable. Oil's wells in our lands. Let earwigger's wivable teach you the dance!

Now their laws assist them and ease their fall!

For they met and mated and bedded and buckled and got and gave and reared and raised and brought Thawland within Har danger, and turned them, tarrying to the sea and planted and plundered and pawned our souls and pillaged the pounds of the extramurals and fought and feigned with strained relations and bequeathed us their ills and recrutched cripples gait and undermined lungachers, manplanting seven sisters while wan warm-wooed woman scrubbs, and turned out coats and removed their origins and never learned the first day's lesson and tried to mingle and managed to save and feathered foes' nests and fouled their own and wayleft the arenotts and ponted vodavalls for the zollgebordened and escaped from liquidation by the heirs of their death and were responsible for congested districts and rolled olled logs into Peter's sawyery and werfed new woodcuts on Paoli's wharf and ewesed Rachel's lea and rammed Dominic's gap and looked haggards after lazatables and rode fourscore odd-winters and struck rock oil and forced a policeman and collaughsed at their phizes in Toobiassed and Zachary and left off leaving off and kept on keeping on and roused up drink and poured balm down and were cuffed by their customers and bit the dust at the foot of the poll when in her deergarth he gave up his goat after the battle of Multaferry. Pharoah with fairy, two lie, let them! Yet they wend it back, qual his leif, himmertality, bullseaboob and rivishy divil, light in hand, helm on high, to peekaboo durk the thicket of slumbwhere, till their hour with their scene be struck for ever and the book of the dates he close, he clasp and she and she seegn her tour d'adieu, Pervinca calling, Soloscar hears. (O Sheem! O Shaam!), and gentle Isad Ysut gag, flispering in the nightleaves flattery, dinsiduously, to Finnegan, to sin again and to make grim grandma grunt and grin again while the first grey streaks steal silvering by for to mock their quarrels in dollymount tumbling.

They near the base of the chill stair, that large incorporate licensed vintner, such as he is, from former times, nine hosts in himself, in his hydrocomic establishment and his ambling limfy peepingpartner, the slave of the ring that worries the hand that sways the lamp that shadows the walk that bends to his bane the busynext man that came on the cop with the fenian's bark that pickled his widow that primed the pope that passed it round on the volunteers' plate till it croppied the ears of Purses Relle that kneed O'Connell up out of his doss that shouldered Burke that butted O'Hara that woke the busker that grattaned his crowd that bucked the jiggers to rhyme the rann that flooded the routes in Eryan's isles from Malin to Clear and Carnsore Point to Slynagollow and cleaned the pockets and ransomed the ribs of all the listeners, leud and lay, that bought the ballad that Hosty made.

Anyhow (the matter is a troublous and a peniloose) have they not called him at many's their mock indignation meeting, vehmen's vengeance vective volleying, inwader and uitlander, the notables, crashing libels in their sullivan's mounted beards about him, their right renownsable patriarch? Heinz cans everywhere and the swanee her ainsell and Eyrewaker's family sock that they smuggled to life betune them, roaring (Big Reilly was the worst): free boose for the man from the nark, sure, he never was worth a cornerwall fark, and his banishee's bedpan she's a quareold bite of a tark: as they wendelled their zingaway wivewards from his find me cool's moist opulent vinery, highjacking through the nagginneck pass, as they hauled home with their hogsheads, axpoxtelating, and claiming cowled consollation, sursumcordial, from the bluefunkfires of the dipper and the martian's frost?

Use they not, our noesmall termtraders, to abhors offrom him, the yet unregendered thunderslog, whose sbrogue cunneth none lordmade undersiding, how betwixt wifely rule and *mens conscia recti*, then hemale man all unbracing to omniwomen, but now shedropping his hitches like any maidavale oppersite orseriders in an idinhole? Ah, dearo! Dearo, dear! And her illian! And his willyum! When they were all there now, matinmarked for lookin on. At the carryfour with awlus plawshus, their happyass cloudious! And then and too the trivials! And their bivouac! And his monomyth! Ah ho! Say no more about it! I'm sorry! I saw. I'm sorry! I'm sorry to say I saw!

Gives there not too amongst us after all events (or so grunts a leading hebdromadary) some togethergush of stillandbutallyouknow that, insofarforth as, all up and down the whole concreation say, efficient first gets there finally every time, as a complex matter of pure form, for those excess and that pasphault hardhearingness from their eldfar, in grippes and rumblions, through fresh taint and old treason, another like that alter but not quite such anander and stillandbut one not all the selfsame and butstillone just the maim and encore emmerhim may always, with a little difference, till the latest up to date so early in the morning, have evertheless been allmade amenable?

Yet he begottom.

Let us wherefore, tearing ages, presently preposterose a snatchvote of thanksalot to the huskiest coaxing experimenter that ever gave his best hand into chancerisk, wishing him with his famblings no end of slow poison and a mighty broad venue for themselves between the devil's punchbowl and the deep angleseaboard, that they may gratefully turn a deaf ear clooshed upon the desperanto of willynully, their shareholders from Taaffe to Auliffe, that will curse them below par and mar with their descendants, shame, humbug and profit, to greenmould upon mildew over jaundice as long as ever there's wagtail surtaxed to a testcase on enver a man.

We have to had them whether we'll like it or not. They'll have to have us now then we're here on theirspot. Scant hope theirs or ours to escape life's high carnage of semperidentity by subsisting peasemeal upon variables. Bloody certainly have we got to see to it ere smellful demise surprends us on this concrete that down the gullies of the eras we may catch ourselves looking forward to what will in no time be staring you larrikins on the postface in that multimirror megaron of returningties, whirled without end to end. So there was a raughty . . . who in Dyfflinsborg did . . . With his soddering iron, spadeaway, hammerlegs and . . . Where there was a fair young . . . Who was playing her game of . . . And said she you rockaby . . . Will you peddle in my bog . . . And he sod her in Iarland, paved her way from Maizenhead to Youghal. And that's how Humpfrey, champion emir, holds his own. Shysweet, she rests.

Or show pon him now, will you! Derg rudd face should take patrick's purge. Hokoway, in his hiphigh bearserk! Third position of concord! Excellent view from front. Sidome. Female imperfectly masking male. Redspot his browbrand. Woman's the prey! Thon's the dullakeykongsbyogblagroggerswagginline (private judgers, change here for Lootherstown! Onlyromans, keep your seats!) that drew all ladies please to our great mettrollops. Leary, leary, twentytun nearly, he's plotting kings down for his villa's extension! Gaze at him now in momentum! As his

582

bridges are blown to babbyrags, by the lee of his hulk upright on her orbits, and the heave of his juniper arx in action, he's naval I see. Poor little tartanelle, her dinties are chattering, the strait's she's in, the bulloge she bears! Her smirk is smeeching behind for her hills. By the queer quick twist of her mobcap and the lift of her shift at random and the rate of her gate of going the pace, two thinks at a time, her country I'm proud of. The field is down, the race is their own. The galleonman jovial on his bucky brown nightmare. Bigrob dignagging his lylyputtana. One to one bore one! The datter, io, io, sleeps in peace, in peace. And the twillingsons, ganymede, garrymore, turn in trot and trot. But old pairamere goes it a gallop, a gallop. Bossford and phospherine. One to one on!

O, O, her fairy setalite! Casting such shadows to Persia's blind! The man in the street can see the coming event. Photo-flashing it far too wide. It will be known through all Urania soon. Like jealousjoy titaning fear; like rumour rhean round the planets; like china's dragon snapping japets; like rhodagrey up the east. Satyrdaysboost besets Phoebe's nearest. Here's the flood and the flaxen flood that's to come over helpless Irryland. Is there no-one to malahide Liv and her bettyship? Or who'll buy her rosebuds, jettyblack rosebuds, ninsloes of nivia, nonpaps of nan? From the fall of the fig to doom's last post every ephemeral anniversary while the park's police peels peering by for to weight down morrals from county bubblin. That trainer's trundling! Quick, pay up!

Kickakick. She had to kick a laugh. At her old stick-in-the-block. The way he was slogging his paunch about, elbiduubled, meet oft mate on, like hale King Willow, the robberer. Cain-maker's mace and waxened capapee. But the tarrant's brand on his hottoweyt brow. At half past quick in the morning. And her lamp was all askew and a trumbly wick-in-her, ringeysingey. She had to spofforth, she had to kicker, too thick of the wick of her pixy's loomph, wide lickering jessup the smooky shiminey. And her duffed coverpoint of a wickedy batter, whenever she druv behind her stumps for a tyddlesly wink through his tunnil-clefft bagslops after the rising bounder's yorkers, as he studd and stoddard and trutted and trumpered, to see had lordherry's blackham's red bobby abbels, it tickled her innings to consort pitch at kicksolock in the morm. Tipatonguing him on in her pigeony linguish, with a flick at the bails for lubrication, to scorch her faster, faster. Ye hek, ye hok, ye hucky hiremonger! Magrath he's my pegger, he is, for bricking up all my old kent road. He'll win your toss, flog your old tom's bowling and I darr ye, barrackybuller, to break his duck! He's posh. I lob him. We're parring all Oogster till the empsyseas run googlie. Declare to ashes and teste his metch! Three for two will do for me and he for thee and she for you. Goeasyosey, for the grace of the fields, or hooley pooley, cuppy, we'll both be bye and by caught in the slips for fear he'd tyre and burst his dunlops and waken her bornybarnies making his boobybabies. The game old merrimynn, square to leg, with his lolleywide towelhat and his hobbsy socks and his wisden's bosse and his norsery pinafore and his gentleman's grip and his playaboy's plunge and his flannelly feelyfooling, treading her hump and hambledown like a maiden wellheld, ovalled over, with her crease where the pads of her punishments ought to be by womanish rights when, keek, the hen in the doran's shantyqueer began in a kikkery key to laugh it off, yeigh, yeigh, neigh, neigh, the way she was wuck to doodledoo by her gallows bird (how's that? Noball, he carries his bat!) nine hundred and dirty too not out, at all times long past conquering cock of the morgans.

How blame us?

Cocorico!

Armigerend everfasting horde. Rico! So the bill to the bowe. As the belle to the beau. We herewith pleased returned auditors' thanks for those and their favours since safely enjoined. Cocoree! Tellaman tillamie. Tubbernacul in tipherairy, sons, travellers in company and their carriageable tochters, tanks tight anne thynne for her contractations tugowards his personeel. Echo, choree chorecho! O I you O you me! Well, we all unite thoughtfully in rendering gratias, well, between loves repassed, begging your honour's pardon for, well, exclusive pigtorial rights of herehear fond tiplady his weekreations, appearing in next eon's issue of the Neptune's Centinel and Tritonville Lightowler with well the widest circulation round the whole universe. Echolo choree choroh choree chorico! How me O my youhou my I youtou to I O? Thanks furthermore to modest Miss Glimglow and neat Master Mettresson who so kindly profiteered their serwishes as demysell of honour and, well, as strainbearer respectively. And a cordiallest brief nod of chinchin dankyshin to, well, patient ringasend as prevenient (by your leave), to all such occasions, detachably replaceable (thanks too! twos intactl). As well as his auricular of Malthus, the promethean paratonnerwetter which first (Pray go! pray go!) taught love's lightning the way (pity shown) to, well, conduct itself (mercy, good shot! only please don't mention it!). Come all ye goatfathers and groanmothers, come all ye markmakers and piledrivers, come all ye laboursaving devisers and chargeleyden dividends, firefinders, waterworkers, deeply condeal with him! All that is still life with death inyeborn, all verbumsaps yet bound to be, to do and to suffer, every creature, everywhere, if you please, kindly feel for her! While the dapplegray dawn drags nearing nigh for to wake all droners that drowse in Dublin.

Humperfeldt and Anunska, wedded now evermore in annastomoses by a ground plan of the placehunter, whiskered beau and donahbella. Totumvir and esquimeena, who so shall separate fetters to new desire, repeals an act of union to unite in bonds of schismacy. O yes! O yes! Withdraw your member! Closure. This chamber stands abjourned. Such precedent is largely a cause to lack of collective continencies among Donnelly's orchard as lifelong the shadyside to Fairbrother's field. Humbo, lock your kekkle up! Anny, blow your wickle out! Tuck away the tablesheet! You never wet the tea! And you may go rightoway back to your Aunty Dilluvia, Humprey, after that!

Retire to rest without first misturbing your nighboor, mankind of baffling descriptions. Others are as tired of themselves as you are. Let each one learn to bore himself. It is strictly requested that no cobsmoking, spitting, pubchat, wrastle rounds, coarse courting, smut, etc, will take place amongst those hours so devoted to repose. Look before behind before you strip you. Disrobe clothed in the strictest secrecy which privacy can afford. Water *non* to be discharged *coram* grate or *ex* window. Never divorce in the bedding the glove that will give you away. Maid Maud ninnies nay but blabs to Omama (for your life, would you!) she to her bosom friend who does all chores (and what do you think my Madeleine saw?): this ignorant mostly sweeps it out along with all the rather old corporators (have you heard of one humbledown jungleman how he bet byrn-and-bushe playing peg and pom?): the maudlin river then gets its dues (adding a din a ding or do): thence those laundresses (O, muddle me more about the maggies! I mean bawnee Madge Ellis and brownie Mag Dillon). Attention at all! Every ditcher's dastard in Dupling will let us know about it if you have paid the mulctman by whether your rent is open to be foreclosed or aback in your arrears. This is seriously meant. Here is a homelet not a hothel.

That's right, old oldun!

All in fact is soon as all of old right as anywas ever in very old place. Were he, hwen scalded of that couverfowl, to beat the bounds by here at such a point of time as this is for at sammel up all wood's haypence and riviers argent (half back from three gangs multaplussed on a twentylot add allto a fiver with the deuce or roamer's numbers ell a fee and do little ones) with the caboosh on him opheld for thrushes' mistiles yet singing oud his parasangs in cornish token: mean fawthery eastend appullcelery, old laddy he high hole: pollysigh patrolman Seekersenn, towney's tanquam, crumlin quiet down from his hoonger, he would mac siccar of inket goodsforetombed ereshiningem of light turkling eitheranny of thuncle's windopes. More, unless we were neverso wrongtaken, if he brought his boots to pause in peace, the one beside the other one, right on the road, he would seize no sound from cache or cave beyond the flow of wand was gypsing water, telling him now, telling him all, all about ham and livery, stay and toast ham in livery, and buttermore with murmurladen, to waker oats for him on livery. Faurore! Fearhoure! At last it past! Loab at cod then herrin or wind thin mong them treen.

Hiss! Which we had only our hazelight to see with, cert, in our point of view, me and my auxy, Jimmy d'Arcy, hadn't we, Jimmy? — Who to seen with? Kiss! No kidd, captn, which he stood us, three jolly postboys, first a couple of Mountjoys and nutty woodbines with his cadbully's choculars, pepped from our Theoatre Regal's drolleries puntomine, in the snug at the Cambridge Arms of Teddy Ales while we was laying, crown jewels to a peanut, was he stepmarm, old noseheavy, or a wouldower, which he said, lads, a taking low his Whitby hat, lopping off the froth and whishing, with all respectfulness to the old country, tomorow comrades, we, his long life's strength and cuirscrween loan to our allhallowed king, the pitchur that he's turned to weld the wall, (Lawd lengthen him!) his standpoint was, to belt and blucher him afore the hole pleading churchal and submarine bar yonder but he made no class at all in port and cemented palships between our trucers, being a refugee, didn't he, Jimmy? — Who true to me? Sish! Honeysuckler, that's what my young lady here, Fred Watkins, bugler Fred, all the ways from Melmoth in Natal, she calls him, dip the colours, pet, when he commit his certain questions vivaviz the secret empire of the snake which it was on a point of our sutton down, how was it, Jimmy? — Who has sinnerettes to declare? Phiss! Touching our Phoenix Rangers' nuisance at the meeting of the waitresses, the daintylines, Elsies from Chelsies, the two legglegels in blooms, and those pest of parkies, twitch, thistle and charlock, were they for giving up their fogging trespasses by order which we foregathered he must be raw in cane sugar, the party, no, Jimmy MacCawthelock? Who trespass against me? Briss! That's him wiv his wig on, achewing of his maple gum, that's our grainpopaw, Mister Beardall, an accompliced burgomaster, a great one among the very greatest, which he told us privates out of his own scented mouf he used to was, my lads, afore this wineact come, what say, our Jimmy the chapelgoer? — Who fears all masters! Hi, Jocko Nowlong, my own sweet boosy love, which he puts his feeler to me behind the beggar's bush, does Freda, don't you be an emugee! Carry-one, he says, though we marooned through this woylde. We must spy a half a hind on honeysuckler now his old face's hardalone wiv his defences down during his wappin stillstand, says my Fred, and Jamessime here which, pip it, she simply must, she says, our pet, she'll do a retroussy from her point of view (Way you fly! Like a frush!) to keep her flouncies off the grass while paying the wetmenots a musichall visit and pair her fiefighs fore him with just one curl after the cad came back which we fought he wars a gunner and his corkiness lay up two bottles of joy with a shandy had by Fred and a *fino oloroso* which he was warming to, my right, Jimmy, my old brown freer? — Whose dolour, O so mine!

Following idly up to seepoint, neath kingmount shadow the ilk for eke of us, whose nathem's banned, whose hofd a-hooded, welkim warsail, how di' you dew? Hollymerry, ivysad, whicher and whoer, Mr Black Atkins and you tanapanny troopertwos, were you there? Was truce of snow, moonmounded snow? Or did wolken hang o'er earth in umber hue his fulmenbomb? Number two coming! Full inside! Was glimpsed the mean amount of cloud? Or did pitter rain fall in a sprinkling? If the waters could speak as they flow! Timgle Tom, pall the bell! Izzy's busy down the dell! Mizpah low, youyou, number one, in deep humidity! Listen, misled peerless, please! You are of course. You miss him so, to listleto! Of course, my pledge between us, there's no-one Noel like him here to hear. Esch so eschess, douls a doulse! Since Allan Rogue loved Arrah Pogue it's all Killdoughall fair. Triss! Only trees such as these such were those, waving there, the barketree, the o'briertree, the rowantree, the o'corneltree, the behanshrub near windy arbour, the magill o'dendron more. Trem! All the trees in the wood they trembold, humbild, when they heard the stop-press from domday's erewold.

Tiss! Two pretty mistletots, ribboned to a tree, up rose libe-rator and, fancy, they were free! Four witty missywives, wink-

588

ing under hoods, made lasses like lads love maypoleriding and dotted our green with tricksome couples, fiftyfifty, their children's hundred. So childish pence took care of parents' pounds and many made money the way in the world where rushroads to riches crossed slums of lice and, the cause of it all, he forged himself ahead like a blazing urbanorb, brewing treble to drown grief, giving and taking mayom and tuam, playing milliards with his three golden balls, making party capital out of landed self-interest, light on a slavey but weighty on the bourse, our hugest commercial emporialist, with his sons booing home from afar and his daughters bridling up at his side. Finner!

How did he bank it up, swank it up, the whaler in the punt, a guinea by a groat, his index on the balance and such wealth into the bargain, with the boguey which he snatched in the baggage coach ahead? Going forth on the prowl, master jackill, under night and creeping back, dog to hide, over morning. Humbly to fall and cheaply to rise, exposition of failures. Through Duffy's blunders and MacKenna's insurance for upper ten and lower five the band played on. As one generation tells another. Ofter the fall. First for a change of a seven days license he wandered out of his farmer's health and so lost his early parishlife. Then ('twas in fenland) occidentally of a sudden, six junelooking flamefaces straggled wild out of their turns through his parsonfired wicket, showing all shapes of striplings in sleepless tights. Promptly whomafter in undated times, very properly a dozen generations anterior to themselves, a main chanced to burst and misflooded his fortunes, wrothing foulplay over his fives' court and his fine poultryyard wherein were spared a just two of a feather in wading room only. Next, upon due reflotation, up started four hurrigan gales to smithereen his plateglass housewalls and the slate for accounts his keeper was cooking. Then came three boy buglehorners who counterbezzled and cross-bugled him. Later on in the same evening two hussites absconded through a breach in his bylaws and left him, the infidels, to pay himself off in kind remembrances. Till, ultimatehim, fell the crowning barleystraw, when an explosium of his distilleries deafadumped all his dry goods to his most favoured sinflute and dropped him, what remains of a heptark, leareyed and letterish, weeping worrybound on his bankrump.

Pepep. Pay bearer, sure and sorry, at foot of ohoho honest policist. On never again, by Phoenis, swore on him Lloyd's, not for beaten wheat, not after Sir Joe Meade's father, thanks! They know him, the covenanter, by rote at least, for a chameleon at last, in his true falseheaven colours from ultraviolent to subred tissues. That's his last tryon to march through the grand tryomphal arch. His reignbolt's shot. Never again! How you do that like, Mista Chimepiece? You got nice yum plemyums. Praypaid my promishles!

Agreed, Wu Welsher, he was chogfulled to beacsate on earn as in hiving, of foxold conningnesses but who, hey honey, for all values of his latters, integer integerrimost, was the formast of the firm? At folkmood hailed, at part farwailed, accwmwladed concloud, Nuah-Nuah, Nebob of Nephilim! After all what followed for apprentice sake? Since the now nighs nearing as the yetst hies hin. Jeebies, ugh, kek, ptah, that was an ill man! Jawboose, puddigood, this is for true a sweetish mand! But Jumbluffer, bagdad, sir, yond would be for a once over our all honoured christmastyde easteredman. Fourth position of solution. How johnny! Finest view from horizon. Tableau final. Two me see. Male and female unmask we hem. Begum by gunne! Who now broothes oldbrawn. Dawn! The nape of his nameshielder's scalp. Halp! After having drummed all he dun. Hun! Worked out to an inch of his core. More! Ring down. While the queenbee he staggerhorned blesses her bliss for to feel her funnyman's functions Tag. Rumbling.

Tiers, tiers and tiers. Rounds.

IV

Sandhyas! Sandhyas! Sandhyas!

Calling all downs. Calling all downs to dayne. Array! Surrection! Eireweeker to the wohld bludyn world. O rally, O rally, O rally! Phlenxty, O rally! To what lifelike thyne of the bird can be. Seek you somany matters. Haze sea east to Osseania. Here! Here! Tass, Patt, Staff, Woff, Havv, Bluvv and Rutter. The smog is lofting. And already the olduman's olduman has godden up on othertimes to litanate the bonnamours. Sonne feine, somme feehn avaunt! Guld modning, have yous viewsed Piers' aube? Thane yaars agon we have used yoors up since when we have fused now orther. Calling all daynes. Calling all daynes to dawn. The old breeding bradsted culminwillth of natures to Foyn Mac-Hooligan. The leader, the leader! Securest jubilends albas Temoram. Clogan slogan. Quake up, dim dusky, wook doom for husky! And let Billey Feghin be baallad out of his humuluation. Confindention to churchen. We have highest gratifications in announcing to pewtewr publikumst of pratician pratyusers, genghis is ghoon for you.

A hand from the cloud emerges, holding a chart expanded.

The eversower of the seeds of light to the cowld owld sowls that are in the domnatory of Defmut after the night of the carrying of the word of Nuahs and the night of making Mehs to cuddle up in a coddlepot, Pu Nuseht, lord of risings in the yonderworld of Ntamplin, tohp triumphant, speaketh.

593

Vah! Suvarn Sur! Scatter brand to the reneweller of the sky, thou who agnitest! Dah! Arcthuris comeing! Be! Verb umprincipiant through the trancitive spaces! Kilt by kelt shell kithagain with kinagain. We elect for thee, Tirtangel. Svadesia salve! We Durbalanars, theeadjure. A way, the Margan, from our astamite, through dimdom done till light kindling light has led we hopas but hunt me the journeyon, iteritinerant, the kal his course, amid the semitary of Somnionia. Even unto Heliotropolis, the castellated, the enchanting. Now if soomone felched a twoel and soomonelses warmet watter we could, while you was saying Morkret Miry or Smud, Brunt and Rubbinsen, make sunlike sylp om this warful dune's battam. Yet clarify begins at. Whither the spot for? Whence the hour by? See but! Lever hulme! Take in. Respassers should be pursaccoutred. Qui stabat Meins quantum qui stabat Peins. As of yours. We annew. Our shades of minglings mengle them and help help horizons. A flasch and, rasch, it shall come to pasch, as hearth by hearth leaps live. For the tanderest stock with the rosinost top Ahlen Hill's, clubpubber, in general stores and. Atriathroughwards, Lugh the Brathwacker will be the listened after and he larruping sparks out of his teiney ones. The spearspid of dawnfire totouches ain the tablestoane ath the centre of the great circle of the macroliths of Helusbelus in the boshiman brush on this our peneplain by Fangaluvu Bight whence the horned cairns erge, stanserstanded, to floran frohn, idols of isthmians. Overwhere. Gaunt grey ghostly gossips growing grubber in the glow. Past now pulls. Cur one beast, even Dane the Great, may treadspath with sniffer he snout impursuant to byelegs. Edar's chuckal humuristic. But why pit the cur afore the noxe? Let shrill their duan Gallus, han, and she, hou the Sassqueehenna, makes ducksruns at crooked. Once for the chantermale, twoce for the pother and once twoce threece for the waither. So an inedible yellowmeat turns out the invasable blackth. Kwhat serves to rob with Alliman, saelior, a turnkeyed trot to Seapoint, pierrotettes, means Noel's Bar and Julepunsch, by Joge, if you've tippertaps in your head or starting kursses, tailour, you're silenced at Henge Ceolleges, Exmooth, Ostbys for ost, boys, each and one? Death banes and the quick quoke. But life wends and the dombs spake! Whake? Hill of Hafid, knock and knock, nachasach, gives relief to the langscape as he strauches his lamusong untoupon gazelle channel and the bride of the Bryne, shin high shake, is dotter than evar for a damse wed her farther. Lambel on the up! We may plesently heal Geoglyphy's twentynine ways to say good-bett an wassing seoosoon liv. With the forty wonks winking please me your much as to. With her tup. It's a long long ray to Newirgland's premier. For korps, for streamfish, for confects, for bullyoungs, for smearsassage, for patates, for steaked pig, for men, for limericks, for waterfowls, for wagsfools, for louts, for cold airs, for late trams, for curries, for curlews, for leekses, for orphalines, for tunnygulls, for clear goldways, for lungfortes, for moonyhaunts, for fairmoneys, for coffins, for tantrums, for armaurs, for waglugs, for rogues comings, for sly goings, for larksmathes, for homdsmeethes, for quailsmeathes, kilalooly. Tep! Come lead, crom lech! Top. Wisely for us Old Bruton has withdrawn his theory. You are alpsulumply wroght! Amsu-lummmm. But this is perporteroguing youpoorapps? Naman-tanai. Sure it's not revieng your? Amslu! Good all so. We seem to understand apad vellumtomes muniment, Arans Duhkha, among hoseshoes, cheriotiers and etceterogenious bargainbout-barrows, ofver and umnder, since, evenif or although, in double preposition as in triple conjunction, how the mudden research in the topaia that was Mankaylands has gone to prove from the picalava present in the maramara melma that while a successive generation has been in the deep deep deeps of Deepereras. Buried hearts. Rest here.

Conk a dook he'll doo. Svap.

So let him slap, the sap! Till they take down his shatter from his shap. He canease. Fill stap.

Thus faraclacks the friarbird. Listening, Syd!

The child, a natural child, thenown by the mnames of, (aya! aya!), wouldbewas kidnapped at an age of recent probably, possibly remoter; or he conjured himself from seight by slide at hand; for which thetheatron is a lemoronage; at milch-goat fairmesse; in full dogdhis; sod on a fall; pat; the hundering blundering dunderfunder of plundersundered manhood; behold, he returns; renascenent; fincarnate; still foretold around the hearth-side; at matin a fact; hailed chimers' ersekind; foe purmanant, fum in his mow; awike in wave risurging into chrest; *victis poenis hesternis*; fostfath of solas; fram choicest of wiles with warmen and sogns til Banba, burial aranging; under articles thirtynine of the reconstitution; by the lord's order of the canon consecrand-able; earthlost that we thought him; pesternost, the noneknown worrier; from Tumbarumba mountain; in persence of whole landslots; forebe all the rassias; sire of leery subs of dub; the Dig-gins, Woodenhenge, as to hang out at; with spawnish oel full his angalach; the sousenugh; gnomeosulphidosalamermauderman; the big brucer, fert in fort; Gunnar, of The Gunnings, Gund; one of the two or three forefivest fellows a bloke could in holiday crowd encounter; benedicted be the barrel; kilderkins, lids off; a roache, an oxmaster, a sort of heaps, a pamphilius, a vintivat niviceny, a hygiennic contrivance socalled from the editor; the thick of your thigh; you knox; quite; talking to the vicar's joy and ruth; the gren, woid and glue been broking by the maybole gards; he; when no crane in Elga is heard; upout to speak this lay; without links, without impediments, with gygantogyres, with freeflawforms;parasama to himself; atman as evars; whom otherwise becauses; no puler as of old but as of young a palatin; whitelock not lacked nor temperasoleon; though he appears a funny colour;stoatters some; but a quite a big bug after the dahlias; place inspectorum sarchent; also the hullow chyst ex-cavement; astronomically fabulafigured; as Jambudvispa Vipra foresaw of him; the last half versicle repurchasing his pawned word; sorensplit and paddypatched; and pfor to pfinish our pfun of a pfan coalding the keddle mickwhite; sure, straight, slim, sturdy, serene, synthetical, swift.

By the antar of Yasas! Ruse made him worthily achieve in-herited wish. The drops upon that mantle rained never around Fingal. Goute! Loughlin's Salts, Will, make a newman if any-

worn. Soe? La! Lamfadar's arm it has cocoincidences. You mean
to see we have been hadding a sound night's sleep? You may so.
It is just, it is just about to, it is just about to rolywholyover.
Svapnasvap. Of all the stranger things that ever not even in the
hundrund and badst pageans of unthowsent and wonst nice or
in eddas and oddes bokes of tomb, dyke and hollow to be have
happened! The untireties of livesliving being the one substrance
of a streamsbecoming. Totalled in toldteld and teldtold in tittle-
tell tattle. Why? Because, graced be Gad and all giddy gadgets,
in whose words were the beginnings, there are two signs to turn
to, the yest and the ist, the wright side and the wronged side,
feeling aslip and wauking up, so an, so farth. Why? On the sourd-
site we have the Moskiosk Djinpalast with its twin adjacencies,
the bathouse and the bazaar, allahallahallah, and on the sponthe-
site it is the alcovan and the rosegarden, boony noughty, all pura-
puthry. Why? One's apurr apuss a story about brid and break-
fedes and parricombating and coushcouch but others is of tholes
and oubworn buyings, dolings and chafferings in heat, contest
and enmity. Why? Every talk has his stay, vidnis Shavarsanjivana,
and all-a-dreams perhapsing under lucksloop at last are through.
Why? It is a sot of a swigswag, systomy dystomy, which evera-
body you ever anywhere at all doze. Why? Such me.

And howpsadrowsay.

Lok! A shaft of shivery in the act, anilancinant. Cold's sleuth!
Vayuns! Where did thots come from? It is infinitesimally fevers,
resty fever, risy fever, a coranto of aria, sleeper awakening, in
the smalls of one's back presentiment, gip, and again, geip, a
flash from a future of maybe mahamayability through the windr
of a wondr in a wildr is a weltr as a wirbl of a warbl is a world.

Tom.

It is perfect degrees excelsius. A jaladaew still stilleth. Cloud
lay but mackrel are. Anemone activescent, the torporature is returning to mornal. Humid nature is feeling itself freely at ease
with the all fresco. The vervain is to herald as the grass adminis-
ters. They say, they say in effect, they really say. You have eaden
fruit. Say whuit. You have snakked mid a fish. Telle whish.

Every those personal place objects if nonthings where soevers and they just done been doing being in a dromo of todos withouten a bound to be your trowers. Forswundled. You hald him by the tap of the tang. Not a salutary sellable sound is since. Insteed for asteer, adrift with adraft. Nuctumbulumbumus wanderwards the Nil. Victorias neanzas. Alberths neantas. It was a long, very long, a dark, very dark, an allburt unend, scarce endurable, and we could add mostly quite various and somenwhat stumbletumbling night. Endee he sendee. Diu! The has goning at gone, the is coming to come. Greets to ghastern, hie to morgning. Dormidy, destady. Doom is the faste. Well down, good other! Now day, slow day, from delicate to divine, divases. Padma, brighter and sweetster, this flower that bells, it is our hour or risings. Tickle, tickle. Lotus spray. Till herenext. Adya.

Take thanks, thankstum, thamas. In that earopean end meets Ind.

There is something supernoctural about whatever you called him it. Panpan and vinvin are not alonety vanvan and pinpin in your Tamal without tares but simplysoley they are they. Thisutter followis that odder fellow. Himkim kimkim. Old yeasterloaves may be a stale as a stub and the pitcher go to aftoms on the wall. Mildew, murk, leak and yarn now want the bad that they lied on. And your last words todate in camparative accoustomology are going to tell stretch of a fancy through strength towards joyance, adyatants, where he gets up. Allay for allay, a threat for a throat.

Tim!

To them in Ysat Loka. Hearing. The urb it orbs. Then's now with now's then in tense continuant. Heard. Who having has he shall have had. Hear! Upon the thuds trokes truck, chim, it will be exactlyso fewer hours by so many minutes of the ope of the diurn of the sennight of the maaned of the yere of the age of the madamanvantora of Grossguy and Littleylady, our hugibus hugibum and our weewee mother, actaman housetruewith, and their childer and their napirs and their napirs' childers napirs and their chattels and their servance and their cognance and their ilks and their orts and their everythings that is be will was theirs.

Much obliged. Time-o'-Thay! But wherth, O clerk?

Whithr a clonk? Vartman! See you not soo the pfath they pfunded, oura vatars that arred in Himmal, harruad bathar namas, the gow, the stiar, the tigara, the liofant, when even thurst was athar vetals, mid trefoils slipped the sable rampant, hoof, hoof, hoof, hoof, padapodopudupedding on fattafottafutt. Ere we are! Signifying, if tungs may tolkan, that, primeval conditions having gradually receded but nevertheless the emplacement of solid and fluid having to a great extent persisted through intermittences of sullemn fulminance, sollemn nuptialism, sallemn sepulture and providential divining, making possible and even inevitable, after his a time has a tense haves and havenots hesitency, at the place and period under consideration a socially organic entity of a millenary military maritory monetary morphological circumformation in a more or less settled state of equonomic ecolube equalobe equilab equilibbrium. Gam on, Gearge! Nomomorphemy for me! Lessnatbe angardsmanlake! You jast gat a tache of army on the stumuk. To the Angar at Anker. Aecquotincts. Seeworthy. Lots thankyouful, polite pointsins! There's a tavarn in the tarn.

Tip. Take Tamotimo's topical. Tip. Browne yet Noland. Tip. Advert.

Where. Cumulonubulocirrhonimbant heaven electing, the dart of desire has gored the heart of secret waters and the poplarest wood in the entire district is being grown at present, eminently adapted for the requirements of pacnincstricken humanity and, between all the goings up and the whole of the comings down and the fog of the cloud in which we toil and the cloud of the fog under which we labour, bomb the thing's to be domb about it so that, beyond indicating the locality, it is felt that one cannot with advantage add a very great deal to the aforegoing by what, such as it is to be, follows, just mentioning however that the old man of the sea and the old woman in the sky if they don't say nothings about it they don't tell us lie, the gist of the pantomime, from cannibal king to the property horse, being, slumply and slopely, to remind us how, in this drury world of ours, Father Times and Mother Spacies boil their kettle with their crutch. Which every lad and lass in the lane knows. Hence.

Polycarp pool, the pool of Innalavia, Saras the saft as, of meadewy marge, atween Deltas Piscium and Sagittariastrion, whereinn once we lave 'tis alve and vale, minnyhahing here from hiarwather, a poddlebridges in a passabed, the river of lives, the regenerations of the incarnations of the emanations of the apparentations of Funn and Nin in Cleethabala, the kongdomain of the Alieni, an accorsaired race, infester of Libnud Ocean, Moylamore, let it be! Where Allbroggt Neandser tracking Viggynette Neeinsee gladsighted her Linfian Fall and a teamdiggingharrow turned the first sod. Sluce! Caughterect! Goodspeed the blow! (Incidentally 'tis believed that his harpened before Gage's Fane for it has to be over this booty spotch, though some hours to the wester, that ex-Colonel House's preterpost heiress is to return unto the outstretcheds of Dweyr O'Michael's loinsprung the blunterbusted pikehead which his had hewn in hers, prolonged laughter words). There an alomdree begins to green, soreen seen for loveseat, as we know that should she, for by essentience his law, so it make all. It is scainted to Vitalba. And her little white bloomkins, twittersky trimmed, are hobdoblins' hankypanks. Saxenslyke our anscessers thought so darely on now they're going soever to Anglesen, free of juties, dyrt chapes. There too a slab slobs, immermemorial, the only in all swamp. But so bare, so boulder, brag sagging such a brr bll bmm show that, of Barindens, the white alfred, it owed to have at leased some butchup's upperon. *Homos Circas Elochlannensis!* His showplace at Leeambye. Old Wommany Wyes. Pfif! But, while gleam with gloom swan here and there, this shame rock and that whispy planter tell Paudheen Steel-the-Poghue and his perty Molly Vardant, in goodbroomirish, arrah, this place is a proper and his feist a ferial for curdnal communial, so be who would celibrate the holy mystery upon or that the pirigrim from Mainylands beatend, the calmleaved hutcaged by that look whose glaum is sure he means bisnisgels to empalmover. A naked yogpriest, clothed of sundust, his oakey doaked with frondest leoves, offrand to the ewon of her owen. Tasyam kuru salilakriyamu! Pfaf!

Bring about it to be brought about and it will be, loke, our lake lemanted, that greyt lack, the citye of Is is issuant (atlanst!), urban and orbal, through seep froms umber under wasseres of Erie.

Lough!

Hwo! Hwy, dairmaidens? Asthoreths, assay! Earthsigh to is heavened.

Hillsengals, the daughters of the cliffs, responsen. Longsome the samphire coast. From thee to thee, thoo art it thoo, that thouest there. The like the near, the liker nearer. O sosay! A family, a band, a school, a clanagirls. Fiftines andbut fortines by novanas andor vantads by octettes ayand decadendecads by a lunary with last a lone. Whose every has herdifferent from the similies with her site. *Sicut campanulae petalliferentes* they coroll in caroll round Botany Bay. A dweam of dose innocent dirly dirls. Keavn! Keavn! And they all setton voicies about singsing music was Keavn! He. Only he. Ittle he. Ah! The whole clangalied. Oh!

S. Wilhelmina's, S. Gardenia's, S. Phibia's, S. Veslandrua's, S. Clarinda's, S. Immecula's, S. Dolores Delphin's, S. Perlanthroa's, S. Errands Gay's, S. Eddaminiva's, S. Rhodamena's, S. Ruadagara's, S. Drimicumtra's, S. Una Vestity's, S. Mintargisia's, S. Misha-La-Valse's, S. Churstry's, S. Clouonaskieym's, S. Bellavistura's, S. Santamonta's, S. Ringsingsund's, S. Heddadin Drade's, S. Glacianivia's, S. Waidafrira's, S. Thomassabbess's and (trema! unloud!! pepet!!!) S. Loellisotoelles!

Prayfulness! Prayfulness!

Euh! Thaet is seu whaet shaell one naeme it!

The meidinogues have tingued togethering. Ascend out of your bed, cavern of a trunk, and shrine! Kathlins is kitchin. Soros cast, ma brone! You must exterra acquarate to interirigate all the arkypelicans. The austrologer Wallaby by Tolan, who farshook our showrs from Newer Aland, has signed the you and the now our mandate. Milenesia waits. Be smark.

One seekings. Not the lithe slender, not the broad roundish near the lithe slender, not the fairsized fullfeatured to the leeward of the broad roundish but, indeed and inneed, the curling, perfect-portioned, flowerfleckled, shapely highhued, delicate features swaying to the windward of the fairsized fullfeatured.

Was that in the air about when something is to be said for it or is it someone imparticular who will somewherise for the whole anyhow?

What does Coemghen? Tell his hidings clearly! A woodtoo-gooder. Is his moraltack still his best of weapons? How about a little more goaling goold? Rowlin's tun he gadder no must. It is the voice of Roga. His face is the face of a son. Be thine the silent hall, O Jarama! A virgin, the one, shall mourn thee. Roga's stream is solence. But Croona is in adestance. The ass of the O'Dwyer of Greyglens is abrowtobayse afeald in his terroirs of the Potter-ton's forecoroners, the reeks around the burleyhearthed. When visited by an independant reporter, "Mike" Portlund, to burrow burning the latterman's Resterant so is called the gortan in quesure he mikes the fallowing for the Durban Gazette, firstcoming issue. From a collispendent. Any were. Deemsday. Bosse of Upper and Lower Byggotstrade, Ciwareke, may he live for river! The Games funeral at Valleytemple. Saturnights pomps, exhabiting that corricatore of a harss, revealled by Oscur Camerad. The last of Dutch Schulds, perhumps. Pipe in Dream Cluse. Uncovers Pub History. The Outrage, at Length. Affected Mob Follows in Reli-gious Sullivence. Rinvention of vestiges by which they drugged the buddhy. Moviefigure on in scenic section. By Patathicus. And there, from out of the scuity, misty Londan, along the canavan route, that is with the years gone, mild beam of the wave his polar bearing, steerner among stars, trust touthena and you tread true turf, comes the sorter, Mr Hurr Hansen, talking allthe-ways in himself of his hopes to fall in among a merryfoule of maidens happynghome from the dance, his knyckle allaready in his knackskey fob, a passable compatriate proparly of the Grimstad galleon, old pairs frieze, feed up to the noxer with their geese and peeas and oats upon a trencher and the toyms he'd lust in Wooming but with that smeoil like a grace of backoning over his egglips of the sunsoonshine. Here's heering you in a guessmasque, latterman! And such an improofment! As royt as the mail and as fat as a fuddle! Schoen! Shoan! Shoon the Puzt! A penny for your thought abouts! Tay, tibby, tanny, tummy, tasty, tosty, tay. Batch is for Baker who baxters our bread. O, what an ovenly odour! Butter butter! Bring us this days our maily bag! But receive me, my frensheets, from the emerald dark winterlong! For diss is the doss for Eilder Downes and dass is it duss, as singen sengers, what the hardworking straightwalking stoutstamping securelysealing officials who trow to form our G.M.P.'s pass muster generally shay for shee and sloo for slee when butting their headd to the pillow for a nightshared nakeshift with the alter girl they tuck in for sweepsake. Dutiful wealker for his hydes of march. Haves you the time. Hans ahike? Heard you the crime, senny boy? The man was giddy on letties on the dewry of the duary, be pursueded, whethered with entrenous, midgreys, dagos, teatimes, shadows, nocturnes or samoans, if wellstocked fillerouters plushfeverfraus with dopy chonks, and this, that and the other pigskin or muffle kinkles, taking a pipe course or doing an anguish, seen to his fleece in after his foull, when Dr Chart of Greet Chorsles street he changed his backbone at a citting. He had not the declaination, as what with the foos as whet with the fays, but so far as hanging a goobes on the precedings, wherethen the lag allows, it mights be anything after darks. Which the deers alones they sees and the darkies they is snuffing of the wind up. Debbling. Greanteavvents! Hyacinssies with heliotrollops! Not once fullvixen freakings and but dubbledecoys! It is a lable iction on the porte of the cuthulic church and summum most atole for it. Where is that blinketey blanketer, that quound of a pealer, the sunt of a hunt whant foxes good men! Where or he, our loved among many?

But what does Coemghem, the fostard? Tyro a tora. The novened iconostase of his blueygreyned vitroils but begins in feint to light his legend. Let Phosphoron proclaim! Peechy

peechy. Say he that saw him that saw! Man shall sharp run do a get him. Ask no more, Jerry mine, Roga's voice! No pice soorkabatcha. The bog which puckerooed the posy. The vinebranch of Heremonheber on Bregia's plane where Teffia lies is leaved invert and fructed proper but the cublic hatches endnot open yet for hourly rincers' mess. Read Higgins, Cairns and Egen. Malthus is yet lukked in close. Withun. How swathed thereanswer alcove makes theirinn! Besoakers loiter on. And primilibatory solicates of limon sodias will be absorbable. It is not even yet the engine of the load with haled morries full of crates, you mattinmummur, for dombell dumbs? Sure and 'tis not then. The greek Sideral Reulthway, as it havvents, will soon be starting a smooth with its first single hastencraft. Danny buzzers instead of the vialact coloured milk train on the fartykket plan run with its endless gallaxion of rotatorattlers and the smooltroon our elderens rememberem as the scream of the service, Strubry Bess. Also the waggonwobblers are still yet everdue to precipitate after night's combustion. Aspect, Shamus Rogua or! Taceate and! *Hagiographice canat Ecclesia.* Which aubrey our first shall show. Inattendance who is who is will play that's what's that to what's that, what.

Oyes! Oyeses! Oyesesyeses! The primace of the Gaulls, protonotorious, I yam as I yam, mitrogenerand in the free state on the air, is now aboil to blow a Gael warning. Inoperation Eyrlands Eyot, Meganesia, Habitant and the onebut thousand insels, Western and Osthern Approaches.

Of Kevin, of increate God the servant, of the Lord Creator a filial fearer, who, given to the growing grass, took to the tall timber, slippery dick the springy heeler, as we have seen, so we have heard, what we have received, that we have transmitted, thus we shall hope, this we shall pray till, in the search for love of knowledge through the comprehension of the unity in altruism through stupefaction, it may again how it may again, shearing aside the four wethers and passing over the dainty daily dairy and dropping by the way the lapful of live coals and smoothing out Nelly Nettle and her lad of mettle, full of stings, fond of stones, friend of gnewgnawns bones and leaving all the messy messy to look after our douche douche, the miracles, death and life are these.

Yad. Procreated on the ultimate ysland of Yreland in the encyclical yrish archipelago, come their feast of precreated holy whiteclad angels, whomamong the christener of his, voluntarily poor Kevin, having been graunted the pravilege of a priest's postcreated portable *altare cum balneo*, when espousing the one true cross, invented and exalted, in celibate matrimony at matin chime arose and westfrom went and came in alb of cloth of gold to our own midmost Glendalough-le-vert by archangelical guidance where amiddle of meeting waters of river Yssia and Essia river on this one of eithers lone navigable lake piously Kevin, lawding the triune trishagion, amidships of his conducible altar super bath, rafted centripetally, diaconal servent of orders hibernian, midway across the subject lake surface to its supreem epicentric lake Ysle, whereof its lake is the ventrifugal principality, whereon by prime, powerful in knowledge, Kevin came to where its centre is among the circumfluent watercourses of Yshgafiena and Yshgafiuna, an enysled lakelet yslanding a lacustrine yslet, whereupon with beached raft subdiaconal bath *propter* altar, with oil extremely anointed, accompanied by prayer, holy Kevin bided till the third morn hour but to build a rubric penitential honeybeehivehut in whose enclosure to live in fortitude, acolyte of cardinal virtues, whereof the arenary floor, most holy Kevin excavated as deep as to the depth of a seventh part of one full fathom, which excavated, venerable Kevin, anchorite, taking counsel, proceded towards the lakeside of the ysletshore whereat seven several times he, eastward genuflecting, in entire ubidience at sextnoon collected gregorian water sevenfold and with ambrosian eucharistic joy of heart as many times receded, carrying that privileged altar *unacumque* bath, which severally seven times into the cavity excavated, a lector of water levels, most venerable Kevin, then effused thereby letting there be water where was theretofore dry land, by him so concreated, who now, confirmed a strong and perfect christian, blessed Kevin, exorcised his holy sister water, perpetually chaste, so that, well understanding, she should fill to midheight his tubbathaltar, which hanbathtub, most blessed Kevin, ninthly enthroned, in the concentric centre of the translated water, whereamid, when violet vesper vailed, Saint Kevin, Hydrophilos, having girded his sable *cappa magna* as high as to his cherubical loins, at solemn compline sat in his sate of wisdom, that handbathtub, whereverafter, recreated *doctor insularis* of the universal church, keeper of the door of meditation, memory *extempore* proposing and intellect formally considering, recluse, he meditated continuously with seraphic ardour the primal sacrament of baptism or the regeneration of all man by affusion of water. Yee.

Bisships, bevel to rock's rite! Sarver buoy, extinguish! Nuotabene. The rare view from the three Benns under the bald heaven is on the other end, askan your blixom on dimmen and blastun, something to right hume about. They were erected in a purvious century, as a hen fine coops and, if you know your Bristol and have trudged the trolly ways and elventurns of that old cobbold city, you will sortofficially scribble a mental Peny-Knox-Gore. Whether they were franklings by name also has not been fully probed. Their design is a whosold word and the charming details of light in dark are freshed from the feminiairity which breathes content. *O ferax cupla*! Ah, fairypair! The first exploder to make his ablations in these parks was indeed that lucky mortal which the monster trial showed on its first day out. What will not arky paper, anticidingly inked with penmark, push, per sample prof, kuvertly falted, when style, stink and stigmataphoron are of one sum in the same person? He comes out of the soil very well after all just where Old Toffler is to come shuffling alongsoons Panniquanne starts showing of her peequuliar talonts. Awaywrong wandler surking to a rightrare rute for his plain utterrock sukes, appelled to by her fancy claddaghs. You plied that pokar, gamesy, swell as aye did, while there were flickars to the flores. He may be humpy, nay, he may be dumpy but there is always something racey about, say, a sailor on a horse. As soon as we sale him geen we gates a sprise! He brings up tofatufa and that is how we get to Missas in Massas. The old Marino tale. We veriters verity notefew demmed lustres priorly magistrite maximollient in ludubility learned. Facst. Teak off that wise head! Great sinner, good sonner, is in effect the motto of the Mac-Cowell family. The gloved fist (skrimmhandsker) was intraduced into their socerdatal tree before the fourth of the twelfth and it is even a little odd all four horolodgeries still gonging restage Jakob van der Bethel, smolking behing his pipe, with Essav of Messagepostumia, lentling out his borrowed chafingdish, before cymbaloosing the apostles at every hours of changeover. The first and last rittlerattle of the anniverse; when is a nam nought a nam whenas it is a. Watch! Heroes' Highway where our fleshers leave their bonings and every bob and joan to fill the bumper fair. It is their segnall for old Champelysied to seek the shades of his retirement and for young Chappielassies to tear a round and tease their partners lovesoftfun at Finnegan's Wake.

And it's high tigh tigh. Titley hi ti ti. That my dig pressed in your dag si. Gnug of old Gnig. Ni, gnid mig brawly! I bag your burden. Mees is thees knees. Thi is Mi. We have caught oneselves, Sveasmeas, in somes incontigruity coumplegs of heoponhurrish marrage from whose I most sublumbunate. A polog, my engl! Excutes. Om still so sovvy. Whyle om till ti ti.

Ha!

Dayagreening gains in schlimninging. A summerwint springfalls, abated. Hail, regn of durknass, snowly receassing, thund lightening thund, into the dimbelowstard departamenty whitherout, soon hist, soon mist, to the hothehill from the hollow, Solsking the Frist (attempted by the admirable Captive Bunting and Loftonant-Cornel Blaire) will processingly show up above Tumplen Bar whereupont he was much jubilated by Boergemester "Dyk" ffogg of Isoles, now Eisold, looking most plussed with (exhib 39) a clout capped sunbubble anaccanponied from his bequined torse. Up.

Blanchardstown mewspeppers pleads coppyl. Gracest goodness, heave mensy upponnus! Grand old Manbutton, give your bowlers a rest!

It is a mere mienerism of this vague of visibilities, mark you, as accorded to by moisturologist of the Brehons Assorceration for the advauncement of scayence because, my dear, mentioning of it under the breath, as in pure (what bunkum!) essenesse, there have been disselving forenenst you just the draeper, the two drawpers assisters and the three droopers assessors confraternitisers. Who are, of course, Uncle Arth, your two cozes from Niece and (kunject a bit now!) our own familiars, Billyhealy, Ballyhooly and Bullyhowley, surprised in an indecorous position by the Sigurd Sigerson Sphygmomanometer Society for bledprusshers.

Knightsmore. Haventyne?

Ha ha!

This Mister Ireland? And a live?

Ay, ay. Aye, aye, baas.

The cry of Stena chills the vitals of slumbring off the motther has been pleased into the harms of old salaciters, meassurers soon and soon, but the voice of Alina gladdens the cocklyhearted dreamerish for that magic moning with its ching chang chap sugay kaow laow milkee muchee bringing beckerbrose, the brew with the foochoor in it. Sawyest? Nodt? Nyets, I dhink I sawn to remumb or sumbsuch. A kind of a thinglike all traylogged then pubably it resymbles a pelvic or some kvind then props an acutebacked quadrangle with aslant off ohahnthenth a wenchyoumaycuddler, lying with her royalirish uppershoes among the theeckleaves. Signs are on of a mere by token that wills still to be becoming upon this there once a here was world. As the dayeleyves unfolden them. In the wake of the blackshape, *Nattenden Sorte;* whenat, hindled firth and hundled furth, the week of wakes is out and over; as a wick weak woking from ennemberable Ashias unto fierce force fuming, temtem tamtam, the Phoenican wakes.

Passing. One. We are passing. Two. From sleep we are passing. Three. Into the wikeawades warld from sleep we are passing. Four. Come, hours, be ours!

But still. Ah diar, ah diar! And stay.

608

It was allso agreeable in our sinegear clutchless, touring the no placelike no timelike absolent, mixing up pettyvaughan populose with the magnumoore genstries, lloydhaired mersscenary blookers with boydskinned pigttetails and goochlipped gwendolenes with duffyeyed dolores; like so many unprobables in their poor suit of the improssable. With Mata and after please with Matamaru and after please stop with Matamaruluka and after stop do please with Matamarulukajoni.

And anotherum. Ah ess, dapple ass! He will be longing after the Grogram Grays. And, Weisingchetaoli, he will levellaut ministel Trampleasure be. Sheflower Rosina, younger Sheflower fruit Amaryllis, youngest flowerfruityfrond Sallysill or Sillysall. And house with heaven roof occupanters they are continuatingly attraverse of its milletestudinous windows, ricocoursing themselves, as staneglass on stonegloss, inplayn unglish Wynn's Hotel. Brancherds at: Bullbeck, Oldboof, Sassondale, Jorsey Uppygard, Mundelonde, Abbeytotte, Bracqueytuitte with Hockeyvilla, Fockeyvilla, Hillewille and Wallhall. Hoojahoo managers the thingaviking. Obning shotly. When the messanger of the risen sun, (see other oriel) shall give to every seeable a hue and to every hearable a cry and to each spectacle his spot and to each happening her houram. The while we, we are waiting, we are waiting for. Hymn.

Muta: Quodestnunc fumusiste volhvuns ex Domoyno?

Juva: It is Old Head of Kettle puffing off the top of the mornin.

Muta: He odda be thorly well ashamed of himself for smoking before the high host.

Juva: Dies is Dorminus master and commandant illy tonobrass.

Muta: Diminussed aster! An I could peecieve amonkst the gatherings who ever they wolk in process?

Juva: Khubadah! It is the Chrystanthemlander with his porters of bonzos, pompommy plonkyplonk, the ghariwallahs, moveyovering the cabrattlefield of slaine.

Muta: Pongo da Banza! An I would uscertain in druidful scatterings one piece tall chap he stand one piece same place?

Juva: Bulkily: and he is fundementially theosophagusted over the whorse proceedings.

Muta: Petrificationibus! O horild haraflare! Who his dickhuns now rearrexes from undernearth the memorialorum?

Juva: Beleave filmly, beleave! Fing Fing! King King!

Muta: Ulloverum? Fulgitudo ejus Rhedonum teneat!

Juva: Rolantlossly! Till the tipp of his ziff. And the ubideintia of the savium is our ervics fenicitas.

Muta: Why soly smiles the supremest with such for a leary on his rugular lips?

Juva: Bitchorbotchum! Eebrydime! He has help his crewn on the burkeley buy but he has holf his crown on the Eurasian Generalissimo.

Muta: Skulkasloot! The twyly velleid is thus then paridi-cynical?

Juva: Ut vivat volumen sic pereat pouradosus!

Muta: Haven money on stablecert?

Juva: Tempt to wom Outsider!

Muta: Suc? He quoffs. Wutt?

Juva: Sec! Wartar wartar! Wett.

Muta: Ad Piabelle et Purabelle?

Juva: At Winne, Woermann og Sengs.

Muta: So that when we shall have acquired unification we shall pass on to diversity and when we shall have passed on to diversity we shall have acquired the instinct of combat and when we shall have acquired the instinct of combat we shall pass back to the spirit of appeasement?

Juva: By the light of the bright reason which daysends to us from the high.

Muta: May I borrow that hordwanderbaffle from you, old rubberskin?

Juva: Here it is and I hope it's your wormingpen, Erinmonker! Shoot.

Rhythm and Colour at Park Mooting. Peredos Last in the Grand Natural. Velivision victor. Dubs newstage oldtime turf-tussle, recalling Winny Willy Widger. Two draws. Heliotrope leads from Harem. Three ties. Jockey the Ropper jerks Jake the Rape. Paddrock and bookley chat.

And here are the details.

Tunc. Bymeby, bullocky vampas tappany bobs topside joss pidgin fella Balkelly, archdruid of islish chinchinjoss in the his heptachromatic sevenhued septicoloured roranyellgreenlindigan mantle finish he show along the his mister guest Patholic with alb belongahim the whose throat hum with of sametime all the his cassock groaner fellas of greysfriaryfamily he fast all time what time all him monkafellas with Same Patholic, quoniam, speeching, yeh not speeching noh man liberty is, he drink up words, scilicet, tomorrow till recover will not, all too many much illusiones through photoprismic velamina of hueful panepiphanal world spectacurum of Lord Joss, the of which zoantholitic furniture, from mineral through vegetal to animal, not appear to full up together fallen man than under but one photoreflection of the several iridals gradationes of solar light, that one which that part of it (furnit of heupanepi world) had shown itself (part of fur of huepanwor) unable to absorbere, whereas for numpa one puraduxed seer in seventh degree of wisdom of Entis-Onton he savvy inside true inwardness of reality, the Ding hvad in idself id est, all objects (of panepiwor) allside showed themselves in trues coloribus resplendent with sextuple gloria of light actually retained, untisintus, inside them (obs of epiwo). Rumnant Patholic, stareotypopticus, no catch all that preachybook, utpiam, tomorrow recover thing even is not, bymeby vampsybobsy tappanasbullocks topside joss pidginfella Bilkilly-Belkelly say patfella, ontesantes, twotime hemhaltshealing, with other words verbigratiagrading from murmurulentous till striduloceĺerious in a hunghoranghoangoly tsinglontseng while his comprehendurient, with diminishing claractinism, augumentationed himself in caloripeia to vision so throughsighty, you anxioust melancholic, High Thats Hight Uberking Leary his fiery grassbelonghead all show colour of sorrelwood herbgreen, again, niggerblonker, of the his essixcoloured holmgrewnworsteds costume the his fellow saffron pettikilt look same hue of boiled spinasses, other thing, voluntary mutismuser, he not compyhandy the his golden twobreasttorc look justsamelike curlicabbis, moreafter, to pace negativisticists, verdant readyrainroof belongahim Exuber High Ober King Leary very dead, what he wish to say, spit of superexuberabundancy plenty laurel leaves, after that commander bulopent eyes of Most Highest Ardreetsar King same thing like thyme choppy upon parsley, alongsidethat, if pleasesir, nos displace tauttung, sowlofabishospastored, enamel Indian gem in maledictive fingerfondler of High High Siresultan Emperor all same like one fellow olive lentil, onthelongsidethat, by undesendas, kirikirikiring, violaceous warwon contusiones of facebuts of Highup Big Cockywocky Sublissimime Autocrat, for that with pure hueglut intensely saturated one, tinged uniformly, allaroundside upinandoutdown, very like you seecut chowchow of plentymuch sennacassia. Hump cumps Ebblybally! Sukkot?

Punc. Bigseer, refrects the petty padre, whackling it out, a tumble to take, tripeness to call thing and to call if say is good while, you pore shiroskuro blackinwhitepaddynger, by thiswis aposterioprismically apatstrophied and paralogically periparolysed, celestial from principalest of Iro's Irismans ruinboon pot before, (for beingtime monkblinkers timeblinged completamentarily murkblankered in their neutrolysis between the possible viriditude of the sager and the probable eruberuption of the saint), as My tappropinquish to Me wipenmeselps gnosegates a handcaughtscheaf of synthetic shammyrag to hims hers, seemingsuch four three two agreement cause heart to be might, saving to Balenoarch (he kneeleths), to Great Balenoarch (he kneeleths down) to Greatest Great Balenoarch (he kneeleths down quitesomely), the sound sense sympol in a weedwayedwold of the firethere the sun in his halo cast. Onmen.

That was thing, bygotter, the thing, bogcotton, the very thing, begad! Even to uptoputty Bilkilly-Belkelly-Balkally. Who was for shouting down the shatton on the lamp of Jeeshees. Sweating on to stonker and throw his seven. As he shuck his thumping fore features apt the hoyhop of His Ards.

Thud.

Good safe firelamp! hailed the heliots. Goldselforelump! Halled they. Awed. Where thereon the skyfold high, trampatrampatramp. Adie. Per ye comdoom doominoom noonstroom. Yeasome priestomes. Fullyhum toowhoom.

Taawhaar?

Sants and sogs, cabs and cobs, kings and karls, tentes and taunts.

'Tis gone infarover. So fore now, dayleash. Pour deday. To trancefixureashone. Feist of Taborneccles, scenopegia, come! Shamwork, be in our scheining! And let every crisscouple be so crosscomplimentary, little eggons, youlk and meelk, in a farbiger pancosmos. With a hottyhammyum all round. Gudstruce!

Yet is no body present here which was not there before. Only is order othered. Nought is nulled. *Fuitfiat!*

Lo, the laud of laurens now orielising benedictively when saint and sage have said their say.

A spathe of calyptrous glume involucrumines the perinanthean Amenta: fungoalgaceous muscafilicial graminopalmular planteon; of increasing, livivorous, feelful thinkamalinks; luxuriotiating everywhencewithersoever among skullhullows and charnelcysts of a weedwastewoldwevild when Ralph the Retriever ranges to jawrode his knuts knuckles and her theas thighs; onegugulp down of the nauseous forere brarkfarsts oboboomaround and you're as paint and spickspan as a rainbow; wreathe the bowl to rid the bowel; no runcure, no rank heat, sir; amess in amullium; chlorid cup.

Health, chalce, endnessnessessity! Arrive, likkypuggers, in a poke! The folgor of the frightfools is olympically optimominous; there is bound to be a lovleg day for mirrages in the open; Murnane and Aveling are undertoken to berry that ortchert: provided that. You got to make good that breachsuit, seamer. You going to haulm port houlm, toilermaster. You yet must get up to kill (nonparticular). You still stand by and do as hit (private). While for yous, Jasminia Aruna and all your likers, affinitatively must it be by you elected if Monogynes his is or hers Diander, the tubous, limbersome and nectarial. Owned or grazeheifer, ethel or bonding. Mopsus or Gracchus, all your horodities will incessantlament be coming back from the Annone Wishwashwhose, Ormepierre Lodge, Doone of the Drumes, blanches bountifully and nightsend made up, every article lathering leaving several rinsings so as each rinse results with a dapperent rolle, cuffs for meek and chokers for sheek and a kink in the pacts for namby. Forbeer, forbear! For nought that is has bane. In mournenslaund. Themes have thimes and habit reburns. To flame in you. Ardor vigor forders order. Since ancient was our living is in possible to be. Delivered as. Caffirs and culls and onceagain overalls, the fittest surviva lives that blued, iorn and storridge can make them. Whichus all claims. Clean. Whenastcleeps. Close. And the mannormillor clipperclappers. Noxt. Doze.

Fennsense, finnsonse, aworn! Tuck upp those wide shorts. The pink of the busket for sheer give. Peeps. Stand up to hard ware and step into style. If you soil may, puett, guett me prives. For newmanmaun set a marge to the merge of unnotions. Inition wons agame.

What has gone? How it ends?

Begin to forget it. It will remember itself from every sides, with all gestures, in each our word. Today's truth, tomorrow's trend.

Forget, remember!

Have we cherished expectations? Are we for liberty of perusiveness? Whyafter what forewhere? A plainplanned liffeyism assemblements Eblania's conglomerate horde. By dim delty Deva.

Forget!

Our wholemole millwheeling vicociclometer, a tetradomational gazebocroticon (the "Mamma Lujah" known to every schoolboy scandaller,be he Matty, Marky, Lukey or John-a-Donk), autokinatonetically preprovided with a clappercoupling smeltingworks exprogressive process, (for the farmer, his son and their homely codes, known as eggburst, eggblend, eggburial and hatch-as-hatch can) receives through a portal vein the dialytically separated elements of precedent decomposition for the verypetpurpose of subsequent recombination so that the heroticisms, catastrophes and eccentricities transmitted by the ancient legacy of the past, type by tope, letter from litter, word at ward, with sendence of sundance, since the days of Plooney and Columcellas when Giacinta, Pervenche and Margaret swayed over the all-too-ghoulish and illyrical and innumantic in our mutter nation, all, anastomosically assimilated and preteridentified paraidiotically, in fact, the sameold gamebold adomic structure of our Finnius the old One, as highly charged with electrons as hophazards can effective it, may be there for you, Cockalooralooraloomenos, when cup, platter and pot come piping hot, as sure as herself pits hen to paper and there's scribings scrawled on eggs.

Of cause, so! And in effect, as?

Dear. And we go on to Dirtdump. Reverend. May we add majesty? Well, we have frankly enjoyed more than anything these secret workings of natures (thanks ever for it, we humbly pray) and, well, was really so denighted of this lights time. Mucksrats which bring up about uhrweckers they will come to know good. Yon clouds will soon disappear looking forwards at a fine day. The honourable Master Sarmon they should be first born like he was with a twohangled warpon and it was between Williamstown and the Mairrion Ailesbury on the top of the longcar, as merrily we rolled along, we think of him looking at us yet as if to pass away in a cloud. When he woke up in a sweat besidus it was to pardon him, goldylocks, me having an airth, but he daydreamsed we had a lovelyt face for a pulltomine. Back we were by the jerk of a beamstark, backed in paladays last, on the brinks of the wobblish, the man what never put a dramn in the swags but milk from a national cowse. That was the prick of the spindle to me that gave me the keys to dreamland. Sneakers in the grass, keep off! If we were to tick off all that cafflers head, whisperers for his accomodation, the me craws, namely, and their bacon what harmed butter! It's margarseen oil. Thinthin thinthin. Stringstly is it forbidden by the honorary tenth commendmant to shall not bare full sweetness against a nighboor's wiles. What those slimes up the cavern door around you, keenin, (the lies is coming out on them frecklefully) had the shames to suggest can we ever? Never! So may the low forget him their trespasses against Molloyd O'Reilly, that hugglebeddy fann, now about to get up, the hartiest that Coolock ever! A nought in nought Eirinishmhan, called Ervigsen by his first mate. May all similar douters of our oldhame story have that fancied widming! For a pipe of twist or a slug of Hibernia metal we could let out and, by jings, someone would make a carpus of somebody with the greatest of pleasure by private shootings. And in contravention to the constancy of chemical combinations not enough of all the slatters of him left for Peeter the Picker to make their threi sevelty filfths of a man out of. Good wheat! How delitious for the three Sulvans of Dulkey and what a sellpriceget the two Peris of Monacheena! Sugars of lead for the chloras ashpots! Peace! He possessing from a child of highest valency for our privileged beholdings ever complete hairy of chest, hamps and eyebags in pursuance to salesladies' affectionate company. His real devotes. Wriggling reptiles, take notice! Whereas we exgust all such sprinkling snigs. They are pestituting the whole time never with standing we simply agree upon the committee of amusance! Or could above bring under same notice for it to be able to be seen.

About that coerogenal hun and his knowing the size of an egg-cup. First he was a skulksman at one time and then Cloon's fired him through guff. Be sage about sausages! Stuttutistics shows with he's heacups of teatables the old firm's fatspitters are most eatenly appreciated by metropolonians. While we should like to drag attentions to our Wolkmans Cumsensation Act. The magnets of our midst being foisted upon by a plethorace of parachutes. Did speece permit the bad example of setting before the military to the best of our belief in the earliest wish of the one in mind was the mitigation of the king's evils. And how he staired up the step after it's the power of the gait. His giantstand of manun-known. No brad wishy washy wathy wanted neither! Once you are balladproof you are unperceable to haily, icy and missile-throes. Order now before we reach Ruggers' Rush! As we now must close hoping to Saint Laurans all in the best. Moral. Mrs Stores Humphreys: So you are expecting trouble, Pondups, from the domestic service questioned? Mr Stores Humphreys: Just as there is a good in even, Levia, my cheek is a compleet bleenk. Plumb. Meaning: one two four. Finckers. Up the hind hose of hizzars. Whereapon our best again to a hundred and eleven ploose one thousand and one other blessings will now concloose thoose epoostles to your great kindest, well, for all at trouble to took. We are all at home in old Fintona, thank Danis, for ourselfsake, that direst of housebonds, whool wheel be true unto lovesend so long as we has a pockle full of brass. Impossible to remember persons in improbable to forget position places. Who would pellow his head off to conjure up a, well, particularly mean stinker like funn make called Foon MacCrawl brothers, mystery man of the pork martyrs? Force in giddersh! Tomothy and Lorcan, the bucket Toolers, both are Timsons now they've changed their characticuls during their blackout. Conan Boyles will pudge the daylives out through him, if they are correctly informed. Music, me ouldstrow, please! We'll have a brand rehearsal. Fing! One must simply laugh. Fing him aging! Good licks! Well, this ought to weke him to make up. He'll want all his fury gutmurdherers to redress him. Gilly in the gap. The big bad old sprowly all uttering foon! Has now stuffed last podding. His fooneral will sneak pleace by creeps o'clock toosday. Kingen will commen. Allso brewbeer. Pens picture at Manchem House Horsegardens shown in Morning post as from Boston transcripped. Femelles will be preadaminant as from twentyeight to twelve. To hear that lovelade parson, of case, of a bawl gentlemale, pour forther moracles. Don't forget! The grand fooneral will now shortly occur. Remember. The remains must be removed before eaght hours shorp. With earnestly conceived hopes. So help us to witness to this day to hand in sleep. From of Mayasdaysed most duteoused.

Well, here's lettering you erronymously anent other clerical fands allieged herewith. I wisht I wast be that dumb tyke and he'd wish it was me yonther heel. How about it? The sweetest song in the world! Our shape as a juvenile being much admired from the first with native copper locks. Referring to the Married Woman's Improperty Act a correspondent paints out that the Swees Auburn vogue is hanging down straith fitting to her innocenth eyes. O, felicious coolpose! If all theMacCrawls would only handle virgils like Armsworks, Limited! That's handsel for gertles! Never mind Micklemans! Chat us instead! The cad with the pope's wife, Lily Kinsella, who became the wife of Mr Sneakers for her good name in the hands of the kissing solicitor, will now engage in attentions. Just a prinche for tonight! Pale bellies our mild cure, back and streaky ninepace. The thicks off Bully's Acre was got up by Sully. The Boot lane brigade. And she had a certain medicine brought her in a licenced victualler's bottle. Shame! Thrice shame! We are advised the waxy is at the present in the Sweeps hospital and that he may never come out! Only look through your leatherbox one day with P.C.Q. about 4.32 or at 8 and 22.5 with the quart of scissions masters and clerk and the bevyhum of Marie Reparatrices for a good allround sympowdhericks purge, full view, to be surprised to see under the grand piano Lily on the sofa (and a lady!) pulling a low and then he'd begin to jump a little bit to find out what goes on when love walks in besides the solicitous bussness by kissing and looking into a mirror.

That we were treated not very grand when the police and everybody is all bowing to us when we go out in all directions on Wanterlond Road with my cubarola glide? And, personably speaking, they can make their beaux to my alce, as Hillary Allen sang to the opennine knighters. Item, we never were chained to a chair, and, bitem, no widower whother soever followed us about with a fork on Yankskilling Day. Meet a great civilian (proud lives to him!) who is gentle as a mushroom and a very affectable when he always sits forenenst us for his wet while to all whom it may concern Sully is a thug from all he drunk though he is a rattling fine bootmaker in his profession. Would we were herearther to lodge our complaint on sergeant Laraseny in consequence of which in such steps taken his health would be constably broken into potter's pance which would be the change of his life by a Nollwelshian which has been oxbelled out of crispianity.

Well, our talks are coming to be resumed by more polite conversation with a huntered persent human over the natural bestness of pleisure after his good few mugs of humbedumb and shag. While for whoever likes that urogynal pan of cakes one apiece it is thanks, beloved, to Adam, our former first Finnlatter and our grocerest churcher, as per Grippiths' varuations, for his beautiful crossmess parzel.

Well, we simply like their demb cheeks, the Rathgarries, wagging here about around the rhythms in me amphybed and he being as bothered that he pausably could by the fallth of hampty damp. Certified reformed peoples, we may add to this stage, are proptably saying to quite agreeable deef. Here gives your answer, pigs and scuts! Hence we've lived in two worlds. He is another he what stays under the himp of holth. The herewaker of our hamefame is his real namesame who will get himself up and erect, confident and heroic when but, young as of old, for my daily comfreshenall, a wee one woos.

Alma Luvia, Pollabella.

P.S. Soldier Rollo's sweetheart. And she's about fetted up now with nonsery reams. And rigs out in regal rooms with the ritzies. Rags! Worns out. But she's still her deckhuman amber too.

Soft morning, city! Lsp! I am leafy speafing. Lpf! Folty and folty all the nights have fallen on to long my hair. Not a sound, falling. Lispn! No wind no word. Only a leaf, just a leaf and then leaves. The woods are fond always. As were we their babes in. And robins in crews so. It is for me goolden wending. Unless? Away! Rise up, man of the hooths, you have slept so long! Or is it only so mesleems? On your pondered palm. Reclined from cape to pede. With pipe on bowl. Terce for a fiddler, sixt for makmerriers, none for a Cole. Rise up now and aruse! Norvena's over. I am leafy, your goolden, so you called me, may me life, yea your goolden, silve me solve, exsogerraider! You did so drool. I was so sharm. But there's a great poet in you too. Stout Stokes would take you offly. So has he as bored me to slump. But am good and rested. Taks to you, toddy, tan ye! Yawhawaw. Helpunto min, helpas vin. Here is your shirt, the day one, come back. The stock, your collar. Also your double brogues. A comforter as well. And here your iverol and everthelest your

619

umbr. And stand up tall! Straight. I want to see you looking fine for me. With your brandnew big green belt and all. Blooming in the very lotust and second to nill, Budd! When you're in the buckly shuit Rosensharonals near did for you. Fiftyseven and three, cosh, with the bulge. Proudpurse Alby with his pooraroon Eireen, they'll. Pride, comfytousness, enevy! You make me think of a wonderdecker I once. Or somebalt thet sailder, the man megallant, with the bangled ears. Or an earl was he, at Lucan? Or, no, it's the Iren duke's I mean. Or somebrey erse from the Dark Countries. Come and let us! We always said we'd. And go abroad. Rathgreany way perhaps. The childher are still fast. There is no school today. Them boys is so contrairy. The Head does be worrying himself. Heel trouble and heal travel. Galliver and Gellover. Unless they changes by mistake. I seen the likes in the twinngling of an aye. Som. So oft. Sim. Time after time. The sehm asnuh. Two bredder as doffered as nors in soun. When one of him sighs or one of him cries 'tis you all over. No peace at all. Maybe it's those two old crony aunts held them out to the water front. Queer Mrs Quickenough and odd Miss Doddpebble. And when them two has had a good few there isn't much more dirty clothes to publish. From the Laundersdale Minssions. One chap googling the holyboy's thingabib and this lad wetting his widdle. You were pleased as Punch, recitating war exploits and pearse orations to them jackeen gapers. But that night after, all you were wanton! Bidding me do this and that and the other. And blowing off to me, hugly Judsys, what wouldn't you give to have a girl! Your wish was mewill. And, lo, out of a sky! The way I too. But her, you wait. Eager to choose is left to her shade. If she had only more matcher's wit. Findlings makes runaways, runaways a stray. She's as merry as the gricks still. 'Twould be sore should ledden sorrow. I'll wait. And I'll wait. And then if all goes. What will be is. Is is. But let them. Slops hospodch and the slusky slut too. He's for thee what she's for me. Dogging you round cove and haven and teaching me the perts of speech. If you spun your yarns to him on the swishbarque waves I was spelling my yearns to her over cottage cake. We'll not disturb their sleeping duties. Let besoms be bosuns. It's Phoenix, dear. And the flame is, hear! Let's our joornee saintomichael make it. Since the lausafire has lost and the book of the depth is. Closed. Come! Step out of your shell! Hold up you free fing! Yes. We've light enough. I won't take our laddy's lampern. For them four old windbags of Gustsofairy to be blowing at. Nor you your rucksunck. To bring all the dannymans out after you on the hike. Send Arctur guiddus! Isma! Sft! It is the softest morning that ever I can ever remember me. But she won't rain showerly, our Ilma. Yet. Until it's the time. And me and you have made our. The sons of bursters won in the games. Still I'll take me owld Finvara for my shawlders. The trout will be so fine at brookfisht. With a taste of roly polony from Blugpuddels after. To bring out the tang of the tay. Is't you fain for a roost brood? Oaxmealturn, all out of the woolpalls! And then all the chippy young cuppinjars cluttering round us, clottering for their creams. Crying, me, grownup sister! Are me not truly? Lst! Only but, theres a but, you must buy me a fine new girdle too, nolly. When next you go to Market Norwall. They're all saying I need it since the one from Isaacsen's slooped its line. Mrknrk? Fy arthou! Come! Give me your great bearspaw, padder avilky, fol a miny tiny. Dola. Mineninecyhandsy, in the languo of flows. That's Jorgen Jargonsen. But you understood, nodst? I always know by your brights and shades. Reach down. A lil mo. So. Draw back your glave. Hot and hairy, hugon, is your hand! Here's where the falskin begins. Smoos as an infams. One time you told you'd been burnt in ice. And one time it was chemicalled after you taking a lifeness. Maybe that's why you hold your hodd as if. And people thinks you missed the scaffold. Of fell design. I'll close me eyes. So not to see. Or see only a youth in his florizel, a boy in innocence, peeling a twig, a child beside a weenywhite steed. The child we all love to place our hope in for ever. All men has done something. Be the time they've come to the weight of old fletch. We'll lave it. So. We will take our walk before in the timpul they ring the earthly bells. In the church by the hearseyard. Pax Goodmens will. Or the birds start their treestirm shindy. Look, there are yours off, high on high! And cooshes, sweet good luck they're cawing you, Coole! You see, they're as white as the riven snae. For us. Next peaters poll you will be elicted or I'm not your elicitous bribe. The Kinsella woman's man will never reduce me. A MacGarath O'Cullagh O'Muirk MacFewney sookadoodling and sweepacheeping round the lodge of Fjorn na Galla of the Trumpets! It's like potting the po to shambe on the dresser or tamming Uncle Tim's Caubeen on to the brows of a Viker Eagle. Not such big strides, huddy foddy! You'll crush me antilopes I saved so long for. They're Penisole's. And the two goodiest shoeshoes. It is hardly a Knut's mile or seven, possumbotts. It is very good for the health of a morning. With Buahbuah. A gentle motion all around. As leisure paces. And the helpyourselftoastrool cure's easy. It seems so long since, ages since. As if you had been long far away. Afartodays, afeartonights, and me as with you in thadark. You will tell me some time if I can believe its all. You know where I am bringing you? You remember? When I ran berrying after hucks and haws. With you drawing out great aims to hazel me from the hummock with your sling. Our cries. I could lead you there and I still by you in bed. Les go dutc to Danegreven, nos? Not a soul but ourselves. Time? We have loads on our hangs. Till Gilligan and Halligan call again to hooligan. And the rest of the guns. Sullygan eight, from left to right. Olobobo, ye foxy theagues! The moskors thought to ball you out. Or the Wald Unicorns Master, Bugley Captain, from the Naul, drawls up by the door with the Honourable Whilp and the Reverend Poynter and the two Lady Pagets of Tallyhaugh, Ballyhuntus, in their riddletight raiding hats for to lift a hereshealth to their robost, the Stag, evers the Carlton hart. And you needn't host out with your duck and your duty, capapole, while they reach him the glass he never starts to finish. Clap this wis on your poll and stick this in your ear, wiggly! Beauties don't answer and the rich never pays. If you were the enlarged they'd hue in cry you, Heathtown, Harbourstown, Snowtown, Four Knocks, Flemingtown, Bodingtown to the Ford of Fyne on Delvin. How they housed to house you after the Platonic garlens! And all because, loosed in her reflexes, she seem she seen Ericoricori coricome huntsome with his three poach dogs aleashing him. But you came safe through. Enough of that horner corner! And old mutthergoosip! We might call on the Old Lord, what do you say? There's something tells me. He is a fine sport. Like the score and a moighty went before him. And a proper old promnentory. His door always open. For a newera's day.   Much as your own is. You invoiced him last Eatster so he ought to give us hockockles and everything. Remember to take off your white hat, ech? When we come in the presence. And say hoothoothoo, ithmuthisthy! His is house of laws. And I'll drop my graciast kertssey too. If the Ming Tung no go bo to me homage me hamage kow bow tow to the Mong Tang. Ceremonialness to stand lowest place be! Saying: What'll you take to link to light a pike on porpoise, plaise? He might knight you an Armor elsor daub you the first cheap magyerstrape. Remember Bomthomanew vim vam vom Hungerig. Hoteform, chain and epolettes, botherbumbose. And I'll be your aural eyeness. But we vain. Plain fancies. It's in the castles air. My currant bread's full of sillymottocraft. Aloof is anoof. We can take or leave. He's reading his ruffs. You'll know our way from there surely. Flura's way. Where once we led so many car couples have follied since. Clatchka! Giving Shaughnessy's mare the hillymount of her life. With her strulldeburgghers! Hnmn hnmn! The rollcky road adondering. We can sit us down on the heathery benn, me on you, in quolm unconsciounce. To scand the arising. Out from Drumleek. It was there Evora told me I had best. If I ever. When the moon of mourning is set and gone. Over Glinaduna. Lonu nula. Ourselves, oursouls alone. At the site of salvocean. And watch would the letter you're wanting be coming may be. And cast ashore. That I prays for be mains of me draims. Scratching it and patching at with a prompt from a primer. And what scrips of nutsnolleges I pecked up me meself. Every letter is a hard but yours sure is the hardest crux ever. Hack an axe, hook an oxe, hath an an, heth hith ences. But once done, dealt and delivered, tattat, you're on the map. Rased on traumscrapt from Maston, Boss. After rounding his world of ancient days. Carried in a caddy or screwed and corked. On his mugisstosst surface. With a bob, bob, bottledby. Blob. When the waves give up yours the soil may for me. Sometime then, somewhere there, I wrote me hopes and buried the page when I heard Thy voice, ruddery dunner, so loud that none but, and left it to lie till a kissmiss coming. So content me now. Lss. Unbuild and be buildn our bankaloan cottage there and we'll cohabit respectable. The Gowans, ser, for Medem, me. With acute bubel runtoer for to pippup and gopeep where the sterres be. Just to see would we hear how Jove and the peers talk. Amid the soleness. Tilltop, bigmaster! Scale the summit! You're not so giddy any more. All your graundplotting and the little it brought! Humps, when you hised us and dumps, when you doused us! But sarra one of me cares a brambling ram, pomp porteryark! On limpidy marge I've made me hoom. Park and a pub for me. Only don't start your stunts of Donachie's yeards agoad again. I could guessp to her name who tuckt you that one, tufnut! Bold bet backwords! For the loves of sinfintins! Before the naked universe. And the bailby pleasemarm rincing his eye! One of these fine days, lewdy culler, you must redoform again. Blessed shield Martin! Softly so. I am so exquisitely pleased about the loveleavest dress I have. You will always call me Leafiest, won't you, dowling? Wordherfhull Ohldhbhhoy! And you won't urbjunk to me parafume, oiled of kolooney, with a spot of marashy. Sm! It's Alpine Smile from Yesthers late Yhesters. I'm in everywince nasturtls. Even in Houlth's nose. Medeurscodeignus! Astale of astoun. Grand owld marauder! If I knew who you are! When that hark from the air said it was Captain Finsen makes cumhulments and was mayit pressing for his suit I said are you there here's nobody here only me. But I near fell off the pile of samples. As if your tinger winged ting to me hear. Is that right what your brothermilk in Bray bes telling the district you were bragged up by Brostal because your parents would be always tumbling into his foulplace and losing her pentacosts after drinking their pledges? Howsomendeavour, you done me fine! The only man was ever known could eat the crushts of lobsters. Our native night when you twicetook me for some Marienne Sherry and then your Jermyn cousin who signs hers with exes and the beard-wig I found in your Clarksome bag. Pharaops you'll play you're the king of Aeships. You certainly make the most royal of noises. I will tell you all sorts of makeup things, strangerous. And show you to every simple storyplace we pass. *Cadmillersfolly*, *Bellevenue*, *Wellcrom*, *Quid Superabit*, villities valleties. Change the plates for the next course of murphies! Spendlove's still there and the canon going strong and so is Claffey's habits endurtaking and our parish pomp's a great warrent. But you'll have to ask that same four that named them is always snugging in your bar-salooner, saying they're the best relicts of Conal O'Daniel and writing *Finglas since the Flood*. That'll be some kingly work in progress. But it's by this route he'll come some morrow. And I can signal you all flint and fern are rasstling as we go by. And you'll sing thumb a bit and then wise your selmon on it. It is all so often and still the same to me. Snf? Only turf, wick dear! Clane turf. You've never forgodden batt on tarf, have you, at broin burroow, what? Mch? Why, them's the muchrooms, come up during the night. Look, agres of roofs in parshes. Dom on dam, dim in dym. And a capital part for olympics to ply at. Steadyon, Cooloosus! Mind your stride or you'll knock. While I'm dodging the dustbins. Look what I found! A lintil pea. And look at here! This cara weeseed. Pretty mites, my sweetthings, was they poorloves abandoned by wholawidey world? Neighboulotts for newtown. The Eblanamagna you behazyheld loomening up out of the dumblynass. But the still sama sitta. I've lapped so long. As you said. It fair takes. If I lose my breath for a minute or two don't speak, remember! Once it happened, so it may again. Why I'm all these years within years in soffran, allbeleaved. To hide away the tear, the parted. It's thinking of all. The brave that gave their. The fair that wore. All them that's gunne. I'll begin again in a jiffey. The nik of a nad. How glad you'll be I waked you! My! How well you'll feel! For ever after. First we turn by the vagurin here and then it's gooder. So side by side, turn agate, weddingtown, laud men of Londub! I only hope whole the heavens sees

us. For I feel I could near to faint away. Into the deeps. Anna-
mores leep. Let me lean, just a lea, if you le, bowldstrong big-
tider. Allgearls is wea. At times. So. While you're adamant evar.
Wrhps, that wind as if out of norewere! As on the night of the
Apophanypes. Jumpst shootst throbbst into me mouth like a
bogue and arrohs! Ludegude of the Lashlanns, how he whips
me cheeks! Sea, sea! Here, weir, reach, island, bridge. Where you
meet I. The day. Remember! Why there that moment and us
two only? I was but teen, a tiler's dot. The swankysuits was
boosting always, sure him, he was like to me fad. But the swag-
gerest swell off Shackvulle Strutt. And the fiercest freaky ever
followed a pining child round the sluppery table with a forkful
of fat. But a king of whistlers. Scieoula! When he'd prop me atlas
against his goose and light our two candles for our singers duohs
on the sewingmachine. I'm sure he squirted juice in his eyes to
make them flash for flightening me. Still and all he was awful
fond to me. Who'll search for *Find Me Colours* now on the hilly-
droops of Vikloefells? But I read in Tobecontinued's tale that while
blubles blows there'll still be sealskers. There'll be others but non
so for me. Yed he never knew we seen us before. Night after
night. So that I longed to go to. And still with all. One time you'd
stand fornenst me, fairly laughing, in your bark and tan billows of
branches for to fan me coolly. And I'd lie as quiet as a moss. And
one time you'd rush upon me, darkly roaring, like a great black
shadow with a sheeny stare to perce me rawly. And I'd frozen
up and pray for thawe. Three times in all. I was the pet of everyone
then. A princeable girl. And you were the pantymammy's Vulking
Corsergoth. The invision of Indelond. And, by Thorror, you
looked it! My lips went livid for from the joy of fear. Like almost
now. How? How you said how you'd give me the keys of me
heart. And we'd be married till delth to uspart. And though dev
do espart. O mine! Only, no, now it's me who's got to give. As
duv herself div. Inn this linn. And can it be it's nnow fforvell?
Illas! I wisht I had better glances to peer to you through this bay-
light's growing. But you're changing, acoolsha, you're changing
from me, I can feel. Or is it me is? I'm getting mixed. Brightening

up and tightening down. Yes, you're changing, sonhusband, and you're turning, I can feel you, for a daughterwife from the hills again. Imlamaya. And she is coming. Swimming in my hindmoist. Diveltaking on me tail. Just a whisk brisk sly spry spink spank sprint of a thing theresomere, saultering. Saltarella come to her own. I pity your oldself I was used to. Now a younger's there. Try not to part! Be happy, dear ones! May I be wrong! For she'll be sweet for you as I was sweet when I came down out of me mother. My great blue bedroom, the air so quiet, scarce a cloud. In peace and silence. I could have stayed up there for always only. It's something fails us. First we feel. Then we fall. And let her rain now if she likes. Gently or strongly as she likes. Anyway let her rain for my time is come. I done me best when I was let. Thinking always if I go all goes. A hundred cares, a tithe of troubles and is there one who understands me? One in a thousand of years of the nights? All me life I have been lived among them but now they are becoming lothed to me. And I am lothing their little warm tricks. And lothing their mean cosy turns. And all the greedy gushes out through their small souls. And all the lazy leaks down over their brash bodies. How small it's all! And me letting on to meself always. And lilting on all the time. I thought you were all glittering with the noblest of carriage. You're only a bumpkin. I thought you the great in all things, in guilt and in glory. You're but a puny. Home! My people were not their sort out beyond there so far as I can. For all the bold and bad and bleary they are blamed, the seahags. No! Nor for all our wild dances in all their wild din. I can seen meself among them, alla-niuvia pulchrabelled. How she was handsome, the wild Amazia, when she would seize to my other breast! And what is she weird, haughty Niluna, that she will snatch from my ownest hair! For 'tis they are the stormies. Ho hang! Hang ho! And the clash of our cries till we spring to be free. Auravoles, they says, never heed of your name! But I'm loothing them that's here and all I lothe. Loonely in me loneness. For all their faults. I am passing out. O bitter ending! I'll slip away before they're up. They'll never see. Nor know. Nor miss me. And it's old and old it's sad and old it's

627

sad and weary I go back to you, my cold father, my cold mad father, my cold mad feary father, till the near sight of the mere size of him, the moyles and moyles of it, moananoaning, makes me seasilt saltsick and I rush, my only, into your arms. I see them rising! Save me from those therrble prongs! Two more. Onetwo moremens more. So. Avelaval. My leaves have drifted from me. All. But one clings still. I'll bear it on me. To remind me of. Lff! So soft this morning, ours. Yes. Carry me along, taddy, like you done through the toy fair! If I seen him bearing down on me now under whitespread wings like he'd come from Arkangels, I sink I'd die down over his feet, humbly dumbly, only to washup. Yes, tid. There's where. First. We pass through grass behush the bush to. Whish! A gull. Gulls. Far calls. Coming, far! End here. Us then. Finn, again! Take. Bussoftlhee, mememormee! Till thousendsthee. Lps. The keys to. Given! A way a lone a last a loved a long the

PARIS,
1922-1939.

FOR THE BEST IN PAPERBACKS, LOOK FOR THE

In every corner of the world, on every subject under the sun, Penguin represents quality and variety—the very best in publishing today.

For complete information about books available from Penguin—including Pelicans, Puffins, Peregrines, and Penguin Classics—and how to order them, write to us at the appropriate address below. Please note that for copyright reasons the selection of books varies from country to country.

In the United Kingdom: For a complete list of books available from Penguin in the U.K., please write to *Dept E.P., Penguin Books Ltd, Harmondsworth, Middlesex, UB7 0DA.*

In the United States: For a complete list of books available from Penguin in the U.S., please write to *Dept BA, Penguin*, Box 999, Bergenfield, New Jersey 07621-0999.

In Canada: For a complete list of books available from Penguin in Canada, please write to *Penguin Books Canada Ltd, 2801 John Street, Markham, Ontario L3R 1B4.*

In Australia: For a complete list of books available from Penguin in Australia, please write to the *Marketing Department, Penguin Books Australia Ltd, P.O. Box 257, Ringwood, Victoria 3134.*

In New Zealand: For a complete list of books available from Penguin in New Zealand, please write to the *Marketing Department, Penguin Books (NZ) Ltd, Private Bag, Takapuna, Auckland 9.*

In India: For a complete list of books available from Penguin, please write to *Penguin Overseas Ltd, 706 Eros Apartments, 56 Nehru Place, New Delhi, 110019.*

In Holland: For a complete list of books available from Penguin in Holland, please write to *Penguin Books Nederland B.V., Postbus 195, NL–1380AD Weesp, Netherlands.*

In Germany: For a complete list of books available from Penguin, please write to *Penguin Books Ltd, Friedrichstrasse 10–12, D–6000 Frankfurt Main 1, Federal Republic of Germany.*

In Spain: For a complete list of books available from Penguin in Spain, please write to *Longman Penguin España, Calle San Nicolas 15, E–28013 Madrid, Spain.*

In Japan: For a complete list of books available from Penguin in Japan, please write to *Longman Penguin Japan Co Ltd, Yamaguchi Building, 2-12-9 Kanda Jimbocho, Chiyuoda-Ku, Tokyo 101, Japan.*